Aircraft of the Spanish Civil War

Frontispiece. *A Dewoitine D.371 of the 1ª Escuadrilla
of Grupo 71 of the Republican air force is shot down over
Catalonia by a Fiat C.R.32 in the spring of 1938.*

Aircraft of the Spanish Civil War 1936–39

Gerald Howson

PUTNAM

©Gerald Howson 1990

First published in Great Britain in 1990 by
Putnam Aeronautical Books, an imprint of
Conway Maritime Press Ltd.
24 Bride Lane, Fleet Street,
London EC4Y 8DR

British Library Cataloguing in Publication Data
Howson, Gerald
Aircraft of the Spanish Civil War 1939–39.
1. Military aircraft, history
I. Title
623.74'6'09

ISBN 0 85177 842 9

Typeset and designed by Swanston Graphics Ltd, Derby
Printed and bound in Great Britain by
William Clowes Ltd, Beccles

Contents

F R A

CATA

Léri

Re

Vinaro

Castellón

Manises
La Señera

VALENCIA

Cabo

Alicante
La Rabasa

Murcia

La Ribera

El Carmolí

Cartagena

Corunna
El Ferrol
Carreño
Gijón
Llanes
Santander
San Sebastian
Biarritz

Oviedo
Albericia
Bilbao
Guernica
Irún

ASTURIAS
SANTANDER
Lamiaco
VIZCAYA
Vitoria
Pamplona

Lugo
Santiago de Compostela

GALICIA

Condor Legion Base
Villafría
Logroño
NAVARRA

León
Gamonal
R Ebro
Huesca

Pontevedra
LEON
Burgos
Tudela
ARAGÓN

Vigo
Gallur
Valenzuela
Sariñena
Sanjurjo
Garrapinillos

Soria
Saragossa
Candasnos

Valladolid
Belchite

Villanubla
Calatayud
Puig Moreno

R Duero
Olmedo
Sigüenza
Alcañiz

CASTILLA LA VIEJA
Mas de las Matas

Salamanca
Segovia
La Cenia

Matacán
Buitrago de Lozoya

Avila
Brunete
Guadalajara
Teruel

Madrid
Barajas

Cuatro Vientos
Alcalá de Henares
Cuenca
Barracas

Getafe

Talavera de la Reina
Torrijos

Navalmoral
CASTILLA LA NUEVA

R Tajo
Toledo

EXTREMADURA
LA MANCHA
San Clemente

Cáceres
Sisante

Herrera del Duque
Tomelloso
Albacete

Las Bardocas
Mérida
Don Benito
Ciudad Real
Los Llanos

Badajoz
Medellín
Almadovar
Hellín

Lisbon
BADAJOZ
Archena

Andújar
Alcantarilla
Murcia

MURCIA
San Javier

Córdoba
R Guadalquivir
Jaén
Totana

PORTUGAL

ANDALUCIA

Tablada
Seville
Guadix

Huelva
El Copero
Granada
Tabernas

Antequera
Armillas

Almería

La Parra
Ronda
Malaga
Cabo de Gata

Jerez de la Frontera
Rompedizos

Cádiz

Algeciras
Gibraltar

Tangiers
Ceuta

Tetuán
Melilla

Sania Ramiel
El Atalayón
Nador

Larache

SPANISH MOROCCO

A

0   50   100   150   200   250 Miles

0   100   200   300   400 Kilometres

N C E
Toulouse-Montaudran
Toulouse-Francazal
Carcassonne
Perpignan
ANDORRA
Vilajuiga △
Bañolas △
Vich △ Gerona
Sabadell △
anudas △ Barcelona
lls
arragona

Division of Spain at beginning of August 1936

El Ferrol • Santander Bilbao
Oviedo
Lugo • Pamplona
Pontevedra • León • Burgos • Logrono Huesca • • Gerona
Saragossa • • Barcelona
Tarragona •
Segovia •
Salamanca • • Madrid Teruel • Menorca
Cáceres • Toledo • Valencia •
Badajoz • Albacete • Ibiza
Alicante •
Córdoba • Murcia •
Huelva • Granada • Cartagena •
Seville • Almería •
Málaga •
Cádiz •

Nationalist Advances
August – October 1936 ---▶

Republican Resistance ⟶

Division of Spain
at beginning of August 1936

Pollensa △
Mahón
mbretes ls.
Son San Juan △ • Porto Cristo
Cabreras ls. △

Antonio

Division of Spain in Spring of 1937

Santander Bilbao
Oviedo • • Vitoria
León •
Burgos • Huesca • • Gerona
Saragossa • Belchite
Segovia • • Barcelona
Tarragona •
Salamanca • Guadalajara
Brunete Madrid • Teruel • Vinaroz
Valencia • Menorca
Mallorca
Albacete • Ibiza
Alicante •
Badajoz • Murcia •
Córdoba • Cartagena •
Huelva • Granada •
Seville • Málaga • Almería •
Cádiz •

Nationalist offensives from
March 1937 to April 1938 ---▶

Republican offensives in 1937 ⟶

Division of Spain
in Spring of 1937

G E R I A

Division of Spain July 1938

Santander
Bilbao •
León •
Burgos • Huesca • • Gerona
Soria • • Barcelona
Saragossa • Tarragona •
Salamanca • Segovia •
Madrid •
Toledo • Menorca
Valencia • Mallorca
Badajoz • Albacete • Ibiza
Alicante •
Córdoba •
Seville • Granada • Cartagena •
Málaga • Almería •
Cádiz •

Republic Offensive of the Ebro
until November 1938
and in Extremandura
January – March 1939 ⟶

Nationalist advances in Catalonia ---▶

Division of Spain July 1938
Battle of The Ebro
and Conquest of Catalonia

Mountains 〰〰
own or city •
irfields or seaplane bases △

Acknowledgements

Mr Richard Sanders Allen, of Albany, New York, was one of the first researchers outside Spain to make a serious attempt to dispel the fog of myth and misinformation that for so long obscured almost every feature of the aerial side of the Spanish Civil War. Today there is not a writer on the subject who is not indebted to him. Most of the information concerning the American aircraft originated from him, but that is only a part of his contribution. I must thank him as well for the many photographs he has provided, and for putting me in touch with many other sources.

Mr James Carmody has given untiring help, particularly in tracing and identifying individually many of the hundreds of miscellaneous aircraft from Great Britain, France, and other European countries that reached Spain through devious channels. I must also thank him for checking large portions of the typescript.

Mr William Green, in addition to giving valuable advice and practical help over many years, provided more than 200 photographs.

General don Jesús Salas Larrazábal has never failed to answer my innumerable questions patiently, courteously and fully, when the answers were known at all. I must equally thank him for his kindness, hospitality and help when I visited Madrid.

Acknowledgements are also due to:

Great Britain
Dr Michael Alpert; Gerry Ames; Brian Bridgeman; Manuel Candelas; the late José-María Carreras, and his widow, María-Pepa Columer; Jerzy Czynk; Paul de Meyer; Dr Jill Edwards; the late Roland Falk; Malcolm Fillmore; Emilio Galera; Air Marshal Sir Victor Goddard; Paul Hayes; Muriel Hughes; the late A J Jackson, and his son Roger Jackson; Philip Jarrett; John King; the late R H McIntosh ('All-Weather Mac'); Jack Meaden; John Pothecary; Dr Paul Preston; Wing Commander Donald Salisbury Green; Air Vice Marshal J de M Severne; Amador Silverio; Winifred Stanynought; and Baron Thomas of Swynnerton, who gave help, advice and encouragement.

Spain
Luis Ignacio de Azaola Reyes; Juan Arráez Cerdá; José Chicharro Villar; Augusto Lecha Vilasuso, a Republican fighter pilot during the civil war; Joan Maluquer i Wahl; Justo Miranda and his wife, doña Paula Mercado; Professor Angel Viñas and Coronel don José Warleta Carrillo.

France
Jean Cuny; Robert Espérou; Patrick Laureau; Jean Liron; Jean Massé; Dr David Wingeate Pike; Rémy Tiger; and, finally, the doyen of the historians of Spanish Anarchism, José Peirats.

Holland
Harm Hazewinkel; Dr Thea Duijker; and the late S A Somberg.

Italy
Angelo Emiliani.

Norway
Ole Nordbø.

Sweden
Lennart Andersson; Benny Karlsson; and Rolf Westerberg.

Canada and the United States
The late C S Ackley; Harry Gann of the McDonnell Douglas Corporation; T R Judge; Joseph P Juptner; Professor Walter Langlois; Tom Sarbaugh; and Dr Richard K Smith.

Introduction

Problems with the history

General

The interval between the end of a war and the time when historians can expect to find the information that will enable them to write reasonably accurate histories is nowadays not usually longer than twenty-five or thirty years. The Spanish Civil War of 1936–39, however, is an awkward exception. It began as a domestic upheaval caused by deep fissures in Spanish society and, since each side had appealed to its natural allies abroad for material aid, rapidly embroiled, or threatened to embroil, the rest of Europe.

Backing the Republican government in Madrid were the Soviet Union, and, in other countries, all those with liberal, democratic or left-wing sympathies. Backing the Nationalist rebels under General Franco were Hitler, Mussolini, fascists everywhere, the Catholic Church, and all those of a conservative or right-wing disposition. Germany, Italy and the Soviet Union sent sizeable expeditionary forces. Tens of thousands of volunteers went to Spain to defend Liberty against Fascist Agression or Christendom against Asiatic Bolshevism. Spain became an arena where every conceivable political theory was to be tested, and where the interfering powers sought to advance their own interests. Outside Spain there developed a war of propaganda no less virulent and reckless in its disregard for facts and truths than the propaganda war between Republicans and Nationalists inside Spain.

The civil war ended on 31 March 1939 with the victory of General Franco and the Nationalists and the departure of half-a-million Republicans into exile. The long years of poverty, exhaustion and international ostracism that followed in Spain were not propitious for the writing of objective histories of the civil war, and although the Franco regime has frequently been blamed, and even ridiculed, for the snail-like pace of its opening-up and liberalisation of the country before Franco's death in 1975, it is hard to see how the pace could have been much faster.

In Spain, the family is the unit of first and greatest importance in all spheres of life, yet there was hardly a family which had not lost someone in the war, more usually before a firing squad, after a denunciation by an informer, rather than on the field of battle. There were, besides, innumerable families which had been broken by the war, with parents and children, husbands and wives, brothers and sisters and cousins finding themselves on opposing sides, often through the accident of where they had happened to be when the war had started on 18 July 1936.

Moreover, during the early 1950s the status of Spain had changed from that of a political pariah to that of a Western ally of the highest strategic importance in the Cold War, and propaganda in defence of this alliance had to be maintained accordingly. Under such circumstances, the Franco government's version of the history of the civil war was the only one permissible in Spain, where thinly concealed hatreds might burst into open violence at the least provocation. When the first attempt at a general and neutral history of the civil war appeared, in 1961, it was written not by a Spaniard but by an Englishman, Hugh Thomas, and it was banned in Spain for a decade. During that decade, however, the book went into several editions, and in each edition an increasing number of parts had to be altered, some of them drastically, in the light of new information. Indeed, through no fault of the author, parts of even the last edition already need revision, for, since the death of Franco, the flow of new information – in the form of memoirs and newly-opened archives – has become a flood.

The Air War in Spain

The Spanish Civil War was the first war in which aircraft played an important, and occasionally decisive, rôle. While the fighting was in progress scarcely any other aspect of the war received more emotive treatment from propagandists and the media, or was more thoroughly misunderstood. At the same time, because the air fighting in Spain brought about the transition from the weapons and tactics of the First World War to those that were to be used throughout the Second World War, it was of momentous importance to the development of military aviation. Nevertheless, of the thousands of books and articles that have been published about the Spanish Civil War, few cover its aerial side seriously or usefully. At the time of writing (1 January 1989), no comprehensive and accurate history of the air war in Spain exists in any language*.

The present book is *not* that history, but is intended to lighten the burden of anyone who may wish to write it in the future. Ever since the civil war began, disagreement and controversy have bedevilled the questions of how many aircraft took part on each side, what they were, where they came from, and who flew them. The discrepancies between estimates offered by different authorities and experts have sometimes verged on the ludicrous. At the start of the war, for example, the French government surreptitiously allowed a number of military aircraft to be flown to the Republicans. According to the French Premier of the time, Léon Blum, they numbered about fifty, and this was the number he gave in an official answer to a state enquiry in 1945. According to some French right-wing politicians, the real number was nearly 500, and in 1987 a young student of the author's acquaintance put the figure at 400 in a dissertation he was writing about the International Brigades in the Spanish Civil War. According to Spanish historians of the 1950s and 1960s, the number was somewhere between 50 and 150, but in a statement written in 1963 the ex-chief of the Republican air forces, General Ignacio Hidalgo de Cisneros, puts it at only 18 – '12 Dewoitine fighters and 6 Potez bombers, and both types were pretty antiquated'. Where does the truth lie? Again, according to some authors, the Russians sent 550 aircraft to Spain, but others set the figure at 806, or 1,200, or 1,400, and differences no less striking can be found among estimates of the numbers of German or Italian aircraft and aircrews sent to the Nationalists.

Since the total number of aircraft of all types, military and civil, that took part in the war on both sides was less than 3,500, such discrepancies are by no means trivial. Until we resolve them our understanding of the air fighting in Spain, and of the Spanish Civil War as a whole, will continue to be impaired. In addition, there is the even more debatable subject of all those aircraft bought clandestinely by both sides, but mainly by the Republicans, in various countries through networks of agencies and front-companies extending round the world, and shipped to Spain by every type of subterfuge to evade the non-intervention embargoes then in force. What, and how many, were they? Where, and how, were they purchased? The search for the answers to these last two questions uncovered a story so complex and so extraordinary that it must be reserved for a separate book. These aircraft, however, have been included here with brief explanations of their provenances. I hope that the list is now nearly complete, and that future additions or corrections will be of only a minor nature.

Where it has been impossible to resolve contradictory statements, as has happened regarding several German and most of the Russian types, I have left the questions open, in the hope that future research among the still uninvestigated records in Germany, Italy and Spain, or after the much hoped-for opening of archives in the Soviet Union, will finally resolve them.

The reader will have noticed that,

although the total number of aircraft that took part in the Spanish Civil War was a mere 3,500 or so, the number of different *types* of aircraft was astonishingly large – more than 280, if we count sub-types. They represent every one of the major aircraft industries of the world except that of Japan, and include some that were in service during or before the First World War, and others that were to continue in service through, and even after, the Second World War. Many of them were of great historical importance or curiosity, either as types or as individual aeroplanes. This was as much the result of the timing of the civil war, which occurred in a decade when the technical development of aircraft advanced more rapidly, and in a manner more varied, than at any time before or since, as of the circumstances in which the aircraft were procured. It is also another reason why the Spanish Civil War offers such an absorbing study to anyone who is interested in the history of civil or military aviation.

* The nearest approach to such a history is *La Guerra de España desde el aire*, by General Jesús Salas Larrazábal, published in the UK in 1969 as *Air War over Spain*. However, it was only the first volume of an intended series that was never completed, and restricted itself to the fighter pilots and fighter aircraft. Moreover, it was written during the 1960s, when the Franco regime was still very much in control and most of the necessary information was not yet available.

Note on Spanish Names

Spaniards employ three names in formal usage:

First Christian
Name
José

Patronym
(Father's surname)
Delgado

Matronym
(Mother's surname)
Durán

All three are used for lists, addresses, and passports, and on formal occasions. For familiar usage, the Christian name and patronym only are employed. Thus 'José Delgado Durán' becomes 'José Delgado', 'Señor Delgado', or 'Delgado', depending on circumstances. Prefixes such as 'de los' are omitted unless the Christian name is used as well. Thus 'Fernando de los Ríos' becomes 'Ríos' (*not* 'de los Ríos' or 'Los Ríos').

However, when a patronym ends in 'z', as in 'Martínez', then the patronym and matronym are used together. Thus 'Alejandro Martínez Alonso' would become 'Martínez

Alonso', rather than 'Martínez'. The same custom is followed when the patronym is 'García', although 'García' is often omitted altogether. Thus the Nationalist air ace Joaquín García Morato is usually referred to as 'Morato', and Andrés García Lacalle as 'Lacalle'.

Needless to say, there are all kinds of exceptions, some bewildering to a non-Spaniard. 'Hidalgo de Cisneros' (the Republican air chief), 'Núñez de Prado' (Director General de Aeronáutica at the outbreak of the civil war), and 'Bermúdez de Castro' are compound patronyms, and must always be written in full.

Spanish aviation on the eve of the civil war

The Air Forces

Since their creation, the Aviación Militar and Aeronáutica Naval had been under the respective control of the Spanish army and navy. In 1933 a Dirección General de Aeronáutica was established as an embryonic air ministry responsible for all technical, administrative, supply and training aspects of both civil and military aviation in Spain, although the Director General himself was always an army officer.

Aviación Militar
Formed as a small unit of the cavalry in 1913, the Spanish Servicio de Aviación Militar was one of the first armed forces in the world to use aircraft in a military operation, when four Farman F.M.7s dropped hand grenades on Moroccan tribesmen on 5 November 1913. Renamed Aeronáutica Militar and then (c.1926) Aviación Militar, the army air service was also referred to in official documents as 'Arma de Aviación', being a

branch of the army comparable with the cavalry or artillery. When the Popular Front government was elected in March 1936, the Order of Battle of the Aviación Militar was as shown on page 6.

The nominal strength of a fighter (caza) escuadrilla was twelve aircraft, and of a Breguet 19 escuadrilla nine aircraft, which gave a first-line strength on paper of seventy-two Nieuport 52s and ninety-nine Breguet 19s. In fact, many of the Nieuports had been withdrawn from service or were under repair. There were, however, about thirty additional Breguet 19s attached to other units.

At Cuatro Vientos, Madrid, were the headquarters of the technical, training and administrative services, as well as three training schools – Escuadrilla Y-1 (elementary flying), Escuela de Observadores (Observer School), and Escuela de Mecánicos – and the central air park. There were regional air parks at León, Seville

and Los Alcázares, near Cartagena. Other training schools were at Alcalá de Henares (Escuela de Vuelo y Combate, or air combat training) and at Los Alcázares, where the Escuela de Tiro y Bombardeo (Aerial Gunnery and Bombing School) and Escuadrilla Y-2 (intermediate flying training) were stationed. The principal training aircraft were about forty de Havilland D.H.9s, eleven D.H.60GIIIA Moth Majors, five D.H.82 Tiger Moths, two Fokker F.VIIb3ms, and eighteen Hispano E.30s. Also based at Los Alcázares was an independent *Grupo* of six Dornier Wal flying-boats, though all but one were without their engines.

There were at least twenty emergency airstrips and landing grounds for military use scattered over every region of Spain. Those with hangars were at Albacete, Alfaro (Logroño), Gamonal (Burgos), Daimiel (Ciudad Reál) and Armillas (Granada).

In April 1936 the newly-elected

Hispano-Nieuport 52s of Grupo 12 of the Aviación Militar at Armilla Aerodrome, Granada, in the spring of 1936. (Arráez)

A CASA-Breguet 19, with a 450hp Elizalde A4 engine, used as a target tug at the Escuela de Tiro y Bombardeo (Gunnery and Bombing School), Los Alcázares, Cartagena. The target, in the foreground, was clearly based on a Fokker F.VII. Four D.H.9s are in the background.

Popular Front government replaced General Goded with General Núñez de Prado as Director General de Aeronáutica. Convinced that a military coup was imminent, he began to concentrate all the best serviceable aircraft on to the aerodromes in the Madrid area. Grupo 12 was disbanded and its aircraft transferred to Getafe (although seven were still under repair at Seville when the civil war broke out). The three de Havilland D.H.89M Dragon Rapides intended for Africa were kept at Cuatro Vientos, while selected machines were transferred from the squadrons at León and Logroño.

NB It will be noticed that the numbering of the Grupos was, although logical, unusual. The numbers 11, 21 and 31 of Escuadra Núm 1 denoted '1st Grupo of Escuadra Núm 1', '2nd Grupo of Escuadra Núm 1' etc., and this system was followed throughout the three Escuadras.

Aviación Militar Order of Battle, March 1936

Escuadra Núm. 1
Getafe
(Madrid) : Grupo 11 – Two escuadrillas of Hispano-Nieuport 52s.
    Grupo 31 – Two escuadrillas of CASA-Breguet 19s.
León   : Grupo 21 – Three escuadrillas of Breguet 19s.

Escuadra Núm. 2
Tablada
(Seville) : Grupo 12 – Two escuadrillas of Hispano-Nieuport 52s, of which one escuadrilla was usually based at Granada.
    Grupo 22 – Two escuadrillas of Breguet 19s.

Escuadra Núm. 3
Prat de Llobregat
(Barcelona) : Grupo 13 – Two escuadrillas of Hispano-Nieuport 52s.
Logroño : Grupo 23 – Three escuadrillas of Breguet 19s.

Fuerzas Aéreas de Africa
Grupo 1 – Three escuadrillas of Breguet 19s distributed as follows: 1a Escuadrilla at San Ramiel, Tetuán; one patrulla (three aircraft) at Larache, and two patrullas of the 2a Escuadrilla at Melilla.
Larache – Four Fokker F.VIIb3m/Ms.
El Atalayón – one escuadrilla of seven Dornier Wals, of which only five were airworthy in 1936. The 3a Escuadrilla of Breguet 19s (Grupo 1) was distributed among various aerodromes in the Spanish Sahara. Ifni and Cabo Cisneros. Of these, the best known was Cabo Juby, since it was also used by l'Aéropostale and, later, Air France and Deutsche Lufthansa.

The Dornier Wal D-8 (EA-AAJ) of the Aeronáutica Naval flying over the Islas Columbretes, off the Valencian coast, shortly before the civil war. A few weeks later D-8 was one of the first aircraft to take part in General Franco's airlift across the Straits of Gibraltar, before the arrival of the Junkers Ju 52/3ms from Germany. (Arráez)

Aeronáutica Naval

The headquarters, depôt, training schools and main aerodrome were at San Javier, 10km north of Los Alcázares. On paper, the most effective units were the three CASA-Vickers Vildebeest-equipped Escuadrillas de Torpederos, two machines of which were fitted with floats. None, however, was as yet equipped with torpedoes. At San Javier there were also two escuadrillas of Savoia-Marchetti S.62s (18 aircraft in all), nine Martinsyde F.4As of the Escuadrilla de Combate y Acompañamiento (Fighter and Escort Squadron), seven Hispano E.30s of the Escuadrilla de Adastramiento (Training Squadron), five Dornier Wal flying-boats and a Cierva C.30A Autogiro. The Aeronáutica Naval had small stations at Barcelona (three Savoia-Marchetti S.62s, one Vildebeest, six Macchi M.18s and one Wal), Marín near Pontevedra in Galicia (five S.62s), Cádiz (two Wals) and Mahón, Menorca (five S.62s). On 18 July 1936 six naval aircraft happened to be at Getafe, Madrid: one Avro 504, one CASA III, one D.H. Moth Major , one Hispano E.30 and one E.34, and the second Cierva C.30A Autogiro.

Civil Aviation

Líneas Aéreas Postales Españoles (LAPE):

Formed in 1932 as a state-controlled airline (see Appendix I, 'Iberia'), LAPE ran services from its central airport at Barajas, Madrid, to Paris, via Toulouse and Bordeaux, Palma (Mallorca) via Valencia and Barcelona, and Gandó, Gran Canaria, via Seville, Tetuán, Cabo Juby, etc. In 1936 work had begun on the construction of a new international airport at Burgos. During the civil war this field was used as a base by the Condor Legion, and after the war the scheme was abandoned.

The aircraft apparently in service in July 1936 are listed on page 8.

In 1935 two Fokker F.VIIb3ms had been transferred to the Aviación Militar and given the military serials 20-5 and 20-6. These were probably

An air meeting in Catalonia before the civil war. Identifiable are the de Havilland Dragon EC-TAT (with Ramón Torres in the cockpit), two Avro Avians, a Cierva C.19 Mk IV, a D.H. Cirrus Moth, a CASA III, and the D.H. Gipsy Moth EC-AQQ, a single-seat conversion which crashed in December 1935. The man on the left is Francisco Pérez Mur, who later wrote a useful memoir of his experiences in the civil war. (Emiliani)

Aircraft in Service with LAPE, July 1936

Type	c/n	Registration	Fleet No
Junkers G 24	835	EC-ADA	1
Junkers F 13	639	EC-BBA	
Savoia-Marchetti S.62P	6205	EC-AMM	9
Fokker F.VIIb3m	5243	EC-AMA	10
Fokker F.VIIb3m	5244	EC-PPA	11
Ford 4-AT-F	71	EC-RRA	12
Fokker F.VIIb3m	5350	EC-AAU	14
Fokker F.VIIb3m	5351	EC-AUA	15
Fokker F.VIIb3m	5352	EC-UAA	16
D.H.60G Gipsy Moth	1274	EC-ALL	17 (?)
Dornier Wal		EC-AAZ	18 (?)
Dornier Wal		EC-YYY	19 (?)
D.H.89 Dragon Rapide	6262	EC-AZZ	20 (?)
Douglas DC-2-115D	1330	EC-XAX *Hercules*	21
Douglas DC-2-115B	1334	EC-AAY *Orion*	22
B.A. Eagle 2	114	EC-CBC	23 (?)
Douglas DC-2-115J	1417	EC-ABB *Sagitario*	24
Douglas DC-2-115J	1521	EC-BFF *Mallorca*	25

c/n 5127, EC-AHH, No 5, and c/n 5201 (or 5211), 'AKK, No 8. Two other Junkers G 24s, EC-AFF and 'FFA, had apparently been withdrawn by July 1936, but not struck off the inventory.

State and Regional authorities
Four D.H.83 Fox Moths and a General Aircraft Monospar ST-12 were operated by the Director General de Aeronáutica for cartographic purposes.

One D.H.85 Leopard Moth was used by the Director General de Seguridad (technically under the authority of the Post Office), and another by the Junta Central de Aeropuertos.

One D.H.80A Puss Moth was owned by the Servicios de Aeronáutica of the Generalitat (the regional government of Catalonia).

One or two R.W.D.9s were under evaluation for the Aviación Militar.

Private Companies
Air Taxi SA of Barcelona operated a D.H.84 Dragon, a D.H.60 Moth, and two Avro Avians.

Automobiles Fernández of Barcelona operated a Beechcraft B.17L as an air taxi from Prat de Llobregat.

CEA (La Compañía Española de Aviación) at Albacete aerodrome operated six Bristol Fighter F2Bs, a Farman F.354, and three Avro Avians for various purposes. Its D.H.60 Moth (EC-ALL) had been sold to LAPE, and its Farman F.200 (EC-LAA) to the Aero Club de Aragón, in 1935.

CTF (La Compañía de Trabajos Fotogramétics) had operated four D.H.60 Moths for commercial map-making, but seems to have sold them all to aero clubs by 1935.

Aero Clubs
Of those in existence by 1936, about thirty can be identified, half of them in Catalonia:-

Barcelona: Aeronautic Club (AC) de Catalunya, AC de Barcelona, Aero Popular de Barcelona, AC de Sant Andreu, AC de Prat de Llobregat, and others at Sabadell, Lérida, Gerona, Cerdunya, Figueras, Puigcerdá, Reus, Seu d'Urgell and Vich.

Madrid: Real Aero Club de España, AC de Madrid, Aero Popular de Madrid.

Valencia: AC de Valencia, AC de Levante. In Aragón, the AC de Aragón (Saragossa) and AC de Huesca.

Andalusia: AC de Sevilla, AC de Cádiz (both at Tablada, Seville), AC de Penibético (Algeciras), AC de Málaga.

On the Canary Islands were the AC de Tenerife and the AC de Las Palmas, and on Mallorca the AC de los Baleares. In 1936, aero clubs and private owners in Spain possessed about 110 light aircraft (see Appendix III).

Aircraft Industry

Aircraft Manufacturers
Construcciones Aeronáuticas SA (CASA), the largest aircraft factory in Spain, was founded in 1923 to produce Breguet 19s under licence for the Aeronáutica Militar, its director being don José Ortíz Echagüe (a distinguished military engineer, aviator and, in later life, genre photographer of Spanish landscapes and regional costumes). Its main plant was at Getafe military aerodrome, Madrid, and there was, and still is, a

The de Havilland D.H.84 Dragon of Air Taxi Barcelona, the Stinson SR Reliant that J-M de la Cuesta had bought for a flight to Egypt, and the Monocoupe 90A De Luxe EC-ZAA from the Aero Club at Seville visit Brooklands Aerodrome, Surrey, in 1934. All three aircraft served in the civil war. (A J Jackson).

smaller factory for building (in those days) flying-boats and seaplanes (Dornier Wal, Vickers Vildebeest) at Puntales, Cádiz. CASA also built a small number of prototypes and the CASA III trainer. In 1936 CASA was making preparations for the production of forty-two Martin 139W bombers and ten Hawker Ospreys.

La Hispano-Suiza, Sección de Aviación, was founded in 1916 by the Hispano-Suiza automobile company under the name 'La Hispano'. The factory was at Guadalajara, and had its own aerodrome. In 1931 it was renamed Hispano-Suiza, Sección de Aviación, and, during the civil war, Hispano Aviación SA (HASA), the title it still holds. Its principal contribution before the civil war was the production of licence-built Nieuport NiD 52s and its own Hispano E.30s, but on the eve of the war it was preparing for the production of fifty Hawker Spanish Furies.

Aeronáutica Industrial SA (AISA) was the Jorge Loring aircraft factory at Carabanchel Alto, Madrid, reconstituted in the 1930s to fulfil a production order for three Fokker F.VIIb3/Ms for the Aviación Militar. During this period Loring built a few

The French air ministry Lockheed 9D Orion F-AKHC, re-engined with a 575hp Hispano-Suiza 9 V engine, in which André Malraux flew to Madrid on 25 July 1936. (P Badré, via R S Allen)

prototypes, but was saved by an order for one hundred González Gil-Pazó GP-1 trainers.

Talleres (Workshops) de la Aviación Militar possessed experimental laboratories and repair and maintainance workshops at Cuatro Vientos (Madrid), Tablada (Seville) and León.

Talleres de la Aeronáutica Naval, the Aeronáutica Naval factory at Barcelona, had been responsible for the production of Savoia Marchetti S.13, S.16 and S.62, and Macchi M.18, flying-boats.

There was in addition a small number of light aircraft built by individual designers such as Adaro, Freuller Valls, Guinea-Severt and Parallols.

Aero-Engines
Elizalde SA, Barcelona, was created in the 1920s by the automobile manufacturer Arturo Elizalde to licence-build Lorraine 12Eb engines

for the CASA Breguet 19s. Later it built other types of Lorraine engines, a number of Walter Juniors, and Dragon radial engines of its own design.

Hispano-Suiza's Guadalajara factory had produced Hispano-Suiza 12HB, 12LB and 12Lbr water-cooled engines for the Nieuport 52s, Dornier Wals and Vickers Vildebeests during the 1920s and 1930s, as well as 9Qd radial engines for the Fokker F.VIIb3m/Ms and Hispano E.30s. In 1936 it was planning to build Wright Cyclone engines for the CASA-built Martin 139Ws.

Re-equipment programme of 1934–35

During the summer of 1934 José-María Gil Robles, Spain's War Minister and a forceful leader of the Catholic party, initiated a programme of general rearmament, including a complete replacement of Spain's obsolete military and naval aircraft by more modern machines. Prime importance was attached to obtaining a strategic bomber, of which Spain had none, and the first choice was the

Martin B-10. Eighty-one of these bombers were ordered at a cost of $5.5 million, but the US Government prevented the sale on the grounds that the type could not be released for export until production for the US Army Air Corps had been completed. Other urgent requirements were for replacements for the Nieuport 52s and the Fokker F.VIIb3m/Ms, and for a new trainer. During the next eighteen months the aircraft listed on page 10 were tested, with varying degrees of thoroughness.

Despite strong pressure to 'buy German', in December 1935 Gen Goded, who was then DG de Aeronáutica and was soon to be one of the principal plotters of the Nationalist rebellion, announced that the new strategic bomber for Spain was to be the Martin 139W, which had now been released for export. Eight pattern aircraft were to be purchased outright and forty-two were to be built under licence by CASA, the total cost being about $12 million. A few weeks before this announcement, Cdte Ramón Franco, Gen Francisco Franco's younger brother and air attaché in Washington (see Dornier Wal), had sent a fulsome report on the Martin after watching US Army exercises to which he had been invited by Gen Douglas MacArthur. The Germans were furious at Goded's sudden decision, and their ambassador in Madrid alleged that, according to his intelligence sources, the contract had been secured through bribery, 'a practice to which the German aircraft industry neither can nor will stoop'.

Under the renovation programme 249 new aircraft were ordered: fifty Martin 139Ws, fifty Hawker Spanish Furies, twenty-eight Koolhoven FK 51s, three de Havilland D.H.89Ms, three Potez 452s, ten Hawker Ospreys, one hundred González Gil-Pazó GP-1s, and five (later raised to thirty) Hispano E.34s. None was notably modern, and of the imported aircraft only three pattern Hawker Spanish Furies, one pattern Hawker Osprey and the three de Havilland D.H.89M military Dragon Rapides had reached Spain by 18 July 1936. Of these, only the D.H.89Ms were in service and armed.

Date	Type	
7.11.34	Marcel Bloch MB 200 Morane Saulnier MS 230E	Three MB 200 medium bombers and three MS 230E trainers were flown briefly by Spanish pilots at Barajas during a goodwill visit by the Armée de l'Air to Spain and Portugal.
10.11.34	Avia B122.2	Trainer. Demonstrated at Getafe by F Novak.
6.1.35	Airspeed A.S.6 Envoy II	G-ACVJ, the *India Demonstrator*, demonstrated at Barajas by Sir Alan Cobham and Flight-Lieutenant R C Hutchinson, during a stop-off on the journey to India. Offered as a replacement to the Fokker F.VIIb3m/M.
18.1.35	Vought V-80 Corsair	At Barajas, by W C Gould (European agent for Vought and Sikorsky) and Burdick, a Vought engineer. After rejection by the Aviación Militar, the Corsair was fitted with a single main float and two wingtip floats and offered to the Aeronáutica Naval as a catapult-launched aircraft for use aboard the two new cruisers then under construction, the *Canarias* and *Baleares*. However, on 30 April 1936 it caught fire and crashed into the sea off San Javier, killing Cdte Leocadio Nardiz and Ten Augusto de la Cierva.
−35	Heinkel He 70A Junkers K 45	As replacement for Breguet 19. Export model of Ju 52/3mg3e.
„ „	Junkers Ju 86 Junkers Ju 160	Offered as a bomber in competition with He 70A. These German aircraft were looked at, if not seriously evaluated, by Cdte Carlos Pastor Krauel while he was air attaché in Germany, 1934–35.
10.4.35	Boeing 281	See section on this aircraft.
10.6.35	Breguet 460	„
6.35	Hawker Spanish Fury	„
6.35	Hawker Osprey	„
6.35	de Havilland D.H.89M	„
7.35	González Gil-Pazó GP-1	„
7.35	Hispano E.34	„
7.35	Loring X	„
7.35	Adaro 1.E.7 Chirta	„
7.35	Potez 452	Single-seat flying-boat fighter, evaluated in France.
16.10.35	Koolhoven FK 51	At Barajas by Dirk Asjes, a Dutch air force pilot who was to achieve distinction in the Pacific War in 1942.
13.12.35	Potez 54	Both flown briefly by Spanish
13.12.35	Amiot 143	pilots during a goodwill visit by the Armée de l'Air.

Outline of the Spanish civil war

The conspiracy

Spain had become a Republic in 1931, and for the next two years the first elected government proposed reforms intended to bring the country into the modern world. The reforms, which were sweeping, were inevitably opposed by the aristocracy, the Church, most officers of the armed services, leaders of finance and industry (which was rudimentary and largely foreign-owned), and a fascist party. The government faltered, and came under attack from the political left, which, accusing it of dragging its feet, tried to force the pace with demonstrations, church burnings, and bombings. As disorder grew, a conservative government under Lerroux in 1933 began to dismantle the reforms of its predecessors. The result was an armed uprising in the Asturias which left 4,000 dead and 30,000 in prison, and an attempt at secession by the Catalonians, who, with the Basques, had long been agitating for independence. Lerroux's government was disgraced by a financial scandal, and a left-wing Popular Front coalition came to power in March 1936. One of its earliest precautionary measures was to send potentially dangerous army generals to far-away garrisons: Franco to the Canaries, Mola to Pamplona, and Goded to Mallorca. These officers promptly started a conspiracy to overthrow the Republic and replace it by a military dictatorship. They gained the support of monarchists, to whom they promised the return of the King, and of the fascists, to whom they promised fascism.

The coup

The coup began during the night of 17–18 July 1936 with a rising in

The Douglas DC-2 Granada *carried the first shipments of Spanish gold to Paris for the buying of arms and aircraft in July and August 1936. This picture was taken on the Aeronáutica Naval base at Prat de Llobregat Airport, Barcelona, probably while the aircraft was refuelling on its way to Paris.* (Arráez)

Below: *anarchist militia wait for the Fokker F.VIIb3m EC-PPA, commandeered from LAPE and converted into a bomber, to take off for a raid on Saragossa in August 1936.*

Spanish Morocco of the Army of Africa, a colonial force which consisted largely of Foreign Legionaries and Moorish Regulares (regular troops), and included many hardened veterans of the Moroccan War of 1909–26. The colony was subdued in a few hours, and on 19 July Gen Francisco Franco arrived from the Canary Islands, in a de Havilland Dragon Rapide hired at Croydon, to take command. Meanwhile, uprisings followed all over mainland Spain on 18 July 1936, and by 21 July Gen Mola had secured most of northern Spain except Catalonia and a strip along the Cantabrian and Biscay coasts. This included the Asturias and three of the Basque provinces, for the Basques, though devoutly Catholic and generally conservative, had sided with the Republic in exchange for a promise of independence.

The uprising failed in Madrid, in all the Mediterranean ports from Barcelona to Málaga, and in most of central and southern Spain. The rebels (or 'Nationalists', as they soon called themselves) and Gen Queipo de Llano did secure the southwest corner of Andalusia, however, and this included the aerodrome and depot at Tablada, Seville. The capture of this aerodrome, which happened more by accident than design, was to produce enormous results, as a few Nationalist leaders may even have foreseen at the time. The crews of Republican warships in the Mediterranean had mutinied against the orders of their officers to join the uprising and, having killed or imprisoned them, now sailed their ships into the Straits of Gibraltar to prevent Franco's army in Spanish Morocco from crossing to Spain. An airlift was proposed, and on 19 and 23 July 1936 Franco despatched emissaries to Mussolini and Hitler with requests for transport and fighter aircraft. Meanwhile, he began to send platoons of troops to Seville in the few aircraft available (three Fokker F.VIIb3m/Ms, a Douglas DC-2, two Dornier Wals and a Fokker F.VIIa bought in Casablanca). These troops strengthened Gen Queipo de Llano's precarious hold on Seville,

Aircraft of the Alas Rojas ('Red Wings') squadron at Sariñena Aerodrome, Aragón, in August 1936: Breguet 19s, a Nieuport 52, a Latécoère 28 and a de Havilland Moth Major.

and established a bridgehead to which the main army could be flown when the German and Italian aircraft arrived.

In Madrid, the embattled government, deserted by most of the armed forces, police, civil and public services, and even by the diplomatic corps abroad, cabled a request for arms and aircraft to Premier Léon Blum of France, who led a Popular Front coalition similar to that in Spain.

Non-intervention

These two appeals, and the very different responses to them by the dictators on the one hand and Blum on the other, made the fighting in Spain a matter of international concern. The dictators sent aircraft to Franco promptly, more indeed than he had asked for, complete with aircrews, armaments, maintainance support and even anti-aircraft batteries to defend the aerodromes: six Heinkel He 51 and twelve Fiat C.R.32 fighters, nine (out of twelve sent) Savoia-Marchetti S.81 bombers and twenty Junkers Ju 52/3mge bomber-transports to Tetuán or Cádiz; and twelve aircraft to Mallor-

ca – three Savoia-Marchetti S.55Xs, three Fiat C.R.32s, three Macchi M.41s, and three Savoia-Marchetti S.81s. These 59 aircraft were followed by a further 82 aircraft between 14 August and 30 September.

Blum's immediate impulse was to grant the Republican request. France depended on Britain as an ally, however, and the British government had other preoccupations. After Mussolini's invasion of Abyssinia and Hitler's march into the Rhineland had failed to inspire serious opposi-

Above: *with all of its markings over-painted, one of the Dewoitine D.372s built for Lithuania prepares to leave for Barcelona on 8 August 1936.* (Laureau)

Two French bombers supplied clandestinely to the Spanish Republic, a Potez 54 and a Bloch MB 210. (Arráez)

tion from any of the western democracies, the British government hoped to conciliate Hitler and woo Mussolini away from him, and an action by France which might be seen as provocative by either of the dictators could not only jeopardise this, but could result in the dividing of Europe into two hostile groups of countries ranked up behind one or the other side in Spain.

Then there was Gibraltar. Since that vital post on the route to India could not be defended against an attack from the land, it was imperative to be on friendly terms with whomsoever might win in Spain. Faced with pressure from Britain and furious opposition from the political right at home, Blum gave in, and proposed instead an International Agreement of Non-Intervention which would bind all signatory governments to prevent the supply of war materials to either side in the Spanish war. While the British were 'welcoming' this proposal, the news was broadcast that three Italian bombers (S.81s) had crashed, two in Algeria and one in the Mediterranean, and that these were part of an expeditionary force which Mussolini was rushing to Gen Franco. Blum secretly authorised the sale of twenty military aircraft (fourteen Dewoitine

D.372 fighters and six Potez 54 bombers) to the Spanish Republicans, provided they were delivered unarmed. The British got wind of this, and Blum was obliged to bring Non-Intervention into effect, unilaterally, at midnight on 8 August 1936. Hours before, however, the aircraft (now nineteen, since a Dewoitine had crashed) were flown to Barcelona by a hastily collected group of mercenaries and a few idealistic volunteers under the nominal command of the writer André Malraux, who knew nothing about aircraft or military aviation. The armaments for the aircraft were never delivered, and substitute armament had to be improvised from old Spanish stock. Thus, in contrast to the eighteen fighters delivered to the Nationalists, the thirteen Dewoitines arrived without arms, spare parts, or trained pilots. Indeed, five of the Dewoitines were damaged on landing at Barcelona, and a team of company mechanics had to be flown in from Toulouse to carry out repairs, a service requiring payment in cash.

During August and September these nineteen military aircraft were followed by seven to twelve more (one Marcel Bloch MB 210, one Potez 544, five or six Loire 46 fighters, and possibly two or four

Marcel Bloch MB 200s), again without arms, aircrews, or spare parts; in short, a total of 26-33 military aircraft, in contrast to the 141 military aircraft received by the Nationalists by 30 September 1936.

These figures are given in detail because, for reasons that are basically political, the whole affair has become concealed in a cocoon of misinformation. Most history books put the number of French military aircraft delivered in August and September at between 38 and 100, while no historian, least of all any who wrote under the eye of the Franco regime in Spain, has bothered to point out that the Nationalists received aircraft that were immediately and effectively usable, and the Republicans did not.

By the beginning of September all the European governments had either signed the Non-Intervention (NI) Agreement or imposed embargoes of their own, and an NI Committee was established in London, with delegates from all of the signatory governments, to monitor progress.

The advance to Madrid

Eleven of the German Ju 52s ferried the greater part of the Army of Africa to Seville or Jerez de la Frontera

Above: *Savoia-Marchetti S.81s and Fiat C.R.32s, complete with crews and armaments, were the first Italian aircraft supplied to General Franco in August 1936.* (Arráez)

during the first three weeks of August 1936, and by the time the transportation was completed, in October, they had moved 13,962 troops and 500 tons of material from Morocco to Spain. The first airlift on such a scale in history, it introduced a new element of mobility into warfare, and was one of the decisive operations, if not *the* decisive operation, of the

Spanish-crewed Ju 52/3ms. The furthest machine, María Magdalena *of the famous* Trés Marías *or 'Three Marys' squadron, was also named* Trechuelo *in memory of a Nationalist pilot killed over Badajoz in August 1936.* (Azaola)

Spanish Civil War. With efficient air support, the Army of Africa marched rapidly northwards, linked up with Gen Mola and, after a diversion to relieve a Nationalist garrison besieged in the Alcázar fortress in Toledo, arrived at the outskirts of

Fokker F.XII G-ADZI, one of four sold by British Airways to General Mola's 'Northern Revolutionary Army', crashed during a thunderstorm over Biarritz while on its way to Burgos, Spain, on 15 August 1936. (Jackaman, via John King)

Madrid by the beginning of November. In the South, Gen Varela had led a motorised column eastwards along the winding roads of the Sierras of Grazalema, Ronda, and Antequera and reached Granada, where Nationalists had taken over the city and surrounding countryside at the time of the uprising. As the Nationalist armies advanced, they pacified the newly occupied country with mass executions, often carried out by 'Black Squads'. Terror reigned on the Republican side, too. In many places where the uprising had been crushed, mobs took control and killed the local gentry, priests,

Above: *SB Katiuskas were the first Russian aircraft to arrive in Spain, and went into action at the end of October 1936. A Hucks starter, based on a Ford Model T chassis, is visible on the left.* (Arraéz)

I-15 Chatos appeared over Madrid for the first time on 4 November 1936. (Azaola)

monks, nuns, police, and anyone else whom they felt deserved death. In the cities, 'death squads' rounded up the 'bourgeoisie' of one district after another and shot them. Estimates of the numbers killed in this way during the first three months vary between 15,000 and 50,000 on each side.

While using the NI Committee as a platform for denouncing France and the Soviet Union as warmongers, Germany and Italy stepped up their aid to the Nationalists. In September 1936 Stalin decided to intervene, and the first Russian expeditionary force of tanks, artillery and 108 aircraft (twenty-five I-15 and thirty-one I-16 fighters, thirty-one SB-2M100A bombers and thirty-one R-5 reconnaissance and ground-attack biplanes) to the main zone, and thirty I-15s to the Basque zone, reached

Republican Spain in October and November 1936. At the same time the first batches of volunteers, from all over the world, were arriving in

Republican Spain to join the International Brigades and 'smash Fascism'. They would eventually total 33,000. The first battalions went into action

A Heinkel He 70 escorted by Fiat C.R.32s. (Arráez)

at the beginning of November, almost simultaneously with the first Russian fighters over Madrid. By 1 November 1936 the fighter defence of the capital had dwindled to a single Hawker Spanish Fury, and the sudden appearance of formations of properly armed and led Republican fighter aircraft threw the Nationalists off balance and so raised the morale of the troops and populace below that it saved the city. By the end of the month the Nationalists were forced to abandon the daylight bombing of Madrid, and in the middle of December their offensive ground to a halt.

World war by proxy

The initial German intervention in Spain, code-named *Unternehmen Zauberfeuer* (Operation Magic Fire), had been organised by a specially created *Sonderstab W* (Special Staff W). To give it the disguise of a commercial undertaking, material was exported by a front-company, ROWAK, in Germany to another, HISMA (La Compañía Hispano-Marroquí), in Tetuán and Seville, and the men had been described on

Ground crews retrieve an S.81 damaged by floods during the Battle of Guadalajara. Madrid, the Nationalist objective during the battle, lies behind the Sierra Guadarrama in the distance. (Emiliani)

their passports as 'tourists'. The Italians, who had not organised their contribution (which was designated 'Operazioni Militari Spagna', or OMS) so thoroughly, had enrolled the men and aircraft into the Spanish Foreign Legion, El Tercio de Extranjeros (i.e. 'the Foreign *Part*, or *Third*, of the African Army'), and the Italian air squadrons were now accordingly styled La Aviación de El Tercio. In November, learning of Soviet intervention, the Germans created a full-scale force in Spain, the Condor Legion, to be kept at a constant strength of 100 first-line aircraft, together with artillery (the new 88mm anti-aircraft guns doubling as field artillery), tanks, communications and extensive training units. In December 1936 Mussolini, not to be outdone, created the Aviazione Legionaria, 250-aircraft strong, as well as the CTV (Corpo Truppi Voluntarii) a ground expeditionary force several divisions strong.

On the Republican side, the International Brigades were controlled, and recruited, by the Communist Party. In addition to the air squadrons, the Russians sent small numbers of tanks and artillery specialists and a thousand or so advisers and secret police (NKVD). Since the start of the war the Republicans had attempted to buy arms and aircraft abroad, and had encountered increasing obstruction from European banks, which either refused to handle

their funds, on the grounds of observing non-intervention, or deliberately sabotaged their transactions. For this reason, after the Russians decided to intervene on the Republican side, Juan Negrín, the Republican Finance Minister, arranged for the transfer of the remaining Spanish gold reserve to the USSR, from where it could be re-exported for arms purchases through Soviet banks. Negrín, however, did not inform the cabinet of his action, and ensured that the move was carried out under conditions of extreme secrecy. As a result, the affair of the 'Moscow Gold' continued to be surrounded by mystery, and to be a subject of bitter accusations and recriminations, for the next half-century. In the eyes of the Franco government it was simply a robbery, albeit the largest single act of plunder in history, carried out by Stalin at gunpoint against his weak and defenceless satellite, and this view was endorsed by many Republican leaders in exile during the years of the Cold War. The researches of Professor Viñas and others, however, have shown that, of the $518,000,000 shipped to Russia, $333,000,000 did in fact find its way back to Paris to pay for arms purchases. For, uncertain of the dependability of Soviet supplies, the Republicans continued to buy arms, aircraft and other material, wherever they could be obtained, through purchasing commissions

Heinkel He 46s of 3-G-11 during fighting near Huesca, Aragón, in 1937. (Arráez)

established in Paris, Prague and New York. The remaining $185,000,000 was retained in the USSR to pay for Soviet material sent to Spain.

The NI Committee was powerless to prevent any of these developments, the only effect of the embargoes being to raise the prices of the materials. Nor did its members dare call to account those who, like the dictators, blatantly violated the agreement, for fear of worsening the already dangerous political situation in Europe.

Jarama and Guadalajara

In February 1937 the Nationalists attacked across the Jarama river in an attempt to encircle Madrid from the south. After fierce fighting on the ground and in the air, the attack had to be abandoned. In March, Italian motorised CTV divisions tried to cut off Madrid from the north-east. Bad weather, and resolute ground-straffing by I-15 squadrons, brought them to a stop, and turned the attack into a rout. Indeed, the only substantial Nationalist gain at this time was the capture of Málaga, and a large area of the surrounding countryside and coast, by a mixed force of Italians and Spanish Nationalists under Gen Queipo de Llano at the beginning of February.

The Northern Campaign – a change of front

With Madrid blocked to them, the Nationalists turned their main attacks on to the Basque zone in the north, starting on 30 March 1937 with an advance against Bilbao. Progress, marked by frequent air raids on defenceless towns and villages (including the notorious bombing of Guernica on 26 April 1937), was slow, and Bilbao did not fall until 19 June 1937.

Political developments

Franco had been named *Generalísimo* and Head of State on 10 October 1936, the intended Head of State,

The Miles Hawk Major of José Rebellho, a Portuguese volunteer, on a liaison mission for the Nationalists.

Gen Sanjurjo, having been killed in an air crash on 20 July 1936. On the Republican side, the loss of Irún and Talavera de la Reina had resulted in the creation, on 4 September 1936, of a new government under the left-wing Socialist Largo Caballero, with, for the first time, two Communist, and even two Anarchist, members in the cabinet. Responsibility for the air forces was given to a new Ministry of Marine and Air under the moderate socialist Indalecio Prieto, who, on 11 November, was also made responsible for the clandestine purchase of war material abroad. The arrival and success of the Russians, however, enormously increased the prestige and power of the Communists in Republican Spain. Trouble

began when, at Stalin's insistence, they demanded that Largo Caballero suppress the non-Communist groups within the Republic and, when he refused, started a campaign to discredit and remove him.

Matters came to a head in May 1937, when the Communists, under Russian direction, violently suppressed the POUM (an anti-Stalinist Marxist party) and, in as much as they were able, the Anarchists in Catalonia. Largo Caballero was forced to resign and was replaced by his Finance Minister, Dr Juan Negrín. Prieto became Defence Minister. Meanwhile, Franco was having troubles of his own with the Falange (the Fascist party) on the one hand and the ultra-Monarchists on the other. Eventually, he succeeded in forcibly removing the leaders and taking control of both movements.

Also in March 1937 the NI Com-

General Mola, the chief planner of the Nationalist uprising, was killed when his Airspeed Envoy crashed into a mountain north of Burgos on 3 June 1937. This photograph is said to have been taken just before departure that day.

Right and below: the first Stukas. The Henschel Hs 123, designed as a dive-bomber, was not used as such in Spain. The three Ju 87As of the special Stukakette of the Condor Legion may have carried out the first true dive-bombing operations in the history of warfare during the Battle of Teruel at the end of 1937. (Ju 87A, Arráez)

mittee at last established a system of controls round Spain, the German and Italian navies covering the Republican coasts, the British and French the Nationalist coasts, and a chain of internationally manned control points being positioned along the French and Portuguese frontiers. The fact that Germany and Italy were actively supporting the Nationalists meant that this system worked in favour of the Nationalists rather than the Republicans, for while German and Italian aircraft had no scruples about attacking and even sinking Republican blockade-runners, French and British warships were hardly able to do the same to German or Italian ships carrying arms and supplies to Nationalist ports. Nevertheless, most of the arms that managed to reach France were sooner or later smuggled across the frontier.

The real problem for the Republicans, especially where aircraft were concerned, was in getting them from their countries of origin to suitable ports of embarkation in secrecy. Occasionally, too, they were faced by manufacturers or intermediaries who, having received substantial advance payments, decided to play safe and not deliver the aircraft.

Republican counterattacks

In an attempt to draw Nationalist forces away from the Basques, the Republicans mounted a series of offensives from the main zone. The first were at Huesca and La Granja (Segovia) in May 1937, both of which failed. They were followed by the Battle of Brunete north-west of Madrid in July. This did succeed, at least, in obliging the Nationalists to transfer most of their air forces to the Madrid sector, but by 26 July 1937 the Republicans had been driven back nearly to their original positions. The Nationalists claimed, in addition, a great aerial victory in which about 160 Republican aircraft were destroyed for the loss of 23, a disaster from which, according to historians writing during the years of the Franco regime, the Republican air forces took six months to recover. The Republicans admitted the loss of only 25 aircraft, however, and Brunete remains one of the many events of the Spanish war about which the truth has yet to be determined.

In August the Republicans attacked at Belchite, near Saragossa, a battle notable for the fierce summer heat in which it was fought, and in September at Jaca, north of Huesca, but achieved few results. By then the Nationalists had captured Santander and were advancing into the Asturias, and they completed their conquest of the northern zone before the end of October 1937.

An I-16 Type 10 of the Republican 4ª Escuadrilla of Grupo 21 on stand-by. The Moscas of this escuadrilla were fitted with clandestinely imported Wright Cyclone F-54 engines for high-altitude fighting, and had distinguishing white propeller bosses. Their emblem was Popeye the Sailor.

Teruel and the Aragon offensive

On 15 December 1937 the Republicans attacked at Teruel, during a snowstorm, and quickly succeeded in surrounding the town. The siege, fought out in temperatures down to 18°C below zero, lasted until the town surrendered on 8 January 1938. On 17 January 1938 the Nationalists counterattacked but were unable to recapture Teruel until the end of February. In March they followed this with a major offensive in Aragon, sweeping all before them and reaching the Mediterranean coast by the middle of April. This opened an eighty-mile-wide corridor between Catalonia and the main, or as it now was, southern, zone of the Republic. In France, Premier Blum, who had fallen from power the previous summer but had recently been re-elected, opened the frontier for the unhindered passage of arms, but was obliged by the British to close it again on 13 June.

The Battle of the Ebro

This battle, a desperate attempt by the Republicans to rejoin the two halves of the Republic or, failing that, at least ensure the survival of the Republic until the expected outbreak of a general war in Europe saved it from otherwise unavoidable defeat, began on 24–25 July 1938 with an attack across the Ebro river. The Republicans advanced about ten miles in six weeks against enormous Nationalist air superiority. Fierce fighting, accompanied by the largest air battles yet seen in warfare as the Republicans threw the whole of their air force into the campaign, continued until the Nationalist counterattacks had driven the Republicans back across the river by 18 November 1938. By this time, too, the Munich crisis had ended with Hitler's triumphant occupation of the Sudetenland.

The end of the civil war

The Nationalists, with overwhelming superiority on land and in the air, opened their offensive against Catalonia on 24 December 1938. Resistance quickly collapsed, and by 10 February 1939 the whole province was captured. With it was lost most of the remaining Republican air force. Apart from a Republican offensive in Extremadura, there was little fighting in March. Instead, a rift occurred on the Republican side between those who, led by Coronel Casado, wished to end the war by negotiation and those who, led by Negrín and the Communists, wished to fight to the end. Street battles in Madrid resulted in the defeat of the Communists, but Casado could extract no terms from Franco other than unconditional surrender. By now, however, the British, French and other governments had formally recognised Franco's Junta as the government of Spain. Isolated, and with

no international standing or hope of help from anywhere, the Negrín government flew into exile, and the Republic surrendered on 31 March 1939. Two weeks before, Hitler had invaded what remained of Czechoslovakia, and in April Mussolini invaded Albania.

The Opposing Air Forces

The division of aircraft

On 18 July 1936 there were 536-553 aircraft of all types, most of them airworthy, in Spain and Spanish Africa, besides 30-40 military aircraft under repair:

Aviación Militar:	191-203
Aeronáutica Naval:	92
Military trainers:	79
Naval trainers:	9

LAPE 15-16 (plus two light aircraft)	
State and Regional authorities:	8-9
Private companies:	14
Privately-owned light aircraft:	126-130

By the end of the first week the Nationalists had captured:

Aviación Militar:	73
	(plus 17 under repair)
Aeronáutica Naval:	5
Military trainers:	19
Naval trainers:	0
State and Regional authorities:	2
LAPE	2
Privately-owned aircraft:	26
Total:	**127**

These included sixty-three Breguet 19s, ten Nieuport 52s (of which seven were under repair), thirteen Dornier Wals (of which ten were under repair), three Fokker F.VIIb3m/Ms and one Douglas DC-2.

The Spanish government retained:

Aviación Militar:	118-130
	(plus at least 15 under repair)
Aeronáutica Naval:	87

A Letov S 231 of the 2ª Escuadrilla of Grupo 71, Republican air force, at Bañolas, near Gerona. Seated on the wheel is José Bastida, the commander, who had recently returned to the Republican zone through an exchange of prisoners. (Arráez)

Military trainers:	60
Naval trainers:	9
LAPE:	13-14 transports and two light aircraft
State and Regional authorities:	6-8
Private companies:	13
Privately-owned aircraft:	105-107
Total:	**412-427**

Personnel
More than 300 airmen were missing from the muster-roll within a week of the uprising. Some, including many of the most skilled and experienced pilots, had joined the Nationalists, some had been killed by one side or the other during the first days of fighting, the Director General de Aeronáutica himself having been executed by the Nationalists at Saragossa. Others had simply deserted and gone into hiding. On the Republican side, command devolved upon Coronel Ignacio Hidalgo de Cisneros, an aristocrat who later joined the Communists, his chief staff officers being Cdte Ángel Pastor Velasco and Cdte Antonio Camacho. On the Nationalist side, Gen Franco appointed Gen Alfredo Kindelán,

one of the first pilots in Spain and an important Monarchist conspirator, as chief of the Arma de Aviación, a post he held throughout the civil war.

The Republican air forces

The Aviación Militar and Aeronáutica Naval retained their separate identities until 19 May 1937, although most surviving naval airmen were transferred to land-based units. During the first three months of the war, the prevailing confusion made it difficult for the Jefatura (headquarters) to maintain effective command beyond the Madrid region. The squadrons in Catalonia acted independently of Madrid, but under the authority of the Generalitat (the semi-autonomous regional government at that time dominated by the local Anarchists) in Barcelona until November 1936. The squadrons in the Basque-Asturian zone, such as they were, were in effect an independent third air force.

The International Squadrons
Such information as exists about these, even fifty years after the events, is usually vague and often contradictory. The small bomber squadron under the nominal command of André Malraux, based first at Cuatro Vientos and then at Barajas, seems to have been designated the Escadre España, the French

word 'Escadre' being used instead of the Spanish Escuadra or Escuadrilla, but one finds all three words used in different accounts. Nor is there agreement over who was in operational command of the Escadre, since Malraux was not an airman. In a memoir, Abel Guidez states that it was he, but in a deposition written in 1973 Col Victor Veniel claims the honour for himself. Reports are equally contradictory regarding Malraux. Some, including Guidez and the mercenary 'François M', praise him highly, while others, including Veniel and Hidalgo de Cisneros, dismiss him as a mere adventurer. The foreign fighter pilots seem to have been formed into a separate unit, the Escadrille Lafayette, operating from Getafe, but, on 3 September, following several complaints against their indiscipline, they were combined with the Malraux sqaudron and placed under a Spanish commander. This may explain why a second influx of foreigners (including several Englishmen) who arrived at this time were, after a brief attempt to form a Deuxième Lafayette, incorporated into the Spanish squadrons. Clearly, if it is not too late, much research is needed to clear up this confusion.

First reorganisation
When Prieto became Minister of Marine and Air in Largo Caballero's government early in September 1936, Coronel Pastor Velasco was appointed to the newly created office

of Subsecretario de Aire, but in October was sent to Prague to buy aircraft and replaced by Camacho. Hidalgo de Cisneros, promoted to general, continued as operational air chief. There was, however, no independent air strategy, and bombing and reconnaissance missions, with tiny fighter escorts when possible, were sent out only in response to demands from army or militia units. Hence the fatal dispersal of forces that was to result in the near-elimination of Republican fighter aircraft in the Madrid sector by the end of October. On 27 September the fighter pilots at Getafe made a gesture of protest against this by flying in a formation of all the available fighters – the Hawker Spanish Fury, the Boeing 281, four Dewoitine D.372s, two Loire 46s and two Nieuport 52s – and successfully drove off a formation of nine Nationalist fighters. Their reward was to be reprimanded for disobedience by the *Jefatura*, and the experiment was never repeated.

In December 1936, foreigners who had not already returned home were re-formed into a single unit, the Escadre André Malraux, and transferred, after a brief stay at Alcalá de Herares, to Albacete. In January 1937 the escadre took part in the disastrous Málaga campaign, after which the remnant was moved to La Señera, Valencia, where it stayed until it was disbanded in the early summer of 1937. Malraux himself left Spain in December 1936, and

returned only to make his film *Sierra de Teruél* in 1937 and 1938.

The Russians
The first Russian contingent was formed into Grupo 12, consisting of eight escadrillas:

Escuadrilla 'Palancar' (Pavel Richagov)	I-15 Chato
Escuadrilla 'Tarkov' (Sergei Tarkhov)	I-15 Chato
1ª Mosca (A Minaev)	I-16 Mosca
2ª Mosca (Pleschenkov)	I-16 Mosca
1ª Katiuska (E Schacht)	SB-2M100A Katiuska
2ª Katiuska (V Khalzunov)	SB-2M100A Katiuska
1ª Rasante (Vochev)	R-5 Rasante
2ª Rasante (?)	R-5 Rasante

Spanish and other non-Russian airmen were incorporated into all units, except the Mosca squadrons, from the beginning. In December 1936 all civil aircraft were incorporated into the Aviación Militar, though LAPE aircraft retained their civil registrations and fleet numbers. In January 1937 Capitán Andrés García Lacalle, a veteran of the early air fighting at Getafe, was appointed to command the 'Palancar' escuadrilla, re-formed with Spanish and American pilots and renamed 'Escuadrilla Lacalle'.

Successive reorganisations
From the fragmentary evidence

A Koolhoven FK 51 of the night-fighting squadron of the Republican air force at Manises, Valencia. (Laureau)

available, it is difficult to form a coherent picture of the organisation of the Republican air forces during 1937 and 1938. For example, at some time in December 1936, or perhaps January 1937, the I-16 Mosca escuadrillas were formed into Grupo 21, the I-15 Chato escuadrillas into Grupo 26, and the R-5 Rasante escuadrillas into Grupo 15, although this last was soon disbanded. Grupo 30 (RZ Natachas) was formed in March or April 1937. However, Largo Caballero's government fell on 15 May 1937 and was succeeded by that of Juan Negrín, with Prieto as Defence Minister, on 17 May. On 19 May 1937 a decree was published abolishing the Aviación Militar and Aeronaútica Naval and replacing them with the Fuerzas Aéreas Republicanas Españolas (FARE). Republican Spain was divided into eight Air Regions (Regiones Aéreas), replacing the Escuadras: Madrid, Guadalajara and Cuenca; Murcia, from Hellin to Almería; Catalonia and eastern Aragon; Valencia, but including Alicante; Cuidad Reál, and parts of Extremadura; the Basque-Asturian enclave; Albacete and La Mancha; and Jaén and eastern Andalusia.

The principal function of these Air Regions was the construction and maintenance of aerodromes. Upon their arrival the Russians had introduced a policy of laying out a vast number of landing grounds, more than 400 being built in the main Republican zone (and more than fifty in the Madrid sector alone) during 1937, most of them camouflaged to appear from the air as farmsteads, abandoned mansions or castles, beside woods. Republican escuadrillas were then constantly kept on the move from field to field, sometimes as often as twice in a day, to minimise the dangers of air attack.

The Escuadra was reinstated as a functional, instead of a geographical, unit, roughly corresponding to the pre-Second-World-War 'Commands' of the Royal Air Force. The structure of the FARE seems, therefore, to have been roughly as follows:

Escuadra Núm 11 de Caza (Fighter Wing No 11):

A Caudron C.600 Aiglon with airmen and two armed Republican militiamen. Although they were employed chiefly as trainers, a few C.600s were used to land agents behind Nationalist lines. Perhaps this was one of them. (Laureau)

Grupo 21 (I-16 Mosca):– At first of four escuadrillas. The 5ª and 6ª Escuadrillas formed in October 1937 and the 7ª in July 1938.

A few Spanish and American pilots joined the Mosca escuadrillas in June 1937. The number of Spanish Mosca pilots rapidly increased thereafter. On 8 October 1937 Manual Aguirre became the first Spaniard to command a Mosca escuadrilla (the 1ª), and in December 1937 he was promoted to command the whole Grupo. The 2ª and 3ª escuadrillas were transferred to the Basque-Asturian zone during the summer of 1937. Most of the aircraft were lost by the end of the campaign, and the units were recreated in the main zone in October 1937. The 5ª Escuadrilla remained all-Russian until its dissolution in August 1938.

Grupo 26 (I-15 Chato): Four escuadrillas. The Escuadrilla *Lacalle* was re-formed with Spanish pilots and transferred to the Basque zone, Lacalle being sent to the USSR in charge of the 2ª Promoción (Training Course). The 1ª Escuadrilla remained largely Russian until May 1938, the other escuadrillas being largely or entirely Spanish from May 1937 onwards.

Escuadra Núm. (?) de Bomardeo

Grupo 12 (SB Katiuska): Three escuadrillas of ten aircraft each. Disbanded October 1937.

Grupo 24 (SB Katiuska): Three escuadrillas of ten aircraft each. A 4ª Escuadrilla was created in November 1937 out of the remains of Grupo 12. (For subsequent history, see SB-2M100A.)

Grupo 30 (Natacha): For history, see RZ Natacha.

Escuadra Núm. 7 Mixto (a mixed wing of three Grupos)

Grupo 71: Created autumn 1937. four escuadrillas: 1ª Escuad. (ten Dewoitine D.371s, two Dewoitine D.510THs, two Fiat C.R.32s).
2ª Escuad. (nine or ten Letov S 231s).
3ª Escuad. (six Gourdou-Lesuerre GL 633s).
4ª Escuad. (Aero A-101s).

Grupo 72: Created autumn 1937. 1ª Escuadrilla (R-5 Rasantes, Vultee V1-As, Northrop 2D and 5B Gamma).
2ª Escuad. (Potez 54, Bloch MB 210, Savoia-Marchetti S.81).

Grupo 73: Vickers Vildebeest *et al*

Independent Grupos: Grupos 28 (Grumman GE-23), 16, 27, 29, equipment not recorded.

The Basque-Asturian zone
Although nominally under the authority of the Republican air forces, in practice the units in this zone were obliged to act independently. Until September 1936 the only aircraft in the north were a D.H.80A Puss Moth and Potez 36/13 at Bilbao, and the little Guinea-Severt 2DDM at Llanes in the Asturias, joined by two Breguet 19s on 4 August, the General Aircraft Monospar ST-12 from the government photographic unit, also on 4 August, and on 14 August by a Miles Hawk Major and a Falcon Major flown, via France, from England. In September and October 1936 there arrived from the main zone the Fokker F.VIIb3m/M No 20/1, the D.H.89M No 22/1, six Breguet 19s, four Savoia-Marchetti S.62s and two CASA-Vickers Vildebeests. In November four Gourdou-Lesuerre GL-32s arrived from France and thirty I-15 Chatos from the USSR, followed in February 1937 by the Lockheed Vega, Sirius, and Orion from Mexico, and in March by seven Letov S 231s from Czechoslovakia. Two Chatos and two Letovs were destroyed in accidents before going into service. Spanish Nationalist authors have added sundry Potez 54s and Bloch MB 200s to the list, but all the evidence is against both assertions, as well as the claim that the Basques obtained four Dewoitine D.373s (naval versions of the D.371s). At the end of June 1937 eight Bristol Bulldogs and eight Potez 25s, bought from Estonia, were unloaded at Musel, in the Asturias. Finally, in response to desperate pleas for aircraft from the Basque President, José Aguirre, the Republicans sent one escuadrilla of Chatos and two of Moscas between May and September 1937. Against the combined strength of the Condor Legion and Aviazione Legionaria, this tiny collection of assorted and mostly obso-

The training base at El Carmolí, near Cartagena, On the left are three I-15 Chatos, two Romano R.82s and three Nieuport 52s, in the middle a line of Caudron C.600s and C.601s, Gil Pazó GP-1s and Miles Hawk Majors, and on the right a line of de Havilland Tiger Moths and Moth Majors. (Arráez)

lete aircraft, operating from primitive airstrips in narrow valleys often within sight of the front, could offer little effective resistance. During the Basque campaign some French sympathisers created the airline Air Pyrenées, whose aircraft are listed in Appendix I.

Training
Most of the Republican training bases were located in the province of Murcia in south-eastern Spain:
Primary Training: Los Gerónimos, El Carmolí, La Ribera and Alcantarilla.

Selection: El Palmar. (D.H.9 *et al*)

Transformation: La Ribera (San Javier) and Lorca. (Breguet 19, D.H.9)

Combat: Archena. (Morane 341, Dewoitine D.372, Focke-Wulf Fw 56, Nieuport 52).

High-speed-fighter training: El Carmolí, near Cartagena, the equipment being four I-16 UTI two-seaters and a few I-16s.

Multi-engined flying-training: Totana, the equipment including Fokker F.VIIb3ms, D.H.84s, D.H.89s and Potez 54s and Bloch MB 210s lent from time to time by the FARE.

Night flying: El Carmolí, the principal aircraft being converted Koolhoven FK 51s, Breguet 19s and Hanriot H-439s.

Aerobatics: Reus, near Tarragona, and Celrá, near the French frontier of Catalonia. Also a school at San Javier (La Ribera). (MS 341/345, MS 181, MS 230, Romano R.82.)

Observers, gunners and armourers: Los Alcázares. (D.H.9, F.VIIb3m)

Radio operators and technicians: Paterna, Valencia.

Mechanics: Godella, Valencia.

Aerial photography: San Clemente, province of Teruél.

Training abroad
USSR: Three courses (*promociones*) of 195-200 airmen each were trained in the Soviet Union, the first leaving Spain in November 1936 and returning in July 1937. The pilots were trained at Kirovabad, in the Caucasus, and the rest at Kharkov. The 2ª Promoción returned to Spain in December 1937,

and the 3ª in the early summer of 1938.

France: About 250 pilots received flying training at various aero clubs and flying schools in France, under what were intended to be conditions of secrecy. The known locations were:

Agen – Aéro-Club Populaire d'Agen, at Villeneuve-sur-Lot. The training was reportedly under the direction of Victor Laffont.

Bourges – École Hanriot at Moulin-sur-Yévre and Lissay-Lochty.

Coulommiers – Le Cercle Aéronautique de Coulommiers et de la Brie. The flying field, 'slightly smaller than a football pitch', was at Boissy-le-Châtel.

Graulhet (Tarne) – Air Languedoc, closed in 1937.

Meaux – Lejeune Aviation, at Isles-Les-Villenoy, near Esbly.

Orly – École Potez and École de Tourisme.

Royan – Aero-Club de Royan.

Aerodrome owned by Caudron, probably leased to Lejeune for training Spanish pilots.

The courses seem to have been established under the auspices of the Federación Populaire des Sports Aéronautiques, originally instituted by the French air minister, Pierre Cot, to provide a reserve of trained pilots in the event of war and analagous, therefore, to the British Civil Air Training Scheme. Its director of training was Joséph Sadi-Lecointe, formerly the setter of several international speed and altitude records and chief test pilot of Nieuport-Delage and Loire-Nieuport. The aircraft employed at the above schools included D.H.60 Moths, Potez 600s, Potez 25s, Hanriot H-437s, Caudron C.272/5 Lucioles, Caudron C.600 Aiglons and Mauboussin trainers. A number of the machines later found their way to Republican Spain, while several of the schools, such as Le

Three de Havilland Dragon Rapides, imported clandestinely from the manufacturer via France, fly over a Dragonfly and another Dragon Rapide at the Escuela de Polimotores (multi-engined flying school) at Totana, Murcia. (Arráez)

Savoia-Marchetti S.79s of the Aviazione Legionaria approach Barcelona through late evening cloud. (Emiliani)

Cercle Aéronautique de Coulommiers, Air Languedoc, and Lejeune Aviation, acted as intermediaries in the purchase of aircraft by the Spanish Republicans.

Aircraft Industry
During the first weeks of the civil war, Hispano-Suiza at Guadalajara and CASA at Getafe concentrated their efforts on the repair of Nieuport 52s and Breguet 19s. In October 1936 both factories were moved for safety to Muscia, being distributed among workshops, churches, monasteries and other convertible large buildings in and around Alicante and Cartagena. Hispano-Suiza was redesignated SAF-1, and CASA SAF-5 ('SAF' has been decoded variously as Servicio de Aviación y Fabricación and Subsecretario de Aire – Fabrica). Early in 1937 they were combined into SAF-15 under a single administration, with its own aerodrome at La Rabasa, Alicante. The work at SAF-15 was multifarious. It included repairing I-16s, re-engining the Fw 56 Stösser, converting the

Vultee V1-As into bombers, and the production of GP-1 trainers, Fokker D.XXIs and C.Xs, and I-16s. Other new factories in Murcia included SAF-2 (the repair of SB Katiuskas, RZ Natachas, etc.), SAF-4 (the repair of engines and the manufacture of armaments and undercarriages), SAF-6 (wheels, propellers, radiators), and SAF-22 (the repair of trainers and production of a small series of D.H.60GIIIA Moth Majors). Another group of aviation factories was established in Catalonia. The first was a workshop on the Air France aerodrome at Barcelona, in which the director, Gaston Vedel, allowed the repair of Potez 54s. The Aeronáutica Naval workshop was moved to a requisitioned cloth factory at Sadadell and, designated SAF-3/16, was used for the repair of aircraft and the production of I-15 Chatos, with subsidiary workshops at Reus, Molins, Villafranca, Rubí and Vich. Until his arrest by the Soviet NKVD in the summer of 1937, on the grounds that a number of Anarchists and other anti-Stalinist left-wingers were employed in the workshops, the German aircraft builder Antonius Raab (late of Raab-Katzenstein) played a leading part in establishing this group of factories.

The Nationalist Air Forces

By 20 July 1936 Gen Mola's air force, based at Gamonal Aerodrome (Burgos), Logroño and León, possessed about thirty Breguet 19s, one D.H.89M, one Junkers F 13 and a few light aircraft, but no fighters. During the first two weeks of August these were reinforced by four D.H.89s, two Fokker F.VIIb3ms and one Fokker F.XII (followed by a second F.XII on 6 September) flown from England, and a few Nieuport 52s, Breguet 19s, a single-engined Fokker F.VIIa, and three Fokker F.VIIb3m/Ms flown up from the south. At the beginning of September 1936 the five D.H.89 Dragon Rapides, four Fokker F.VIIb3ms (one F.VIIb3m/M having crashed at Jerez in August), the F.VIIa and two F.XIIs were formed into the Grupo Fokker-Dragon under the command of Maj J A Ansaldo. He was one of four monarchist brothers, all pilots, and had been badly burned in the crash that had killed Gen Sanjurjo (see D.H.80A Puss Moth).

In the south, Gen Franco's rather ramshackle collection of aircraft, many of which had been under repair or had been sabotaged during the uprising on 17-18 July 1936, was augmented from the beginning of August by aircraft and airmen from Germany and Italy:

11 Junkers Ju 52/3ms: Flown from Germany, via Italy, to Spanish Morocco, 28 July – *c* 10 August.

9 Junkers Ju 52/3ms: By sea to Cádiz, arrived 6 August 1936.

6 Heinkel He 51s: By sea to Cádiz, arrived 6 August 1936.

9 (out of 12) Savoia-Marchetti S.81s: By air to Spanish Morocco, 30 July 1936.

12 Fiat C.R.32s: By sea to Spanish Morocco, 13-14 August 1936.

9 Heinkel He 51s: Arrived 17 August 1936, via Portugal.

9 Fiat C.R.32s: 28 August 1936, arrived Vigo.

3 Fiat C.R.32s: 3 September 1936, arrived Vigo.

9 Heinkel He 51s: Arrived early September 1936, via Portugal.

20 Heinkel He 46s: Arrived mid-September 1936, via Portugal.

9 Heinkel He 46s: Arrived late September 1936, via Portugal.

1 Cant Z.501: Arrived Cádiz, *c* 20 September 1936.

10 IMAM Ro 37s: Arrived 29 September 1936.

12 Fiat C.R.32s: Arrived 29 September 1936.

The chief uncertainty in the above figures concerns the Fiat C.R.32s, for which some authors have given a smaller number. At the same time, the number of C.R.32s that arrived on 3 September has sometimes been given as nine. An Italian official document quoted by Angelo Emiliani, however, states that the number of Fiat C.R.32s delivered from 14 August to 3 September 1936 was twenty-four, or two *squadriglii*. This seems rational and, to square with it,

the delivery on 3 September has been reduced to three, on the assumption that there must have been confusion between the two deliveries of 28 August and 3 September 1936.

In all, then, there is a total of 129 military aircraft, of which 73 came from Germany and 56 from Italy, delivered to the Nationalists on the Spanish mainland between 28 July and 29 September 1936. In addition, the following were delivered to Mallorca:

3 Savoia-Marchetti S.55X: Arrived 18 August 1936.

3 Fiat C.R.32: Arrived 27-28 August 1936.

3 Macchi M.41: Arrived 27-28 August 1936.

3 Savoia-Marchetti S.81: Arrived early September 1936.

These bring the total to 141, which may be broken down as follows:

From Germany, 73 aircraft
20 Junkers Ju 52/3m
24 Heinkel He 51
29 Heinkel He 46

From Italy, 68 aircraft
39 Fiat C.R.32 (36 to the mainland)
12 Savoia-Marchetti S.81 (9 to the mainland).
10 IMAM Ro 37
1 Cant Z.501
3 Savoia-Marchetti S.55X (Mallorca)
3 Macchi M.41 (Mallorca)

As explained earlier, the Italians were incorporated into the Spanish Tercio de Extranjeros, or Foreign Legion, the 1ª Escuadrilla de Caza (the Fiat C.R.32 squadron) being nicknamed La Cucaracha, or 'Cockroach', probably after the song. The Germans remained under Operation Magic Fire (*Unternehmen Zauberfeuer*) with strict orders to avoid combat with the enemy, but after three Heinkel He 51s had been damaged by Spanish pilots they managed to have this order rescinded. The raid on Getafe and Barajas, on 23 August 1936, was carried out entirely by Spaniards,

however. A few of the best Spanish fighter pilots – Joaquín García Morato, Ángel Salas, Julio Salvador and Miguel García Pardo – were allowed to fly with the Cucaracha escuadrilla from time to time. The Heinkel He 46s were handed straight over to the Spaniards.

After the link-up between Gen Franco's and Gen Mola's armies in the latter part of August 1936, the Nationalist Breguet 19s were formed into a single Escuadra A and the Junkers Ju 52/3ms, both Spanish- and German-flown, into Escuadra B. Both units were disbanded in November, followed by the Fokker-Dragon group in December 1936. The Spanish Nationalists purchased three He 51s by public subscription, but all three were destroyed on 29 December 1936 during an attack on their aerodrome at Caudé (Teruel) by I-15s.

With the creation in November and December 1936 of the Condor Legion and Aviazione Legionaria, the Nationalist air force became three distinct entities.

Condor Legion (Commander: Gen Hugo von Sperrle, replaced on 30 October 1937, by Gen Helmuth Volkmann). All wings, squadrons and units were designated by a letter, followed by the number '88':

Jagdgruppe 88 (J/88):
1.J/88: He 51 until Sep 37, then Bf 109B.
2.J/88: He 51 until Mar 37, then Bf 109B.
3.J/88: He 51 until Apr & Jul 37, then Bf 109C & D.
4.J/88: He 51. Disbanded Mar 37; re-formed, with He 51, Oct 37; disbanded Jul 38.
VJ/88: Bf 109 V3, V4; He 112 V5; Hs 123.

Kampfgruppe 88 (K/88):
1.K/88: Ju 52 until Mar 38, then He 111E-1.
2.K/88: Ju 52 until summer 37, then Do 17E, then He 111E-1.
3.K/88: Ju 52 until Jul 37, then He 111B, then He 111E-1.
4.K/88: Formed Jun 37 on He 111B, then He 111E-1.
VB/88: Formed Feb 37, He 111B, Do 17E, Ju 86D. Disbanded Jul 37.

Aufklärungstaffel 88 (A/88):
A/88: He 70E and He 70F until May 37, then Do 17F; later Do 17P, Hs 126. Also one kette of He 45 throughout.

See-Aufklärungstaffel 88 (AS/88):
AS/88: He 59B-2, He 60E, Arado 95E (transferred to Grupo 64).

Other sections were:
S/88: (*Stab*) Command and HQ.
LN/88: Radio communications etc.
F/88: (*Flak*) Anti-aircraft batteries.
P/88: (*Park*) Maintenance and supply. There were also units of armoured cars, transports, naval patrol and for training.

Aviazione Legionaria (Commanders: Col Vicenzo Velardo, replaced in June 1937 by Gen Mario Bernasconi)

3° Stormo Caccia (3rd Fighter wing):
VI Gruppo: Gamba di Ferro (Iron Leg) 31ª, 32ª, 33ª Squadriglia (C.R.32).
XVI Gruppo Cucaracha (Cockroach) 24ª, 25ª, 26ª Squadriglia (C.R.32).
XXIII Gruppo Asso di Bastoni (Ace of Spades) 18ª, 19ª, 20ª Squadriglia (C.R.32).
XXII Gruppo Auton. Osservazione Acrea Linci (Lynx), 120ª, 128ª Squadriglia (Ro 37). These two squadriglie were originally the 1ª and 2ª Escuadrillas de Reconocimiento of the Aviación de El Tercio.
Squadriglia Autonoma Mitragliamento 'Frecce' (Arrows) (C.R.32bis).

21° Stormo Bombardamento Pesante (21st Heavy Bomber Wing):
XXIV Gruppo Pipistrelli (Bat) 213ª, 214ª Squadriglia (S.81).
XXV Gruppo Pipistrelli (Bat) 215ª, 216ª Squadriglia (S.81). The 216ª Squad. formed in 1938 out of aircraft transferred from Mallorca. Disbanded, and aircraft transferred to Spaniards, on 30 September 1938.

111° Stormo Bombardamento Veloce (111th High Speed Bomber Wing):
XXIX Gruppo Sparvieri (Sparrow Hawk) 280ª, 289ª Squadriglia (S.79).
XXX Gruppo Sparvieri 281ª, 285ª Squadriglia (S.79).
The 111° Stormo was formed in April 1938 with the arrival of the XXX Gruppo.
XXXV Gruppo Auton. Misto. 230ª, 231ª Squadriglia (B.R.20). 65ª Squadriglia (Ba 65).
  Gruppo Sperimentale Caccia. Formed Mar 39 (G.50).

Aviazione Legionaria delle Baleari
X Gruppo Auton. Caccia Baleari 101ª, 102ª Squadriglia (C.R.32).
XXV Gruppo Bombardamento Notturno Pipistrelli delle Baleari ('Bats of the Balearics') 215ª, 252ª Squadriglia (S.81).

8° Stormo Bombardamento Veloce:
XXVII Gruppo Falchi delle Baleari ('Falcons of the Balearics') 18ª, 52ª Squadriglia (S.79).
XXVIII Gruppo Falchi delle Baleari ('Falcons of the Balearics') 10ª, 19ª Squadriglia (S.79).
The XXVIII Gruppo arrived in 1937, and the 8° Stormo became a complete unit after the arrival of the XXVII Gruppo in January 1938.

Spanish Nationalist Arma de Aviación
As on the Republican side, the creation of a Spanish-manned air arm progressed as trained crews and aircraft became available. The list on page 28, based on information collected and published by Gen Jesús Salas Larrazábal, deals with the Grupos only. Details of the Escuadrillas will be found under the respective aircraft types.

Training
In August 1936 the Nationalists organised a few intensive courses for air gunners, observers and navigators at Tablada, Seville. Meanwhile, hurried preparations were made for a flying training school at an aerodrome built on the land of El Copero, an estate 15km south of Seville, and another on an aerodrome which had been built at La Parra, 10km north of Jerez de la Fontera, as a landing ground for the airlift in August 1936. El Copero opened in November 1936, and here the 1ª Escuela Elemental de Vuelo (1st Elementary Flying School) was established, with a second school at Cáceres in Extremadura. The driving force behind the extremely efficient Nationalist flying training organisation was Comandante Gerardo Fernández Pérez, who took command at El Copero and Jerez at the beginning of 1937. From the spring of 1937 onwards the Nationalist training schools were:

Primary: El Copero. Cáceres was moved in April 1937 to Las Bardocas, an island on the Guadiana River, near Badajoz.
Selection: El Copero
Transformation: Jerez de la Frontera.
Aerobatics and fighter: El Copero, Jerez, Villanubla (Valladolid), Gallur (Saragossa).
Observers, bombardiers, navigators etc: Logroño, Tetuán, Los Rompedizos (Málaga).
Blind and night flying: Olmedo, later Matacán (Salamanca).

Aircraft used for pilot training

A Heinkel He 60E of 2-G-62-73 over the Mediterranean shortly before the end of the civil war. (Arráez)

Fighter:

1-G-2	May 37	He 51
2-G-3	May 37	C.R.32
3-G-3	Jan 38	C.R.32
4-G-2	Jul 38	He 51
5-G-5	Jan 39	He 112B & Bf 109B

Army Co-operation

1-G-10	Oct 36	Bre 19	Disbanded Jun 37, became 5-G-17 (Aero A-101).
2-G-10	Oct 36	Bre 19	Disbanded Jun 37, became 6-G-15 (He 45).
3-G-10	Oct 36	Bre 19	Renamed 1-G-10 Jun 37.
4-G-10	Oct 36	Bre 19	History as 3-G-10.
5-G-10	Oct 36	Bre 19	Became 2-G-10 (Bre 19) Jun 37.
1-G-11	Jan 37	He 46	Became 3-G-11 Jun 37.
2-G-11	Jan 37	He 46	History as 1-G-11.
1-G-12	Feb 37	Ro 37bis	Became 2-G-12 Jun 37.
7-G-14	Oct 37	He 70E	
8-G-18	Oct 38	Ca 310	
9-G-18	Oct 38	Ca 310	

Bomber:

Grupo Fokker-Dragon: Disbanded Dec 36.

1ªGrupo de Ju 52, formed Nov 36, disbanded May 37, became 3-G-28 (S.79) Aug 37.

2ª Grupo de Ju 52, formed Nov 36, became 1-G-22 May 37 (Ju 52).

3ª Grupo de Ju 52, formed Dec 36, became 2-G-22 May 37 (Ju 52).

3-G-28	Aug. 37	S.79
4-G-28	Oct 37	S.79
5-G-28	Oct 37	S.79
6-G-28	Jun 38	S.79
7-G-20	Jun 38	Fokker F.VIIb3m, F.XII. Disbanded by Sep 38.
8-G-27	Jul 38	Do 17E
10-G-25	Aug 38	He 111B
11-G-25	Feb 39	He 111B
15-G-21	Sep 38	S.81
16-G-21	Sep 38	S.81
17-G-21	Sep 38	S.81
18-G-21	Sep 38	S.81

Seaplanes and Flying-boats:

1-G-70 Oct 36 Dornier Wal. Disbanded Apr 38, re-formed Oct 38.

2-G-62 Apr 37 Cant Z.501. Became 2-G-62-70 (Cant Z.501 and Dornier Wal) Apr 38, and 2-G-62-73 (Cant Z.501 and Z.506B) in Oct 38.

E-60 Jun 37 He 60. Incorporated into 2-G-62-73 in Nov 38.

During the second half of 1938 the Nationalist air arm was reorganised into four divisions consisting of two Air Brigades, a fighter Escuadra, and a division containing the remaining independent groups and small units:

1ªBrigada Aérea Hispana
1ª Escuadra 1-G-27 (Do 17E), 2-G-22 (Ju 52).
2ª Escuadra 16-G-21 (S.81), 17-G-21 (S.81)
5ª Escuadra 15-G-21 (S.81), 18-G-21 (S.81), 7-G-14 (He 70E).

2ª Brigada Aérea Hispaña
3ª Escuadra 3-G-28 (S.79), 4-G-28 (S.79).
4ª Escuadra 5-G-28 (S.79), 6-G-28 (S.79).
6ª Escuadra 8-G-18 (Ca 310), 9-G-18 (Ca 310).
7ª Escuadra de Caza 2-G-3 (C.R.32), 3-G-3 (C.R.32), 5-G-5 (He 112B and Bf 109B), Jan 39.

Independent groups:
1-G-2 and 4-G-2 (He 51); 1-G-8 (captured I-15 Chatos); 2-G-10 (Bre 19); 4-G-12 (Ro 37bis); 6-G-15 (He 45 and two He 46); 5-G-17 (Aero A-101); 10-G-25 and 11-G-25 (He 111B); 8-G-27 (Do 17E); 1-G-70 (Dornier Wal); 6-G-62-73 (Cant Z.501, Z.506B and He 60).

Independent Escuadrillas
8-E-3 (C.R.32); 3-E-14 (He 70E); 4-E-14 (He 70E), as part of Grupo Mixto 86-70 (Hs 123 and Ju 86).

included D.H. Moths, D.H.9s, Arado Ar 66s, Bücker Jungmanns and Jungmeisters, Ro 41s, PWS 10s, Gotha Go 145s and Breguet 19s. Aircraft for aircrew training included Fokker F.VIIb3ms, Ju 52s and D.H.89s.

Aircraft Industry
At the beginning of the civil war the Nationalists captured the Regional Air Parks at León, and Tablada, Seville, of which the second was by far the more important. During the first nine months of the war all assembly and repair work was carried out in the depôt workshops at Tablada until, in the summer of 1937, the assembly of German aircraft was transferred to León. The Hawker Spanish Fury captured near Badajoz in August 1936 was rebuilt at Tablada and, after a crash, rebuilt again. It was here, too, that José Pazó, who defected to the Nationalists, designed and built his P.IV monoplane (See González-Gil-Pazó aircraft).

Meanwhile, personnel of the Hispaño-Suiza concern who had been in the zone occupied by the Nationalists during the first weeks of the war founded a new factory in the Triana district of Seville, where Fiat C.R.32s which had suffered major damage were rebuilt, about fifty being completed by the end of the war. At Cádiz, CASA undertook the repair of Dornier Wals and the replacing of their Lorraine engines by Isotta-Fraschinis. In 1938 CASA bought land alongside Tablada Aerodrome and signed contracts for the production of He 111s at Tablada and Bücker Bü 131 Jungmanns at Cádiz. None were completed, however, before the end of the civil war. These three factories, and that at Getafe after the end of the war, provided the basis of Spain's post-war aircraft industry. In 1938 an Experimental Aircraft Centre was established at Jerez de la Frontera. This became responsible for the completion of I-16s recovered at the end of the war, production lines being set up in requisitioned sherry bodegas near the town.

Colours, camouflage, registrations and insignia

Prewar

Military and naval aircraft were painted with aluminium dope, the metal surfaces being left plain and polished. The national insignia of the Spanish Republic consisted of red, yellow and purple roundels on the outer wings and red, yellow and purple bands on the rudder.

Registrations
The Spanish word for 'registration' is *matriculación*, (plural *matriculaciones*), but it also denotes any kind of military serial.

Civil:
Until 1931 the Spanish national letter was 'M'. This was followed by four letters which identified the individual aeroplane. In 1931 this became 'EC-' ('España: Civil') with three letters. Thus the registration of the Fokker F.VIIb3m M-CAKK was changed to EC-AKK. Letters were allocated *not* in alphabetical sequence, but by a permutation method intended to facilitate quick recognition from a distance. Thus three F.VIIb3ms acquired in 1933 were registered EC-AAU, 'AUA and 'UAA, and other aircraft registered at

about the same time became 'UUA (D.H. Fox Moth), 'AUU (Potez 36) and 'UAU (D.H. Moth).

Government-owned machines were marked EC- followed by a number and a second -E (e.g. the D.H.85 Leopard Moth EC-5-E belonging to the Dirección General de Aeronáutica). This system continued to be applied to many civil aircraft imported clandestinely during the civil war (perhaps all, except those transferred to LAPE). Before the war, civil aircraft imported were temporarily registered EC-W followed by a 'ferry number'. While under evaluation as a military liaison (*enlace militar*) aircraft, a Polish R.W.D.9 carried the registration EM-W46 ('España: Militar').

Military and Naval:
Until about 1926, military and naval aircraft were likewise registered by a letter system, the M being followed by a second M and a letter denoting the type of machine, and two more letters for individual identification. For example, a de Havilland D.H.9 would be M-MH- and a Dornier Wal M-MW-. However, some also received serial numbers, which were painted on the rudder, so that the D.H.9 M-MHAS was also H-19. In 1926 the Aviación Militar changed to a number system, and the Aeronáutica Naval to a modified letter system.

Aviación Militar:
Each type of aircraft was allotted an identifying type-code number, which was followed by a serial num-

The strange and shapely Fairchild 91 was captured en route to Spain by the Nationalists and used for coastal reconnaissance.

ber assigned to each aircraft as it entered service. This service serial number was painted in *black* on the middle, yellow, band on the rudder: e.g. the Breguet 19 with 12-162 on the rudder was the 162nd Breguet 19 to be taken into service. In addition, the Grupo number and the number of the aircraft in the Grupo were painted in large black figures on the fuselage sides, and sometimes on the top surface of the upper wing as well. Thus the Breguet 19 12-162 was also 23-32, denoting it to be the 32nd Breguet 19 of Grupo 23. There were exceptions to this practice, however. Neither the Fokker F.VIIb3m/Ms nor the D.H.89M Dragon Rapides, for example, had Grupo numbers, but simply type and serial numbers painted in white on the fuselage. (Thus the Fokkers were registered 20-1 to 20-4 (and 20-5 and -6 after the transfer of two from LAPE in 1935), and the D.H.89Ms were 22-1 to 22-3.)

Known pre-civil-war type-code numbers are:

3	Nieuport 52	22	D.H.89M
4	Hawker Spanish Fury	32	D.H.60 Moth
12	Breguet 19	33	D.H.82 Tiger Moth
15	D.H.9	34	D.H.60 Moth Major
20	Fokker F.VIIb3m/M	49	Junkers F 13 and K 30

The Cierva Autogiros (C.19 Mk.IV and C.30A) were originally registered 41-1 to 41-3. Photographic evidence shows that in 1935 they bore the registrations Y-1-1 to Y-1-3, and 21-1 to 21-3, though which they bore in July 1936 is not certain.

Finally, the fighter Grupos bore the following emblems:

Grupo 11: a black panther, *passant*, on the fin.

Grupo 12: a black stag, leaping, in a circle, on the fuselage.

Grupo 13: a four-leaf clover on a black disc, on the fin.

Aeronáutica Naval:

The naval aircraft, likewise, had two sets of registrations, EA- followed by three letters and a type-letter followed by a serial number. Thus the Hispano E.30 EA-HAA was also H-1, and the Savoia-Marchetti S.62 EA-BAB was also S-1. By 1936 the EA- registrations were no longer painted on the flying-boats or Vildebeests.

Known type codes are:

Dornier Wal	D
Hispano E.30	H
Macchi M.18	M
Martinsyde F.4	MS
Savoia-Marchetti S.62	S
Vickers Vildebeest	T

The S.62s had an emblem painted on the prow, depicting a witch seated on a flaming exahust pipe and looking through a telescope. The emblem of the Vildebeest *escuadrillas* was a plunging dolphin.

Civil War

Republicans

By the beginning of August 1936 it had become practice to overpaint the roundels with broad red bands. Similar, or broader, bands were painted round the rear fuselage, and sometimes the whole of the fuselage from the cockpit or the wing trailing-edge to the tail was painted red. A primitive camouflage of green or ochre blotches was often dabbed on the bare metal or doped surfaces not already covered with red, though degree and pattern seem to have been left to the inventiveness of the mechanic detailed to do it. As the war progressed, the camouflage of all aircraft became more thorough, though there seems to have been no regulated system. Individual variations, when known, are mentioned under the types concerned. The Loire 46s, which arrived on 7 September 1936, had their French roundels painted over as red discs, *á la Japonnaise*, though this was probably changed later. The Dewoitine D.371s diverted from the Armée de l'Air in 1937 kept their French colouring (dark green, with sky blue undersurfaces) and even their Armée de l'Air *matriculations*, though for how long is again uncertain. The Swissair Lockheed Orions retained their bright red livery until at least June 1937, while other aircraft were painted dark grey or blue (Seversky SEV-3, D.H.90 Dragonfly). The Russian fighters retained their V-VS regulation dark green, with sky blue undersides, throughout the war, though I-15s and I-15s built in Spain were given wavy or mottled camouflage. The camouflage of the SB Katiuskas varied according to the terrain surrounding the base from which they were operating at any particular time.

Type codes:

The Republicans adopted a letter system based on that of the old Aeronáutica Naval, the letters and numbers being painted in black, or white, on the fuselage sides. When this system came into effect is not certain, but it probably began tentatively early in 1937 and was applied systematically after the creation of the FARE in May 1937.

Known type codes are:

Fighters:

CA	I-15 Chato
CC	I-152 Super-Chato
CM	I-16 Mosca
CH	I-16 (Spanish-built)
CN	Nieuport 52
CD	Dewoitine D.371/372
CE	Dewoitine D.500 (ordered Dec 1936, none delivered)
CW	Dewoitine D.510TH
CF	Fokker D.XXI
CL	Letov S 231, 331, 431
CS	Seversky P-35 (project to build in Spain cancelled)

Bombers:

BB	Marcel Bloch MB 210
BF	Fokker F.XVIII
BK	SB-2M100 Katiuska
BP	Potez 54
BV	Vultee V1-A

Reconnaissance:

RR	R-5 Rasante
RB	Breguet 19 (night-flying training)
RH	D.H.9 (trainer)

Attack:

AD	Grumman GE-23 Delfin

Light Bombers and Liaison:

LA	Airspeed Envoy or Aero A-101
LB	Bellanca 28/70 and 28/90 (28/90, none delivered)
LD	D.H.84 Dragon
LF	Fokker C.X
LG	Gourdou-Leseurre GL 633 B1
LL	Aero A-101 and Ab-101
LN	RZ Natacha
LR	D.H.89 Dragon Rapide
LY	D.H.90 Dragonfly

Transports:

TA	Avia 51
TC	Caudron Göeland
TD	Douglas DC-2
TF	Farman F.402
TG	Northrop 2D Gamma
TH	D.H.87B Hornet Moth
TK	Lockheed Orion
TL	Latecoère 28
TM	General Aircraft Monospar ST-25
TN	Northrop Delta
TP	Spartan Executive
TS	Stinson Reliant
TV	Breguet 470 Fulgur

Ambulance:

SF	Farman F.402 (and probably F.190 etc.)
SM	General Aircraft Monospar ST-25

Flying-boats and seaplanes:

HD	Dornier Wal
HM	Macchi M.18
HS	Savoia-Marchetti S.62
HV	Vickers Vildebeest (seaplane)

Captured aircraft:

FF	Fiat C.R.32
FH	Heinkel He 111B
FM	Messerschmitt Bf 109B
FS	Savoia-Marchetti S.81

Trainers:

EA   Caudron C.600 Aiglon
EC   Saab-SEMA 12
EE   Hispano E.30
EF   Hispano E.34
EG   Gil-Pazó GP-1
EJ   Koolhoven FK 51
EK   Koolhoven FK 51bis
EL   Caudron C.272 Luciole
EM   D.H.60 Moth
EN   Miles aircraft (M2H Hawk Major, M23 Hawk Speed Six, M3 Falcon)
EP   D.H.82 Tiger Moth
EQ   Monocoupe 90-A
ER   Romano R-82
ES
ET
EU   Morane-Saulnier MS 140, MS 230 etc
EW   Focke-Wulf Fw 56 Stösser
EX   Bücker Bü 133 Jungmeister
EY   I-16UTI two-seat trainer
EZ   Hanriot H-182

Amphibian:
XA Reserved for the Fairchild 91 bought from Robert Cuse but captured by the Nationalists on the *Mar Cantábrico*.

The Potez 54s pose a special problem. Those delivered in 1936 were identified by a single letter (See Potez 54). This letter seems to have been retained on the few that survived until late 1937, so that BP-002, for example, still had R painted in white on its fin. A similar 'carry-over' may explain why a D.H.82 Tiger Moth with EM-016 on the fuselage had a large P on its fin.

Some time in 1937, aircraft began to carry individual numbers within the squadron on their fins, usually in white, but sometimes in yellow or orange. Thus the SB Katiuska BK-024 had a large 3 painted in white on its fin. Other machines had this white number only. Similar anomalies can be found among the I-15s and RZ Natachas. On a flight (patrulla) leader's machine, this number was inside a white triangle. A squadron leader's aircraft was identified by a white square, outline only, on the fin, with no number inside.

LAPE aircraft retained their civil registrations, though these do not seem to have been painted on the aircraft at all times. The Fokker F.XX seems to have kept its govern-

The 'Double-Six' emblem of the 3ª Escuadrilla de Moscas.

ment registration EC-45-E for months after it arrived in Spain. Again, LAPE Fleet numbers were usually, but not always, painted on the fin or rudder. Some machines were camouflaged (wavy or mottled); others were painted grey, green or blue, and some (Northrop 1C Delta) left in plain metal finish.

Only the fighter squadrons seem to have employed squadron emblems, and these are briefly described under I-15 and I-16.

Nationalists

Distinctive markings:

At the end of July 1936, Nationalist commanders gave *ad hoc* local instructions that aircraft should be marked in as distinctive a manner as possible, and suggested rows of black bars, black discs, St Andrew's Crosses, etcetera. There followed a short period of considerable confusion, during which aircraft were painted with an extraordinary variety of insignia. Despite regulations issued early in August, variations can be seen in photographs of Nationalist aircraft throughout the war. However, in general, Nationalist insignia consisted of white St Andrew's Crosses on upper and lower surfaces of the

wings, sometimes on black discs. Sometimes there were two or three black stripes between the crosses and the wingtips, or the wingtips were painted white. On each fuselage side was a black disc, sometimes bearing a unit emblem, or (later), the Nationalist Yoke and Arrows device, and sometimes left blank. The rudder was white, with a black St Andrew's Cross on each side. Photographs of Fiat C.R.32s, nevertheless, show some painted as above, others with the St Andrew's Crosses painted on top of the black stripes on the top surface of the upper wing, and with three black stripes against a white ground on the undersurfaces of the lower wings, and with squadron emblems painted on squares, or rectangles, or straight on to the camouflage, in front of the black discs on the fuselage sides, or on the fins. Italian flying-boats and some other aircraft (perhaps while crossing the Mediterranean to Spain, such as He 111s) carried three black stripes on a white ground round the entire rear fuselage.

Camouflage:

At first this was improvised, as on Republican aircraft. The first Italian Fiat C.R.32s to arrive seem to have borne the mottled camouflage of the Regia Aeronautica, while the S.81s were painted cream-yellow. The Balearic squadrons can be identified

Above: *Oblt Knüppel's 'Zylinder Hut' (Top Hat) blazon was adopted by 4.J/88 until March 1937, when it was transferred to 2.J/88, then newly re-equipped with Messerschmitt Bf 109Bs.*

The 'Cadena' (Chain) emblem of the Spanish ground-attack group 1-G-22.

in photographs by their wave-band camouflage, as distinct from the mottled or narrow wavy-stripe camouflage of the Italian mainland units. The Fiat C.R.32s on the Balearics were left, at least until the summer of 1937, in plain aluminium finish.

The German fighters retained the plain light grey of the Luftwaffe fighter units until the spring of 1937, when the grey was blotched over with green. In the Spanish units they were painted with ochre and green wave-band camouflage. Other German aircraft, including those of the He 51 ground-attack staffel 4.J/88, retained their Luftwaffe 'splinter'

camouflage. Thus one can tell from a photograph whether an He 51 was serving with a fighter staffel of J/88 (light grey, later blotched over with green), or 4.J/88 ('splinter' camouflage), or one of the Spanish units (wave-band camouflage). A curious exception was the Heinkel He 70s of A/88 (qv). Aircraft attached to the Condor Legion (including at least two Vultee V1-As) were usually painted with 'splinter' camouflage.

Type-code numbers:
The Nationalists adopted a number system based on that of the old Aviación Militar. The numbers were divided into sequences of about nine,

according to category:

Fighters:
1 Nieuport 52 (later Fiat G.50)
2 Heinkel He 51
3 Fiat C.R.32
4 P.W.S.10
5 Heinkel He 112 V5 and He 112B
6 Messerschmitt Bf 109
7 IMAM Ro 41
8 Breda Ba 64, Heinkel He 112 V9 and captured I-15 Chatos
9 Arado Ar 68E

Attack:
10 CASA-Breguet 19
11 Heinkel He 46
12 IMAM Ro 37bis
13 Not used
14 Heinkel He 70E and He 70F
15 Heinkel He 45
16 Breda Ba 65
17 Aero A-101
18 Vultee V1-A, later Caproni Ca 310
19 Henschel Hs 126

Bombers:
20 Fokker F.VIIb3m and F.XII
21 Savoia-Marchetti S.81
22 Junkers Ju 53/3m
23 Fiat B.R.20
24 Henschel Hs 123
25 Heinkel He 111
26 Junkers Ju 86D
27 Dornier Do 17
28 Savoia-Marchetti S.79
29 Junkers Ju 87A and Ju 87B

Light Aircraft and Trainers:
30 Single-engined light aircraft

Capitán Joaquín García Morato, the highest-scoring fighter pilot of either side in the civil war, with forty accredited victories, and, behind, Capitán Ángel Salas Larrazábal, another distinguished Nationalist pilot and a future Spanish air minister. The circular emblem on the tail of the C.R.32 shows a falcon, a bustard and a blackbird, with the words 'Vista, suerte y al toro' ('A glance, luck and at the bull!'), a bullfighter's saying used at moments of danger and uncertainty. Originally the emblem of the first Spanish Fiat C.R.32 flight, the Patrulla Azul *('Blue Patrol'), it was adopted by the Spanish Fiat C.R.32 groups 2-G-3 and 3-G-3 and, after the war, by the fighter regiments of the Ejercito del Aire.* (Arráez)

31 Twin-engined light aircraft
32 Caproni AP.1
33 Bücker Bü 131 Jungmann
34 Breda Ba 28
35 Bücker Bü 133 Jungmeister
36 Arado Ar 66
37 Light fighter trainers
38 Gotha Go 145

Transports:
40 D.H.89 Dragon Rapide
41 Airspeed Envoy
42 Twin-engined transports
43 Single-engined transports
44 Messerschmitt Bf 108 Taifun
45 Fokker F.VIIb3m and F.XII
46 Fieseler Fi 156 Storch
47 Consolidated Fleetster (post-war)

Flying-boats and seaplanes:
50 Macchi M.41
60 Heinkel He 60
61 Savoia-Marchetti S.62
62 Cant Z.501
63 Fairchild 91
64 Arado Ar 95
70 Dornier Wal
71 Heinkel He 59
72 Junkers Ju 52/3mW
73 Cant Z.506

Captured aircraft (except I-15 Chato):

1W I-16 Mosca (Rata)
2W I-152 (post-war)
3W Letov S.231
4W Hawker Spanish Fury
5W Grumman GE-23
16W R-5 Rasante
17W RZ Natacha
20W SB Katiuska

These type-code numbers were applied to the grupos and escuadrillas of the Spanish Nationalist air arm. However, 2-G-3 should be read as meaning 'Second Group – Fiat C.R.32s', rather than as 'the Second Group *of* Fiat C.R.32s'. A glance at the list of Grupos given earlier will make this clear. The same, of course, applies to the escuadrillas.

The type numbers were painted, in black or white, on the fuselage sides of each aircraft, often (but not always) to the left of the black disc. The serial number of the individual aeroplane (*matriculación* being the word used for this as well) was painted to the right of the disc, or, if not, the two numbers were joined by a hyphen. Thus, 3 ● 51, or 3-51, meant that this was the fifty-first Fiat C.R.32 to be taken on strength by the Nationalist air forces, regardless of whether it was serving with an Italian or a Spanish unit. The squadriglia

numbers of the Aviazione Legionaria Fiat C.R.32 units were painted on the wheel spats – a practice not applied to Spanish-flown C.R.32s until the summer of 1938. When transferred from a German or Italian to a Spanish squadron, an aeroplane usually kept its original serial number, although there was a considerable amount of changing of the numbers of the Junkers Ju 52/3ms. The first batch of Heinkel He 46s, however, which went directly to Spanish units, were serialled from 11-150 to 11-169.

Another source of confusion has been the Grupo 30 of single-engined light aircraft. The codes 30-1 to 30-49 seem to have been allotted to those that were in the northern half of Nationalist Spain (Burgos and Logroño) at the start of the civil war, while those at Seville started at 30-50 (a de Havilland Gipsy Moth). Thus the Leopard Moth captured at Seville on 18 July became 30-56. After the two Nationalist zones were joined, and more light aircraft came into Nationalist possession, this distinction was not strictly adhered to. The four Polish R.W.D.13s, for example, which arrived several months after

A Heinkel He 111 displays the 'Komet' emblem of 1.K/88.

the start of the war, became 30-2, -3, and -4 (perhaps replacing aircraft that had been written off) and -14. The last wartime serial was 30-74, allotted to a Spartan Executive brought over by a defector. Republican aircraft recovered by the Nationalists after the war began at 30-75 and continued until 30-188 (a Tiger Moth).

The Aircraft

Adaro 1.E.7 Chirta

Designed and built in 1934 by Julio Adaro Tarradillos, an instructor at the Escuela Superior Aerotécnica, the Adaro 1.E.7 was a two-seat sesquiplane of wood and metal construction intended for fighter training and aerobatics. It was powered by an inverted in-line Walter Junior air-cooled engine rated at 105-120hp. Fuel was stored in a tank in the centre-section of the upper wing, an unusual feature of which was the ailerons, which extended along the whole of the trailing edge from the centre-section to the wingtip. In the competition for a new trainer for the Aviación Militar, held at Cuatro Vientos in 1935-36, the Adaro proved less efficient than the González Gil-Pazó GP-1 and Hispano E.34, and was not ordered. When the Nationalists captured Cuatro Vientos in November 1936, they found the Adaro, undamaged, in a hangar.

Span 10m; length 6.5m; height 2.5m; wing area 17.7sqm.
Empty weight 480kg; loaded weight 730kg; wing loading 37kg/sqm.
Maximum speed 180km/h; stalling speed 70km/h; take-off distance 70m; landing distance 62m; ceiling 5,050m.

Aero A-101 and Ab-101

In 1933 the Czechoslovakian Ministry of National Defence held a competition for a two-seat light day-bomber to replace the obsolescent Aero A-30/330 series. The winner was the Aero A-100, a large, two-seat, unequal-span biplane of wood and metal construction, powered by a 650-750hp Avia Vr.36 liquid-cooled engine. Forty-four were built for the

Czechoslovakian air force in 1934-35. The A-101 was a version fitted with an Isotta-Fraschini Asso 1000 eighteen-cylinder liquid-cooled W engine rated at 800hp, with a maximum output of 1,000hp, and the first production examples reached the service late in 1935. The enormous weight (278.9kg) of this powerplant resulted in a very disappointing performance, and replacement of the A-101s by Letov S 238s started in 1936.

In October 1936 a Spanish Republican purchasing commission arrived in Czechoslovakia, and among the first aircraft it was offered were forty or so of the Aero A-101s then being withdrawn from service. Since the International Non-Intervention Agreement, to which Czechoslovakia was a signatory, prohibited the direct export of war material to Spain, several months passed while the Spanish Republicans devised ways of smuggling the aircraft to their destination under the pretence of exporting them to a third country. After unsuccessful attempts to arrange this

The Adaro 1.E.7. (Arráez)

through China and Iraq, the Republicans eventually agreed a deal with the Estonian government, and on 8 April 1937 the first twenty-two Aero A-101s left the Polish port of Gdynia on board the *Hordena*, a ship belonging to the Scotia Line (a company created in Paris for running arms to Republican Spain) and supposedly bound for Tallinn, Estonia. The *Hordena*, however, was captured by the Nationalist cruiser *Canarias* in the Bay of Biscay on 16 April 1937, and, after assembly, the Aeros were formed into two escuadrillas of the Spanish Nationalist air arm.

The first escuadrilla (1-E-17, '17' being the Nationalist type code allotted to the Aero A-101) was based at León, under the command of Capitán Cárdenas, the Aeros replacing the Breguet 19s of 2-G-10. Almost immediately it was employed in the Battle of La Granja, a Republican attack directed at Segovia which was opened on 29 May 1937 and was intended, like other Republican offensives that summer, to draw Nationalist pressure away from the north. On 5 June in particular, the Aeros, in conjunction with the

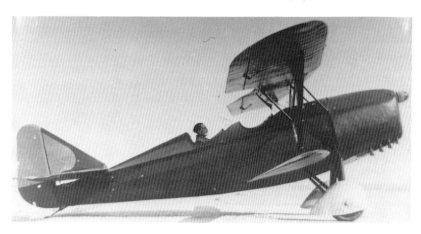

A Republican Aero A-101 of the 2ª Escuadrilla of Grupo 72.

publican Aeros were formed into the 2ª Escuadrilla of Grupo 72 and relegated to coastal patrol duties.

The Republicans nicknamed their Aeros 'Pragas' (Pragues). The Nationalists called their Aeros 'Ocas' (Geese), and Republican Aeros 'Felipes' (Philips) or, more disparagingly, 'Papagayos' (Parrots), a term used indiscriminately for the R-5s, RZs and Aeros. Sixteen Republican

A Nationalist Aero A-101 of 5-G-17. ▷

Ro-37bis of 4-G-12, distinguished themselves by flying, almost at ground level, through the passes and gorges of the Sierra Guadarrama to locate and harrass Republican troops being brought up to the attack. The second escuadrilla (2-E-17), replacing the Breguet 19s of 1-G-10 at Logroño, was moved to Vitoria and employed with the air units supporting the Nationalist advance on Bilbao. At the end of June the two Aero-equipped escuadrillas were formed into a single group; 5-G-17, under the command of Comandate Llorente Solá. After continuous operations in Biscaya, at the Battle of Brunete (on the Madrid front), and in the Santander and Asturian campaigns until October 1937, the Aero group was transferred to the quieter fronts of southern Spain, where it continued operations until the end of the civil war.

Meanwhile, sixteen Aero Ab-101s (Hispano-Suiza 12Ydrs vee engines rated at 725hp) arrived in the Republican zone during the summer of 1937 and were assembled in an underground workshop built in caves near Madrid. Bearing the type code 'LN' (or 'LA' according to some sources), they took part in their first action during the Battle of Belchite in August 1937. On at least one occasion, while bombing Nationalist troop positions at the front, they shared the sky with the Nationalist Aero A-101s engaged in bombing Republican troop positions in the same sector, to the utter confusion of everyone concerned, not least the anti-aircraft gunners below.

A third batch of nine Aeros, probably A-101s, arrived in France

An Aeronca C.3. (A J Jackson)

during the summer of 1937 and was impounded by the French authorities. When the Franco-Spanish frontier was opened from 19 March to 13 June 1938, however, they were allowed to cross into Spain and were assembled at Figueras, in Catalonia, in May. Capitán Santiago Capillas, who tested them at Toroella de Montgris (also called Vergès), remembers that they were so heavy that they could take off safely in a strong crosswind, but that in the air they were sluggish and almost unmanoeuvrable. All of the remaining Re-

Aeros were renovated by the Nationalists after the war. In March 1940 thirteen were still flying in the Ejercito del Aire, the rest having been scrapped or cannibalised for spare parts, but all had been withdrawn from service by 1946.

Aero A-101

Span 17m; length 12.09m; height 3.7m.

Empty weight 2,578kg; loaded weight 4,345kg.

Airspeed A.S.6J(I) Envoy G-ADBB Wharfedale *of Northeastern Airways, on hire in 1936 to Air Dispatch of Croydon.*

Maximum speed 256km/h; cruising speed 225km/h; ceiling 5,500m; range 845km.

Aero Ab-101
Span 17m; length 12.4m; height 3.7m.
Empty weight 2,330kg; loaded weight 4,199kg.
Maximum speed 259km/h; cruising speed 204km/h; ceiling 7,499m; range 949km.

Aeronca C-3
In 1928 the Aeronautical Corporation of America, based at Cincinnatti, Ohio, produced a near-ultra-light high-wing monoplane, the Aeronca C-2, of which two examples were imported into Britain in 1930 and 1931. From this was developed the C-3, a side-by-side two-seat version, which was both built under licence and assembled from American-built parts by Light Aircraft Ltd at Hanworth between 1935 and 1939.
In March 1936 one of these Aerona C-3s (registration unreported) was flown across France to Spain for the Aero Club de Madrid by J D Kirwin of Aircraft Exchange and Mart, and was presumably still at Madrid when the civil war broke out in July.

Powerplant: 40hp Aeronca E.113C twin-cylinder, dual-ignition, engine.
Span 36ft; length 20ft; height 7ft 10in; wing area 142.2sq ft.
Empty weight 569lb; loaded weight 1,005lb.
Maximum speed 95mph; cruising

speed 87mph; ceiling 12,000ft; range 200 miles.

Airspeed A.S.5 Courier, A.S.6 Envoy and A.S.8 Viceroy
The Airspeed Courier, a single-engined low-wing cantilever monoplane which carried four passengers, has a place in history as the first British aircraft with a retractable undercarriage to go into production. Appearing first in 1933, the Courier achieved some success, and helped to establish the reputation of Airspeed as a small but progressive aircraft manufacturer. Sixteen were built, most of them being used on domestic air services in the United Kingdom. The prototype, G-ABXN, was used for early in-flight-refuelling experiments, and the first production model, G-ACJL, came third (after the de Havilland D.H.88 Comet and Douglas DC-2) in the MacRobertson England–Australia air race of October 1934.
The A.S.6 Envoy was an enlarged, twin-engined, and aesthetically more appealing development of the Courier, carrying six or eight passengers, and was designed by A H Tiltman and N S Norway, now better known as the novelist Nevil Shute. Twenty-five were built altogether. The A.S.8 Viceroy was a one-off Envoy modified for the MacRobertson race and powered by two Armstrong Siddeley Cheetah VI supercharged radial engines with long-chord NACA cowlings. All three types were built of wood, with stressed-ply-covered fuselages and fabric-covered outer wings and tail surfaces.
In his autobiography *Slide Rule*, Nevil Shute writes that in 1936 six Couriers were sold at better than

their original prices and went by devious routes to Spain, and that Airspeed '... made a bulk sale of practically the whole of our stock of unsold Couriers and Envoys to one British sales organisation and heard no more of them'. In fact, no Couriers went to Spain. In August 1936 the Spanish Republican agent Comandante Carlos Pastor Krauel bought four Couriers (G-ACLR, 'SZ, 'VE and 'VF) and the Envoy G-ADBA through Union Founders' Trust (UFT), a City company specialising in the setting up of 'industrial and commercial projects all over the world'. The Envoy G-ADBA, which belonged to Cobham Air Routes, was on lease to Olley Air Service at the time, and was in the Airspeed hangar for an engine refit. It can be safely assumed that it was sold to UFT with the consent of Capt Olley, whose D.H.89 Dragon Rapide G-ACYR had flown Gen Franco from the Canary Islands to Spanish Morocco on 17-19 July 1936, for at about this time he sold D.H.84 Dragon G-ACNA to the same company.
On 20 August 1936, two young Airspeed employees tried to take off in the Courier G-ACVE, with the intention of flying it to France and selling it to the Spanish government, but they crashed, and one of them was killed. This alerted the authorities who, in obedience to the Non-Intervention regulation introduced the previous day, grounded the other three Couriers, and Envoy G-ADBA, and placed the Airspeed hangars under police guard. This unhappy situation prevailed for six months, while acrimonious correspondence passed between Airspeed and HM Government.
Before the misadventure of 20 August, however, three Envoy IIs had already left for Spain, the first two on 9 August 1936. Envoy G-AEBV was sold to Cdte Pastor, via UFT, by Brian Allen Aviation at Reading. G-ADBB *Wharfedale* of North Eastern Airways was at that time on hire to Air Dispatch, of which the Hon Mrs Victor Bruce was a director, and left Croydon for France on the same day. The third Envoy, G-ACVJ *India Demonstrator*, belonged to Commercial Air Hire, of which Mrs Bruce was also a director, and departed on

Envoy G-ADBB, with hastily-painted Nationalist markings, at Burgos in August 1936.

Although it went to the Republicans, Shute's statement that this was the machine in which Gen Mola (a Nationalist) was killed is partly true. At Barcelona, for some reason, its wings were removed and replaced by those of G-AEBV, and in this hybrid machine the well-known Spanish aviator Fernando Rein Loring (a relation of Jorge Loring, the aircraft builder) defected from Barajas on 26 September 1936. At Pamplona it was painted with St Andrew's Crosses which did not wholly obliterate its mixed British registration, given the Spanish Nationalist registration 41-1, and sent to Burgos to replace G-ADBB as Mola's personal aeroplane. On 3 June 1937, while taking Mola and other officers to Burgos, it crashed into the side of a hill under low cloud and everyone on board was killed. There were many rumours of conspiracy and sabotage, some blaming the Germans and others Franco himself, and for years Coronel Chamorro, the father of the dead pilot, kept two loaded pistols on a table in his home in readiness for the day when he should confront his son's murderers.

During the winter of 1936-37 Airspeed was involved in another intrigue. On 28 August 1936 UFT sold all of its aircraft, including the Envoy II and four Couriers, to la Fédération Populaire des Sports Aéronautiques, which was then procuring aircraft for the Spanish Republicans, and in October 1936 FPSA sold them to Air Taxis Vienna through Josef Hermann, a Paris dealer. In November Baron Pfyffer of Altishofen, Lucerne, representing Air Taxis Vienna, arrived in London to buy the Courier G-ACLT from PSIoW and the two Envoy IIs 'DAZ and 'BZ from NE Airways. The British Government prohibited the sale on learning that Air Taxis Vienna did not exist, and that the man handling all these deals was Louis Balfour of PSIoW. Another Austrian, Eric Michel Hoffman, immediately offered £90,000 for 'AZ and 'BZ, as well as three brand new unregistered Envoy A.S.6JIIIs (c/ns 61, 62 and 69)

The Airspeed A.S.8 Viceroy.

12 August 1936. However, while 'EBV and 'CVJ were safely on the Republican aerodrome of Prat de Llobregat, Barcelona, by 22 August, G-ADBB was at Gamonal aerodrome, Burgos, where the Nationalist Gen Mola had his headquarters. *Wharfedale* allegedly carried out one bombing raid on Barajas Airport, Madrid, before being used by Mola as his personal transport.

On 13 August the Viceroy slipped out of Croydon, flown by Ken Waller and Max Findley, who had bought it for the Schlesinger Trophy race to South Africa and then sold it to Cdte Pastor on being offered £9,500 – the price of the aircraft (£5,500) plus the first prize (£4,000) as compensation for not competing in the race. On its arrival at Barcelona the Republicans named the Viceroy *Arturo González Gil*, after the Socialist aircraft designer recently killed during the fighting against Mola's army in the Sierra Guadarrama (see González Gil-Pazó GP-1). Its final disposition is unknown.

The Envoy II G-ADCA of Portsmouth, Southsea and Isle of Wight Aviation (PSIoW) happened to be at Heston on the day of the Courier crash (20 August 1936), and so escaped being grounded. It was therefore flown to Croydon, where Capt A Rollason, of Rollason Aircraft Service, bought it and sold it to l'Office Générale de l'Air (OGA), which was then procuring aircraft for the Spanish Republicans. A Foreign Office attempt to hold the Envoy failed, and Rollason flew it to Paris on 21 August. A week later it crashed near Alès on its way to Barcelona and was written off.

Rollason also bought the prototype Envoy, G-ACMT, which, despite Shute's statement, was the only previously unsold Envoy to go to Spain. Some Envoys, however, were still on the 'tenuous' hire purchase arrangements Shute mentions, and there is evidence to suggest that G-ACVJ, for example, was re-appropriated by Airspeed on the pretext that an instalment was late so that the company could sell it to Pastor. Rollason flew 'CMT from Lympne (not Croydon, as Shute states) to the Potez field at Meaulte (OGA being a Potez selling organisation) on 29 August 1936, and from there it was flown to Barcelona.

and two Avro Ansons, on behalf of the famous arms magnate Fritz Mandel (husband of Hedy Lamarr), for use by an oil company based in Trieste. It is now known that the Spanish Republicans, who were the real buyers, wanted these aircraft for flying gold and valuables out of Spain for sale abroad, allowing the Douglas DC-2s which were then being used for this purpose to be freed for other duties.

The Republican official handling the affair, Cdte Jácome, paid Hoffman £17,241 deposit against a contract stipulating that the aircraft must be delivered before 6 March 1937, when new Non-Intervention controls were to come into force. Hoffman applied for licences to export the Envoys c/n 61 and 62, and the Foreign Office, although warned by intelligence sources of the true destination of the aircraft, granted them. Even more strangely, the British government did not inform the Belgian government about what was afoot until the two Envoys were actually *en route* for Antwerp. When the ship docked, however, the Envoys, although impounded, were

Airspeed Envoy prototype G-ACMT, married to the wings of another Envoy sold to the Republicans, G-AEBV, was brought over to the Nationalists and became General Mola's personal transport, with the military serial 41-1. Mola was killed in an accident to this aeroplane.

freed by some mysterious means, shipped to Rotterdam, and re-sold to one D H Reinders (or Reynders). The Envoys were assembled at Ypenbourg Aerodrome, where the Dutch government, duly alerted, impounded them. They were allotted the registrations PH-ARK and 'ARL, but these were never taken up. When 6 March 1937 passed, Jácome, unable to recover the deposit because the contract was now void, and already in trouble over his mishandlig of other transactions (see Vultee V1-A), was alleged to have absconded with the balance of 7 million pesetas.

Meanwhile, the Republicans were told by their intelligence service that although Hoffman was working for Mandel (a Jew), he was reported to be a Gestapo agent. At this period the Nationalists and their allies were making strenuous efforts to infiltrate the Republican arms procurement organisation to create as much mischief as possible. It is said that the two Envoys remained at Ypenbourg until they were destroyed by the Luftwaffe in May 1940. However, in a photograph showing a line of Messerschmitt Bf 109Es on a Dutch aerodrome in the summer of 1940, two aircraft in the background appear to be Airspeed Envoys. If these are the same machines, and it is reasonable to suppose they are, then they were not destroyed in the bombing, and their final disposition remains unknown.

In his book *Airspeed Aircraft Since 1931* (Putnam, 1970) the late H A

Taylor tentatively identified the two Envoys bought by Hoffman and impounded in Holland as the A.S.6JII/IIIs G-AEGF (c/n 55) and 'GG (c/n 56). These had been registered on 29 and 30 December 1936 respectively, and sold to British Scandinavian Airways. The sale was cancelled, and the two aircraft seem to have vanished into thin air. Since there is now no doubt that the two in Holland were c/ns 61 and 62, the fate of this other pair remains a mystery, for a Spanish connection, though possible, is unlikely in view of the lack of evidence.

On 5 March 1937 the last of Hoffman's Envoy IIIs, (c/n 69), which was still at Portsmouth, was sold to Auguste Amestoy, who immediately had it registered as F-APPQ and so established as French property. The fact that Amestoy gave his address as 55 Avenue George V, Paris, which was that of the Spanish Republican Arms Purchasing Commission, prompted the British authorities to place a guard on the Envoy at Portsmouth, but the British Government had no legal means of preventing its departure, and was obliged to allow the French pilot Leopold Galy to fly it to Biarritz on 19 March. There it joined the ranks of Air Pyrénées (see Appendix I). F-APPQ, with Galy at the controls, was shot down over the Basque country by five Heinkel He 51s on 26 May 1937, but Galy and his passengers escaped with minor injuries. Airspeed used a photograph of the crashed Envoy in

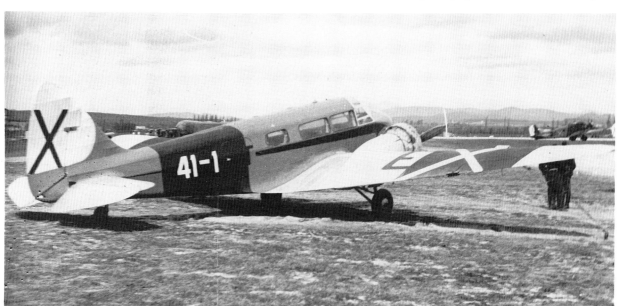

An A.S.6J(III) Envoy transferred from Air Pyrénées to LAPE as Fleet No 32. The photograph is dated 11 July 1938. (Azaola)

The Envoy III F-AQAA on Barcelona Airport after its undercarriage collapsed. (Arráez)

its next publicity brochure as proof of the aeroplane's structural strength.

Airspeed built five more Envoy IIIs for Air Pyrénées:

c/n	Registration	Export licence date	Joined Air Pyrénées
70	F-AQAA	28 Jun 37	8 Jul 37
71	F-AQAB	31 Jul 37	17 Sep 37
72	F-AQCR	31 Jul 37	10 Aug 37
73	F-AQCS	31 Aug 37	4 Sep 37
74	F-AQCT	31 Aug 37	6 Sep 37

As mentioned in Appendix I, the adventurous history of this airline would require a book to itself, the Envoys and other aircraft, flown by daring pilots, carrying out innumerable dangerous missions along the Bay of Biscay coast. On 7 September Abel Guidez, late of the Malraux squadron, was flying to Gijón, in the Asturias, to rescue some Russian airmen before they fell prisoner to the advancing Nationalists, when his Envoy III F-AQCS (which had joined the airline only three days before) was caught by a *schwarm* of Messerschmitt Bf 109s and shot down, Guidez being killed.

After the collapse of the northern Republican zone, some of Air Pyrénées' remaining Envoys were transferred to LAPE (the state airline) in the main zone, one being registered EC-AGE, Fleet No. 32. After the war the Nationalists recovered one from Oran, Algeria. It was given the military serial 41-1, and in 1946 was renumbered C 11.

Powerplants: A.S.6 Envoy I/II – two 185hp Wolseley A.R.9 Mk. I.
A.S.6A Envoy II – two 220hp Armstrong Siddeley Lynx IVC.
A.S.6J Envoy III – two 350hp Armstrong Siddeley Cheetah IX.
A.S.8 Viceroy – two 290hp Armstrong Siddeley Cheetah VI.
Envoy I, II, III and Viceroy: span 52ft 4in; length 34ft 6in; height 9ft 6in; wing area 339sq ft (Viceroy 299sq ft).

Empty weights Envoy I, 3,442lb; Envoy II, 3,780lb; Envoy III, 4,340lb; Viceroy, 3,900lb.

Loaded weights Envoy I, 5,300lb; Envoy II, 5,830lb; Envoy III, 6,600lb; Viceroy, 6,300lb.

Envoy I   Maximum speed 170mph; cruising speed 150mph; initial climb 850ft/min; ceiling 17,000ft.

Envoy II   Maximum speed 174mph; cruising speed 153mph; initial climb 1,020ft/min; ceiling 16,500ft; range 650 miles.

Envoy III   Maximum speed 203mph; cruising speed 170mph; ceiling 22,000ft; range 620 miles.

Viceroy   Maximum speed 210mph; cruising speed 190mph; initial climb 1,000ft/min; range 1,400 miles.

American Eagle-Lincoln Eaglet B.31

Almost every book or article listing the types of aircraft used in the

Spanish Civil War includes an American Eagle A or A129, which was said to be awaiting registration in July 1936. The only machine of this type in Spain was the American Eagle-Lincoln Eaglet B.31 (NC12559, c/n 1109), powered by a 45hp Szekely S.R.3.0. three-cylinder radial engine. Exported from the USA in 1933, it did not reach Spain until 1935, when it was bought by Estéban Fernández of Barcelona. On 16 September 1935, when it was the property of Sr Gastoñado, it crashed on Prat de Llobregat Aerodrome. It is not known whether it was repaired before the outbreak of the civil war.

Span 34ft 4in; length 21ft 7in; height 8ft 4in; wing area 164sq ft.

Empty weight 509lb; loaded weight 922lb.

Maximum speed 90mph; cruising speed 75mph; ceiling 14,500ft; range 240 miles.

Arado Ar 66C

Designed by Walter Rethel before he left the Arado Handelgesellschaft (which became the Arado Flugzeugwerke Gmbh in 1933), the Arado Ar 66 was a single-bay, two-seat training biplane. The prototype Ar 66a first flew in 1932. A second prototype, the Ar 66b, was fitted with

An American Eagle-Lincoln Eaglet B.31. (Peter M Bowers, Seattle, via Jos P Juptner)

floats, but the third, the Ar 66c, which had a 240hp Argus As10C liquid-cooled engine, reverted to a wheeled undercarriage. This was the version, designated Ar 66C, ordered into production in 1933. It had wooden wings and a fuselage of welded steel tube, with fabric covering. The Ar 66C's most curious feature was its tail assembly, in which the one-piece tailplane sat on top of a truncated fin in front of the rudder. Several thousand Ar 66Cs were built as primary trainers for the Luftwaffe between 1933 and 1938, and in 1943 some were fitted with bomb racks and pressed into service on the Eastern Front with the Störkampfstaffeln, or nocturnal ground-attack squadrons.

Six Ar 66Cs were delivered to Spain early in 1937 to join the Bücker Jungmanns and other trainers at the

Arado Ar 66 36-2 of the Escuela de Transformación (Intermediate Training) at La Parra, Jerez de la Frontera. (Arráez)

Nationalist Escuela de Vuelo (flying school) at El Copero, 15km south of Seville. They were allotted the military serials 36-1 to 36-6 and used for gunnery and photo-reconnaissance instruction. One crashed in 1937, and a second in 1938. The remaining four continued flying (after 1941 with the new type code ES-7) until at least 1946.

Span 10m; length 8.30m; height 2.93m; wing area 26.63sq m.

Empty weight 885kg; loaded weight 1,185kg.

Maximum speed 210km/h; cruising speed 175km/h; climb 1,000m in 4.1min; ceiling 4,500m.

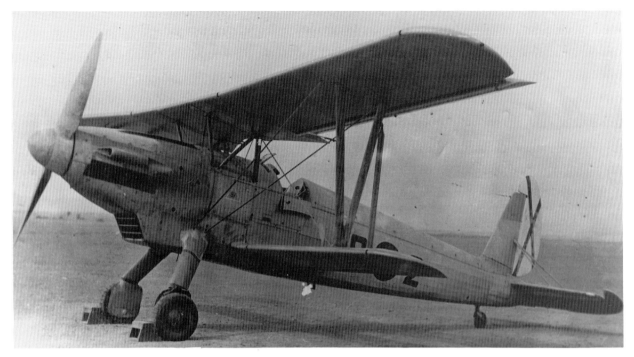

An Arado Ar 68E at the Condor Legion base of La Cenia. (Arráez)

Arado Ar 68E-1

During air combat over the Madrid front in September 1936, Republican pilots, including the South African ex-RAF fighter pilot Vincent Doherty, reported several alarming encounters with a Nationalist 'Arado fighter' equipped with a 20mm cannon firing through the propeller boss. It would keep well above a dogfight until its pilot saw a Republican fighter in difficulties, when he would dive down and deliver the *coup de grâce.* Doherty even went so far as to tell Wg Cdr Medhurst at the Air Ministry in London that he had seen the Arado blow the fuselage of a De-woitine D.372 in half. These stories were printed in European newspapers, and were still being repeated in the 1970s. How they originated is not clear, for no Arado fighter armed with a 20mm cannon existed in 1936, and no Arado fighters of any description arrived in Spain until three Arado Ar 68Es were delivered to the Condor Legion early in 1938.

The Arado Ar 68 was the last of the line of single-seat fighters developed by Walter Rethel and, later, Walter Blume, between 1928 and 1934. In the course of tests during 1935 and 1936 it showed itself to be superior to the Heinkel He 51 in all

An Arado Ar 95A of AS/88.

respects except for speed on the level. Powered by a Junkers Jumo 210Ea (680hp) liquid-cooled engine, it was armed with two 7.9mm machine guns mounted above the engine to fire through the propeller arc, and six 10kg SC10 fragmentation bombs under the lower wings. Although substantial numbers were built for the Luftwaffe, none was sent either with Operation Magic Fire or with the first consignments of aircraft to the Condor Legion. The poor showing of the He 51 against the Russian I-16 during the winter of 1936-37 convinced the Luftwaffe operations staff that the time of the fighter biplane was passing, and the air ministry instructed Arado to abandon

all further work on the Ar 68. Nevertheless, three Ar 68E-1s were sent to Spain for trials as night fighters, and, with the Nationalist military serials 9-1, 9-2 and 9-3, were based at La Cenia in southern Catalonia. Nothing is recorded of their night-flying operations, but it is known that they were occasionally used for ground attack during the Battle of the Ebro and the advance into Catalonia in January and February 1939. At the end of the war they were handed over to the Nationalists and placed under the command of Capitán Javier Murcia. Two were still flying in 1945, when their code serial was changed to C-11.

Span 11m; length 9.5m; height 3.3m; wing area 27.3sq m.

Empty weight 1,600kg; loaded weight 2,020kg.

Maximum speed 335km/h at 2,650m; climb 6,000m in 10min; ceiling 8,100m; range 415km.

Arado Ar 95A

Designed under the direction of Dipl-Ing Walter Blume in 1935, the Arado Ar 95 torpedo bomber was intended to operate either from wheels, aboard a German aircraft carrier, or from floats. The prototype Ar 95 V1 (D-OLVO) was a two-seat, single-bay staggered biplane with a metal monocoque fuselage and aft-folding wings, powered by a 845hp BMW 132 nine-cylinder air-cooled engine. Its armament consisted of one fixed forward-firing 7.9mm MG 17 machine gun on the left side of the forward fuselage, an MG 15 7.9mm gun on a movable mounting in the rear cockpit, one 700kg torpedo, or one 375kg bomb under the fuselage, and six 50kg bombs under the wings.

Trials with five Ar 95 prototypes revealed an unsatisfactory performance, and the type was released for export. Six Arado Ar 95A-0 three-seat seaplanes, which differed from the prototypes in having a continuous canopy to protect the crew and the more powerful 880hp BMW 132Dc radial engine, were built in 1937. In August 1938 they were sent to the Condor Legion seaplane base at Pollensa Bay, Mallorca, where they constituted a separate squadron, Grupo 64. They played a minor part in operations, and at the end of the civil war three were handed over to the Spanish Navy, serialled 64-1 to 64-3. In 1945 the group was redesignated HR-3 and was disbanded shortly afterwards.

Span 12.5m; length 11.1m; height 5.2m; wing area 45.4sqm.

Empty weight 2,450kg; loaded weight 3,570kg.

Maximum speed 275km/h at sea level; 302km/h at 3,000m; ceiling 7,300m; range 1,094km.

Avia BH-33.3

During 1925-27 the Belgian company SABCA had built fifty Czechoslovakian-designed Avia BH-21 fighters for the Belgian Aéro-

An Avia BH-33

nautique Militaire. In 1928, encouraged by this success, the Avia company at Skoda sent three prototypes of an improved version, the BH-33, powered by the 490hp Walter-Bristol Jupiter VI radial engine, for evaluation by the Belgians. No order was placed, and the three fighters (BH-33.1, registered U1, BH-33.2/U2, and BH-33.3/U3) were subsequently used by Belgian air force pilots for aerobatic practice.

In the summer of 1936 the BH-33.3/U3 was refurbished by the Mulot-Ertag company at Brussells-Evère, builders of the Mulot Sport light aircraft and, perhaps through the intercession of a Comintern agent named as Georges Djoumkowski, was bought by one R Vandevelde on behalf of the Spanish Republicans. The Avia was repainted white with all registrations concealed, the gun-troughs were covered over and the gun synchronisation mechanisms removed and hidden in the fuselage. On 26 August 1936 it was ferried across France to Spain by ex-air force pilot André Autrique. The flight was an adventurous one, and clearly well organised, for Autrique landed twice in the countryside to refuel from vans that were waiting for him. Unfortunately he lost his way, came down in a field at Ste-Foy-la Grande near Libourne (Bordeaux), was arrested, and was released only through the personal intervention of the French air minister, Pierre Cot. When he landed at Barcelona on 27 August he discovered that someone had stolen the gun-synchronisation mechanisms. What happened to the Avia BH-33.3 after that is not known.

Span 8.9m; length 6.85m; height 2.74m; wing area 22.2sqm.

Empty weight 830kg; loaded weight 1,250kg.

Maximum speed 269.5km/h at ground level; 248km/h at 5,000m; climb 5,000m in 8min 38sec; ceiling 7,500m; range 450km.

Avia 51

In 1929 the small aircraft section of the famous Skoda arms company was transferred to Cakovice, near Prague, and combined with the Avia factory. The chief designer, Dr Ing Richard Nebesar, was sent to the USA to gain experience in the latest engineering techniques and, while there, worked with the Glenn Martin company and the Lockheed Division of the Detroit Aircraft Corporation.

Returning to Czechoslovakia in 1931, Nebesar began work on the Avia 50, an abortive project, and the Avia 51, a six-passenger transport which clearly owed much to the Lockheed Vega. Powered by three 200hp Avia RK-12 radial engines, it was a cantilever high-wing monoplane with an all-metal monocoque fuselage and fabric-covered metal wings and tail assembly. It proved unstable to fly and was prone to flutter, but in 1934 three were acquired by CLS, an airline owned by Skoda. After they had been in service for a short time the pilots refused to fly them, so the three Avia 51s were among the aircraft sold, via Estonia, to the Spanish Republicans. Only one reached Spain, however, and it is believed that the ship carrying the other two was sunk in the Mediterranean by Nationalist warships. In Spain, the Avia 51 was usually flown by the LAPE pilot Jorge

An Avia 51.

Xuclá, although, since it bore the military registration TA-1, it does not seem to have joined the LAPE fleet. To Xuclá's relief it was soon grounded owing to a lack of spares.

Span 15.1m; length 10.75m; height 3.5m; wing area 38sq m.
Empty weight 2,520kg; loaded weight 3,790kg; wing loading 100kg/sq m.
Maximum speed 273.55km/h; cruising speed 225km/h; ceiling 5,000m; range 780km.

Avro 504K

Remembered by many who flew it as the nearest thing to the 'perfect aeroplane' that they ever encountered, the Avro 504, of which the 504K was the classic variant, was certainly one of the greatest aircraft of all time. The prototype first flew in 1913, more than 10,000 were built altogether, and some were still serving as trainers, in the RAF and in foreign air forces and flying schools, at the beginning of the Second World War.

Of the fifty or so Avro 504Ks imported by Spain during the 1920s, two, both belonging to the Aeronáutica Naval, were still flying in July 1936. One happened to be at Getafe military aerodrome, and the other at San Javier, Cartagena. Nothing

The Avro 504K of the Aeronáutica Naval, EC-FAE, flying near Cartagena. (Arráez)

further is known of them. A note in the log book of the (then) student pilot Gabriel Allés, recording that he flew an 'Avro' at La Ribera (the training school at San Javier) on 28 June 1937, has been assumed to refer

to this Avro 504K. La Ribera, however, was the base for intermediate and night-flying training, and the Avro was therefore almost certainly the Avro 626 or the 643 Cadet imported clandestinely in January 1937.

Span 36ft; length 29ft 5in; height 10ft 5in; wing area 330sq ft.
Empty weight 1,231lb; loaded weight

1,829lb; wing loading 5.542lb/sq ft.

Maximum speed 95mph; cruising speed 75mph; climb 700ft/min; ceiling 16,000ft; range 225 miles.

Avro 594 Avian

The prototype Avro 581 Avian (G-ABOV), built for the *Daily Mail* light aeroplane competition in 1926, was a two-seat biplane with square-cut wingtips and the characteristic Avro circular rudder without a fin. The production Avro 594 Avian had rounded wingtips, a triangular fin, and an enlarged rudder with a straight trailing edge, and used a variety of air- and water-cooled engines. The wings were of wood with fabric covering. The fuselage was a welded-steel-tube girder with wooden formers, covered over the upper part with plywood and over the lower with fabric. At least fifteen Avians were imported into Spain between 1927 and 1932, of which eleven were still flying in July 1936, six of them in Catalonia.

Aero Club de Barcelona at Prat de Llobregat Airport
Avian IVM (90hp Renault) c/n 529, EC-ATA
Avian IV (105hp ADC Cirrus Hermes) c/n 304, EC-FAF
Avian IIIA (95hp Cirrus III) c/n 198 EC-PAA

Air Taxi SA, at Prat de Llobregat
Avian III (95hp Cirrus III) c/n 326, EC-AIA
Avian III (95hp Cirrus III) c/n 108, EC-CAC

José Canudas flying school, at a field near the airport
Avian IV (90hp Fiat A-50) c/n 325, EC-IAA

Real Aero Club de España, Barajas, Madrid
Avian II (85hp Cirrus II) c/n 292(4), EC-EEE
Avian III (95hp Cirrus Hermes) c/n 405, EC-FAA

Getafe military airfield, Madrid
Avian IIIA (95hp Cirrus III) c/n 151, EC-AAE (ex-G-EBYM). This was the property of Comandante Juan Ortiz Muñoz, commander of the air base at Los Alcázares, Cartagena. He

was on leave when the uprising occurred, hastily flew down to Los Alcázares in this machine on 18 July, and played a leading role in saving the base for the Republicans.

The tenth and eleventh Avians were at San Bonet, near Palma, Mallorca, and belonged to the recently created *Aero Club de los Baleares*
Avian IIIA (95hp Cirrus III) c/n 594, EC-AAI
Avian IIIA (95hp Cirrus III) c/n 465, EC-EAA

On 18 July 1936 the five Avro Avians at Barcelona were impressed, along with all other available aircraft, performing every kind of duty until September or October, and were then sent to serve as trainers at the flying schools in Murcia. The fate of the Avians at Madrid is not recorded, but those which were not destroyed by Nationalist bombing were presumably sent to Murcia as well.

Of the Balearic Islands, only Minorca stayed loyal to the Republic, and, while planning an expeditionary force to recapture Mallorca and Ibiza, the Republicans kept up sporadic air attacks on Palma and other targets with a force of about twenty Savoia-Marchetti S.62 and Macchi M.18 flying-boats. During this period, the Nationalist air force in the Balearics consisted of the two Avro Avian IIIAs and de Havilland D.H.60X Moth EC-CCA, which, manned by five members of the Aero Club in rotation, maintained a series of nearly continuous patrols over the coasts and even as far as Minorca. At the end of July Avian EC-AAI was machine-gunned by a Republican S.62 while on the ground and immobilised. In the other Avian, EC-EAA, Juan Crespi Fornán (who later became a Heinkel He 45 pilot) flew numerous missions, even drop-

ping bombs by hand on a Republican submarine and a landing-craft during the Republican capture of Ibiza on 9 August 1936. On 15 August Crespi's Avian, returning home from a raid on the island of Cabrera, made a forced landing near Colonia de Campos, on the south coast of Mallorca, and was wrecked. The Moth survived the campaign.

Span 28ft; length 24ft 3in; height 8ft 6in.
Empty weight (MkIIIA) 935lb; (MkIV) 1,005lb; Loaded weight (MkIIIA) 1,435lb; (MkIV) 1,523lb.
Maximum speed (MkIIIA) 102-105mph; cruising speed 87-90mph; ceiling 18,000ft; range 360-400 miles.

Avro 626

The Avro 626, of metal construction and powered by a 277hp Armstrong Siddeley Cheetah V radial engine fitted with a Townend ring, was a variant of the Avro 621 Tutor, one of the standard trainers of the RAF. It had a third cockpit and a Scarff gun-ring. One 626, the demonstrator G-ABRK (c/n533), which had been a familiar sight at air displays in Britain for several years, was sold by

The Avro 594 Avian IIIA MC-CAAE (later EC-AAE) bought by Alvaro García Orgara (left). Leaning on the wing is Carlos de Haya, who was to become one of the most distinguished Nationalist pilots in the civil war. The Avian was later sold to Capitán Juan Ortiz Muñoz, commander of the air base at Los Alcázares, and it was in this machine that he flew from Madrid to Los Alcázares on 18 July 1936 to save the aerodrome for the Republicans. (A J Jackson)

Avro 626 demonstrator G-ABRK was smuggled into Republican Spain in January 1937. (A J Jackson)

W R Westhead, of Heston Aerodrome, to Leslie Stanynought (alias Leslie Charles Lewis) in December 1936. It presumably passed into Spain early in January 1937, together with two of Stanynought's other aircraft, the Avro 643 Cadet and the Miles M23 Hawk Speed Six (which see). It was employed as a gunnery trainer at the school for observers and bombardiers at Los Alcázares.

Span 34ft; length 26ft 6in; height 9ft 9in; wing area 300sq ft.
Empty weight 2,010lb; loaded weight 2,667lb.
Maximum speed 130mph; cruising speed 108mph; ceiling 16,000ft; range 200 miles.

Avro 643 Cadet

The Avro 631 Cadet was produced in 1931 as a scaled-down Avro Tutor, with its wings, which had rounded tips, and movable control surfaces built from wood instead of metal. The Avro 643 Cadet was an im-

The Avro 643 Cadet G-ADEX was also smuggled into Spain in January 1937. (A J Jackson)

proved version of the 631, with a raised rear seat and other modifications. In 1935 CASA procured a licence to build a series of 631 Cadets at their Puntales factory in Cádiz, and a pattern aircraft, c/n778, with the ferry registration EC-W26, was flown to Spain in December 1935. The Spanish Cadets were to be fitted with 105hp Walter Junior inverted in-line engines in place of the 135hp Armstrong Siddeley Genet Major radials of the British aircraft. The project was ended by the outbreak of the civil war, and it is not known what became of the pattern aircraft. There has been confusion between this machine and the Avro 631 Cadet EC-DBD which had belonged to the Real Aero Club de España and had been destroyed in a crash during an air display at Los Llanos, Albacete, in 1935.

One Avro 643 Cadet that certainly reached Republican Spain during the civil war was G-ADEX (c/n820). Belonging originally to the Hon H F Watson, it was bought in December 1936 by Leslie Stanynought (alias 'LC Lewis') and, with an Avro 626 and a Miles Hawk Speed Six, flown to France. It was reported at Toulouse-Montaudron aerodrome on its way to Spain on 8 January 1937. In Spain it was used at La Ribera flying field, San Javier (Cartagena), as an intermediate and night-flying trainer. It dit not survive the war.

Span 30ft 2in; length 24ft 9in; height

A B.A. L25C Swallow flying a businessman to a meeting: an early 'executive transport'. (Philip Jarrett)

8ft 9in; wing area 262sq ft.
  Loaded weight 2,000lb.
  Maximum speed 118mph; cruising speed c100mph; ceiling c13,000ft; range c350 miles.

B.A. (B.K.) L25C-1A Swallow

In March 1929 Maj E F Stephen began importing Klemm L25 monoplanes into Britain, and, having successfully sold twenty-seven by 1933, later decided to build the type under licence. Accordingly the British Klemm Aeroplane Company was established at Hanworth Aerodrome, with GH Handasyde, designer of the Martinsyde fighters of the First World War, as works manager. The B.K. L25C-1A Swallow differed from the Klemm L25 in minor structural details, and in having a 90hp Pobjoy Cataract III radial engine in a blistered cowling, or a 90hp Blackburn-built Cirrus Minor inverted in-line engine. In 1935 the company was reorganised as the British Aircraft Manufacturing Co, and subsequent production aircraft were designated B.A. Swallow 1s and Swallow 2s.

In 1934 a B.K. L25C-1A Swallow (90hp Pobjoy Cataract III) was bought by the Aero Club de Valencia

and registered EC-XXA. Shortly after the outbreak of the civil war, the Basque civil pilot F Lezama Leguizamón used it to cross over to the Nationalists. In Nationalist service, with the military serial 30-22, it seems to have been employed on liaison duties. In 1940 it was returned to civil flying as the property of Lezama at Bilbao, registered EC-CAP. In 1950 it was sold to the Aero Club de Lérida, and in 1962, registered EC-ACC, to A Méndez of Seville.

Two American pilots who flew in the Republican air force, Edwin Liebowitz (also known as Ed Lyons) and Abraham Schapiro (alias Art Vasnit) have recalled that, while ferrying a B.A. Swallow to Barcelona, they were forced down near Narbonne, in France, when its propeller flew off. This clearly refers to the Maillet 21, but it is possible that they flew a Swallow to Spain on another occasion. The most likely candidate would be G-ADMB (c/n405), registered to Col H L Cooper until August 1936 and the only Swallow to have been sold abroad at that time.

Span 42ft 8½in; length 26ft; height 7ft; wing area 215sq ft.
  Empty weight 990lb; loaded weight 1,500lb.
  Maximum speed 112mph; cruising speed 88mph; ceiling 17,000ft; range 420 miles.

B.A. Eagle 2

One of the most impressive and

The B.A. Swallow EC-XXA after being brought over to the Nationalists by its owner, Sr Lezama. The registrations have been concealed beneath sheets of newspaper glued over the fabric. (Azaola)

handsome of the British light aeroplanes produced in the 1930s, the B.A. Eagle 2, designed by G H Handasyde, was a wooden low-wing cantilever monoplane powered by a 130 h.p. de Havilland Gipsy Major engine and accommodating a pilot and two passengers in a spacious, sound-proofed, cabin. Unlike the generally similar Miles Falcon and Percival Gull, however, it possessed a manually operated, outwardly retracting undercarriage. 'British Klemm Eagles', as they were usually called, were regular competitors in races and rallies held in Britain, Europe and the Commonwealth from 1934 until the outbreak of the Second World War. Several were adapted for long-distance flying, and in 1935 EC-CBA(?), c/n 108, was bought by Juan Ignacio Pombo for an attempt on the trans-south-Atlantic record. This machine, named *Santander*, crashed at Bathurst (now Banjul, Gambia) on 26 May 1935,

and Pombo bought a second Eagle 2, c/n114, EC-CBB, in June 1935. In this machine he made a successful twenty-stage flight from Santander, Spain, to Mexico City. The civil war broke out before the Eagle 2 could be returned to Spain, and Pombo, whose father and brother were both pilots, eventually joined the Nationalists. Meanwhile, a third B.A. Eagle 2 (c/n115) was bought by LAPE in 1935, registered EC-CBC, and allotted the Fleet No 23. It was customarily flown by Luis Ruano Beltrán, who was to die in the

The B.A. Eagle 2 EC-CBC of LAPE at Barajas. (Arráez)

massacre of the Nationalist prisoners at Paracuellos, outside Madrid, in November 1936. The Eagle, which was at Barajas in July 1936, was used by the Republicans for liaison duties, and became a particular favourite of senior Russian air staff. It did not survive the war.

Span 39ft 3in; length 26ft; height 6ft 9in; wing area 200sq ft.
Empty weight 1,450lb; loaded weight 2,400lb;
Maximum speed 148mph; cruising speed 130mph; ceiling 16,000ft; range 650 miles.

Beechcraft 17

The attractive Beechcraft 17 'Staggerwing' biplane, so called because its upper wing was back-staggered to increase the pilot's range of vision, was one of the most successful light aeroplanes ever built, and was the design by which its manufacturers became famous. The prototype, with a fixed and trousered undercarriage, first flew on 4 November 1932, and the first production aircraft won the Texaco Trophy the next year. The fixed undercarriage was soon replaced by one that retracted inwardly, and was operated manually. The cabin accommodated the pilot and three (in some versions, four) passengers. The usual powerplant of the earlier versions was the Jacobs L-4 (225hp) radial on the 17L series, the Jacobs L-5 (285hp) on the 17B series, and the Wright R-975-E (420hp) on the 17R series, all engines being mounted in long-chord NACA cowlings. Some Beechcraft 17Rs were fitted with extra fuel tanks to increase their range to a remarkable 850 miles. Construction was of wood and metal, the forward fuselage and

leading edges of the wings and tail surfaces being covered with plywood, and the rest with fabric. The Beechcraft 17 was produced in twenty civil, military, landplane and seaplane versions between 1932 and 1945, and several are still flying.

At least seven, and possibly ten, Beechcraft 17s were involved directly or indirectly in the Spanish Civil War, and their identities and histories have been the cause of considerable confusion among aviation historians.

Beechcraft B17L c/n 33, NC14454: (Jacobs L-4).
Sold to Automobiles Fernández SA of Barcelona as an air taxi in 1935. Registered EC-BEB. Impressed into Republican service on 18 July 1936, but damaged when Ramón Torres landed with the undercarriage retracted on Prat de Llobregat, Barcelona, on 4 August. Repaired and transferred to the Alas Rojas (Red Wings) group at Sariñena, Aragon, it was wrecked in November when a storm turned it over and blew it into a Potez 43.

Beechcraft B17R c/n 66, NC15811 (Wright R-975).
Bought in France in 1935 by Réne Drouillet, ostensibly for use by Movietone News. In fact, Drouillet had been an adviser to Haile Selasse, the Emperor (or Negus) of Ethiopia, but had become involved in an Italian plot to kidnap the Emperor and fly

Beechcraft 17R NC15816 was brought to Europe on the airship Hindenburg *and used by Owen Cathcart-Jones and Victor Urrutia for liaison between the Nationalists and the ex-King of Spain, Alfonso XIII, in Czechoslovakia.*

him as a prisoner to Italy. The Beechcraft was impounded at Villacoublay after an over-zealous Italian embassy official, not privy to the plot, reported that it was being illegally exported to Ethiopia, which was then being invaded by Italy. Drouillet was arrested and briefly imprisoned, and in 1937 he sold the Beechcraft, through various intermediaries, to Air Pyrénées (see Appendix I). Registered F-APFD, it was painted beige, with black stripes and various emblems (the Lion of Juda and a four-leafed clover, among others), and was flown by Basque nationalist Georges Lebeau. F-APFD took part in many dangerous missions to the Basque and Asturian zones of Republican Spain, where it was popularly believed to have once been the personal aeroplane of Haille Selasse, and was thus called *El Avion Negus* (The Negus Aeroplane), one of several machines so named as a result of a similar misunderstanding. The Basque President, José Aguirre, finally escaped to France in this Beechcraft, which remained at Briscous after the civil war. It was discovered by the Germans in 1940 and wrecked during a test flight.

Beechcraft C17L c/n 83, NC15813 (Jacobs L-4).
Possibly the machine bought by C E Gardner, the 1936 King's Cup winner, in December 1936, and sold abroad immediately. (Gardner had previously sold his de Havilland D.H.89 Dragon Rapide G-ADFY to the Nationalists). It is also possible that this was the light blue Beechcraft (allegedly F-APFB, though this registration also belonged to a Potez 25) that served with the Beechcraft *Avión Negus* through the spring and summer of 1937, as part of the small fleet of Air Pyrénées. It was often flown by Jean Dary, who had previously flown for the Republicans with the Escadrille Lafayette and the Escuadrilla Palancar (I-15 Chatos) on the Madrid front. Dary wrecked the Beechcraft while landing at Parme-Biarritz Aerodrome in September 1937.

The following Beechcraft 17s were bought by, or for, the Spanish Republicans:

Beechcraft B17R, c/n 50 (Wright R-975).
Bought by Sir Harold Farquhar, Secretary at the British Legation, Mexico City, and given the British registration G-ADLE. In 1935, fitted both with wheels and floats, it was used for a flight from Mexico to Heston, London, via Alaska, the USSR and Europe, the pilot being Fritz Bieler, a German ex-patriot in Mexico who was later to procure

aircraft for the Spanish Republicans. At Croydon, G-ADLE was bought by Surrey Flying Services (SFS), the UK agency for Beechcraft. In March-April 1937 SFS sold G-ADLE to the Dutchman Frank ten Bos, proprietor of Aero Industries, but it was registered to an English employee, AGA Fisher. When the authorities learned that it was to be re-sold to the Spanish Republicans, the export was prohibited. Nevertheless, the aircraft had been cleared for flying by the end of 1938, for on 20 January 1939 it came down with wing icing in a cabbage patch on Laaland Island, Denmark (curiously, it had previously come down in a cabbage patch at East Farleigh, Kent). It was still flying at the beginning of the Second World War (it was not written off in January 1939, as has been stated), but nothing further is known of it.

Beechcraft B17R c/n 52, NC15403 or 15413 (Wright R-975).

This is believed to have been one of two Beechcraft 17s bought by the Spanish Republican agent Teniente Francisco Corral from the Lion Oil Refining Co, Eldorado, Arkansas, on 21 November 1936, ostensibly for an ambulance service at Tabasco, Mexico. It is reported to have crossed into Mexico without an export permit about 1 January 1937, although Lion Oil claimed that it was still at Eldorado on 28 April 1937. Be that as it may, a Beechcraft 17 *was* delivered to the Spanish Republican ambassador in Mexico some time in 1937, and was given the registration XA-BEV or 'BEY. Apparently, however, it was not shipped abroad the *Ibai* (See Appendix II).

Beechcraft B17R, c/n 71, NC15816 (Wright R-975).

This aircraft was brought to Europe as cargo on board the airship *Hindenburg* in 1936 by James Haizlip, the well-known Shell company and racing pilot. In July 1936 it was bought in France by Victor Urrutia, a Spanish Monarchist and member of the Nationalist conspiracy, who employed Owen Cathcart-Jones (who had come fourth in the England-Australia MacRobertson Air Race in 1934) to fly him on various missions carrying messages between Gen Mola at Burgos and the ex-King Alfonso XIII in Czechoslovakia. Pursued by the authorities of several countries, Cathcart-Jones and Urrutia were forced to abandon the Beechcraft at Innsbruck Aerodrome, Austria. When he was eventually able to recover it, Urrutia sold the Beechcraft to Alitalia. It was re-registered I-IBIS, and was still flying at the beginning of the Second World War.

Beechcraft C-17R c/n 118, (Wright R-975).

Brought to Europe by James Haizlip on board the airship *Graf Zeppelin* and based at Frankfurt, Germany, this aircraft was used by Alec Ulmann (European Manager of Aviquipo – Aviation Equipment and Export) and Haizlip for marketing tours round Europe. When Haizlip and Cathcart-Jones became interested in trying to sell aircraft to either side in the Spanish war, the Beechcraft was shipped to Tilbury, London, bought by Surrey Flying Services, and registered G-AESJ, one of the intermediaries being Brian Allen (see Percival Gull and Airspeed Envoy). It was then bought by Miss Pauline Thomson, acting for Haizlip, who in turn was acting for the Belgian company LACEBA (see Fokker D.XXI and C.X, and Romano R-82 and R-83), which had been set up, or assisted, with Spanish Republican funds. Thomson/Haizlip then sold it to Frank ten Bos (see previous entry), and the British authorities, now suspicious, withdrew its general licence. The Air Ministry believed that the importing of the aeroplane into England, and the registration and subsequent selling and re-selling, were simply manoeuvres to raise the price at which it would be sold to the Spanish Republicans. Nevertheless, ten Bos was allowed to display G-AESJ at the First International Aircraft Exhibition in Brussels during May and June 1937, under pain of heavy penalties should he sell it to a Spanish agent. It returned to Britain after the show, and was still there at the end of the Spanish Civil War. At the outbreak of the Second World War it was the only Beechcraft 17 in British ownership. After impressment it may have become the famous Beechcraft DR628, flown by Prince Bernhardt of the Netherlands.

Four other Beechcraft 17s should be mentioned in connection with the Spanish Civil War.

Beechcraft B17L, c/n 23, G-ADDH (Jacobs L-4).

This was owned by Amy Johnson (Mollison), who had held the Beech concession in England for a time, and was 'sold as spares' to Thor Solberg, a Norwegian, in July 1937. It never reached Norway, however, and is suspected to have been sold as spares to Air Pyrénées.

Beechcraft E17B, c/n 141, NC16449.

Taken to France in May 1937 by Gloria Bristol, a famous beautician and friend of Amy Johnson, this aircraft disappears from records thereafter.

Beechcraft C17B, c/n 127, NC17062 (Jacobs L-5).

This aircraft was sold in France by Charles C Grey of Kansas after a forced landing at Cennevières-sur-Marne in April 1937. No further record of it has been found.

It is true that Haile Salasse had briefly owned a Beechcraft 17, sold to him in fact by Réné Drouillet (see above). This was the 17L c/n 24, NC14405 (Jacobs L-4), bought by Drouillet to fly two journalists (H R Knickerbocker and Henri de Vilmorin, a friend of Malraux) to Addis Ababa to cover the Italian invasion of Ethiopia in 1935. Drouillet made a wheels-up landing at Cairo Airport and sold the Beechcraft to Haile Selasse for £12,000. The Beechcraft served in the Ethiopian (Abyssinian) air force for six weeks, but was either destroyed by bombing or captured by the Italians. It could not, therefore, have been the *Avion Negus* (see above), although no doubt the two aircraft were confused later.

Beechcraft B17L

Span 32ft; length 24ft 6in; height 8ft 6in; wing area 273sq ft.

Empty weight 1,800lb; loaded weight 3,150lb.

Maximum speed 175mph at sea level; cruising speed 162mph at 5,000ft; ceiling 15,500ft; range 560 miles.

Beechcraft C17R

Span 32ft; length 24ft 5in; height 8ft 2in.

Empty weight 2,250lb; loaded weight 3,900lb.

Maximum speed 211mph at sea level; cruising speed 195mph at 10,000ft; ceiling 21,500ft; range 800 miles.

Bellanca 28-70 and 28-90

Guiseppe Mario Bellanca emigrated from Italy to the United States in 1911. By the end of the 1920s he had achieved distinction as an aircraft designer with his Wright-Bellanca WB-2 Columbia, in which Clarence D Chamberlain and Charles A Levine flew from New York to Eisleben, Germany, on 4-6 June 1927, barely two weeks after Charles Lindbergh's epic flight to Paris, and for his series of Pacemaker, Airbus and Aircruiser high-wing transports, characterised by their idiosyncratic high-lift struts and 'bow-legged' landing gear. The Bellanca 77-140 bomber, a twin-engined development of the Airbus and Aircruiser, was built in 1934 to meet a requirement of the Columbian Fuerza Aérea. The numbers '77-140' referred to the wing area (770sq ft) and the total horsepower of two 700hp Wright Cyclone engines (1,400hp). Four were delivered in 1935, and two more were ordered in 1936. On 25 August 1936 a Mr van Merkensteijn of Rotterdam, Holland, made an offer for these two aircraft on behalf of the Spanish Republicans. Negotiations continued until 10 September, when Guiseppe Bellanca, a warm supporter of the Spanish Republican cause, reluctantly turned down the proposal after being warned by the US State Department of the disapproval such a sale would incur from the government.

The Model 28-70 (280sq ft/ 700hp), Bellanca's first attempt at a high-performance aircraft, was commissioned for entry in the Mac-Robertson England–Australia Air Race of 1934 by an Irish consortium headed by Col James C Fitzmaurice of the Irish Free State Army Air Corps, who, with Hauptmann Hermann Koehl and Baron Gunther von Huenefeld, had made the first successful east-west crossing of the North Atlantic in the Junkers W 33 *Bremen* in April 1928. The Bellanca 28-70, powered by a 700hp Pratt & Whitney Twin Wasp Junior S1AG radial engine in a long-chord NACA cowling, was a sizeable low-wing monoplane with an unusually wide-track retractable undercarriage. The two crew members, who had dual controls, occupied an enclosed cabin to the rear of the fuselage, close to the large, rounded fin and rudder. The fuselage was built of welded chrome-molybdenum tubing with wooden

The Bellanca 28/70 The Irish Swoop.

stringers and fabric covering. The wings were of braced two-spar wooden construction with fabric covering. The bracing was effected by a system of tie-rods to the top of the fuselage and to a pair of faired kingposts projecting in tandem below the fuselage, a curious feature which caused many misgivings, in some minds, over the damage the posts might cause in the event of a wheels-up landing.

When the Bellanca 28-70, bearing the Irish registration EI-AAZ, arrived at Mildenhall in October 1934 for the start of the race, its fuselage was painted white, its wings green, and its cowling yellow. The name *The Irish Swoop*, over a horseshoe, was painted on the cowling and fuselage sides below the cockpit, for Fitzmaurice hoped to gain additional publicity for the Irish Sweepstake. The air race committee judged the Bellanca unsafe and disqualified it. Fitzmaurice and his copilot, Jock Bonar, started off for Australia nonetheless, but cowling troubles over Belgium forced them to return to Britain. Further problems developed with the landing gear, and the machine was shipped back to Bellanca at Newcastle, Delaware, where it was wrecked by a freak wind in April 1935. After rebuilding and considerable modification (though it was not, contrary to many published assertions, re-engined with a 900hp Twin Wasp), the Bellanca 28-70

The Bellanca 28/90B.

Flash, as it was now called, was registered NR190M and offered to James Mollison for his next (and fourth) transatlantic flight. Mollison bought the *Flash*, which he re-named *The Dorothy* in honour of his girlfriend, the actress Dorothy Ward, and repainted it garish green and orange. Wearing a dress-suit under his flying clothes, he took off from Floyd Bennett Field, New York, on 28 October 1936, and landed at Croydon after a flight of 13 hours 7 minutes, breaking the record set only six weeks before by Merrill and Richman in the Vultee V1-A *Lady Peace* (q.v.). A month later Mollison and Edouard Corniglion-Molinier (see Lockheed Orion and Potez 54) made an unsuccessful attempt to break the London–Cape Town record set by Mollison's estranged wife, Amy Johnson. After returning to England, *The Dorothy* was re-registered G-AEPC. Mollison described the aeroplane as a 'brute', though he professed much affection for it, despite its alarming character, and claimed that he had touched 272mph in it on more than one occasion. On 17 April 1937 he flew it to Paris with Baron Segonzac to plan an east-west Atlantic crossing with Beryl Markham, a project for which she was soon to buy the Northrop 1C Delta SE-ADI. Henceforth, the history of the Bellanca 28-70 becomes suspiciously obscure. According to reports in *Les Ailes*, after two trips to London he made a dead-stick landing at Meaux, Esbly, either on 24 April or 24 May 1937. Thereafter,

French newspapers printed several stories that he had sold his Bellanca to the Spanish Republicans via SFTA (see Appendix II), an assertion supported by persistent Spanish claims during the next 45 years that a Bellanca did, indeed, fly in the Spanish Republican air force, and that it was shot down, or caught fire in the air, over the Madrid sector.

That Mollison did sell the Bellanca to an agent for the Spanish Republic seems probable. Meaux was the aerodrome of Lejeune Aviation, which not only trained Republican pilots in France, but procured a considerable number of Caudron, Morane-Saulnier and Potez aircraft for the Republican government. It was from Meaux that Beryl Markham's Northrop Delta disappeared to Spain, and it was also from Meaux that the Bellanca disappeared from view as well. Moreover, Mollison spent the next two years in France, living well but with no visible means of support, which might suggest that a high sum was paid for the Bellanca. In September 1939 the UK Air Ministry was impressing all aircraft on the British civil register, and demanded to know the whereabouts of G-APEC, whose last Certificate of Airworthiness had expired on 23 October 1937. Mollison's solicitor told them it had been sold on 23 June 1939. Such statements are all too familiar when aircraft that were sold to Spain are concerned, and this one cannot be accepted as any more trustworthy than the others.

After Mollison's transatlantic flight in October 1936, Miles Sherover, whose Hanover Sales Corporation had just been created with

Spanish Republican funds to function as an American counterpart to SFTA in France (see Appendix II), approached Guiseppe Bellanca in November and discussed the possibility of producing a military version of the 28-70. The result was the 28-90, powered by a 900hp Twin Wasp Senior driving a three-blade Hamilton propeller. Its armament consisted of two machine guns in the wings, a single gun in the observer's cockpit and eight 54.5kg bombs carried on external racks under the wings. This armament, with a top speed of 280mph, a cruising speed of 250mph, a ceiling of 30,500ft and a range of 800-1,000 miles claimed by the manufacturer, made the 28-90 an impressive warplane, with a performance higher than that of any other aircraft in Spain at that time. The Spanish government placed an order for twenty straight off the drawing board. The ostensible purchaser was Air France, which pretended that they were mailplanes, but the US State Department, seeing that the agent was the by-now-notorious SFTA, prohibited the sale. After a long delay the aircraft were sold to China, where they were soon destroyed, some by Japanese air attacks on aerodromes, but most by Chinese pilots.

In December 1937 an order for twenty-two Bellanca 28-90Bs (with flaps and improved undercarriage fairings) was received from an agency in Athens, apparently connected with, or founded by, Antonius Raab (see Potez 54, Introduction and Appendix II), on behalf of a 'Reservist School' in Greece. The scheme was supported in America by Hall Roosevelt, President Franklin Roosevelt's brother-in-law. The discovery that the Greek import licences and other documents were forged put paid to the transaction, however, and the Bellancas remained in crates on the dockside at Wilmington.

During the last weeks of the civil war the Republican Premier, Juan Negrín, tried to sustain morale by claiming that American aircraft, including large numbers of '*el rapidísimo Bellanca*', would soon arrive to turn the tide of fortune in favour of the Republic. Two ace Republican fighter pilots, who had been sent to Paris to plead with the French government to

A Blackburn L.1C Bluebird IV.

allow all of the (mostly Russian) aircraft held in France to be shipped to Spain before it was too late, claimed that they had seen these aircraft in France. This gave rise to a story, still believed by some writers, that the Bellancas were unloaded at Le Havre and returned to the United States when their crossing to Spain was prohibited. In reality, on 27 February 1939 (even before he made his promises about the Bellancas) Negrín ordered Coronel Francisco León Trejo, chief of the Republican Purchasing Commission in the United States, to sell all aircraft not yet delivered at fifty per cent of their purchase price. Sherover offered a mere ten per cent, which was refused. Eventually, President Cárdenas of Mexico, whose government had been the only one in the world openly to support the Republicans throughout the civil war, bought the aircraft at full cost price, the money being used to pay for the sustenance of Republican refugees arriving in Mexico. After two accidents, the Bellancas were withdrawn from Mexican service in 1940.

Bellanca 28-90

Span 46ft 2in; length 25ft 11in; height 8ft 8in; wing area 279sq ft.

Loaded weight 6,755lb.

Maximum speed 280mph; ceiling 30,500ft; range 800-1,000 miles.

Blackburn L.1B Bluebird III and L.1C Bluebird IV

The original Blackburn Bluebirds (Mks. I, II and III), which were of wooden construction with fabric covering, were the first British side-by-side two-seat sporting aeroplanes to go into production. Although they were built only in small numbers, they achieved a considerable degree of popularity in the late 1920s. One L.1B Bluebird III, G-AABC (80hp Armstrong Siddeley Genet II), was sold to the Spanish pilot Fernando Pedioza in 1929, but, since there is no trace of it in Spanish registration records after 1930, one must assume that it took no part in the Spanish Civil War.

The L.1C Bluebird IV was not so much a development of its predecessors as a new aeroplane, being larger, of metal construction, and having radically different wings and empennage. The only feature retained from the earlier Bluebirds was the side-by-side seating. The Bluebird IV, however, was an outstanding light aeroplane, and was used by many famous pilots of the day. In G-ABDS (120hp de Havilland Gipsy II) the Hon Mrs Victor Bruce made the first solo flight (interrupted by sea-passages across the Pacific and Atlantic oceans) round the world in 1930. One, G-AAOC, was taken to Spain by its owner, Mrs Elizabeth Scott, and there sold to A Fernández Matamoros of the Aero Club de

Madrid in 1933. It was in the Republican zone at the start of the civil war and, if not destroyed in one of the Nationalist air raids on Barajas, was presumably flown down to Los Gerónimos or Alcantarilla and used as a primary trainer.

Bluebird IV:

Span 30ft; length 23ft 2in; height 9ft; wing area 246sq ft.

Empty weight 1,070lb; loaded weight 1,750lb.

(Gipsy I): Maximum speed 120mph; cruising speed 85mph; initial climb 730ft/min; range 320 miles.

Blériot SPAD 51, 91 and 510

Two Blériot SPAD 51s, and one Blériot SPAD 91, were in Spain during the civil war, and at least two of these aircraft engaged in several combats during October 1937. Because there is still some confusion over which individual aeroplanes they were, and because their presence gave rise to one of the more enduring myths of the air war in Spain – namely that fifteen or twenty-seven Blériot SPAD 510 fighters fought on the Republican side – it is convenient to deal with all three types together.

When Blériot absorbed the SPAD company, in 1921, André Herbemont (designer of the famous SPAD fighters of the First World War) designed a series of biplane and

Blériot SPAD 51-01.

sesquiplane single- and two-seat fighters which began with the Blériot SPAD 41 and ended with the Blériot SPAD 710 in 1934. Most of them were intended for the French *Léger*, or 'Jockey', lightweight fighter programme of the late 1920s and early 1930s, and most bore a strong family resemblance, notably in the shape of the fin and rudder, and in having a swept upper wing and unswept lower wing and deep-chord interplane I-struts.

The Blériot SPAD 51/1, with its fabric-covered metal wings and wooden monocoque fuselage, appeared in 1924. It was powered by an uncowled 420hp Gnome-Rhône Jupiter radial engine, and was armed with two 7.7mm MAC (Vickers) guns in the upper wing. Fifty 51/2s were built for the Polish air arm in 1925-26, and ten 51/4s (600hp Jupiter, and two additional guns in the fuselage) for Turkey. About a dozen were built for aerobatic displays, and one of these was bought by the Aero Club de Aragón and registered EC-BCC in 1935. On 26 December 1935 the Aero Club advertised both that aircraft and their Farman F.200 (EC-LAA) for sale in the French journal *Les Ailes*. Since

neither aircraft was in flying condition, however, there were no buyers, and both were still in Spain when the civil war broke out six months later. They somehow must have been refurbished, for both were removed to the aerodrome at Barracas, a village near the coast in the province of Castellón. When the Nationalists captured the aerodrome in July 1938 the two machines were among the wrecked aircraft, which included the Potez 54 'O', scattered about the field. Later, the Italian press published photographs of the Blériot

SPAD 51 and, despite its civil registration and obvious antiquity, claimed that it was a Communist fighter shot down by the Nationalists.

There exists another photograph of what is almost certainly a Blériot SPAD 51 after it had apparently

A wrecked Blériot SPAD 51 with Republican markings and a red star on its fin. This was presumably one of the two Blériot SPAD fighters, the other being a 91, brought to Getafe, Madrid, in the autumn of 1936. (Azaola)

suffered a violent ground-loop, bearing Republican markings, a red star on the fin, and covered with a mottled camouflage. The man standing beside it resembles the French volunteer pilot Abel Guidez. It is not known for certain which Blériot SPAD 51 this is (it is possibly F-AIVS), how or when it reached Spain, or where and when the accident occurred, except that it was probably at Getafe (see below).

The Blériot SPAD 91, sixth in the lineage, went into nine different prototype versions between 1927 and 1932, but none received a production order. It was an all-metal, fabric-covered biplane powered by a Hispano-Suiza 12Hb liquid-cooled engine. The 91/6, with rounded wingtips, a lengthened fuselage, its tailplane lowered to the base of the fuselage, and a 500hp Hispano-Suiza 12Mb engine, appeared in 1931. After its test flights, during which its tailplane was restored to a higher position, it remained in a hangar until September 1936, when some company workers asked Louis Blériot if they could recondition it and present it to 'the Heroic Spanish People in their Struggle for Liberty'. He made no objection, provided that they did this in their spare time and at their own expense. On 30 September 1936, piloted by M Landry and bearing the Spanish government registration EC-12-E, it left Toulouse-Montaudran (the Air France airport) for Barcelona, whence it was taken on to Getafe, Madrid, by Abel Guidez, a French volunteer in the Malraux squadron who had transferred to the Escadrille Lafayette. In his memoirs, the Spanish fighter pilot (and later chief of Spanish Republican fighters) Andrés García Lacalle wrote that its arrival was preceded by exaggerated tales of its effectiveness and modernity, 'no doubt occasioned', he mistakenly presumed, 'by the enormous price paid for it'. He states that there was much delay in arming it with two guns bolted to the undersurface of the lower wings to fire outside the propeller arc, owing to the difficulty of improvising an effective firing mechanism. He ends by saying that, after a few test flights, a foreign pilot landed it heavily, and it was wrecked in a 'violent ground-loop'.

Lacalle, who was writing thirty-

The Blériot SPAD 91.

five years afterwards in exile, might have confused this with the Blériot SPAD 51 shown in the photograph, for on 21 October 1936, according to Nationalist historians, a 'Blériot SPAD 510' was shot down over Getafe by the Italian pilot Tenente Montagnacco in a Fiat C.R.32 of the *Cucaracha* squadron. The matter is further confused, however, by the testimony of Maurice Chauvenet, a young French pilot of the Escadrille Lafayette, who wrote an account of his experiences shortly after leaving Spain in November or December 1936. In this, he describes a skirmish between two 'Spads', one of which he was flying, and four Fiats protecting some Junkers Ju 52s. Guidez, in a similar account written at about the same time, mentions a similar skirmish on 2 October 1936 with four Fiats in which, 'thanks to the marvellous manoeuvrability of the Spad', he was able to 'disperse' his opponents after twenty minutes of combat. Both accounts seem to have been written for propaganda purposes, and are not exactly trustworthy, but they are probably correct in establishing that there were two Blériot SPAD fighters in active service at Getafe for a time.

Montagnacco's unconfirmed victory on 21 October is probably the source of the stories concerning the presence of Blériot SPAD 510 fighters in Spain, the numbers delivered varying, in different sources published until the 1970s, between fifteen and twenty-seven. The origin of these two figures seems to have been a Republican document, stolen and published by the Nationalists in 1938, concerning an unsuccessful

attempt to buy fifteen Blériot SPAD 510s, twenty-one Dewoitine D.371s and six Dewoitine D.510s in January 1937. According to the Republican buying agent, Teniente Coronel Juan Ortiz Muñoz (who had been the commanding officer of Los Alcázares air base in July 1936), the deal fell through because its sponsor, the famous First World War air ace Col Réné Fonck, demanded two million French francs in cash for himself before signing the contract. However, since only sixty Blériot SPAD 510 fighters were built, and all can be accounted for in service with the Armée de l'Air, it is almost certain that none was ever delivered to Spain, especially since no Republican pilot can be found who remembers seeing one, let alone flying one.

There are rumours that the Blériot SPAD 91/8 F-ALXC, an inverted-sesquiplane version of 91/4 and 91/6 fitted with an Hispano-Suiza 12Xbrs engine and a 20mm *moteur-canon*, went to Spain. These can also be discounted, for such an unusual machine would have attracted a great deal of notice, and would have been remembered by all who saw it.

Blériot SPAD 51/6:

Span 9.49m; length 6.45m; weight 3.1m; wing area 24.27sq m.

Empty weight 990kg; loaded weight 1,360kg; wing loading 56kg/sq m.

Maximum speed 230km/hr; climb to 4,000m in 9min 2sec; ceiling 9,000m.

Blériot SPAD 91/6:

Span 8.8m; length 6.48m; height 3.1m; wing area 22sq m.

Empty weight 1,160kg; loaded weight 1,440kg.

Maximum speed 244km/hr; ceiling 8,700m.

Blériot SPAD 56 and 111

During the 1920s André Herbemont, the chief designer of Blériot Aéronautique, experimented with a series of single-engined passenger-carrying biplanes of the 'type-berline', so named (after the old-fashioned coach) because the pilot's cockpit was located behind the passenger cabin – a format continued in the 1930s in the Northrop Alpha, de Havilland D.H.83 Fox Moth and Consolidated 20A Fleetster. Among these was the Blériot SPAD 56, of which eighteen were custom-built in six different versions between 1923 and 1929 (only the 56/4 and 56/5 had cockpits in front of the passenger cabins). The two Blériot SPAD 56/6s (c/n 19/4442, F-AJVA, and c/n 20/4443, F-AJTN), both powered by 420hp Gnome-Rhône 9 Ab uncowled radial engines, were built for AIR-publicité in 1929 to tow advertising banners, though provision was made for four passengers. Their construction was of wood, the monocoque fuselage being built of ply and the wings and tail covered with fabric. Two petrol tanks sat on top of the upper wing centre section, and the outer wings were braced by a pair of deep-chord I-struts.

In 1927 Herbemont began work on a wooden (later wood and metal) single-engined, low-wing, six-to-eight-passenger monoplane, the Type 111, of which only five were built. The somewhat unsightly undercarriage-bracing V-struts of the prototype were replaced in subsequent models by two pairs of parallel struts – no less unsightly or drag-

A Blériot SPAD 56. (A J Jackson)

creating – slanting down from the fuselage shoulders to the upper surface of the wings. The Blériot SPAD 111/3 (c/n 3/4443, F-ALND), powered by an uncowled 470hp Gnome-Rhône Jupiter 9 Ady radial engine and with a capacity for eight passengers, first flew in 1930. It was used for two or three years by Louis Blériot, as a vehicle for publicising his company.

The Blériot-SPAD 111/4 was the first of the series to have a retractable undercarriage. In 1932 there appeared the Blériot SPAD 111/5 *Sagittaire*, in which Herbemont had redesigned the fuselage to follow the 'berline' layout of the biplanes, with the pilot occupying an open cockpit behind the passenger cabin. Financial difficulties delayed development and testing until 1934, when, after further modifications, the Blériot SPAD 111/6 (as the 111/5 now was), fitted with a 760hp Gnome-Rhône 14 Kdrs radial engine in a long-chord cowling and with extra tanks, was entered for the MacRobertson England–Australia air race. An accident at Le Bourget prevented its taking part, however, and the 111/6 *Sagittaire*, F-ANJS, spent the next two years standing in a hangar.

In the last week of August 1936 the French press reported that the Fédération Nationale des Travailleirs du Bâtiment (the National Federation of Building Workers) had bought four aircraft for the Spanish Republic, of which the first two, 'ancient and decrepit Blériots', had already left for Spain on 20 August. The first, the Blériot-SPAD 56 F-AJTN, piloted by Louis Clément, carried an unnamed passenger who made no secret to reporters, when the

aircraft staged at Limoges, of his strong Anarchist views. The Blériot 111/3 F-ALND, piloted by Rémy Clément (perhaps a relative of Louis and certainly involved in procuring aircraft for the Spanish Republicans), had taken as passengers the General Secretary of the Fédération, Réné Arrachard, and his deputy, Lucien Labrousse. What happened to the two Blériots in Spain is not recorded.

The second Blériot SPAD 56/6, F-AJVA, did not leave France. The fourth aircraft, the Morane-Saulnier MS 233 F-AJLH, did not leave either, and was sold by Arrachard to the Aéro Club Lyonnaise in 1938.

In a deposition written in 1973, Col Victor Veniel (late of the Malraux squadron) states that he personally flew the Blériot 111/6 *Sagittaire* in Republican Spain, adding that it was procured through Lucien Boussot-rot, the well-known transatlantic flyer and Socialist Deputy, whom he accuses of profiteering on the sale. He further states that two weeks after it had arrived in Spain he was ordered to take off on a propaganda and fund-raising tour. Shortly after leaving Prat de Llobregat Airport, Barcelona, the engine burnt out and he was forced down on a beach on the Costa Brava.

Blériot SPAD 56/6 F-AJTN:

Span 13.3m; length 9m; height 7.3m; wing area 48.6sq m.

Empty weight 1,462kg; loaded weight 2,244kg.

Maximum speed 180km/h; range 600km.

Blériot SPAD 111/3 F-ALND:

Span 16m; length 10.4m; height

The Blériot SPAD 111/3 F-ALND. (Liron)

3.15m; wing area 33.1sq m.

Empty weight 1,588kg; loaded weight 2,618kg.

Maximum speed 231km/h; range 1,100km.

Blériot SPAD 111/6 *Sagittaire* F-ANJS:

Span 17m; length 10.66m; height 4.03m; wing area 34.56sq m.

Empty weight 2,136kg; loaded weight 3,400kg.

The Blériot SPAD 111/6 F-ANJS Sagittaire. (Liron)

Maximum speed 370km/h; range 1,800km.

Bloch MB 200 and MB 210

Although books or articles about aircraft of the Spanish Civil War usually devote some space to the Bloch MB 200, there is no clear contemporary evidence, in the form of documents, eyewitness accounts, or photographs, to show that any bombers of this type were delivered to, or used by, the Spanish Republicans.

The Bloch MB 200 was an all-metal, high-wing monoplane, powered by two 725hp Gnome-Rhône 14 Kirs/Kjrs radial engines, built to a French air ministry specification of 1932. With its severe angularity, its slab-sided fuselage, its generous glasshouse fenestration and birdcage-like turrets, it was a typical French bomber of the early 1930s. It had a crew of four, and its defensive armament comprised three 7.5mm MAC 1934 machine guns, one each in nose, dorsal and ventral turrets. It could carry up to 1,000kg of bombs, either as twenty 50kg bombs carried in vertical racks internally, or as 100kg or 200kg bombs externally beneath the fuselage. Between 1934 and 1936 a total of 208 MB 200s was built, and they equipped twelve Armée de l'Air squadrons.

It is said that, when the Spanish Dirección General de Aeronáutica

A Bloch MB 200.

turned its attention to the selection of a new medium bomber in 1934, the Bloch MB 200 'tested' at Barajas, Madrid, on 7 November 1934 was among the unsuccessful competitors. What actually happened in November 1934 was that a flight of three MB 200s of GB 11/22, based at Chartres, and three Morane MS 230E trainers from Étampes, flew to Lisbon for a benefit air display, organised by *Le Petit Parisien* and Air Propagande on behalf of the widow of a popular Portuguese pilot recently killed in France, and during the return flight stopped for a few hours at Barajas. There was an official reception, graced by the French ambassador and numerous Spanish air officers, and during the afternoon three Spanish pilots were allowed to try the controls of the Bloch in flight. The celebration ended with a dinner. At that time the Spanish government had all but finalised a contract to buy eighty-one Martin 139Ws (the agreement broke down later but was revived in December 1935), and it is unlikely that, whatever the French might have hoped, the Spaniards had any thought of testing, let along ordering, the Bloch MB 200.

It is said that two Bloch MB 200s were flown to Prat de Llobregat, Barcelona, on 20 August 1936 (that is, a month after the start of the civil war), and that two more were delivered in crates shortly afterwards. It is further said that these four participated in a few bombing missions over the Madrid front before disappearing without trace. Research has revealed only two items of information, both dubious, which might support this. On 24 November 1936 the British Air Attaché in Paris, Grp Capt Douglas Colyer, visited the CEMA (test centre) at Villacoublay, and afterwards talked to Col Jauneaud, chef-de-cabinet for civil aviation to the air minister, Pierre Cot. When the conversation turned to stories in the French press about aircraft supplied to the Spanish Republicans, Jauneaud said that only one Bloch MB 200 (now shot down) had gone to Spain, and no Bloch MB 210s, the proof being that only a single pro-

totype MB 210 existed, and Colyer himself had seen it at Villacoublay that morning. Jauneaud was obviously lying so far as the MB 210 was concerned (see below), so it is impossible to say whether or not he was telling the truth about the MB 200.

The second source is a verbal statement on a cassette kindly sent to the author by Hilaire du Berrier, an American pilot who flew for the Republicans during the winter of 1936-37. According to du Berrier, Vincent Schmidt, a fellow American pilot (and painter) living in Paris, encountered difficulties in the autumn of 1936 in enrolling in the Spanish Republican air force. Comandante Jácome, at the Spanish Republican Purchasing Commission, invited Schmidt to ferry a 'Marcel Bloch night bomber', which had just been bought, to Spain, because no Spanish pilot was available. Schmidt carried out his assignment and, having been allowed to join the Republican air force in return, actually flew the Bloch in Spain for a time, with 'a bullfighter for a rear gunner'. This may have been the MB 200 referred to by Jauneaud, for, as shown below, it cannot have been an MB 210. A summary of war material received between 11 November 1936 and 17 March 1937, drawn up by the Republican Commisariat for Armaments and Munitions, includes '1 Marcheli Bloch', which again presumably refers to the same machine. This would mean, though, that the MB 200 was shot down (if it

A Bloch MB 210.

was shot down) within a day or two of its arrival in Spain, that Schmidt could hardly have flown it for long, and that the Republicans, if the other reports are true, received a total of five MB 200s. Nevertheless, it is difficult to believe that five such large and distinctive bombers could have disappeared without leaving some trace. Some sources have stated that Schmidt flew his Bloch in the northern, or Basque, zone. However, had it been shot down by the only Nationalist fighters in the area at the time, three He 51s, it would surely have been prominent in the German list of victories.

The Bloch MB 210, of which the prototype first flew in 1934, was a low-wing, twin-engined, all-metal monoplane with retractable undercarriage, yet nevertheless bore a close relationship to the MB 200 in its construction and uncompromisingly unaesthetic appearance. Like the MB 200, it was powered by two Gnome-Rhône 14 Kirs (starboard) /Kjrs (port) radial engines, improved to give 820hp at 10,550ft and 900hp at 13,820ft, and carried a crew of five. Defensive armament consisted of a single 7.5mm Darne (or MAC 1934) machine gun in the manually-operated Type A nose turret, a similar weapon in the semi-retractable dorsal Type B turret, and a third in the retractable ventral turret. Up to 1,600kg of bombs could be carried internally. One hundred and thirty MB 210 night bombers were ordered for the Armée de l'Air in 1935, the production being sub-contracted to five different companies, including Hanriot, which was to produce twenty at its Bourges factory. Owing to the delays then plaguing the French aircraft industry, only two of the entire order had been built by July 1936, while the first Hanriot-built example was still on the stocks.

After the outbreak of the war in Spain and the French declaration of Non-Intervention on 8 August 1936, a group of senior Air France officials – notably Edouard Serre, the technical director, Col Victor Poirier and Lionel de Marmier, the chief test pilot – began to devise clandestine ways of exporting aircraft to Spain, and one of their plans involved the Bloch MB 210. Five Bloch 220s

(civil versions of the MB 210, of more streamlined appearance) had been ordered by Air France the previous winter and were nearing completion. The workers at the Hanriot factory suddenly started working round-the-clock shifts to complete the first production MB 210, which was flown to Villacoublay for testing on 29 July. On 26 August de Marmier obtained permission to fly the MB 210 on a trial circuit round France, via Toulouse–Montaudran and Bordeaux, to familiarise himself with the handling characteristics of the basic 210/220 design. After taking off from Toulouse, however, he flew south to Barcelona, where a Spanish pilot, under his tuition, took it on to Albacete. Unfortunately the Bloch damaged its nose after a few sorties and, because the company engineer sent to supervise the repair injured his back in a fall, the bomber was immobilised for more than two months.

At the end of October 1936 the next three Hanriot-built MB 210s to be completed were packed into crates and sent by lorry across the frontier to Spain, instead of being flown to Villacoublay for trials. Outraged at the subterfuge, of which they had had no inkling, the Hanriot directors resigned in protest. At that time the Hanriot company was being nationalised under the regional authority of an administrative council nominated by the strongly pro-Rebublican air minister, Pierre Cot, and it was they, in collusion with Air France, Marcel Bloch (today better known as Marcel Dassault), and Boris Lesk, a Bloch company engineer, who had organised the conspiracy. When the row abated, the directors rejoined the company. It is probable that these four MB 210s were not given construction numbers, for later records seem to show that the first Hanriot-produced MB 210 did not leave the factory until November 1936, and that the 'single prototype' seen by Colyer at Villacoublay on 24 November was therefore this machine. Some sources say that seven Bloch MB 210s, all without construction numbers, were built for the Spanish Republicans, a story obviously impossible to verify. What does seem possible is that the story of the four

MB 200s delivered in August 1936 may have originated from confusion with the MB 210s.

The four MB 210s known to have been delivered to Spain suffered so many mechanical faults in their Gnome-Rhône 14 K engines that they were repeatedly immobilised for weeks at a time. Armament, as usual, was improvised and often limited to a single Lewis gun of First World War vintage in the dorsal turret. Very few factual details are known of their military operations. One, perhaps the first, is believed to have been with the Escadre André Malraux for a time, after which two (or four) were incorporated into an ephemeral 'Grupo Bloch'. On 1 March 1937 two MB 210s joined Grupo 11, based at Lérida, a night-bombing squadron additionally equipped with the Fokker F.IX, F.XVIII and two to four Potez 54s. One MB 210 was wrecked in a heavy landing by the Czech pilot Kozek, its starboard undercarriage leg and wing being damaged beyond repair, and the other was transferred to the 2ª Escuadrilla of the mixed bomber group Grupo 72. With the four Potez 54s acquired in 1937, it continued flying night missions until the summer of 1938. It had a large white 'M' painted on its fin. It was not flying at the end of the war, however. At some unrecorded date the other two MB 210s were transferred to the multi-engined flying school at Totana.

In the light of the known information, therefore, the safest assumption would be that only one Bloch MB 200 and four MB 210s took part in the Spanish Civil War.

Bloch MB 200:

Span 22.45m; length 16m; height 6.92m; wing area 66.75sq m.

Empty weight 4,195kg; loaded weight 6,785kg.

Maximum speed 230km/h; cruising speed 215km/h; ceiling 8,000m; range 1,000km.

Bloch MB 210:

Span 22.81m; length 18.9m; height 6.15m; wing area 75sq m.

Empty weight 5,990kg; loaded weight 9,746kg; wing loading 130kg/sq m.

Maximum speed 335km/h; cruising speed 250km/h; ceiling 9,900m; range 1,700km.

Bloch 300 Pacifique

Intended as a thirty-passenger air-liner for far-eastern service with Air France, the Bloch 300 was a much enlarged, three-engined, aero-dynamically-refined development of the Bloch MB 210 bomber and MB 220 transport. Only one was built, and during initial trials in November 1935 it received the registration F-AONB. Further trials resulted in modifications to the fusel-age and tail unit, and in the reduction of the number of passengers which could be carried from thirty to twenty-four. The first-class (eight-seat) and second-class (sixteen-seat) cabins were separated by a commod-ious cocktail bar, with four stools.

In October 1937 the Bloch 300, officially called *La Pacifique* and unofficially *La Grosse Julie*, was re-registered F-AOUI and leased to Air France for a 100-hour endurance flight on a circuit encompassing Paris, Toulouse and Marseilles. It is said that, during this flight, the aircraft made an unauthorised detour to Barcelona, where it delivered a cargo of arms. Plausibility is lent to this allegation by the fact that the pilot was Lionel de Marmier, the chief test pilot of Air France, who had already delivered a Bloch MB 210 and (perhaps) a Douglas DC-2 to Barcelona, and that the radio oper-ator was Edouard Serre, the tech-nical director of the airline, who did everything in his power to assist the Spanish Republicans throughout the civil war. It seems that clandestine flights to Spain continued until *La Pacifique* was formally handed over to Air France in January 1938. Finally, the fact that it disappears from French records after 11 April 1938 has led to the belief that it ended its life in Spain. However, as no ex-LAPE pilot remembers having seen

The Bloch 300 Pacifique. (Jack Meaden)

so enormous an aeroplane in Repub-lican service (it would have been by far the largest to fly on either side in the civil war), the question must be left open. It is possible, for instance, that it was operated by the FARE, used to evacuate Republican govern-ment officials from Albacete to France at the very end of the war, and then put away in a hangar in France to avoid reclamation by the Franco government.

Powerplants

F-AONB – three Gnome-Rhône 14 Kfrs-1 Mistral Major radial engines, rated at 1,000hp each.
F-AOUI – three Gnome-Rhône 14 N16/17 radial engines, rated at 1,000-1,100hp each.

Span 25.89m; length 23.3m; height 6.25m; wing area 97.7sq m.

Empty weight 8,875kg; loaded weight 13,055kg.

Maximum speed 329km/h; cruising speed 290km/h; ceiling 4,000m; range 1,400km

Boeing 281

The little Boeing P-26A 'Peashoo-ter', as it was nicknamed by its pilots in the US Army Air Corps (USAAC), was one of the most famous and distinctive fighters of the years between the two world wars. It was also, like its contemporary the Martin B-10, transitional, in that it incorporated new concepts and fea-tures without itself being radical or especially advanced in its construc-tion and design for an aeroplane of the early 1930s. Although it was a low-wing monoplane, its wings were externally braced instead of cantile-vered, and its undercarriage was fixed instead of retractable; com-

promises which were forced on the Boeing design team by traditionalists in the USAAC Materiél Division. Nonetheless, when the P-26A began to enter service in December 1933, the Air Corps pilots were proud to be flying what they regarded, and what was described by the American press, as the most modern fighter in the world. In reality, with a top speed of 225mph and a climb of 20,000ft in 12.5 minutes, its performance was in no way superior to fighters then entering service in Europe.

In 1934 Boeing built an export version, the Model 281, of which, out of twelve built, ten were exported to China in 1936. Meanwhile, the Spanish Dirección General de Aero-náutica, in search of a new fighter to replace the ageing Hispano-Nieuport 52s, invited Boeing to send a Model 281 for demonstration in Spain, and a contract was signed on 16 January 1935 by the Boeing company and one Alfonso Albéniz, for which he received an advance of 5 per cent of the unit price. The Boeing 281, NX12275 (the fourth in the production series) arrived at Barajas, Madrid, on 10 March 1935, and was put through its paces by company pilots Eric Nelson and Les Towers, and afterwards by the Spanish milit-ary pilots Gonzálo García Sanjuán, Fernández Pérez Acedo and Ramón Puparelli. The deciding factor against the aircraft, however, is said to have been the unit price of 500,000 pesetas (£19,825) that the Boeing company was asking. Instead, in June 1935 the Spanish government signed a contract with the Hawker Aircraft Company of Kingston, England, for fifty Spanish Fury biplanes to be built under licence by Hispano-Suiza at Guadalajara.

The Boeing 281, however, re-mained at Barajas, and was still there when the civil war erupted on 18 July 1936. It was transferred to Cuatro Vientos and, after failures of the gun gear had twice resulted in the propeller being nearly shot away, was flown over the front without armament for a few weeks to raise the morale of the armed Republican militia facing Gen Mola's forces in the Sierra de Guadarrama. Eventually two Vickers guns, operated by an improvised firing mechanism of rods and wires, were mounted under the wings to fire outside the propeller arc. Thereafter, based at Gatafe, the Boeing 281 took part in numerous missions and combats, on one occasion flying in an extraordinary mixed formation with a Spanish Fury, four Dewoitine D.372s, two Loire 46s and two Nieuport 52s. It was flown by various pilots in turn, and the American volunteer Eugene Finnick described it as 'an old rattletrap'. By the third week of October 1936 it was one of only three Republican fighters remaining airworthy at Getafe, the others being a Dewoitine and a Fury, and on 21 October it was shot down in a combat over the aerodrome with three Fiat C.R.32s. The pilot, Ramón Puparelli (one of those who

The Boeing 281. (Philip Jarrett)

had originally tested it in 1935), managed to bale out. Some time later, the Spanish Republican embassy in Paris paid a Boeing representative, Wilbur Johnson, $20,000 (£4,016) for the aircraft.

Span 27ft 11⅝in; length 23ft 7¼in; height (tail up) 9ft 4½in; wing area 149.5sq ft.
Empty weight 2,271lb; loaded weight 3,360lb.
Maximum speed 234mph; cruising speed 199mph; initial climb 2,360ft/min; normal endurance 1hr 54min; maximum range with auxiliary fuel 570 miles.

Breda Ba 25

The Società Italiana Ernesto Breda turned to aircraft manufacture in 1917, when it received a contract to build multi-engined Caproni bombers. Its first military aircraft, the Breda Ba 19 single-seat fighter-trainer biplane, appeared in 1930. The Breda Ba 25, a two-seat development, became the most widely used trainer in the Regia Aeronautica until 1939, and small numbers were exported to Afghanistan, Ethiopia, China and Paraguay. The standard engine was a 240hp Alfa Romeo D2 radial, sometimes fitted with a Townend ring, but other engines included a licence-built (Alfa Romeo)

Armstrong Siddeley Lynx, an Issotta-Fraschini Asso liquid-cooled vee engine and (on the Ba 25I seaplane version) a Walter Castor. There is no written record of any Breda Ba 25s in Spain, but a documentary programme about the Spanish Civil War shown on French television in 1988 showed what appeared to be a Ba 25 in Spanish Nationalist colours dropping two light bombs, the film clip probably being taken from a training or propaganda film made during or shortly after the civil war. The number of Breda Ba 25s sent to Spain was presumably very small.

Span 10m; length 8m; height 2.90m; wing area 25sq m.
Empty weight 750kg; loaded weight 1,000kg.
Maximum speed 205km/h; cruising speed 160km/h; ceiling 6,200m; range 500km.

Breda Ba 28

Derived from the Breda Ba 25, the Breda Ba 28 was a single- or two-seat (dual-control) aerobatic trainer biplane of wood and metal construction, powered by a 370hp Piaggio P.VII (Licence-built Gnome-Rhône 7 K) radial engine. Six Breda Ba 28s

A Breda 28 trainer at Villanubla, near Valladolid. (Emiliani)

were delivered to the Spanish Nationalists during the civil war. They were allotted the type-code number 34, and numbers 34-1 and 34-2 were still in service with the Escuela de Caza (fighter school) at Villanubla, Valladolid, in March 1940. The longest-serving Ba 28 was 34-2, which was withdrawn in September 1945.

Span 10m; length 7.8m; height 3.1m; wing area 30sq m.

Empty weight 960kg; loaded weight 1,200kg.

Maximum speed 240km/h; cruising speed 200km/h; ceiling 7,500m.

Breda Ba 33

When it first appeared in 1929, the Breda Ba 33 low-wing two-seat cabin monoplane was one of the most advanced light aircraft in the world. It was powered by a 120hp D.H. Gipsy III inverted in-line engine, and was of mixed construction. The welded-steel-tube fuselage was fabric co-vered with the exception of the metal-covered curved deck behind the enclosed cockpit. The outer wing panels, which folded, were of wood with a plywood skin, and the centre section was of steel, with a ply skin. The wings were braced to the upper longerons of the fuselage by a pair of inverted vee struts, and the under-

carriage legs consisted of a pair of streamlined pyramidal spats. With a remarkable range of 1,200 to 1,800km, the Breda Ba 33 was used for numerous long-distance flights during the early 1930s.

One Breda Ba 33, I-AAUW (c/n 3206), which belonged to the Conti Leonardo Bonci of Milan, was sold to José-María Malagrida, a Spanish aristocrat resident in Italy and a supporter of Gen Franco, in August 1936. The sale was arranged by Corina Negrone, the wife of the Marquese de Negrone and herself holder of the Italian high-altitude record. Bonci flew the Breda Ba 33 from Milan to Oran, Algeria, and, on the pretence of flying to Fez, took it via Spanish Morocco to Seville, where he presented it to Gen Queipo de Llano. It was employed on various reconnaissance missions and, on 17 November 1936, flew over the San-tuario de la Cabeza, near Córdoba, to drop messages of encouragement to the beseiged Nationalist garrison. It was christened *Arriba España.*

Span 9.4m; length 6.8m; height 2m; wing area 15sq m.

Empty weight 430kg; loaded weight 730kg (long range, 830kg).

Maximum speed 230km/h; cruising speed 200km/h; ceiling 7,000m; range 1,200km; maximum range 1,800km.

Breda Ba 39

The Breda Ba 39 two-seat mono-

plane was a heavier version of the Ba 33, powered by a 140hp Colombo S.63 six-cylinder in-line engine and fitted with flaps and slots, the slots extending along the outer wing panels and having automatic control for high-incidence landings. The two cockpits had sliding canopies. The Ba 39 was an easier aeroplane to fly than the Ba 33, and in 1934 one example, flown by Folonari and Malinverni, achieved fame by making a circuit of the Mediterranean from Turin and back. One Ba 39, reg-istered I-MASS but bearing Spanish Nationalist markings, was used in the civil war by the reporters of the Italian newspaper *Corriere della Sera.*

Span 10.11m; length 7.8m; height 2.9m; wing area 17.5sq m.

Empty weight 430kg; loaded weight 730kg.

Maximum speed 220km/h; climb to 4,000m in 21min; ceiling 6,000m; range 900km.

Breda Ba 64

Designed in accordance with the theory of the Italian Gen Auredeo Meccozi, that the ideal military air-craft should be able to perform a wide variety of functions, the Breda Ba 64 was a single-seat all-metal low-wing cantilever monoplane intended to fulfil the rôles of fighter, light bom-ber, army co-operation and photo-reconnaissance. The prototype was powered by a 700hp Alfa Romeo (licence-built Bristol) Pegasus radial

A Breda 33. (A J Jackson)

engine in a long-chord cowling. The undercarriage retracted rearwards into the wings, and the headrest of the open cockpit was extended as a streamlined fairing along the fuselage top-decking as far as the tail. Its armament consisted of four 7.7mm machine guns in the wings and up to 400kg of bombs in racks under the wings. A small number was built for the Regia Aeronautica, some remaining in service until the outbreak of the Second World War. Two were purchased by the USSR in 1938. One example served with the Aviazione Legionaria in Spain, arriving in June 1937 and receiving the military serial 8-1. It had an anti-crash pylon above the windscreen, into which was fitted a rear-view mirror.

The Breda 39 I-MASS, used by Cor-riere della Sera in Spain. (Emiliani)

Span 12m; length 9.6m; height 3.3m; wing area 23.4sq m.

Empty weight 1,496kg; loaded weight 2,494.8kg.

Maximum speed 360.4km/h; ceiling 8,000m; range 900-1,500km, according to load.

Breda Ba 65

Evolved from the Breda 64, the Ba 65 was a low-level assault aircraft. The prototype, which was powered by a 1,000hp Fiat A.80 RC 41 radial engine, first flew in 1935. Of all-metal construction, it was a single-seat, low-wing cantilever monoplane with an aft-retracting undercarriage, a wing-mounted armament of two 12.7mm and two 7.7mm Breda SAFAT machine guns, and an internal bay for 450kg of bombs. The Ba 65 could be converted into a two-seater, the second crew member sitting in an open cockpit behind the pilot's cabin. An initial order for 81 Ba 65s, powered by 900hp Isotta-Fraschini K-14 (licence-built

Gnome-Rhône 14 K) radial engines, was placed by the Regia Aeronautica, and production began in 1936. Although it was not, in the event, very effective in the face of fighter opposition, the Ba 65's aggressive, somewhat bull-like silhouette made it a favourite subject in the propaganda posters of the day, by which Mussolini was attempting to instil a warlike spirit into the Italian people.

Following Mussolini's decision in December 1936 to establish a 250-aircraft Aviazione Legionaria in Spain, four Breda Ba 65s (probably the first four to reach the Regia Aeronautica) were despatched by sea and unloaded at Palma, Mallorca, on 28 December 1936, where they were joined by a further eight on 8 January 1937. Perhaps because they were not considered high-priority aircraft, in view of the limited shipping space available they remained on Mallorca until the end of March, when they were transported to Cádiz in lots of four (together with Fiat C.R.32s in

A Breda 64.

lots of twenty) on the SS *Arienne*, the first four arriving at Tablada, Seville, for assembly on 7 April. The second four were unloaded at Cádiz on 19 April, and the third batch on 3 May 1937 – the dates being recorded in British Intelligence reports. The Breda Ba 65 was assigned the type-code number 16, and the twelve aircraft (16-1, –3, –5, –7, –11, –12, –15, –16, –18, –23, –29 and –31; nos –13 and –17 being omitted owing to superstition) were formed into the 65ª Squadriglia Autonoma di Assalto, under the command of Capitano Vittorio Desiderio, and based at Soria in northern Spain. The squadron emblem, a black dragon breathing a red flame and, underneath, the words *Mi fanno un baffo* ('they're bluffing me') were painted on the fin. Aircraft 16-29 was wrecked in a landing accident, and during June and July 1937 the squadron was plagued by teething troubles in the new and still-experimental aircraft. As a result, they did not begin military operations until August 1937, and on 24 August scored their first and, so far as is known, only aerial victory in the civil war when Sergente Dell'Aqua encountered a

solitary SB Katiuska over Soria aerodrome and shot it down.

During the northern campaign several Ba 65s were converted into two-seaters and one, 16-5, was fitted with an A360 two-way radio for trials in radio telegraphy. At the end of the campaign, in October 1937, the 65ª Squadriglia, now commanded by Capitano Duilio Fanali and part of the Gruppo Autonomo Misto of Fiat B.R.20 bombers, was transferred to Tudela in Navarra, and in December, despite appalling weather conditions that grounded many aircraft on both sides, the Bredas were em-

Isotta-Fraschini K-14-powered Breda 65s of the 65ª Squadriglia Autonoma di Assalto. (Azaola)

ployed in the bitter battles for Teruel. In January 1938 a reinforcement of four K-14-powered Ba 65s arrived from Italy (16-35, -38, -39, and -41) and joined the squadron at Tudela in the first week of February. After the capture of the city, the Nationalists launched their major offensive in Aragón, which by 15 April carried them through to the Mediterranean coast and cut the Republic in two. During the advance the Ba 65s were employed constantly in attacking the retreating enemy troops, railway and road junctions, artillery batteries and landing grounds.

During the Battle of the Ebro, in July 1938, the Ba 65s, now based at Puig Moreno in the province of Teruel and commanded by Capitano Antonio Miotto, were employed for

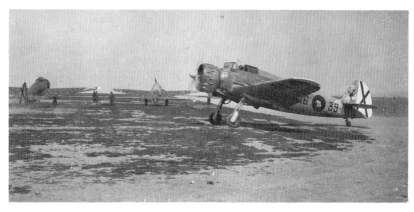

One of the six Fiat A-80-powered Breda 65s that arrived in Spain in September 1938, at Puig Moreno Aerodrome. (Arráez)

the first time as dive bombers, launching attacks against the pontoon bridges that the Republicans had thrown across the River Ebro. In one attack the aircraft of Capitano Miotto and Sergentos Piccolomini and Marinelli scored six direct hits with 100kg bombs. By September, when the battle was approaching its climax, only eight Ba65s were still operational, and it was fortunate that a reinforcement of six Fiat A.80-powered aircraft arrived. When taken on strength, these were given the military serials of Ba65s previously lost: 16-1, -7, -11, -16, -18 and -35.

In January 1939 the 65ª Squadriglia was place under the command of Capitano Giorgio Grossi and transferred to Logroño for the final offensive against Catalonia. During the campaign the squadron was divided into two flights, one of K-14-powered Ba65s and the other of Fiat A.80-powered aircraft. The last operational flight was carried out by four aircraft from Olmedo on 24 March 1939, five days before the end of the war. When the Italian Aviazione Legionaria returned to

Italy, in May 1939, the eleven surviving Breda Ba65s were handed over to the new Spanish Ejercito del Aire. During the Spanish Civil War the Breda Ba65s of the 65ª Squadriglia had flown 1,921 sorties, including 368 ground-straffing and 59 dive-bombing attacks. Of the twenty-three sent, twelve had been lost, but whether the number shot down by Republican aircraft was three or six is not clear from surviving records. The Breda Ba65s in Spanish service were transferred to the Academia de Aviación at León in 1940, and were withdrawn from service before the beginning of 1946 owing to a lack of spares.

A two-seat version, the Ba 65bis, with a Breda L hydraulically-operated dorsal turret mounting a 12.7mm Breda SAFAT machine gun, had

been developed early in 1937. It was supplied in small numbers to the air forces of Iraq and Portugal, as well as to the Regia Aeronautica, but none went to Spain.

Span 11.9m; length 9.6m; height 3.33m; wing area 252.95sq m.
Empty weight 1,950kg; loaded weight 2,950kg.
Maximum speed 415km/h at 5,000m; cruising speed 360km/h; ceiling 7,800m; range 750km.

Breguet 27S

The Breguet 27, a two-seat recon-

Maryse Hilz, flying the Breguet 27S F-AKFM Jöe III, *takes off on her flight to Tokyo in January 1934.* (Liron)

Breguet 460 Vultur. (Philip Jarrett)

naissance bomber built in substantial numbers for the Armée de l'Air during the 1930s, was a sesquiplane of quite distinctive appearance. Behind the gunner's cockpit the fuselage curved down steeply into a thin boom which carried the tail assembly, a configuration that gave the gunner a good field of fire. A small number of Breguet 27s were adapted for long-distance flying, and in one of these, the Breguet 27S (or Breguet 330) F-AKFM *Jöe III*, powered by a 650hp Hispano-Suiza 12Nb liquid-cooled engine, the famous woman pilot Maryse Hilsz made a remarkable flight to Tokyo in January 1934. On the return she flew from Saigon to Paris in 5 days 10 hours. The Breguet 27S, which was the property of the Ministère de l'Air, remained at Villacoublay until October 1936, after which it no longer appears in any records. The Right-Wing newspaper *l'Action française*, however, reported on 4 October that 'La Compagnie Achat', at the Hôtel Commodore in Paris, had bought it for 210,000 francs (£2,000) and re-sold it for 360,000 francs (£3,428) to an architect, Imrat-Rachon, and one Mirabel, who, the newspaper alleged, were buying arms for the Spanish 'Reds'. No details of its subsequent history are known.

Military version: span 17.01m; (lower wing 7.58m); length 9.76m; height 3.58m; wing area 49.67sq m.

Empty weight 1,756kg; loaded weight 2,393kg (A2 version), 2,893kg (BN2 version).

Maximum speed 236km/h at ground level, 275km/h at 3,500m; ceiling 7,900m; range 1,050km.

The Breguet 460 at Rosas aerodrome, Catalonia, in December 1936. (Arráez)

Breguet 460 M4 Vultur

The Breguet 460 all-metal, low-wing cantilever monoplane medium bomber, which carried a crew of four and was powered by two 850hp Gnome-Rhône 14 Kdrs radial engines, was an updated version of the unsuccessful series of *multi-place de combat* sesquiplanes, the Breguet 411 to 420. With the abandonment of the *multi-place de combat* programme in 1932 (see Junkers K 30 and Potez 54), the Breguet design team was able to concentrate on producing a bomber pure and simple. Nevertheless, the resulting 460 retained some of the unattractive features of the cumbrous 'aerial cruisers' that the French had built in the late 1920s and early 1930s, including a slab-sided fuselage, unsightly angles, and large generous transparencies in the forward fuselage. It also retained the thin rear fuselage of its predecessors

and the Breguet 27. The undercarriage legs retracted rearwards into the engine nacelles, but left the wheels half-exposed. The defensive armament consisted of three machine guns, one in a curious fenestrated turret in the nose, and one each in the dorsal and ventral gun positions, and it could carry up to 1,076kg of bombs.

The CEMA test pilot Louis Bonte remembers that, during trials at Villacoublay, the Breguet 460 was found to be 'a very bad machine, difficult and dangerous to fly, with a tendency to "vault" when landing and subject to fits of "flutter"'. So alarming was the vibration on one occasion that the crew decided to bale out, only to find that they could not open the escape hatches. A complete redesign produced the Breguet 462, which turned out to be excellent, but in the meantime the company tried to recoup its loss by selling the 460 abroad. On 10 June 1935 Louis Breguet himself, accompanied by his sales chief, Willemetz, and the famous transatlantic flyer Dieudonne Costes, arrived at Barajas Airport to demonstrate the Vultur, as the 460 was now called, to the Director General de Aeronáutica, Gen Goded, and his advisers. Although .hey were politely enthusiastic, the Spaniards placed no order, and the machine would probably have remained in the 'graveyard' at Villacoublay until scrapped but for the Spanish Civil War. Possibly through the intercession of Raoul Delas, a French airman who had flown a Latécoère 28 in Spain and procured two or three Dewoitine D.53s for the Spanish Republicans from the same Villacoublay 'graveyard', the Breguet 460 was acquired by the Republicans in November 1936, given a brief retesting by Breguet company pilot Raoul Ribière on 20 November, and flown to Barcelona four days later.

Based at Prat de Llobregat, the Vultur was used for coastal patrol. Nobody liked it, for, in addition to its other defects, it was slow. On 7 March 1937 the Breguet was fired at by a Nationalist warship off the Costa Brava. A piece of shrapnel must have caused some damage, for the Breguet turned away, descended towards the shore, and crashed into the water a few yards out from the beach of the Bay of Rosas. The pilot, Ramón Torres (a well-known long-distance flyer before the war) and the crew of three were killed. Later, the Nationalist propaganda office claimed that Torres, whose political sympathies were known to have tended more to the right than to the left, had been forced to fly at pistol-point, and had tragically died while attempting to escape to Nationalist territory.

Span 20.5m; length 12.94m; wing area 56.25 sq m.
Empty weight 4,668kg; loaded weight 7,686kg.
Maximum speed 384km/h; climb 3,000m in 7min 15sec; ceiling 5,300m.

Breguet 470 Fulgur

A wooden mockup of the Breguet 460T, a civil version of the 460M4 bomber, was exhibited at the Salon de l'Aéronautique in Paris in November 1934. The failure of the bomber, however, led to the cancellation of the 460T and the development of the Breguet 470 Fulgur (Lightningflash) airliner, based on the Breguet 462. Similar in format to the Douglas DC-2, though lacking its pleasing lines, the Fulgur was powered by two 804hp Gnome-Rhône 14 Kirs radial engines, and accommodated a crew of four and twelve passengers. In the hope of enticing orders, Breguet entered the prototype, F-APDY, in the Paris-Saigon air race in 1936, with Michel Detroyat as pilot. No orders were forthcoming, and in the spring of 1937 the Fulgur was sold to SFTA (see Appendix II), which passed it on to the Spanish Republicans. In August 1937, however, Pierre Cot, the French air minister, asked the Spanish Republicans to return the Breguet temporarily so that it could take part in the forthcoming Istres-Damascus air race, because the Amiot 370, the only French entry that could hope to beat the Italian Savoia-Marchetti S.79, was not ready. Fitted with two 940hp Gnome-Rhône 14 N-O radial engines borrowed from the Breguet-Wibault 670T, the Fulgur, flown by Codos, Arnoux and Agnus, was the first aeroplane to land at Damascus, but on the return fell back to sixth place, the winner being the S.79.

Returned to Spain, the Fulgur flew for LAPE as EC-AHC: its fleet number is not known. According to José-María Carreras, an ex-LAPE

The Breguet 470 Fulgur in LAPE service.

pilot (and later personal pilot to Lord Beaverbrook and a transatlantic pilot for the Air Transport Auxiliary), the Breguet was not popular with the pilots, a particular source of irritation being the retracting mechanism of the undercarriage, which 'took forever to pull the legs up and chuffed like a steam engine while doing so'. After being used to evacuate Spanish government personnel to France during the fall of Catalonia in February 1939, the Fulgur did not return to Spain.

Span 20.5m; length 15.32m; height 5.93m; wing area 56.25 sq m.
Empty weight 4,840kg; loaded weight 8,200kg; wing loading 145.5kg/sq m.
Maximum speed 320km/h; cruising speed 285km/h; ceiling 6,000m; range 2,000km.

Breguet-Wibault 670T

Although it is sometimes confused with the preceding Breguet 470, which it superficially resembled, the 670T, designed by Michel Wibault, was an altogether larger machine with a different wing shape and tail assembly. Only one example, F-ANNT, was built, and its career was unhappily short. One day in June 1936 a mechanic reported that, when he had opened the passenger door, it had come away from the fuselage and nearly fallen on top of him. It was found that the adhesive used for binding the sound-proofing material inside the passenger saloon was dissolving the alloy of the fuselage. After a complete rebuild and the transfer of its 940hp Gnome-Rhône

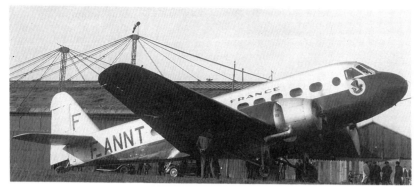

The Breguet-Wibault 670T. (Philip Jarrett)

14 N-O engines to the Breguet 470 Fulgur, the 670T, now fitted with two 14 Ks, was sold to SFTA (see Appendix II) in March 1938. Apart from the fact that it is said to have been registered EC-AGI, no record of its service in Spain has survived, and it is possible that it was used merely as a source of spares. Another story says that it was destroyed in Catalonia by bombing.

Span 24.86m; length 18.74m.
Empty weight 5,536kg; loaded weight 9,500kg; wing loading 121.6kg/sq m.
Maximum speed 340km/h; cruising speed 280km/h; range 2,000km.

Bristol Fighter F.2B

After the First World War a number of Bristol F.2Bs, powered by 200hp Hispano-Suiza engines, as well as Bristol Tourers of various types, were bought by the Spanish armed services and civilian aero clubs. Fifteen F.2Bs were used extensively by the Spanish army during the Moroccan war in the first half of the 1920s, and seven were used as trainers by the Escuela de Bombardeo y Tiro (Bombing and Gunnery School) at Los Alcázares near Cartagena. In 1936 six Bristol F.2Bs, with 300hp Hispano-Suiza 8Fb engines, were still on register to the Compañía Española de Aviación at Albacete Aerodrome: EC-AAJ, c/n 2301; 'AJA, c/n 2601; 'IAI, c/n 1916; 'IIA, c/n 2300; 'III, c/n 1982; 'JAA, c/n 2199.

What part, if any, they played in the opening stages of the civil war is not recorded.

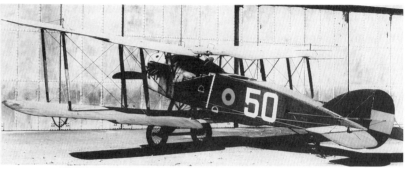

A Bristol Fighter F.2B (300hp Hispano-Suiza 8Fb engine) of the Aviación Militar. (Instituto de Historia y Cultura Aeronautica)

Bristol F.2B with 300hp Hispano-Suiza 8Fb engine: span 39ft 3in; length 24ft 10in; height 9ft 6in; wing area 405sq ft.
Empty weight 2,070lb; loaded weight 3,000lb.
Maximum speed 120mph; ceiling 20,000ft; endurance 3hr.

Bristol Bulldog II

The Bristol Bulldog, designed by Capt Frank Barnwell to meet Air Ministry Specification 9/26, was one of the classic single-seat fighters of the late 1920s. It was sturdy, extremely manoeuvrable, and easy to handle in the air and maintain on the ground. It had a pugnacious, businesslike look about it which exactly befitted its purpose and bolstered the confidence of those who flew it.

The prototype Bulldog I made its first flight on 17 May 1927, and a modified version, the Bulldog II, was ordered into production for the RAF the following year. Powered by an uncowled 470hp Bristol Jupiter VII, it was of all-metal construction, fabric covered with the exception of the forward fuselage. Its armament

consisted of two Vickers .303 machine guns mounted on either side of the cockpit and synchronised to fire between the propeller blades. A slightly improved version, the Bulldog IIA, with a 490-510hp Bristol Jupiter VIIF engine, appeared in 1931. When production ceased in 1934, 440 Bulldogs had been built, of which 361 (49 Bulldog IIs, 253 Bulldog IIAs, and 59 Bulldog TM two-seat trainers) had been built for

the RAF, at one time equipping no fewer than ten of the thirteen squadrons forming the Air Defence of Great Britain. Among those exported were twelve to Latvia, twelve to Estonia, eleven to Sweden, four to Denmark, and seventeen to Finland. In accordance with an agreement by which Gnome-Rhône manufactured all Bristol engines for aircraft exported to Europe, the Bulldogs for Latvia, Estonia and Sweden were fitted with the 425hp Gnome-Rhône Jupiter VI engines.

By the beginning of 1937 the Estonian government was anxious to replace the ageing equipment of its air force, and the Chief of Staff, Col Richard Tomberg, was especially keen to purchase a squadron of Supermarine Spitfires. A chance to fund this purchase arose when representatives of the Spanish Republican government came to an agreement whereby they would buy most of the airworthy material of the Estonian air force, in return for which the Estonian government would act as the ostensible buyer of about ninety aircraft purchased by the Spanish Republicans in Czechoslovakia, but still held in that country because of the Non-Intervention agreement, plus twenty-five Fokker G-1s ordered in Holland. According to Col Tomberg's admission to Wg Cdr West, the British Air Attaché at

Helsinki, on 28 July 1937, eight Bulldogs and eight Potez 25s had left the country for Spain by the end of May. In fact, these sailed from Tallinn, hidden beneath bales of potatoes, on the SS *Viuu*, of the A Nelberg (or A Trueberg) Shipping Company, about 20 June 1937, and arrived at El Musel, Gijón, in the Asturias, on 5 July 1937. The Bulldog IIs were formed into an escuadrilla under the command of José González Feo.

Nothing is recorded of their military operations in the northern zone, where they faced an enemy vastly superior in numbers and equipment, but by September the few survivors had been collected into a squadron of assorted obsolete aircraft, nicknamed, with a mixture of pity and admiration for the luckless pilots, *El Circo Krone* (The Krone Circus), after a well-known travelling circus of the time. At the end of the northern campaign in October 1937, one relatively undamaged Bulldog airframe, shorn of its fabric covering, was recovered by the Nationalists and exhibited, with other captured Republican aircraft and weapons, at the Gran Kursaal exhibition in San Sebastián in 1938.

According to a report by the Basque General Mariano Gamir Ulibarri, dated 3 August 1937, eleven Bristol aircraft were still in service at that time. This might be a confusion of two aircraft types, referring to eight Bristol Bulldogs and three Letov S 231s, or it might mean that not eight, but twelve Estonian Bulldogs were sold to the Basques, the other four perhaps sailing in a different ship. (This, however, raises the question of which ship, for no other vessel sailing from Tallinn to Spain during this period seems to have carried aircraft). Clarification of this enigma is probably no longer possible, but, as a point of information, the Bristol construction numbers of the 12 Estonian Bulldogs were 7447-7458.

Span 33ft 10in; length 25ft 0in; height 9ft 10in; wing area 306.5sq ft.

Empty weight 2,412lb; loaded weight 3,530lb.

No performance figures for the Bulldog II with a 425hp Gnome-Rhône Jupiter VI are available, but they were

The Bristol Bulldog II.

appreciably lower than those of the Bulldog IIA (490hp Jupiter VIIF), which were: maximum speed 178mph at 10,000ft; climb to 20,000ft in 14.5min; ceiling 29,000ft; range 350 miles at 15,000ft.

The maximum speed of the Bulldog IIs in Spain would have been in the region of 165mph.

Bücker Bü 131 Jungmann

The Bücker Jungmann shares, with the de Havilland Moth and Tiger Moth, the honour of being one of the greatest elementary training biplanes ever built. Designed by Carl Clemens Bücker, the Bü 131 was an equal-span biplane with wood and metal wings and a metal fuselage, fabric covered with the exception of

A Bücker Bü 131 Jungmann (Azaola)

the metal-skinned forward fuselage and cockpit surrounds. The upper and lower wing panels, both of which were fitted with ailerons, were interchangeable. The powerplant used in the majority of the production aircraft was the 105hp Hirth 504 A2 inverted in-line engine. In the Luftwaffe and in the air forces of Japan (where 1,254 were built under licence), Switzerland and Spain (production continued in both countries until the 1950s) the Jungmann served as a primary, transformation, and elementary-aerobatic trainer.

The first Bü 131s arrived in Nationalist Spain in November 1936, and were assigned to the Escuela Elemental at El Copero, a country estate 15km south of Seville, whose grounds had been converted into an aerodrome. A second batch arrived in February 1937, and these aircraft were distributed between the Escuela de Transformación at Jerez de la Frontera and the second Escuela

A Bücker Bü 133 Jungmeister.

Elemental at Cáceres, which, in the summer of 1937, was moved to Las Bardocas Aerodrome, located on an island in the Guadiano river near Badajoz. Fifty Bücker Jungmanns were delivered to Spain altogether, and were given the military serials 33-1 to 33-50. Forty-nine were flying at the end of the civil war. In 1940 the rebuilt CASA factory at Getafe began production of a series built under licence, deliveries starting in 1941 and enabling the motley assortment of trainers then in service to be handed over to the aero clubs and private owners. Two hundred Hirth-powered Jungmanns (designated CASA C-1131) were produced during the next two years. A second series of 300 was begun in 1950, these being fitted with the Spanish ENMASA Tigre G.IVA inverted in-line engine of 125hp, which was also fitted in thirty of the original German-built aircraft. The 530 post-civil-war Jungmanns were given the serials 33-101 to 33-630.

With Hirth 504 A2: Span 7.4m; length 6.62m; height 2.25m; wing area 13.5sq m.
Empty weight 390kg; loaded weight 680kg.
Maximum speed 183km/h; cruising speed 170km/h; climb 192m/min; landing speed 82km/h; ceiling 4,000m; range 650km.

Bücker Bü 133 Jungmeister

The prototype of this famous single-seat trainer, powered by a 140hp Hirth inverted in-line engine, first flew in December 1935 and, refitted with a 160hp Siemens Sh14A-4 radial in a blistered cowling, made its début at the Berlin Olympic Games in July 1936. During the next three years Bücker Jungmeisters became familiar and popular participants in aerial competitions and displays in Europe and the USA, winning numerous awards and generally being regarded as the best aerobatic aircraft in the world. In design and construction the Jungmeister was similar to the Bü 131 Jungmann, of which it was essentially a scaled-down version.

Twenty Bücker Bü 133s were delivered to Nationalist Spain at the beginning of 1937 and, bearing the military serials 35-1 to 35-20, they were employed at the Escuela de Transformación at Jerez de la Frontera. One example, with the type-code EX, is known to have served in the Republican air forces, though how it came into their hands is not recorded.

In 1941 CASA produced a series of twenty-five Jungmeisters, designated CASA C-1133s and powered by 160hp Hirth HM 506 inverted in-line engines. In 1945 the Jungmeister received the new type code ES-1 (Escuela Superior tipo 1), changed in December 1953 to E-1 (Siemens engine) and E-1B (Hirth).

Span 6.6m; length 5.9m; height 2.35m; wing area 12sq m.
Empty weight 410kg; loaded weight 585kg.
Maximum speed 225km/h; landing speed 80km/h; climb to 2,000m in 3min; ceiling 6,000m; range 500km.

Cant Z.501 Gabbiano

In 1931 the Cantière Navale Triestino (Trieste Naval Shipyard) in northern Italy acquired the services of the aeronautical engineer Filippo Zappata and changed its name to the Cantière Riuntini dell'Adriatico (United Adriatic Shipyard), or CRDA. Perhaps because it was easier to say, however, the contraction 'Cant' was given to all the aircraft produced by the company. Zappata's first design for the CRDA was the Cant Z.501 Gabbiano (Seagull) flying-boat, which made its maiden flight at Monfalcone, Trieste, in 1934. Bearing the civil registration I-AGIL, this aeroplane established a new long-distance record for seaplanes when it flew 4,120km (2,560 miles) from Monfalcone to Manawa, Eritrea, in October of the same year. A French aircraft broke this record shortly afterwards, but the Z.501 regained it in July 1935 by flying 4,957km (3,080 miles) from Monfalcone to Berbera, Somaliland. The Cant Z.501, however, was designed as a naval reconnaissance bomber, and the first examples entered service early in 1936. A wooden single-engined parasol monoplane, its two-step hull, fuselage, floats and fin were covered with stressed plywood, and the wings and control surfaces with fabric. The wing was of constant chord, but the outer panels beyond the junction points of the main bracing struts had elliptical taper. Power was provided by an 835hp Isotta-Fraschini Asso XI R2C15 liquid-cooled vee engine housed in a nacelle above the wing, driving a three-blade variable-pitch metal propeller. Up to 500kg of bombs could be carried on underwing racks, and the defensive armament comprised three 7.7mm Breda SAFAT flexibly-mounted machine guns; one in a gunner's position in the bow, another in a semi-enclosed turret in the rear of the engine nacelle and the third in a similar turret in the rear fuselage.

Shortly after the outbreak of the Spanish Civil War, the Aero Club de Cádiz raised sufficient money by public subscription to buy a single flying-boat from the Italian government, and in the middle of September 1936 a Cant Z.501, flown by an Italian ferry pilot, landed in Cádiz

Bay. The name *Cádiz* was painted on its fuselage in honour of the donors, and the machine, bearing the military serial 62-1, was entrusted to two Spanish pilots, Tenente Ruiz de la Puente and Alférez Bay Wright. Impatient to go into action, the pilots, with a radio operator and a mechanic, took off on their first mission of war on 22 September. After half an hour, unfamiliarity with the throttle controls brought the *Cádiz* down on to a choppy sea and the aircraft broke its back. The two pilots clung to the tail, which remained afloat, and the other two crew members took to the dinghy. All were eventually rescued by passing ships.

In December 1936 three Cant Z.501s with Italian crews arrived at Palma, Mallorca, and, with the three Macchi M.41 flying-boats, were formed into a squadron commanded by Tenente Carlo Rinaldi (whose pseudonym in Spain was 'Revello'). After a month or so of reconnaissance flights the Z.501s were handed over to the Spanish Nationalists, who formed them into the group 2-G-62, based at Pollensa, Mallorca, and commanded by Comandante Luis Rambaud, who had led the ephemeral unit of He 51s in August 1936. Before it began operations, 2-G-62 suffered its first casualty. On 1 February 1937, 62-1, piloted by Ruiz de la Puente, struck the mast of a tobacco ship while taking off, and crashed. Ruiz de la Puente was killed, along with his copilot, Antonio Melendreras Sierra, whose brother, Cdte José Melendreras Sierra, was with the Republicans and had been sent to the USA to buy aircraft (see Appendix II, Vultee V1-A, and other American aircraft). The cause of this accident was the tendency of the Cant Z.501 to throw up an immense spray during take-off, which under certain conditions made it impossible for the pilot to see forwards.

In March 1937 Rambaud was replaced by Cdte Federico Noreña, and the group was reinforced by five more aircraft (62-4 to 62-8), the seven aircraft being divided into two escuadrillas. The 1ª Escuadrilla, under Capitán Carlos Pombo, adopted as its unit emblem a diver riding a broomstick, and the 2ª, under Capitán Fernando Morenas Carvajal (succeeded by Capitán

Soriano Muñoz), chose a diver riding a grotesque fish and carrying a bomb on his shoulders. Both emblems were painted in white on a white-ringed black disc. At this time the Z.501s had the upper surfaces of their wings painted with black 'sunbeams' splayed outwards and backwards from the leading edges, similar to those on the He 70s. In August 1937 this scheme was replaced by a pair of black stripes on the upper surface of the wing, either side of the nacelle, and three black and two white stripes round the upper rear fuselage. November 1937 saw the arrival of the last two Z.501s (62-9 and 62-10).

The principal duty of 2-G-62 was to locate and follow the courses of Republican and other ships bringing supplies from France and the Soviet Union, and among its notable successes were the spotting of the *Mar Blanco* on 15 June 1937, which was subsequently forced to take refuge in Oran, Algeria, and, on 9 October 1937, of the *Cabo Santo Tomé*, a 16,000-ton motor-ship carrying six aircraft, fifty tanks, seventy-five lorries, 2,600 tons of war materials, and 2,700 tons of foodstuffs and general supplies. As a result of the tracking by 2-G-62, the ship was attacked by two Nationalist frigates and driven ashore on the Algerian coast. When carrying out reconnaissance over Republican ports, Z.501 pilots would usually climb to 4,000m, dive down to 1,000m over the town, and then turn out to sea to make their escape. In

A Cant Z.501.

August 1937 2-G-62 worked in close co-operation with three Cant Z.501-equipped squadriglie of the Regia Aeronautica based in Sardinia, the 142ª, 145ª and 188ª, and on one occasion 62-2 flew to Elmas, Sardinia, where it was fitted with a brand new engine. These were curious episodes indeed, considering the accusations that the Italian government was then levelling against other countries, especially France, for violating Non-Intervention.

Maritime and coastal reconnaissance by the Spanish groups was arduous and dangerous work, and it was claimed, no doubt truthfully, that the Z.501s of 2-G-62 logged more operational flying hours than any other aircraft of the Nationalist air forces, including the Ju 52s. Losses, more through wear and tear than enemy action, were correspondingly heavy, and by the beginning of 1938 only five of the original ten delivered were still flying. In March these were combined with the Dornier Wals of 2-E-70 to form the mixed group 2-G-62-70. With the arrival of six Cant Z.506Bs in September, the Z.501s joined them to form a new mixed group, 2-G-62-73, 73 being the type code for the Z.506B, and the Wals regained their independence. By April 1939, however, only three Z.501s were still flying, and these were transferred to Spain to take part in various victory ceremonies, notably the formal farewell to the Condor Legion on 1 May, and a flypast over Valencia on the following day. With the creation of the Ejercito del Aire, it was planned to transfer the

A Cant Z.506B of 1-E-73 at El Atalayón, Melilla, Spanish Morocco, in 1938. (Arráez)

Z.501s and Z.506Bs to Atalayón, Spanish Morocco, but this was abandoned and the squadron returned to Pollensa. In September 1939 the squadron was redesignated the 53ª Escuadrilla of the 51 Grupo Mixto de Hidros. Little is recorded of the Cant Z.501s after that, and they were probably withdrawn from service before the end of 1940.

Span 22.5m; length 14.30m; height 4.24m; wing area 62sq m.
Empty weight 3,850kg; loaded weight 5,950kg; maximum weight 7,050kg.
Maximum speed 275km/h; cruising speed 240km/h; range 1,000km.

Cant Z.506B Airone

In the summer of 1937 Teniente-Coronel Ramón Franco, Gen Francisco Franco's younger brother and overall commander of the Región Aérea de los Baleares (the Nationalist air forces stationed on Mallorca), sent a report to the Nationalist air chief, Gen Kindelán, giving the reasons why the Cant Z.501 flying-boats were inadequate for the heavy duties demanded of them. They were slow and, being single-engined, the failure of an engine would usually result in the loss of the aircraft and its crew. Besides, they were too few in number to cover the vast areas of sea over which the ships supplying the enemy sailed, and he asked Kindelán to start negotiations for the purchase of more modern aircraft. After vainly trying in Germany for six months,

Kindelán turned to Italy, and by June 1938 had received an offer of eight Cant Z.506B Airone (Heron) tri-motor seaplanes new from the CRDA factory at Monfalcone near Trieste. After further negotiations, the Spaniards settled for four.

After the Z.501, Zappatta's next successful design for CRDA had been the Z.506, a twin-float commercial monoplane powered by three Pratt & Whitney Hornet radial engines and carrying twelve passengers. The prototype, I-CANT, first flew early in 1935, and two production series were built for Ala Littoria: the Z.506A, powered by 760hp Wright Cyclone engines, and the Z.506C, powered by 680hp (750hp for take-off) Alfa Romeo 126 RC34 radial engines (licence-built Bristol Pegasus). The airliners operated mainly on the Adriatic service between Trieste and Brindisi, but in 1936 Z.506As established no fewer than sixteen world records in their class, including eleven speed records with load, three closed-circuit speed records, and two load-to-altitude records. In regular service the Z.506A cruised at 259km/h (161mph). Meanwhile, CRDA had developed a military version, the Z.506B Airone, which had the same powerplant as the Z.506C but differed from the civil models principally in having a long underbelly gondola faired into the lower fuselage to house the bomb aimer, bomb bay and ventral gunner, who operated a pair of twin 7.7mm Breda machine guns firing downwards, as well as a manually-operated dorsal turret, with twin 12.7mm machine guns, in line with the wing trailing edge. Construction was en-

tirely of wood, with fabric covering.

On 6 August 1938 four complete Spanish aircrews, led by Comandante Federico Moreña (commander of 2-G-62-70, see Z.501), were flown in a bright red Ala Littoria Z.506A to Monfalcone for a ten-day course of conversion training. The first two Z.506Bs were ferried to Pollensa, Mallorca, on 21 August, and the second two on 27 August. The Cant Z.501/Dornier Wal group 2-G-62-70 was now disbanded and a new group, 2-G-62-73 (73 being the type code of the Z.506B) was formed. This unit consisted to two escuadrillas, 1-E-73, equipped with the Z.506Bs under the command of Capitán Antonio Soriano, and 2-E-62, equipped with Z.501s. The Z.506Bs were painted light blue-grey, with sky-blue undersurfaces. Their serial numbers (73-1 to 73-4) were painted in black in front of the black disc, on which was painted, in white, the squadron emblem of a bomb with a mast and a dhow sail.

Most of September 1938 was spent in training, and the Z.506Bs did not carry out their first war operation until 6 October 1938, when they flew over Alicante and dropped sacks of bread as a propaganda gesture to the starving populace. On 28 October 1938 Ramón Franco and his crew perished when his machine, 73-1, dived and crashed into the Mediterranean while on a dawn bombing raid on Valencia and Denia. Ramón Franco had been an equivocal figure in the civil war. A national hero (and until 1936 far more famous than his brother) since his crossing of the South Atlantic in the Dornier Wal *Plus Ultra* in 1926, he had not pleased his conservative family by his involvement with freemasonry and the extreme political Left during the 1930s until, while he was air attaché in Washington, friendship with Gen Douglas MacArthur had turned his sympathies in the opposite direction. Even so, he had not returned to Spain until November 1936, and then with apparent reluctance, and Gen Franco had posted him to Mallorca to avoid the embarrassment of the intense hostility of prominent Nationalist air force officers. After the crash there were the inevitable rumours of sabotage and planned assassination.

The remaining three Z.506Bs

continued bombing and reconnaissance missions until, on 21 January 1939, 73-4 was brought down in bad weather by failure of the starboard engine. After five days, during which it successfully weathered several storms, the seaplane was towed to Porto Cristo, but was so badly damaged that it had to be written off. The last mission of the civil war to be flown by a Cant Z.506B occurred on 16 March 1939, when 73-2, piloted by Cdte Noreña, carried out a search for a Nationalist ship which, after being set on fire by Republican shore batteries during the Nationalist Fifth Column attempt to take over the port of Cartagena, had run aground near Cabo de Gata on the south-eastern corner of Spain. The seaplane found the wreck, but was driven off by Republican fighters.

After the civil war the remaining two Z.506Bs and three Z.501s continued general maritime duties, and in September 1939 were re-formed into the 53ª Escuadrilla del 51° Group Mixto de Hidros, still stationed at Pollensa, which was now being extended into a large naval base. The type code of the Z.506B was simultaneously changed to 53. During the Second World War, and especially after the fall of France, the two Z.506Bs carried out numerous reconnaissance missions over the Algerian coast and central Mediterranean. On 15 July 1942 the port engine of 53-2 (the original 73-2), commanded by Cdte Ignacio Ansaldo (brother of J-A Ansaldo – see D.H. Dragon Rapide, D.H. Puss Moth and IMAM Ro 37bis), suddenly exploded and threw its propeller while on patrol near the Balearic Island of Cabrera. After alighting, the aircraft was destroyed when the ammunition began to explode and shortly after blew up the petrol tanks. The crew, who were floating in lifejackets, the dinghy having been burnt, were rescued half an hour later by a passing RAF Short Sunderland and taken to Gibraltar. The last Z.506B, 53-3, remained in service until July 1943, after which it stood as a monument at the end of the main esplanade of the seaplane base,

A Caproni Ca 100 in Nationalist service. (Emiliani)

where it remained for several years.

Span 26.5m; length 19.24m; height 7.45m; wing area 87sq m.
Empty weight 8,300kg; loaded weight 12,300kg.
Maximum speed 360km/h; cruising speed 300km/h; ceiling 8,000m; range 2,000km.

Caproni Ca 100

An extremely popular little sports aeroplane and trainer of the late 1920s and early 1930s, the Caproni Ca 100 biplane was unusual in having an upper wing of less span than the lower. Of wooden construction, with a ply-covered fuselage and fabric-covered wings, it had Handley Page slots in the leading edge of the upper wing. The Ca 100 could also be used as a night-flying and parachute trainer. Its powerplant could be a 94hp Colombo S.53, a 150hp Colombo

The Caproni Ca 100.

S.63, an 85hp de Havilland Gipsy, a 90hp ADC Cirrus III or a 120hp Isotta-Fraschini Asso 80 inverted in-line air-cooled engine. Two Ca 100s were delivered to Nationalist Spain during the civil war, one of them being given the military serial 30-70.

Span (top) 8.35m, (bottom) 10m; length 7.3m; height 2.73m; wing area 24.4sq m.
Empty weight 400kg; loaded weight 680kg.
Maximum speed 164km/h; climb to 1,000m in 7min 4sec; ceiling 4,000m; range 700km.

Caproni AP.1 'Apio'

Designed by Cesare Pallavicino for the Compagnia Aeronautica Bergamesca (CAB) division of the Caproni group of companies, the AP.1 first appeared in 1934 as a low-level-attack aircraft in the same category as the Breda Ba 64. A single-seat, low-wing cantilever monoplane of

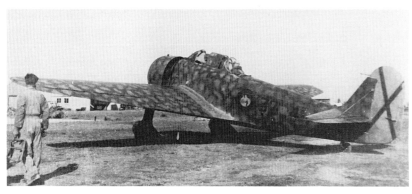

A Caproni AP.1 in Nationalist service.
(Emiliani)

wood and metal, with a thick-section wing, a braced tailplane and a trousered undercarriage, it was powered by a 700hp Piaggio PX RC 35 radial engine. The production model was a two-seater, with a spatted undercarriage, and was powered by a 680hp Alfa Romeo 125 C 34 radial in a long-chord cowling. Two fixed 7.7mm machine guns were mounted in the wings, and a movable Lewis gun was operated by the gunner in the rear cockpit. Small numbers of AP.1s were built for the Regia Aeronautica, Paraguay and El Salvador. The Paraguayan order, for eighteen landplane and four seaplane versions, was cancelled in June 1938, and ten of the landplanes (c/ns 75300 to 75309) were diverted to Nationalist Spain, where they were assigned to the Escuela de Caza (Fighter School) at Villanubla, near Valladolid, and given the military serials 32-1 to 32-10. The Spanish nickname 'Apio' (celery) was a play on 'AP.1' and the yellow-green colouring of their camouflage.

In 1940 the AP.1s moved with the School to Reus (Tarragona) and then in 1941 to Morón de la Frontera (Seville), where they were redesig-nated ES-4 in 1945. A veteran of those years remembers that, until the 1950s, a Caproni AP.1 used to take a priest on his rounds from Morón to Seville and Jerez de la Frontera every Sunday morning.

Span 13m; length 9.3m; height 3.2m; wing area 28sq m.
Loaded weight 2,850kg; wing loading 102kg/sq m.
Maximum speed 375km/h; ceiling 7,500m; range 1,200km.

Caproni Ca 135S Tipo Spagna

Designed, like the Caproni AP.1, by Cesare Pallavicino of the Bergamasca division of the Caproni company, the Ca 135 twin-engined medium bomber was a mid-wing cantilever monoplane of wood and metal. The prototype, powered by two 836hp Isotta-Fraschini Asso XI RC 40 water-cooled engines, made its maiden flight on 1 April 1936, and during the next few months modified versions were ordered in small numbers by the Regia Aeronautica (thirty-two) and the Peruvian air force (six). The Ca 135, however, was beset by troubles of every kind, to

The Caproni Ca 135S, Tipo Spagna.

the extent that Count Caproni caustically remarked that it was obviously 'not a *using*, but a *selling*, aeroplane'. This remark may explain why, through extremely convoluted and secret channels in the spring of 1937, some Ca 135s were actually offered for sale to the Spanish Republicans.

Meanwhile, the Regia Aeronautica ordered eight examples, powered by 1,000hp Fiat A80 RC 41 radial engines and designated Ca 135 S (Tipo Spagna), for service with the Aviazione Legionaria in Spain. The Ca 135S, which differed from all other variants in having engine nacelles that projected behind the wing trailing edges, had a crew of four and a defensive armament of one 7.7mm machine gun in the nose turret, a 12.7mm gun in the ventral position, and another 12.7mm gun in the dorsal turret, which was fitted with a steel tube projecting from the rear and guided by a rail which prevented the gunner from shooting through either of the twin rudders. The bomb load could be made up of various combinations of 800-50kg bombs, or two torpedoes, to a maximum load of 1,862kg.

The first Ca 135S was tested in February 1938, and in August seven aircraft, with crews detailed from the 11° Stormo, were ordered to Ciampino in preparation for transfer to Spain. One aircraft slewed round on taking off from the Caproni aerodrome at Taliedo and wrecked its undercarriage, and a second damaged its tail on landing. A month later, on 9 September 1938, the seven Caproni Ca 135Ss, accompanied by the first three Caproni Ca 310s intended for the Spanish Nationalists, took off from Alghero for Son San Juan, Mallorca. The formation ran into a violent storm. Two Ca 135Ss turned back with ice

A Caproni Ca 310 of 8-G-18.

in their carburettors, and three, as well as a Ca 310, crashed into the sea with the loss of nineteen lives (each aircraft carried a mechanic for the ferry flight). The two Ca 135Ss that reached Mallorca stayed at Son San Juan, unused, almost until the end of the civil war, their crews being transferred to other units. The three Ca 135Ss remaining in Italy were used for training. Two improved variants, the Ca 135bis and Ca 135bisU, had more success, thirty-two being built for the Regia Aeronautica and thirty-six for Hungary. They served on the Eastern Front in the Second World War.

Span 18.96m; length 14.5m; height 3.5m; wing area 61.5sq m.
Empty weight 6,063kg; loaded weight 9,063kg.
Maximum speed 408km/h at 4,000m; cruising speed 348km/h at 4,000m; ceiling 7,500m; range with 1,200kg of bombs 1,000km, with 500kg of bombs 2,000km.

Caproni Ca 310 'Capronchino'

In 1936-36 Cesare Pallavicino designed two twin-engined, low-wing cantilever monoplanes intended for policing and general duties in the Italian colonies overseas, the Caproni Ca 309 Ghibli (Desert Wind) and the Ca 310 Libeccio (South West Wind). The Ca 309, which had a fixed undercarriage and was powered by two 185hp Alfa Romeo 115 inverted in-line engines, was produced in several versions for the Regia Aero-

nautica. The Ca 310, with a retractable undercarriage and powered by two 450hp Piaggio P. VII C 16 radial engines, had cleaner aerodynamic lines and better performance than the Ca 309, but won no production order in Italy. Several orders were received from abroad, however, (Croatia, Yugoslavia, Hungary, Norway and, curiously, one for 200 from the RAF, which was cancelled by the outbreak of the Second World War), and sixteen, powered by Piaggio 500hp P.VII C35 engines, were purchased by the Spanish Nationalist Arma de Aviación. The Ca 310 was of wood and metal construction and could carry a variety of armaments, including two fixed 7.7mm machine guns in the wings, a 12.7mm gun in a shallow dorsal turret behind the pilot's cabin, and 320kg of bombs.

The first ten Ca 310s arrived in Mallorca between 9 September 1938 (when one was lost on the ferry flight, but was replaced, see Caproni Ca 135S) and 1 November 1938. They were in service, nine based at Candasnos and one at Logroño, from 20 December 1938 onwards. The ten Ca 310s (nicknamed *Capronchinos* and with the type code 18) were incorporated in 8-G-18 (Cdte Félix Bermúdez de Castro) and 9-G-18 (Cdte Rafael Martínez de Pisón, recovered from the wounds received while leading the Ro 37bis group the previous summer) as a part of the Escuadra Núm. 6, commanded by Cdte J-A Ansaldo, itself a part of the 2° Brigada Aérea Hispana. After quite extensive action in the Catalonian campaign, while based at Candasnos, Logroño and Bell-Puig, the two Ca 310 groups were transferred to Extremadura to counter the last

Republican offensive of the war. The remaining six aircraft arrived in 1939, after the end of the civil war. Twelve were still in service on 1 March 1940, incorporated into Grupo 43 (small transport aircraft). At the end of 1945 the type code was changed to A3.

Span 16.2m; length 12.2m; height 3.52m; wing area 38.4sq m.
Empty weight 3,040kg; loaded weight 4,205kg.
Maximum speed 347km/h at 3,000m; cruising speed 305km/h at 3,000m; range 1,025km.

CASA III

Designed in 1928-29 by Luis Bousa Peco, the CASA III was a two-seat light parasol monoplane, built of metal and fabric covered, except for the metal-covered control surfaces and forward fuselage. About nine were built. The prototype, M-CAGG (EC-AGG after 1931), powered by a 90hp ADC Cirrus III engine, first flew on 2 July 1929, piloted by Carlos de Haya and Arturo Alvarez-Buylla Godino. During the next six months it was used for a series of races and highly successful cross-country flights, including the first by a light aircraft to the Canary Islands. In 1937 it was bought by Comandante Juan Ortiz Muñoz and it was sold to Vicente Valles at Prat de Llobregat, Barcelona, in 1935. The second aircraft, powered by a 100hp Isotta-Fraschini Asso 80A in-line engine, was unregistered, and appears to have done little flying. The third, likewise unregistered, had greater wing area, which perhaps explains why, during an aerobatic display, first one wing and then the other broke away. The pilot, Alejandro Gómez Spencer, escaped by parachute. The fourth, M-CMAM (later EC-MAM), was powered by a 100hp D.H. Gipsy I in-line engine, and, like subsequent CASA IIIs, had a strengthened outer undercarriage leg. Piloted by Haya, it took part in the 2me Challenge de Tourism Internationale in 1930.

Five more CASA IIIs were built during the early 1930s: EC-ARA, with a 110hp Elizalde A-6 uncowled radial engine, belonged to Antonio Revenga at Barajas, Madrid, and was later fitted with wheel spats. At

The CASA III M-CMAM brought to England by Carlos de Haya during the 2me Challenge de Tourisme Internationale in 1930. Its engine was a 100hp de Havilland Gipsy I. (A J Jackson)

Barajas also were EC-RAA (120hp D.H. Gipsy II) belonging to Rafael Belmonte, EC-RRR (120hp D.H. Gipsy II) belonging to Francisco Sotomayor, and EC-XAC (120hp Walter Venus radial with a Townend ring). The ninth, EA-GCA, belonged to the Aeronáutica Naval, and was at Getafe on 18 July 1936. It was powered by a 120hp D.H. Gipsy III which, curiously, had been re-inverted so that the cylinders faced upwards.

During the civil war the CASA IIIs were impressed by the Republicans into service as trainers, though none are listed as still flying in 1939.

Span 10.5m; length 7.5m; height 2.5m; wing area 16.8sq m.
Empty weight 450kg; loaded weight 790kg.
Maximum speed 170km/h; cruising

speed 150km/h; ceiling 5,000m; endurance 4hr 30min.

CASA-Breguet 19

The Breguet 19 sesquiplane, which was designed to replace the Breguet 14 two-seat light bomber of 1916, first appeared in 1921 and soon gained a reputation as one of the best and most versatile general-purpose military aircraft of its day. About 2,000 were built in France, of which 706 were exported (including 25 to Argentina, 6 to Belgium, 15 to Bolivia, 5 to Brazil, 4 to China and 70 to the Manchurian war-lord Chang Tso Lin, 30 to Greece, 2 to Japan, 2 to Persia, 250 to Poland, 30 to Spain, 70 to Turkey, 12 to Venezuela and 185 to Yugoslavia). A further 649 were built under licence in Belgium, Greece, Japan, Spain and Yugoslavia. Some of Chang Tso Lin's Bre-

A CASA III, EC-ARA, with a 110hp Elizalde A4 radial engine. (CASA, via José Warleta)

guet 19s saw brief action during the Japanese takeover of Manchuria in 1931, and some of the Bolivian machines were used intermittently during the Gran Chaco War between Bolivia and Paraguay (1932-35), but it was not until the Spanish Civil War that the type was used operationally in considerable numbers, by which time it was thoroughly outdated. Yet, despite working under every conceivable disadvantage and facing opposition far more formidable than its designers could have envisaged fifteen years before, it acquitted itself remarkably well.

The Breguet 19 (often written XIX) had a metal airframe which was fabric covered with the exception of the corrugated metal skinning of the forward fuselage and cockpit surrounds. Its wings were braced by a single I strut on either side, and the centre section of the upper mainplane was supported by two thick streamlined struts mounted in tandem along the upper fuselage centreline, directly in front of the cockpit, which must have seriously impaired the pilot's forward view. In the Breguet 19B2 two-seat bomber version, up to 400kg of bombs were carried on racks beneath the lower wings. The defensive armament consisted of two 7.7mm drum-fed Lewis guns on a Scarff ring fitted to the observer's cockpit. Optional weapons were a fixed forward-firing synchronised machine gun mounted above the engine, and a fourth Lewis gun firing through a hatch in the rear fuselage floor. The Breguet 19A2 reconnaissance version had provision for a fixed camera mounted vertically in the fuselage, and a second in the

CASA-Breguet 19 powered by a 500hp Hispano-Suiza 12Hb engine.

observer's cockpit on a movable mount for oblique photography. The undercarriage was of the cross-axle type, and consisted of two faired legs braced by tie rods. The Breguet 19 was designed to accommodate almost any engine of between 300hp and 800hp.

In 1923 the Spanish government decided to build a series of Breguet 19s under licence for the Aeronáutica Militar and, since no suitable facilities for production existed, Construcciones Aeronáuticas SA (CASA) was created under the direction of Comandante José Ortiz Echagüe, with a factory at Getafe military aerodrome, south of Madrid. Meanwhile, thirty Breguet 19s powered by 500hp Hispano-Suiza 12 HB liquid-cooled vee engines were bought from Breguet for immediate service in Spanish Morocco, where the war against the Riff rebels was drawing to its close. The first sixteen arrived at Melilla, Spanish Morocco, in June 1925, and another nine towards the end of the year. Breguet also supplied three pattern aircraft for the CASA production series, two powered by 450hp Lorraine-Dietrich 12 Eb water-cooled broad-arrow engines, and one by an Hispano-Suiza 12 HB, together with components for the first twenty-six machines. The Lorraine engines were to be produced by the Elizalde automobile factory in Barcelona, under the designation 'Elizalde A4'. Altogether, 200 Breguet 19s of the A2 and B2 type were built in Spain, at least fifty of them with Hispano-Suiza engines, between 1926 and 1933.

Much of the fame attached to the Breguet 19 owes it origin to a number of spectacular long-distance flights made by pilots of various air forces during the late 1920s. One Greek Breguet 19, for example, flew a 12,000-mile (19,300km) circuit via Athens, Casablanca, Paris and Bucarest in 1927, while the year before three Spanish aircraft, piloted by González Gallarza, Lóriga, and Martínez Estéve, and known collectively as *La Patrulla Elcano*, attempted a 10,595-mile (17,050km) formation flight from Madrid to Manila. Only

CASA-Breguet 19 number 12-5 (22-41) (450hp Elizalde 12Eb engine) of Grupo 22 at Seville.

Gallarza managed to reach the Philippines, Estévez and Loriga being forced down en route. A by-product of these flights was the development of the Breguet 19GR (*Grand Raid*) and 19TR (*Transatlantique*) 'Bidon' and 'Super Bidon' aircraft ('bidon' meaning 'fuel can'), with greater wingspans, rounded wingtips, and redesigned fuselages and tail units, for long-distance record breaking.

In 1930 a Breguet 19TR Super Bidon crewed by Costes and Codos, and with a question mark painted in white on its fuselage, made the first east-west flight from Paris to New York. Two Breguet 19 Bidons and one Super Bidon were built by CASA: No 71, in which Capitán Haya and Capitán Rodríguez broke three international records; No 72 *Jesús del Gran Poder*, in which

Jiménez and Iglesias flew from Seville to Bahia in 1929; and the Super Bidon *Cuatro Vientos*, in which Barbarán and Collar flew from Seville to Cuba in 1933.

During the 1930s, under the Republic, Breguet 19s equipped five bomber groups of the Aviación Militar: Grupo Núm. 31 (two escuadrillas) at Getafe, Madrid, and Grupo Núm. 21 (three escuadrillas) at León; Grupo Núm. 22 (two escuadrillas) at Tablada (Seville); Grupo Núm. 23 (three escuadrillas) at Logroño; and Grupo Núm. 1 at Melilla, in Spanish Morocco, with independent patrullas (three aircraft each) at Larache and Cabo Juby. In addition, twenty or more were used for liaison duties and by the Y-1 and Y-2 gunnery and bombing schools at Alcalá de Henares and Los Alcázares respectively. The Breguet 19s were given the type code 12, which, followed by the service reception (*matriculación*) number, was painted in black on the rudder and sometimes

A line-up of Nationalist Breguet 19s.

A Nationalist Hispano-powered Breguet 19. The airmen are Baltasar Farriols (left) and Teódoro Anton (right). (Azaola)

on the top surface of the upper mainplane. The aircraft were painted in an aluminium finish overall, with the Grupo and Grupo serial numbers in black on the fuselage sides. Thus the fifth Breguet 19 to be taken into service had 12-5 on the rudder and upper wing and, since it belonged to Grupo 22, 22-41 on the fuselage. Some Breguets of Grupo 1 and Grupo 22 had a black or red flash along the centreline of the fuselage sides. The defensive armament of the Spanish Breguets consisted of a single 7.69mm drum-fed Vickers K gun on the observer's ring mounting.

When delays in the re-equipment programme of 1934 made it apparent that the Breguet 19s would not be replaced until the end of 1938 at the earliest, thirty aircraft were rebuilt by CASA and returned into service in 1935, which brought the number of first-line Breguets to about 100, with about 20 more in miscellaneous units. In the weeks preceding the Nationalist uprising, the Director General de Aeronáutica's policy of concentrating aircraft in the Madrid

sector did not give the Breguets high priority. As a result the Nationalists, by capturing the aerodromes at Logroño, León, Seville and in Spanish Africa, came into possession of sixty-three Breguet 19s, of which six were brought across during the first week by defectors, including two pilots – Angel Salas and Miguel Garciá Pardo – who were to become leading air aces in the war. One or two Breguets also crossed in the opposite direction, flown by pro-Republican pilots who had found themselves on the wrong side. The most notable was Féliz Urtubi, who shot his Falangist observer while patrolling over the Mediterranean and flew to Getafe.

The Nationalist Breguet 19s

In Spanish Africa a number of Breguet 19s were sabotaged by pro-Republican groundcrews during the Nationalist takeover, but some of these seem to have been repaired. At that time Gen Franco had eight in flying condition, and these were used to harass Republican ships in the Straits of Gibraltar and to fly officers

to Seville. There, Gen Queipo de Llano had between twenty and twenty-five at his disposal. In the north, Gen Mola had about thirty, spread between León in the west and Saragossa and Logroño in the east. These were used on reconnaissance and bombing missions over the Basque country and the Sierra de Guadarrama north of Madrid, and in attacks on the Anarchist columns approaching Saragossa and Huesca from Catalonia. Because armament was in short supply, some observers had only a hunting rifle, and it was with one of these that Julián del Val, with an extraordinarily lucky shot, hit and wounded the pilot of an attacking Nieuport 52, José Corranchano, over the Somosierra Pass, forcing him to break off the attack and land violently in a field below.

After the link-up between Franco's and Mola's armies during the third week of August 1936, all the Breguet 19s were formed into a single Escuadra A, consisting of ten escuadrillas (the Junkers Ju 52/3ms formed Escuadra B). Two escuadrillas were retained at Seville for the fighting in the Sierra de Grazalema, near Ronda, where the Nationalists were widening the corridor they had opened from Jerez to Granada, and six escuadrillas were employed in covering the combined advance on Madrid through Talavera de la Reina and Toledo. The remaining two were kept at Saragossa, where they occasionally found themselves in confusing aerial combat with Republican Breguet 19s, Vickers Vildebeests, and other assorted aircraft which were then making repeated attacks on the city.

In October 1936 Escuadra A was dissolved and re-formed into five Grupos numbered 1-G-10 to 5-G-10 (10 being the type code now assigned to the Breguet 19), of two escuadrillas each, but the escuadrillas numbered consecutively through the groups. For example, 1-G-10 consisted of 1-E-10 and 2-E-10, and 2-G-10 of 3-E-10 and 4-E-10. With the arrival of Heinkel He 46 and IMAM Ro 37bis aircraft in October, and of Russian fighters over Madrid in November, the venerable Breguets were moved to safer sectors: 1-G-10 to the Basque front, 2-G-10 to León, 3-G-10 to Seville and Córdoba, 4-G-10 to Granada, and 5-G-10 to Spanish Morocco. On 30 November 1936 five Breguets from 1-G-10 (then at Vitoria), together with a de Havilland Dragon Rapide and a Fokker F.XII from Cdte Ansaldo's Fokker-Dragon group, were largely responsible for preventing a Republican attack in the Villareál sector by attacking and causing great damage to a column of forty troop-carrying lorries in a narrow pass beside Monte Arlabán. At the end of December 3-G-10 was heavily engaged in fighting near Córdoba, and in January 1937 3-G-10 and 4-G-10 covered Gen Queipo de Llano's successful attack on Málaga, which resulted in its capture. At the end of February, on the northern front, the Breguets of 2-G-10 at León and Navia, led by Capitán Eyaralar, took part in a drive to break through Republican lines and relieve the Nationalists besieged in the town of Oviedo, in the Asturias.

In May and June 1937 the Breguet groups were reorganised, some being re-equipped and renamed in the process: 1-G-10 (by then at León) was re-equipped with Heinkel He 45s and became 6-G-15, and 2-G-10, re-equipped with Aero A-101s, became 5-G-17. The third and fourth groups were combined into a single group, renamed 1-G-10, with an escuadrilla at Córdoba and another at Granada. In October 1937 the Aero A-101 group was disbanded, its crews sent to other

Four Hispano-engined Breguet 19s in Republican markings.

units, and the aircraft sent south to re-equip the Breguet group 1-G-10, which now became the new 5-G-17. The airworthy Breguets remaining in Nationalist Spain were either scrapped or relegated to the Escuela de Transformación (Transformation School) at Jerez de la Frontera, where they flew until replaced by Gotha Go 145s in 1938 and 1939. The group in Africa, 2-G-10 (the old 5-G-10), kept its Breguets until the end of the war, and took part in the victory parade at Barajas on 12 May 1939. Ten Nationalist Breguet 19s were lost in action or through accidents during the civil war.

According to the Polish air historian Andrez Glass, twenty ex-Polish Breguet 19s were sold through SEPEWE (or SPV), a sales agency in Danzig, to the Spanish Nationalists via Portugal in July 1936, together with the Polish P.W.S. 10s and R.W.D. 13s. There is as yet no evidence to corroborate or disprove this story.

The Republican Breguet 19s

On 18 July 1936 there were about thirty Breguet 19s at Getafe, Cuatro Vientos, and Barajas. Five were at Barcelona, with five more under repair, and the remaining twenty or thirty were divided between Manises (Valencia), and Los Alcázares, Cartagena. Breguet 19s made some decisive interventions during the opening stages of the war, more through their effect on morale among people generally unfamiliar with aeroplanes than through physical damage. A single bomb dropped by a Breguet 19 persuaded the Nationalist officers and troops in the Montaña barracks, Madrid, to surrender, and other Breguets did much to bring about the surrender of the artillery barracks at Carabanchel, in the suburbs, whose commanders had also joined the rebellion. In August 1936 Breguets were sent south to Andújar and Herrera del Duque to provide air support to the Republican militia retreating before Franco's columns driving up from Seville, and a number were shot down or destroyed on the ground. Breguet 19s did score one success on 16 August when five, in company with Potez 54s of Malraux's newly-arrived Escadre España and a Douglas DC-2, attacked a Nationalist motorised column commanded by Coronel Asensio outside Medellín, in Extremadura, and reportedly scattered it. At the time this was believed to be the first occasion in which an 'army' had been defeated solely by air power, and André Malraux included a vivid account of it in his novel L'Espoir. Nevertheless, the Republicans wasted their brief numerical superiority, which was much exaggerated by Nationalist propagandists, by distributing their aircraft over a wide front and employing them in a large number of small and ineffective attacks, instead of concentrating them upon a few important targets. In the opinion of Lacalle, the Republican pilot whose memoirs are often cited in this book, the mere sound of the engines of forty Breguets flying in formation over Avila on the first day would have kept that city loyal to the Republic.

Some of the Breguets at Valencia were moved north to Barcelona, and on 1 August two of them flew to San Sebastián to establish contact with the Basques, for whom, as fellow separatists, the Catalonian Generalitat, or regional government, had much sympathy. To avoid Nationalist-held territory the Breguets crossed into France and staged through Toulouse and Biarritz, an action which provoked much complaint in the newspapers of the French Right-wing opposition. On 4 August 1936 nine Breguets from Barcelona were moved to Sariñena, in Aragón, where a new aerodrome had been hurriedly laid out under the direction of Capitán Amador Silverio, 'El Dibujante' ('The Draughtsman'), and these formed the nucleus of the so-called *Alas Rojas* (Red Wings) group led by Isidoro Giménez. Together with a Fokker F.VIIb3m (ex-EC-PPA from LAPE), a Latécoère 28, the de Havilland D.H. 89M No 22-2, four D.H.84 Dragons and other machines (even including some D.H.9s for a time, it is said) the Breguet 19s, some of which had *Aviación del Pueblo* ('Aviation of the People') painted in large red letters on the undersurfaces of the lower wings, carried out repeated attacks on Saragossa and Huesca.

In October 1936 six more Breguet 19s, with two Vickers Vildebeests and four Savoia-Marchetti S.62s, were flown across to Bilbao to create a more substantial Basque air force. One of the Breguets and a Vildebeest were shot down over Eiber by Heinkel He 51s on 21 October, less than a week after arrival. In December the Breguets were the subject of indignant comment from such American mercenaries as Maj Fred Lord and Bert Acosta (the pilot on Commander Byrd's famous transatlantic crossing in a Fokker F.VIIb3m in June 1927), who were outraged at being ordered to fly such ancient machines. All were destroyed during the northern compaign of 1937.

Early in September 1936 the vanguard of the large number of Soviet personnel that was to be sent to Spain arrived in Madrid, and two Soviet engineers, Ioffe and Zalesski, fitted forward-firing machine guns on some of the Breguets at Barajas, with which they then launched a low-level attack against Nationalist troops at Villalengua, north of Toledo. Without fighter escorts, however, such an attack could not be repeated. In November 1936, after the arrival

of R-5s and SBs from Russia, the Breguet 19s were relegated, like their Nationalist counterparts, to quieter fronts, and, during 1937, to the training schools in Murcia. A photograph taken in October 1937 at the Escuela de Vuelo de Noche (Night Flying School) at El Carmolí, near Cartagena, shows a line of Breguet 19s. The nearest machine has RB-024 painted in white on its fuselage, while another has a large capital letter A. If any Republican Breguet 19s survived the civil war, the Nationalists do not seem to have bothered to list them. The last recorded miliary action by Breguet 19s in any war took place as late as April 1945, when two were still serving with Josip Tito's partisans in Yugoslavia against the Chetnik forces of Gen Mikhailovich.

Span 14.83m; length 9.51m; height 3.69m; wing area 50sq m.

With Elizalde A4 engine: loaded weight 2,096kg;
Maximum speed 222km/h; ceiling 6,300m; range 800km.

With Hispano-Suiza 12HB: loaded weight 2,200kg;
Maximum speed 230km/h.

CASA-Breguet 26T

The Breguet 26T was a passenger-carrying version of the Breguet 19, retaining the wings and tail of the military version but with a redesigned fuselage. The pilot sat in an open

A CASA-Breguet 26T ambulance.

cockpit in a high position in front of the upper-wing centre section, and the cabin, accommodating six passengers, had four rectangular windows on each side. The 26T was powered by an uncowled 430hp Gnome-Rhône Jupiter radial engine. From the 26T was developed the Breguet 280T, with a 600hp Hispano-Suiza water-cooled engine, an enclosed pilot's cockpit, the wings and tail of the Breguet 19 TR Super Bidon, and four arched windows in the fuselage sides. At least one 26T and four 280Ts were used by Air Union during the late 1920s and early 1930s.

In 1928 CASA built two aircraft designated Breguet 26T, the design being a compromise between the two French types. The fuselage was that of the 26T, with the rectangular windows and open cockpit, but the wings and tail were those of the 280T, and it was powered by a 450hp Elizalde A4 (licence-built Lorraine 12Eb) water-cooled engine. The first machine, c/n 113, M-CEAE, was converted into an ambulance and handed over to the Aviación Militar, and the second, c/n 114, M-CHHA (later EC-HHA), was delivered to CLASSA, and so passed on to LAPE in 1931.

The ambulance was still flying in July 1936, and was handed over to the Escuela de Polimótores (School for Multi-engined Aircraft) at Totana, Murcia, in 1937.

CASA-Vickers Vildebeest

The Vickers Vildebeest, of which the prototype first flew in April 1928, was

*The first production CASA-Vickers
Vildebeest, T-1.* (CASA, via José
Warleta)

a single-engined, two-seat torpedo-
bomber biplane designed to replace
the Hawker Horsley. It was a solidly
built, rugged machine of metal construction with fabric covering, in
which the pilot's cockpit was set
immediately behind the engine and
in front of the leading edges of the
single-bay, square-tipped wings.
The wide-track undercarriage could
be replaced by twin floats. Either a
single 18in torpedo or 1,000lb of
bombs in underwing racks could be
carried. The pilot was armed with a
single fixed synchronised Vickers
gun in the port side of the fuselage,
and the observer-gunner, whose
cockpit was located behind the wing
trailing edges, had a single Lewis gun
mounted on a Scarff ring. Between
1932 and 1935 209 Vildebeests, in
four production versions, were built
for the RAF, the most handsome
version being the Mk IV, with an
825hp Bristol Perseus VIII radial
engine in a long-chord cowling and
streamlined spats over the wheels.
Twenty-six were built under licence
by CASA in Spain. It was the
misfortune of the Vildebeest that, in
the two theatres of war in which it saw
action, in Spain in 1936 and in
Malaya in 1942, it was obsolete and
completely outclassed and outnumbered by the enemy it had to face –
disastrously so in Malaya.

The prototype, serial number
N230 (later G-ABGE) was demons-
trated before a Spanish delegation at
Brooklands, Surrey, on 22 July 1929.

The Spaniards expressed an interest
in placing an order, provided that
their version was fitted with an
Hispano-Suiza engine which could
be produced in Spain. Accordingly,
the 600hp Hispano-Suiza 12Lbr
liquid-cooled engine that had been
installed in the second, private-
venture, airframe was transferred to
N230, which was then fitted with
floats and given the 'B conditions'
marking O-3. After testing a Blackburn Ripon, the Spaniards decided
on the Vildebeest, and acquired a
licence for twenty-five to be built by
Construcciones Aeronáuticas SA
(CASA) at their factory at Getafe,
Madrid. After a tour of the Baltic, in
which it met with various misadven-
tures, N230 was sold to Spain and
ferried there in March 1932 by HWR
Banting, its Spanish ferry registration
EC-W11 being wrongly painted on
its fuselage as EC-WLL. A second

*A Vildebeest seaplane with 'water-ripple'
camouflage.*

Vildebeest was sent from Weybridge
in parts and reassembled at Getafe,
bringing the total for Spain to twenty-
seven. For so small a number of
aeroplanes production cannot be said
to have been rapid, for the last of the
twenty-five built did not reach the
Aeronáutica Naval base at San Javier
(Cartagena), where they were to
equip Escuadrillas de Torpederos
Núm. 1, 2 and 3, until April 1936.
Indeed, the last two escuadrillas were
still being formed when the civil war
broke out on 18 July 1936. The
Vildebeests were serialled T-1 to
T-27, their identities being painted
in black on the silver fuselage sides.
The group emblem, a black and
yellow dolphin leaping over a black
ball, was painted on either side of the
engine cowling. It had been intended
to equip seven aircraft as seaplanes,
fourteen sets of floats having been
built by the CASA factory at Puntales, Cádiz. In the event, only two of
the Vildebeests (T-16 and T-17) had
been so fitted by 18 July, the rest of
the floats being at Cádiz and in the
possession of the Nationalists.

The Vildebeests could carry
725kg of bombs, a heavier load than
that of any other aircraft in Spain at
the time, and accordingly they were
hastily fitted with every bomb rack
available, some, together with
machine guns and ammunition,
being rushed down from Madrid in
the prevailing confusion. Improvised
bomb sights were fitted, and holes
cut in the cockpit floors through
which the pilots could aim. Unfortunately, instead of being concentrated
together, which would have enabled
them to be effective, the Vildebeests
were dispersed as soon as possible,

some being sent to Calalonia, others to Madrid, and two to the isolated Basque-Asturian enclave in the north.

The first casualty occurred on 23 July 1936, when José-María Freire, flying the seaplane T-17, bombed Palma, Mallorca, and became lost while trying to return to Barcelona. Freire alighted on the water beside the Spanish steamship *Ayala Mendi* to determine his position, but as he took off again the floats struck a high wave and the machine crashed. The crew was saved, but an attempt to hoist the Vildebeest aboard had to be abandoned. The other seaplane, T-16, survived until February 1937, when it struck a jetty while taking off in Barcelona harbour. The pilot, Barón, was killed, and his observer, Godia, was gravely injured.

Meanwhile, the Vildebeest land-planes played a prominent, though not very effectual, part in the opening phases of the civil war, during which seven (or, according to the Nationalists, nine) were shot down, the first on 28 July 1936 over Teruel. In twos and threes they carried out raids on Saragossa, Granada and Córdoba. A Vildebeest which was shot down by a Heinkel He 51 over Antequera on 12 August was the first of the forty victories accredited to the Nationalist pilot Joaquín García Morato, the highest-scoring ace of the war. One Vildebeest pilot, Antonio Gómez Baños, saved himself when attacked by a Nationalist Nieuport 52 by opening the Handley Page slots and reducing his flying speed to 70km/h every time the Nieuport got into position to attack, thus forcing the enemy pilot to overshoot. The Vildebeest returned to base riddled with bullet holes, but the two crew members were unhurt. In the Basque zone, one Vildebeest was shot down by Heinkel He 51s over Eibar on 21 October 1936. The second was still flying in December, when it took part, with two Breguet 19s, a General Aircraft Monospar ST-25, two Miles Hawks and a Miles Falcon, in an attack on the Condor Legion base at Vitoria, and survived.

By the end of the year the remaining Vildebeests were relegated to training duties, from which they were brought back into action during the Republican retreat from Málaga in February 1937. They were also used during the Republican victory over the Italians at Guadalajara in March, when every available aircraft was mustered to attack Italian troops while the bad weather prevented the Nationalist air forces, whose aerodromes were mostly waterlogged, from taking to the air. Thereafter, little more is heard of the CASA-Vickers Vildebeests. At least six, as a part of Grupo 73, were still flying in April 1938 – three at Barcelona, two at Los Alcázares and one at El Carmolí, Cartagena. One must have been refitted as a seaplane, perhaps using the floats of the crashed T-17, for such a machine was on the inventory of Grupo 73 in the summer of 1938. The Nationalists recovered two Vildebeests at the end of the war, one of them being T-23, and continued flying them until the 1940s.

Landplane: span 14.93m; length 11.22m; height 4.47m; wing area 67.75sq m.

Empty weight 1,990kg; loaded weight 3,850kg.

Maximum speed 220km/h; cruising speed 180km/h; ceiling 4,350m; range 1,200km.

Caudron C.59 and C.490

The Caudron C.59, a two-seat, two-bay biplane powered by a 180hp Hispano-Suiza 8Ab water-cooled engine, first appeared in 1922 and became one of the most successful French trainers and sports aeroplanes of the 1920s. Altogether, 1,800 were built for the French military and naval air services, and for flying schools in France and abroad.

During 1937 and 1938 Lejeune Aviation, which ran a flying school at Esbly, Meaux, north-east of Paris and was engaged in procuring assorted aircraft for the Spanish Republicans, bought ten Caudron C.59s from the École Caudron at Ambérieu and exported them all, or all but one, to Spain. One, possibly F-AJPU, which was flown from Toulouse–Montaudran on 17 February 1937 by Réné Imbert, made a forced landing in Catalonia on the way to Barcelona. After the aircraft was repaired, the Catalonian authorities allowed Imbert to continue his flight inland.

During the Nationalist advance through Aragón and southern Catalonia to the coast in the spring of 1938, three Caudron C.59s were involved in a dramatic incident. On the afternoon of 25 March, after machine-gunning a column of lorries, the Fiat C.R.32s of the Spanish Nationalist group 2-G-3 were turning for home when their commander, Capitán Angel Salas, saw three Republican biplanes coming in to land on Mas de las Matas Aerodrome, near Alcorisa in the province of Teruel. Noticing that Nationalist troops were less than a kilometre away and advancing rapidly across country towards the field, he landed beside the Caudron C.59s, as they turned out to be. While the other C.R.32s kept away any retreating Republican soldiers in the vicinity, he held the pilots of the Caudrons at pistol point until the arrival of the Nationalist soldiers, who promptly tried to seize him, too, as a prisoner of

A Caudron C.59. (Liron)

war. The Caudrons belonged to a flight of four aircraft which, under the leadership of Teniente Momblona, were being evacuated from the Escuela de Vuelo (Flying School) at Reus, Tarragona. The pilot of the fourth machine had seen what was happening before he touched down, and made good his escape. The captured C.59s were: F-AJOS (c/n 1110/6475); F-AJPV (c/n 1096/6481) and, probably, F-AOTN (c/n 926/–).

The other C.59s sold to the Spanish Republicans were:

F-AISR (c/n –/6195) Caudron–Lejeune before 1 Jan 1938, to Spain shortly after.

F-AJMU (c/n 1101/6463) Caudron–Lejeune before 1 Jan 1938, absent 1939.

F-AJPU (c/n 1097/6474) Caudron–Lejeune before 25 Mar 1937 (1938?).

F-ALGC (c/n 1098/6550 Caudron–Lejeune, 10 Sept 1937, to Spain after 1 Jan 1938.

F-ALGD (c/n 2/6551) Caudron–Lejeune, 10 Sept 1937.

F-AINA (c/n 2/6174) Caudron–Lejeune, before 1 Jan 1938, to Spain shortly after.

Of uncertain disposition is F-AIOR (c/n 4/6177), bought by Lejeune Aviation on 10 September 1937. The last Bureau Veritas inspection date is 10.2.37, but it was 'Réformé' on 10 June 1937.

The history of the Caudron C.490, developed from the C.59, is curious. In 1932 Caudron began work on a machine to replace the ageing C.59s that still comprised the majority of the equipment of the Caudron flying schools, but, since the C.59 was still a popular machine, nothing more radical was envisaged than the installation of a more powerful Anzani engine. The resulting C.157, built round a C.59 airframe, proved a disappointment, since its performance was no better than that of the aircraft it was intended to replace. In July 1933 Caudron was bound by contract to buy all future engines from Renault, and the C.157 was re-engined with a 250hp Renault 9A radial engine and redesignated C.320. Although nine C.320s were built, they, too, were unsatisfactory, and five were converted back to C.59s. In 1935, one of these (C.157/

320, No. 5, F-AJAE) was re-engined yet again with a 170hp Renault 6 Pfi Bengali inverted in-line engine from a Caudron Simoun and redesignated C.490. Thus in 1935 there rolled out of the hangar a 'new' prototype which appeared, except for its engine, to belong to the early 1920s, complete with two-bay, square-cut wings with scalloped trailing edges and a straight-axle undercarriage. Nevertheless, the type went into production in four versions (C.490, C.491, C.493 and C.493), the last two having their wings set at a dihedral angle.

On 10 September 1937 Lejeune Aviation bought three C.490s, re-engined with 170hp Renault 6TF engines, from the École Caudron at Royan: F-AODD (c/n 3/7162), F-AODF (c/n 4/7164), and F-AODK (c/n 7/7169). These were still at Esbly for the Bureau Veritas visit on 13 October 1937, but had vanished by the time of the next visit on 25 March 1938, which almost certainly means that they had slipped across the frontier to Republican Spain.

Caudron C.59

Span 10.2m; length 7.8m; height 2.9m; wing area 26sq m.

Empty weight 700kg; loaded weight 988kg.

Maximum speed 170km/h; endurance 3.3hr.

Caudron C.490

Span 10.23m; length 8.60m; height 2.55m; wing area 26sq m.

Empty weight 644kg; loaded weight 1,022kg.

A Caudron C.272 Luciole.

Maximum speed 180km/h; range 450km.

Caudron C.272–C.276 Luciole

Designed by Paul Deville, who was responsible for the creation of no fewer than fifty-eight prototypes in the course of his productive career, the Caudron C.270 Luciole (Firefly) was a two-seat, single-bay, equal-span wood and metal biplane intended for training, sports flying and tourism. The prototype, F-ALIK, powered by a 95hp Salmson 7Ac uncowled radial engine, appeared in 1930 and, the following year, flown by Maurice Finat and his wife, won the French Concours national téchnique des avions de Tourisme. The Luciole was highly successful, and during the next nine years 724 were built in at least a dozen versions, designated according to the engine fitted and modifications to the tail assembly. All had dual controls and folding wings.

The first Luciole to reach Spain was a C.270 (95hp Salmson engine), bought by E Fernández of Barcelona in 1932 and registered EC-SSS. It survived the civil war, during which it had been used as a trainer, and for a while became 30-186 of the Ejercito del Aire. Handed over to the Aero Club de Barcelona in 1940, it was re-registered EC-CAT, and in 1946 became EC-ABJ. It was written off after an accident in 1949. A C.272 Luciole (95hp Renault 4Pb inverted in-line), EC-ADE, was acquired by the Aero Club de Barcelona in 1935, but does not appear to have survived the civil war. In 1936 three more C.272 Lucioles were bought by the Escuela Catalana de Aviación.

Further Lucioles were imported clandestinely during the civil war, some having already been used to train Spanish Republican pilots in France, though the exact number is not known. The accompanying list shows all the Caudron Lucioles that disappear from the records without clear reason between July 1936 and March 1939.

The C.272/2s had 100hp Renault 4Pei inverted in-line engines, the C.272/3 had a 120hp Renault 4Pdi, and the C.276 a 105hp de Havilland Gipsy III.

Two of the listed Lucioles, though it is not known which, survived the civil war and became 30-171 and 30-172, the latter being withdrawn from service in 1940 and 30-171 in 1946.

Span 9.9m; length 7.61m; height 2.76m; wing area 25sq m.
Empty weight 450kg; loaded weight 870kg.

A Caudron C.282/8 Phalène. (Liron)

Maximum speed 150-170km/h; cruising speed 135-145km/h; stalling speed 75km/h; landing speed 59-62 km/h; ceiling 4,000m.

Caudron C.282 Phalène and C.510 Pélican

As the Caudron Luciole was in-

Type	c/n	Reg'n	Owner	Last Bureau Veritas inspection	Location
C.272	2/6560	F-ALMN	V Laffont	11.04.37	AC Populaire d'Agen
C.272	5/6564	'MR	V Laffont	25.05.37	AC Populaire d'Agen
C.272	9/6604	'VL	L Lejeune	21.09.37	Esbly
C.272	19/6679	'AMFH	L Lejeune	28.07.37	Esbly
C.272	21/6701	'FJ	L Lejeune	28.07.37	Esbly
C.272	24/6704	'FM	L Lejeune	21.09.37	Esbly
C.272/2	26/6574	'ALRG	L Lejeune	28.07.37	Esbly
C.272/2	17/6977	'ANKH	Sté.Caudron		To Barcelona, 24-25.08.36
C.272/3	2/6851	'ALSM	L Lejeune	18.06.37	Esbly
C.272/5	8/7146	'AOAG	L Lejeune	13.07.37	Esbly
C.273	5/7415	'APBN	V Laffont		
C.273	19/7420	'BR	L Augiere	19.06.37	Villeneuve-sur-Lot, sold to SFTA
C.273	21/7493	'HL	P Legastelois	26.05.37	
C.273	22/7494	'HM	P Legastelois	27.05.37	

Most of the above owners were involved in procuring aircraft for the Spanish Republicans at that time. Other Caudron Lucioles whose final disposition is uncertain are:

Type	c/n	Reg'n	Owner	Remarks
C.272	15/6642	F-AMAB	Ailes Catalanes	Sold abroad 1938
C.272/2	19/6978	'ANKI	Sté.Caudron	Last BV 22.07.35
C.272/2	20/7043	'TA	Sté.Caudron	Sold abroad 12.36
C.276	7/6794	'AMMD	AC L'Ile de France	Sold abroad 04.37, but also 'Destroyed' 25.04.37
C.273	15/7431	'APEO	A Garnier	Sold abroad 07.37

tended as a rival to the de Havilland Moth and Tiger Moth, so the C.280 Phalène (Moth) was designed as a rival to the de Havilland Puss Moth, which it closely resembled. Built entirely of wood, with plywood covering the forward fuselage and fabric the rear fuselage, wings and tail, it was a four-seat high-wing cabin monoplane which could be powered by a variety of engines, the most usual being the 120hp or 140hp Renault Bengali or the 120hp de Havilland Gipsy III inverted in-lines. A pair of ailerons extended the entire length of the wing trailing edges. Like the Luciole, the Phalène was produced in several versions, designated according to the engine fitted.

In 1935 Caudron C.282 Phalène c/n 35/6572, with a Gipsy III engine, was bought by Alberto Salinas of Burgos, registered EC-ZZZ, and kept at Gamonal Aerodrome, a few miles east of the city. By a curious coincidence, the only other Phalène to take part in the Spanish Civil War landed at this same aerodrome on 17 July 1936, the day before the uprising, in mysterious circumstances. The pilot was Henri Rozés, who had not long before been chief of the Caudron flying school at Toulouse-Francazal Aerodrome. Rozés was now a freelance pilot, and had been hired to fly Antonio de Lizarza, a leading Carlist (adherents to the cause of Alfonso Carlos, one of the pretenders to the Spanish throne) and Nationalist conspirator, from Biarritz to Lisbon to confer with Gen Sanjurjo (see de Havilland Puss Moth). The machine used for this flight was the C.282/2 Phalène III F-AMMO (c/n 26/6812, D.H. Gipsy III). While crossing Castile en route to Lisbon, Rozés told Lizarza

One of the two Caudron Phalènes on the Nationalist aerodrome at Burgos in the early weeks of the war. (Arráez)

that they would have to land at Burgos because strong headwinds had used up too much fuel. At Burgos, Lizarza and Rozés were arrested as suspicious persons and, together with the military governor of Burgos and others thought to be planning rebellion, were taken to Guadalajara prison (Lizarza's life was eventually saved by the intervention of a Communist who, providentially, had been a school friend).

Rozés, however, was secretly taken from Guadalajara to Madrid, whence he returned to France and became active in ferrying aircraft to Republican Spain. In the 1970s it was alleged that Rozés was a Left-Wing activist or Freemason who had infiltrated the conspiracy, and that the landing at Burgos was pre-planned in order to deliver Lizarza into the hands of the Republican authorities. Be that as it may, when the Nationalists took over Burgos on 18 July 1936, two Caudron Phalènes were already on Gamonal Aerodrome. A few days later the British adventurer-pilot Rupert Bellville (see D.H. Leopard Moth) arrived at Burgos and used one of the Phalènes to fly a senior Nationalist officer on a reconnaissance flight over Madrid. Both of these Phalènes were incorporated into Grupo 30 (for light aircraft). After serving as 30-8, EC-ZZZ was sold to P Fuster of Seville in 1942 and registered EC-BAK. In 1945, as EC-ABU, it became the private aeroplane of the Governor General of Spanish Guinea in West Africa, being based at Santa

Isabel Aerodrome, Bata. The other Phalène, F-AMMO, became 30-30, but was withdrawn from service before being returned to civil flying. A third aircraft, 30-23, is also said to have been a Phalène. The only possible candidate is the C.282/8 F-ANLU (c/n 38/6786), which belonged to the Société Caudron and was sold abroad in November 1936. Since all other Société Caudron aircraft went to the Republicans, however, there is a need to know how this machine came to be sold to the other side.

The Caudron C.510 Pélican, powered by a 140hp Renault Bengali 4Pei, was a Phalène with a lengthened cabin and increased wing area to carry a pilot, ambulanceman and stretcher case. The C.510 F-AOFR (c/n 39/7221) belonging to Rémy Clement was 'sold abroad' in September 1936. Since Clément purchased several aircraft on behalf of the Spanish Republicans and was a Resistance fighter working with the SOE during the Second World War, there can be little doubt concerning its destination.

Left: the Caudron C.510 Pélican.

C.282

Span 11.54m; length 8.25m; height 2m; wing area 23.41sq m.

Empty weight 500kg; loaded weight 950kg.

Maximum speed 180km/h; cruising speed 150km/h; ceiling 4,500m; range 825km.

C.510

Span 11.82m; length 8.5m; wing area 23.75sq m.

Empty weight 626kg; loaded weight 1,140kg.

Maximum speed 185km/h; cruising speed 165km/h; range 1,000km.

Caudron C.440–C.448 Göeland

Designed by Marcel Riffard, the Caudron Göeland, a twin-engined, low-wing cantilever monoplane carrying a crew of two and six passengers in an air-conditioned cabin, was one of the most successful aircraft produced by the Caudron company in the interwar years. It was built of wood and, except for the duralumin-covered nose-cone, was skinned with stressed ply. The prototype, C.440 F-ANKV, first flew in 1934 with the celebrated test and record-breaking pilot Raymond Delmotte at the controls, and during the next three years Caudron Göelands achieved great distinction both in French and international air races.

The Göeland was produced in several modified versions, which included:

The Caudron Göeland prototype, C.440-01 F-ANKV (200hp Renault Bengali 6 engines), sold to Air Pyrénées in February 1937. (Liron)

C.440, of which two were built, powered by two 200hp Renault Bengali Six inverted in-line engines.

C.441, powered by two 220hp Renault 6Q-01 engines angled 3° outwards from the fuselage centreline.

C.444, powered by two Renault 6Q-00 engines.

C.445, powered by two 220hp Renault 6 Pdi engines angled 4° outwards. A trainer version, the C.445M, was produced for the Armée de l'Air.

C.448, powered by two 240hp Renault 6Q-02 or 6Q-03 engines.

Air France was among the operators of both the C.444 and C.445. During the Occupation of 1940-45, Göelands were produced for the Luftwaffe, and in one of these Marcel Florein, who had flown in Spain with the Malraux squadron and in China with the 14th Squadron under Vincent Schmidt (see Bloch MB 200 and Vultee V1-A), and Georges Klein, a mechanic, escaped to England on 10 December 1941.

At least six Caudron Göelands flew in the Spanish Civil War:

C.440 F-ANKV (c/n 1/6905), the prototype, was sold by Société Caudron to August Amestoy and used by Air Pyrénées from February 1937 (see Appendix I).

C.444 F-ANKX (c/n 1/6906), the second prototype, was sold by Société Caudron to August Amestoy in April 1937 and used by Air Pyrénées.

C.448 F-AOMX *Ric et Rac* (c/n 1/7272) was built for the Paris-Saigon air race of October 1936, and had a slightly lighter structure than the series models and a range of 4,640km (2,900 miles). Flown by R Bril and Capitán Challe in the race, it failed to complete the course owing to engine trouble. According to some French newspapers it was sold to the Spanish Republicans via a company named Arc-en-Ciel, though it has been impossible to verify the existence of such an agency. Be that as it may, it was sold to SFTA (see Appendix II) in February 1937 and to Air Pyrénées in March, allegedly for 500,000 French francs. On 22 June 1937, shortly after the fall of Bilbao, this Göeland landed on the beach at Zarauz, a seaside resort near San Sebastián, and fell into Nationalist hands. Numerous propaganda stories were woven around this incident. According to C G Grey, the editor of *The Aeroplane*, the pilot was accompanied by a Russian general and a French colonel, as well as the jewels belonging to the effigy of the Virgen de la Begoña, which were presumably being taken to France to pay for arms purchases. In fact the prisoners were Coronel Aguirre, chief of the Basque artillery, Señor Espinosa, the Basque minister of health, and a French reserve officer. It seems improbable that the jewels were aboard the aircraft, for the Euskadi Republic and its president, José Aguirre, were officially and devoutly Catholic. The pilot was José Yanguas Yañez, who, the previous autumn, had caused amusement while flying a de Havilland Puss Moth over Vil-

One of the two Caudron C.445 Göelands, with redesigned tail assemblies and 220hp Renault 6 Pdi engines, used by LAPE. (Liron)

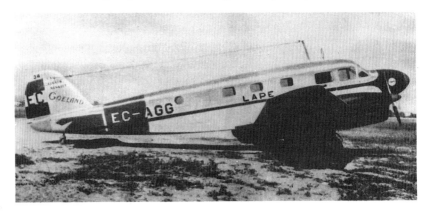

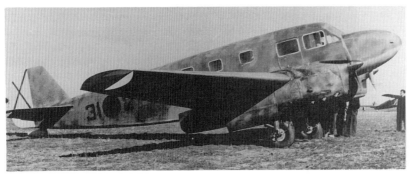

The Caudron C.448 F-AOMX Ric et Rac, *built for the Paris-Saigon air race of October 1936, with a further modified fin and rudder and powered by 240hp Renault 6 Q engines. Used by Air Pyrénées, it was captured by the Nationalists and became 31-2. (Arráez)*

lareal by emptying a bag of stones on to a group of Requetes (Carlist militia) drilling in the town square. Deliberate treason on the part of Yanguas therefore seems unlikely. The ex-LAPE pilot José-María Carreras told the author, however, that he had spotted Yanguas in a café in France in 1938 and wondered why the Nationalists had released him. Later, the Basque president, Aguirre, spoke of Yanguas's 'treason'. In the Nationalist air arm F-AOMX became 31-2, and was attached to the Fiat fighter group 2-G-3 commanded by García Morato. It was out of service before the end of the war.

C.445 F-AOYP (c/n 4/7347), was sold by Air France to SFTA on 25 September, and then went to Republican Spain, where it served in the FARE as a transport.

C.445 F-AOYQ (c/n 5/7348) and F-AOYR (c/n 6/7349), were sold to SFTA by Air France on 25 September 1937; they then went to Republican Spain, where they were incorporated into LAPE with the registrations and fleet numbers EC-AGG/34 and 'AGF/33 respectively. At the end of the civil war they were among the transports used to fly Republican officials and ministers to France, and during the summer of 1939 both SFTA, which was facing liquidation, and the new Spanish government laid claim to them. Another Göeland, probably ex-F-AOYP, was recovered from Oran, Algeria, in May 1939, and became 31-7 in the Ejercito del Aire. It continued serving until the early 1940s.

Two aircraft reported as Göelands that had been flown to Spain in August and October 1936 (one flown by Faicré and Carriaga and the other by Chace) were Lucioles. Similarly, two Göelands reported in *l'Action française* as being flown by Lionel de Marmier and Georges Cornez to 'Bulgaria' (by which the paper meant 'Red Spain'), did indeed go to Bulgaria.

Span 17.6m; length 13.8m; height 3.5m; wing area 40sq m.

Empty weight 7,300kg; loaded weight 3,500kg.

Maximum speed 300km/h; cruising speed 260km/h; landing speed 100km/h; ceiling 5,600m; range 560m.

Above: *a Caudron C.600 Aiglon.* (Liron)

Caudron C.600 and C.601 Aiglon

One of the best-known light aeroplanes designed by Marcel Riffard, the Caudron C.600 Aiglon (Eaglet) was a slender, clean-lined, wooden low-wing cantilever monoplane which first appeared in 1935. It gained international renown in the same year when André Japy flew the specially modified C.601 F-ANSI, with a transparent canopy over the cockpits, from Istres to Saigon in five days at an average speed of 125km/h. Aiglons continued to break long-distance speed records until the Second World War. The Aiglon was built in several versions, designated according to the type of Bengali Junior engine fitted (100-140hp). The C.600G had a 120hp de Havilland Gipsy III or 130hp Gipsy Major.

At least twenty, and probably more, C.600 and C.601 Aiglons (and one C.600G) were imported into Republican Spain during the civil war and used as transformation trainers at La Ribera (San Javier, Cartagena), Lorca and Archena (see table below).

In Spain, several were fitted with 'trousered' undercarriages.

The following Aiglons are suspected to have been imported, because none appear to have been officially registered: F-AQKG (7621), 'H (-2), 'K (-5), 'L (-6), 'M (-7).

Other suspects are F-APCV, bought by SFTA in March 1938, F-AOGS, 'ANVO (sold in 'Roumania' 9.36), 'AOKC, 'AOKN, 'AOVI,

Type	c/n	Reg'n	
C.600	2/7027	F-ANSC	Cercle Aér. Coulommiers, 9.36; SFTA 3.38
C.600	27/7055	F-ANVC	P Berson; SFTA
C.600	72/7067	F-ANVD	To Republican Spain, 29.9.36
C.600	35/7132	F-ANZR	M Cayre, 9.36
C.600G	74/7203	F-AOGY	Cie France Navigation 8.38
C.600	103/7241	F-AOKF	V Laffont, 5.37. 'Destroyed' 1938
C.600	116/7246	F-AOKK	L Lejeune 9.37. Disappeared 2.38
C.600	124/7248	F-AOKM	L Lejeune 9.37. Disappeared 2.38
C.600	120/7305	F-AOVE	L Maniglier, sold abroad 9.36
C.600	114/7307	F-AOVG	L Lejeune 9.37
C.600	117/7308	F-AOVH	Sté Caudron, sold abroad 9.36
C.600	144/7443	F-APCA	P Casau; disappeared 1937
C.601	9/7437	F-APCE	Sold to J-A Ansaldo (Nationalist) after 1 Nov 1936; became *Nationalist* 30-6
C.600	152/7444	F-APCL	V Laffont, disappeared by 2.38
C.600	159/7432	F-APCT	AC Guyancourt, last seen 8.37
C.600	160/7453	F-APCU	SFTA 5.37 – 3.38
C.601	12/7457	F-APCZ	A Rodier 3.37. SFTA 3.38
C.601	13/7615	F-AQKA	P Legastelois 3.37. SFTA

'APCI, 'APCY, 'AOKJ and 'APCG. While it is not suggested that *all* of these went to Republican Spain, some very probably did.

A number of Aiglons were recovered by the Nationalists after the civil war, and seven became 30-140 to 30-144 and 30-164 to 30-166. With the delivery of the CASA-built Bücker Jungmann to the Ejercito del Aire in 1941-42, the Aiglons were handed over to civil flying clubs, and 30-166 became EC-CAD (later 'AFR, written off in 1964), and two others became 'CAC and 'CAE.

C.600

(100hp Renault Bengali 4Pqi)
Span 11.4m; length 7.6m; height 2m; wing area 14.5sq m.
Empty weight 560kg; loaded weight 865kg.
Maximum speed 211km/h; cruising speed 190km/h; ceiling 360m in 1.6min; range 630km.

C.601

(140hp Renault Bengali 4Pei)
Empty weight 580kg; loaded weight 880kg.
Maximum speed 225km/h; cruising speed 200km/h; ceiling 6,000m; range 540km.

Caudron C.635 Simoun

A low-wing, cabin light aeroplane and air taxi, the Simoun became well-known in the later 1930s for long-distance flights and other achievements when piloted by such figures are Maryse Hilz, André Japy and Antoine de Sainte Exupéry. One air taxi C.635, F-ANCG (c/n 17/6975), is believed to have been used by Jean Dary (the highest-scoring fighter pilot of the International Squadron in September 1936) when he was flying for Air Pyrénées in 1937, and therefore can be said to have participated in the Basque campaign. It was, however, inspected by the Bureau Veritas on 19 September 1938, so its Spanish involvement was presumably over by then.

Incidentally, when André Malraux flew from Paris to take his

Caudron C.600 and C.601 trainers at El Carmolí, Cartagena. The C.601s have trousered undercarriages. (Arráez)

squadron of volunteers and mercenaries in their Potez 54s to Barcelona on 8 August 1936, he arrived at Toulouse-Francazal in a Caudron C.635 air taxi.

Span 10.4m; length 8.97m; height 2.15m; wing area 16sq m.
Empty weight 978kg; loaded weight 1,675kg.
Maximum speed 300 km/h; ceiling 5,600m; maximum range for long-distance flying, 5,350km.

Cierva C.19 and C.30A Autogiro

Don Juan de la Cierva Codorníu, who with Pablo Picasso and Pablo Casals is properly revered in Spain as one of the true Spanish geniuses of this century, was the inventor of the first practical rotating-wing aircraft, the 'Autogiro', and in the interwar years his name was almost synonymous with machines of this category. Many of the prototype and production Autogiros were built by A V Roe and Co Ltd at Manchester, although Cierva established his own company

at Hanworth in 1932. The C.19 was the first Autogiro to have automatic rotor-starting. In the C.19 Mk IV the twin-rudder box tail of the Mks I-III was replaced by a monoplane tail and a single rudder. The Cierva C.30A was the most elegant, as well as the most successful, of all the Autogiros, and the first to dispense with the stub wings of earlier designs.

Two Cierva C.19 Mk IVs and five Cierva C.30As were in Spain at the start of the civil war. One C.19 Mk IV, G-ABXI (c/n 5159), was bought from Avro by the Aviación Militar on 4 October 1932 and, bearing the registration 49-1 (in error for 41-1, 49 being the type code for the Junkers F 13 and K 30), left Heston for Spain on 7 October 1932. Later, the serial 41-1 was changed to 21-1, and then to Y-1-1. The second C.19 Mk IV, c/n 5158, completed on 4 October 1932, was bought by Andrés Lasso de la Vega, the Marqués de Torres de la Pressa, and left

Below: *the Caudron Aiglon 30-6, one of the very few French aircraft sold to the Nationalists. (Arráez)*

A Caudron 630 Simoun. (Liron)

Heston on 7 December 1932 bearing the ferry registration EC-W13. In Spain it was registered EC-ATT. Serving in the Republican zone from 1936-39, it survived the civil war and became 30-62 in the Ejercito del Aire. Upon return to the Marqués in the 1940s it was re-registered EC-CAB, and, in the 1950s, EC-AIM. It is now in the Museo del Aire at Cuatro Vientos, Madrid.

Two Cierva C.30As (the C.30 with a wide-track undercarriage) were acquired by the Aeronáutica Naval and flown from Hanworth to San Javier by Teniente de Navio Antonio Guitián and Ten de Nav José de la Guardia in September 1934: c/n 756, registered EA-SCA, and c/n 757, EA-SCB. Two weeks later, in October 1934, near-civil-war broke out in northern Spain when the Asturian miners rose in armed revolt, and EA-SCB was sent to join the Breguet 19s of Grupo 21 at León on the 8 October. During the next ten days EA-SCB, piloted by Guitián, spent more than fifty hours on reconnaissance and liaison missions, accompanying the army column advancing on Oviedo under the command of Gen Yagüe (who in the civil war was to be one of Franco's most successful generals), and thus became the first rotary-winged aircraft in the world to be employed on military operations.

Two C.30As, bought by the Aviación Militar, arrived in Spain in

The Cierva C.30A of the Aviación Militar, 41-2. (Instituto de Historia y Cultura Aeronautica)

December 1934: c/n 781, which became 41-2, then 21-2, and finally Y-1-2; and c/n 782, serialled 41-3, 21-3 and Y-1-3. The fifth C.30A, bought by the González Byass company to publicise its sherries, cannot

A Cierva C.19 Mk IV. (A J Jackson)

be identified with certainty, and seems to have had no Spanish registration. It might have been c/n 706, G-ACVC, sold abroad in August 1934, but more probably was c/n 744, G-ACXV, sold abroad in December 1935. All five C.30As were in the Republican zone throughout the civil war, but, since most of the qualified Spanish Autogiro pilots were in the Nationalist zone, it is unlikely that the machines took to the air. None survived the war.

C.19 MkIV

(105hp Armstrong Siddeley Genet Major I radial).

Rotor diameter 34ft; length 19ft 9¾in; height 10ft 3in.

Empty weight 975-1,050lb; loaded weight 1,550lb.

Maximum speed 102mph; cruising speed 90mph; climb 630ft/min; range 230 miles; rotor speed 180rpm.

C.30A

(140hp Armstrong Siddeley Genet Major IA radial).

Rotor diameter 37ft; length 19ft 8½in; height 11ft 1in.

Empty weight 1,220lb; loaded weight 1,800lb.

Maximum speed 110mph; cruising speed 95mph; climb 700ft/min; range 285 miles; rotor speed 180rpm.

Comper CLA.7 Swift

The Comper Swift, a diminutive single-seat high-wing monoplane, became almost synonymous with air racing all over the world in the decade before the Second World War, and achieved the most extraordinary feats of long-distance touring. It was constructed of wood and, except for the plywood rear decking, was covered with fabric. Power could be provided by a variety of engines in the 40-130hp range: the 40hp ABC Scorpion II, 50hp British Salmson AD 9, 75hp Pobjoy R, 120hp de Havilland Gipsy III or 130hp Gipsy Major.

In 1933 the Spanish flyer Fernando Rein Loring (see Airspeed Envoy) bought Swift c/n S.33/12 (Pobjoy R5), which was delivered to Barajas, Madrid, on 18 March 1933 with the ferry registration EC-W12. After it was registered EC-AAT, he flew it from Madrid to Manila and back later in the same year. It was still at Barajas on 18 July 1936, and was

The prototype Consolidated 20A Fleetster, one of the three Fleetsters of TWA that were sold to the Spanish Republicans in December 1936. (Larry Peterson, via Ed Peck and R S Allen)

Fernando Rein Loring and his Comper Swift, EC-AAT, after his flight from Madrid to Manila and back in 1933. (A J Jackson)

used for liaison. It does not seem to have survived the civil war, however, and was probably destroyed by bombing in October 1936.

Span 24ft; length 17ft 8½in; height 5ft 3½in; wing area 90sq ft.

Empty weight 540lb; loaded weight 985lb.

Maximum speed 140mph; cruising speed 120mph; ceiling 22,000ft; range 380 miles.

Consolidated 20A Fleetster

The original Consolidated Model 17 Fleetster was a near contemporary of the more famous Lockheed Vega, which, though slightly larger, it much resembled, and was intended to serve

on feeder lines supporting the main air routes of the New York, Rio and Buenos Aires Line (NYRBA). Ten Model 17s, one 17-2C, and three 17As, all named 'Fleetster' after Reuben Hollis Fleet, the founder and President of the Consolidated Aircraft Corporation, were built between 1929 and 1932. In 1930 the team under the company's chief designer, I M Laddon, produced the Model 20, a parasol monoplane variant similar to the Lockheed Air Express, to take better advantage of the space inside the fuselage. As in the French Blériot SPAD 'berline', the pilot's cockpit was placed behind the passenger cabin. Only four were built. This layout was retained in the Model 20A, although the cantilever wing was enlarged, the undercarriage made taller and the overall weight increased by 900lb. The airframe was metal throughout, the monocoque fuselage being covered with metal stressed skin, the tail assembly with corrugated metal skin, and the wing with fabric. The pilot was protected by a sliding canopy, and the undercarriage wheels had large spats, these being replaced in service by 'super-balloon' tyres. There was accommodation for seven passengers and 335lb of baggage. Power was provided by a 575hp Pratt & Whitney Hornet B1 radial in a long-chord cowling. Seven 20A Fleetsters were built, and all were sold to Trans-Continental and Western Air (TWA) in 1933. Of these, five were still on the inventory of TWA in 1936, though they were no longer in use owing to a ban on single-engined passenger aircraft in commercial air-

lines. In August 1936 a company named Condor Airlines was created on the promise of being able to buy all TWA's remaining single-engined aircraft (one Lockheed Orion and the five Fleetsters), which it would use for a freight and mail service along the Californian coast. Condor Airlines started in business with the first two Fleetsters, but in September 1936 aircraft dealer Charles Babb bought the remaining three Fleetsters and the Orion at prices Condor could not match. As related elsewhere (see Vultee V1-A, Lockheed Orion, and Appendix II), the Fleetsters sailed with the Wolf shipment in December 1936, and the Orion crashed en route to New York. Condor Airlines folded shortly afterwards for lack of suitable aircraft.

With the other Wolf shipment aircraft, the three 20A Fleetsters – c/n 1, NC13208 (the prototype); c/n 4, NC13211; and c/n 6, NC13213 – were assembled at Bléville Aerodrome, near Le Havre, France, and flown to Toussus-le-Noble, south of Paris. One Fleetster was tested at Villacoublay by CEMA while waiting to be re-exported, ostensibly to 'Bulgaria', by la Société Française des Transports Aériens (SFTA), the agency that took over the aircraft from Daniel Wolf and bought Toussus Aerodrome as well. It was found to be in such a deplorable condition that SFTA did not dare submit the other two. Two, or perhaps all three, of the Consolidated 20A Fleetsters flew to Spain in August and September 1937.

The last Fleetster to be built, c/n 7, NC13214, had been sold by TWA to Gordon Mounce, the Consolidated company agent, who in turn sold it on 17 December 1936 to D Morgan Hackman, an American dealer in Mexico. Hackman had previously been among the agents competing to buy the Vultees for the Spanish Republicans, and was now ostensibly acting for Coronel Alfredo Lezama of the Mexican army. The aircraft was re-registered XA-BER. Thus this last Fleetster joined the Spanish ambassador's collection of twenty-eight aircraft at Vera Cruz, was shipped to Bordeaux aboard the *Ibai* in December 1937, and crossed into Spain in the spring of 1938.

In Spain, at least one of the Fleetsters was taken on by LAPE, and another was used by the FARE as a troop transport. However deplorable their condition, the Fleetsters were very popular with the Spanish pilots, who found them stable, easy to handle, and excellent for use from primitive airfields, roads, and beaches. Two were recovered after the war from Oran, Algeria, by the Nationalists and, bearing the military serials 47-1 and 47-2, were employed by the Ejercito del Aire. In 1945 they were reclassified as L17-1 and L17-2, and were still flying in the early 1950s.

Span 50ft; length 33ft 9in; height 12ft; wing area 361.5sq ft.

Empty weight 3,850lb; loaded weight 6,800lb.

Maximum speed 175mph; cruising speed 160mph; cruising range 800 miles.

Couzinet 101

Of the various unusual, and occasionally bizarre, aeroplanes that found their way to Republican Spain as a result of the haphazard buying by agents who often knew little or nothing about aircraft, few were stranger than the little Couzinet 101 trimotor, F-AMIJ, that landed at Barajas, Madrid, on 22 August 1936. It was in essence a scaled-down version of the large Couzinet 70/71 *Arc en Ciel* trimotor in which Jean Mermoz had made a famous crossing of the South Atlantic in January 1933. The most striking feature of Réné Couzinet's trimotors, which some regarded as revolutionary pointers to the future, was the design of

Two Consolidated Fleetsters in Spanish Republican service. (Arráez)

the monocoque fuselage, in which the fin and rudder were blended with the structure as a progressively flattened extension of the fuselage shell, with the aim of minimising the drag of a conventional tail assembly. In the ultimate model, the Couzinet 10, the streamlining of the undercarriage trousers and engine nacelles, and of the enormously thick-section wing, was carried almost to the extent of imitating the flowing concrete forms becoming fashionable in the Art Deco style of architecture of the period.

The Couzinet 101, which retained the same general shape and elliptically tipped wings of its bigger relatives, was powered by three 75hp Pobjoy R radial engines in Townend-ring cowlings, driving four-bladed propellers, and the undercarriage wheels were protected, as in the Couzinet 71, by large spats. The cabin, which was provided with ample windowing, accommodated a pilot and two passengers, with a spacious luggage cupboard behind. It may have been the 'large sports tourist aircraft' advertised for sale for 260,000 French francs in August 1936, but what became of it after its arrival at Barajas is not recorded.

Span 13.5m; length 10.05m; wing area 20sq m.

Empty weight 900kg; loaded weight 1,420kg.

Maximum speed 250km/h; cruising speed 220km/h; ceiling 6,300m; range 885km.

De Havilland D.H.9

The de Havilland D.H.4, the D.H.9's predecessor, was the first British aeroplane designed specifi-

The Couzinet 101. (Laureau)

cally for high-speed day-bombing and, during its 18 months' active service over the Western Front from March 1917 to November 1918, proved to be one of the best combat aircraft, and certainly the best day-bomber, used by either side in the First World War. Its only serious defect was the excessive distance between the rear gunner and the pilot, whose cockpit was placed rather far forward under the upper wing centre-section to provide him with a good forwards and downwards field of view. This made communication between the two crew members almost impossible. In the D.H.9, intended as a long-range day-bomber capable of reaching targets inside Germany, this defect was remedied by placing the pilot's cockpit behind the trailing edge, but unfortunately this otherwise excellent aeroplane was spoilt by the low power and unreliability of its 230hp BHP water-cooled engine. Nevertheless, the D.H.9 was produced in large numbers, over 2,000 being built in 1918 alone. Some were fitted with 240hp Siddeley Pumas or the much better 450hp Napier Lions, and the type saw considerable service during the last months of the war. Contrary to general belief, the D.H.9A was not simply an improved D.H.9, but an entirely new design, employing different methods of construction and having wings of greater span and chord. Powered usually by the famous 400hp American Liberty engine, but otherwise by a 350hp

Rolls-Royce Eagle VIII or Napier Lion, the D.H.9A continued in RAF service until 1931, and was exported to several countries. Postwar civil variants included the D.H.9B, a three-cockpit version of the D.H.9, and the D.H.9C, a D.H.9A in which the rear cockpit was replaced by a cabin for two passengers or a compartment for mail.

Following the visit to Spain of Hereward de Havilland (the brother of Capt Geoffrey de Havilland) in 1919, a number of D.H.4s and sixteen surplus D.H.9s, fitted with 300hp Hispano-Suiza 8Fb engines, were acquired by the Aeronáutica Militar. A production series of some 130 D.H.9s was built under licence by La Hispano at Guadalajara, deliveries starting in 1922. They equipped six bomber squadrons on main-

A de Havilland D.H.9 of the Aviación Militar. (Azaola)

land Spain, and, when replaced by Breguet 19s, were relegated to the conversion training school at Cuatro Vientos (Madrid) and the Gunnery and Bombing School at Los Alcázares, Murcia. About 1926 their original M-MH- type code was changed to '15'. La Hispano also assembled eight D.H.9As with Napier Lion engines, and these saw service in the Moroccan war. Meanwhile, two D.H.9Cs, M-AAAG and 'AAGA, had been bought by La Compañía Española de Tráfico Aéreo (CETA), and were used as mail carriers between Seville and Larache (Spanish Morocco). In June 1923 a D.H.9B, ex-H9128 and G-EAUN, was bought by Joaquín Cayón of Seville and registered M-AGAG (later EC-FFF). Finally, an unspecified de Havilland aircraft was bought by José Escobar González, also of Seville, and registered EC-AQA in 1931. Since it does not appear to have been a Moth, it was

Two Spanish de Havilland Cirrus Moths of the Real Aero Club de España, M-CACC and M-CCAA, during a visit to Britain. (A J Jackson)

Gipsy Moth c/n 1098 was custom-built, with enclosed cockpits, for the Duque de Estremera in 1929. (A J Jackson)

possibly an ex-military D.H.9.

About forty D.H.9s of various types appear to have been flying in Spain in July 1936, as well as others in service but not airworthy. At least eighteen were taken over by the Nationalists at the beginning of the war and, with the type code 34, were used as trainers. The highest military serial of which there is a record is 34-19 (13 had presumably been omitted, as usual), but it is known that numbers 34-2, -4, -6, -7 and -9 were still in use by the Escuela de Vuelo (Flying School) at El Copero, south of Seville, in the summer of 1937, and that others were at the Escuela de Transformación at Jerez de la Frontera as late as March 1938. On the Republican side, at least twenty-one D.H.9s were at Los Alcázares in July 1936. On 1 August three were transferred to Guadix Aerodrome, east of Granada, where, in company with a flight of Vickers Vildebeests, they carried out reconnaissance and bombing missions until the 25 August, this presumably being the last occasion on which D.H.9s were employed on military operations in any theatre of war. At Los Alcázares the first groups of Republican pilots received their conversion training on D.H.9s during the early months of the war. Later, D.H.9s were used as gunnery trainers until all but one were phased out of service. This solitary survivor was recovered by the Nationalists after the civil war and continued flying, as 38-14, with the Gotha Go 145 training squadron until the 1940s. Nothing is recorded of the fate of the civil D.H.9B and D.H.9Cs.

La Hispano-built D.H.9

(300hp Hispano-Suiza 8Fb water-cooled engine)

Span 13.99m; length 8.89m; height 3.45m; wing area 45.21sq m.

Empty weight 1,355kg; loaded weight 2,183kg.

Maximum speed 197km/h; cruising speed 140km/h; ceiling 5,790m; endurance 4hr.

De Havilland D.H.60 Moth, Gipsy Moth, and Moth Major

When the de Havilland D.H.60 Moth prototype G-EBKT made its first flight, with Capt Geoffrey de Havilland at the controls, on 22 February 1925, it set a new style in the configuration of light aeroplanes which was to have a world-wide influence. Since so much has been published on the history and achievements of this estimable family of aeroplanes, this section concentrates only on those forty-five or so which were caught up in the turmoil of the Spanish Civil War.

The earliest Moth to arrive in Spain that can be traced is the D.H.60X (c/n 497, 90hp ADC Cirrus III engine) that was registered M-CACC (EC-ACC after 1931) and delivered to the Real Aero Club de España at Barajas, Madrid, in March 1928. The 'X' meant 'Experimental' and denoted some modifications to the design, but after 1928 it denoted the split-axle, or X-type, undercarriage fitted on all subsequent members of the Moth family. Another four or five were delivered to Spain during the next two years, the doubtful fifth one being c/n 558, G-ABWS, which was exhibited in Barcelona in June 1928 and reportedly sold there in January 1929, but for which no Spanish registration can be found. One (c/n 634, EC-DDA) was fitted with a Fiat A.12 engine. Seventeen D.H.60G Gipsy Moths (100hp D.H. Gipsy I or 120hp Gipsy II engines), of which at least one was an early D.H.60X with a cross-axle undercarriage but refitted with a Gipsy engine, arrived between February 1929 and December 1933, one of them (c/n 1224, EC-ALL) being used by the state airline LAPE. Another arrival was a single D.H.60M, or Metal Moth, with a steel-tube, instead of wooden, fuselage frame. This was c/n 1541, and carried the ferry registration MW-131. In addition, at the end of

1929 the Aviación Militar acquired two Metal Moths (c/ns 1427 and 1428, ferry registrations MW-124 and -125). These were given the military serials 32-1 and 32-2, and were employed by the Escuela Elemental de Pilotos (Pilots' Basic Training School) at Alcalá de Henares, which is now a north-eastern suburb of Madrid.

The D.H.60GIII Moth was powered by a D.H. Gipsy III engine – a 120hp Gipsy II inverted to allow the cowling to conform to the shape of the fuselage and to give the pilot a better forward view. An improved version of the Gipsy III, the Gipsy IIIA of 130hp, went into production as the Gipsy Major, and the D.H.60GIIIA, fitted with this engine, was accordingly called the de Havilland Moth Major.

Two D.H.60GIIIs (c/ns 1916 and 5180) and three D.H.60GIIIA Moth Majors (c/ns 5008, 5075, and 5076) arrived in Spain between July 1930 and October 1934. In addition, in December 1934 twelve Moth Majors (c/ns 5101 to 5112, ferry registrations EC-W28 to -W39) were acquired by the Aviación Militar and employed by the Escuela de Combate y Vuelo (Air Combat Training School) at Alcalá de Henares. These were given the military serials 34-1 to 34-12, but on 29 January 1935 34-11 (presumably c/n 5111) crashed at Alcalá, killing the pilot, Comandante Martínez de Aragón. Also in January 1935, a single Moth Major (c/n 5141) was acquired by the Aeronáutica Naval.

The 1936 Bureau Veritas register of Spanish civil aircraft lists only twenty-four Moths and Moth Majors in Spain, which leaves four or five unaccounted for. This register, which was compiled in France, was certainly imperfect however, for one Metal Moth (c/n 1541) and two Moth Majors (c/ns 5075 and 5139) known to have arrived in Spain are not on any of the registers of the 1930s. It may be assumed, therefore, that a minimum of forty-five Moths, Metal Moths, and Moth Majors were in Spain on 18 July 1936: thirty civil Moths and Moth Majors and one Metal Moth; eleven military Moth Majors and two Metal Moths; and one naval Moth Major. The details are given in the table on these pages.

c/n	Date of delivery	Ferry registration	registration	Owners and details
D.H.60 and D.H.60X Moth				
497	3.28		M-CACC EC-ACC	Real Aero Club de España (RACE)
498	3.28		M-CCAA EC-CAA	RACE. Crashed at Barajas 1.5.36; pilot, Enrique Vinet, pass. Sta Lucía Fernández, injured
499	3.28(?)		M-CCCA EC-CCA	i) Duque de Extremera ii) Juan de Bustos (1931-1934)
558	1.29(?)		G-EBWS	Exhib. Barcelona 6.28, sold 1.29
624 (Fiat A.12)	7.30		M-CDDA EC-DDA	i) Nelia SA ii) Air Taxis Barcelona
644	1.29		G-EBZF(?) M-CAAK EC-AAK	Antonio Habsburg Borbón
D.H.60G Gipsy Moth				
831	2.29		G-AACK EC-DAA	Enrique Ansaldo
919 (Single-seater)	31		EC-AQQ	i) Wilfredo Ricart Medina ii) Ramón Arqués Valverda (1934). Crashed 12.35
1013	11.29	MW-113	MC-CGAG EC-GAG	i) Compañía de Trabajos Fotogramétricos (CTF) ii) JA Ansaldo
1014	10.29	MW-114	M-CGGG EC-GGG	i) CTF ii) Aero Club de Málaga
1015	10.29	MW-115	M-CAAH EC-AAH	CTF (sold by 1936)
101-	10.29	MW-116	M-CAHA EC-AHA	i) CTF ii) Alfonso Casas Gutiérrez
1029	?	?	?	Imported by Carlos de Salamanca (an aircraft dealer), 1929
1075	1.31	MW-118	M-CAPA EC-CAPA	Alfonso Casas Gutiérrez
1076	4.30	MW-119(?) MW-120(?)	M-CHAA EC-HAA	i) RACE ii) Aero Club de Andalucía
1086	7.31	MW-121	EC-QAA	Jesús Martínez San Vicente
1098	7.29	MW-117	M-CGAA EC-GAA	i) Ivan Bustos, Duque de Estremera ii) Manuél Peña Martínez
1133	12.29	MW-122	M-CKAA EC-KAA	Francisco Habsburgo Borbón; *not in civil war*, reg. cancelled before July 1936
1218	3.30	MW-128	M-CLAL EC-LAL	i) A de la Čuesta ii) Jesús Martínez San Vicente
1223	7.30	MW-123	EC-LLA	Compañía Española de Aviación (CEA). Re-engined with Cirrus III

1224	7.30	MW-130	M-CALL EC-ALL	i) CEA ii) LAPE
1253	6.30	MW-133	G-AAZG EC-MMA	i) Antonio Rexach ii) Augusto Puaga iii) 30-94 (1939) iv) EC-AAE (c1940)
1293	1.31	MW-134	M-CNAN EC-NAN	i) Aero Club de Andalucía ii) 30-64 (1936) iii) EC-AAN (cancelled 1957) iv) Rebuilding 1986 (see below)
N/A	N/A	N/A	EC-NAA(?)	i) Aero Club de Andalucía ii) 30-52 (1936) iii) EC-BAU iv) EC-ABX (c1961)
1916	4.33		EC-TTA	i) Aero Club de Andalucía ii) 30.54 (1936) iii) EC-BAV (1940) iv) EC-ACN (1953)
1918	6.33		EC-UAU	i) Real Aero Club de España ii) Crashed in Madrid street 6.3.35. Rebuilt iii) 30-88 (1939) iv) EC-CAA (1942) v) EC-ACO (1951) Probably re-engined with Gipsy Major
	7.30		M-CANN(?)	Alfonso Alarcón, Barajas. Possible confusion with EC-ANN (Metal Moth) below.

D.H.60M Metal Moth

1427	12.29	MW-124		Aviación Militar (32-1)
1428	12.29	MW-125		Aviación Militar (32-2)
1541	7.30	MW-131	EC-ANN(?)	A. García, Valencia, or Alfonso Alarcón, Bilbao

D.H.60GIIIA Moth Major

5075	26.6.34	EC-W24	EC-XAA	Juan Pruneda, Madrid
5076	7.7.34	EC-W25	EC-AXX	i) J-M de la Cuesta, Madrid ii) 30-92 (?) (1939) iii) EC-BAL (1946) iv) EC-BAV(?) (1953)
5098	31.10.34		EC-YAY	i) Aero Club de Andalucía ii) 30-53 (1936) iii) EC-BAX (1943) iv) EC-ABY (1951)
5101- 5112	12.34	EC-W28- EC-W39		Aviación Militar (Nos 34-1 to 34-12)
5139	1.35	EC-W47	EC-BBD	Patronata de la Expedición Iglesias (an Amazonian expedition aborted because of the civil war).
5141	11.34		M-1	Aeronáutica Naval, delivered in crates without engine

At present there is no means of resolving the inconsistencies in this list. As the list of post-war Moths shows, one was registered for a time as 30-52 (supposedly ex-EC-NAA) and another as 30-64 (supposedly ex-EC-NAN). EC-NAA, however, is not in any Bureau Veritas register of 1931-36. Similar confusion exists over EC-ANN. If this was 1541, then it was the Metal Moth listed above, but in the Bureau Veritas it is listed as a Gipsy Moth with the construction number 5180 (which, in fact, was Queen Bee K8647 in the RAF). Aircraft c/n 5108 was one of the Moth Majors delivered to the Aviacíon Militar in 1934, which eliminates the possibility of a misprint.

The civil war years
Between thirty and thirty-six airworthy de Havilland Moths, Gipsy Moths, Metal Moths and Moth Majors were on the aerodromes that remained in Republican hands. During the first few weeks of fighting, some of those in Catalonia were used for liaison and reconnaissance, but by November all of them, except perhaps EC-ALL belonging to LAPE, were transferred to the flying schools in Murcia where, in the summer of 1937, they were given the type code EM and numbered accordingly. One or two Morane-Saulnier MS 60s (Morane-built D.H.60Xs) may have been imported into Republican Spain during the civil war, and a small series of Moth Majors was built at the SAF 22 factory in 1937 and 1938, perhaps utilising spare engines bought before the war.

The Nationalists appear to have come into possession of ten aircraft of the Moth family (EC-CCA, -HAA, -QAA, -LAL, -NAA, -NAN, -TTA, -YAY and two others, one of which later became 30-1 and the other 30-50), and during the first few weeks those in Andalusia were used for military missions such as reconnaissance and grenade-dropping, as was EC-CCA in Mallorca (see Avro Avian). On 28 July 1936 EC-HAA was shot down by groundfire over La Roda, near Córdoba, the two crew members, Recasens Serrano and Tomás Muruve, being taken prisoner and executed by Republican militia. On Mallorca, EC-CCA survived the Republican invasion of the island

A hybrid Moth in Republican service. This is a D.H.60X of the first type ('X' denoting 'experimental' and not a split-axle undercarriage) to which a Gipsy engine has been fitted. The undercarriage bungees have lost their springiness. (Emiliani)

Moth Majors and Tiger Moths at El Carmolí, Cartagena. (Arráez)

and, despite a crash at Palma on 16 August 1938, outlasted the civil war, finally being withdrawn from flying in 1976.

At the end of August 1936 the Nationalist Moths on the mainland were relegated to the Escuela Elemental de Vuelo (Elementary Flying Training School) at El Copero, south of Seville, and, later, to the Escuela de Transformación at Jerez de la Frontera. In 1937 one or two were flying at the 2ª Escuela Elemental at Las Badocas, Badajoz. They were given the type code 30 (single-engined light aircraft) and numbered 30-7, -8, -50, -51, -52, -53, -54 and -64. At the end of the civil war the Nationalists still possessed three Gipsy Moths, 30-52 (EC-NAA?), 30-64 (EC-NAN?) and 30-54 (EC-TTA), and a Moth Major (30-53, EC-YAY), as well as 30-50 (unknown). In addition, they recovered nineteen Moths of various types from the Republicans and incorporated them all into Grupo 30.

It should be noted that the first aircraft to receive a postwar military

Post-war survivors (in alphabetical order of their last registrations)

Military serial	First registration	Second registration	Withdrawn
30-94 (ex-'MMA)	?	EC-AAE	EC-1962
30-64 (ex-'NAN)	?	EC-AAN	1957
30-92 (ex-'AXX)	EC-BAL	EC-ABV	1951
30-52 (ex-'NAA?)	EC-BAU	EC-ABX	1962
30-53 (ex-'YAY)	EC-BAX	EC-ABY	1961
30-54 (ex-'TTA)	EC-BAV	EC-ACN	
30-88 (ex-'UAU)	EC-CAA	EC-ACO	1976
30-83	EC-BAZ	EC-ADE	1961
30-75 (ex-'CCA?)	EC-BAJ	EC-AEC (or EC-AEL)	1976
30-76	EE1-76	–	1949
30-91	–	EC-AEQ	
30-81	EE1-81	EC-AFK	1962
30-89	EE1-89	EC-AFQ	Ministerio del Aire, 1962
30-78		EC-AFS	1958
30-79	EE1-79	EC-AFT	1960
30-80		EC-AFU	1960
30-86		EC-AFV	1958
30-77	EE1-77	EC-AFX	1961
30-82		EC-AIT	1960
30-85	EE1-85	–	1949
30-90			1946
30-93			1946

serial in Grupo 30 is believed to have been the D.H.60X Moth EC-CCA, which had been at Son San Juan, Mallorca, throughout the war and in 1939 became 30-75, although some sources list 30-75 as a Gipsy Moth. During the 1940s, as the Spanish-built Bücker Jungmanns reached the flying schools of the Ejercito del Aire, all but four of the Moth-family aircraft (30-76, -85, -90 and -93) were handed over to civil aero clubs, from which some were later bought by private owners. Some received 1940-system civil registrations, and were re-registered in the late 1940s or early 1950s, and others received only the later registrations.

The EE1 type code was given to the few Moths that remained in military service between 1946 and 1950. In 1962 EC-AFQ (ex-30-89 and EE1-89) was acquired by the Ministerio el Aire, rebuilt, and presented to the Museo del Aire in 1975, where it is on permanent exhibition.

One Moth omitted from the lists is the machine now belonging to John Pothecary and kept at Shoreham Airport, Sussex, England. He found it in a shed in a village near Lérida, in a fairly parlous state. Its fuselage appeared to be that of a Moth Major, but it had a Gipsy I engine and EC-AAO painted on its fuselage and wings. Research has revealed that it was built at Seville in 1944 out of parts of various other Moths. Its registration had belonged to a pre-war Klemm L.25 before being transferred to a González Gil-Pazó GP-1 (ex-30-98?). When the GP-1 was destroyed in an accident in 1947, the registration was transferred to this hybrid Moth. It is now registered G-AAOR and is, at the time of writing (October 1989), in flying condition.

D.H.60X

Span 30ft; length 23ft 8½in; height 8ft 9½in; wing area 243sq ft.

Empty weight 955lb; loaded weight 1,750lb.

Maximum speed 98.5mph; cruising speed 85mph; ceiling 14,000ft; range 290 miles.

D.H.60G

Span 30ft; length 23ft 11in; height 8ft 9½in; wing area 243sq ft.

Empty weight 962lb; loaded weight 1,650lb.

Maximum speed 98mph; cruising speed 83mph; ceiling 18,000ft; range 290 miles.

D.H.60GIIIA

Dimensions as for D.H.60G.

Empty weight 1,040lb; loaded weight 1,750lb.

Maximum speed 112mph; cruising speed 96mph; ceiling 20,000ft; range 300 miles.

De Havilland D.H.80A Puss Moth

By the end of the 1920s sport flying had reached the stage at which prospective buyers of light touring aeroplanes were demanding cabin aircraft which would do away with the need for themselves and their passengers to wear uncomfortable flying suits, helmets and goggles. De Havilland offered the D.H.80, a high-wing cabin monoplane powered by a Gipsy II inverted in-line engine, seating a pilot and a passenger in tandem. The wooden-framed slab-sided fuselage was plywood covered, and the wings and tail-assembly had fabric covering. The prototype, G-AAHZ, first flew in September 1929. The D.H.80A Puss Moth, the production model, had a fuselage of more pleas-

A de Havilland Moth Major captured by the Nationalists at the end of the civil war and re-serialled 30-78. (A J Jackson)

ing shape, built of welded steel tube with fabric covering. Seating was staggered to allow its use as an occasional, though rather cramped, three-seater, and the engine was the familiar 120hp Gipsy III or 130hp Gipsy IIIA (Gipsy Major). When the aircraft was landing, the streamlined fairings over the two undercarriage shock-absorber struts could be turned 90° to serve as rudimentary airbrakes. Between 1930 and 1933 a total of 259 Puss Moths was built, several of them achieving fame as record breakers. The best known was G-ABXY, *The Heart's Content*, in which James Mollison made the first flight from England to South America and the first solo crossing of the South Atlantic in February 1933.

Three Puss Moths were imported into Spain during the 1930s. The first, c/n 2064, was bought by the trophy-winning Spanish pilot Gómez del Barco in 1931. It wore the ferry registration MW-135 and was then registered as EC-NNA. In 1934 it was sold to the Basque pilot José Yanguas Yañez.

The second, c/n 2223, EC-AAV, was bought through José Canudas in 1933 by the Servicios de Aeronáutica de la Generalitat de Cataluña (the air service of the Catalonian regional government).

The third Spanish Puss Moth was c/n 2246, EC-VAA, bought by Teódoro Martel of Madrid in 1934 and sold to Francisco Moreno in 1936.

On 20 July 1936, two days after the beginning of the Nationalist uprising, Major Juán-Antonio Ansal-

do, a military pilot and ardent monarchist, flew in EC-VAA from Biarritz to a Portuguese military aerodrome near Lisbon. His orders were to convey the exiled monarchist leader, Gen Sanjurjo, whom the conspirators had nominated as the future Head of State, to Pamplona, where Gen Mola had taken control. On learning of Ansaldo's arrival at Lisbon, the embattled Spanish government in Madrid made a formal complaint to the Portuguese government, which, though sympathetic to the uprising, thereupon insisted that Sanjurjo depart from a private flying field. The chosen field, at Marinla, was small and surrounded by pine trees. To Ansaldo's alarm, Gen Sanjurjo insisted on taking aboard a heavy suitcase containing his full ceremonial dress as Head of State. The Puss Moth had some difficulty in getting into the air, its undercarriage struck a tree-top, and the machine crashed into a stone wall and burst into flames. Ansaldo was thrown out and badly burned, though he recovered to take command of the Fokker-Dragon group at the end of August. Sanjurjo was killed, opening the way for Gen Franco to become both Commander-in-Chief and Head of State, and thus the dictator of Spain until his death in 1975. Franco's propaganda chief, Luis Bolín, attributed the crash to engine

failure, which seems unlikely in view of the lengendary reliability of the Gipsy Major. There were also rumours of sabotage. The plain truth seems to be that the Puss Moth was overloaded with the suitcase.

Sanjurjo had been offered the use of a 'splendid bimotor' aircraft by another monarchist conspirator, Fal Conde, but had rejected it as too showy. This was probably the D.H.84 Dragon G-ACZZ belonging to Crilly Airways, and no doubt Sanjurjo was anxious about the effect of landing on Spanish soil, on so nationally important an occasion, in a British registered, owned and piloted aeroplane.

Puss Moth EC-NNA was used by José Yanguas, who was then flying with the tiny Basque air arm, for reconnaissance missions and attacks on Nationalist troops which were more comic than militarily effective. On one occasion in the autumn of 1936 he emptied a bag of stones on to the heads of some Requetes (Monarchist militia, distinguished by their red berets) who were parading in the town square of Villareal. He did this in revenge for an incident in which an aircraft bearing Republican roundels had dropped six light bombs on Republican militia in Ochandiano.

Puss Moth EC-AAV, used by Republican officers in Catalonia, did not survive the war.

Two British-owned Puss Moths were also involved in the Spanish Civil War. The first was G-ABYW, in which Tom Campbell-Black (the co-winner, with C W A Scott, of the speed prize in the great Mac-Robertson England–Australia air race of 1934) made an adventurous flight from Heston to Paris and thence, via Biarritz and Burgos, to Lisbon on 28-30 July 1936. He and

his Puss Moth had been chartered by the Spanish Nationalists to fly the Marqués de Rivas de Linares and other conspirators, who were acting as liaison between various Nationalist groups and carrying funds to pay for aircraft bought in Britain (including four Fokker F.XIIs belonging to British Airways).

The second was G-ABWA, used by Charles Kenneth Apjohn-Carter (alias Charles Kennett) and Robert Bannister-Pickett, both of whom had briefly flown for the Republicans in September and November 1936. In December they found further employment in smuggling out of Republican Spain jewellery confiscated from aristocrats and other wealthy people who had been executed or had fled abroad. It was a hazardous trade, on the one hand organised by the Soviet NKVD (forerunner of the KGB) and on the other employing wealthy playboys such as the (then) young Porfirio Rubirosa. On 30 December 1936, however, while returning from Spain to Abridge, Essex, the Puss Moth crashed in the water just off the beach on the French Channel coast. Kennett and Bannister-Pickett swam ashore easily, but Kennett claimed that the jewellery, which was supposed to be handed over to the Spanish Embassy in London to pay for the purchase of aircraft, had been lost. Since he emigrated to Canada shortly afterwards, allegedly an inexplicably wealthy man, there were those who doubted his story.

The D.H.80A Puss Moth G-ABWA in which Charles Kennett and others flew jewellery confiscated by the Spanish Republicans to France and Britain to pay for arms purchases. On 30 December 1936, during a flight from Albacete to West Malling, the Puss Moth came down in the sea off Le Havre, and, although Kennett and his passenger were saved, the machine and, allegedly, its cargo, were lost. (A J Jackson)

Span 36ft 9in; length 25ft; height 7ft; wing area 222sq ft.

Empty weight 1,265lb; loaded weight 2,050lb.

Maximum speed 128mph; cruising speed 108mph; ceiling 17,500ft; range 300 miles.

De Havilland D.H.82A Tiger Moth

In 1931 de Havilland produced the final variant of the 60G Gipsy Moth, the D.H.60T Moth Trainer. This was re-engined with a 120hp Gipsy III engine, and the centre-section cabane struts were moved forward to improve the instructor's escape in the event of an emergency. After tests, the wings were swept back to re-establish the CG position and the new design was named the D.H.60T Tiger Moth, a designation changed in September 1931, after the first eight had been built, to D.H.82 Tiger Moth. Finally, the production version was fitted with a 130hp Gipsy IIIA Major engine and designated D.H.82A. Production began in 1932 and continued until 1945. The Tiger Moth was undoubtedly one of the greatest trainers of all time, and numerous examples are still flying sixty years after the maiden flight of the prototype.

In December 1933 D.H.82A G-ACBN (c/n 3148) was sold to the Spanish Government, and was followed by four more at the end of the month, c/ns 3192 to 3195. These were intended for the Escuela Elemental de Vuelo (Elementary Flying Training School) at Alcalá de Henares, and left Hatfield bearing the Aviación Militar serials 33-2, -3, -4, and -5. It is reasonable to suppose, therefore, that when G-ACBN had previously arrived at Alcalá it had become 33-1. During the revolt in the Asturias in October 1934, an armed rebellion in which 4,000 people died, the Tiger Moths, under the command of Capitán Ibarra, were employed on liaison duties. In 1935 33-5 was stationed at Cabo Juby in Spanish West Africa. In July 1936 it was flown to Republican-held Ifni by a defector, and after the civil war became 30-104.

During the first weeks of the civil war the Tiger Moths, which were all in Republican hands, were flown on reconnaissance and liaison missions. In September 1936 they were transferred to the flying schools at Los Alcázares and San Javier, near Cartagena in Murcia, and the following spring received the type code EP. Between March and July 1938 seventeen new Tiger Moths were,

A de Havilland D.H.82A Tiger Moth. (A J Jackson)

however, sold individually to various Frenchmen, some of them dealers or agents and some members of le Cercle Aéronautique de Coulommiers et de la Brie, a flying club near Paris which trained Spanish Republican pilots and procured aircraft for the Republican government. These are listed in Table A.

In 1938 all except F-AQOS were sold to SFTA (see Appendix II), and twelve of them (including F-ARAR) exported to Republican Spain. F-AQOV was eventually sold back to an English buyer and became G-AGAP.

After the civil war the Nationalists recovered twelve Tiger Moths and incorporated them into Grupo 30 (single-engined light aircraft) as trainers. In 1942-46 eleven were handed over to flying clubs and, of these, seven continued flying long enough to receive civil registrations. They are listed in Table B on page 100.

Span 29ft 4in; length 23ft 11in; height 8ft 9½in; wing area 239sq ft.

Empty weight 1,115lb; loaded weight 1,825lb.

Maximum speed 109mph; cruising speed 90mph; ceiling 18,000ft; range 300 miles.

De Havilland D.H.83 Fox Moth

The de Havilland Fox Moth, which appeared in March 1932, was a successful attempt to convert the Tiger Moth into a light transport aircraft that combined economic

Table A

c/n		
3655	F-AQJU	Dr Réné Arbeltier, CA de Coulommiers
3656	F-AQJV	Dr Pierre Berson, CA de Coulommiers
3657	F-AQJX	Alfred Rodier, CA de Coulommiers
3658	F-AQJY	Paul Legastelois (dealer)
3659	F-AQJZ	Rémy Clément (agent for Republicans)
3665	F-AQNF	Henry Compare, CA de Coulommiers
3666	F-AQNG	Robert Peitz
3667	F-AQNH	Marc Cayre (agent for Republicans)
3668	F-AQNI	Paul Legastelois
3669	F-AQNJ	Lucien Augier, CA de Coulommiers
3686	F-AQOQ	Paul Legastelois
?	F-AQOS	Roger Levy
3687	F-AQOV	Paul Legastelois
3685	F-AQOZ	Paul Legastelois
3688	F-AQOX	Paul Legastelois
3691	F-AQOY	Paul Legastelois
3692	F-ARAR	Dr Réné Arbeltier, CA de Coulommiers

Table B

30-100	EE1-100	Aero Club de los Baleares. Withdrawn 1948
30-101		AC de Valencia. Withdrawn ?
30-102	EC-AFL	i) AC de Valencia
		ii) AC de Madrid
		iii) AC de los Baleares
		iv) AC de Zaragoza
		v) Real Aero Club de España (1953)
		Withdrawn 1965
30-103		i) AC de Madrid
		ii) AC de Valencia
		Withdrawn 1946
30-104	EC-AGB	i) AC de Madrid (c/n 3195, ex-33-5)
		ii) AC de Barcelona
		iii) Ministerio del Aire to USA, reg. N182DH (1969)
		iv) To UK, Ian Grace, 1986, G-ACMD
30-107		
30-116	EC-AIU	i) AC de Madrid
		ii) AC de Valencia
		iii) AC de Vigo (1955)
		Withdrawn 1965
30-154	EC-AFN	i) AC de los Baleares
		ii) RAC de España (1953)
30-162	EC-AFM	i) AC de Valencia
		ii) AC de Madrid
30-169		AC de Valencia
30-170	EC-AHY	AC de Madrid
30-188	EC-AEV	i) AC de los Baleares
		ii) RAC de España. This was the last aeroplane to be incorporated into Grupo 30. Withdrawn 1963

One of the above was, at some time, registered EC-EAA.

running with the highest performance possible within the basic formula. Retaining the mainplanes, tail assembly, engine mounting and undercarriage of the Tiger Moth, designer A E Hagg placed the passenger cabin within the fuselage and in front of the pilot's cockpit. Powered by a 120hp Gipsy III engine, the D.H.83 could carry a pilot and four passengers on short trips, and a pilot and three passengers on longer journeys up to its maximum range of 360 miles. In July 1932, four months after the first flight of the prototype, a Fox Moth won the King's Cup Air Race, and the type was largely responsible for the initial success of such small airlines as Hillman's Airways and Portsmouth, Southsea and Isle of Wight Aviation. Ninety-eight Fox Moths were built altogether, of which forty-eight went to British owners, some examples being powered by the 130hp Gipsy Major, and others by the 140hp Gipsy Major IC.

Six Fox Moths were exported to Spain, five of them for photographic survey work. The first of these, c/n 4066, EC-AVA, ferry registration EC-W15, was bought in 1933 by the Compañía española de Trabajos fotogramétricos (CETF), and in 1935 was sold to Arturo Zúniga of the Aero Club de Cataluña.

The next four were purchased in 1934 by Avance Cadastral, a company established under the aegis of the Dirección General de Aeronáutica to produce a photographic map of the whole of Spain. As government-owned aircraft, they were registered as follows:

c/n	Ferry registration	Registration
4073	EC-W19	EC-1-E
4074	EC-W20	EC-2-E
4075	EC-W21	EC-3-E
4076	EC-W22	EC-4-E

The last Fox Moth to be imported was c/n 4087, ferry registration EC-W23, EC-VVA, fitted as a seaplane and bought by the Patronato Expedición Iglesias for an intended survey of the Amazon basin (see D.H.60 Moth).

During the civil war the six Fox Moths were used by the Republicans as light transports. One aircraft, EC-VVA, which had been converted into a landplane, survived the war. After recovery by the Nationalists it became 30-147 and, finally, EC-AEI, and was the property of the Aéro Club de Sadadell and a succession of private owners. It continued flying until the mid-1960s.

At the start of the civil war, British and US diplomatic correspondence makes several references to a British aeroplane, G-AECX, which was at Granada for unclear reasons and was described as a 'de Havilland Fox Moth'. In fact, it was a D.H.90 Dragonfly.

Span 30ft 10½in; length 25ft 9in; height 8ft 9½in; wing area 261 sq ft.

Empty weight 1,100lb; loaded weight 2,070lb.

Maximum speed 113mph; cruising speed 96mph; ceiling 12,700ft; range 360 miles.

The four de Havilland D.H.83 Fox Moths purchased by Avance Cadastral for aerial mapping, before leaving for Spain in 1934. (A J Jackson)

The Fox Moth seaplane EC-VVA, bought for a survey of the Amazon basin in April 1934. During the civil war EC-VVA was converted into a land-plane. (A J Jackson)

De Havilland D.H.84 Dragon 1 and Dragon 2

In the summer of 1932 Edward Hillman, pleased that the Fox Moths were making a success of his cut-price internal air services, asked de Havilland for a twin-engined equivalent with which to open a service to Paris. At about the same time the Iraqi government asked de Havilland for a twin-engined general-purpose military aircraft armed with three machine guns and sixteen 20lb bombs. The result was the D.H.84 Dragon biplane, powered by two 130hp Gipsy Major engines. It had a wooden airframe, the fuselage being covered with plywood and the tail unit and wide-span, narrow-chord wings with fabric. The prototype made its maiden flight under 'B' conditions as E-9 on 12 November 1932 and, registered G-ACAN, was delivered to Hillman in December. The Dragon's ability to carry six passengers, each with 45lb of luggage, at 109mph for an hourly petrol consumption of only 13 gallons guaranteed its immediate popularity with small airlines, and the type quickly went into quantity production. The sixty-seventh Dragon, G-ACKU, was the first of an improved version, the Dragon 2, with individually framed passenger windows replacing the single window-strip in each fuselage side, larger wheel spats and fully faired undercarriage struts. Altogether, 206 Dragons were built; sixty-six Dragon 1s, fifty-three Dragon 2s, and eighty-seven built under licence in Australia. The Dragon 1s included eight military aircraft for Iraq with elongated dorsal fins to counter the aerodynamic effect of the dorsal gun position, a modification later applied to the military and seaplane versions of the D.H.89 Dragon Rapide.

The first D.H.84 to arrive in Spain was the Dragon 1 c/n 6020 (ferry registration EC-W14), registered EC-TAT and bought in 1933 by Automobiles Fernández of Barce-

De Havilland D.H.84 Dragon G-ACNA joined the Alas Rojas ('Red Wings') group at Sariñena, Aragón, in August 1936 and served as a bomber. (A J Jackson)

lona for use on their newly created Aerotaxi service. Some Spanish sources state that one, or even two, Dragons were acquired by LAPE in 1933-34, but there is no trace of them in any surviving British or Spanish records.

At the start of the civil war EC-TAT was immediately requisitioned by Comandante Díaz Sandino, who was scraping together an air force at Prat de Llobregat Airport, Barcelona, and used for every kind of duty to which it could be adapted. According to the memoirs of the Spanish pilot Francisco Pérez Mur, a de Havilland Dragon was flown from England to Prat de Llobregat on 20 July 1936, two days after the outbreak of the war, by Jaime Camarasa, an instructor at the Escuela de Aviación de Barcelona. Again there is no evidence of this, and it is hard to see which Dragon it

could have been. The only remotely possible candidate would seem to be G-ACMC, which had belonged to Jersey Airways. It had been bought by Airwork on 23 July 1936, and the only subsequent record is a question mark at '8.36'. A number of machines bought by Airwork in August 1936 did later pass to one side or the other in Spain, and dates of sale recorded at this period were often after the machines had actually flown to Spain. Nevertheless, the date of arrival seems too early.

During August and September 1936 the Spanish air force officer Comandante Carlos Pastor Krauel, acting through Union Founders Trust Ltd (see Appendix II), bought about thirty aircraft in Britain, including twelve Dragon 1s and 2s. Two of them, piloted by two airmen hired at £120 a flight, G W Haigh and P de W Avery, flew to Paris on 13 August but were obliged by the authorities at Le Bourget to return next day. By then Pastor had collected three more Dragons at Croydon and, to avoid a repetition of the episode at Le Bourget, all five were fitted with enough five-gallon petrol tanks – strapped into the passenger seats and stacked on the floor, and connected to the main tanks by rubber hoses and a hand-pump – to enable them to reach Barcelona in a single hop. The five Dragons were:

c/n 6106 G-ACDL, bought from Luxury Air Tours, Worthing
c/n 6023 G-ACEV, bought from Airwork, Heston
c/n 6056 G-ACKC, bought from Commercial Air Hire, Croydon
c/n 6066 G-ACKU, bought from Wrightways, Croydon
c/n 6067 G-ACNA, bought from Olley Air Service, Croydon

The quintet (flown by Haigh, Lloyd, Alfred Jaffe, and seven others whose names are not recorded) took off together before daybreak on Saturday 15 August 1936. Two, 'KC (a Dragon 1) and 'NA (a Dragon 2), reached Barcelona at 7.30am and were spotted by a British destroyer as they came down to land on Prat de Llobregat. Dragon G-ACDL landed undetected. The other two, 'EV and 'KU (the first Dragon 2), staged at Paris, and on 17 August 'EV flew down to Barcelona accompanied by a General Aircraft Monospar ST-25 and two Airspeed Envoys. On 19 August G-ACKU flew back to Croydon because its engines were giving trouble. (An engineer who was involved in this business says that some Dragons and Dragon Rapides were given a quick going-over before departure by the repair company for which he worked, and that if their engines were new and in good condition they were removed and, unknown to Comandante Pastor, replaced by old or worn-out units). At Croydon the authorities immediately grounded G-ACKU, claiming that the petrol tanks that were strapped in the seats, and were leaking, made it completely unsafe.

On 19 August the British government, alarmed by the sudden exodus of aeroplanes, brought in a regulation prohibiting the export of civil aircraft to Spain, and the remaining eight Dragons (including 'KU) never left the country. De Havilland, which had sold three Dragon 1s (G-AEMI, 'J and 'K) to UFT, cancelled the sale before the aircraft had left Hatfield. The remaining four were G-ACBW *Neptune*, 'CEK *Leicestershire Vixen*, 'HV and 'KB. Of the four Dragons that reached Spain and the five held at Croydon, 'DL, 'KC, 'BW and 'KB had been owned by the Air Dispatch group of companies, the managing director of which was the Hon Mrs Victor Bruce (see Airspeed Envoy), who had also allegedly acted as an intermediary between UFT and Wrightways in the sale of G-ACKU. Dragons 'NA and 'EK had belonged to Olley Air Service, and 'EV to Airwork. Despite the most complicated manoeuvres on the part of the vendors to get them out of the country, all eight Dragons were held under an export ban by having their General Licences revoked, which in practice grounded them for months at a time, until the end of the Spanish Civil War.

On 18 August 1936 the four Dragons at Barcelona (G-ACDL, 'EV, 'KC and 'NA) were transferred to the newly-prepared and primitive flying ground at Sariñena, near Zaragoza in Aragon. Fitted with rudimentary armament, they were incorporated into the Alas Rojas (Red Wings) squadron of assorted aircraft, which included a Fokker F.VIIb3m, a Latécoère 28, nine Breguet 19s, a D.H.89M, a Beechcraft 17, a D.H. Fox Moth, two Nieuport 52s, a Potez 36, a Caudron Luciole, some Moth Majors and an old Farman F.194, EC-AAR. As a regular component of the mixed formation known jocularly as *La Balumba* (The Midden Heap), the Dragons were used continuously on military operations, albeit of a somewhat amateurish kind, until the squadron was disbanded at the end of October. The Hon Mrs Bruce is mistaken in her assertion, in her autobiography, that her Dragons were used only as ambulances, although it may well be true that some of the D.H.84s later served in that rôle.

In 1937 the surviving Dragons, bearing the type code LD, were relegated to the Escuela de Polimótores (Multi-engine Flying Training School) at Totana, Murcia. If the Nationalists recovered any D.H.84s after the war, they would have incorporated them into Grupo 40 or 42. Owing to their habit of referring both to D.H.84s and D.H.89s as 'Dragon', Spanish records are of no help here. Thus the several D.H.84s referred to in the Civil Aviation Authority *Gazeteer* for Spain during 1939-51 were probably, and in some cases certainly, D.H.89 Dragon Rapides.

Span 47ft 4in; length 34ft 6in; height 10ft 1in; wing area 376sq ft.

Dragon 1

Empty weight 2,300lb; loaded weight 4,200lb.

Maximum speed 128mph; cruising speed 109mph; ceiling 12,500ft; range 460 miles.

De Havilland D.H.85 Leopard Moth G-ACLN was used by Rupert Bellville to fly journalists about Nationalist Spain until he inadvertently landed on a Republican aerodrome. The aeroplane was taken over by the Republican air force. (A J Jackson)

Dragon 2

Empty weight 2,336lb; loaded weight 4,500lb.

Maximum speed 134mph; cruising speed 114mph; ceiling 14,500ft; range 545 miles.

De Havilland D.H.85 Leopard Moth

The de Havilland Leopard Moth, which first flew on 27 May 1933, was designed as a successor to the Puss Moth. The most notable differences to its predecessor were its tapered wings; the undercarriage shock-absorber legs, which were carried to a bolt below the front of the windscreen instead of to the upper longerons; and the wooden (instead of metal) fuselage frame. It seated a pilot and two passengers, was powered by a 130hp Gipsy Major engine, and was of pleasing appearance. During the next three years 131 were built, many for export, and two of these were sold to Spanish buyers. The first was c/n 7047, which left Heston on 19 April 1934, piloted by Alejandro Arias Salgada y de Cubas, chief of the Sección del Dirección General de Aeronáutica (DGdeA). As a government aeroplane it was registered EC-5-E and was used by the Junta Central del Aéropuertos for photographic surveying to find suitable sites for new aerodromes, and as a runabout by officials of the DGdeA. The second was c/n 7108, which left Britain on 8 August 1935, bearing the ferry registration EC-W49, and was used by the Director General de Seguridad.

On 18 July 1936 EC-5-E passed into Nationalist possession when Capitán Antonio Rexach, a military pilot and (at that time) left-wing activist, flew it from Barajas to Tablada, Seville, to ensure that this important base remained in government hands. Finding the aerodrome in turmoil, he dismissed the commanding officer, Cdte Estévez, and replaced him, without any authority to do so, by another officer who had been a long-time friend. Then, in-

stead of staying to ensure that Tablada remained under Republican control, he boarded a Douglas DC-2 that was about to take off to bomb Tetuán. Without Rexach's knowledge, the officer who replaced Estévez had recently joined the Falange (Fascist movement), and some hours later the aerodrome and all the aircraft on it, including the Leopard Moth, were taken over by the Nationalists. Being at Seville, the D.H.85 received the military serial 30-56 and was used as an officers' transport for two weeks, until it crashed on the aerodrome at Cáceres, killing the pilot, Manuel Camino Parludé. Of EC-W49, which flew on the Republican side, nothing is known except that it did not survive the civil war.

A second Leopard Moth came into Republican possession during the civil war, however. This was G-ACLN, belonging to Mrs Edwin Montagu, for whom Rupert Bellville had been pilot during her tour of Russia in 1931. In July 1936 Bellville flew the Marquis of Donegal, who was then working as a journalist, to Burgos in this aeroplane to interview Gen Mola, and later visited the Republican side at Barcelona. In August 1937, having returned to the Nationalist side, Bellville and Ricardo González Gordón, a member of the sherry family, landed at Albericia Aerodrome, Santandar, believing that it had been captured by the Nationalists. It had not, and the two were taken prisoner. Released by the Nationalists after the capture of Gijón in October, Bellville said he had seen his Leopard Moth flying southwards a few days previously, from his prison-cell

window, and had later heard that the Governor of Gijón had used it to escape to the main Republican zone. This Leopard Moth likewise did not survive the civil war.

Span 37ft 6in; length 24ft 6in; height 8ft 9in; wing area 206sq ft.

Empty weight 1,405lb; loaded weight 2,225lb.

Maximum speed 137mph; cruising speed 119mph; ceiling 21,500ft; range 715 miles.

De Havilland D.H.87A and D.H.87B Hornet Moth

The de Havilland D.H.87 Hornet Moth originated in 1934 as an experimental design for research into a biplane replacement of the Gipsy Moth, combining a cabin arrangement resembling those of the Puss Moth and Leopard Moth with a wing planform similar to that of the D.H.86 four-engined airliner. It was powered by a 130hp Gipsy Major engine. After a year of teething troubles the wing was redesigned with an even more pronounced, almost elliptical, taper, and the resulting model, the D.H.87A, went into quantity production. Early in 1936 a modified version with square-cut wings, designated D.H.87B, replaced the D.H.87A as the standard production model.

Three D.H.87As and three D.H.87Bs were bought in Spain before the civil war, and some uncertainty still exists concerning the histories of several of them. (See table below.)

The last three arrived too late to receive registrations. Indeed, it is not clear that c/n 8050 EC-W54 arrived

A de Havilland D.H.87A Hornet Moth recovered by the Nationalists at the end of the civil war. (Arráez)

at all, for it is believed to have gone to Switzerland, where it became HB-OMI.

A second puzzle concerns EC-BBF, owned by Cornago Pruneda. In July 1936, shortly before the civil war, Joaquín García Morato (the future leading Nationalist air ace) and Pruneda visited England in a square-tipped Hornet, EC-BBF, for a weekend rally organised by the Royal Aero Club. Possibly the *Flight* correspondent reporting the occasion confused this aircraft with the Austrian Hornet brought by Stephen Kaspeler-Schenke (OE-DAK), or c/n 8043 was in fact a D.H.87B. A third puzzle is posed by a photograph taken at the Republican aerodrome at Sariñena, in Aragon, the base of the Alas Rojas group, in September or October 1936 after the start of the civil war. It shows a D.H.87B, which suggests that it was one of the two bought by the Workers' Co-operative (Co-operación del Traball) in May 1936, but also shows on the fuselage the registration EC-E or F, followed by what may be a B (EC-FB-?). The LAPE pilot J-M Carreras has told the author, however, that neither of the Co-operative Hornet Moths were registered, and that the Hornet Moths used in Barcelona and Madrid had tapered wings. Possibly, as happened with Airspeed Envoys G-ACMT and 'EBV, the fuselage of D.H.87A EC-FBB was married to the wings of a D.H.87B, perhaps after an accident.

On 18 July 1936 the second of the Co-operative-owned Hornet Moths happened to be at La Guardia, near Pontevedra, Galicia, on the Atlantic coast, where it was destroyed before it could be taken to the Republican zone. The other Hornet Moths were used throughout the civil war, bearing the type code TH, for liaison and transport duties, and the first Co-operative-owned D.H.87B survived the war and was captured by the Nationalists at Vich aerodrome in February 1939, during their conquest of Catalonia. Hornet Moth c/n 8039 was also recovered after the war. It became EC-CAI, being bought by J Balcells (see Farman F.194), and was re-registered EC-AKA after 1946 and, in 1950, was sold to the Aero Club de Vizcaya.

D.H.87A

Span 32ft 7in; length 24ft 11½in; height 6ft 7in; wing area 220.5sq ft.

Empty weight 1,240lb; loaded weight 1,950lb.

Maximum speed 131mph; cruising speed 111mph; ceiling 17,800ft; range 640 miles.

D.H.87B

Span 31ft 11in; length 24ft 11½in; height 6ft 7in; wing area 244sq ft.

Empty weight 1,304lb; loaded weight 2,000lb.

Maximum speed 124mph; cruising speed 105mph; ceiling 14,800ft; range 620 miles.

De Havilland D.H.89, D.H.89A and D.H.89M Dragon Rapide

The de Havilland Dragon Rapide is one of the most famous and longest-enduring piston-engined airliners ever built. The design, carried out under the supervision of A E Hagg, was originally intended as an improved Dragon powered by the new 200hp Gipsy Six engines, but as work progressed it acquired more and more of the features of its larger contemporary, the four-engined D.H.86, including tapered wings, the construction and shape of the fuselage, and a pair of trousered undercarriage legs integrated with the two engine nacelles. The cabin accommodated a pilot and six or eight passengers, according to the fuel load. The prototype, E.4, which was initially named Dragon Six to denote the engines, made its maiden flight in April 1934 and was still being used for joy rides in Zurich in 1958. As with the Dragon, the first order for the Dragon Six came from Hillman's Airways, which bought seven, but within five years more than twelve British and thirteen foreign airlines and charter companies were operating the type. The name was changed to Dragon Rapide (commonly abbreviated to Rapide) in 1935. In the summer of 1936 c/n 6309 G-ADWZ, belonging to Personal Airways of Croydon, was fitted with a nose landing light, thickened wing-tips and small trailing-edge split flaps on the lower mainplanes, and thus became the first D.H.89A. This became the standard production version thereafter, and most earlier Rapides were converted to this form.

In the autumn of 1934 the Spanish state airline LAPE acquired c/n 6262, which flew to Spain with the ferry registration EC-W27 and received the registration EC-AZZ. Its LAPE fleet number is not known for certain, but was probably 20. In 1935 the Aviación Militar, seeking a replacement of the four obsolescent Fokker F.VIIb3m/Ms serving with the Fuerzas Aéreas de Africa, tested an Airspeed Envoy and a D.H.89M.

The D.H.89M was chosen, partly on price and partly because the Rapide, with Gipsy Six engines and fixed undercarriage, promised to be more reliable than the Envoy in the gruelling conditions of the Western Sahara. Three D.H.89Ms (c/n 6310 G-ADYK, c/n 6311 'YL and c/n 6312 'YM) arrived at Cuatro Vientos, Madrid, in January 1936. Like the D.H.84M Dragons built for Iraq (and seaplane versions of both the D.H.84 and D.H.89), they had extended dorsal fins to counter the aerodynamic effect of the dorsal gun position. A ventral Vickers F machine

Model	c/n	Ferry registration	registration	Date	Owner
D.H.87A	8039	EC-W51	EC-EBE	12.35	Federico Valles Dolz, Marqués de San Joaquín
D.H.87A	8043	EC-W52	EC-BBF	12.35	Juán Cornago Pruneda
D.H.87A	8049	EC-W53	EC-FFB	12.35	Conde de Piniers
D.H.87B	8050	EC-W54		5.36	Conde de Soriano
D.H.87B	8079	EC-W55		5.36	Escuela de Aviación de Barcelona; Co-operación del Treball Aérei
D.H.87B	8083	EC-W56		5.36	As above

One of the three D.H.89M militarised Dragon Rapides, number 22-1, supplied to the Aviación Militar in January 1936. (Instituto de Historia y Cultura Aeronáutica)

The D.H.89 Dragon Rapide G-ADCL was flown to the Nationalists on 1 August 1936. (A J Jackson)

gun was mounted to fire through a hatch in the fuselage floor behind the trailing edge, and bomb racks were mounted under the fuselage to carry a dozen 12kg bombs. The pilot was provided with a fixed forward firing Vickers F mounted in the port side of the fuselage, and the bombardier/ rear gunner had a Marconi AD 6Mt/r wireless. There was provision for aerial cameras to be mounted vertically in the fuselage. The D.H.89Ms could easily be converted, when necessary, into troop transports or ambulances. The three D.H.89Ms (which the Spaniards simply called Dragons) were given the military serials 22-1, -2 and -3. Their fuselages, engine and undercarriage nacelles and inner lower wings were painted black, and the wings and tail surfaces (including the dorsal fins) pale ochre. After the election of the Popular Front government in March 1936, Gen Nuñez de Prado, the Director General de Aeronáutica, decided that, in view of the danger of a military coup, these modern aircraft would be safer near Madrid. He therefore stationed them, not in Africa, but at the Escuela de Vuelo y Combate (Air Combat Training School) at Alcalá de Henares. When it was discovered that the senior officers at the school were involved in a conspiracy (see Fokker F.VIIb3m), the D.H.89Ms, which had carried out several flights to Africa and back, were transferred to Getafe.

De Havilland Dragon Rapides were instrumental in some crucially important events at the start of the Spanish Civil War. The most famous by far is G-ACYR (c/n 6261), which was chartered from Olley Air Service, Croydon. In this Rapide the Spanish journalist Luis Bolín and three English 'holidaymakers' (Maj Hugh Pollard, his daughter Diana and her friend Dorothy Watson) flew from Croydon to Gandó aerodrome, Las Palmas, on the Canary Islands during 11-14 July 1936 to provide Gen Franco with an aircraft capable

of flying him to Tetuán, Spanish Morocco, where he could take command of the Spanish African Army and raise the standard of rebellion. This dramatic flight has been described in several books and need not be recounted here, except to mention that the person who had recommended the Dragon Rapide in the first place had been Juan de la Cierva, that the pilot was Capt C W R Bebb, his flight mechanic was Mr Bryers, and that the radio operator, whose name is not recorded, had been sent home from Casablanca before reaching La Palmas. Rapide G-ACYR was used to fly Bolín from Tetuán to Lisbon (where Bolín conferred with Gen Sanjurjo – see D.H. Puss Moth) and thence to France, from where Bolín continued to Rome by commercial airline with a request to Mussolini for aircraft (see Savioa-Marchetti S.81). The Rapide returned to Croydon a week or so later, and continued flying until 1953. In the 1960s it was restored, presented

to the Spanish government, and placed on display at the Museo del Aire, Cuatro Vientos, Madrid.

On 18 July 1936 General Núñez de Prado was ordered by Premier Casares Quiroga to fly to Saragossa and try to persuade the garrison commander, Gen Cabanellas (an old friend of Núñez de Prado since the Moroccan war), to stay loyal to the Republic. On landing at Saragossa in the D.H.89M 22-3, however, the general, his adjutant and the pilot were arrested. A few days later they were shot and, it is alleged, their bodies placed by the roadside as a discouragement to Republican sympathisers. The D.H.89M passed into Nationalist hands. On 20 July the LAPE Dragon Rapide EC-AZZ flew two air force officers, Comandantes Juan Aboal and Ismael Warleta, to Paris to negotiate the first purchase of military aircraft in France, and on the same day a British Airways Rapide (probably G-ACPN) landed at Burgos, piloted by the celebrated R H McIntosh ('All-weather Mac') and with three distinguished journalists on board – Sefton Delmer, H R Knickerbocker and Louis Delaprée – who wanted to interview the rebel

A Dragon Rapide of Cdte Ansaldo's 'Grupo Fokker-Dragon' at Olmeda. Probably ex-G-ADFY or 'DCL, it was named Capitán Vela *in memory of a Nationalist officer killed when his Dragon Rapide was shot down in error by German fighters.*

D.H.89A Dragon Rapides, imported via SFTA, at the Escuela de Polimotores (multi-engined flying school) at Totana, Murcia, in 1938. A D.H.90 Dragonfly is visible in the distance on the left.

leader Gen Mola, an episode that led to the Fokker F.XII affair (see relevant entry).

Meanwhile, in England, Cierva and Tom Campbell-Black purchased four D.H.89s through Airwork at Heston. The first to leave Heston, on 1 August, was G-ADCL (c/n 6277), piloted by Lord Malcolm Douglas-Hamilton and with Richard L'Estrange Malone (European sales manager of Airwork and son of Col Cecil L'Estrange Malone, a Communist Member of Parliament in the 1920s) as navigator. This aircraft had been damaged in an accident in June 1935 and completely rebuilt by de Havilland. For the journey the passenger cabin was almost filled with five-gallon petrol tanks, leaving only a small gap through which the two airmen had to crawl to reach the pilot's cabin. False registrations were painted on the wings and fuselage, over which the true registrations were painted in lamp black, the idea being that the genuine registrations could be scrubbed off in the event of a forced landing in the wrong place. At Burgos G-ADCL was converted into a fighter-bomber by Capitán Angel Salas. A forward-firing Vickers gun was fitted beside the pilot's seat, and a hole cut in the floor through which the bombardier could kick out bombs with his feet.

The second Rapide to leave, on 4 August, was G-ADFY (c/n 6291), bought from the recent King's Cup winner Charles Exton Gardner and flown to Burgos by A Rowley. The third and fourth, which left on 13 August, were the dark green (with red trim) G-ADAO (c/n 6275), bought from Ethyl Export, and (probably) the dark blue G-ACPN

(c/n 6252) of British Airways, which McIntosh had brought back to Gatwick a few days before.

In the Nationalist air arm these Rapides were given the type code 40 and, together with the D.H.89M (ex-22-3) captured at Saragossa and renumbered 40-5, were numbered 40-1, 40-2 (ex-G-ADCL), 40-3 and 40-4. Number 40-1 was used as a staff transport, and the other four were incorporated into the Fokker-Dragon group at Olmedo under the command of Mayor J-A Ansaldo. The group began intensive operations from about 20 August, but on 26 August 40-5 (the D.H.89M) was inadvertently shot down near Segovia by Heinkel He 51s. The two occupants, Capitán Pouzo and Capitán Vela, were killed, and their names were painted on the fuselages of 40-1 and 40-2, respectively, as a memorial. After the group disbanded, in December 1936, Ansaldo continued flying in his beloved 40-2, even when leading his Ro 37 group. This veteran Rapide survived the war, and on

2 October 1945 became EC-AAY of Iberia. It crashed in Spanish Guinea in June 1946. The other three Rapides were relegated to transport or training duties.

On the Republican side, EC-AZZ remained with LAPE throughout the war. The Republicans acquired another civil Rapide, the Italian-owned I-DRAG (c/n 6260), which happened to be at Le Bourget in August 1936. It was bought through Rollason Air Service of Croydon, and flown by Corniglion-Molinier (see Lockheed Orion) to Barcelona on 14 August, though whether it joined LAPE or the air force is not known. It was reportedly wrecked in a taxiing collision with a captured Fiat C.R.32. On 30 July D.H.89M 22-2 was transferred from Madrid to Barcelona, and on 5 August from there to Sariñena, where it served as an escort fighter to the Alas Rojas group. Because of its black fuselage it was called *El Avión Negus* by the populace, who mistakenly believed it had once been the private aeroplane of Emperor Haile Selasse of Ethiopia, whom they saw as a fellow victim of Mussolini's aggression. It was shot down on 19 October 1936 when its pilot, Luis Aguilera Cullell, bravely attacked a patrol of Heinkel He 51s to draw them away from the Fokker F.VIIb3m and Latécoère 28 he was escorting. Dragon Rapide 22-1 was transferred to the Basque front and was destroyed, together with the Douglas DC-2 c/n 1527, by Nationalist bombing at Albericia Aerodrome, Santander, on 6 April 1937.

In August and September 1936 three Dragon Rapides were purchased by Republican agents in England, but, despite much manoeuvring by the vendors and intermediaries, were prevented from reaching their intended destinations:

G-ADAK: Sold by British Continental Airways to Cecil Herbert Stone (who also bought the D.H.84 G-ACEK) and then to Union Founders' Trust (see D.H.84) in August 1936. Sold to Le Fédération Populaire des Sports Aéronautiques on 28 August. Three Frenchmen attempted to steal this Rapide from Croydon, where it was being kept under guard with four suspect D.H.84s in the Air Dispatch hangar, on 5 September 1936.

G-ADWZ: The first D.H.89A, of Personal Airways, Croydon, and G-ACTU, belonging to Lord Forbes (see Douglas DC-1) were both kept in the Personal Airways hangar. Repeated attempts were made to buy these two, the intermediaries being the pilot Eric Cummings and the Frenchmen Marc Cayre, Pierre Legastelois and M Rousseau. G-ADWZ was indeed flown to Paris and re-registered F-APES, but was obliged to be returned to England. Both sales were eventually dropped.

G-AEMH: Bought directly from de Havilland in August 1936, but the company cancelled the sale before delivering the aircraft.

The surviving records of two D.H.89s suggest that they reached Republican Spain. The first is c/n 6284 G-ADDF, which Airwork sold to Lejeune Aviation shortly before 7 September 1937. The second is one entered in a Nationalist post-war report on Republican aircraft purchased abroad as 'one secondhand Dragon, 14.3.37', the name Dragon being applied to D.H.84s and D.H.89s alike. The most likely candidate is OO-JFN (c/n 6273) *Bwana Roleke*, registered to the Belgian L J Mahier and recorded as 'sold in France 25.4.37'. It did not enter the French register, however, and seems to have disappeared into the blue. Sales recorded as taking place after the departure of aircraft for Spain were quite common at this time.

Finally, in December 1937 and through 1938 ten D.H.89A Dragon Rapides were bought directly from de Havilland by a number of Frenchmen, at least two of whom (Dr Arbeltier and A Rodier) were members of Le Cercle Aéronautique de Coulommiers et de la Brie (see D.H.82 Tiger Moth). As the French buyers received the Rapides they sold them to SFTA (see Appendix II), which in turn organised their transfer to Republican Spain. From a report in Spanish archives and other sources, it appears that nine were delivered, four bearing their French registrations:

number 41 on its rudder and registered EC-AGO, but it is impossible to determine its original identity. It is known that a number of Rapides were used by the Republican Escuela de Polimótores (multi-engined flying school) at Totana, Murcia, in 1938-39, but those which arrived after November 1938 could have done little but assist in the evacuation of Republican personnel to France at the end of the war. Eleven (including six that had taken refuge at Oran, Algeria) were recovered by the Nationalists after the war, but these may have included a D.H.84 or two. Five were used by SAETA (which became TAE in April 1940), and were passed to Iberia in December 1940. One Rapide was employed on an inter-island service between Las Palmas and Tenerife in the Canary Islands in 1940, but crashed in May 1941. So great was the fuel shortage during the winter of 1941-42 that the D.H.89s, which could run on automobile petrol, were the only Iberia aircraft able to fly regular schedules, several being used to keep open the route from Tangier to Málaga via Melilla. As they became unairworthy they were replaced by D.H.89s from the Ejercito del Aire. When the situation improved, in the spring of 1942, three were transferred to Spanish Guinea (now Equatorial Guinea) and maintained a service between Santa Isabel, on Fernando Póo island, and Bata. The following Iberia D.H.89s can be identified:

EC-BAC (c/n 6420, ex-F-ARII), became EC-AAR in June 1942, scrapped 1960.

EC-AAS, acquired March 1941,

c/n	Ostensible buyer	French C of A	Reg'n	Delivery in Spain
6382	Paul Legastelois	2.12.37	F-AQIL	18.01.38 (?)
6383	Paul Legastelois	1.12.37	F-AQIM	10.12.37
6393	Paul Legastelois	4.01.38	F-AQIN	5.01.38
6395	Dr Réné Arbeltier	21.01.38	F-AQJH	22.02.38 (?)
6396	A Rodier	16.03.38	F-AQJI	
6420	Paul Legastelois	11.11.38	F-ARII	Delivery confirmed
6424	Paul Legastelois	22.11.38	F-ARIJ	Delivery confirmed
6425	Paul Legastelois	25.11.38	F-ARIK	Delivery confirmed
6427	Paul Legastelois	28.11.38	F-ARIL	Delivery confirmed
6428	Paul Legastelois	7.12.38	F-ARIM	Delivery confirmed

From this point it is difficult to disentangle the individual histories of the Spanish Dragon Rapides. A photograph shows, for example, a Rapide in LAPE colours, with fleet

sold to Belgian Congo, February 1957.

EC-CAQ (c/n 6425, ex-F-ARIK), became EC-ABG in January 1943, sold abroad 1954.

The D.H.90 Dragonfly c/n 7529 bearing one of its post-civil-war registrations.

EC-AAY (c/n 6277, ex-G-ADCL, 40-2) acquired in October 1945, crashed in Spanish Guinea, June 1946.

EC-AAV, acquired January 1943, withdrawn 1957.

EC-AAX, on Santa Isabel–Bata route, January 1942.

Span 48ft; length 34ft 6in; height 10ft 3in; wing area 236sq ft.

Empty weight 3,230lb; loaded weight 5,500lb.

Maximum speed 157mph; cruising speed 132mph; ceiling 16,000ft; range 520 miles.

De Havilland D.H.90 Dragonfly

Although it resembled a cross between a scaled-down D.H.86 and D.H.89 Dragon Rapide, the Dragonfly four-passenger luxury tourer (two 130hp D.H. Gipsy Major engines) differed structurally from both. The fuselage was a monocoque shell of pre-formed ply stiffened with spruce stringers, and the thick, ply-covered centre-section of the lower wing eliminated the need for bracing struts or wires and improved both performance and cabin access. The prototype, E-2 (later G-ADNA), first flew in September 1935, and sixty-six production aircraft were built.

Three Dragonflies flew in Republican service during the Spanish Civil War, and a fourth was briefly involved at the very beginning. This was G-AECX (c/n 7505), registered to Arthur Henry Youngman of Self-

ridges, the famous London department store. At the end of July 1936 this aeroplane landed at Gamonal aerodrome, near Burgos, where Gen Mola had established his headquarters. The pilot was the Vicomte de Sibour, representing the Socony-Vacuum Oil Company (Mobiloil), and the passengers were his sister and her husband, Gordon Selfridge and Peggy Shannon, 'a girl from Rochester' (whether this was Rochester, Kent, or Rochester, New York is not clear). After discussions, Mola allowed them 85 gallons of petrol to fly to Granada, where, in reply to anxious queries from United States and British consular staff, they explained that they had come to evacuate Socony employees. Although they did fly four American ladies from Granada to Tangiers before returning to England, there is reason to suspect that the true purpose of the flight to Spain was to arrange the covert supply of petroleum to the Nationalists by Socony – supplies which, it is now known, were indeed expedited. Mola, who needed every drop of petrol he could get, would hardly have given away 85 gallons without a stronger reason than the evacuation of foreigners, whose evacuation was already being organised by the American consulates and Nationalist authorities in Andalusia.

The first Dragonfly sold to the Republicans seems to have been G-AEBU (c/n 7501), which is recorded as being sold in France in May 1938, apparently to Pierre Legastelois, and re-registered F-AQEU. When three Frenchmen – Marc Cayre, Alfred Rodier and Dr René Arbeltier – arrived at Newhaven on 2 March 1938 to visit Nash

Aircraft and Sales regarding the repair of B.A. Eagle G-ADJO, which Cayre had bought, the police, knowing the connection of these men with the Spanish Republicans, searched them and found a cheque book, one of the stubs of which recorded the payment to Paul Legastelois of £419.14s.10d for a Dragonfly, which suggests that the money was being paid in instalments. F-AQEU was flown to Barcelona by A Boyer, who also flew the Sikosrky S.38B to Bilbao.

The second Dragonfly was c/n 7529, which was sold to Gustav Wolf some time in 1937 and registered F-APDE. Whether or not Gustav was related to Daniel and Marcel Wolf (Vultee V1-A) is not known, but in 1938 he sold the Dragonfly, which was at Constantine, Algeria, to SFTA (see Appendix II). Although the sale is recorded as being made in October 1938, the Dragonfly probably reached Spain some months earlier.

The identity of the third Dragonfly in Republican Spain is uncertain. The only likely candidate seems to be G-AFAN (c/n 7556), which was sold by de Havilland to Devlet Hava Yollair, the Turkish state airline, in September 1937. At that time certain Turkish officials were acting as illicit intermediaries of the Spanish Republic (see Grumman GE-23 and Hawker Spanish Fury), and the aircraft might thus have found its way to Spain.

In the Republican Fuerzas Aéreas the Dragonflies were given the type code LY and were used as liaison transports and as trainers at Totana, Murcia. Two were recovered by the Nationalists at the end of the war and, sharing the type code 40 (later L-9) with D.H.84s and D.H.89s, were used by the Ejercito del Aire before being handed over to Iberia in the 1940s. Dragonfly c/n 7529 (ex-F-APDE) became EC-BAA, then EC-AAQ, before being sold in Belgium as OO-PET in 1949. It was then sold in France, becoming F-OAMS, and in August 1954 was flown from Toulouse-le-Noble to Jersey. Dismantled, it was flown to England in a Bristol Freighter, rebuilt as a D.H.90A with Gipsy 10 engines, and registered G-ANYK. It resumed flying in March 1959, and

Marcel Doret's Dewoitine D.530.

in January 1961 was bought by Metropolitan Air Movements. It crashed on landing at Le Baule, France, on 22 June 1961.

Span 43ft; length 31ft 8in; height 9ft 2in; wing area 256sq ft.

Empty weight 2,500lb; loaded weight 4,000lb.

Maximum speed 144mph; cruising speed 125mph; ceiling 18,100ft; range 625 miles.

Dewoitine D.27 and D.53

The predecessor of the Dewoitine D.371, the D.27 parasol monoplane single-seat fighter appeared in 1928. Sixty were built for the Swiss air force, seven for export (three to Yugoslavia, three to Rumania, and one to Argentina) and four for the Dewoitine company itself. The D.53 of 1931 was a D.27 with a strengthened wing and a 500hp Hispano-Suiza 12Md vee engine in place of the 12Mb of the D.27. Seven D.53s, of different variants, were built altogether.

In September 1936 three D.27s or D.53s were offered to a Spanish Republican agent in France, and, according to a Spanish Nationalist intelligence dispatch, two flew from Toulouse-Montaudran to Barcelona on 7 February 1937. Raoul Delas, a French pilot who had flown the Latécoère 28 of the Alas Rojas (Red Wings) squadron at Sariñena the previous autumn, was allegedly a party to the transaction, as well as to the theft of a Potez 43 and two Potez 58s from the Aveyron flying club (for

which, since he was still in Spain, he was sentenced *in absentia* to two years' imprisonment). The identity of these Dewoitines, however, is still uncertain. It is unlikely that they were any of the Dewoitines exported to Rumania or Yugoslavia, as has been suggested, because the governments of both countries were strongly antagonistic to the Spanish Republic. More probably they were from the eight D.27s or seven D.53s, all civil aircraft, flying in France in 1936. The most likely candidates are:

D.53-01, F-AMQX (C of A 3343), which disappeared from the Bureau Veritas register after 1936.

D.272 F-AJTE, and/or D.53-06 F-ANAX (C of A 3568), both used by Marcel Doret, the Dewoitine company test pilot, for aerobatic displays. In 1937 he ordered a new D.53 (C of A 1758) from Lioré-et-Olivier, which handled most Dewoitine production, and had this, too, registered as F-AJTE. The other two, he later explained, had been cannibalised to build the new aircraft, an assertion for which no evidence has been found. Moreover, neither of the earlier two can be found on the registers after 1936.

A third possibility is that the Spanish aircraft were the three original D.27s of the pre-production series rejected by the French Service Téchnique de L'Aéronautique in 1929, and redesignated D.53s after having their wings strengthened. In 1936 these were still at Villacoublay, from where a number of aircraft disappeared to Spain during the first months of the civil war.

In Spain, the two (or three) D.27/D.53s were used as formation

and aerobatic trainers at San Javier, near Cartagena, where they were called *Dewoitinillos* or *Dewoitine pequeños* (little Dewoitines), to distinguish them from the D.371s.

Span 10.30m; length 6.56m; height 2.78m; wing area 17.55sq m.

Empty weight 1,038kg; loaded weight 1,415kg.

Maximum speed 291km/h; climb to 2,000m in 3min 6sec; ceiling 9,200m.

Dewoitine D.31-01

The Dewoitine D.30, which appeared in 1931, continued the line of high-wing monoplane transports built by the Société Aéronautique Française Dewoitine during the 1920s. A three-engined version, the D.31-01, was built from the second prototype D.30, but did not make its maiden flight until 21 January 1932, bearing the registration F-AKFE. Power was provided by three 230hp Hispano-Suiza 9Qa radials, but in 1935 these were replaced by 320hp 9Qbs, the central engine being enclosed in a long-chord NACA cowling. It carried a crew of two and ten passengers, and was of metal contruction with fabric covering. The property of CEMA at Villacoublay, the D.31-01 was last registered by the Bureau Veritas in June 1935 at Le Bourget, but does not appear in the 1937 register. This raises the possibility that it was among the various aircraft flown, or transported in crates, to Republican Spain during the winter of 1936-37.

Span 24.99m; length 14.86m; height 4.15m; wing area 68sq m.

Empty weight 3,273.4kg; loaded weight 5,280kg.

Maximum speed 235km/h.

Dewoitine D.35

The Dewoitine D.35 was a four-passenger monoplane with a high, strut-braced wing and wide-track undercarriage, intended as a 'limousine' for flying Dewoitine employees between Toulouse and Paris on company business. Only one was built, powered by an uncowled 230hp Hispano-Suiza 9Qb radial engine (later replaced by a 370hp 9Qd), and after a year's trials it was registered

A Dewoitine D.35. (J Cuny)

F-ALNC in February 1932. In 1933 it was placed at the disposition of Marcel Doret, the chief company test pilot, but no trace of it can be found in the Bureau Veritas register after 1937 (see Dewoitine D.27). It is not unreasonable to suppose, therefore, that it was yet another of the various obsolete or rejected prototypes that were retrieved from the backs of hangars and sold to the Spanish Republicans.

Span 12.16m; length 9.18m; wing area 24.6sq m.
Empty weight 895.7kg; loaded weight 1,612kg.
Maximum speed 205km/h at ground level; 195km/h at 2,000m.

Dewoitine D.371 and D.372

When the Service Téchnique de l'Aéronautique, the technical branch of the French Ministère de l'Air, issued specifications for a new single-seat fighter in 1930, the French aircraft manufacturers invited to take part in the 'C 1' competition submitted no fewer than ten official and five unofficial en-

trants. Nine were high-, shoulder-wing or parasol monoplanes; five were low-wing monoplanes, of which one, the Hanriot-Biche 110, was a pusher with its tail supported by twin booms; and only one, the Blériot-SPAD 510, was a biplane. The winner was the Dewoitine D.500, an elegant low-wing monoplane with an open cockpit and a fixed, wide-track undercarriage, from which were developed two higher-powered versions fitted with the Hispano-Suiza 12Xcrs *moteur-canon*, the D.501 and D.510. A total of 336 of the three versions was built for the Armée de l'Air between 1933 and 1938.

Meanwhile, Les Établissements Lioré et Olivier, a large company famous for its heavy bombers and airliners, saw the 1930 'C 1' competition as an opportunity to break into the fighter market. Since it handled most of the Dewoitine production orders and was building a number of D.27s and D.53s, it decided to redesign the D.27 parasol monoplane to modern requirements and enter it as an unofficial contender. The resulting D.370-01, initially fitted with an uncowled 725hp Gnome-Rhône 14Kbr radial engine, was a disappointment and many critics, with the benefit of hindsight, have wondered why Lioré chose to enter a field in which it had

no experience with a fighter based on an obsolescent formula. At that time, however, much uncertainty prevailed over what form the single-seat fighter of the next generation should take, for the well-tried virtues of the conventional biplane, above all its manoeuvrability and ruggedness, were by no means offset by the advantages of speed on the level, and in the dive, claimed for the low-wing cantilever monoplane. Nor, for that matter, was speed always evident. The winner of the exactly comtemporary F.7/30 fighter competition in Britain, the Gloster Gladiator biplane, was some 20mph faster on the level than the Supermarine F.7/30, which was a low-wing monoplane of the inverted-gull-wing type. Some designers, especially in France, still favoured the parasol monoplane, with its wing strut-braced above the fuselage, as the best compromise between minimum airframe weight, relatively low airframe cost, and acceptable aerodynamic qualities. As if to prove the point, when the second prototype, the Dewoitine D.371-01, flew at last in March 1934, having had to wait nearly a year for its 770hp Gnome-Rhône 14Kds engine, its top speed of 380km/h and rate of climb of 5,000 metres in 5 minutes 33 seconds exceeded even those of the D.500 (364km/h and 5,000 metres in 6 minutes 38 seconds). Being a private venture, the D.371 was available for export, and in June 1934 the Lithuanian government ordered fourteen, slightly modified and designated D.372.

Following the collapse of the International Disarmament Conference in October 1934, the French government announced a rapid expansion of air strength under 'Plan I', and, questioning the wisdom of depending entirely on low-wing monoplane fighters, the Armée de l'Air ordered sixty Blèriot SPAD 510 biplanes, sixty Loire 46 gull-wing monoplanes and twenty-eight Dewoitine D.371 parasol monoplanes. The Aéronavale likewise ordered twenty D.373s for service on the carrier *Béarne*, and in 1936 ordered a further twenty-five, fitted with fold-

ing wings and designated D.376. Production of the four series was undertaken by the Lioré et Olivier factory at Clichy, Paris.

The basic D.371, with less wing area and a narrower fuselage than the D.370, followed the Dewoitine practice of marrying an all-metal fuselage to fabric-covered wings and tail surfaces, with the difference that the leading edges of the wing and tail surfaces were now also metal covered. All four production versions were powered by 880hp Gnome-Rhône 14Kfs radial engines in long-chord blistered cowlings, and the undercarriage wheels were protected by shapely spats, features that enhanced the machine's seductively attractive appearance. The French versions were armed with four MAC 34 7.69mm machine guns, mounted under the wing on the D.371 and in the wing on the D.373 and D.376. The D.372 had two Darne 7.69mm machine guns in the wing and two Browning .303in machine guns mounted in the upper forward fuselage, synchronised to fire between the propeller blades. It also had parking brakes and a slightly different arrangement of cockpit controls.

The D.372 contract, however, was soon to cause serious trouble. Production was delayed, first by the

A Dewoitine D.372 in Lithuanian markings.

repeated strikes then disrupting French industry and, second, by numerous changes insisted upon by the Lithuanians. For example, they wanted to install six machine guns to make the D.372 the most heavily-armed fighter in the world. Then, after the appearance of the D.501 with the Hispano *moteur-canon* (a

An ex-Lithuanian D.372 in Republican service, probably at Manises, Valencia, in 1937.

20mm shell-firing cannon mounted between the cylinder blocks to fire through the propeller boss), they asked to be allowed to cancel the contract, on grounds of late delivery, and to order D.501s instead. When this move failed, they demanded that the D.372s be armed with two 20mm cannon in the wing and two machine guns in the fuselage. The D.371-01 was used as a test bed for the twin-cannon installation, but during a power dive on 5 December 1935 the wingtips tore away after violent buffeting, and the pilot, Lepreux, was barely able to land safely. The Service Téchnique de l'Aéronautique therefore ordered that the fourteen

D.372s and twenty-eight D.371s had their wings strengthened. As a result, and thanks to yet more strikes, the D.372s did not emerge from the factory until May 1936, and the D.371s until December. The Lithuanians now rejected the D.372s on the grounds that, as a result of the weight added by the strengthening of the wings, performance no longer matched that specified in the contract.

On 4 June 1936 the Front Populaire (Popular Front) was elected in France, and two days later the new air minister, Pierre Cot, resolved the deadlock by offering to replace the unwanted D.372s by fourteen D.501s. The Lithuanians accepted with alacrity. On 18 July civil war broke out in Spain, and it is often stated that it was only then that the strongly pro-Republican Pierre Cot persuaded the Lithuanians to relinquish the D.372s, which he wanted to send to Spain, in exchange for the D.501s. Although this is demonstrably untrue, there is little doubt that the Spanish Civil War unexpectedly solved the question of what to do with the fourteen D.372s now looking for a purchaser.

The political machinations that surrounded the export of these and other French military aircraft to the Spanish government are too complicated to describe here, and all that need be said is that the fourteen D.372s were ostensibly sold to the Spanish journalist and author Corpus Barga at a unit price of 610,000 French francs, which was more than twice the 278,000 French francs each they would have cost the Lithuanians. They were flown from Villacoublay to Toulouse-Francazal, one crashing en route, and from there departed for Republican Spain on 8 August 1936, a few hours before the French unilateral declaration of Non-Intervention in the Spanish war came into effect. Three more were damaged on landing at Prat de Llobregat Aerodrome, Barcelona. A small team of Dewoitine company mechanics which arrived the day after found that the spats had been scraping the tyres, and removed them, along with the parking brakes, as a safety measure. An equally probable cause of the accidents, however, is that few of the pilots, who were mostly mercenaries or volunteers contracted to join the Republican air force, had flown the D.372 before.

A great deal of misinformation, most if it politically motivated, has been published about the number of French military aircraft, and Dewoitine fighters in particular, that fought in Spain during the first weeks of the civil war. The Nationalists, and their supporters round the world, published highly exaggerated figures which remained in circulation until the late 1970s. Most authorities now believe that the number of D.372s and D.371s sent to Spain in August 1936 was twenty-six, with another four or fourteen delivered during the next six months. Others put the number sent in August at twenty-three – thirteen D.372s as well as ten D.371s diverted from the Armée de l'Air. This ignores the fact that only twenty-eight D.371s were built. The strengthening of their wings was not completed until December 1936, during the course of which the gun arrangement was altered to two mounted in the wing centre section and two under the wing just outside the cabane struts, and on 16 December all were offered for sale, through an intermediary, to the Spanish government. The correspondence shows that they were ready for delivery to the Armée de l'Air in December 1936, and that negotiations with the Spaniards were still in progress in March 1937, when the letters cease in mid-flow.

In May 1937, eighteen only were delivered to GARALD 574, a French fighter squadron at Bizerte, Tunis, in North Africa, where they served (but did little flying, owing to endless trouble with the engines) until 1939. That the other ten were secretly diverted to Spain, still displaying their intended Armée de l'Air numbers, is beyond doubt, for in October 1937 the Italian anti-Fascist volunteer Guiseppe Krizai (who had been shot down and taken prisoner by the Nationalists and later exchanged) returned to Spain to take command of a newly-created squadron equipped with D.371s, the 1ª Escuadrilla of Grupo 71. Photographs of his personal D.371 show it still bearing the French military serial R-913 in black on the underside of its wing. Since it is also known that, by March 1937, the handling of the negotiations for the D.371s had passed to a group of Italian anti-Fascists in Paris (who were also negotiating for fifty Potez 54s, of which only four were finally bought in October 1937), it seems that they were bought either in small lots during the course of 1937 or as a single lot in October.

Finally, it is probable that two Dewoitines reported to have been smuggled to Spain a year earlier, in October 1936, were the D.370-01 and D.371-01 prototypes, there being no record of what otherwise became of them, and that the D.372 that had crashed in France in August 1936 was repaired and sent on later. Thus the total of twenty-six would be correct not for those sent in August 1936, but for those supplied throughout the war.

It is difficult to determine how these Dewoitines actually performed in Spain, because there is a plethora of conflicting reports, most of them politically inspired. The Nationalists dismissed all the French aircraft in Spain as 'bad', and claimed that twenty Dewoitines were shot down before 30 October 1936. On the Republican side the Russians and the Spanish Communists, determined to argue the superiority of Soviet technology, dismissed them as 'antiquated'.

It is true that, by 28 October, the Republican fighter force on the Madrid front had dwindled to a single Hawker Spanish Fury, but the blame for this lay not with the Dewoitines and Loire 46s as aircraft, but in the manner they were delivered and used. They were delivered unarmed, and the armaments were either stopped at the frontier or purloined by the People's Militia in Catalonia. On 16 August one D.372 was sent to Guadix in the south, where, still unarmed, it was shot down by Fiat C.R.32s over its own aerodrome on 27 August. The pilot, Capitán de Haro, one of the most experienced of Spanish airmen, was killed. The other twelve were sent to Madrid, where they had to be fitted with old Vickers guns, of which there were not enough to permit more than two to each machine. Because Lioré et Olivier had thoughtfully removed

the firing mechanisms, mounting plates, synchronising mechanisms and even the gunsights (though some of these were delivered in November or December), everything had to be made from scratch, but the firing devices, improvised from rods and wires, were unreliable and the guns, many of them rusty, usually jammed after a few rounds.

Even so, when the first two D.372s to be armed went into action, together with the remaining Hawker Fury, on 31 August 1936 and encountered three Fiat C.R.32s, they shot down two without loss. This success was not repeated, for the Republican Jefatura (Command), instead of concentrating its fighters, sent them out singly or in pairs to spread them as widely as possible. Another difficulty was that the D.372 was unforgiving to a novice, and the pilots were either foreign mercenaries and volunteers, few of whom had flown fighters, or Spaniards who had flown nothing more modern than Hispano-Nieuport 52s. In his memoirs, Lacalle, who rose to command the Republican fighter force later in the war, criticises the Dewoitine for its heaviness on the controls. In a letter to the author, however, Augusto Lecha Vilasuso, who had been at Madrid with Lacalle and flew D.371s from October 1937

One of the ten D.371s delivered to Republican Spain not, as is usually supposed, in August 1936, but probably in October 1937. The picture was apparently taken shortly after delivery, for the French military serial R-913 (another photograph shows '13' under the port wing) has not yet been painted over. This machine became the commander's aircraft of the 1ª Escuadrilla of Grupo 71.

until the end of the war, explained that, 'whereas in most aircraft, when you turn you move the stick and rudder bar simultaneously, in the Dewoitine and Loire 46 you had to move the rudder bar first and then the stick, otherwise the machine immediately became very heavy, and the muscular effort to hold it in the turn, or roll etc., became extremely painful'. Once this was learned, the Dewoitine was docile and manoeuvrable.

Two foreign volunteers, Vincent Doherty, an ex-RAF fighter pilot, and Jean Dary, a First World War minor ace who was credited with four victories in Spain in September 1936, both testify that the high speed and rate of climb of the Dewoitine gave it a decisive advantage over the Fiat C.R.32, for which it would have been more than a match but for its defective armament and the lunatic

policy of dispersal imposed by the Jefatura. Dary did, however, feel that it was not quite rugged enough for the primitive conditions in Spain. Curiously, the Gnome-Rhône 14Kfs engine, which kept the Dewoitines in French service earthbound for long periods of time because of its unreliability, gave no trouble in the Dewoitines in Spain.

In fact, only three Dewoitines on the Madrid front, and Haro's machine at Guadix, were shot down. Five were destroyed or damaged by bombing and six by landing accidents, but, of all of these, five were repaired and transferred in the winter to Manises aerodrome, Valencia, and later to the air combat school at Archena. According to Lecha, five of the ten D.371s of Grupo 71 were lost by June 1938. Two well-known photographs of a Dewoitine being shot down in flames, which were published in the Italian press in the summer of 1938 (and in the *Illustrated London News* of 25 June 1938 and 21 January 1939), and are usually said to show a scene over the Madrid front in the autumn of 1936, almost certainly show a D.371 (the aircraft has spats) of Grupo 71. The photographs were taken within seconds of each other over the same landscape, and depict one and the same aeroplane.

A Dewoitine D.510TH. (J Cuny)

The remaining five D.372s, with two captured Fiat C.R.32s and a Dewoitine D.510TH, were employed on coastal patrol, convoy protection and city defence, operating from Vilajuiga on the Costa Brava. Two of the D.371s were fitted with 20mm Oerlikon cannon for use against ground targets and shipping, and thus became the most heavily-armed fighters in the Republican FARE. All of these aircraft were destroyed on 5 February 1939, during the Republican collapse in Catalonia when, while landing at Bañolas aerodrome before an intended evacuation to France, they were caught by a squadron of Heinkel He 111s and two squadrons of Messerschmitt Bf 109s of the Condor Legion.

Span 11.22m; length 7.44m; height 3.42m; wing area 17.45sq m.
Empty weight 1,295kg; loaded weight 1,725kg.
Maximum speed 385km/h; climb to 5,000m in 5min 40sec; range 830km.

Dewoitine D.510TH

As related in the section on the D.371, the winner of the 1930 'C 1' competition for a new French single-seat fighter was the Dewoitine D.500, a shapely low-wing cantilever monoplane powered by a 600hp Hispano-Suiza 12Xbrs liquid-cooled engine and armed with two fixed 7.7mm machine guns mounted inside the cowling above the engine. The D.501, which appeared in 1933, had the more powerful, though still experimental, armament of a Hispano-Suiza 12Xcrs *moteur canon*,

in which a 20mm licence-built Oerlikon shell-firing cannon was mounted in the vee between the cylinder banks to fire through a hole in the propeller boss, plus the two machine guns. The D.500 and D.501 were of all-metal, stressed-skin construction and, although they retained the fixed undercarriage and open cockpit still preferred by fighter pilots, they were considered, when they entered service in 1934-35, to be among the best and most advanced fighters in the world.

The D.510 was essentially a D.501 with a more powerful 860hp Hispano-Suiza 12Ycrs, a three-bladed variable-pitch propeller, and a strengthened undercarriage. It appeared in 1934, and the first production examples began to enter service in the autumn of 1936. By then, however, so hectic had become the pace of technical development in the last three years before the Second World War that they were already outdated.

If the D.510 was obsolescent, its *moteur-canon* was not, and it was precisely to evaluate this that the air ministries of the USSR and Great Britain ordered single examples, and Japan two. The D.510 that finally arrived at Martlesham Heath in June 1937, after long delays, was discovered to have been sent with the cannon carefully removed. All Air Ministry enquiries to Lioré et Olivier, which had built the aeroplane, were met with expressions of bewilderment over what could have happened to it. It was never supplied.

This detail is mentioned because it is relevant to the story of the two D.510s that found their way to Republican Spain.

In December 1934 the Turkish government ordered thirty-six D.510s from Lioré et Olivier, which was building the series for the Armée de l'Air. Lioré et Olivier failed to produce them on time and, after mutual acrimony, the order was cancelled. A second contract for thirty-six adapted for dive-bombing was likewise cancelled after a prototype had been tested and rejected. The Turkish D.510s (designated D.510T) were, in fact, D.500s, with D.500-type undercarriages and two-blade wooden propellers, fitted with Hispano-Suiza 12Xcrs engines from which the cannon had been removed. For this reason the unfinished D.510Ts at the factory were rejected by the Armée de l'Air as being incompatible with the D.510s already in French service.

On completing the first order of twenty-five D.510s for the Armée de l'Air in October 1936, Lioré et Olivier brought to completion two of the D.510Ts, c/ns 26 and 27. With the assistance of Jean Moulin (Pierre Cot's chef-de-cabinet at the Ministère de l'Air and later hero of the Resistance under the German Occupation), and probably through SFTA (see Appendix II), the company sold them to the 'Kingdom of Hédjaz' (Saudi Arabia), a channel to Spain which had already been used for the Loire 46s and the two pre-series D.371s. The two Dewoitines, stripped of armament and now called D.510TH ('Turquie-Hédjaz') No 1 and No 2, were tested at Villacoublay by Doumerc (for Lioré et Olivier) and Lepreux (for Dewoitine) on 30 November 1936.

On 18 December 1936 Roger Nouvel, a wealthy sports pilot engaged in ferrying aircraft to Barcelona, flew D.510TH No 2 to Toulouse, whence Henri Rozés flew it to Barcelona on 19 December 1936. There it was photographed by a French reporter, and the photograph raised a storm in the French parliament four days later. In the midst of the shouting, a deputy tried to defend Pierre Cot by arguing that the 'TH' on the rudder denoted that the aircraft was a civil machine, for everyone knew that civil aircraft were registered by letters and not by numbers! On 24 December Georges Delage took off from Villacoublay in D.510TH No 1, but was forced down near Limoges after losing his way in thick fog. Damage was slight, and the Dewoitine was dismantled, crated and taken to Barcelona by lorry. Meanwhile, in the French Chambre de Députés the row continued with increasing violence, the Right arguing that Pierre Cot was weakening French air power by selling more than 500 aircraft, including the most modern and secret French fighters (Dewoitine D.510s) to the Spanish Communists and their Soviet masters. As a result, the French government insisted that the Spanish Republicans return the two Hispano-Suiza 12Xcrs engines lest the Russians should get their hands on them. This was despite the fact that the Russians had already taken their D.510R (which, unlike the two in Spain, or the one sent to England for that matter, did have its cannon) to the USSR for testing in September.

Without their engines, the D.510THs languished at Barcelona for the next six months, until they were fitted with Russian M-100A (licence-built Hispano-Suiza 12Y engines) taken from a written-off SB Katiuska. After a few months with the Escuela de Alta Velocidad (High Speed Flying School) at El Carmolí, in Murcia, the two D.510s were transferred to the 1ª Escuadrilla of Grupo 71, a group equipped besides with the ten newly-arrived Dewoitine D.371s and two captured Fiat C.R.32s. The squadron was relegated to coastal patrol and city defence duties, and during the spring of 1938 José Corral, flying one of the D.510s (armed with two Russian PV-1 machine guns mounted in the wings), is believed to have been responsible for shooting down a Heinkel He 59B-2 seaplane during the night of 21-22 March 1938. By June 1938 the squadron, reduced to five or six D.371s, one D.510, and one Fiat C.R.32, was based at Vilajuiga on the Costa Brava. All of these aircraft were destroyed by the Condor Legion while they were landing at Bañolas aerodrome, Catalonia, on 5 March 1939.

The Spanish Republican pilot Francisco Pérez Mur has written that in January 1937 he saw three low-wing Dewoitine fighters in Prat de Llobregat aerodrome, Barcelona, and it has been assumed that the third was a D.500 brought by a French deserter from Toulouse-Francazal military aerodrome. Nonetheless, all the oft-repeated stories of numerous Dewoitine D.500s and D.510s in Spain, and especially reports of air combats involving these aircraft over the Madrid front during the autumn of 1936, should be discounted once and for all. So should the report concerning the testing and use in action of the D.510 with *moteur-canon* in Spain, which the American volunteer pilot Albert ('Ajax') Baumler wrote for the US Army Air Corps Intelligence Section after his return to America in 1938.

Span 12.092m; length (without cannon) 7.85m; height 3.625m; wing area 16.16sq m.
Empty weight 1,399kg; loaded weight 1,873kg.
Maximum speed (with two-blade propeller) 390km/h; climb to 5,000m in 6min 14sec; ceiling 10,500m.

Dornier Do J Wal

During the First World War Professor Claudius Dornier, then head of the experimental division of the German Zepplin-Werke at Lindau, had produced a series of large flying-boats incorporating what were then modern concepts and had been among the first to experiment with metal stressed skin, a system by which the covering of an aircraft became an integral part of its load-bearing structure. After the Armistice Dornier created his own company, but two projects for commercial aircraft, the Gs I and Gs II, were cancelled by the Allied Control Commission on the grounds of their size. To evade this restriction Dornier founded an Italian subsidiary at Marina di Pisa, the Società di Costruzioni Meccaniche di Pisa (later changed to Costruzioni Meccaniche Aeronautiche SA, or CMASA), specifically for developing the Dornier Gs II. When the resulting prototype, the Dornier Do J Wal (Whale), made its first flight, on 6 November 1922, it immediately impressed all who saw it as representing a remarkable advance in the design of seaborne aircraft. It was a slender all-metal cantilever monoplane with metal skinning, powered by two 'push-pull' tandem engines in a nacelle mounted on the centre-section of the rectangular parasol wing.

The conventional method of improving the stability of a flying-boat on water was to provide a pair of auxiliary floats beneath the wingtips, but Dornier used a pair of aerofoil-section sponsons projecting from the lower hull at the CG, which offered reduced drag, increased stability and could also serve as fuel tanks. The sponsons were braced to the mainplane by two pairs of angled struts. The Wal carried a crew of four: two pilots side by side, a navigator/gunner in the nose cockpit, and a mechanic/gunner in the midships cockpit, each gunner operating a pair of twin Lewis guns on a Scarff ring. Up to 700kg of bombs could be carried on racks under the wings.

More than 300 Wals, in many different versions, were eventually built, 150 of them in Italy and the rest in Spain, the Netherlands, Japan and, after 1933, Germany. Merely to chronicle their record-breaking and pioneering achievements would require a book in itself. Spain was the first foreign country to become aware of the potentialities of this great aircraft, for a technical commission headed by Gen Francisco Echagüe Santoyo had visited the factory at Marina di Pisa in the autumn of 1922 and, before the prototype had even flown, placed an order for six aircraft at a unit price of 300,000 pesetas. Indeed, the original prototype, powered by two 300hp Hispano-Suiza water-cooled engines, was the first of the six to be delivered. The Wals, reinforced by a further seven in 1925 and three more in 1929, gave distinguished service in the Moroccan War, and in February 1926 Mayor Ramón Franco (younger brother of Gen Francisco Franco), Capitán Ruiz de Alda and Serjento Pablo Rada made the first flight in history across the South Atlantic in the Dornier Wal M-WAL *Plus Ultra*.

Late in the 1920s licences were obtained for twenty-nine to be built by Construcciones Aeronáuticas SA

Dornier Wal D-8, of the Aeronáutica Naval, at Alcudia, Mallorca, before the civil war. (Arráez)

(CASA) at their factory at Puntales, Cádiz: seventeen for the Aviación Militar, ten for the Aeronáutica Naval and two nine-passenger transports for the airline CLASSA (which became LAPE under the Republic). The military Wals were powered by 450hp Elizalde A5 (licence-built Lorraine 12Ed) engines, the naval Wals by 600hp Hispano-Suiza 12 Lbr engines, and the LAPE aircraft by 550hp Napier Lions. In prewar service the military Wals were given the type code 6, and the naval Wals the code D. The two LAPE aircraft were registered EC-AAZ (fleet No 19) and EC-YYY (fleet No 20).

On 18 July 1936 twenty-six Wals remained in service, including the two LAPE machines, and the Nationalists managed to gain possession of thirteen of these in the first two days. None, however, was in flying condition. Of the Republican thirteen, eight were airworthy: 6-15 of the Aviación Militar was at Los Alcázares, Murcia; D-1, -2, -3, -6 and -7 of the Aeronáutica Naval were at San Javier, and the two LAPE Wals were at Barcelona. The other five (6-19, -22, -28, -30 and -32) were without their Elizalde A5 engines, which had developed faults in their reduction gears. For reasons never explained, and which seem more puzzling still considering the desperate need the Republicans had for

open-sea reconnaissance aircraft, the Republicans made no apparent effort to put the engineless Wals back into service, and failed to put the airworthy aircraft to any useful purpose. Wal D-1, piloted by Capitán Beneito, carried out four raids on Mallorca at the end of July before it was brought down on the sea off Cabrera, D-2 made an abortive attempt to supply arms to a few Republican militia cornered on the Mallorca coast, and a third Wal was shot down by a Nieuport 52 near Cádiz on 25 July 1936. On 15 December 1936, Antonio Blanch Rodríguez, a naval auxiliary flying with the Nationalist forces in Spanish Morocco, flew across to Republican Spain in the Wal 70-31 (originally 6-31 of the Aviación Militar). This aircraft was powered by

A Dornier Wal in Nationalist service. (Arráez)

Isotta-Fraschini Asso Ri engines installed by Italian mechanics at el Atalayón, and was soon withdrawn from service for lack of engine parts. In May 1937 only four Dornier Wals were in service, and these, with the new serials HD-001 to HD-004, were formed into the 2ª Escuadrilla of Grupo 73, based at San Javier. They were used for training, and by the end of the war only HD-002 and -004 were still serving.

By contrast, the Nationalists managed to put all thirteen of their Wals back into service, and exploited them to the full throughout the civil war. At Cádiz, D-4, -5 and -8 were under repair, but by 20 July D-8 was already participating in the first airlift, carrying twelve soldiers per flight from Ceuta to Cádiz, and was joined by D-5 three days later. After the arrival of the Junkers Ju 52/3ms at the end of the month and at the beginning of August, the Wals returned to their

more appropriate duties of long-distance reconnaissance and bombing attacks on Republican ships. Later in August, the arrival of twenty 500hp Isotta-Fraschini Asso 500 engines from Italy made it possible to put back into service the ten Wals belonging to the Aviación Militar at El Atalayón (6-16, -17, -18, -21, -24, -25, -26, -27, -29 and -31), which, like those at Barcelona, had been grounded pending replacement Elizalde engines.

In September 1936 all of the Nationalist Wals (including D-5, whose repairs were completed on 15 August) were formed into 1-G-70 (70 being the Nationalist type code for the Wal), commanded by Cdte Luis Rambaud and divided into two escuadrillas, 1-E-70 (Teniente Naval Ruiz de la Puente) and 2-E-70 (Capitán Julio Meléndez Machado), the crews being ex-naval and ex-Aviación Militar personnel. For an emblem, 1-G-70 adopted the same Mah Jong 'Red Dragon' that the Wals had displayed during the Moroccan War. For the rest of the civil war the Dornier Wals, which became the workhorses of the Nationalist naval air services, moved between the bases at Cádiz, El Atalayón and Pollensa, Mallorca, often leaving detachments of two or three aircraft at all three stations simultaneously. In May 1937 three Wals (70-21, -24 and -27) led by Cdte Martínez Merino were trans-

A Dornier Do 17E No 27-4 was one of the first to arrive in Spain to serve in the experimental unit VB/88 of the Condor Legion. When this photograph was taken, at La Parra, Jerez de la Frontera, in March 1939, it was serving with the Spanish Nationalist group 8-G-27. (Arráez)

ferred to El Ferrol, Galicia, to participate in the northern campaign, where, for the first time, they found themselves under occasional attack by formations of I-15 fighters. Merino soon discovered, however, that the best defence against fighters was to dive down to sea level and twist and turn just above the water, the I-15 pilots being afraid to dive close enough to deliver accurate fire lest they failed to pull out in time and hit the sea. From El Ferrol the Wals moved to Bilbao and thence to Santander, before returning to the Mediterranean after the end of the campaign. In January 1938 the two escuadrillas were redesignated 2-E-70 and 3-E-70, but in October 1938 they returned to their original numbers. During that period the group had been integrated with the Cant Z.501s to become 1-G-62-70.

After the arrival of the Cant Z.506Bs and the formation of 1-G-62-73, the old group 1-G-70 was recreated. It continued giving service until the end of the war, its last mission being the rescue, by 70-7, of the crew of an He 59 which had come down near Ibiza on 22 March 1939. On 1 April 1939 ten Wals remained in service, to which were added HD-002 and -004 (ex-LAPE, EC-YYY) recovered from the Republicans. Another two were put back into service in 1940, bringing the total strength to fourteen aircraft, all in the 51ª Escuadrilla de Hidros based at El Atalayón. In 1945 they received the new type code HR-1 (HR-2 being assigned to the He 60), and in 1946 seven were still in service, including HR-1-4, -17, -21 and -34, the serials being the same as their original D-, 6- and 70- numbers. There seems to be no record of when they were finally withdrawn, but it is known that HR-1-34 was

written off after an accident on 25 September 1950. This Wal, however, was not the last in service even then.

Span 22.5m; length 17.25m; height 4.8m; wing area 96sq m.
Empty weight 3,250kg; loaded weight 5,750kg.
Maximum speed 180km/h; cruising speed 150km/h; ceiling 5,000m; range 1,000km.

Dornier Do 17

During the first year of the Second World War, the Dornier, Heinkel and Junkers bombers of the Luftwaffe became household names all over Europe and were often cited as salient examples of Nazi duplicity and aggression. To evade the Versailles restrictions on German rearmament, it was said, they had been designed as airliners and mailplanes which could, without difficulty, be converted into bombers, and as airliners and mailplanes they had been passed off on a gullible public to disguise the Nazis' warlike intentions. The truth, as always, is more complicated and more interesting, for the origins of these aircraft actually antedate the coming to power of Hitler in January 1933.

In July 1932 the Inspection Department of the Army Ordnance Office of the Weimar Republic secretly drew up outline specifications for a high-speed twin-engined all-metal monoplane, and issued them to the Dornier, Heinkel and Junkers companies. The proposal was that the new aircraft, utilising the most modern structural and aerodynamic techniques, should be suitable for service both as a medium bomber in the embryonic and still clandestine Luftwaffe and as a prestige-gaining

Dornier Do 17Fs of A/88.

passenger- or mail-carrying aircraft in the national airline, Deutsche Lufthansa, but that, in any problems arising from the attempt to reconcile these contradictory demands, the military requirements should always take precedence. With the advent of the Third Reich, this programme was taken over, and accelerated, by the Technical Division (Abteilung Tecknik) of the new State Air Ministry (Reichsluftfahrtministerium), and by the end of 1934 all three prototypes – the Dornier Do 17, the Heinkel He 111 and the Junkers Ju 86 – had made their first flights.

Of the three, the Dornier Do 17 evinced the least concession to any but a purely military purpose, and it is hard to understand how informed aviation journalists of the day, upon seeing this clean-lined shoulder-wing monoplane with its extraordinarily slender fuselage, could have believed otherwise. Yet they did, and the story was put out, and later universally accepted as historical fact, that the Dornier Do 17 had been conceived to meet a requirement of Deutsche Lufthansa for a fast mail-plane capable of carrying six passengers, that it had been rejected as unsuitable, and that its later conversion into a bomber had come about only by chance. This myth, carefully cultivated by the German organs of propaganda, persisted until the 1980s. It was not dispelled until the researches of Karl Kössler proved that, as early as May 1933, Erhard Milch, the new Secretary of State for Air, had ordered that the first Do 17 prototype was to be the military version, that the second prototype

was to be for Lufthansa, and that the differences between the two were to be so minimal that the civil version could be easily adapted to a military rôle.

The Dornier Do 17c, later re-designated Do 17 V1 to comply with the newly standardised Versuchs (experimental) numbers assigned to prototypes, first flew on 23 November 1934. With a single fin and its thin fuselage unbroken by any glazing except that of the pilot's cabin, the door, and four tiny portholes on each side of the fuselage behind the wing trailing edge, it did indeed merit the 'Flying Pencil' epithet that was within two years to become the Do 17's popular nickname. The second, 'civil', prototype Do 17 V2, with twin rudders, flew in May 1935 and, after testing, the twin-rudder assembly was fitted to the V1 and adopted as standard for all subsequent models. Various prototypes followed until production lines for two versions ordered in quantity by the Luftwaffe, the Do 17E bomber and Do 17F photographic reconnaissance aircraft, were laid down during the course of 1936. Both versions were powered by BMW VI 7,3 twelve-cylinder liquid-cooled vee engines rated at 550hp at 1,530rpm and 750hp for take-off. The Do 17E carried a crew of three: the pilot, a navigator/bomb-aimer seated behind, and a radio operator/gunner who operated a 7.9mm MG 15 machine gun on a movable mounting in a dorsal cockpit protected by a blister housing behind the pilot's cabin, and a similar gun which could be fired down through a sliding hatch in the floor. The crew were accommodated in the forward part of the fuselage. The pilot and bomb-

aimer could see downwards and forwards through the glazed panels of the nose section, and the Zeiss bombsight stood in a small canoed housing that projected below the floor. The Do 17E had a maximum cruising speed of 315km/h, a top speed of 354km/h at sea level, a tactical radius of 500km while carrying 500kg of bombs, and could dive at speeds of up to 550km/h. The Do 17F differed from the Do 17E principally in having three continuous-strip cameras (one RB 10/18, one RB 20/30, and one RB 50/30) installed in the bomb bay, no bombsight or bomb-release mechanism, and provision for an auxiliary fuel tank. The first Do 17Es joined 1/KG 153 at Meersburg and 1/KG 155 at Giebelstad (these being the original bomber groups of the infant Luftwaffe in 1934) early in 1937, while Aufklarung G.(F)/22 and Aufkl. G.(F)/122 received their first Do 17Fs in October, not reaching full statutory strength until April 1938. By this time, however, considerable real operational experience with both subtypes had been gained in the Spanish Civil War.

Although the Republican fighter forces on the Madrid front had been almost obliterated by the end of October 1936, the arrival of two squadrons each of Russian I-15 and I-16 fighters during the first fortnight of November quickly redressed the balance. As a result, the slow and poorly-armed Ju 52/3ms were unable to operate except with strong fighter escorts, and since the Heinkel He 51s were found, to the great surprise and chagrin of the Germans, to be outclassed in all respects by the Russian fighters, the escorts had to be provided by the Italians in their Fiat C.R.32s. The situation was as alarming as it was humiliating, and early in December Haupt Rudolf Freiherr von Moreau, commander of the bomber group (K/88) of the Condor Legion, was recalled to Germany to report the facts in detail. Von Moreau proposed that an experimental bomber group (Versuchs-bomberstaffel), equipped with the three latest bomber types entering service with the Luftwaffe, should be formed in Spain to enable the aircraft to be evaluated in genuine conditions of war. The proposal was enthusiastically backed by Goering, and picked crews were summoned from Spain for intensive conversion courses on the new machines.

Early in February 1937 four Heinkel He 111B-1s, three or four Do 17E-1s and four Ju 86D-1s were unloaded at Cádiz and assembled in the 'Zeppelin Hangar' on Tablada Aerodrome, Seville, the Dorniers being under the technical supervision of the company engineer, Junginger. The twelve bombers were then flown to Salamanca and incorporated into VB/88 under the command of von Moreau. The Do 17E-1s were assigned the Nationalist type code 27 and, as the He 111B-1s were nick-named 'Pedros' in commemoration of von Moreau's previous bomber group of Ju 52s, so the Do 17s were nicknamed 'Pablos'. Whether or not the Do 17Es joined the He 111Bs of VB/88 in attacks on Republican aerodromes and troop concentra-tions at the beginning and end of the Battle of Guadalajara in mid-March is not recorded, but it would be reasonable to suppose that they were. On 26 March 1937 the entire Con-dor Legion was moved north to take part in the Nationalist offensive against Bilbao, the bomber units being based on a specially prepared field near Burgos, which had been under construction as the projected Aeropuerto Nacional before the civil war. On 31 March the offensive began, and at 0710hrs twenty Ju 52s made a concentrated bombing raid on the Basque village of Ochandiano, which was followed at 0900hrs by a second raid by three He 111s and two Do 17Es. The Dorniers, escorted by Bf 109s of J/88, carried out a second mission over Jacinto, 40km south-east of Bilbao, later the same day. Since the effective Republican opposition consisted only of a single squadron of I-15 Chatos, which were not fast enough to intercept the Heinkels and Dorniers of VB/88, the German crews soon came to believe that they could fly over enemy terri-tory unescorted. During a raid on Bilbao by a mixed formation of He 111Bs, Do 17Es and Ju 86Ds on 18 April, however, it happened that six Chatos were patrolling directly above. These dropped down on the bombers and their leader, Teniente Felipe del Rio, was credited with

A Dornier Do 17P of A/88 in 1938.

shooting down a Dornier Do 17, the first combat loss of this type of aircraft in the war. Rio was promoted to Capitán, but was shot down and killed two days later by a Bf 109 (not accidentally by anti-aircraft fire from a Republican destroyer, as is usually stated). The loss of the Do 17 has additional interest, however, for pap-ers found on the body of the pilot, Oberleutnant Hans Sobotka, showed that the aircraft had reached Spain from Germany only thirteen days before, having staged at Rome on 15 April 1937. This might support the contention that the number of Do 17E-1s delivered to Spain was twenty, and not, as some authorities state, twelve.

Meanwhile, fifteen Do 17Fs ar-rived in batches throughout the spring and summer of 1937 to replace the Heinkel He 70F-2s of A/88, which in turn were handed over to the Spanish Nationalists. During this period reinforcements of He 111s enabled K/88 to transfer its Do 17Es to A/88 as well, though these continued to be used as bom-bers when the occasion demanded. During the Battle of Brunete, for example, Do 17Es and Ju 52/3ms carried out night raids on Madrid and Republican aerodromes. In the spring of 1938 Spanish crews were enrolled into K/88 and A/88 for familiarisation, those in the Do 17s being under the command of Cdte Luis Rambaud (see He 51 and Cant Z.501). At the end of July 1938, five Do 17Es were formed into 8-G-27, commanded by Rambaud, the first unit of the Spanish Nationalist air arm to be equipped with this type.

Rambaud was killed when his Do 17 crashed on 28 October 1938, one Do 17 was shot down during the Catalonian Campaign, and two more lost in a collision on 4 April 1939, five days after the end of the civil war. Meanwhile, a small number of Do 17Ps (some sources say four, and others ten) had arrived in Spain in October 1938 to reinforce the Do 17Fs of A/88. These were powered by BMW 132M B/1 radial engines rated at 870hp for take-off and 665hp at 1,250rpm, which increased the maximum speed to 400km/h. Although the Dornier Do 17 partici-pated in all the major battles and campaigns of the civil war from March 1937 onwards, it was soon found that, when faced with a fast fighter such as the Russian I-16, its light defensive armament made it dangerously vulnerable. This experi-ence led to the complete redesign of the forward fuselage. The Spaniards nicknamed the Do 17 *Bacalao*, be-cause its thin profile and 'flattened-out' planform reminded them of the yellow-brown strips of dried and salted cod (bacalao) seen hanging in every grocery.

The total number of Do 17s delivered to Spain is still uncertain. Some authorities put it at thirty-one (twelve Do 17E-1s, fifteen Do 17Fs and four Do 17Ps), and others at forty-seven. Nor, in the absence of Condor Legion records, are there accurate figures for losses, although an estimate of ten is usually agreed. It is known, however, that in March 1940 41 Escuadrilla (later Grupo 44) of the Ejercito del Aire still had thirteen Do 17s on strength. If the total number delivered was thirty-one, and wartime losses were only ten, then eight must have been lost in

The Douglas DC-1 at the Grand Central Air Terminal, Los Angeles. (Douglas Historical Foundation, via Harry Gann)

peacetime duties in a single year. For reasons such as this, the figures available at the time of writing are clearly unsatisfactory.

Span 18m; length 16.25m; height 4.32m; wing area 55sq m.

Empty weight 4,500kg; loaded weight 7,040kg.

Maximum speed 354km/h at sea level, 310km/h at 4,000m; cruising speed 315km/h at sea level, 263km/h at 4,000m; range 1,000km; maximum range without bomb load, 1,590km.

Douglas DC-1

In the summer of 1932 rumours began to circulate through the American aviation world that the Boeing company was developing a revolutionary all-metal twin-engined twelve-passenger monoplane with a retractable undercarriage. It was said that companies of the United Airlines Group, of which Boeing was a member, had already placed a tentative order for the first sixty production machines, should the prototype prove successful, on condition that Boeing should refuse orders from rival airlines. Since it was unlikely that the new Boeing would be a failure, it was clear that within two years United Airlines would possess machines that would outperform all other airliners in the world, and

The DC-1 in LAPE service in January 1939. (Emiliani)

would have a monopoly on them.

Deciding that the only way to counter this threat was to beat it with something better, Jack Frye, vice-president of operations at Transcontinental and Western Air (TWA), wrote to other leading aircraft manufacturers on 2 August 1932, giving specifications for a three-engined airliner able to carry twelve passengers in maximum comfort for 1,000 miles at a cruising speed of 150mph. Its gross weight was not to exceed 14,200lb, it was to climb at 1,200ft/min, and it would have all the latest navigational aids. Five days later Donald Douglas, founder and President of the Douglas Aircraft Company, went to New York to meet the board of TWA, and within three weeks secured a contract for a single test aircraft. During exhausting haggling over technical details, TWA agreed that the aircraft should be powered by two engines instead of three, but Charles Lindbergh, TWA's technical adviser, insisted

that it be able to take off on one engine with a full load. The Boeing monoplane, the Model 247, first flew on 8 February 1933 and earned its place in aeronautical history as the world's first modern airliner, but was overshadowed by the Douglas DC-1 (Douglas Commercial One), which flew for the first time on 1 July 1933.

The Douglas DC-1 (c/n 1137, registration NC223Y), powered by two 710hp Wright Cyclone SGR-1820-F1 radial engines developed especially for the prototype, possessed all the refinements of the Boeing and several more – notably the rigid and light Northrop multicellular wing and a remarkably streamlined aerodynamic shape. The passenger cabin, which accommodated twelve passengers in cushioned high-backed seats, was heated and sound-proofed, and performance, despite a gross weight of 17,500lb, comfortably exceeded the TWA requirements. The DC-1's cruising speed was 198.8mph, and its range 1,000 miles. The production version, designated DC-2, had its fuselage lengthened by 2ft to accommodate two more passengers, and its range was increased to 1,060 miles.

In 1934, when DC-2s began to enter service with TWA, Pan American Airlines, Eastern Airlines, Western Airlines and American Airlines in the USA, and with KLM and Panagra abroad, it was evident that nothing could match them for speed or comfort. In October 1934 the KLM DC-2 PH-AJU *Uiver* caused a sensation by winning the handicap section of the great MacRobertson

Mildenhall–Melbourne air race while carrying three passengers and 30,000 airmail letters, and in competition with other aircraft especially built or converted for the race. An enlarged, sleeper-accommodation version of the DC-2 with re-designed wings and tail, the Douglas DST (later DC-3), appeared in 1934. It was to become one of the most successful aircraft of all time.

Having fulfilled its experimental purpose with TWA, the one-and-only DC-1 was sold to Howard Hughes, TWA's largest stockholder, in January 1936 and re-engined with 875hp Wright Cyclone F-52s for an attempt to break the round-the-world record set by Wiley Post. Its wings were replaced by those of a DC-2 (c/n 1292), the fin and rudder were enlarged, and the fuselage, with the windows skinned over, was filled with petrol tanks to extend the range to 6,000 miles. For some reason Hughes abandoned this plan, and in December 1936 the DC-1 became one of the eighteen aircraft for which Robert Cuse applied for an export licence to ship to Republican Spain (see Appendix II). It was valued on the licence at $70,000, though the sum paid by the Spanish Republicans was probably larger. Its real market value was in the region of $50,000. It did not sail aboard the *Mar Cantábrico*, however, and its history over the next eighteen months is obscure. Indeed, it is not even certain that the sale to Cuse was finalised. According to some reports, it was used briefly by the US Army Air Corps.

On 27 May 1938 the DC-1 was bought by Lord Forbes (see de Havilland D.H.89 Dragon Rapide), who wanted to fly the Atlantic in it. Howard Hughes dissuaded him, and the aircraft, which by then had flown 1,370 hours, was shipped to London on the deck of a freighter. Too big to pass through the dock gates, the aircraft was transferred to a lighter and unloaded at the Ford factory at Dagenham. After assembly by KLM engineers, it was re-registered G-AFIF. In September 1938 Lord Forbes used it to fly parties of journalists to Munich to cover the Sudetenland crisis and then, because he found it too large to retain as a private aircraft, it was sold, possibly through a dealer, to SFTA (see

Appendix II). It seems to have crossed to Republican Spain in November 1938 and, re-registered EC-AGN, it served with LAPE as Fleet No 39. The DC-1 probably assisted in evacuating Republican members of government to France during the collapse of Catalonia in February 1939, but must have returned to Spain, for on 23 March it was the aircraft in which two Republican officers, Coronel Ortega and Coronel Garijo, flew from Madrid to Burgos in a vain attempt to negotiate peace terms more honourable than the unconditional surrender demanded by Gen Franco.

During the last week of the civil war the DC-1 flew parties of senior Republican officials to France. It was returned to Spain, with the DC-2s and other aircraft, in May 1939, and on 7 July was transferred to Iberia, re-registered EC-AAE, and christened *Manuél Negrón* after Comandante Manuél Negrón de las Cuevas, the Nationalist airman killed during the Battle of Teruel. In December 1940 the DC-1 made a belly-landing on Málaga Aerodrome and was wrecked beyond repair. It had happened, however, that during the civil war the wooden float on which the effigy of Nuestra Señora de la Esperanza (Our Lady of Hope) used to be carried through the streets of Málaga during Holy Week had been burned by an anti-clerical mob, and in 1941 a new, aluminium float (or *andas*) was made from the fuselage of the DC-1. It is all that remains of the progenitor of the most famous

Douglas DC-2 c/n 1330, EC-XAX Hercules. (Iberia, via R S Allen)

and successful line of civil aircraft ever produced.

Span 85ft 11in; length 59ft.
Empty weight 11,780lb; loaded weight 17,500lb.
Maximum speed 210mph; cruising speed 200mph; ceiling 23,000ft; range 1,000 miles.

Douglas DC-2

The genesis and early history of this famous aeroplane are summarised in the section on the Douglas DC-1. In 1933 the Dutch aircraft manufacturer Anthony Fokker secured the rights to import, assemble and distribute the DC-2 in Europe. Forty DC-2s were sold in this way: nineteen to KLM and three to KNILM; a few to private owners in Holland; and others to Switzerland, Spain, Poland, Germany, France, Italy, Austria and Czechoslovakia. Thus the DC-2 began to revolutionise civil aviation in Europe just as it was doing in the Americas. The various export versions were designated DC-2-115, with a capital-letter suffix to denote the internal modifications required by particular customers, and each aircraft was assigned a Fokker import number on leaving the Douglas factory – two small details that have proved helpful in trying to sort out the confusion that has prevailed over the history of the six DC-2s in the Spanish Civil War.

Throughout 1934 there had been debate in Spanish aeronautical circles over whether to re-equip the state airline Líneas Aéreas Postales Españolas (LAPE) with Douglas DC-2s or cheaper, but smaller, Lockheed Electras. The Director General de Aeronáutica, Com-

This photograph purports to show Orion *(LAPE No 22), but in fact shows* EC-XAX Hercules - *note '-AX' under the wing and the lettering above the windows. Why it was so retouched is a puzzle.* (José Warleta, via R S Allen)

The DC-2 c/n 1334, EC-AAY Orion.

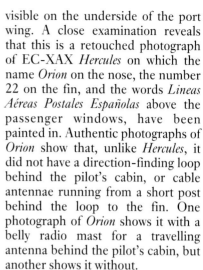

visible on the underside of the port wing. A close examination reveals that this is a retouched photograph of EC-XAX *Hercules* on which the name *Orion* on the nose, the number 22 on the fin, and the words *Lineas Aéreas Postales Españolas* above the passenger windows, have been painted in. Authentic photographs of *Orion* show that, unlike *Hercules*, it did not have a direction-finding loop behind the pilot's cabin, or cable antennae running from a short post behind the loop to the fin. One photograph of *Orion* shows it with a belly radio mast for a travelling antenna behind the pilot's cabin, but another shows it without.

3   DC-2-115J c/n 1417; Douglas Export No E-1762, Fokker No 29. This aircraft left the Douglas factory on 26 November 1935. It

andante Ismael Warleta, advocated the DC-2 on the grounds that it would put LAPE not only on a competitive footing with KLM and Swissair, but in a position of advantage over French and British airlines, which had no modern airliners at all. The issue was decided by the outstanding performance of the KLM DC-2 in the MacRobertson England–Australia air race in October 1934, and, on the very night that the news of this achievement reached Europe, Warleta authorised Vicente Roa, who was in Amsterdam, to place an order with Fokker for five DC-2-115s. The order was on cigarette-paper written in a café. The first four were delivered as follows:

1   DC-2-115D c/n 1330; Douglas Export No E-1321, Fokker No 8. Accepted by Fokker at the Douglas factory on 12 January 1935, it left the USA 11 March 35 for Cherbourg, and was assembled at Quérqueville, to where it had been trans-

The DC-2 c/n 1417, EC-EBB Sagitario. (Iberia, via R S Allen)

ported by lighter. Bearing the temporary Dutch registration PH-AKF, it flew to Spain in April, where it was registered EC-XAX and named *Hercules* after the constellation. It made its inaugural flight to Paris on 29 May 1935 as LAPE fleet No 21.

2   DC-2-115B c/n 1334; Douglas Export No E-1330, Fokker No 12. Accepted by Fokker on 1 March 1935, it reached Spain on 29 May 1935. Registered EC-AAY, it was christened *Orion* and given LAPE fleet No 22. The first seeds of the confusion alluded to above were sown by the publicity agents for LAPE, who issued a photograph purporting to show *Orion*, with 22 on the fin, in which, however, AX is

was flying for LAPE by the beginning of March 1936, although its Spanish certificate is dated 31 March 1936. Registered EC-EBB and named *Sagitario*, it was given LAPE fleet No 24. This DC-2 is distinguishable by an enlarged fin, the leading edge of which continues in a thin strip to the top of the curve of the rudder. It had black propeller spinners.

4   DC-2-115J c/n 1521; Douglas Export No E-1906, Fokker No 30. This machine left the Douglas factory on 24 April 1936, arrived

at Cherbourg aboard the *Europa* on 15 May 1936, was at Le Bourget on 16 June, and reached Barajas, Madrid, a day or two later. Although there is no doubt that it became LAPE fleet No 25, there was for many years uncertainty over its registration and name. Until 1979, in view of the lack of official registration records for the weeks immediately preceding the civil war, Spanish authorities agreed that it was registered EC-BBE and named *Granada.* More recent researches in post-war Spanish registration records show, however, that it was registered EC-BFF, and this is confirmed by Douglas records, which state that it was painted EC-BFF before leaving the factory. Moreover, a recently discovered photograph shows that it was named *Mallorca,* not *Granada.*

The Spanish Civil War broke out a month after the arrival of the fourth DC-2, EC-BFF. One DC-2 at Le Bourget, Paris, was hastily summoned to Madrid and arrived early on the morning of 18 July, without passengers. At the same time, two DC-2s, No 22 ('AAY) and No 25 ('BFF), were sent to Tablada Aerodrome, Seville, under the command of LAPE operations manager Joaquín Mellado, who had orders to load them with bombs and bomb Tetuán, where the uprising against the Madrid government had just been proclaimed. Douglas DC-2 No 25 ('BFF) was immobilised when a monarchist officer, Capitán Vara de Rey, fired his shotgun into one of the engines. The other DC-2, with a pair of Fokker F-VIIb3ms, flew on to bomb Tetuán and returned directly to Madrid. That night Tablada was taken over by the rebels, and DC-2 No 25, EC-BFF *Mallorca,* which was repaired by 25 July, became Nationalist property.

From this point an almost inextricable confusion has existed concerning the names, registrations, and identities of the (eventually five) Douglas DC-2s that were in Republican service. The history of the Nationalist DC-2, on the other hand, presents no problems. As soon as it was repaired it made a few flights ferrying Nationalist troops from Spanish Morocco to the mainland, and on 6 August, with Capitán

Carlos de Haya as pilot, it was the aircraft in which Gen Franco himself flew from Spanish Morocco to Seville. Thereafter, Haya flew the DC-2 on numerous bombing and reconnaissance missions and, most notably, used it to drop supplies to the Nationalists besieged in the monastery and shrine of Santa María de la Cabeza in the mountains of Córdoba. Eventually, bearing the military serial 42-1 and renamed *Capitán Vara de Rey* in honour of its captor, it became Franco's personal transport, and remained so for the rest of the civil war. An Irishman, William Winterbottom, is said to have served as copilot for a time.

The three Republican Douglas DC-2s (LAPE Nos 22, 21 and 24) were used on a great variety of missions as bombers, troop transports, civil transports and for flying cargoes of Spanish gold to Paris to pay for armaments – a service which began on 25 July 1936, before Non-Intervention was declared, and continued intensively until the bulk of the remaining Spanish gold reserve was shipped to the Soviet Union at the end of October 1936. Thereafter, these flights (carrying gold, jewellery and valuables) continued intermittently until the middle of 1938. Conversion for the bombing rôle was primitive in the extreme, but could be effected in an hour or

The DC-2 c/n 1521, EC-BFF, was hitherto said to have been named Granada, *but this picture, taken on 20 July 1936 at Tablada, Seville, after its capture by the Nationalists, shows that it was named* Mallorca. *(Arráez)*

two. The passenger door was removed and a slanting wooden chute, rather like a washboard, was affixed to the floor. Seventy to eighty 24lb bombs were laid on the seats and passed by hand to the bombardier, who slid them down the chute at a signal from the bomb aimer, who was equipped with a Warleta bombsight on the flightdeck. Heavier bombs of 110lb to 220lb were laid on the floor and swung into position by rope and tackle. A window on each side was removed for the mounting of two machine guns and, thus equipped, the Republican DC-2s carried out frequent raids on such targets as Tablada Aerodrome, the Campamento barracks outside Madrid (briefly held by the rebels), the Loyola barracks at Oviedo, the Pelayo barracks at San Sebastián, the Alcázar at Toledo, Granada, Algeciras, La Linea, and various aerodromes in Spanish Morocco. On 4 August, during a raid on Badajoz, EC-EBB *Sagitario* encountered the Nationalist DC-2 EC-BFF, and the two converted airliners flew round while their gunners fired through the cabin windows. It has been said that one of the DC-2s had a hole cut in the roof behind the pilot's cabin for a dorsal gunner equipped with a Lewis gun on a Scarff ring, but no photograph exists to confirm this.

Two more DC-2s joined the Republican forces during the civil war:

DC-2-115M c/n 1527; Douglas Export No E-1910, Fokker No 31; accepted by Fokker on 17 August 1936. Company records do not spe-

Ex-EC-BFF Mallorca *as General Franco's personal transport, 42-1.*

cify this DC-2's destination, but note that it was painted with zinc-chromate to resist pitting by blown sand, which suggests that it was the fifth of the DC-2s intended for LAPE. On 9 September 1936 Louis de Marmier, the chief test pilot of Air France, who had recently deli-vered a Bloch MB 210 to Republi-can Spain, flew a DC-2 from Le Havre to Le Bourget, Paris. This must have been c/n 1527, since no other DC-2 was shipped to Europe between April and November 1936. It became LAPE No 26, and as such made its first gold run to Paris ten days later (17 September 1936), a second on 22 September, and a third on 7 October.

DC-2-115D c/n 1320; no traceable Douglas export number, Fokker No 2. This, only the second DC-2 imported into Europe, had been ordered as the personal aeroplane of President Dollfuss of Austria. By the time Fokker had accepted it on 22 September 1934, however, Dollfuss had been murdered by the Nazis (25 July 1934) and, when it arrived in Holland, Fokker retained it as an unregistered demonstrator. In 1935 the Austrian government bought it after all as a ministerial transport, with the registration A-500 painted on wings and fuselage. On 5 April 1936 it was bought by Swissair and registered HB-ISA, though whether or not this was applied to the aircraft is uncertain. In October 1936 it was sold to the Spanish Republicans as part of a complicated deal organised by the celebrated Swiss-Lithuanian barrister Vladimir Rosenbaum, the other aircraft in the deal being two Swissair Lockheed Orions and the sole surviving General Aviation Clark GA 43A. The ostensible buyer

was Air France, and the intermedi-ary the Spanish novelist Antonio Espina, whose rôle in the transaction was similar to that of the other Spanish novelist, Corpus Barga, in the purchase of the Dewoitine D.372s and Potez 54s in August 1936. When Rosenbaum was brought to trial and gaoled for this transaction in 1937, Swissair denied all knowledge of a 'Spanish connec-tion' to the deal. José-María Carrer-as, the LAPE pilot who ferried the DC-2 from Le Bourget to Barcelona on 26 October 1936, told the author, however, that, according to Espina, Swissair had agreed to sell the DC-2, which the Spaniards wanted, on condition that the Spaniards also bought the other three aircraft, which they did not want. In Spain, A-500 was used for a time as a flying headquarters by the Commander-in-Chief of the Russian units in Spain, Maj-Gen Jacob Smush-kievich, who was given (perhaps for this very reason) the nom-de-guerre 'General Douglas'. In the summer of 1937 the DC-2 was transferred to LAPE (No 27, EC-AGA), and made three gold runs to Paris in Septem-ber and October. In 1938, after suffering serious damage in an acci-dent, it was rebuilt, and on 20 November it was photographed on Malta, where it had landed while taking Republican officials to Ank-ara for the funeral of Kemal Atatürk, the founder of modern Turkey.

Long after the civil war, Republi-can airmen and mechanics remem-bered the DC-2s with great admira-tion and affection. Their high speed, rate of climb and ceiling enabled them to escape all Nationalist fight-ers except the Messerschmitt Bf 109, and their ruggedness was nothing short of astonishing. They

operated from secret fields in moun-tain valleys, or on beaches, and were never in hangars at any time during the war. As troop transports they could carry up to thirty-five soldiers at a time, and on one occasion, while landing on Tarragona aerodrome with such a load, a DC-2 struck a bomb crater and bent its wing seven-teen degrees out of true, yet it was able to take off again and return safely to base. On another occasion an ammunition box exploded while being unloaded and blew a wide hole in the side of the fuselage, warping the structure so badly that the crew thought that the Douglas would never fly again. Nevertheless, work-ing through the night in the open air, they patched up the hole and found, after a test flight, that the machine flew as well as ever. In his memoirs the Republican air chief Gen Hidal-go de Cisneros recalls the amaze-ment of visiting Douglas engineers during the civil war upon discover-ing that the DC-2s had been flown, with no ill effects, with their passen-ger doors removed.

Much of the confusion over the histories of the individual Republi-can DC-2s derives from four state-ments made at different times and by different writers. The first is that c/n 1521 EC-BFF, LAPE No 25, captured by the Nationalists on 18 July 1936, was named *Granada* when in fact it was named *Mallorca*, though why it should have been named after a Balearic island when its predecessors were named after constellations is still a puzzle. The second statement is that, after the loss of No 25 to the Nationalists, the Republicans renamed No 22 ('AAY *Orion*) *Granada*. The third is that the Republican DC-2 destroyed by bombing at La Albericia aerodrome, Santander, on 6 April 1937 was 'EC-BFF *Granada*'. The fourth is that No 22 'EC-AAY *Granada* (ex-*Orion*)', was destroyed by sabotage in France in October or November 1936.

The first piece of evidence that sheds some light on this tangle is a report in the Paris newspaper *Le Temps* for 30 July 1936, which says that on 29 July a Spanish transport aircraft named *Granada* brought a cargo of gold to Le Bourget. This proves that one of the Republican DC-2s had been so renamed by that date. Granada had been captured by the Nationalists on 23 July, and had been bombed several times since, and the new name perhaps commemorated a raid carried out by this aircraft. Most of the gold flights at this period were made by No 22 ('AYY *Orion*), the log book of the LAPE mechanic Macías recording flights on 30 July, and 3, 5, 6 and 12 August. The first gold flight, however, was made on 25 July, and there may have been others before the 30th. On the other hand, in the only photograph of a DC-2 with *Granada* painted on the nose (a group of Republican militiamen in the foreground are making defiant clenched-fist salutes – see p.11), the machine has the red nose and Douglas flash down the fuselage seen in photographs of No 24 *Sagitario* and No 25 *Mallorca*, but not on *Hercules* or *Orion*. Moreover, it has a belly mast for a trailing aerial, which most photographs of *Orion* do not show. Nevertheless, a note in the British Foreign Office correspondence on the Spanish Civil War reports that, on 29 September 1936, a DC-2 registered EC-XAX (No 21 *Hercules*) and named *Toledo* landed at Parme-Biarritz en route from Santander to Paris. It had a red flash down the fuselage and a 'gun turret' in the nose (which might have been the nose landing-lights misconstrued by the eyewitness, or a machine gun projecting out of the window of the pilot's cabin). Apparently, then, *Hercules* had been painted with a red flash shortly before the outbreak of the civil war to match the two later arrivals, and presumably the same had been done to *Orion*, to which a radio mast might have been added as well. It is possible that the assertion that *Orion* was renamed *Granada*, first made by the aviation writer Miguel Sanchís in

an article in *Avion* in February 1970 (and since then much doubted by other investigators, including the author) was correct after all. As to the name *Toledo*, the Republicans had frequently bombed the Nationalist garrison besieged in the Alcázar fortress in Toledo during August and September, and the new name perhaps commemorated a raid carried out by *Hercules*.

Neither No 22 *Orion/Granada* nor No 26 (c/n 1527, which arrived in Republican Spain in September 1936) survived the war. If the story that No 22 *Orion/Granada* was destroyed by sabotage in France in the autumn of 1936 is true, why was the incident not reported, and in a sensational fashion, by the French right-wing press? According to ex-LAPE pilot J-M Carreras, the DC-2 destroyed by bombing at Santander in April 1937 was the last to arrive – that is No 26. As to the assertion that it was EC-BFF *Granada*, without some supporting evidence one can only keep an open mind.

EC-XAX Hercules *in Republican service during the civil war. Sitting on the wing is the pilot, Jorge Xuclá.*

Reports that the French air ministry DC-2, c/n 1333 F-AKHD, was sold to the Spanish Republicans can be discounted. Although it may have flown to Spain at some time, it was still in France in 1939. Finally, on the official registration list of the surviving Douglases in 1940 (four DC-2s and the DC-1), one machine is given the construction number 'A-540'. This is a confusion with A-500, the original Austrian registration of c/n 1320, which it is now known became 42-5 after the civil war.

In the winter of 1939-40 the five Douglases, of which four had been returned from France, were acquired by Tráfico Aéreo Español, which was taken over by Iberia in June 1940. The DC-2 histories may thus be summarised:

No 21: DC-2-115D, c/n 1330, EC-XAX *Hercules/Toledo*; Nationalist 42-3; Iberia 1940, EC-AAD *Carlos de Haya*; last service 8 September; w/o 25 September 1947.
No 22: DC-2-115B, c/n 1334, EC-AAY *Orion/Granada*(?); destroyed during civil war.

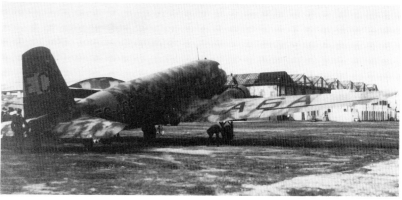

The DC-2 c/n 1320 (ex-Swissair and re-registered EC-AGA) at Malta on 20 November 1938, while taking Republican officials to Ankara to attend the funeral of Kemal Atatürk.

No 24: DC-2-115J, c/n 1417, EC-EBB *Sagitario/Granada* (?); Nationalist 42-4; Iberia 1940, EC-AAB *Ramón Franco*; last service 19 October 1945; w/o 25 September 1947.

No 25: DC-2-115J, c/n 1521, EC-BFF *Mallorca);* Nationalist 42-1 *Vara de Rey*; Iberia 1940, EC-AAC *Vara de Rey*, but later renamed *Tajo*; destroyed in crash at Barcelona 3 February 1944, two crew and six passengers killed, one crew and two passengers injured; w/o 25 September 1947.

No 26: DC-2-115M, c/n 1527, registration and name uncertain; destroyed at Santander 6 April 1937.

No 27: DC-2-115D, c/n 1320, A-500, HB-ISA, EC-AGA; Nationalist 42-5; Iberia 1940, EC-AAA *García Morato*; last service 11 April 1946; w/o 25 September 1947.

Assuming that all the Spanish DC-2s had 720hp Wright Cyclone SGR-1820-F2 engines, the following data apply: span 85ft; length 62ft; height 16ft 3in; wing area 939sq ft.

Empty weight 12,010lb; loaded weight 18,200lb; useful load 6,190lb; payload 3,405lb or 16 passengers and 685lb baggage (with 360gals fuel).

Maximum speed 213mph; cruising

The Fairchild K.R.22 EC-VAV at Tablada, Seville, on 20 July 1936. (Arráez)

speed 200mph at 14,000ft; landing speed 63mph; ceiling 23,000ft; range 700–1,016 miles.

Fairchild K.R.22C-7E

A light, parasol-winged two-seat sports monoplane, the Fairchild K.R.22 was a creation of the Kreidner-Reisner Aircraft Company absorbed by Fairchild in 1929. The wing, which had wooden spars and metal ribs, was covered with fabric and had a metal-reinforced leading edge. The ailerons extended the entire length of the trailing edge except for the cut-out above the rear cockpit. The fuselage was of metal tubing with fabric covering, and the wheels of the wide-track undercarriage were housed in streamlined spats. In the K.R.22C-7E version, the 125hp Warner Scarab radial engine was housed in a long-chord NACA cowling. The Fairchild K.R.22 carried a pilot, passenger and 65lb of luggage.

In May 1934 Pablo Atienza Benjumea, of the Aero-Club de Andalucía at Seville, bought a K.R.22C-7E (c/n 1008) which was registered EC-VAV. During the first few weeks of the civil war it was employed on numerous military missions, on one occasion scattering a platoon of Republican militia when the observer hurled some pumpkins down upon their heads. It was damaged when it collided with a Heinkel He 51 while taxiing, but was repaired and survived the war. It bore the serial 30-60 and continued flying until 1949, when it was written off after an accident.

Some Spanish aviation writers have said that a K.R.22C-7F (145hp Warner Super Scarab) was employed on the Republican side as a trainer at the elementary flying school at La Ribera, San Javier, and have suggested that it must have been one of the six K.R.22C-Fs supplied to the Mexican government in 1934. No such aircraft appears in any of the lists of the aeroplanes collected by the Spanish Republican ambassador at Vera Cruz, or in lists of those that were shipped on board the *Ibai* in December 1937. If one did reach Republican Spain, therefore, it must have been embarked on some other ship, undetected by the FBI or the Mexican authorities.

Span 32ft 10in; length 22ft; height 7ft 11in; wing area 170sq ft.

Empty weight 1,102lb; loaded weight 1,750lb.

Maximum speed 130mph; cruising speed 110mph; landing speed 48mph; climb 650ft/min; ceiling 17,300ft; range 380 miles.

Fairchild 91

At the time of its first appearance, early in 1935, the graceful Fairchild 91 (originally Model XA-492), designed by Armand Thiebolt of the Fairchild Manufacturing Corporation at Hagerstown, Maryland, was the largest, fastest and most advanced single-engined amphibian flying-boat in the world. Of all-metal stressed-skin construction, it was powered by a 750hp Pratt & Whitney Hornet S2E-G nine-cylinder radial engine housed in a nacelle above the fuselage, angled to give downthrust. The undercarriage retracted outwards into the wing, and eight passengers were accommodated in two cabins divided by a watertight bulkhead. Six examples were ordered off the drawing board by Pan American Airlines for use by their subsidiaries in China and Brazil, but, after the passing of US safety regulations proscribing the use of single-engined machines on commercial passenger services, the order was cancelled. Nevertheless, of the seven Fairchild 91s built, two were used by Panair do Brazil, two were exported to Japan, one was sold to a private owner, and one to

the Museum of Natural History, New York, for exploration in New Guinea.

In December 1936 the prototype, c/n 9401 NC14743, was bought by Robert Cuse of the Vimalert Corporation (see Vultee V1-A and Appendix II), and was one of the eight aircraft shipped aboard the *Mar Cantábrico* and captured by the Nationalists in the Bay of Biscay on 8 March 1937. After assembly at El Ferrol, Galicia, the Fairchild 91 was used, along with three Dornier Wals of 1-E-70, for reconnaissance patrols along the Biscay coast. Because there was no possibility of arming it, however, the Fairchild was soon relegated to safer transport and liaison duties. After the end of the northern campaign in October 1937 it was transferred to Cádiz, where, in the complete absence of Republican aircraft, it resumed naval reconnaissance duties. In December 1938 it joined the Heinkel He 60/Dornier Wal squadron 1-E-70 at El Atalyón, near Melilla in Spanish Morocco, where it remained until it was withdrawn from service in 1941. Besides the usual Nationalist markings (St Andrew's Cross on the rudder, black discs and black and white stripes on the wings), the Fairchild 91 carried the legend *Virgen de Chamorro* on the rear fuselage sides, the military serial 63-1 in black under the cabin and on the fin, and a painting of Popeye the sailor, throwing down a bomb, on each side of the nose.

Span 56ft; length 46ft 8⅓in; height 4ft 8in; wing area 483sqft.

Empty weight 6,596lb; loaded weight 10,500lb.

Maximum speed 166mph; cruising speed 151mph; ceiling 15,600ft; range 665 miles.

Farman F.190/291 series

At the end of the 1920s several French aircraft manufacturers, inspired by the success of small four-passenger monoplanes in the USA, decided to venture into the market. The Farman contribution, the F.190, displayed all the angularity, including a perfectly rectangular wing with square-cut tips, that characterised the products of this company. Constructed of wood, with

The Fairchild 91 in Nationalist service.

fabric covering, and powered by a 230hp Gnome-Rhône 5 Ba Titan uncowled radial engine, the prototype first flew in July 1928. In November, after extensive trials, the wing was changed to a hexagonal trapezoid planform, and the rudder enlarged and counterbalanced accordingly. Fifty-seven F.190s were produced, at least four of which found their way to Spain during the civil war, and from among the large family of derivatives (of which a further fifty or so were built), those that also concern us are the F.191/1, F.192/1, F.193, F.194, F.291/1, and F.391.

Of these, one was in Spain when the war began. This was an F.194 powered by a 250hp Hispano-Suiza 6Mb in-line liquid-cooled engine. Only four of this version were built, and the last was sold directly to José Canudas (pilot and owner of an aerodrome bearing his name near Barcelona) in 1932 and registered EC-AAR. In 1936 Canudas, by now Director General de Aeronáutica to the Generalitat (the regional government of Catalonia) resold the Farman to José-Maria Carreras, a LAPE pilot and head of an aeronautical co-operative society. After the outbreak of fighting the F.194 was commandeered by the Servicios de Aeronáutica de la Generalitat and used on reconnaissance and transport duties. On 21 August 1936, however, the civil pilot Juán Balcells decided he was on the wrong side and absconded to France in it, landing at La California Aerodrome,

Nice. While Balcells made his way, through Italy, to Nationalist Spain, the F.194 was returned to Barcelona, where it was destroyed shortly afterwards.

The other members of the F.190 family in the Spanish Civil War seem to have been:

To the Republicans
1   F.190 c/n 43/-, F-AJMV, 230hp Gnome-Rhône 5 Ba radial. Sold by Marcel Avignon of Montpelier to an untraceable buyer in Marseilles, this aircraft disappears from the records in August 1936.
2   F.190 c/n 55/7299, F-ALQK. Rémy Clément's personal aeroplane, this was sold abroad, almost certainly to Spanish Republicans, in October 1936 (see F.192/1 below).
3   F.190 c/n 11/7147, F-AIYM *Paris-Saigon*. Once used for a long-distance flight to Saigon by Bailly and Goullet, this F.190 was sold by Lucien Maniglier to SFTA in January 1937, converted to an ambulance and sent to Republican Spain (?).
4   F.190 c/n 32/7153, F-AJIA. Registered to Constant Cresty, it was 'sold abroad' on 25 September 1936.
5   F.192/1 c/n 2/7467, 230hp Salmson 9Aba radial. Only two F.192s were built (in 1935), and the second, F-ANNV, was bought by Rémy Clément on 25 September 1936 (see F-ALQK and F-AJIA, above). Clément, who was then procuring aircraft for the Spanish Republicans and was to serve with distinction in the Résistance, sent it to Barcelona on 20 October 1936.
6   F.193 c/n 3/7267, F-ALFB, 230hp Farman 9Ea radial. Con-

A Farman F.193 captured by the Nationalists at the end of the war. (Arráez)

The Farman F.190 No 11, F-AIYM, in which Bailly and Goulette had made a flight from Paris to Saigon, went to Republican Spain in January 1937. (Liron)

verted from F.197 c/n 5/7267 with a 240hp Lorraine 7Me radial in 1929, this aircraft was sold to R Peitz in November 1936, but had probably left for Spain at end of September. This is presumably the Farman, bearing the Nationalist insignia and the postwar military serial 30-112, shown in a much-reproduced photograph and often identified as an F.402.

7   F.193 c/n 6/7421, F-AMXL. Owned by Albert Bucciali and kept at Toussus, Paris, this machine disappears from records after March 1937. It may, however, have gone to the Nationalists.

8   F.291/1 c/n 4/7335, F-ALUI *Jöe II*. This aircraft was custom-built for Maryse Hilz in 1935 as an F.291 and converted to an F.291/1 with a 350hp Gnome-Rhône radial for long-distance flying. It was sold to R Guilloux, a member of the Escadre España, and was probably in Spain by September 1936. The Registration was cancelled on 25 March 1937. Maryse Hilz's Breguet 27S *Jöe III* is believed to have gone to Republican Spain as well.

To the Nationalists

9   F.191 *Aquila Branca* (White Eagle), powered by a 230hp

Gnome-Rhône 5 Ba Titan IV radial engine. A one-off long-distance version, built to the order of the Portuguese government for a proposed record-breaking flight that was never made, the *Aquila Branca* had no windscreen, there being a large petrol tank in the front part of the cockpit. The pilot, who sat in the passenger cabin, looked forwards through a periscope and sideways through two square windows cut in the fuselage sides. Painted white, it was transferred to the Cia Portuguesa de Aviaco for photographic survey duties. On 26 August 1931 it was commandeered by a group of revolutionaries, led by Ten Cor Sarmento de Beires, opposing the Salazar dictatorship, and used in a bombing raid against the Almada fortress outside Lisbon. The coup failed, and the rebels flew to Seville. The Farman was returned to Portugal, but in July 1936 was lent to the Spanish Nationalists and used for liaison duties, usually piloted by the Marqués de Merito. On 28 August 1936 Capitán José Larrauri Mercadillo (see Heinkel He 46 and Junkers Ju 52/3m) flew Gen Franco to Saragossa, and on the 30th returned to Seville with the money donated by the province of Aragón to pay for

three He 51 fighters. It returned to Portugal, where it was destroyed when it crashed into the sea off Praia de Santa Cruz on 8 August 1937, its five occupants being killed.

10   F.391 c/n 3/7385, F-AMTH. This Farman was registered to Henry Lévêque de Vilmorin, who was the *Le Jour* correspondent in Nationalist Spain, where he was regarded with especial favour. The last Bureau Veritas check in which it appears was on 5 September 1936, and the registration was cancelled on 23 March 1937. A Condor Legion photograph showing the rear half of a Farman of the F.190 type with 30-5 on the fuselage could possibly be this aeroplane (if it is not F-AMXL, above), especially since the low military serial number indicates that it must have reached Burgos early in the civil war. This would make it, together with the Caudron Aiglon F-APCE (30-6) and perhaps the F.193 F-AMXL, one of the very few French aircraft delivered to the Nationalists during the civil war. Whether it was sold or presented is not known.

One other F.291, c/n 1/7265, F-ALEZ, was indirectly involved in the Spanish Civil War. Originally owned by Edouard Corniglion-

A Farman F.231/354. (Liron)

A Farman F.200. (Philip Jarrett)

Maximum speed 170km/h; ceiling 3,500m; range 400km.

Farman F.354

Both the Farman F.230/239 and F.350/359 families of light sports aeroplanes of the early 1930s were derived from the F.200 low-wing monoplane of 1923. One of these, the F.231 c/n 1/7294, F-ALIL, was converted to an F.354 (95hp de Havilland Gipsy I) in 1931, sold to the Compañía Española de Aviación at Barajas Airport, and registered EC-AVV. During the first weeks of the civil war it was used by Republican officers as a runabout and, if it was not destroyed in a bombing raid, was later transferred to one of the flying schools in Murcia.

Span 9.14m; length 6.40m; height 2.2m.
Empty weight 452kg; loaded weight 678kg.
Maximum speed 210km/h; ceiling 5,000m; range 500km.

Farman F.401 and F.402

In the same category of touring aeroplanes as the Caudron Phalène, de Havilland Puss Moth and R.W.D.13, the Farman F.400 was a small, high-wing cabin monoplane accommodating a pilot and two passengers. Of fabric-covered, wooden construction, and adaptable to a variety of liquid- or air-cooled engines, its most novel feature was the replacement of the traditional joystick and rudder bar by two hand-operated control levers – a system that did not prove popular and was abandoned in most of the production aircraft. One F.401 and four F.402s with 110hp Lorraine 5 Pb engines are suspected of having been smuggled into Republican Spain during the civil war:
1   F.401 c/n 1/7360, F-AMNZ. Owned by Marcel Demeny but sold abroad in October 1936; buyer untraceable.
2   F.402 c/n 45/7422, F-AMXY. Owned by Marcel Demeny but sold abroad in October 1936; buyer untraceable.

Molinier (airman, journalist, soldier and, later, Gaullist politician), it was bought by Paul L Weiller, owner of the Gnome-Rhône company, converted to a 291/1 with a 350hp Gnome-Rhône 7Kd radial engine, and used in 1934 by Corniglion-Molinier and André Malraux for a flight to the Yemen in search of the lost city of Queen Balkis of Sheba. It was also the aeroplane in which Malraux and Corniglion-Molinier intended to fly to Madrid for the first time after the outbreak of the civil war, but it developed engine trouble and the French ministerial Lockheed Orion was put at their disposal instead. A week later, however, Corniglion-Molinier used the F.291/1 to fly Antoine de Saint-Exupéry and a party of journalists to Barcelona.

Farman F.190
Span 14.38m; length 10.4m; height 2.52m.
Empty weight 913kg; loaded weight 1,700kg.

Farman F.200
The designation Farman F.200 was originally given to a single-seat low-wing monoplane in 1923, but in 1929 was reassigned to a small two-seat parasol-winged trainer derived from the F.190 and powered by a 120hp Salmson 9Ac radial engine. One F.200, registered EC-LAA, was bought by the Compañía Española de Aviación and kept at Los Llanos Aerodrome, Albacete. In 1935 it was bought by the Aero Club de Aragón, but, together with the Blériot SPAD 51 EC-BCC, was put up for sale in December of that year, the asking price being 10,000 French francs for the pair. There were no takers, and both machines were found by the Nationalists when they captured Barracas Aerodrome (in the province of Castellón) in April 1938.

Span 11.2m; length 8.2m; height 2.48m.
Empty weight 617kg; loaded weight 980kg.
Maximum speed 200km/h; ceiling 5,150m; range 850km.

Farman F.402 F-AMZY was one of the aircraft procured for the Spanish Republicans by Rémy Clément. (Liron)

3   F.402 c/n 52/7430, F-AMZY. Belonging to Rémy Clément, this aircraft was last inspected by the Bureau Veritas on 10 November 1936.
4   F.402 c/n 55/7436, F-ANBV. Owned by Mlle Marotte and sold abroad in April 1937.
5   F.402 c/n 58/7441, F-ANDU. Belonging to Marc Cayre, this machine is listed as being converted into an ambulance and sold abroad in December 1936.

Both Clément and Cayre were active in procuring aircraft for the Spanish Republicans. On 16 December 1936, *Le Jour*, in a report that 'two Farmans with Lorraine engines have departed for Spain', probably referred to F-AMZY and the F.193 F-ALFB, which left for Spain at about that time. Finally, the Farman F.406, a single example fitted with a 125hp de Havilland Gipsy Major, is reported to have been sold to SFTA and then sent to Spain. Its registration is unknown.

F.400

Span 11.72m; length 8.17m; height 2.14m.
Empty weight 608kg; loaded weight 1,198kg.
Maximum speed 215km/h; ceiling 4,000m; range 1,000km.

Farman F.430, F.431 and F.432

The Farman F.430 was a twin-engined, five- or six-passenger low-wing monoplane in the same category as the Airspeed Envoy and de Havilland D.H.84 Dragon. Constructed entirely of wood, with stressed ply skinning, it had a fixed undercarriage and two de Havilland 135hp Gipsy Moth I inverted in-line engines (replaced in the F.431 by 180hp Renault 6 Pdi, and in the F.432 by 180hp Renault 6 Q 06-07 engines of the same format). The F.430 series was not successful, and only the prototype and four production aircraft were built, the F.431s No 2 and No 3 being converted into the first two F.432s, and three seem to have been sold off to the Spanish Republicans:
1   F.430 prototype, c/n 1/7438,

Farman F.430 F-ANBY.

F-ANBY. Used by Farman Air Service for flying sardines to Paris; sold via Rémy Clément and SFTA (see Appendix II) after September 1936.
2   F.432 c/n 2/7466, (ex-F-431 No 2) F-ANOY. Used for six weeks by Farman Air Service on its Biarritz–Bordeaux route; sold to Marc Cayre and SFTA 23-24 September 1936.
3   F.432 c/n 2/7510, F-APEA. Registered to Lucien Maniglier, and sold abroad without C of A on 10 November 1936.

All of the above owners were occupied in procuring aircraft for the Spanish Republicans. The Farmans were probably all used as ambulances, and in Spain may have been confused with General Aircraft Monospars.

Span 15.45m; length 12.06m; height 2.82m; wing area 36.11sq m.
Empty weight (F.430) 1,306kg, (F.431) 1,573kg, (F.432) 1,776kg; loaded weight (F.430) 2,190kg, (F.431) 2,666kg, (F.432) 2,713kg.
Maximum speed (F.430) 220km/h, (F.431) 230km/h, (F.432) 230km/h; ceiling (F.430) 5,000m, (F.431 and F.432) 5,300m; range (all versions) 980km.

Farman F.480 Alizé

The Farman F.480 was a two-seat parasol monoplane of similar layout and size to the F.200, but whose designer had made a few concessions to aerodynamics, such as rounded wingtips and a curved fuselage top-decking. These concessions, however, were offset by the usual Farman clutter of struts, and the uncowled 110hp Lorraine 5 Pb radial engine contributed to the impression that it was an aeroplane of the mid-1920s rather than the mid-1930s. The prototype, F-AOXQ, named *Alizé* (Trade Wind), first flew in May 1936, and eleven production examples followed in the next four months. In December 1936 these were bought by SFTA and flown to Spain, the first two (F-AOXQ and 'PHU) on 24 December 1936 and the remainder four days later: F-AOXT, 'PHV, 'PIB, 'IC, 'ID, 'IE,

'IF, 'IM, 'IN, and 'IO. They were used by the training schools at Los Alcázares and La Ribera (San Javier) in Murcia, and no doubt some survived the war.

Span 11.6m; length 7.38m; height 2.6m.
Empty weight 544kg; loaded weight 845kg.
Maximum speed 215km/h; ceiling 3,000m; range 585km.

Fiat A.S.1

The Fiat A.S.1 was a small two-seat parasol monoplane of wooden construction, with fabric-covered wings and tail and a ply-covered fuselage. Its engine was an uncowled 150hp Fiat A-50 radial. Three A.S.1s went to Spain in the 1930s:

1   c/n 101, EC-ALA, bought by Gerardo Besterrechea of the Aero-Club de Andalucía, at Tablada, Seville, in March 1930.
2   c/n 304, EC-QQA, bought by Bernardo Rodríguez Morgado, of the Real Aero-Club de España, Barajas, Madrid, in November 1931.
3   Details unknown, but was in Republican territory throughout the civil war.

In the autumn of 1936 EC-QQA was removed to Murcia, where it was used as a primary trainer at Los Gerónimos. Fiat A.S.1 EC-ALA, at Seville, was impressed into military service for reconnaissance duties, given the military serial 30-61, and later used as a runabout by Nationalist pilots. After the war the Nationalists recovered the two Republican Fiat A.S.1s, allotting them the serials 30-150 and -151. Aircraft 30-61 continued in service until 1949. The final disposition of the other two is not recorded.

Span 10.4m; length 6.1m; height 2.53m; wing area 17.6sq m.
Empty weight 410kg; loaded weight 700kg.
Maximum speed 144km/h; climb to 1,000m in 6.52min; ceiling 6,800m; range 1,000km.

Fiat B.R.20

One of the most significant results of

A Fiat A.S.1.

the revolution in aircraft design that occurred during the first five years of the 1930s was the advent of the fast twin-engined bomber monoplane with cantilever wings, retractable undercarriage, enclosed accommodation for the crew, and modern radio and direction-finding equipment. The first to appear, in February 1932, was the Martin 123, which became the Martin B-10 in the US Army Air Corps. It was followed two years later by the Russian ANT-40 (or Tupolev SB), and in rapid succession by the Bloch MB 210, Junkers Ju 86, Heinkel He 111 and Dornier Do 17, all of which flew in the Spanish Civil War. Although the Fiat B.R.20 was, therefore, hardly a leader of this new trend, it possibly holds the record, in its period, for the speed and efficiency with which it was designed and put into service. C R Rosatelli, best known for his fighter biplanes, did not begin design work until the late autumn of 1935, yet the prototype Fiat B.R.20 (MM274) made its first flight on 10 February 1936. A production series was ordered within six weeks, and

A Farman F.480 Alizé. (Liron)

the first production example reached the 13° Stormo Bombardamento Terrestre of the Regia Aeronautica in September 1936.

The B.R.20 had a steel-tube fuselage, the front half of which was covered by duralumin sheeting and the rear by fabric. The all-metal wings, fins and tailplanes had fabric-covered control surfaces. It could carry up to 1,600kg of bombs, stored horizontally inside the fuselage, the bomb doors being pneumatically operated. The defensive armament comprised a single Breda-SAFAT 7.7mm machine gun in an hydraulically operated turret in the nose, twin 7.7mm guns in a similarly powered, semi-retractable dorsal turret, and a manually movable gun mounted on a ventral hatch that could be lowered and raised hydraulically. The bombardier used a Jozza U3A bombsight, and the navigator/radio-operator had an RA 5301 transmitter, an AR5 receiver and a P.3N direction-finding aerial. For photographic missions an AGR61 camera was mounted in the bomb bay. The undercarriage retracted rearwards into the engine nacelles. The B.R.20, named Cigogne (Stork), was popular with

Fiat B.R.20s of the XXXV Grupo Auton. Misto, Aviazione Legionaria. (Arráez)

the service pilots for its sturdiness and pleasant flying qualities, the only source of problems being the two Fiat A.80 RC 41 radial engines (885hp, or 1,030hp for take-off), which vibrated badly at high revolutions and were unreliable in hot or dusty locations, such as North Africa.

In June 1937 three B.R.20s from the 13° Stormo were transferred to Spain for evaluation under war conditions, but one of these was damaged when an engine developed a violent vibration on approaching Tablada aerodrome, Seville, and forced the pilot to come down in an orange grove, creating, as he put it, a 'boulevarde' that destroyed twenty-five orange trees. Based at Soria in northern Spain, the remaining two, with the military serials 23-21 and 23-23, flew occasional missions during the Battle of Belchite, in Aragón, in July and August 1937. With the return of the repaired 23-22 to service and the arrival of three more B.R.20s (23-24, -25, and -26) from the 7° Stormo on 21 August 1937, the Grupo XXXV Autonomo Misto *Cigogne* was formed, with the 65ª Squadriglia *Il Baffo* of Breda 65s, based at Tudela, in Navarra, and under the overall command, first, of Col Sergio Lalatta and then of Maggiore Enrico Ciguersa. Throughout the Battle of Teruel in the winter of 1937-38 and the Nationalist offensive through Aragón in March and April 1938, the six

B.R.20s were employed on bombing missions, occasionally in conjunction with the low-flying Breda 65s but usually at altitudes of 4,800 to 5,000m, where their cruising speed of 343km/h enabled them to operate without fear of serious Republican fighter opposition. During this period their only casualty was due to a collision on Tudela Aerodrome.

On 4 June 1938 the Gruppo was transferred to Puig Moreno, north of Teruel, where it received a reinforcement of seven more B.R.20s (Nos. 23-1 to 23-7), these being formed into the 231ª Squadriglia under the command of Capitano Roberto Giannoni, the command of the 230ª Squadriglia meanwhile having passed to Capitano Lamberto Fruttini. The new aircraft differed from the earlier arrivals in possessing a new, and smaller, Breda M1 dorsal turret, equipped with a single Breda-SAFAT heavy-calibre 12.7mm machine gun with 350 rounds. On 25 July 1938, during the opening phase of the Battle of the Ebro, the two B.R.20 squadrons attacked the pontoon bridges that the Republicans had built across the Ebro river, and succeeded in destroying several of them, but suffered their first and only battle casualty when the aircraft of Capitano Fruttini was hit by anti-aircraft fire. Fruttini managed to fly the damaged bomber over Nationalist lines before ordering the crew to bale out, but he and Maresciallo Moro, who refused to obey the order, were killed when the aircraft crashed. Command of the 230ª Squadriglia passed to Capitano Ettore Fargnoli. At the end of 1938 the Gruppo transferred to

Valenzuela, near Saragossa, whence, under the command of Tenente Colonnello Ugo Rampelli (later replaced by Col Impevi), it carried out daily sorties during the conquest of Catalonia.

Of the thirteen (some say sixteen, and others nineteen) Fiat B.R.20s delivered, ten were still in service when the civil war ended. They were transferred to the Ejercito del Aire, joining Grupo 11 of the Regimiento Mixto Num.1 at Alcalá de Henares and at Barajas, where they remained until withdrawn from service in the late 1940s, their type code having been changed to B-3.

Span 21.56m; length 16.17m; height 4.30m; wing area 74sq m.
Empty weight 6,739kg; loaded weight 10,339kg.
Maximum speed 430km/h (some authorities give c.390km/h) at 4,000m; cruising speed 343km/h; ceiling 7,200m; range 3,000km; endurance 5.5hrs.

Fiat C.R.20 and C.R.30

The distinguished series of single-seat fighter biplanes designed by Celestino Rosatelli for the Aeronautica d'Italia, the aviation division of the huge Fiat conglomerate, between the two world wars represented a line of development in pursuit of a machine combining maximum strength with maximum agility. To this end, all of his fighters had Warren girder-type interplane bracing, a characteristic that came to be regarded as Rosatelli's 'trade mark'. The first of the line was the Fiat C.R. (Caccia Rosatelli, or Rosatelli Fighter) of 1923, which differed from its successors in having an upper wing of less span than the lower. The C.R.10 of 1924 was a failure, chiefly because of its engine cooling system, but its successor, the C.R.20 of 1926, was the first of the truly classic Fiat fighters, and the first to have an all-metal airframe. It was powered by a 410hp Fiat A.20 engine, and armed with two fixed forward-firing 7.2mm Vickers guns mounted above the engine. There was also provision for two Darne guns in the fuselage sides. The C.R.30 of 1932 was really the C.R.20 brought up to date and more

A Fiat C.R.20.

robustly built. It was powered by a 600hp Fiat A.30 liquid-cooled engine driving a two-blade metal propeller, and its armament consisted of two fixed forward-firing 7.7mm or 12.7mm synchronised machine guns above the engine. Streamlined spats protected the main and tail wheels. The C.R.30 equipped several fighter squadrons of the Regia Aeronautica and, besides gaining the Bibescu Cup and other international trophies, was chosen, like earlier and later Fiat fighters, for the famous *Pattuglie Acrobatiche* aerobatic squadron. Although the C.R.30 was soon superseded by the C.R.32, a few remained in service until the end of the Second World War.

Six Fiat C.R.20s were sent to Spain, three in February 1938 and three in March. Two Fiat C.R.30s, both two-seat trainers, were sent, one in January 1938 and the second in June. The eight aircraft served as trainers with the Escuela de Caza (Fighter School) at Gallur, near Saragossa, moving with the school to Villanubla (Valladolid) after the civil war and, in 1942, to Morón de la Frontera, near Seville.

Fiat C.R.20

Span 9.8m; length 6.7m; height 2.75m; wing area 25.65sq m.

Empty weight 980kg; loaded weight 1,400kg.

Maximum speed 250km/h; ceiling 5,000m; range 500km.

Fiat C.R.30

Span 10.5m; length 7.8m; height 2.6m; wing area 27sq m.

Empty weight 1,345kg; loaded weight 1,895kg.

Maximum speed 351km/h; climb to 4,000m in 8.5min; ceiling 8,700m; range 850km.

Fiat C.R.32

One of the truly great among fighter biplanes, the Fiat C.R.32 bore the brunt of air combat for the Nationalists through all but the first five weeks of the Spanish Civil War, and contributed more than any other aeroplane type, with the possible exception of the Junkers Ju 52/3m,

Fiat C.R.30 No 37-4.

to their eventual victory. Its pedigree has been briefly described in the section on the Fiat C.R.20 and C.R.30, of which it was a marginally scaled-down and refined development.

The prototype C.R.32 (MM201) first flew on 28 April 1933, and trials soon showed that it had all the classic Fiat virtues – supreme agility, sensitive handling characteristics, stability, and an excellent dive – as well as an improved all-round performance. Like the C.R.20 and C.R.30, it was a staggered sesquiplane of all-metal construction with fabric covering. The wings, which were based on two tubular duralumin spars, were braced by the now traditional Warren-girder strut system. Ailerons were fitted to the upper wing only, and balanced by 'park-bench' tabs, while the rudder and elevators were statically and dynamically balanced. The cockpit

and windshield of the C.R.30 had been redesigned to improve the pilot's view, and the wheel spats enlarged and better streamlined. Armament still consisted of two fixed, synchronised, 7.7mm or 12.7mm machine guns (or one of each). Power was provided by a 592bhp Fiat A.30 RA liquid-cooled vee engine driving a Fiat two-blade metal propeller, the pitch of which could be adjusted on the ground.

Before the end of 1933 the Regia Aeronautica placed an initial order for fifty, and a second for 232 followed in 1934, while export orders were received from China (twenty-four) and Hungary (fifty). In the event, the first nine built went to China, but, after the majority had been lost in accidents caused by the poor training of the Chinese pilots, the remainder of the order was cancelled. By the summer of 1936 the Fiat C.R.32 was numerically the most important fighter in the Italian air force, and a four-gun version with an improved A.30 RAbis en-

Fiat C.R.32 No 3-51, the machine in which Joaquín García Morato scored most of his forty accredited victories. (Azaola)

gine, the C.R.32bis, was already in production.

Following Mussolini's decision to give armed support to Gen Franco, twelve Savioa-Marchetti S.81s were flown, with crews, direct to Spanish Morocco on 30 July 1936, three being lost en route. At the same time, twelve Fiat C.R.32s, the equivalent of a single squadriglia but drawn from different units, were embarked on the SS *Nereid*, together with volunteer pilots and a small number of mechanics. These were disembarked at Melilla, at the eastern end of Spanish Morocco, during the night of 12-13 August to ensure secrecy and, after assembly and test flying, seven were flown to Tablada, Seville, on the 18 August. The rest followed on 21 August, and the whole fighter unit, commanded by Capitano Vincenzo Dequal (late of the 1° Stormo Caccia at Campoformido, Italy), was given the new title '1ª Escuadrilla de Caza de la Aviación de El Tercio' – the 1st Fighter Squadron of the Foreign Legion Air Arm. The C.R.32s received the type code 3 and were nicknamed *Chirris* by the Spaniards, from the Italian pronunciation of the letters 'CR'. By the end of August 1936 the Italian-flown Fiats had had several encounters with the enemy, shooting down a Nieuport 52 near Córdoba and a solitary, unarmed, Dewoitine D.372 over Guadix aerodrome. On 31 August, however, three Fiats met two Dewoitine D.372s and a Hawker Spanish Fury (flown by Lacalle) near Talavera de la Reina, and in the ensuing dogfight two Fiats were shot down without loss to the Republicans. One pilot, Sergente Castellani, escaped by parachute and managed to regain Nationalist territory, but the other, Tenente Monico, was captured and shot by Republican militia. The third Fiat was damaged on landing at its base. In addition, six others had been damaged in accidents, rendered *hors de combat* by forced landings, or grounded through a temporary lack of spares, leaving only three serviceable. At least two of the Fiat C.R.32s came down in Portugal, the Portuguese authorities promptly returning both the aircraft and their pilots to Nationalist Spain.

Since Cádiz was considered unsafe for disembarkation at that time, owing to the proximity of Republican warships, a second batch of nine C.R.32s was taken by ship round to Vigo, in the north-west of Spain, at the end of August 1936. They were transported by rail to Seville, a journey made possible by the fact that Franco's and Mola's armies had linked up two weeks previously and cleared western Spain of Republican forces. Another batch of nine followed on 3 September 1936. There is disagreement over the number of Fiat C.R.32s delivered between 12 August and 28 September 1936. Most Spanish historians list the deliveries as twelve to Melilla on 12 August, three (and three Macchi M.41s) to Mallorca on 27 August, nine to Vigo on 28 August, and twelve to Vigo (with twelve Ro 37bis)

on 23 September, making thirty-three to the mainland and three to Mallorca. However, two Italian documents in the Archivio Centrale di Stato in Rome call this into question. The first states that twenty-seven fighters (twenty-four Fiat C.R.32s and three Macchi M.41s) were delivered to Spain by 28 August 1936; the second that thirty-six Fiat C.R.32s had been delivered by 3 September. This must raise the number of C.R.32s delivered to metropolitan Spain by mid-September 1936 to thirty-three, not twenty-one, and by mid-October to forty-five, and not thirty-six, as usually stated.

When the nine Fiats bought via Vigo were ready for service, in the middle of September, the nineteen or twenty aircraft were formed into two escuadrillas, the 1ª still under the command of Dequal, and the 2ª under Capitano Dante Olivera. It was about this time, too, that the 1ª Escuadrilla adopted the nickname *La Cucaracha* (The Cockroach), probably after the song, which was then at the height of its popularity, and its personnel strength was augmented by three Spanish pilots: Capitán Joaquín García Morato (who was to become the highest scoring ace of the war on either side, nearly all his accredited victories being scored in Fiat C.R.32 No.3-51), Capitán Ángel Salas Larrazábal, and Teniente Julio Salvador Díaz-Benjumea. In October 1936 a fourth, Teniente Miguel García Pardo, joined the group. From time to time these Spaniards also flew He 51s with the German squadrons.

Since the start of the campaign Tenente Colonnello Bonomi, the overall commander of the Aviación de El Tercio, had argued that the available fighters should be concentrated rather than dispersed over a wide front in small patrols. The losses to the Dewoitines on 31 August conclusively supported his reasoning, and henceforth the two escuadrillas operated from the same aerodromes, first at Cáceres, then at Salamanca and, after its capture on 4 September, Talavera de la Reina, about 120 kilometres from Madrid. They flew in formations of at least six, and usually of eight or twelve aircraft, and, when escorting bombers, in three flights, one at the same altitude as the bombers, and the others stepped above at intervals of 1,000m.

During the advance on Madrid in September and October 1936, the two Fiat squadrons were opposed by an ever-diminishing number of Dewoitine D.372s (of which there were only twelve at the beginning), five Loire 46s, a Hawker Spanish Fury and a Boeing 281, all with weak and defective armament, and between thirty and forty old Nieuport 52s which, although properly armed, were so outclassed by the Fiats, and even by the Heinkel He 51s, that they scarcely counted at all. Moreover, while the Italian pilots were well trained, thoroughly familiar with their aircraft and belonged to a cohesive military formation, the Republican pilots included a high proportion of volunteers or mercenaries of many nationalities, few of whom had any military training or even spoke a common language. It is hardly surprising, therefore, that the Republicans were reduced to a solitary Hawker Spanish Fury by the time the Soviet aircraft appeared on

Fiat C.R.32s of the X Gruppo Auton. Caccia Baleari, *based on Mallorca.* (Emiliani)

the scene at the beginning of November. Nevertheless, since more than half the Republican fighters were lost in accidents or bombing attacks on their aerodromes, the claim by C.R.32 pilots of seventy-five 'kills' between 18 August and 4 November 1936 can be disregarded.

The C.R.32s achieved a decisive success in the part they played in repelling the Republican invasion of Mallorca. Three had been disembarked at Palma on 27 August, and by the end of the next day they had destroyed or neutralised the Republican Savoia-Marchetti S.62s covering the invasion. The Republicans withdrew on the 29 August, leaving the Nationalists with an invaluable naval and air base in the Mediterranean.

On 28 October 1936 four Russian SB-2M100A bombers, led by Lt Col Ernst Schacht, attacked Tablada air base, Seville, where the 3ª Escuadrilla of Fiats was being formed from the aircraft delivered on 28 September. Although a C.R.32 patrol was airborne at the time, the speed of the SBs enabled them to make good their escape, although one was damaged by anti-aircraft fire. During their return flight the Spanish Nationalist pilot Capitán Angél Salas, who happened to be patrolling in a Fiat over the

front lines, spotted the formation and, in a single diving pass, damaged a second SB. During the next few days SBs flying in ten-aircraft formations repeated their attacks on Nationalist aerodromes, severely damaging six C.R.32s on Gamonal Aerodrome, Talavera, on 1 November. Ten Col Bonomi ordered the redeployment of his remaining Fiats to Torrijos, and during the transit flight the Fiat fighters vainly tried to intercept two SBs, Morato finding himself in the novel situation of being chased by a bomber. The alarm felt by the Italians at being confronted by a bomber they could not intercept was briefly allayed next day when two Fiat pilots, Mantelli and Delicato, spotted an SB (which was by now being mistakenly identified as a 'Martin') circling below over Torrijos, obviously looking for their aerodrome. They immediately dived and shot it down in flames. Their sense of triumph was cut short next day, when two Fiats were attacked by ten unfamiliar biplanes. Shortly afterwards, nine Fiats were attacked by another ten of these biplanes, two being so badly damaged that they crashed on landing at Torrijos. The arrival over the Madrid front of twenty-four Polikarpov I-15 fighters – soon dubbed Chatos (Snub Noses) by the Republicans

Fiat C.R.32s of the 26ª Squadriglia of the XVI Gruppo Cucaracha *taxi to take off on patrol.* (Emiliani)

and 'Curtiss' by the Nationalists – and, two weeks later, of thirty-one Polikarpov I-16 fighter monoplanes, with a top speed of 454km/h, dramatically swung the balance of air power in the Republicans' favour. After a series of gruelling air battles, Bonomi ordered that C.R.32 pilots would henceforth engage the enemy only when possessing numerical superiority. As this never occurred, it was impossible to escort Nationalist bombers over Madrid, and daylight bombing of the Spanish capital was abandoned.

With the creation of the Aviazione Legionaria in December 1936, the C.R.32 escuadrillas were disbanded and re-formed as the 24ª, 25ª and 26ª squadriglie of the XVI Gruppo *Cucaracha* under Maggiore Tarscisco Fagnani, Dequal having been recalled to Italy. Attached to this Gruppo was a flight of three Spaniards (Morato, Salvador and Bermúdez de Castro) who called themselves *La Patrulla Azul* (The Blue Patrol), and these were detached with the squadriglia sent to cover the Nationalist advance on Málaga in January 1937. Meanwhile, during the Battle of La Jarama, south of Madrid, the two Italian squadriglie of C.R.32s were, after sustaining losses, ordered by Gen

Velardi (commander-in-chief of the Aviazione Legionaria) not to cross into Republican airspace. The Nationalist air chief, Gen Kindelán, had long been trying to persuade the Italians to equip all Spanish fighter units with C.R.32s, and saw Velardi's order as a chance to force his hand. He instructed the *Patrulla Azul* to transfer to the Jarama front and, at the first opportunity, attack the enemy regardless of the order. On 18 February 1937, when two large formations of C.R.32s and I-15s were flying parallel along the front, both refusing combat, the three C.R.32s of the *Patrulla Azul* appeared and flew straight into the enemy formation, forcing the Italians to come to their rescue. Kindelán had made his point, and the first all-Spanish C.R.32 escuadrilla, 1-E-3, was formed with six aircraft on 30 March 1937. On 30 April 2-E-3 was formed, the two escuadrillas being combined into the all-Spanish group 2-G-3 on 4 May 1937. In the same week two new Italian gruppos were created as more aircraft arrived from Italy – the VI Gruppo (31ª, 32ª and 33ª Squadriglie) and the XXIII Gruppo (18ª, 19ª and 20ª Squadriglie), named *Asso di Bastoni* (Ace of Clubs). A year later the VI Gruppo was named *La Gamba di Ferro* (Iron Leg) in honour of Capitano Ernesto Botto, who, having lost a leg in action in 1936, returned to Spain to command a squadron at the end of 1937. Meanwhile, the Fiats of the

XVI Gruppo had been deployed to Vitoria to participate in the offensive against Bilbao, and it is not generally known that the ten C.R.32s of the 25ª Squadriglia, led by Capitano Mario Viola, provided escort to the Junkers Ju 52/3ms of the Condor Legion when they bombed Guernica on 26 April 1937.

To follow the history of the C.R.32s in the civil war hereafter would simply be to retell the history of the air war itself, for they took part in every operation until the end: the whole of the northern campaign, the Battles of Huesca, Brunete, Belchite and Teruel in 1937, the advance to the Mediterranean coast, the Valencia offensive and the Battle of the Ebro in 1938, and the Catalonian offensive and the fighting in Extremadura in 1939. In November 1937, after a series of raids by SBs and Potez 54s on Palma, a Fiat group, the X Gruppo Autonomo *Baleari* (101ª and 102ª Squadriglie), comprising some thirty fighters, was formed on Mallorca, based at Son San Juan. While the C.R.32s on the mainland were painted with mottled camouflage, the Italian-flown aircraft having their squadriglia numbers painted on the wheel spats, the C.R.32s on Mallorca had the waveband camouflage of the bombers on the island. In January 1938 a second Spanish C.R.32 Grupo of three escuadrillas, 3-G-3, was formed, and at the same time the Aviazione Legionaria received twelve examples of the four-gun C.R.32bis. These equipped the Squadriglia Autonomo Mitragliamento *Frecce* (Arrows) under Capitano Gosilla, which was to specialise in close support of ground operations, and carried out its first mission on 12 March 1938. By this time, 297 C.R.32s had been delivered to Nationalist Spain: 184 C.R.32s, twelve C.R.32bis, thirty-seven C.R.32ter, and sixty-four C.R.32quater (a further forty-five C.R.32quater were to follow in April 1938 and a last batch of thirty-five in July 1938, bringing the total delivered during the civil war to 377). In August 1938, during the Battle of the Ebro, the VI Gruppo *Gamba di Ferro* was disbanded, and its aircraft transferred to the Spanish Nationalist air arm, six being used to create a seventh squadron, 8-E-3, commanded by Capitán José Pazó, the co-designer of the González Gil-Pazó monoplanes.

The C.R.32ter and C.R.32quater, which began to arrive in the summer and autumn of 1937, were equipped with twin 12.7mm Breda-SAFAT machine guns (the C.R.32quater differing from the C.R.32ter only in minor details that reduced the empty weight from 1,450kg to 1,386kg). By then, the Fiat pilots had learned to match the superior manoeuvrability of the Fiat against the superior speed of the I-16, and in the frequent dogfights losses were about even, or marginally in favour of the Italian fighter. In head-on passes the 12.7mm guns outranged the 7.62mm Shkas 35 guns of the I-16 Moscas, enabling the Fiat pilots to open fire first, but at close range the high rate of fire of the light-calibre Shkas (1,800 rounds per minute) was more destructive than the lower firing rate and muzzle velocity of the heavy-calibre Breda-SAFAT guns. The I-15 biplane, which had four 7.62mm PV-1 (880 rounds per minute) to the two of the Fiat, could outclimb the Fiat and had a slightly smaller turning radius, but the C.R.32 was slightly faster and could easily outdive the I-15.

The Germans, still smarting from the failure of the Heinkel He 51 as a fighter, could not resist the temptation to make some adverse remarks about the Fiat C.R.32 in a report on the Battle of Brunete: 'This is one of the most employed, and most criticised, aircraft in Spain. It would be perfect but for the forward placing of the oil and water cooling systems and the location of the fuel tank, all of which are vulnerable to enemy fire. The enemy always fires from in front or beneath. Fiats invariably catch fire when shot down. In order to present the enemy with the narrowest possible target, Italian pilots have developed a fine skill in aerobatics and flying.'

The outstanding quality of the C.R.32, however, was its sturdiness, which enabled it to take an astonishing amount of damage and remain airborne. On 1 November 1938, during one of the innumerable dogfights over the Ebro, Guiseppe Baylon of the *Cucaracha* group collided with an I-16 (probably CM-276 flown by Teniente Cortizo). One wing of the I-16 was shorn off, and the fighter, subject to the powerful torque of its large engine, shook itself to pieces and exploded. The Fiat lost half its lower port wing, but was able to return to base. These dogfights over the Ebro and the Costa Brava in 1938 were the largest air battles that had occurred in warfare up to that time, with as many as 100 aircraft involved on each side. Formations of seventy-two Fiat C.R.32s were common. Perhaps the most remarkable group of 'kills' by a Fiat pilot was that of Capitán Angel Salas, who, on 2 September 1938, dived down on a formation of nine SBs over Monterubio and shot down three in six minutes. The last aircraft of either side to be shot down in the war was a Fiat C.R.32 piloted by Asiedo of the *Asso de Bastoni* group, on 31 March 1939, the very last day of the civil war. It was brought down after the order to surrender had been accepted and many Republican aircraft had already landed on Nationalist aerodromes. On 4 April 1939, while giving a celebratory solo display of aerobatics in his Fiat No 3-51 to assembled air officers, Joaquín García Morato was killed.

The very success of the Fiat C.R.32 in Spain was, paradoxically, to have an adverse effect on the fighting capability of the Regia Aeronautica. When touring Nationalist Spain in May 1938, the British air attaché in Paris, Grp Capt Douglas Colyer, heard heartfelt praise of the Fiat from Italian and Spanish pilots who 'were unanimous in their preference for an open cockpit for a fighting aeroplane'. He wrote in his report to the Air Ministry, 'If one can draw a lesson from this war, it would seem that great manoeuvrability and sturdiness are still the greatest assets of the fighter aeroplane, and that the sacrifice of these qualities to mere speed on the level and in the climb may be mistaken policy'. This was precisely the view of the Italian air staff, who ordered the Fiat C.R.42, a biplane with an open cockpit and fixed undercarriage, into mass production. With a top speed of only 397-430km/h, depending on altitude, it was, despite its otherwise superb qualities, completely unable to sustain combat against the Spitfires, or even the Hurricanes, of the RAF during the Second World War.

Of the 377 Fiats delivered, 96 were serving with Italian units and 89 with Spanish units when the civil war ended, plus 14 Spanish Fiats at the Escuela de Caza and others under repair. A total of 115 Fiats was transferred by the departing Italians to the Spaniards in May 1939. This leaves 159, of which 27 had been lost by Spanish units and, presumably, 132 by Italian units. To these must be added 49 damaged and rebuilt by the Hispano-Suiza factory at Triana, Seville, during the war.

Six Fiat C.R.32s were captured intact by the Republicans during the war. One of the earliest was 3-6, piloted by Tenente Giorgio Franceschi, which force-landed at Don Benito on 16 September 1936. A photograph shows that it had '451' painted on its fin, a '4' on its wheel spats and, most curiously, a machine gun mounted above the lower starboard wing (this may have been added by its Republican captors). After testing, it was wrecked when it collided with a Dragon Rapide (probably the ex-I-DRAG) at Alcalá de Henares in November 1936. A second crashed in December 1936, and a third was shipped to the Soviet Union. Of the remaining three, two served with the 1ª Escuadrilla of Grupo 71 at Vilajuiga from October

A Fiat G.R.8 under repair.

Span 8.75m; length 6.99m; height 2.94m; wing area 18.92sqm.

Empty weight 558.8kg; loaded weight 835.5kg.

Maximum speed 212km/h; cruising speed 183.43km/h; ceiling 5,200m.

Fiat G.50

Inappropriately named Freccia (Arrow), the Fiat G.50 was the first single-seat, low-wing, cantilever retractable-undercarriage monoplane to enter service with the Regia Aeronautica. In its first form it even had an enclosed cockpit as well. In 1936 the Italian Ministerio dell' Aeronautica issued specifications for three categories of single-seat fighter: a lightly armed interceptor, a longer-ranged escort fighter, and a fighter-bomber. While the other five designs submitted by Italian manufacturers were intended to meet one or another of these distinct requirements, the Fiat G.50 was designed by Guiseppe Gabrielli to satisfy all three. It was, moreover, designed round the new 840-960hp Fiat A.74 RC 38 two-row fourteen-cylinder radial engine: hence its somewhat un-arrowlike silhouette.

The prototype first flew on 26 February 1937 and, after initial appraisal, forty-five pre-series aircraft were ordered. Following the crash of the second prototype G.50 in September 1937, the competing Macchi C.200 was judged the better fighter, but production of the Fiat was continued as an insurance against possible difficulties in the production of the Macchi.

In October 1937 the Nationalist air ace Capitán Joaquín García Morato tested a G.50 at Guidonia, while visiting Italy at the invitation of the Regia Aeronautica. The first (or 1ª Serie) Fiat G.50s, armed with twin 12.7mm Breda SAFAT machine guns mounted in the upper forward fuselage, began to reach the Regia Aeronautica at the end of 1938, and ten were immediately shipped to Spain, where the civil war was drawing to its close. They were unloaded at Tarragona and taken by lorry to Reus, in southern Catalonia, only recently captured by the Nationalists. The ten G.50s, allotted the type code

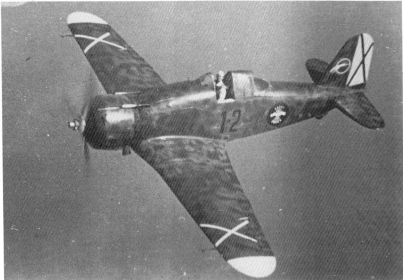

A Fiat G.50. (Azaola)

1937, one being shot down in April 1938 and the other surviving until it was destroyed, with the Dewoitines of the squadron, at Bañolas Aerodrome on 5 February 1939. The third was found by the Nationalists at the end of the war at the Republican Escuela de Caza at Archena.

After the civil war, Hispano-Suiza built a series of 100 Fiat C.R.32quaters, and the 300 or so aircraft continued serving in Grupos 21, 22, 23 and 26, or as trainers, until the late 1940s.

Span 9.5m; length 7.45m; height 2.63m; wing area 22.1sqm.

Empty weight (C.R.32) 1,450kg; (C.R.32quater) 1,386kg; loaded weight (C.R.32) 1,900kg; (C.R.32quater) 1,905kg.

Maximum speed (C.R.32) 354km/h; (C.R.32quater) 356km/h; climb to 3,000m (C.R.32) 1.5min; (C.R.32quater) 1.3min; ceiling (C.R.32) 7,700m; (C.R.32quater) 7,500m; range (C.R.32) 780km; (C.R.32quater) 796km.

Fiat G.8

Designed by Guiseppe Gabrielli, the G.8 was a two-seat training biplane which first flew in 1934. It had the same Warren-girder interplane bracing as the Fiat C.R.30 and C.R.32 fighters, and a 135hp Fiat A.54 radial engine in a Townend-ring cowling. Two Fiat G.8s were delivered to Spain in January 1938, and were used by the Nationalist Escuela de Caza (fighter school) at Gallur, Saragossa, and later at Villa-nubla (Valladolid).

1 (which previously denoted the Nieuport 52), were formed into the Gruppo Sperimentale di Caccia (Experimental Fighter Group), under the command of Maggiore Mario Bonzano, and transferred to Escalona, the base of the famous Fiat C.R.32 group, the XXIII Gruppo *Asso de Bastoni* (Ace of Spades). Because Bonzano had previously belonged to this group, at least some of the G.50s were painted with the coveted 'Bastoni' emblem on their fuselage sides. Although the Fiat G.50 group flew a number of patrols during the last fortnight of the war, usually flying at 8,000m as escorts to Fiat C.R.32 groups and throttled fully back to maintain position above their slower charges, they encountered no Republican fighters. At this high altitude one pilot, Maresciallo (Sgt-Maj) Pongiluppi, lost consciousness over Madrid. The aircraft landed itself in a wheatfield, suffering only minor damage.

Two more G.50s arrived at the end of March 1939, bringing the total delivered to twelve. Operational experience in Spain, and especially strong criticism of the cockpit canopy by the pilots, led to various alterations to the production aircraft, the most important being the reversion to a traditional open cockpit, retained by the Fiat G.50s that fought on many fronts throughout the Second World War. The 1ª Serie Fiat G.50s in Spain were handed over to the Ejercito del Aire in 1939 and, with the Heinkel He 112Bs, assigned to Grupo 27 of the Regimiento Mixto Núm. 2, based at Melilla in Spanish Morocco. The lack of spares caused increasing maintenance difficulties, however, and the last G.50s were withdrawn from service in 1943.

Span 11m; length 7.8m; height 3.3m; wing area 18.25sq m.
Empty weight 1,965kg; loaded weight 2,400kg.
Maximum speed 473km/h at 6,000m; climb to 6,000m in 7.5min; ceiling 10,750m; range 700km.

Fieseler Fi 156 Storch

The Fieseler Storch was known to millions of people, especially German and Allied soldiers in every European, Russian or Mediterranean theatre of the Second World War, who otherwise knew little about aircraft. A thin-fuselaged high-wing monoplane of gawky appearance, whose wings seemed to consist largely of high-lift devices, the Storch was the first really practical short take-off and landing (STOL) aeroplane, for it made its maiden flight in the summer of 1936, nearly twenty years before the acronym was thought of. Powered by a 240hp Argus As 10 C-3, and fitted with full-span Handley Page automatic slats along its wing leading edges and Fieseler-Rollflügel extendable high-lift flaps from the ailerons to the fuselage, the Storch could take off in 50m and land in a mere 15m in a mild 13km/h headwind. In a medium headwind it could land within a space of five yards – almost vertically.

The Storch was present wherever the Wehrmacht operated, and featured in several melodramatic episodes, such as the rescue of Mussolini from imprisonment in the hotel on the top of the Gran Sasso Massif, and Hanna Reitsche's landing in front of the Führerbunker in an attempt to rescue Hitler from Berlin. Nearly 2,900 were built, and the type was used, copied or built under licence in a dozen other countries, including France, Italy, Bulgaria, Croatia, Finland, Hungary, Japan, Rumania, Sweden and Switzerland. Despite its odd appearance, the Fieseler Fi 156A-1, the first production model, was of thoroughly conventional construction. It had a fabric-covered welded steel tube fuselage, two-spar fabric-covered wooden wings, and a plywood-covered wooden tail unit. The tall, long-stroke undercarriage was designed to absorb shocks when landing on rough ground. The glazing of the three-seat cabin was angled outwards from the fuselage sides to allow the maximum downwards field of view. In the later Fi 156C series provision was made for a defensive MG 15 machine gun and racks to carry three 50kg bombs or a 135kg mine, or for conversion into an ambulance.

The first use of Storchs in military operations was during the last months of the Spanish Civil War, when, towards the end of 1938, four were delivered to the Condor Legion. Numbered 46-1 to 46-4, they were used as staff transports and for liaison duties by S/88 (Staff Section) and P/88 (Technical Section, or Park) until they were handed over to the Spaniards after the war. Seventeen more arrived in 1939-40. In 1945 their type code was changed to L.16, and in 1956 to L.6. One, employed by the military authorities in Spanish Guinea and bearing the military serial G.6, received the civil registration EC-AAX in 1946. It was scrapped in 1951. Another, used by the Dirección General de Aviación Civil and registered EC-ADM, was still flying in the 1960s.

Span 14.25m; length 9.9m; height 3.05m; wing area 26sq m.
Empty weight 910kg; loaded weight 1,219kg.
Maximum speed 175km/h at sea level; take-off distance into wind 75m; to clear obstacle 20m high, 200m; landing distance from 20m, no wind, 190m; landing run, 26m; range at 150km/h, 350km; at 95km/h, 380km.

Fleet 10

The Fleet 10 was one of a series of closely similar two-seat trainer and

The Fieseler Fi 156 Storch.

aerobatic biplanes produced by the Fleet Aircraft Company at Lake Erie, Ontario, during the 1930s. Of wood and metal construction, it was powered by an uncowled 125hp Kinner 125 B5 six-cylinder radial engine. Two, and possibly three, were imported into Spain during the years of the Republic, one being delivered from Tetuán, Spanish Morocco, to Toledo, Spain, by Reuben Hollis Fleet himself, the president of the company and guiding hand of the Consolidated Aircraft Corporation. This may have been the Fleet 10 c/n 377, registered in Spain as EC-AAQ and bought by a Sr Garrido in 1931. At least one other was purchased by the Aeronáutica Naval in 1934, possibly one of two demonstrated in Portugal by the company agent, Gordon Mounce. In June 1935 one of these aircraft took part in an aerobatics competition during an aviation festival at Barajas, Madrid, the pilots being Capitán José Ibarra Montis and Capitán Joaquín García Morato, the future Nationalist air ace. Ibarra won by one-and-a-half points. In July 1936 two Fleet 10s were at San Javier, the base and HQ of the Aeronautica Naval, and one at least was still flying in the spring of 1937, when it was seen by the American

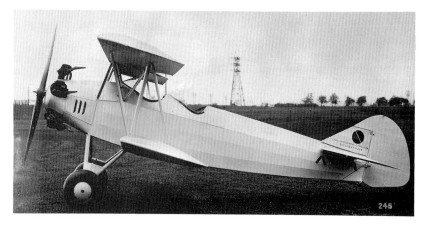

A Fleet 10.

mercenary pilot Frank Tinker.

Span 28ft; length 21ft 6in; height 8ft; wing area 195sq ft.
Empty weight 1,221lb; loaded weight 1,931lb.
Maximum speed 115mph; cruising speed 95mph; landing speed 55mph; ceiling 12,500ft; range 620 miles.

Focke-Wulf Fw 56A-1 Stösser

Conceived to meet the specifications of a German lightweight 'Home Defence Fighter' programme of 1933, in which the contending pro-

totypes were to be powered by the 240hp Argus As 10C eight-cylinder inverted-vee air-cooled engine, the Focke-Wulf Fw 56 Stösser (Falcon Hawk) was one of the first aircraft designed by Dr Kurt Tank for the Focke-Wulf company, which he had joined in 1932. It was a single-seat parasol monoplane of wood and metal, fabric covered with the exception of the forward fuselage, which was skinned with detachable alloy

One of the three Focke-Wulf Fw 156 Stössers in Republican service, shortly after assembly at San Javier, November 1936. (Arráez)

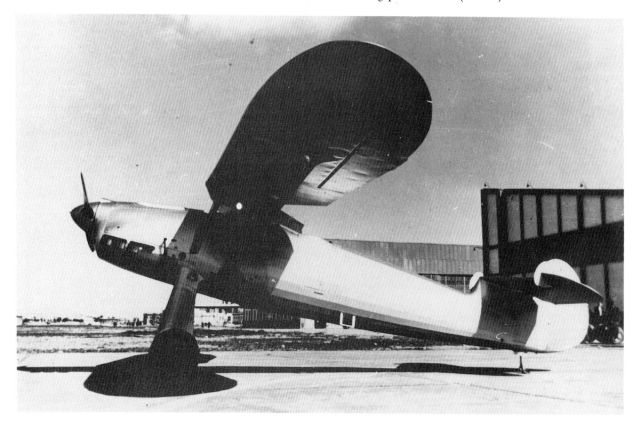

sheet. It had a narrow-track two-leg undercarriage, and a curious tail assembly, the rudder being positioned behind the tailplane and elevators, which were mounted on top of a truncated fin extruded from the fuselage. Despite its fragile appearance, the Stösser proved both sturdy and remarkably agile in the air and, after the shelving of the Home Defence Fighter scheme in 1935, was ordered in quantity by the Luftwaffe and the paramilitary NSFK (National Socialist Flying Corps) as an advanced fighter-trainer. Early in 1936 the second prototype (Fw 56 V4 D-IIKA) was fitted with bomb racks and used for demonstrations of dive-bombing techniques. The type was released for export in 1937, twelve being bought by Austria, eighteen by Hungary, and others by Bolivia and Bulgaria. Spectacular aerobatic displays by Stösser often provided the high points of flying displays in Europe and the United States.

The fact that three Focke-Wulf Stösser were used as trainers at Le Ribera (San Javier) and Archena by the Republicans during the civil war was forgotten until photographs of them were discovered in the early 1960s. The question then arose as to how such modern German aircraft could have come into Republican possession. The proffered explanation – that they had been on board a German or Nationalist ship captured by the Republicans – was clearly untrue. Only one enemy ship was ever captured at sea by the Republicans, the *Palos*, and she had no aircraft on board. The puzzle was solved in 1979 by James Carmody, although some details of the extraordinary story are still obscure. During the Italian invasion of Abyssinia (Ethiopia), the British arms dealer Capt John Ball (trading as the Soley Arms Company) provided the Abyssinian emperor, Haile Selasse, with several consignments of arms. The last of these, loaded on board the *Santa Maria* at Antwerp on 4 April 1936, included three Focke-Wulf Fw 56A-1 Stösser, complete with six

machine guns, ammunition and bombs, and three German pilots hired to fly them. Ball was alleged to have bought the aircraft through a Swiss agency. If that is true, then it might explain how the purchase was possible at a time when the Stösser was not yet released for export, and had only just begun to reach the Luftwaffe. Swiss agencies, unlike agencies elsewhere in Europe, were always able to pay for aircraft in hard currency, which perhaps persuaded the Nazi government to turn a blind eye to the transaction, even though the aircraft were being sold to the enemy of Mussolini. By the time the *Santa Maria* reached Gibraltar, however, the Abyssinian war had ended, and Capt Ball spent the next three months trying to find a buyer for the arms and aircraft while the

ship sailed from port to port, only to be refused permission to dock wherever it went.

Ball seems to have been in touch with Spanish Nationalist conspirators in England and Belgium at least three weeks before the uprising, for at the end of June 1936 the *Santa Maria* returned to Antwerp and the aircraft were transferred to the *Stanhope*, one of three old ships belonging to Jack Billmeir, a near neighbour of Ball's in Highgate, London, who had been trading with Spain for fifteen years. The *Santa Maria* sailed for Cádiz, Spain, where the customs authorities confiscated some crates of Focke-Wulf spares which had been inadvertently left on board, and which passed to the Nationalists when they took over the port on 18-19 July. For some reason

A Focke-Wulf Stösser undergoes the engine change that nearly resulted in the engineers being shot for treason. (Arráez)

the *Stanhope* did not sail for Spain when the civil war broke out, and the Belgian authorities impounded the machine guns, gun mounts, ammunition and bombs and transferred them to a lighter. Somebody stole these weapons during August, and the Nationalists, who no longer wanted unarmed aircraft, cancelled the sale. Ball then sold the aircraft to a Republican agent, probably Ten Cor Luis Riaño. One of the aircraft was transferred to the *Stanmore*, a sister-ship to the *Stanhope*, and the two vessels surreptitiously left Antwerp on 1 October 1936, delivering the Focke-Wulf Stösser at Alicante on 10 October. One effect of this incident was that Billmeir, who had intended to trade with both sides in the civil war, felt let down by the Nationalists and henceforth traded exclusively with the Republicans. By 1938 he was the largest single shipper of supplies to the Republicans, with six companies and thirty-one ships, all financed by the Spanish government. This enabled him to become one of the foremost shipowners in Britain after the Second World War, and a Commodore of the Royal Yacht Club.

The Stösser were assembled at San Javier, where the American pilot-of-fortune Hilaire du Berrier saw them in November 1936, and were later used for aerobatic training at La Ribera (a flying school adjacent to the main field at San Javier) and for combat training at Archena. After several months' intensive use their Argus engines became worn out and were replaced by Hispano-Wright Whirlwind 9D radial engines from written-off Hispano E.30 trainers. The conversion, which was carried out at the SAF-15 aircraft factory at La Rabasa (Alicante), created problems of longitudinal stability and, after the first flights, the test pilot, Paco Piedra, reported 'They don't fly well'. The Chief Political Commissar of SAF-15 promptly arrested the engineers who had carried out the conversion and charged them with sabotage, for which the penalty was death. Their lives were saved only by the fortuitous arrival, during the hearing, of Coronel Alejandro Gómez Spencer, Chief of the Material Division of the air forces and one of the most experienced and re-

spected airmen in Spain. He insisted the hearing be adjourned until he had tested the machines himself. After the test flights he declared the machines so safe that they could fly by themselves, and to prove the point took off again in one of them and flew low across the aerodrome, his arms held high above his head and his feet placed on the rim of the cockpit. The engineers were acquitted and later promoted. The Commissar, who was extremely unpopular owing to his propensity for seeing traitors everywhere, lost much of his authority thereafter, and was later arrested as a Fascist spy. The final disposition of the three Stösser is not recorded.

Span 10.55m; length 7.62m; height 2.44m.
Empty weight 755kg; loaded weight 995kg.
Maximum speed (with Argus 10C engine) 285km/h at sea level; ceiling 6,200m; range 460km.

Fokker C.X and D.XXI

On 24 August 1936 the Netherlands government signed the International Agreement of Non-Intervention, which included a ban on the sale of all aircraft, civil or military, to either side in the Spanish Civil War. However, this did not prevent the sale of four ex-KLM Fokker trimotors to Republican Spain a month later. Then, at the end of October 1936, the Fokker company received a purchasing commission of Spanish Republi-

The prototype Fokker C.X, sent to Spain in 1937.

can officers and agents, described as 'South Americans', at its Amsterdam factory, and agreed a contract for the sale of twenty examples of the still secret Fokker G.1 twin-boom fighter-bomber, an order later increased to twenty-five. In the event, none of these was delivered. Meanwhile, Fokker signed contracts for the manufacture under licence in Republican Spain of twenty-five Fokker C.Xs and fifty Fokker D.XXIs.

The Fokker C.X was a sturdy, handsome, unequal-span wood and metal biplane, carrying a crew of two and powered by a 650hp Rolls-Royce Kestrel V liquid-cooled engine. Designed for reconnaissance and ground-attack duties, it had two 7.9mm forward-firing machine guns mounted on top of the engine cowling, and a movable gun in the observer's cockpit. Two 175kg bombs, or four of 100kg, could be carried on underwing racks. In 1935 ten C.Xs had been ordered for the Netherlands East Indies Army Air Services, and, in the summer of 1937, a further twenty for the home-based LVA (Royal Dutch Air Force).

The Fokker D.XXI single-seat fighter had been designed for East Indies service and, since it was mistakenly believed that Japan would lack modern military aircraft for the forseeable future, emphasis had been placed on ruggedness, manoeuvrability and ease of maintenance under primitive conditions, rather than on high performance. The result was a tough-looking low-wing monoplane with an enclosed cockpit for the pilot but a fixed and spatted undercarriage. Power was provided by a 645hp

Bristol Mercury VI radial engine, and armament consisted of four 7.9mm machine guns, two in the upper fuselage and two in the wings. The project fell into temporary abeyance when the Dutch air staff decided that bombers should take priority over fighters in the East Indies, but in the summer of 1937 the LVA placed an order for thirty-six D.XXIs, to be powered by 850hp Bristol Mercury VIII engines.

It seems that Fokker finalised the Spanish contract shortly after receiving the orders for the C.X and D.XXI from the LVA. A pattern C.X, probably the original prototype, PH-ALX, arrived in Spain on 15 September 1937. Although neither Fokker nor Spanish Republican records mention the delivery of a pattern D.XXI, an aircraft did arrive in 1937. This was almost certainly the original prototype, which, despite the change of air-staff policy, had been sent to the East Indies for testing and was then returned to the Netherlands. There is no record that it reached Holland, and it appears to have been trans-shipped somewhere en route and unloaded at Alicante.

Production of both series was started by SAF-15; the C.Xs were built in the church of San Vicente in the village of Floreal de Raspeig (near Alicante), and the D.XXIs in the convent of Santa Faz, a famous shrine on the Alicante-Valencia road, built to house one of the three handkerchiefs of Saint Veronica. In overall charge of the project was Comandante Carlos Pastor Krauél, who was assisted by de Vries, a Fokker company engineer. Engines, instruments, undercarriages and some other vital parts were to be smuggled into Spain by LACEBA of Brussels (see Appendix II). Many of these failed to arrive, however, and by mid-summer 1938 only one example of each aircraft had been completed. The D.XXI, powered by a Russian M-25 radial engine taken from a written-off I-16, was tested by Mario Palacios in the presence of Gen Emilio Herrera, chief of the Technical Advisory Board of the Republican air forces and a mathematician of world renown. The C.X was fitted with an M-100A engine from a Russian SB bomber.

When the Nationalists occupied

The Fokker D.XXI prototype, which was sent to Spain in 1937.

Alicante at the end of the civil war, they found fifty sets of wings, twenty-five fuselages and twenty-five undercarriages for the D.XXIs, and twenty-five sets of wings, twenty-five fuselages and twenty-five undercarriages for the C.Xs, as well as the two complete C.Xs (the price for the fifty undercarriages was £13,302). The two complete D.XXIs had disappeared, and it seems that they were deliberately destroyed by the Republicans before the surrender. The undercarriages of the uncompleted D.XXIs, however, were used on the Hispano HS 42 trainers that Hispano Aviación built in the 1940s. The two Fokker C.Xs, bearing the military serials R.7-1 and R.7-2, remained in Spanish service until the end of the 1940s.

Fokker C.X

Span 12m; length 9.2m; height 3.30m; wing area 31.7sq m.
Empty weight 1,450kg; loaded weight 2,300kg.
Maximum speed 320km/h; cruising speed 270km/h; ceiling 8,200m; range 850km.

Fokker D.XXI

Span 11m; length 8.2m; height 3m; wing area 16.2sq m.
Empty weight 1,450kg; loaded weight 2,050kg.
Maximum speed 425km/h; cruising speed 340km/h; climb to 6,000m in 7.5min; ceiling 11,000m; range 950km.

Fokker F.VIIa

Anthony Fokker achieved fame, and notoriety, through his brilliantly conceived fighters built for the Imperial German Military Air Service during the First World War. Obliged by the defeat of Germany to return to his native Holland, he created a new company, with branches in Germany and the USA, and produced a series of single-engined commercial transport aircraft of which the last, the Fokker F.VIIa (an extensive redesign of the F.VII of 1924), first flew in March 1925. Although only thirty-five were built, the F.VIIa was the progenitor of a long line of highly successful trimotor commercial transports which began with the F.VIIb3m and ended with the F.XX. The F.VIIa was a typical Fokker concept: a high-wing cantilever monoplane with a thick-section, plywood-skinned, two-spar wooden wing and a fabric-covered, welded steel tube fuselage. There was accommodation for a pilot, copilot and eight passengers, and power was provided by a 400hp Gnome-Rhône Jupiter radial engine. Six F.VIIas built for the Polish airline LOT were fitted with 450hp Lorraine 12 Ed water-cooled 'broad-arrow' engines, and another three with Lorraine 12 Ed engines were sold to Le Société de Transports Aeriens Rapides (STAR) of France for its Paris–Cherbourg–Deauville and Le Touquet services.

Two Fokker F.VIIas flew in the Spanish Civil War, and both were 'mystery' aeroplanes in almost every

A Fokker F.VIIa with a Lorraine 12 Ed engine.

The mysterious history of Fokker F.VIIa PH-EHE is related in the text. (Ole Norbø, via R S Allen)

sense. The first to arrive, which flew with the Nationalists, took part in the airlift over the Straits of Gibraltar. In August 1936 it was transferred to the Fokker-Dragon group of bombers that was being formed, under the command of Mayor Juan-Antonio Ansaldo, at Olmedo, in Castile. Thirty years later a survivor of the group remembered that, although he had no idea where this F.VIIa had come from or what had happened to it afterwards, it had been known in the squadron as *Carlanco*. It was given this name, he said, because its cumbrous undercarriage legs reminded pilots of the wading bird of that name found in the marshes south of Seville. There can be little doubt that *Carlanco* was of French origin. On 23 July 1936 the Casablanca-based airline Compagnie des Transports Aériens Moroccains placed an advertisement in the 'Aircraft Wanted' section of *Les Ailes* for a 'Fokker monomoteur, en bon état', and within a day to two a Frenchman from Casablanca sold an

aeroplane to the Nationalists at Tetuán for 80,000 French francs in cash.

In July 1936 there were only three Fokker F.VIIas still in French ownership – the Lorraine-powered machines bought by STAR in 1930. Two, c/n 5226 F-AJUB (a three-seater) and c/n 5227 F-AJUC (an eight-seater), belonged to Photos Aériennes Moreau, and the third, c/n 5228 F-AJUD, to LANA at Algiers. When checked by Bureau Veritas in 1939, 'UC was at Le Bourget and 'UD still at Algiers. However, F-AJUB disappears from the register after its last inspection at Oran (Algeria) in 1936, and is the obvious candidate. Additional evidence is provided by the fact that Moreau's photo-survey aircraft were all painted light blue: F-AJUC, for

instance, was *Avion Bleu V*. A Carlanco is not, in fact, a wading bird at all, but the European Roller *Coracias garullas garullus*, a jay-like bird of which the male is light blue in colour with a reddish beak. Migrating from Russia and northern Europe to North Africa, it is more common in southern Spain and Morocco than in Britain. After mating, the pair start a raucous 'clacking' duet – hence the name '*garullus*', and hence, too, probably, its Spanish name Carlanco. A light blue Lorraine-powered Fokker F.VIIa (especially if its propeller-boss was painted red and its engine was old and noisy) would bear a striking resemblance to the Carlanco. This seems a more likely explanation of its nickname, and probably solves the problem of its identity as well.

The Republican Fokker F.VIIa, a standard version with a Gnome-Rhône Jupiter radial engine, was c/n 4984, originally registered H-NADN and then PH-ADN. In June 1936 Professor Gilbert Murray bought it from KLM on behalf of the League of Nations Union and handed it over to the Swedish adventurer Count von Rosen for Red Cross work in Abyssinia, during which period it carried the British registration G-AEHE. On 21 September 1936 von Rosen sold it to Henk J Warnikoff, a KLM sales agent, who in turn sold it to SFTA (see Appendix II), which was then, using the front-name 'Air Tropic', in the process of buying four Fokker trimotors from KLM for the Spanish Republicans. For the next three months it flew to and fro over the Pyrenees, bearing red crosses on wings and fuselage and a new Dutch registration, PH-EHE. On 20 March 1937 it landed in a field near Béziers, France, but the police arrested the pilot, Josef Schumaker, before he could meet the people sent to contact him. Two nights later the F.VIIa was set on fire, while still on the field, and destroyed. Later, von Rosen was told that the pilot, masquerading as a Red Cross official, had been flying gold and valuables out of Spain for sale in France to pay for arms purchases, and using this as a cover for drug smuggling.

Span 19.31m; length 14.35m; wing area 58.5sq m.

Empty weight 1,950kg; loaded weight 3,650kg.

Maximum speed 185km/h; cruising speed 150km/h; ceiling 3,125m; range 900km.

Fokker F.VIIb3m

During the summer of 1925 Reinhold Platz, who had supervised the redesign of the Fokker F.VII as the F.VIIa, studied the possibility of converting the F.VIIa into a trimotor. The project was hastily brought to reality when Henry and Edsel Ford announced a 1,900-mile Ford Reliability Tour for commercial aircraft in the USA, due to start at the end of September 1925. Because time was short, Platz's original plan to build the two outboard engine nacelles into the wings was shelved, and the two engines were mounted beneath the wings, their nacelles being braced by struts to the wing spars and fuselage frame. Although this was aesthetically less pleasing, it had the advantage of placing all three engines in the same horizontal plane, minimising trim changes under various power settings. The Fokker F.VIIa3m, as it was later designated, performed so well in the Ford Reliability Tour, and Anthony Fokker exploited the opportunity so skilfully, that journalists sourly called it the 'Fokker Publicity Tour'. This event, and a number of spectacular record-breaking and pioneering flights across the north and south Altantic, the Pacific and the North Pole during the next three years, not only won numerous orders for the Fokker company, but started a vogue in trimotor airliners that continued for the next seven years and produced such celebrated aircraft as the Ford 4-AT and the Junkers Ju 52/3m. At least twenty-one F.VIIas were converted into F.VIIa3ms. The third F.VIIa3m airframe (c/n 4954) was built with a greater span, increasing the wing area from 58.5sq m to 67.6sq m, and a longer fuselage. This variant, later designated F.VIIb3m, became the standard production version. Sixty-one F.VIIb3ms were built, and these, together with the F.VIIa3ms, became the most widely used commercial aircraft in the world during the early 1930s.

In 1929 the Spanish airline CLASSA bought a Fokker F.VIIb3m (c/n 5127) from the Swiss company Balair. It bore the Swiss registration CH-160 and was powered by three 215hp Armstrong Siddeley Lynx radial engines. In Spain it was re-registered M-CAHH (later EC-AHH). During the next eighteen months three F.VIIb3ms, powered by 300hp Wright Whirlwind J 6 radials, were bought direct from Fokker: c/n 5201 (or 5211), M-CAKK (EC-AKK); c/n 5243, M-CAMA (EC-AMA); and c/n 5244, M-CPPA (EC-PPA), the last arriving in January 1931. With the creation of LAPE they received the fleet numbers 5, 8, 10 and 11 respectively. Three more F.VIIb3ms joined LAPE in 1933, all powered by 340hp Armstrong Siddeley Serval engines: c/n 5350, EC-AAU, LAPE No. 14; c/n 5351, EC-AUA, LAPE No. 15; and c/n 5352, EC-UAA, LAPE No. 16.

In 1933 the Spanish government agreed a contract for a series of Fokker F.VIIb3m/Ms (bomber versions of the F.VIIb3m) to be built under licence by the Loring factory at Carabanchel, Madrid. A pattern aircraft, c/n 5353, fitted with three 325hp Hispano-Suiza 9Qd (licence-built Wright Whirlwind J 9/R 975) radial engines, was delivered in January 1934. The economic and political troubles of 1934 nearly brought about the cancellation of this programme, but eventually Comandante Ismael Warleta, then Director General de Aeronáutica, arranged a compromise

Fokker F.VIIb3m/M No 20-1 of the Aviación Militar.

by which three were constructed, and the four F.VIIb3m/Ms were delivered to the Fuerzas Aéreas de Africa at Cabo Juby, in Spanish West Africa. They bore the military serials 20-1 to 20-4.

With the entry of the first two Douglas DC-2s into LAPE service in 1935, two F.VIIb3ms, probably EC-AHH, No. 5 and 'AKK, No. 8, were transferred to the Aviación Militar and based at the Escuela de Vuelo y Combate at Alcalá de Henares, where they received the serials 20-5 and 20-6. After the election of the Popular Front in March 1936, the commander of the base at Alcalá, Cdte Jordana (whose brother, the Conde de Gómez Jordana, was to become Gen Franco's foreign minister), joined the conspiracy to overthrow the Republic. Early in July 1936, in preparation for the coup, the two F.VIIb3ms 20-5 and 20-6 were fitted with bomb racks. This was discovered by Coronel Hidalgo de Cisneros (who later became a Communist and chief of the Republican air forces) during a spot inspection, and the two Fokkers, together with the three de Havilland D.H.89Ms, were loaded with all the arms and munitions found on the base and transferred to Getafe. The government, however, felt that the political situation was too tense at that time (June 1936) to allow the taking of any measures against the officers at the training school.

On the eve of the rebellion, Capitán Félix Sampil, pilot of the F.VIIb3m/M 20-1, was ordered to bring his aircraft to Madrid. Next morning (18 July 1936) the same order was sent to the remaining three Fokkers at Cabo Juby. The pilot of

one, Teniente Ureña, decided to join the rebellion and landed his machine, 20-2, at Larache in Spanish Morocco. The other two, 20-3 and 20-4, were flown to Tablada Aerodrome, Seville, and, when the base was taken over by the Nationalists during the night of 18-19 July, both Fokkers were captured and their crews shot. On 20 July they were flown to Tetuán, and the next day they brought the first platoons of Franco's crack Foreign Legion troops across from Spanish Morocco to Seville. Thus, by enabling the Nationalist General Queipo de Llano to consolidate his hold on the city, which until then had been precarious, the three Fokker F.VIIb3m/Ms played a decisive part in this stage of the war. With Tablada Aerodrome safely in their hands, the Nationalists had a landing field to which they were able to fly the whole of the Army of Africa from Morocco (see Junkers Ju 52/3m), a move which quickly altered the balance of the fighting in their favour.

Throughout the remainder of July the three F.VIIb3m/Ms, which the Nationalists nicknamed *Veterano* (20-2), *Abuelo* (20-3, 'Grandfather') and *Anciano* (20-4, 'Old Man'), were used to fly troops across the Straits of Gibraltar, but they also participated in eleven bombing attacks on the Republican fleet between 21 July and 5 August. By the beginning of August a new flying ground had been completed near Jerez, and it was here that 20-4 came to grief. The Fokker was carrying one of Franco's ablest commanders, Mayor (later General) Carlos Asensio, from Africa, when it crashed on landing and was written off. On 6 August 20-2 *Veterano* was flown to Gamonal Aerodrome, Burgos, to join the air component of the Nationalist forces commanded by Gen Mola in northern Spain, and was shortly followed by 20-3 *Abuelo*.

On 13 August 1936 the Nationalist squadron at Gamonal received a welcome reinforcement in the form of two ex-KLM F.VIIb3ms flown from Croydon, London: c/n 5187 PH-AGR *Reiger* (Heron) and c/n 5263 PH-AFS *Specht* (Woodpecker). These had been bought for 37,000Fl (£5,000) by the Spanish ex-air-attaché in Paris and London, Comandante Carmelo de las Morenes Alcalá, who had joined the National-

ists. At first KLM had refused to sell because of Non-Intervention, but eventually agreed provided the aircraft were sold to Crilly Airways and flown to Croydon by KLM pilots. The two F.VIIb3ms, with additional petrol drums strapped into the passenger seats, were flown non-stop from Croydon to Burgos by T Neville Stack and Donald Salisbury Green in a hazardous journey lasting 7hours 15 minutes. They were converted into bombers with the military serials 20-1 and 20-4 (to replace the 20-1 that had gone to the Republicans and the 20-4 that had crashed) and, with two F.XIIs, the F.VIIa, and four Dragon Rapides flown from England, were formed into a 'Fokker-Dragon' Grupo under the command of Mayor J-A Ansaldo, based at Olmedo. The group, which moved from aerodrome to aerodrome in northern Spain, performed bombing missions until the end of the year. During these actions 20-3 *Abuelo* (piloted by a German named Schleicher) was forced down over Jaca, near the French frontier, on 7 October 1936, and 20-1 (Ex-PH-AFS *Specht*) was lost, though whether in action or from some other cause is not known.

After the disbanding of the group, 20-2 *Veterano* and 20-4 (renamed *Abuelo*) were transferred to the Escuela de Tripulantes y Observadores (Observer and Air Crew Training School) based first at Tablada, Seville, and then at Rompedizos Aerodrome, Málaga. Shortly before the end of the civil war, 20-4 *Abuelo* (ex-PH-AGR *Reiger*) was withdrawn from service, but 20-2 *Veterano* continued flying until the early 1940s, bearing the new military serial 45-2.

At the start of the civil war the Republicans possessed the F.VIIb3m/M 20-1, the five F.VIIb3ms of LAPE (of which only three, apparently, were airworthy) and the two F.VIIb3ms at Getafe, which had been thoughtfully provided with bomb racks by the Nationalist conspirators. On 18 July 1936 these two, accompanied by a 'converted' DC-2, bombed the aerodrome and the port at Tetuán. The chief effect of this raid, since the bombs intended for the docks fell on the Sultan of Morocco's palace and killed fifteen people, was to bring the

Moors into the war on the side of Gen Franco. One LAPE F.VIIb3m, which had returned from the Canaries to Seville a few days before the revolt, was flown to Madrid late on 18 July by a Republican crew who were able to take off from Tablada thanks to the clouds of dust thrown up by the propellers, which temporarily blinded their pursuers. A second, EC-PPA, arrived at Barcelona from Mallorca just before the island was taken over by the Nationalists. Nicknamed *Abuelo*, like 20-3 of the Nationalists, it was converted into a bomber. Two steel tubes were slung across the passenger saloon to project out of the windows, and another tube was attached on each side, from which three 50kg bombs were suspended. On the night of 2-3 August EC-PPA *Abuelo*, piloted by Manuél Gayoso, made a raid on Saragossa. Of the six 50kg bombs dropped, three struck the cathedral of the Virgen del Pilar, a venerated shrine, but failed to explode. The bishop and the devout citizens of Saragossa proclaimed a miracle. Later, however, Gayoso caustically observed that, since the bombs were of surplus First World War stock, the miracle was that any had exploded at all. On 8 August EC-PPA was transferred to the so-called *Alas Rojas* (Red Wings) group at Sariñena in Aragon and became, literally, the flagship of the bomber formation popularly called 'La Balumba' (The Midden Heap) by the Anarchist militia holding this sector of the front. The formation consisted of the F.VIIb3m, a Latécoère 28, two or three D.H.84 Dragons, six Breguet 19s, a Vickers Vildebeest and occasionally one or two light aeroplanes, fighter escort being provided by the D.H.89M No. 22-2 and four Nieuport 52s. As 'La Balumba' approached the target, Eladio Pericás, the bomb aimer in the Fokker (which led the formation), would tug on a rope attached to the foot of the gunner, Serjento Prieto, who would raise a red flag. Thereupon the formation would close up and await the signal to drop its bombs, which in theory came when Pericás tugged twice and the gunner raised a green flag. However, Pericás was a large and strong man and Prieto rather small, and in his excitement Pericás sometimes tugged so hard that Prieto was pulled down into the fuselage before he could raise his flag, which would necessitate a second pass over the target.

Early in September 1936 a second F.VIIb3m from LAPE and the F.VIIb3m/M that had remained in Republican hands, the original 20-1, joined EC-PPA to take part in the brief Republican offensive against Huesca, during which they occasionally came face to face with the Nationalist F.VIIb3ms and F.XIIs of the 'Fokker-Dragon' group, which had been temporarily transferred to this sector. On the Madrid front, another ex-LAPE Fokker F.VIIb3m, the rear half of its fuselage painted bright red and flown by the flamboyant, publicity-seeking military pilot Capitán Antonio Rexach, was used daily to bomb the Nationalist garrison besieged in the Alcázar fortress at Toledo. His gunner, and inseparable companion, was Pablo Rada, who had been flight mechanic on the Dornier Wal *Plus Ultra* in which Ramón Franco and Ruiz de Alda had made the first crossing of the South Atlantic in 1926. This Fokker was damaged by a heavy landing at Herrera del Duque and written off, after which Rexach and Rada went to France on the pretext of buying new aircraft, and from there, with the money entrusted to them, absconded to Cuba. Early in October 1936 the LAPE pilot José-María Carreras ferried the F.VIIb3m/M to Bilbao to reinforce the tiny Basque air arm. It was still flying in December 1936, but its ultimate fate is unrecorded. On 19 October 1936 EC-PPA narrowly escaped destruction when 'La Balumba' was attacked by a number of Heinkel He 51s. It was saved by Luis Aguilera, who, flying the black-painted D.H.89M *Avion Negus* (22-2), drew the Germans away, at the cost of his own life, while the Fokker escaped into cloud.

Little is known of the activities of the Republican Fokker F.VIIb3ms after November 1936. Two were lost when, having been severely mauled in an encounter with Italian-flown Fiat C.R.32s on 4 February 1937, they made an emergency landing on Rompedizos aerodrome, Málaga, which was captured by the Nationalists four days later. At least one more F.VIIb3m was acquired abroad, c/n

5136 F-AJCH *Le Radieuse* of Air France, which was bought for 120,000 French francs (£1,621) through SFTA in the spring of 1937. (Some sources have said that F-AJCH was sold in Switzerland, registered CH-193, and written off in 1935, but this is disproved by a Republican document.) On 6 May 1937 EC-UAA (LAPE No. 16) flew gold from Valencia to Paris, and was wrecked while landing in a snowstorm in the south of France on 22 December 1937. On 3 June 1937 two F.VIIb3ms, the F.XII and the F.IX, together with seventeen Russian R-5 biplanes escorted by nineteen fighters, flew daylight sorties against La Granja de Revenca and Hill 1220 in the Sierra de Guadarrama, and similar operations continued for two more weeks. Thereafter, the F.VIIb3ms, like the other Fokker trimotors, were relegated to training duties at the Escuela de Polimótores (Multi-engined Flying School) at Totana in Murcia. One was shot down in 1939, and must have been the last airworthy F.VIIb3m in Republican service, for none survived the war.

Span 21.71m; length 14.56m; height 3.88m; wing area 67.6sq m.

Empty weight 2,900kg; loaded weight 5,000kg.

Maximum speed 185km/h; cruising speed 150km/h; ceiling 3,100m; range 775km.

Fokker F.IX

The F.IX, of which only two were built, was Fokker's largest trimotor transport, and was intended to carry six passengers in sleeping accommodation on the Holland–Dutch-East-Indies route. The prototype,

c/n 5106, PH-AGA *Adelaar* (Eagle), powered by three 480hp Gnome-Rhône Jupiter VI radial engines, first flew on 26 August 1929, and was delivered to KLM on 5 October. The second, PH-AFK, which had a larger fuselage and could seat up to 20 passengers, entered service in May 1930, but was destroyed in a crash in August 1931. After a proving flight to Batavia (Jakarta), PH-AGA was converted to an ordinary airliner with seating for seventeen passengers, and, re-engined with three 650hp Pratt & Whitney Hornet T1C1 radials with Townend rings, was used only on European routes, chiefly from Amsterdam to London. Twelve examples of a bomber version, designated F.39, were built by Avia for the Czechoslovak air force.

The Fokker F.IX was one of the four trimotors sold to the Spanish Republicans in October 1936 (see Fokker F.XII for details) and, while in transit through France, received the registration F-APFA. There is no record of its Spanish service until 1 March 1937, when it was incorporated into a night-bombing unit, Grupo 11, under Comandante Juan Armario, along with the F.XII, F.XVIII, two Bloch MB 210s and four Potez 54s. It was fitted with vertical bomb racks inside the passenger cabin, from which the bombs could be released only in pairs. It was probably this aircraft that, with the racks removed, flew a large cargo of food and medicine from Lérida to Bilbao on 3 March 1937. Having crossed 350km of Nationalist terri-

Fokker F.VIIb3m PH-AGR of KLM was flown from Croydon to Burgos on 13 August 1936 by Donald Salisbury Green, and became 20-4 in Ansaldo's 'Grupo Fokker-Dragon'.

The Fokker F.IX PH-AGA Adelaar.

tory, it overflew France and reached Bilbao from the Bay of Biscay. The pilot was Armario, and his copilot was Francisco Pérez Mur. After returning on 21 March it was refitted as a bomber, its first mission being an attack on the artillery barracks at Saragossa. Night bombing missions continued through April and May, the squadron moving from Sariñena to Lérida, Balaguer, Castejón and Alcañiz. On 28 April the F.XII was damaged during a night landing. Two F.VIIb3ms were added to the squadron, now designated Grupo 15, and in June the four trimotors, together with seventeen R-5s and escorted by nineteen fighters, carried out daylight missions over the Segovia front. On 18 June 1937 five Fokker trimotors (the F.XII having been repaired) bombed Saragossa aerodrome, and on 19 June the F.IX and F.XVIII, having sufficient range, bombed Pamplona railway station. Whether the F.XI continued as a bomber or reverted to its transport rôle shortly thereafter is not clear, but it was certainly a transport by 1938. It survived the civil war, was recovered by the Nationalists, and soldiered on for a few years in Grupo 45 of the Ejercito del Aire.

Span 27.17m; length 19.42m; wing area 103sq m.

Empty weight 5,150kg; loaded weight 9,350kg.

Maximum speed 235km/h; cruising speed 210km/h; ceiling 3,000m; range 1,480km.

Fokker F.XII

The Fokker F.XII, larger than the F.VIIb3m but smaller than the F.IX,

One of the four Fokker F.XIIs sold to the Nationalists by British Airways, G-ADZK crash-landed at Lagord Aerodrome, near La Rochelle, France, on 15 August 1936, and never reached Spain. (A J Jackson)

was a three-engined development of the twin-engined F.VIII, powered by 425hp Pratt & Whitney Wasp C radial engines in Townend-ring cowlings and seating 16 passengers. Eleven were built in 1931 and 1932, and four of these were bought from KLM by Crilly Airways to fly on a proposed route from Croydon to Lisbon in December 1935. These were: c/n 5284, PH-AFV *Valk* (Falcon), which became G-ADZH; c/n 5285, PH-AFU-II *Uil* (Owl), which became 'ZI; c/n 5292 PH-AIE *Ekster* (Magpie), which became 'ZJ; and c/n 5301 PH-AII *Ibis*, which became 'ZK. When this plan failed, owing to opposition by the Spanish government, Crilly sold them to British Airways for £15,000 in February 1936. Keen to open a route to South America via Portugal, British Airways tried to revive the London–Lisbon project, and meanwhile employed the four F.XIIs on its Paris and Scandinavian services. At the same time the aircraft were put up for sale, but, since they were now obsolescent, their asking price dropped to £2,000 each.

On 20 July 1936 Robert Henry McIntosh landed at Gen Mola's headquarters on Gamonal aerodrome, Burgos, in a British Airways de

Havilland D.H.89 Dragon Rapide. He brought three journalists, and, at Mola's request, arranged for the purchase of the four F.XIIs through the British Airways agent in Lisbon, James Rawes and Co. The price of £38,000 was to be paid in advance, in gold coins. This transaction was spoilt by the folly of the managing director of British Airways, Maj MacCrindle, who, against McIntosh's express warnings, decided to stage the ferry flight via Paris and

Bordeaux, and by the malice of the company's representative in Paris. This man had wanted to buy the airliners himself and resell them to Mola for £60,000. In pique, he informed the pro-Republican French air minister, Pierre Cot, of what was afoot. Accordingly, when the four F.XIIs were about to leave Bordeaux, they were impounded and held until 1 August, when only the personal intervention of the British Foreign Secretary, Anthony Eden, secured their release on the promise that they would not be sold to any Spanish buyer.

No sooner had they landed at Gatwick than British Airways received an offer of 1,000,000 French francs (£13,157) each for them from l'Office Générale de l'Air (see Dewoitine D.371 and Potez 54), which was then, under Pierre Cot's supervision, procuring aircraft for the Spanish Republicans. This offer was refused, but on 10 August 1936 an

Fokker F.XII ex-PH-AIJ IJsvogel *serving with the night-bombing unit Grupo 11 in June 1937.*

offer of £33,000 for the four was made by Stefan Czarniecki, a Polish arms dealer, on behalf of C Morawski, who represented a Danzig (Gdansk) firm named 'West Export' which in turn was acting for a mining company at Katowice in southern Poland. On 12 August four Polish pilots arrived to fly the F.XIIs to Katowice. When the aircraft took off next morning, however, it transpired that the pilots had never flown large, multi-engined aircraft before, and, moreover, instead of flying towards Poland, they headed south across France. Thunderstorms over the Pyrenees turned three of the Fokkers back. One, 'ZK, crash-landed at Lagord aerodrome, near La Rochelle, a second, 'ZJ, landed safely at Bordeaux, but the third, 'ZI, piloted by Count Kazimiercz Lasocki, was apparently struck by lightning while trying to land at Parme-Biarritz, and was destroyed, the pilot (and, it was believed, C Morawski) being killed instantly. The fourth, 'ZH, piloted by Adam Szareck (winner of the 1935 light aeroplane contest in Poland) managed to cross the Pyrenees and land in the grounds of a sanatorium at Barañan, near Vitoria. Szareck refused to fly it further, and the F.XII was flown to Burgos by Capitán Ángel Salas, who had had some experience with the F.VIIb3m/Ms of the Aviación Militar in Africa.

On 6 September 1936 the French authorities released G-ADZJ. On arriving at Burgos it was incorporated into Mayor Ansaldo's Grupo Fokker-Dragon, the two F.XIIs receiving the military serials 20-5 and 20-6. Each was fitted with bomb racks and a rudimentary dorsal gun position. The F.XIIs operated with the group on the northern front until December. On one occasion (11 October), while dropping supplies to the Nationalist garrison beseiged in Oviedo, the two F.XIIs were attacked by German He 51s, whose pilots mistook them for Republican aircraft. One of the Fokker pilots, Rodríguez Carmona, was so badly wounded that his arm had to be amputated. On 30 November 1936

20-6, flown by Julián del Val, in company with a Dragon Rapide and some Breguet 19s, succeeded in blocking a narrow pass and trapping forty Republican lorries and several thousand troops on the south side of Arbalán mountain. In 1937 both F.XIIs were relegated to transport duties and, later in the year, to the aircrew training school at Tetuán, Spanish Morocco, with the new military serials 45-5 and 45-6. The latter was written off after an accident, but 45-5 survived the war.

One Fokker F.XII, c/n 5306, PH-AIJ *IJsvogel* (Kingfisher), flew on the Republican side. This aircraft was sold on 12 September 1936 by KLM to Alfred Pilain, a Frenchman acting for the newly created SFTA. Ostensibly the buyer was 'Air Tropic', a non-existent airline which was supposed to be opening a service between Dakar and Gao (near Timbuctu) in French West Africa. On 25 September Pilain bought three more Fokker trimotors, the F.IX, an F.XVIII and the F.XX, the total cost of the four being given as 12 million French francs, which was then registered as the nominal capital of SFTA. After refurbishing and repainting, the four Fokkers arrived at Le Bourget, Paris, on 23 October, all bearing French registrations, that of the F.XII being F-APET. There was loud denunication in the French pro-Nationalist press, and the British air attaché in Paris informed the Foreign Office of this breach of Non-Intervention. On Saturday 25

October SFTA announced that, before they went to Africa, the four Fokkers would be flown to Madrid by volunteer pilots (Antoine, Chailloux, Cornet and Chase) to bring out French citizens who wished to leave. The aircraft took off next morning, before the British Foreign Office could protest to the French government. During the spring and summer of 1937 the F.XII joined the night-bomber squadron at Sariñena. In July it was relegated to transport duties, and it may have been the Fokker reputedly damaged or destroyed by the Cagoulards (a French Fascist terrorist group) at Toussus on 19 August 1937. At any rate, it disappears from the records about this time, and did not survive the war.

Span 23.02m; length 17.8m; height 6.3m; wing area 83sq m.

Empty weight 4,359kg; loaded weight 7,250kg.

Maximum speed 230km/h; cruising speed 205 km/h; ceiling 3,400m; range 1,300km.

Fokker F.XVIII

The F.XVIII was the last trimotor to follow the traditional Fokker pattern set by the F.VII, and five, powered by 420hp Pratt & Whitney Wasp C radials, were built in 1932-33 for the Holland–Dutch-East-Indies route. One of these, c/n 5309, PH-AIP *Pelikaan*, flew to Batavia (Jakarta, Indonesia) and back, a total of over 29,000km, in four days in December

Fokker F.XVIII PH-AIP Pelikaan *after its record-breaking 'Christmas Mail' return flight to Batavia (Indonesia) in December 1933, which took four days each way. Left to right: Capt Boris Smirnoff, copilot Soer, Grosfeld and Van Beukering.* (Jack Meaden)

1933, with four passengers in sleeping accommodation and a heavy load of mail. It continued to fly this arduous route until it was transferred to European service in 1935. In October 1936, together with the F.IX, an F.XII and the F.XX, PH-AIP was sold to the Spanish Republicans (see Fokker F.XII), re-registered F-APIP in France, and, after serving as a bomber, was used as a transport until the fall of Catalonia. It was destroyed when the Condor Legion attacked Vilajuiga aerodrome on 6 February 1939. A photograph of its burnt-out wreckage was published in the German and Italian newspapers as proof that the Dutch were flouting Non-Intervention, but the captions did not mention that this had once been the world famous *Pelikaan* of KLM.

Span 24.5m; length 18.5m; height 4.57m; wing area 84sq m.
Empty weight 4,590kg; loaded weight 7,550kg.
Maximum speed 240km/h; cruising speed 210km/h; ceiling 4,800m; range 1,820km.

The F.XX in Republican camouflage, on a French aerodrome.

Fokker F.XX

The last trimotor to come off the Fokker drawing boards, the F.XX was an attempt to modernise the formula by adopting a more streamlined form and a retractable undercarriage (manually operated by two large wheels to the rear of the flightdeck). The traditional ply-covered wooden wing and fabric-covered steel-tube fuselage were retained, and power was provided by three 640hp Wright Cyclone R-1820-F radial engines, later replaced by three 690hp Cyclone R.1820-F2s. There was accommodation for a crew of three, twelve passengers and an unusually large quantity of baggage, part of which was stored in the wing centre section.

The F.XX was the second largest of the Fokker trimotors after the F.IX, and perhaps its greatest asset was its useful load of 3,500kg, which gave it an excellent tare:load ratio of 39.5:61.5. Its handling qualitites in the air, however, left much to be desired, and, after prolonged trials, including a flight to the Dutch East Indies and back, no production order was received.

The sole F.XX, c/n 5347 PH-AIZ *Zilvermeeuw* (Silver Gull), was kept on KLM European services until it was sold, along with the F.IX, an F.XII and an F.XVIII, to SFTA in October 1936 on behalf of a non-existent airline, 'Air Tropic', its temporary French registration being F-APEZ. It crossed into Spain on 26 October 1936, but nothing more is heard of it until 6 January 1937, when it was seen at Toulouse-Francazal aerodrome, France, en route to or from Barcelona, painted with wave-band camouflage and bearing the governmental registration EC-45-E in yellow on its fuselage. On 1 March it was forced down by a snowstorm at Feytiat Aerodrome, Limoges. On 4 and 14 June, and 8 August, 1937, it carried gold bullion and jewellery to Paris, and was described in some French newspapers as a 'Russian bomber'. It was not popular with Republican pilots and, after two of its engines had been replaced by a Russian M-25 from an I-16 and a Walter Merkur from a Letov S 231, which caused it to yaw viciously on take-off, it became even less popular. In the first week of February 1938 the

The Fokker F.XX.

LAPE pilot Eduardo Soriano crashed it on Prat de Llobregat Airport, Barcelona. His colleagues were so relieved that they refused to believe that he had not done it 'accidentally on purpose'.

Span 25.7m; length 16.7m; height 4.55m; wing area 96sq m.
Empty weight 5,350kg; loaded weight 8,850kg; wing loading 92.12kg/sq m.
Maximum speed 305km/h; cruising speed 250km/h; ceiling 6,600m; range 1,660km.

Ford 4-AT-F and 5-AT-B Trimotor

The Ford Trimotor belongs in the gallery of immortals in air transport history. For more than forty years Trimotors served with over a hundred different operating companies all over the world, performing every kind of duty from passenger-carrying to fire-fighting, crop-spraying and even occasional rather stately exhibitions of aerobatics. The 4-AT-A was developed from the Ford 2-AT and 3-AT transports built by the Stout Metal Airplane Company Division of the Ford Motor Company, and its layout was probably influenced by the success of the Fokker F.VIIb3m in the Ford Reliability Tour of September 1925. The prototype first flew on 11 June 1926. Powered by three uncowled 200hp Wright Whirlwind J-4 radial engines, the 4-AT-A was built of duralumin, with a skinning of corrugated Alclad (a three-ply having a duralumin centre layer and aluminium outer coverings). By the 1950s its structure had earned the Trimotor the affectionate nicknames of 'Tin Goose' and 'Tin Lizzie'. Most of the 4-AT series, of which seventy-one were built in six variants (4-AT-A through to 4-AT-F) carried twelve passengers.

The first Ford Trimotor to reach Spain was the Ford 4-AT-E-68 (US registration NC8406), bought by the Spanish airline Compañía de Líneas Aéreas Subvencionadas SA (CLAS-SA) in 1929 and delivered to Barajas by the ferry pilot Van Zahn. Once there, however, it was grounded for nearly a year. First, the Junkers company in Germany had brought a suit against Ford for infringement of patent by employing corrugated metal skinning, an invention which had become almost the trademark of Junkers aircraft since the J.4 of 1917. While the case was being heard, all Ford Trimotors were grounded. Second, through some carelessness the Ford had been transported across the Atlantic lashed on the deck of the ship, and seawater had corroded areas of its Alclad skin. This provoked a second lawsuit against Ford. By May 1930 the Junkers case was resolved and the Ford, which had been repaired in the meantime, made its first flight from Getafe to Gandó, Gran Canaria, on 20 May, with José-María Ansaldo (brother of J-A Ansaldo – see D.H. Puss Moth, D.H. Dragon Rapide and IMAM Ro 37bis) as pilot and Eduardo Soriano (see Fokker F.XX) as copilot. The aircraft, registered M-CKKA (later

Ford Trimotors at the Ford factory, Dearborn, Michigan. Aircraft EC-W10, the last 4-AT to be built, became EC-RRA.

EC-KKA), remained in service with CLASSA (and, after 1931, with LAPE) on the Spain–Morocco–Canary Islands route until 1933. After an accident it was shipped to England, repaired, re-registered G-ACAK and resold to Holden's Air Transport, New Guinea, where it remained at work as VH-OSZ until it was destroyed by Japanese bombers in March 1942.

In 1931 production of the Ford 4-AT series ceased, though the slightly larger 5-AT series remained in production until 1932. The last 4-AT to be built, the 4-AT-71 (the one and only Model 4-AT-F), was completed in July 1931 and registered NC9656. It had three 300hp Wright Whirlwind J-6 (R-975) engines, with NACA cowlings on the outboard engines, and seating for eleven passengers. Cabin décor, comfort, heating and ventilation were improved. This aeroplane was sold to LAPE and, bearing the ferry registration EC-W10, was delivered by J Parker Van Zandt, a well-known pilot and aviation writer from Arizona. It was registered EC-RRA, and its LAPE fleet number may have been 12. Like EC-KKA, it flew on the Madrid–Barcelona–Valencia–Seville–Canary Islands routes. During the civil war it continued to serve as a general transport. In his book *Some Still Live* (New York, 1938), Frank Tinker mentions that the American volunteer pilot Albert J Baumler (who later flew with Chennault's 'Flying Tigers' in China) flew in the Ford from Madrid to Valencia on 30 July 1937. After the civil war the Ford was taken over by the Nationalists and incorporated into the Ejercito del Aire with the military serial 42-8. In February 1941 it was transferred to Iberia, registered EC-BAB, and used on the Tangiers–Tetuán–Melilla route in Spanish Morocco for three months. On 17 May 1941, however, it was sent to replace a D.H.89 Dragon Rapide (or D.H.84 Dragon) which, with Junkers Ju 52 No. 67, had been employed on trial flights to reopen the Madrid–Las Palmas (Canary Islands) route but had crashed at Tenerife in the first week of May. The Ford continued in this service until it was returned to the Ejercito del Aire in 1942. It was used as a transport by the

The Freüller Valls MA, apparently the aircraft in which Arthur Koestler was flown to Gibraltar by Carlos de Haya after an international press campaign had secured his release from a Nationalist prison. He was exchanged for Haya's wife, until then a prisoner of the Republicans. (José Warleta)

Estado Mayor del Aire (General Air Staff) until withdrawn from duties, probably in 1945.

Some researchers believe that a second Ford Trimotor joined the Republican air forces during the civil war, although the author has found no surviving ex-LAPE pilots who remember it. The most likely candidate would be the Ford 5-AT-B c/n 42, ex-NC9676, which was sold as a photo-survey aircraft to Royal Dutch East Indies Airlines (KNILM) in September 1935 and re-registered PK-AKE. The airline thought it unsuitable, and bought three D.H.89 Dragon Rapides instead. The Ford remained at Schiphol until at least 26 August 1936, when its registration was cancelled. According to contemporary rumours, it was bought either by a company in England or by the Bataafische Petroleum Maatschappi in what is now Indonesia, but it never reached either country. Indeed, because it disappears from all records without explanation after August 1936, the supposition that it went to Spain is not absurd. It might have been destroyed in one of the Nationalist bombing attacks on Barajas or Getafe before its presence became generally known.

Ford 4-AT-F

Span 74ft; length 49ft 10in; height 11ft 9in; wing area 785sq ft.

Empty weight 6,929lb; loaded weight 11,000lb.

Maximum speed 138mph; cruising speed 113mph; landing speed 52mph; ceiling 14,000ft; range 540 miles.

Freüller Valls MA

A tiny low-wing monoplane with an enclosed cabin for two occupants seated side-by-side, a trousered undercarriage, and a 90-95hp Pobjoy radial engine in a long-chord cowling, the MA was the third aeroplane to be designed and built by the Malagueño aristocrat José Freüller Valls, the Marqués de la Paniega. The airframe was of fabric-covered light alloy tubing, and the wings were braced by a pair of inverted V-struts. Registered EC-BBC, the MA first flew in 1935, and, with a top speed of 220km/h, so impressed Joaquín García Morato that he planned to enter it for the International Light Aeroplane Contest in 1936. This hope was dashed by the outbreak of the civil war, and the aeroplane, which Freüller had presented to the Aero Club de Málaga, remained on Rompedizos Aerodrome. When the Nationalist uprising was crushed in the city, in July 1936, nearly every member of Freüller Valls's family was executed. Freüller himself, perhaps because of his prestige as an aeronautical engineer, was kept under house arrest until Nationalist troops reached the outskirts of Málaga on 7 February 1937, when a squad of Republican militia took him from his home and shot him.

It seems that, after the capture of Málaga, the Freüller Valls MA was transferred to Tablada air base, Seville. In his autobiography *The Invisible Writing* (London, 1954), Arthur Koestler describes how, after he had been condemned to death as a spy by the Nationalists and held in Seville prison, a press campaign in

The General Aircraft Monospar ST-12 G-ADDY, sold to the Nationalists in August 1936. (A J Jackson)

Monospar ST-25 Jubilee G-AEGX Florence Nightingale was the first Monospar ambulance. In February 1937 it was acquired by the confidence trickster 'Mick' Corrigan, flown to France by 'Charles Kennett', and sold to the Republicans via SFTA. (Philip Jarrett)

England influenced Gen Franco to release him in exchange for a prisoner held by the Republicans, the wife of the distinguished Nationalist pilot Carlos de Haya. Haya himself flew Koestler to Gibraltar, where the exchange was made, in an aeroplane called 'The Baby Douglas'. On being questioned about this by the author, Koestler said that the one fact he was sure of was that he had sat next to Haya, not behind or in front of him. On being shown photographs of various types of light aircraft known to have been at Seville at the time, but without being told which had side-by-side seating, he picked out the Freüller Valls as the aircraft that jogged his memory most strongly. As it was the only machine in the selection with side-by-side seating, this seems to establish the identity of the 'Baby Douglas' beyond reasonable doubt.

Dimensions and weights: none available.

Maximum speed 220km/h.

General Aircraft Monospar ST-12 and ST-25

Until the early 1930s, the chief objection to the cantilever monoplane was that, in order to possess the required strength, its wing had to be extremely thick, and therefore excessively heavy. One solution to this problem, invented by the Swiss engineer H J Steiger, was to build the wing round a single duralumin spar of the Warren girder type, braced by load-bearing tie-rods, the whole being covered with fabric. The British Air Ministry was sufficiently interested to commission two 'Monospar' wings and to test one of them on a Fokker F.VIIb3m.

The first aircraft designed on this principle was the ST-3, built for the Monospar Wing Company by Gloster Aircraft in 1931. It showed sufficient promise to justify the formation of General Aircraft Ltd, at Croydon, for the purpose of developing further aircraft using the Monospar formula. The General Aircraft Monospar ST-4, a scaled-up ST-3, was a four-seat low-wing cabin monoplane with a fixed wide-track undercarriage, powered by a pair of uncowled 85hp Pobjoy R radial engines. Four were built, followed by twenty-six ST-4 Mk IIs with minor internal modifications and nose landing-lights. The ST-6 was a five-seater with a redesigned forward fuselage, a retractable undercarriage and cowled 90hp Pobjoy Niagara Is. The ST-10, while reverting to the fixed undercarriage, introduced further aerodynamic refinements in the fuselage and tail unit. Twenty-two were built, and one of these, G-ACTS, won the King's Cup air race in July 1934. The ST-12 was

powered by two 130hp de Havilland Gipsy Major inverted in-line engines, and possessed the highest performance of all Monospars. Four were built for British owners, and several for export, including one, c/n 43, sold in 1935 to the Spanish Dirección General de Aeronáutica for photographic survey work. Its ferry registration was EC-W43, but its Spanish registration is not known (EC-6-E?). The Monospar ST-18 Croydon, which appeared in 1935, was a ten-passenger commercial airliner with a retractable undercarriage, powered by two 450hp Pratt & Whitney Wasp Junior radial engines. Only one, G-AECB, was built (see below). The ST-25, with 90hp Pobjoy Niagara II engines, was the last Monospar built in quantity. It was produced in three versions: the ST-25 Jubilee (1935, the year of its appearance, was the Jubilee year of King George V), carrying a pilot and five passengers; the ST-25 De Luxe (95hp Niagara IIIs) with four seats and an enlarged fin; and the ST-25

A General Aircraft Monospar ST-25 Universal captured by the Nationalists after the civil war.

Universal, with twin fins and rudders, which was convertible to serve as a transport carrying a pilot, three passengers and baggage; as a freighter; or as an air ambulance. S J Noel-Brown, who was secretary to General Aircraft (which built a new factory at Hanworth Aerodrome in 1936), was also a part-time official of the British Red Cross, and he was the moving spirit behind the project to build a series of Monospar ambulance aircraft. The first Monospar to be converted was one of the two ST-25 De Luxes, G-AEGX, which was christened *Florence Nightingale* by Amy Johnson during a ceremony at Hanworth in June 1936. The ten other air ambulances built were ST-25 Universals.

In June 1935 don Carlos Muntadas Salvadó-Prim, the Marqués de Prim, bought the ST-25 Jubilee c/n 53 G-ADMZ, which was re-registered EC-AFF. Early on the morning of 18 July 1936, while news of the rebellion in Spanish Morocco was being announced over the wireless, the Marqués and two relatives took off from Barcelona for Biarritz, to take part in the Rally Côte Basque on the 20th, but returned to Spain to join the uprising on 22 July, landing the ST-25 in the grounds of the Piedra monastery south of Calatayud. The next Monospar to reach Spain during the civil war likewise went to the Nationalists. This was the ST-12 G-ADDY (c/n 39), registered to R J B Seaman. Probably procured through Tom Campbell Black, it was flown to Burgos, via France, by the company's chief test pilot, Capt H C MacPhaill, with L T C Castlemaine as navigator, leaving Heston at 10.15am on 2 August 1936. This ST-12 was later attached to the Condor Legion as a utility aeroplane.

On 4 August 1936 the ST-12 (c/n 43) of the photographic unit at Cuatro Vientos, Madrid, was flown, via France, to San Sebastián by Teniente Coronel Antonio Sanjuán Canete.

The next three Monospars to arrive from abroad went to the Republicans. The ST-25 Jubilee G-ADPI (c/n 54), registered to Hubert Holliday of Mobiloil (see D.H.90 Dragonfly) and the ST-25 Jubilee G-ADVG (c/n 61), bought from General Aircraft through Aircraft Exchange & Mart, were seen at Barcelona on 22 August 1936. A second Jubilee bought from Aircraft Exchange & Mart, G-ADSN (c/n 58), arrived at Bilbao, in the Basque zone, before 12 August. It was quickly converted into a 'bomber', and on 16 August Eloy Fernández Navamuel bombed the Nationalist patrol boat *Tiburón*, forcing it to sail into Santander and surrender. G-ADSN and the ST-12 took part in the Republican offensive in the Villareal sector and, together with other assorted aircraft flown by volunteers of various nationalities (including a Miles Hawk Major and a Miles Falcon), carried out a 'forlorn hope' raid on 11 December 1936 against Vitoria Aerodrome, which was being enlarged to accommodate the fighter- and He 70-equipped units of the Condor Legion. One Monospar (probably ex-G-ADSN), flown by the Englishman Sydney Holland, was shot down over the aerodrome, the pilot and his Russian observer being killed. The ST-12 (if that was the survivor) was later converted into an ambulance, and was still flying in September 1937, towards the end of the northern campaign.

In February 1937 the original Monospar ambulance, G-AEGX *Florence Nightingale*, somehow came into the hands of the confidence trickster Denis 'Mick' Corrigan, who sold it to SFTA. Charles Kennett, who had flown for the Spanish Republicans in September 1936 and then been employed in smuggling jewellery confiscated in Republican Spain into France and England (see D.H.80A Puss Moth), flew G-AEGX from Hanworth to Meaulte, the Potez company aerodrome near Albert in northern France, without clearance on 17 February. At that time Meaulte was a chief staging post for aircraft on their way to Spain from Britain and the Low Countries. When Kennett and his partner Bannister-Pickett tried to deliver two more Monospar ST-25s (G-AEVN and 'WN) in March, however, the authorities grounded both machines. Despite this, General Aircraft apparently did succeed in exporting seven more ST-25s to Republican Spain:

G-ADLT c/n 50, Jubilee, F-AQAC (May 1937), SFTA, Spain Sept.1937.

G-ADWH, c/n 63, Jubilee,

	ST-12	Jubilee	De Luxe	Universal
Span	40ft 2in	40ft 2in	40ft 2in	40ft 2in
Length	26ft 4in	26ft 4in	26ft 4in	25ft 4in
Height	7ft 10in	7ft 10in	7ft 10in	7ft 10in
Wing area	217sq ft	217sq ft	217sq ft	217sq ft
Empty weight	1,840lb	1,680lb	1,758lb	1,818lb
Loaded weight	2,875lb	2,875lb	2,875lb	2,875lb
Maximum speed	158mph	142mph	135mph	131mph
Cruising speed	142mph	130mph	123mph	115mph
Ceiling	21,000ft	16,000ft	12,000ft	15,300ft
Range	410 miles	585 miles	496 miles	419 miles

F-AQAD (May 1937), SFTA, Spain Sept.1937.

G-ADWI, c/n 64, Jubilee, F-AQCL (June 1937). SFTA, Spain Sept.1937.

— —. c/n 67, Universal F-AQOL. Unconfirmed.

G-AEPG, c/n 87, Universal F-AQOM, date unknown.

G-AEMN, c/n 88, Universal. Departed Nov.1937.

G-AFDC, c/n 98, Universal. Unconfirmed.

Of the above, F-AQOM either never reached Spain or escaped to France in 1939, for it was still flying in France in 1945. In Republican service, the Jubilees were given the type code TM (Transporte Monospar) and the Universals SM (Sanitario Monospar).

Five Monospars of various types survived the civil war, of which four were given the military serials 31-2, 31-3, 31-5 and 31-6. In 1940, 31-3 (Later L.8-2) was returned to civil ownership with the registration EC-AHE, and it was still flying in 1956. In 1945 31-6 was sold to CETFA for photographic survey work, receiving the registration EC-CAR (later EC-ABH). Monospar 31-5 continued as a staff transport in the Ejercito del Aire until it was withdrawn in 1947.

Finally, eight Pratt & Whitney Wasp Junior engines intended for production ST-18 Croydons that were never built (the prototype was lost when returning from a flight to Australia, and production was cancelled) were sold by General Aircraft to a Spanish Republican agent in London in May 1937. They were probably used for the Romano R.83s delivered to Spain.

General Aviation Clark GA 43A

In 1931 Col Virginius Clark, who had been Chief Aeronautical Engineer to the US Army during the First World War, was hired by Aviation Corporation, a holding company which had recently acquired the Fairchild aircraft and engine manufacturing companies, to design a fast single-engined low-wing ten-passenger monoplane to compete with the Northrop Alpha, Boeing Monomail and Lockheed Orion. The result was the Fairchild-Pilgrim 150, powered by a 650hp Wright F radial engine, which was of all-metal construction except for the fabric covering the outer wing panels, and had a fixed, spatted undercarriage. It first flew on 22 May 1932. In September, General Aviation, a subsidiary of General Motors, acquired all rights and patents for the Pilgrim 150 prototype, which was redesignated Clark GA 43 and fitted with a semi-retractable undercarriage. Only four examples of the extensively redesigned, all-metal production aircraft, the Clark GA 43A, were built, and three of them were sold to Swissair:

c/n 2202, 715hp Wright Cyclone R-1820 F-1; X82Y, later CH-169 (Swiss) and HB-LAM (Swiss).

c/n 2203, X13901, sold as a bare airframe.

c/n 2204, 710hp Wright Cyclone R-1820 F-3; NC13903, HB-ITU.

Clark GA 43A CH-169 entered Swissair service in the spring of 1934 on the Zurich–Frankfurt route, and

The Swissair General Aviation Clark GA-43A sold to the Republicans in October 1936. (R S Allen)

was the first Swissair machine to carry a two-way radio. It was re-registered HB-LAM in 1935. The second complete aircraft, HB-ITU, entered service in the spring of 1935, and was used on the Basle–Frankfurt–Geneva–Vienna routes until it crashed on Mount Rigi on 30 April 1936. In September 1936 Vladimir Rosenbaum, a celebrated Swiss barrister of Lithuanian origin who was engaged in the clandestine procurement of arms for the Spanish Republicans, Max Brunner, a leading Swiss Communist, and Antonio Espina, a Spanish novelist, organised the sale of four Swissair aircraft (a Douglas DC-2, two Lockheed Orions and the surviving Clark GA 43A) to the Spanish Republicans. The ostensible buyer was Air France, and an ephemeral front company, Mecklerfirma, was created for the transaction. The total price was $138,250 (£28,742), plus a two per cent commission to Rosenbaum. This was an extremely modest percentage at a time when many dealers and intermediaries were extorting from the Spanish Republicans commissions of between twenty and thirty per cent on the sale of aircraft already priced at three to five times their market value. In 1937 Rosenbaum and Brunner were tried and imprisoned for contravening Non-Intervention by this sale.

The DC-2 flew to Le Bourget and left for Spain on 23 October 1936, but whether the other three aircraft

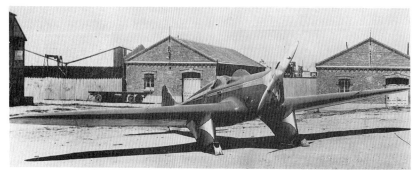

The González Gil-Pazó GP-1. (Instituto de Historia y Cultura Aeronáutica, vía José Warleta)

flew to Spain, or went in crates by road or rail, is not certain. In Republican Spain the Clark GA 43A joined the LAPE fleet, though its registration and fleet number are not recorded. It was found to be a fairly good aeroplane, with a load-carrying capacity equal to that of the Vultee V1-A, though it was considerably slower. Late in 1937 it was sent to SAF-5 at La Rabasa, Alicante, for a thorough overhaul, but nothing more is heard of it after that.

Span 53ft; length 43ft 1in; height 12ft 6in; wing area 464sq ft.

Empty weight 5,283lb; loaded weight 8,750lb.

Maximum speed 190mph; cruising speed 170mph (in Spain, about 150mph); ceiling 18,000ft; range 850 miles.

González Gil-Pazó No. 1, GP-1, GP-2 and GP-4

Arturo González Gil y Santibañez, an army captain in the Cuerpo de Inginieros (Engineer Corps) and civil aviator, studied aeronautical engineering in Paris and worked for Caudron before returning to Spain in 1925. He retired from the army in 1933 to become technical director at the Loring aircraft factory. José Pazó Montes, also an Engineers captain, and chief of the Land Survey Aerial Photographic Service, had worked with Guinea and Severt (see Guinea-Severt 2DDM) in 1931-32. Gil and Pazó's first joint creation was a low-wing, two-seat cantilever monoplane with a fixed unspatted undercarriage, designated the Gil-Pazó No. 1. Of wood and metal construction with plywood skinning, and powered by an ADC Cirrus engine, it was similar in appearance to the Miles M2 Hawk. It first flew in June 1932, receiving the registration

EC-VVC, and was at Cuatro Vientos, Madrid, in July 1936. No technical data other than its loaded weight of 778kg are available, and nothing is recorded of its history during the civil war.

Their next venture, designed to meet the specification for a two-seat trainer issued by the Director General de Aeronáutica in 1934, was the GP-1, a supremely elegant open-cockpit, low-wing cantilever monoplane superficially resembling the Miles M2H Hawk Major. The wing trailing edges were slightly curved, however, giving the wing a semi-elliptical planform, and the head-rest behind the cockpit was extended in a gentle curve to the root of the fin. The undercarriage wheels were housed in streamlined trousers. The wings, which had flaps, were built of wood with a stressed-ply covering, and the fuselage was of welded steel tube, covered with fabric over the rear part and with dural sheeting over the fore part. The prototype, EC-VVV (c/n 1), first flew in June 1934, powered by an ADC Cirrus engine. A 195hp Walter Junior inverted in-line engine was installed for the competitive trials, and the GP-1 emerged the clear winner against the Loring X, Hispano E.34 and Adaro 1.E.7.

In 1936 González Gil and Pazó received an order for 100 GP-1s, to be built by AISA (as the Loring factory was now called) at Carabanchel Alto, Madrid, for a total price of 1,900,000 pesetas (£76,000, or £760 each). The Walter Junior engines were to be built by Elizalde under licence. None of these aircraft was completed by July 1936, and in October, when Nationalist troops were approaching Madrid, AISA was evacuated to Alicante. By then, Arturo González Gil, a dedicated Socialist, had been killed while lead-

ing a platoon of Socialist Youth militia in the Sierra Guadarrama (an Airspeed Viceroy was renamed in his honour). José Pazó, however, had opposite political views and had escaped to the Nationalist side.

Before politics ended their relationship, Gil and Pazó had built three derivatives of the GP-1. The first was the GP-2 two-seat cabin monoplane EC-EEB, powered by a 130hp de Havilland Gipsy Major engine, in which Ramón Torres and Carlos Coll made a record-breaking flight from Barcelona to Agadir, Morocco, in January 1936. The second was a special single-seat version of the GP-2, EC-BEE, in which Lorenzo Richi made a return flight from Madrid to Bata in Spanish Guinea (now Equatorial Guinea) at an average speed of 187km/h in March 1936. The third was the GP-4, a four-seat cabin monoplane prototype, registered EC-AFM. In September 1936 José Pazó was instructed to fly a cracked cylinder block from the engine of a Potez 54 to Barcelona for urgent repair. After taking off from Cuatro Vientos in the GP-4, he turned westwards instead, continuing his flight as far as his native village in Galicia, on the Atlantic coast, where he could be identified by people who knew him. There he landed on a beach, from where, eventually, he was ordered to fly the GP-4 to Tablada, Seville. Bearing the military serial 30-20, the GP-4 was employed on liaison and transport services.

Despite his duties in the Nationalist air arm, in which he served as a pilot in the He 70 group, as a Fiat C.R.32 pilot in 8-E-3, and as a test pilot of captured SBs, Pazó managed to design and build another cabin monoplane, the P-IV, which made its first flight early in 1939. After the end of the war, its trials completed, the Pazó P-IV was incorporated into the Ejercito del Aire as 30-177. Diplomatic and administrative duties prevented Pazó from returning to design work until the 1950s.

In the Republican zone, AISA,

A González Gil-Pazó GP-2. (Instituto de Historia y Cultura Aeronáutica, via José Warleta)

The GP-2 Especial in which Lorenzo Richi made a record-breaking return flight from Spain to Bata (Equatorial Guinea) in March 1936. (Instituto de Historia y Cultura Aeronáutica, via José Warleta)

evacuated to Alicante and combined with Hispano-Suiza to form SAF-15 in 1937, is said to have produced about forty GP-1s during the civil war, of which about thirty were recovered by the Nationalists and incorporated into Grupo 30. Of these, the following received civil registrations during the 1940s:

30-96   EC-BAO, withdrawn 1956
30-98   EC-AAO, withdrawn 1947. Destroyed in accident
30-113 EC-AFY, withdrawn 1960
30-114 EC-AFZ, withdrawn 1958
30-115 EC-BAR/'AGA, withdrawn 1961
30-120 EC-ADF, withdrawn 1952
30-125 EC-AAP/'ADD, withdrawn 1952. Destroyed in accident
30-126 EC-AFP, withdrawn 1951
30-129 EC-BAT/L.3-129, withdrawn 1955
30-149 EC-AAQ, withdrawn ?
30-153 EC-CAH/'ACY, withdrawn 1956
30-155 EC-CAM/'AGF, withdrawn 1961

The GP-1 30-40, flown to the Nationalists by a defector, was written off in 1946 and received no registration. A second GP-2, EC-FFB, became 30-159 after the war, then EC-AAM, and was written off in 1957. The GP-4 EC-AFM/30-20 became EC-AAZ, and was withdrawn in 1961.

GP-1

Span 11.6m; length 8.5m; wing area 18sq m.

Empty weight 525kg; loaded weight 880kg.

Maximum speed 212km/h; minimum speed 69km/h; ceiling 7,500m; range 1,000km.

GP-4 (130hp Walter Major)

Span 12.146m; length 8.9m.

Maximum speed 210km/h; cruising

The GP-4, brought over to the Nationalists by its co-designer, José Pazó, at Seville in 1938. (US Air Force photo, via Dr R K Smith)

speed 180km/h; ceiling 5,000m; range 1,400km.

Gotha Go 145A

A product of the Gotha Waggon-fabrik, builders of the famous heavy bombers of the First World War, the Gotha Go 145 was a single-engined two-seat biplane of wood and metal construction, powered by a 240hp Argus As 10C Series III inverted-vee air-cooled engine. It first flew in February 1934 and, as the Go 145A, was ordered in quantity by the Luftwaffe for intermediate and gunnery training. The aircraft had a swept-back upper mainplane and a split-axle undercarriage, the wheels being provided with hydraulic brakes; its tailskid consisted of a flat, diamond-shaped piece of metal attached by a ball-and-socket joint to a sprung leg and a bracing arm. For gunnery training a 7.9mm ring-mounted machine gun was installed in the rear cockpit.

The first eight Gotha Go 145As were unloaded at Vigo on 28 May 1938. They were followed shortly afterwards by a further thirteen, and were sent to replace the P.W.S.10s of the Escuela de Transformación at Jerez de la Frontera, being given the military serials 38-1 to 38-21. One was lost in an accident. A further twenty-five were built under licence by Construcciones Aeronáuticas SA at its rebuilt factory at Getafe, Madrid, in 1940-41. These received the serials 38-22 to 38-46, and were employed at the transformation and

A Gotha Go 145 at La Parra, Jerez de la Frontera. (Arráez)

gunnery schools at Gallur, in the province of Zaragoza. They received the new type code ES-2 in 1945, and were withdrawn from service in 1950, though officially not until some years later.

Span 9m; length 8.7m; height 2.9m; wing area 21.75sq m.

Empty weight 870kg; loaded weight 1,350kg.

Maximum speed 212km/h; cruising speed 180km/h; landing speed 90km/h; climb 170m/min; ceiling 3,700m; endurance 4 hrs.

Gourdou-Leseurre GL-32 C1, GL-410, GL-482 C1 and GL-633 B1

Charles Gourdou and Jean Leseurre began their collaboration in the designing and building of aircraft with the Gourdou-Leseurre C1 single-seat fighter of 1917. It was a high-wing parasol monoplane with a steel-tube fuselage and a wing with metal spars and wooden ribs. The airframe was fabric covered with the exception of the forward fuselage.

Gourdou and Leseurre continued to produce fighters to this formula, with little basic variation, for the next eleven years, but the only one to

achieve real success was the GL-32 C1 of 1925. Powered by an uncowled 420hp Gnome-Rhône 9 Ac Jupiter radial engine, the GL-32 was designed to participate in the 1923 C1 programme, in which it was judged runner-up to the Nieuport-Delage NiD 42 (see Hispano-Nieuport 52). It began to enter French squadron service in September 1927. From the sixth production aircraft onwards the Gnome-Rhône 9 Ac was replaced by the 9 Ad of similar horsepower. Its armament consisted of two fixed forward-firing 7.7mm machine guns. The Aéronautique Militaire took delivery of 380 GL-32s, 15 were supplied to the Aviation Maritime, 50 to Rumania and 12 to Turkey. Because Gourdou-Leseurre operated as a subsidiary of the Atéliers et Chantiers de la Loire from 1925 until 1928, 415 GL-32s were built at the Loire factory at Saint Nazaire, and the type was often referred to as the Loire-Gourdou-Leseurre LGL-32 C1. By 1934 all GL-32s had been relegated to training squadrons, and about 130 remained in service by 1936.

Meanwhile, Gourdou-Leseurre

A Gourdou-Leseurre GL-32.

had been using two of its unsuccessful prototypes for experiments in dive-bombing techniques, with the intention of designing a specialised dive-bomber. These were the GL-410 parasol monoplane and the GL-482 C1, a cumbersome gull-winged monoplane designed for the C1 programme of 1930 (see Dewoitine D.371 and D.510). The GL-410 differed from the GL-32 chiefly in having swept-back wing leading edges, a wider-track, split-axle undercarriage, and a supercharged Gnome-Rhône 9 Asb Jupiter of 480hp. Two GL-410s were built, one being used by the company for the dive-bombing trials, and the other being left at Villacoublay (see below). The GL-482, the last Gourdou-Leseurre fighter to be built and the first to diverge from the parasol monoplane configuration, was also the first to use all-metal construction. It was powered by a 690hp Hispano-Suiza 12Xbrs supercharged liquid-cooled engine, the radiator for which was placed midway along the fuselage beneath the pilot's cockpit. The complex arrangement of bracing struts, a shortcoming common to most gull-wing fighters, created so much drag that the aircraft's performance was unacceptably low, and the GL-482 was rejected early in the C1 competition.

Reports concerning the Gourdou-Leseurres of various type that took part in the Spanish Civil War are confusing and often contradictory, and what follows is merely an attempt to correlate those that appear reliable with the few that can be supported with documented evidence. The frequently published statement that four Gourdou-Leseurre GL-32s were delivered to Barcelona on 4 August 1936 and operated in the fighting over Aragón during the next few weeks cannot be corroborated, and seems to be quite untrue. However, in October 1936, through the personal intercession of the Technical Director of Air France, Edouard Serre, and Ernest Vinchon, the husband of the flyer Adrienne Bolland, the Basque government bought four old GL-32s from one of the flying schools of the Armée de l'Air. These arrived, armed, in November (according to reports by the Basque President, don José Aquirre, dated 31 October and 13 November 1936). After they had proved satisfactory, or at least airworthy, the Basques contracted with Gourdou-Leseurre for a new production series to be built, on the assurance that these slow and obsolete fighters could still be serviceable as dive-bombers against Nationalist ships blockading the Cantabrian coast and troops in the narrow passes of the mountainous Basque country. The number ordered is usually put at twelve, but, to judge by the known construction numbers of the aircraft built, it seems to have been at least fifteen. While they were in production, however, Edouard Serre received a direct appeal from the Plenary Committee of the FAI (Federación Anarquista Ibérica, the inner core of the Spanish Anarchist movement), who said that they urgently needed aircraft for a flying school they were trying to establish in Catalonia. Accordingly, Serre came to an arrangement with the Basques by which some of the GL-32s would be diverted to the main zone. The politics of the affair were complicated, but no doubt the non-Basque representatives on the Republican Comisión de Compras (Purchasing Commission) in Paris had their say in the matter, too.

Since the aircraft were to be dive-bombers, the new-series GL-32s were built with the split-axle undercarriages of the GL-410 type, to allow for the fitting of a bomb rack and a 100kg bomb under the fuselage. In addition, two racks for small bombs were fitted, one on each of the two horizontal connecting struts between the parallel wing-bracing struts. As the GL-32s were completed they were tested, though not apparently by the CEMA at Villacoublay, and given civil registrations before being ferried to Spain. The transfer of all but three was handled by SFTA (see Appendix II).

Besides the new aircraft, a single old GL-32 was acquired and flown to Spain. This was c/n 5, which had been kept by Gourdou-Leseurre and, with the civil registration

A Gourdou-Leseurre GL-482.

F-AJHV (1930), had been used for aerobatic displays by the celebrated Marcel Bapt. Finally, to complicate the matter yet further, some French newspapers reported in November 1936, and again in April 1937, that the prototype GL-410 was among the aircraft smuggled to Spain. Gourdou-Leseurre published an indignant denial, pointing out that the prototype was still at the company aerodrome and being used for experimental trials. This was true, but the company omitted to mention the second prototype, which had been left at Villacoublay since 1933 and used for joyrides by CEMA test pilots, notably Jacques Lecarme (see Romano R.82). This machine does seem to have disappeared from Villacoublay, along with several other discarded prototypes, during the autumn of 1936, and may have been one of the four Gourdous bought by the Basques in October. The deliveries to Spain can be summarised, with reasonable accuracy, as follows:

In November 1936, four:
Four ex-Armée de l'Air GL-32s, or three GL-32s and one GL-410.
In March 1937, two:
c/n 452 F-APPX: Del. Marcel Serre, 16 March 1937.
c/n 453 F-APPZ: Del. Ulysse Gorsse, 16 March 1937. (For Gorsse, see Potez 56).
In April 1937, five or six, of which one was lost en route:
c/n 5 F-AJHV: Del. after 2 April 1937, when it was last checked at Orly by Bureau Veritas.
c/n 455 F-APYB?:

c/n 456 F-APYC?: 'YB and 'YC are blank in Bureau Veritas, but would seem probable for these two aircraft. Both were exported by SFTA in April 1937.
c/n 457 F-APXU: Via William Domènge (see Percival Gull Six), but crashed in the sea, probably shot down by Nationalist fighters during delivery flight, 21 April 1937. The pilot, Armand Meillorat, was killed.
c/n 458: Nothing known, but possibly delivered in April 1937.
c/n 459 F-APYD: Del. via SFTA, April 1937.
In May 1937, four, of which one was lost en route:
c/n 454 F-APYA: Del. Marie-Joseph Grand, 8 May 1937, but crashed near Bordeaux on delivery flight. Machine taken back to Sté-Gourdou-Leseurre and rebuilt as GL-633 by July 1937 (see below).
c/n 460 F-APYE: 10 May 1937, SFTA.
c/n 461 F-APYF: 14 May 1937, SFTA.
c/n 463 F-APYH: 22 May 1937, SFTA.
In June 1937, three:
c/n 464 F-APYI: 3 June 1937, SFTA.
c/n 465 F-APYJ: 3 June 1937, SFTA.
c/n 467 F-APYK: 15 June 1937, SFTA.

The missing aircraft in the above list, c/n 462 F-APYG, was not delivered, but was retained by Gourdou-Leseurre for conversion into a dive-bomber (see below). This makes a total of 16-17 GL-32s, plus perhaps the GL-410, actually delivered to Spain, though it is not possible to know exactly which went to the Basque and which to the main zones. However, it is known that, on 30 April 1937, six GL-32s, each carrying a 100kg bomb, attacked the Nationalist battle-cruiser *España*, which later sank. Several authors, and one of the pilots who took part in this attack, have stated that the battle cruiser was sunk by the Gourdous. Indeed, this was reported at the time, and was claimed as the first occasion in which a major naval vessel had been sunk by aircraft in genuine conditions of war. This so alarmed the British Admiralty that an inquiry was ordered, for, if true, it was ominous news for the Royal Navy. The inquiry found that the *España* had been chasing a British merchant ship making for Bilbao when she had struck a mine laid by a *Nationalist* minelayer a few days before, and had begun to list. Some aircraft had flown over, reported the British crew of the merchantman, but had dropped no bombs. Their Lordships at the Admiralty breathed a sigh of relief. In fact the *España* took a long time to sink and was attacked, both by GL-32s and Breguet 19s, several hours after the British ship had lost sight of her. Some direct hits were claimed, but it must still be doubted whether they constituted the decisive *coup de grâce* that sent her to the bottom.

Little is heard of the Gourdous in the northern zone after this, although seven were still flying on 3 August 1937. These were based at La Albericia, near Santander, and made up two patrullas under the command of Juan Carrasco Martínez and Pedro Lambas Bernal. By the time the northern campaign ended, in October 1937, however, all the Gourdous had been destroyed. The GL-32s delivered to Catalonia were not used by the Anarchist flying school because the Anarchists had ceased to be an independent force in the Republic after the armed clashes with the Communists during May 1937, and the flying school was never established. The GL-32s were therefore incorporated into the 3ª Escuadrilla of Grupo 71, based at Cervera on the Barcelona-Lérida road and commanded by Capitán Roque Carrión. One of the flight leaders (and squad-

The Gourdou-Leseurre GL-633B1 prototype. (Liron)

ron commander in Carrión's absence) was the Belgian André Autrique (see Avia BH-33). Nothing is recorded of their military operations, if indeed there were any.

The GL-32 c/n 462 F-APYG was extensively remodelled as a dive-bomber and redesignated GL-633 B1. The undercarriage was greatly widened and strengthened by additional bracing struts, two struts were added to the cabane, the wingtips were rounded, the fuselage was strengthened and metal-skinned from the engine to the rear of the pilot's cockpit, and a headrest was added, with a fairing from the cockpit to the leading edge of the fin. Power was provided by an uncowled 480hp Gnome-Rhône Jupiter 9 Ady radial engine driving a variable-pitch two-blade metal propeller in place of the wooden propeller of the GL-32. A rack for a single 250kg bomb was mounted between the legs, with a pair of arms to swing the bomb clear of the propeller arc before releasing.

This machine was demonstrated at Barcelona in December 1936 by company test pilot Jérôme Cavalli, who had been a sergeant-pilot in a French GL-32 squadron during the 1920s, and was well-known as an aerobatic display pilot in the same type of aircraft. The dive-bombing demonstration so impressed the Spaniards that they placed a preliminary order for six aircraft, which included the prototype. According to

a postwar Nationalist report based on captured Republican documents, these were delivered on 7 and 20 July, 29 and 30 September, and 13 and 27 October 1937. Curiously, the registrations of the last four only are given, and, moreover, as F-APYS, 'YA, 'YA and 'YS respectively. However, 'YA was the GL-32 that had crashed in France on 8 May 1937 and, like F-APYG, it had been rebuilt as a GL-633 B1. On the other hand, 'YS was not a Gourdou-Leseurre at all, but a Caudron Göeland which had no connection with the Spanish war. Nothing is known of the use of the six GL-633s in Spain. One, with the military serial LG-008 on the fuselage sides, has been recorded in a photograph, and may have been the aircraft recovered intact after the fall of Catalonia in February 1939. The rest, together with the GL-32s, seem to have been destroyed on the ground by the Condor Legion at Bañolas on 5 February 1939, or at Vilajuiga next day. According to some French newspaper reports of December 1937, the GL-482 gull-winged fighter, which, like the GL-410, had been used for dive-bombing trials, was tested at Villacoublay in October 1937 by the chief test pilot of the CEMA, Capitaine Constantin Rozanoff, before being sent to Spain. If this is true, it presumably joined the squadron at Cervera.

The Republicans also ordered fifteen Gourdou-Leseurre GL-601 B1 dive-bombers, derived from the GL-432 and GL-521 dive-bomber projects. None was built, but drawings show that the GL-601 would have been a neat parasol monoplane with a Gnome-Rhône K 9 radial engine in a long-chord NACA cowling, a spatted undercarriage and an enclosed cockpit. The armament of two wing-mounted Hispano-Suiza 20mm cannon was intended for attacking ground targets. The machine was designed to have the unusually long range, for a single-seater, of 1,200km at a cruising speed of 240km/h. Its top speed was estimated (optimistically, perhaps) at 400km/h. Such a large single-seater, weighed down by its bomb and heavy armament, would have been extremely vulnerable to enemy fighters and would have required strong fighter escorts, a factor which may have persuaded the Spanish Republicans to cancel the order.

Gourdou-Leseurre GL-32 C1

Span 12.2m; length 7.55m; height 2.95m; wing area 24.9sq m.

Empty weight 963kg; loaded weight 1,376kg.

Maximum speed 250km/h at sea level; climb to 5,000m in 12min; ceiling 8,750m; range 500km.

Gourdou-Leseurre GL-410

Dimensions as GL-32.

Empty weight 970kg; loaded weight 1,380kg.

Maximum speed 280km/h at 5,000m; range 600km.

Gourdou-Leseurre GL-482 C1

Span 9.86m; length 7.28m; height 2.8m; wing area 17.75sq m.

Loaded weight 1,580kg.

Maximum speed 300km/h at 4,000m; ceiling 10,750m.

Gourdou-Leseurre GL-633 B1

Span 12.2m; length 7.58m; height 3.1m; wing area 24.8sq m.

Empty weight 1,017kg; loaded weight 1,680kg.

Maximum speed 250km/h; climb to 2,000m in 3min; ceiling 10,000m; range 600km.

Grumman GE-23

In October 1936 the leading maker of railway rolling-stock in Canada, the Canadian Car & Foundry Company (CC & F) of Montreal, announced that it was going to reopen its long-disused factory at Fort William, Ontario, and expand into aircraft production. To the people of Ontario, where there was much unemployment, this was good news. No one, even in the aeronautical press, asked why the aeroplane chosen to launch this hazardous attempt to break into a new market should be the Grumman FF-1, an obsolescent six-year-old two-seat biplane designed specifically for carrier-borne operations, which, after only two years in service, had been withdrawn from first-line duties by the US Navy six months previously. In a world where the major powers already had their own shipboard aircraft and the smaller countries had no aircraft carriers, who was going to buy it?

The Grumman FF-1 was the design on which the Grumman Aircraft Engineering Corporation had founded its fortunes, and the first of the long line of aircraft that would make its name almost synonymous with US naval aviation for the next forty years. The prototype G-5, or XFF-1, had first flown on 29 December 1931. It embodied many features, such as all-metal construction (only the wings being fabric covered), an enclosed cockpit for pilot and observer, and a retractable undercarriage, that were then considered innovatory. To house the retractable undercarriage, which re-

Grumman GE-23 Delfín No AD-012. (Azaola)

quired thirty-five vigorous turns of a hand-crank to raise or lower, the ventral part of the forward fuselage was enlarged, giving the XFF-1 that high-breasted, portly look which was to characterise the whole family of Grumman naval aircraft, through several generations. During its trials the XFF-1 showed that it could outfly even the fastest single-seat fighters then in service, and twenty-seven were ordered for use on the carrier *Lexington*.

The FF-1, known in the US Navy as 'Fifi', was powered by a 675hp Wright Cyclone R-1820-78 radial engine in a Townend-ring cowling, and its armament consisted of two fixed forward-firing 7.62mm Browning M-2 machine guns in the upper fuselage and a movable M-2 gun in the observer's cockpit, the canopy of which could be raised on hinges. Two inflatable flotation bags were installed in the upper wing to keep the machine temporarily buoyant should it come down on water. The US Navy also ordered thirty-four examples of a scout version, the SF-1, which had only a single fixed gun, increased fuel capacity, a longer-chord NACA engine cowling and a Hamilton variable-pitch propeller. By the middle of 1935, however, Grumman had produced the F2F-1 single-seat fighter and its development, the F3F-1. The US Navy had ordered both and, as these reached the squadrons during the autumn of 1935 and spring of 1936, the FF-1s and SF-1s were relegated

to land stations as utility aeroplanes.

Meanwhile, the company had been rebuilding the second G-5 prototype (re-designated GG-1) to combine the armament of the FF-1 with the refinements of the SF-1. This was the aircraft, powered by an 860hp Wright Cylcone R-1820-F-52 radial engine and called the G-23, for which CC & F acquired the manufacturing rights. On 20 November 1936 the G-23, registered NR2V and with 'Grumman Canadian Fighter' painted on its fin, was flown from New York to Montreal in a record-breaking 1 hour and 40 minutes by Harold Klein, who had recently been taken on by CC & F as company test pilot.

Within three weeks Klein was back in New York, demonstrating the G-23 at Floyd Bennett Field on 15 December to Teniente Coronel Francisco León Trejo, a Spanish Republican air force officer who had been sent to America to buy aviation material. On 7 January 1937, as a result of the Cuse affair (see Appendix II), the US Congress voted to embargo the sale of all war material to either side in Spain. Notwithstanding this, three agents of the Spanish government – Dr Alejandro Otero, Dr Leo Katz, and Martin Licht – travelled to Montreal to place an order with CC & F for forty Grumman GE-23s (the 'E' denoting 'España'), complete with arms and ammunition. It was proposed that they be exported via China or Turkey. Negotiations broke down when CC & F declared itself unable to meet the early delivery date demanded by Otero, and also partly because the company did not wish to get into difficulties with the Canadian government, which had just decided to tighten its own regulations concerning non-intervention in Spain. For the next six months little was heard of the Grumman 'Canadian Fighter' or of aircraft production at Fort William, for, despite considerable advertising, no further orders were received. In July 1937, however, CC & F received an order for forty Grumman GE-23s from Turkey, accompanied by confirmatory letters from the Turkish ministries of foreign affairs, defence and protocol. The agent handling the transaction was the same Dr Leo Katz who had

visited Montreal the previous January. Contracts were finalised in Paris in September 1937 and, in view of the early delivery date insisted on by Turkey, CC & F decided to subcontract the manufacture of all the components to US companies, and use the factory at Fort William to assemble the complete aircraft. Grumman itself undertook to build the semi-monocoque fuselages, the Brewster Aeronautical Corporation the wings, tail units and struts, Bendix Products the undercarriages, Moore and Eastwood the bomb racks, and the Aerial Machine and Tool Corporation the gun mounts.

From October 1937 onwards these components, plus the engines from Curtiss-Wright and the propellers from Hamilton Standard, converged on the Fort William factory. They were assembled under the supervision of a woman engineer, Miss Elsie MacGill, and her assistant Michael Gregor, who had formerly worked for Seversky. Owing to delays occasioned by Brewster's failing to deliver on time, the first GE-23 (c/n 101) was not completed until 3 February 1938.

Meanwhile, the Nicaraguan government had bought the original prototype XFF-1, and the Mexican government was considering the purchase of a GE-23. Unfortunately the XFF-1 had crashed in the sea on 29 September 1938, and CC & F decided to send c/n 101 as a replacement in the hope of keeping Central American countries interested until the Turkish contract was fulfilled. The Turkish order had in the meantime been increased to fifty aircraft. By 22 March 1938 the Fort William plant had completed much of the assembly work, and eighteen aircraft had been finished and flight-tested. Another sixteen were complete but for the wings and tail units awaited from Brewster and, since the contract had not specified flight-testing, CC & F decided to save time by shipping these with the eighteen completed aircraft without delay, ordering Brewster to send the wings and tails to St Johns, where they could be picked up en route. In April 1938 the components for thirty-four aircraft thus sailed for Le Havre, France – where they were to be accepted by the agent, Katz – aboard three Norwe-

gian freighters, the *Hada County*, *Bant County* and *August*, hired and renamed by Intercontinental Transport Services (familiarly called 'the County Line').

Shortly before the last consignment was due to leave Montreal, on 20 May, the American commercial attaché in Ankara, while on a visit to New York, had heard mention of this sale of Grumman aircraft to the Turkish government. He told the US State Department that, so far as he was aware, no such order had ever been placed. Enquiries elicited a strong denial from the Turkish government, and the remaining sixteen aircraft, which were already being loaded on the *Hada County* at Montreal, were impounded. Investigations revealed that all the papers supposedly from the Turkish government had been forged by two bribed Turkish officials. Canadian Car & Foundry strenuously denied any complicity, and, despite its temporary embarrassment, the affair did not turn out too badly for it in the end. With its huge floorspace at Fort William, the largest in Canada, already laid out for aircraft production at the expense of the Spanish government, it was able to embark on the production of Hawker Hurricanes for the RAF, being the first factory in Canada to do so. The sixteen surplus Grumman GE-23s were taken over by the RCAF, by whom they were called Goblins.

Many aspects of this extraordinary affair are still obscure, but all the evidence now suggests a sequence of events somewhat different from that described by CC & F at the time of the scandal. The Spanish Republicans in Paris had been establishing a connection with certain Turkish high officials, for the purpose of obtaining arms, since September 1936, and one of its results was an attempt to buy Fury IIs from the Hawker company in the summer of 1937. The Grumman affair was another.

A key figure in both seems to have been Fuat Baban, a Levantine arms dealer who (according to the Gestapo) was organising a drug-smuggling chain on behalf of none other than Hermann Goering. He also happened to be the Lockheed agent in Turkey, Greece and the Middle East, with contacts in all the governments in the region. Meanwhile, Frank Ambrose, a Long Island agent for Grumman and other aircraft companies, was trying to procure aircraft for Comandante Sanz Sainz, the Republican buying agent in New York (see Vultee V1-A and Seversky SEV-3), and suggested the Grumman FF-1 as a possible purchase. So the original proposal that CC & F should go into aircraft production with this type of machine appears to have come, not from the company directors in October 1936, as they claimed, but from the Spaniards themselves at least a month earlier, in September 1936. The choice of Turkey as a viable channel to circumvent Non-Intervention was the result of natural communications between aircraft and arms dealers on both sides of the Atlantic. As for Dr Katz, he seems to have belonged to the circle of Soviet NKVD agents in western Europe that was controlled by Walter Krivitsky, who defected in 1937. Thus the purchase of the Grummans was one link in a chain of interwoven conspiracies involving, as always, political idealists, serving officers doing their duty, opportunistic profiteers and professional criminals.

The thirty-four Grumman GE-23s (c/ns 102-135) reached France when the Spanish frontier was briefly open for the passage of war material, and they were hurriedly transported across the border to Vich, where SAF-3/16 had a workshop for the production of I-15 Chatos. After assembly, arming and testing, they were flown to Cardedeu-La Garriga Aerodrome, near Granollers, north of Barcelona, on 7 May 1938. Officially named Delfin (Dolphin) and assigned the type code AD (Asalto Delfin), followed by the serial numbers 001 to 034, they were formed into a new independent unit, Grupo 28, under the command of the veteran and ace pilot Comandante Andrés García Lacalle. The Grupo was divided into two twelve-aircraft escuadrillas, plus one staff aircraft and nine held in reserve.

The 1ª Escuadrilla was commanded by Capitán Santiago Capillas, who had recently led the Escuadrilla Independiente Núm 50 of RZ Natachas, and the 2ª Escuadrilla was commanded by Capitán Santiago

Sánchez Calvo. By this time Catalonia was isolated from the main southern zone by a ninety-mile-wide corridor of Nationalist-held territory between the River Ebro and Valencia. Lacalle imposed a rigorous training programme, including night flying and a course of aerobatics, for the Delfines were intended to fulfil the secondary rôle of fighter. On one exercise Capillas suffered the embarrassment, and fright, of seeing both his flotation bags suddenly inflate after he had accidentally touched the release handle. With its more powerful Cyclone F-52 engine, and shorn of naval equipment, the GE-23 had a performance superior to that of the FF-1 and SF-1, being able to attain 218mph at 4,200ft and possessing a climb of 1,600ft/min. The chief complaint against it by Spanish pilots was its broad side-profile and narrow undercarriage, which made it difficult to land in a crosswind and prone to *caballitos* (ground loops) and *capotajes* (nose-overs).

The first offensive operations were restricted to ground attacks (there was provision for two 50kg or twelve 10kg bombs on underwing racks) in sectors free of fighter opposition. On several occasions Lacalle removed the RCA radio from his staff aircraft and, installing it in his car, directed operations from a high point overlooking the front. Two Delfin pilots nevertheless became disoriented during these missions and landed behind Nationalist lines, their machines being AD-001 and -005. The second of these two aircraft was displayed with other captured Republican aircraft at the Gran Kursaal exhibition in San Sebastián in the late summer of 1938, where it provoked much comment from German and Italian visitors regarding US policy in the Spanish Civil War.

While the 2ª Escuadrilla was transferred to the southern zone, the 1ª Escuadrilla was heavily employed throughout the Battle of the Ebro (25 July to 16 November 1938), one machine being fitted with a motorised camera for hazardous missions to obtain photographic coverage of the front. When attacking ground targets, the Delfines would approach in a shallow dive, release their bombs at about 1,500ft, and race for home

individually at treetop level. Three were lost in accidents, and two were shot down on 1 September by Capitán Miguél García Pardo and Rudolphe Henricourt (a Belgian volunteer flying with the Nationalists), both of whom were flying Fiat C.R.32s. On 24 December 1938 Lacalle was appointed Jefe de la Escuadra de Caza (Chief of Republican Fighters), and command of Grupo 28 passed to José Riverola. One patrulla of three aircraft was assigned to night flying in defence of Barcelona, and the other two to coast patrols and the daylight defence of the city. During the collapse of Catalonia one of the eight remaining Grummans was lost in an accident, four were captured on Barcelona aerodromes, and three were destroyed by the Condor Legion on Vilajuiga Aerodrome on 6 February 1939.

In the southern zone the Delfines of the 2ª Escuadrilla took part in the Republican counter-offensive in Extremadura during January-February 1939. During the last fortnight of the war the five remaining Grummans were transferred to El Carmolí, Cartagena, to protect the withdrawal of the remnants of the Republican fleet to French North Africa, on one occasion claiming their only 'kill' of the war, a Heinkel He 59 seaplane. This loss was not admitted by the Condor Legion. On 7 March 1939 the five GE-23s and twenty I-15 Chatos straffed two Nationalist ships laden with Spanish troops which were sailing into Cartagena harbour in the mistaken belief that the port had been taken over by the Nationalist Fifth Column. One ship, the *Castillo de Olite*, was sunk, and the other, the *Castillo de Peñafiel*, withdrew, badly damaged and with many dead and wounded. On 30 March, when the Republican air forces were ordered to surrender, the five Delfines, led by José Riverola, took off from La Aparecida Aerodrome in company with the last five I-15 Chatos of the 3ª Escuadrilla of Grupo 26 and flew instead to Oran, Algeria. The five Grummans were returned to Nationalist Spain in May 1939.

During the civil war the Nationalists had nicknamed the Grumman 'Pedro Rico' on account of its uncanny resemblance to the corpulent

Mayor of Madrid, whom the Nationalists regarded almost as a figure of fun. In June 1939 the nine surviving Grummans, still retaining the more dignified name of Delfin and with the new type code 5W (later changed to R.6), were formed into a squadron based in Spanish Morocco. Five were still flying in February 1946, and continued in service until 1955.

Span 34ft 6in; length (tail up) 24ft 6in; height (tail up) 11ft 1in; wing area 310sq ft.

Empty weight 3,076lb; loaded weight 4,975lb.

Maximum speed 218mph; cruising speed 200mph; initial climb 1,600ft/min; ceiling 25,017ft; range (at 167mph) 646 miles.

Guinea-Severt 2DDM

This charming two-seat monoplane, powered by an uncowled 75hp Pobjoy R radial engine, was designed and built in spare time by Capitán José Luis Severt y López Altamirano and Teniente Miguel Guinea Elorza in one of the hangars of the Servicios Técnicos at Cuatro Vientos military air base, Madrid, in 1934. It made its first flight in 1935 and, registered EC-ZAZ, was subsequently sold to don Julio Alegría of Bilbao. During the civil war it was used for reconnaissance by the Basque air arm. By a curious coincidence, Ten Guinea himself, who was with the Nationalist forces that captured Bilbao in June 1937, saw the little aeroplane he had built burning by the side of a road.

No data available.

Hanriot HD-14 and HD-17

The most successful aircraft ever produced by the celebrated father-and-son team of aeronautical pioneers, Réné and Marcel Hanriot, the HD-14 first flew in 1920, two years after the end of the First World War. Designed by Réné Hanriot and Pierre Dupont, and clearly a descendent of their first joint venture, the HD-1 single-seat fighter of 1916, the HD-14 was a

two-bay, two-seat trainer biplane, equipped with dual control. A curious feature was its two separate twin-wheel undercarriages, one under each inner lower wing, fitted with large ski-like skids projecting forwards to ensure safer landings by beginners. Altogether, 2,001 HD-14s were built, and one HD-14 and one closely similar HD-17 were imported into Spain in 1930:
HD-14, c/n 573, EC-AAN, powered by a 95hp Gnome-Rhône rotary engine. Owned by Alfonso Alarcón Artal of Barcelona.
HD-17, c/n 263, EC-AII, powered by a 70hp Clerget rotary engine. Owned by Julio Torrens Solor of Castellar del Valles, Catalonia.

Both were kept at Prat de Llobregat Airport, Barcelona, and were flying in 1936. Neither survived the civil war.

Span 10.4m; length 7.25m; wing area 34.5sq m.

Empty weight 516kg; loaded weight 710kg.

Maximum speed 116km/h; ceiling 2,000m.

Hanriot H-437 and H-439

The Hanriot H-43 was a sturdy two-seat military training biplane which first appeared in 1927. Altogether, 144 were built in nine versions, designated H-431 to H-439 according to the powerplant fitted. Except for its wooden wing ribs and fabric wing covering, the H-43 was built of metal, and had a split-axle undercarriage. One H-437 and six H-439s appear to

have found their way to Republican Spain during the civil war:
H-437ter F-ALQZ, the original H-431 prototype transformed into an H-437/1 (240hp Lorraine 7Me radial) and then re-engined with a 280hp Salmson 9Aba radial engine.
H-439 prototype F-AJSM, (240hp Lorraine 7Mb radial). First flew in 1933, and withdrawn from service at the École d'Aviation de la SGA at Bourges in April 1936.
H-439 F-AJVX, 'XM, 'LBN, 'BP, and 'BR. All used for training Republican pilots at Bourges from December 1936 until July 1937.

These and F-AJSM (which was refurbished and put back into flying condition) were bought from Hanriot by Air Languedoc between 1 August and 30 November 1937 (F-ALQZ on 25 October 1937) and resold to SFTA (see Appendix II) on 19 November 1937. Shortly thereafter they were flown to Spain and used by the Escuela de Transformación at La Ribera, San Javier aerodrome, Cartagena, and by the Escuela de Vuelo Nocturno (Night Flying School) at El Carmolí, also near Cartagena.

Span 11.40m; length 7.98m; height 3.16m; wing area 30.24sq m.

Empty weight 958kg; loaded weight 1,300kg.

Maximum speed 184km/h; ceiling 5,300m.

Hanriot H-182

Derived from the Hanriot H-180 tourer, the H-182 was a two- or

The Guinea-Severt 2DDM. (José Warleta)

Above: *a Hanriot HD-14.* (Liron)

three-seat sesquiplane trainer of mixed construction, powered by a 140hp Renault 4 Pei inverted in-line water-cooled engine. The undercarriage consisted of two compression legs mounted beneath the short stub wings extending from the lower fuselage longerons and braced to the upper wing by a pair of vee struts. The rear of the cabin was open behind the cut-out upper wing centre section. The prototype H-182, F-ANAU, first flew in 1935, and 346, including fifty for Turkey, were built altogether. In the autumn of 1936 six (some sources say ten) H-182s were delivered to Republican Spain. Although nothing is known of how or through whom the sale was effected, it is reasonable to suppose that it occurred at the same time as the sale of the four Bloch MB 210s which were built under subcontract by Hanriot, and was negotiated by the same people. In Spain the aircraft received the type code EZ and were employed at the flying schools in Murcia, mostly for night-flying instruction. Meanwhile, a few were used for training Spanish Republican pilots at the École d'Aviation de la SGA (École Hanriot) at Bourges, France.

Span 12m; length 7.22m; height 3.15m; wing area 18.97sq m.
Empty weight 612kg; loaded weight 888kg.
Maximum speed 215km/h; ceiling 5,000m; range 650km.

Hawker Osprey

The Osprey, the naval version of the Hawker Hart day-bomber of the Royal Air Force, was a two-seat carrier-borne fighter-reconnaissance biplane which first entered service with the Fleet Air Arm in November 1932. The wings were built of stainless steel and duralumin with fabric covering, and the fuselage was a braced stainless-steel box girder faired to an oval section and fabric covered with the exception of the area forward of the pilot's cockpit. The structure was stronger than that of the Hart, to permit catapulting, and the fuselage housed flotation bags. The Fleet Air Arm operated 127 Hawker Osprey Mks I, II, III and IV, the last having 640hp uprated Rolls-Royce Kestrel V engines in place of the 525hp Kestrel IIMs of the earlier models. The Osprey's armament consisted of

A Hanriot H-437. (Philip Jarrett)

A Hanriot H-182. (Liron)

The pattern Hawker Osprey delivered to Getafe in May 1936. (A J Jackson)

eight 20lb bombs, or two 112lb bombs, carried on racks under the wings, a fixed forward-firing Vickers Mk IIA .303 machine gun mounted on the port side of the fuselage, and a ring mounted Lewis gun for the observer.

In 1934 the Hawker Osprey demonstrator, G-AEBD, made a sales tour round Spain and was evaluated at San Javier, Cartagena, by a Junta Técnica of the Aeronáutica Naval, which had been considering replacements for the long-obsolete Martinsyde F.4s and Macchi M.18s still in service. As a result, CASA received a contract to build ten Osprey seaplanes under licence at Getafe, Madrid, the floats to be built, like those for the CASA Vickers Vildebeests, at Puntales, Cádiz. Four of the Ospreys were intended for use aboard the new cruisers *Canarias* and *Baleares* then under construction.

In the winter of 1935-36 the Hawker works at Brooklands re-engined G-AEBD with a 620hp Hispano-Suiza 12Xbr, the same engine as that to be fitted on the Spanish Fury, and this pattern aircraft (c/n 41), bearing both the British registration and the Spanish naval registration EA-KAJ, was delivered to Getafe early in the summer of 1936. (The frequently published statement that it was delivered to Guadalajara with the three Spanish Furies is erroneous). By July 1936 several sets of floats had been completed at Cádiz, and a few fuselages and sets of wings at Getafe. Throughout the first months of the civil war the Osprey, its registrations overpainted with red bands, was employed on bombing and recon-

naissance missions, usually alone, but sometimes in conjunction with Breguet 19s. According to one much-repeated story, in the spring of 1937 it made a forced landing in Portugal, whence it never returned. There is no evidence to confirm the truth or untruth of this.

Hawker Osprey landplane

Span 37ft; length 24ft 4in; height 12ft 5in

Maximum speed 176mph; ceiling 22,000ft; range about 450 miles.

Hawker Spanish Fury

The Hawker Fury I, designed by Sir Sydney Camm, was the first RAF aircraft capable of maintaining a speed of over 200mph in level flight, and when it entered service in 1931 it was generally regarded as the best interceptor fighter in the world. It was powered by a 525hp Rolls-Royce Kestrel I liquid-cooled engine, and its fuselage was basically a braced metal Warren-type girder faired with oval dorsal frames and wooden stringers. The forward fuselage was covered by detachable alloy panels, and the rear by fabric. The biplane wings, which were of unequal span and braced by N struts, had metal spars and wooden ribs, and were fabric-covered. The Fury's armament consisted of two Vickers Mk. II or IIID .303 machine guns in the upper forward fuselage, synchronised to fire between the propeller blades. Its top speed was 207mph, and it could climb to

10,000ft in 4 minutes 25 seconds. Altogether, 146 were built, and Fury Is remained in front-line service until 1939.

Hawker produced a number of experimental Furies embodying various modifications to the wings and undercarriage and powered by different engines. One of these eventually became the Fury II, similar in major respects to the Fury I, but fitted with wheel spats and powered by a 640hp Kestrel VI engine which raised its maximum speed to 224mph. The ninety-nine that were built for the RAF and entered service in 1937 were intended as stop-gaps and transition trainers until they were replaced by Hawker Hurricanes and Supermarine Spitfires.

It seems likely that this was also the plan that the Spanish Dirección General de Aeronáutica had in mind when, after evaluating a Fury II at Brooklands in June 1935, it agreed a contract for fifty to be built under licence by Hispano-Suiza at Guadalajara, to replace the ageing and outdated Hispano-Nieuport 52s of the Aviación Militar. At the insistance of don Miguel Mateu, the director of Hispano-Suiza, the 'Spanish Fury', as it was called at Hawkers, was to have the new 612hp Hispano-Suiza 12Xbr engine, the reduction in power being more than compensated for by the fact that it weighed 67kg less than the Kestrel VI. The proposed armament was two fixed heavy-calibre 13.2mm Hispano guns in the upper fuselage, but mounts were installed to take these, 7.92mm Hispano-Suiza guns, or Vickers Mk 5 guns of similar calibre. The most conspicuous change, however, was the adoption of single-strut cantilever undercarriage legs and large-diameter Dowty internally-sprung wheels, which, combined with the graceful lines of the long engine cowling, made the Spanish Fury one of the most beautiful biplane fighters ever built.

Before delivery, the three pattern Spanish Furies, in aluminium dope and polished metal finish, were painted with the Spanish red, yellow and purple roundels on the wings and horizontal bands on the rudder. The military serials of the three aircraft, 4-1, 4-2 and 4-3, were stencilled in black on the yellow

The Hawker Spanish Fury No 4-3.

rudder bands. Accompanied by Hawker test pilot and engineer P C Lucas and two mechanics, the three Spanish Furies arrived in crates at Guadalajara in June 1936, probably on the 11 June (according to Mr Lucas – the hitherto published date of 11 July, only one week before the outbreak of the civil war, is erroneous, as is the assertion that he was accompanied by J S Hindmarsh and P W S Bulman, two senior Hawker test pilots). By the end of the month the three aircraft were assembled and tested, and the three Englishmen returned to London. They did not, as usually stated, return hurriedly after the fighting had broken out.

When fighting did break out on 18 July, and both Guadalajara and the Madrid aerodromes had been secured by government supporters, the three Furies were transferred to Getafe. They were not yet armed, but, since there were no Nationalist fighters in the vicinity at the time, they were sent out on patrols to boost the morale of the Republican militia gathering in the Guadarrama mountains to oppose Gen Mola's forces advancing on Madrid from the north. After difficulty with the synchronisation mechanisms was resolved, the Furies were armed in the first week of August. However, a duel between a Fury and a Nationalist de Havilland Dragon Rapide (40-2) piloted by Capitán Angél Salas, on 10 August 1936, lasted 15 minutes without result, which suggests that the armament was still not functioning. One Fury (4-2) was lost on 19 August when the pilot, Félix Urtubi (who had just defected from the Nationalists at Tetuán in a Breguet 19 after shooting his Falangist observer with a pistol), was so intent on chasing a Nationalist Junkers Ju 52/3m as far as the Portuguese border that he ran out of fuel and was forced to land in Nationalist territory near Badajoz. His attempt to set fire to the Fury was interrupted by the approach of National-ist soldiers, and, although Urtubi escaped back to Republican territory disguised as a coalman driving a donkey, the Fury passed into Nationalist possession. It was exhibited at Badajoz, and its photograph was published in newspapers all over the world. The second Fury was lost when it was sent to Guadalajara for repair after Lacalle had landed it heavily.

At Getafe, the remaining Spanish Fury was proudly pointed out to the deputations of foreign politicians, journalists, and other privileged sightseers who visited the aerodrome daily, but was jealously guarded from the host of foreign pilots who arrived at the beginning of September. As a result, it became the subject of some strange legends. One, circulated round several chanceries and embassies in Europe, maintained that Britain had sent its newest Hawker Fury fighter, and its top pilot, to test it in battle, but that the Italians had at last succeeded in shooting it down. In reality, the claim of Joaquín García Morato

The Spanish Fury No 4-2 on show in Badajoz after it had come down without fuel in Nationalist territory. Its pilot, Félix Urtubi, escaped to Republican territory disguised as a coalman leading a donkey. (Arráez)

notwithstanding, no Fury was shot down in the Spanish civil war. On 29 August 1936 Lacalle, in this Fury, led the first two armed Dewoitine D.372s into action, when they encountered three Fiat C.R.32s. In the ensuing brief dogfight the Dewoitine pilots shot down two Fiats without loss. Thereafter the Fury was in constant action, usually flown by Lacalle or (until his death) Urtubi, sometimes alone and sometimes leading a small patrol made up by a pair of D.372s, Loire 46s or Nieuport 52s. It continued to fly through the whole of September and October 1936, and became a familiar sight escorting, usually alone, patrols of Breguet 19s or single Potez 54s in the *estilo Lacalle* ('Lacalle style'), no more than 100 metres above its charges.

The policy of the Jefatura (com-mand) of sending fighters out singly or, at most, in threes against enemy formations of six or nine Fiat C.R.32s and Heinkel He 51s so angered Republican pilots that, on 27 September, the day Toledo fell, they staged a protest by sallying forth in a formation of every fighter available – the Fury, the Boeing 281, two Loire 46s, three D.372s and a pair of Nieuport 52s. They spotted a force of nine Fiats and three Heink-els, who refused to give combat, but in the afternoon the Fury, three D.372s and a Loire 46 attacked a formation of Ju 52/3ms, only to be bounced by nine C.R.32s led by Capitano Vicenzo Dequal. One Ju 52 was claimed shot down and two Dewoitine pilots, Vincent Doherty and Eric Griffiths, were severely wounded.

The Fury continued to lead a charmed life. By 23 October the fighter force at Getafe had almost vanished, the Boeing, Loires, and most of the Dewoitines having been shot down, destroyed by bombing, lost in accidents or sent away for repair. The day soon arrived when the Republican air chief, Gen

Hidalgo de Cisneros, 'was reduced to giving the order, in response to yet another air raid alarm, "send out the fighter!"' 'The fighter' was the Fury, flown in rotation by Lacalle and Javier Jover Rovira, a naval pilot seconded to Getafe. Lacalle was sent on leave on 28 October, before joining a newly-arrived Russian escuadrilla of I-15 Chatos on 5 November, and when Getafe came under artillery fire as Nationalist troops approached Madrid, Jover and the Fury were evacuated to Alcalá de Henares. There, a day or two later, the Fury struck a high-tension cable after taking off and was badly damaged.

Thus ended the fighting career of the only Hawker Fury to see sus-tained action in any theatre of war. Between 18 July and 2 November 1936 it flew more than 150 combat missions. The 'victories' scored in the Fury during this time are not recorded. When he joined the Chato squadron on 5 November, however, Lacalle was already credited with eleven victories (a fact he does not mention in his memoirs), some of which must have been scored in the

Fury, and this takes no account of possible victories scored by other pilots. Lacalle, who later rose to command the whole Republican fighter force, wrote that the Fury was in a class by itself compared with all the other fighters in Spain on either side; dependable, free of vices and wonderfully sensitive to the controls. His only criticism concerned the top speed, which, he believed, never reached the 360km/h (224mph) claimed by the manufacturer. The only occasion on which the airspeed indicator crept over 300km/h (187mph) was when, escaping from a formation of He 51s after his guns had jammed, he put the Fury into a full-power vertical dive and pulled out just above the ground. A possible explanation of this is that the indicator may have been a British instrument recording not kilometres, but miles per hour. Nevertheless, when he saw 'his' Fury at Alcalá, minus wings, damaged and filthy, he made a promise to write a letter of praise and gratitude to the Hawker company at Brooklands. It was only the hectic pressure of subsequent events that prevented his doing so.

The two damaged Furies were taken to La Rabasa, near Alicante, after Hispano-Suiza was evacuated there in October, 1936, and were cannibalised to make one good aeroplane. Señor Marcelino Viejo, an engineer at Hispano since 1926, relates that he made the ribs for the upper mainplane and other components with his own hands, because Non-Intervention prohibited Hawker from sending the special material, despite the fact that it had already been paid for. He has also explained the well-known photograph of a Spanish Fury in which a section of the upper half of the fuselage behind the cockpit is painted red, producing a curious chequered pattern. This was the result of marrying the fuselages of the two Furies. When the Republican red bands had been painted on shortly after the outbreak of the war, one machine had received a narrowish red band behind the cockpit, and the other a broad band in front of the tail. Shortly after Viejo took the photograph at La Rabasa the Fury was given an overall mottled camouflage. The Fury was then taken over by one of the Sampil brothers (see Fokker F.VIIb3m) and probably transferred to the Combat Training School at Archena.

The Spanish Fury captured by the Nationalists was likewise rebuilt at Tablada, Seville, under the supervision of José Pazó Montes (see González Gil-Pazó GP-1), but was damaged after a test pilot inadvertently shot off the propeller as a result of a fault in the synchronisation gear. It was rebuilt a second time, and C G Grey, the editor of *The Aeroplane*, reported in June 1938 that Hawker would have been proud of the skill with which it had been done. When the Republicans surrendered, on 31 March 1939, the Nationalists flew in mass formation over Madrid. The Fury, piloted by Gen José Rodríguez Díaz y Lecea, was in one of the fighter squadrons. Both Furies continued flying in the Ejercito del Air until 1948, first with the type code 4W, and then as C.2 after November 1945.

No data available.

Heinkel He 45

Until the advent of the He 70 in December 1932, the name of Ernst Heinkel was associated with solidly built, rugged and practical aircraft that were advanced in neither conception nor construction. In this respect, the cumbrous Heinkel He 45 was representative of the whole family. Designed in parallel with the He 46 for a secret programme instituted in contravention of the Paris Air Agreement of 1926 – to say nothing of the Versailles Treaty – the He 45 was a two-seat, single-engined light bomber and long-distance-reconnaissance aircraft. The two-spar wings were of wood, with fabric covering, and the fuselage was built of welded steel tube, the forward part and upper decking being covered with light metal and the rest with fabric. The armament consisted of a single fixed forward-firing 7.9mm MG 17 machine gun on the starboard side above the 660hp BMW VI 6,0 ZU engine, and an MG 15 gun on a Scarff-type ring in the observer's cockpit. Behind the observer's position was a bay for a camera or ten 10kg bombs. A further 200kg of bombs could be carried on underwing racks. The observer also had a FuG VI radio powered by a wind-driven generator.

The He 45 was often considered, especially by Spanish pilots, to be almost excessively large for a two-seat biplane. In reality it was not much larger than a Hawker Hart, and the illusion was caused by the height of its undercarriage, necessitated by the truly enormous propeller. The prototype first flew in the spring of 1932, and a production order was placed during the following autumn, three months before Hitler became Chancellor of Germany. During the next three years 512 Heinkel He 45s were built, making the He 45 for a time the numerically most important aircraft in service with the Luftwaffe.

The first Heinkel He 45s for Spain, between fifteen and twenty-one in number, arrived in November 1936 to form the Aufklärungsgruppe (Reconnaissance Wing) of the Condor Legion, A/88. The He 45 was assigned the type code 15, and A/88 took some part in the Battle of La Jarama south of Madrid in February 1937. With the arrival of the first Dornier Do 17s in February and March 1937, the Condor Legion handed over six He 45s to the Spanish Nationalists, who formed them into a single escuadrilla attached to the Breguet 19 group 1-G-10 at León under Comandante Eyaralar. The first commander of the Heinkels was Capitán Francisco Iglesias, the same who had made, with Jiménez, the famous flight from Seville to Bahia in the Breguet 19 Bidon *Jesús del Gran Poder* in 1929.

Having already nicknamed the Heinkel He 46s 'Pavas' (Turkey Hens), the Spaniards promptly dubbed the larger He 45s 'Pavos' (Turkeys). The Breguet-Heinkel group was at first called the 2° Grupo de Bombardeo Táctico, a name changed soon afterwards to the 1° Grupo de Asalto. Transferred to Vitoria, the group was employed intensively throughout the Viscaya campaign – that is, the drive to capture Bilbao – but early in June 1937 was returned to León to counter the Republican offensive at La Granja, Segovia.

Heinkel He 45s of 6-G-15. (Azaola)

During the second half of June, with the delivery of six more He 45s, a separate group, 6-G-15, was formed at León under the command of Cipriano Rodríguez, another veteran long-distance pilot of the Breguet Bidon in the late 1920s. After actions in the Asturias and the Santander sector, 6-G-15 was transferred to Avila for the Battle of Brunete in July 1937, two Pavos being lost in ground loops during the first days. In August the He 45s returned to the northern front, being employed chiefly in the mountainous Asturian region until the end of September. By this time, casualties were beginning to mount, five aircraft having been shot down in September alone. After the conclusion of the northern campaign, and a rest period at Burgos, 6-G-15, now commanded by Félix Bermúdez de Castro (nicknamed 'El Chili'), took part in the hard-fought Battle of Teruel in December 1937 and January 1938. By this time reinforcements had brought the group strength up to fifteen aircraft, with twelve more under repair or otherwise out of service.

During the Nationalist drive through Aragón to the Mediterranean coast in March and April 1938, the He 45s, based at Sanjurjo, Saragossa, were in such constant action that by 26 March only three of the entire group of fifteen aircraft were in flying condition. Nevertheless, the group was in action again by 1 April, though seriously under strength, and was one of the air units detailed to cover Gen Aranda's final breakthrough to the coast at Viñaroz, which was captured on Good Friday, 15 April 1938. During heavy fight-

A Heinkel He 45 of A/88 at Le Cenia, during the Battle of Brunete. (Azaola)

ing round the Pyrenean town of Bielsa in May 1938, the group lost another four aircraft, two of which were shot down.

Throughout the period since June 1937, A/88 of the Condor Legion retained two *ketten* (flights of three aircraft each) of He 45s, employing them chiefly for artillery spotting. Three were shot down: one by anti-aircraft fire over Aviles, in the Asturias, on 22 October 1937, the pilot (Lt Friedrich Schwanengel) being killed, and two over Cabells on 7 April, also by anti-aircraft fire, all four crew members being killed. The three aircraft must have been

replaced, for in June 1938, after the arrival of Henschel Hs 126s, A/88 handed over six He 45s to 6-G-15. The heaviest actions involving He 45s, however, were undoubtedly those during the Battle of the Ebro (25 July to 16 November 1938), at the height of which every aircraft was logging more than four hours' operations a day. On 23 September the He 45s, by now led by Comandante Antonio Llop Lamarca, were transferred to Posadas, near Córdoba. After a brief rest period at Burgos in November, 6-G-15 embarked on its last major operation of the war, the conquest of Catalonia, which began on 23-24 December 1938. At this time two He 46s were added to the group. The last He 45 to be destroyed was 15-15, which had been damaged several times previously. On 28 March 1939, three days before the end of the war, it was blown up during a ferry flight between Saragossa and León, the pilot, Teniente Moro Diez, being killed. The cause was probably a bomb planted by a saboteur.

Altogether, twelve Heinkel He 45s appear to have been shot down, including the three belonging to A/88, and a further nine seriously damaged. The number of He 45s delivered to Spain is usually put at thirty-three (15-33 being the highest serial number found on any records), though some authors put the total at forty-one. However, if the Condor Legion handed over twenty-seven in 1937, kept six until 1938 but lost three of these in action, yet handed six over in June 1938, then the total must be at least thirty-six. A further fifteen were delivered in 1939, and on 1 March 1940 twenty-five were still in service with the Ejercito del Aire, the majority with Grupo 41 at Málaga and San Javier, Cartagena. In 1945 their type code was changed to A.2. They continued in service until about 1950. A vivid, informative, and sometimes amusing account of life as an He 45 pilot during the civil war can be found in *Cadenas del Aire* by Dr J L Jiménez-Arenas Martín (Madrid, 1973).

Span 11.5m; length 10m; height 3.6m; wing area 34.59sq m.
Empty weight 2,105kg; loaded weight 2,745kg.
Maximum speed 290km/h; cruising speed 220km/h; ceiling 5,500m; range 1,200km.

Heinkel He 46C

Whereas the Heinkel He 45 was developed for long-range reconnaissance, the He 46 was designed for short-range reconnaissance. Both were conceived as biplanes. The He 46a, in fact, made its maiden flight in 1931 before the He 45. It differed from the He 45 mainly in having a swept-back upper wing, a smaller lower wing to give the observer a better downwards view, and a Siemens-built Bristol Jupiter radial engine. When trials showed that the lower wing seriously restricted the observer's field of view forwards, it was removed, and the upper wing enlarged to increase the gross wing area from an original 31.6sq m to 32.9sq m (reduced in the He 46C to 32.3sq m).

The He 46C, which was ordered into quantity production in 1933 and began to enter Luftwaffe service early in 1935, was a two-seat parasol monoplane with a fabric-covered wooden wing and a metal fuselage, the fore-part of which was covered by light metal panels and the rest by fabric. Its armament consisted of a single 7.9mm MG 15 machine gun on a ring mounting in the observer's cockpit and twelve 10kg bombs in vertical racks inside the fuselage,

behind the observer's cockpit. There were two levers, one for releasing the bombs singly and a second for releasing them in salvo. The bombsight was mounted on the starboard side of the fuselage floor, and demanded a certain amount of contortion on the part of the observer when he was centring his target. Alternatively, the bomb bay could be converted to house a Zeiss aerial camera, supplemented by a hand-held camera which the observer worked, leaning over the fuselage side.

The chief defect of the He 46C-1 (580hp BMW Bramo 22B radial engine), apart from its leisurely performance, was its distracting vibration, which Heinkel's engineers had been unable to cure. Some 215 were built altogether for the Luftwaffe, besides 18 for Romania and 36 for Hungary. The last He 46s in Luftwaffe service were replaced by Henschel Hs 126s after the Polish campaign, but those in Bulgarian and Hungarian service flew in the Russian campaign until 1943.

In September 1936, by secret arrangement between the Spanish Nationalists and the Portuguese government of Dr Salazar, a batch of twenty Heinkel He 46C-1s was unloaded at Lisbon and transported to Tablada, Seville, for assembly. They received the type code 11 but, perhaps to confuse the enemy as to the true number in Spain, were serialled 11-150 to 11-169. The He 46s were handed over to the Spanish Nationalists and formed into three escuadrillas – 1-E-11, 2-E-11 and

A Heinkel He 46.

3-E-11 – and, as they offered little improvement on the Breguet 19s, were assigned to quieter sectors. Escuadrilla 1-E-11, commanded by Capitán Manrique Montero, was based at Saragossa, and 2-E-11 and 3-E-11 were at León. The He 46s of 1-E-11 began operations on 2 November 1936 with flights over Huesca. The next day they were attacked by three Republican Nieuport 52s, from which they escaped with little damage, the Nieuports being scarcely faster than the Heinkels. At the end of the month Montero was replaced by Capitán Gancedo, and the squadron transferred to Vitoria to counter the Republican offensive at Villareal in Navarra. Escuadrilla 2-E-11 (Capitán Vara de Rey, the same who had immobilised the Douglas DC-2 at Seville on 18 July 1936) and 3-E-11 (Capitán Jiménez Ugarte) operated from León during this period. With the arrival of ten more He 46s in November 1936, 4-E-11 (Capitán Laurrari) was formed and combined with 2-E-11 into the Grupo de Asturias 1-G-11 under Vara de Rey, the other two squadrons being formed into the Grupo de Aragon 2-G-11 (Comandante Pérez Pardo), based at Saragossa.

In June 1937 both groups were combined into a single group of two escuadrillas of twelve aircraft each, 3-G-11, under the command of Pérez Pardo. The group performed with distinction in the Battle of Belchite, but suffered heavy casualties, Pérez Pardo himself being among those killed. After the winter battle of Teruel 3-G-11 was dis-

banded, and the He 46s were relegated to the Escuela de Tripulantes (Aircrew Training School) at Málaga, under Cdte Iglesias. Ten He 46s survived the civil war, and three of them (with the new code R.1) continued flying until 1946. According to some sources the total number of He 46s sent to Spain was not thirty but forty-six, but as this would mean that thirty-six were shot down or otherwise lost, the lower figure seems more probable.

Span 14m; length 9.5m; height 3.4m; wing area 32.3sq m.

Empty weight 1,765kg; loaded weight 2,300kg.

Maximum speed 215km/h at 800m; ceiling 6,000m; range 1,050km.

Heinkel He 50G

Although the development of the dive-bomber in Germany as an important tactical weapon is usually counted as having begun with the Sturzbomber-Programm of 1933 (see Henschel Hs 123), the first German dive-bomber was built and flown two years earlier, in response to a Japanese order placed with Heinkel for a two-seat dive-bomber capable of carrying a bomb load of at least 250kg, stressed for catapult launching from warships, and adaptable as a seaplane or landplane. The Heinkel He 50 first flew in the summer of 1931 and, after acceptance by the Japanese Navy, was produced in Japan as the DIAI Type 94 and DIAI Type 96 carrier-bombers, entering service in 1935.

Twelve examples of a modified version, the He 66aCh (He 50B), were built for China, but in the spring of 1935 these were transfer-

red before delivery to various Luftwaffe flying schools and, on 1 October, to the Fliegergruppe Schwerin, the Luftwaffe's first dive-bombing unit. As Henschel He 123s became available the He 50s were relegated once more to the A/B Schulen.

The He 50 was a strong twin-bay fabric-covered biplane with wooden wings and a steel-tube fuselage with wooden formers. It was powered by an uncowled 580hp (at 1,000m) Siemens SAM 22 radial engine. In October 1936 one He 50G arrived at Tablada, Seville, where it was flown by a civil pilot named Zitzewitz. It was not used in action, and was grounded after a few months.

Span 11.5m; length 9.76m; height 4.4m; wing area 34.8sq m.

Empty weight 1,600kg; loaded weight 2,620kg.

Maximum speed 235km/h; ceiling 6,400m; range 600km.

Heinkel He 51

In the chronicles of military aviation there appear from time to time types of aeroplane which, having failed lamentably in the rôles for which they were intended, were relegated by necessity to others which their designers had never envisaged for them, but in which, to everyone's surprise, they achieved distinction. The history of the He 51 is an example.

The prototype He 51a was based directly on the He 49, the first design for Heinkel by the brothers Siegfried and Walter Günter (see He 70 and He 111), and underwent its initial flight tests in the summer of 1933. A pre-production series of nine He 51As, built for the Deutschen Luftsports-verband (German Air Sports League, the nucleus of the still clandestine Luftwaffe), was followed by an order for 141, which began to enter service with 1 Gruppe of the Jagdegeschwader 132 *Richthofen* and 1/JG 134 *Horst Wessel* in the spring of 1934. These were soon replaced by the marginally improved He 51B, which, by the summer of 1936, had become the first standard fighter of the Luftwaffe.

Dr Goebbels' propaganda ministry publicised it as a fighter second to none among the world's service

A Heinkel He 50.

A Heinkel He 51 of 4.J/88 in November 1936.

fighters. This task was facilitated by the shape of the aeroplane itself, for, although it revealed hints of the aerodynamic refinement and elegant curves that characterised the Günter brothers' later designs, the Heinkel He 51, with its menacing nose and wide-spread undercarriage legs ('like hungry stamens', in the words of a Spanish Republican fighter pilot), undoubtedly had the look of a killer. Nevertheless, it was a conventional, unequal-span biplane of fabric-covered metal construction, belonging to a tradition that was already obsolescent, and its 550hp BMW VI 7,32 liquid-cooled vee engine was thoroughly outdated. Its armament consisted simply of twin 7.9mm MG 17 machine guns mounted above the engine and synchronised to fire between the blades of the wooden propeller. Between the splayed, wire-braced undercarriage legs was mounted a 170-litre drop-tank to increase the range from 550km to 740km at 85 per cent full power.

Following Hitler's decision to assist Gen Franco, six He 51Bs, with their pilots, maintenance crews and other personnel recruited for 'Operation Magic Fire', were dispatched to Spain aboard the *Usaramo*, the aircraft and equipment being ostensibly exported through the spe-

cially created company HISMA (Compañía Hispano-Marroquí). When the *Usaramo* reached Câdiz, late on 5 August 1936, Republican ships were preparing to shell the city in retaliation for the passage of a Nationalist convoy of small boats that had managed to bring some 3,000 troops across from Morocco that day, and the German ship was able to steal into port only under cover of darkness. The six Heinkels were disembarked next morning during a Republican bombardment, but the firing was so inept, there being few officers on board the warships, that the uncrated Heinkels were loaded on to a train and taken along the isthmus to the mainland under the very barrels of the Republican guns without being damaged.

At Tablada Aerodrome, Seville, the aircraft were assembled, assigned the type code 2, and then tested by their German pilots: Oblt Eberhardt, Hptm von Houwald, Hptm Knüppel, Hpt Trautloft, Lt Klein and Lt Hefter. The pilots flew their first 'display' patrol over Seville on 12 August and, since they were under orders to avoid combat with Republican aircraft, spent the next few days training five selected Spanish pilots: Luis Rambaud, Joaquín García Morato, Miguel García Pardo, Julio Salvador and Ramiro Pascual. On 18 August, while on solitary patrols, Morato claimed the destruction of a Republican fighter over

Loja, and of a Potez 54 over Antequera, and Salvador shot down a Nieuport 52 and a Breguet 19 (with a second probable) over Mérida.

The He 51, however, presented difficulties to pilots unfamiliar with it, in particular a tendency to bounce and veer on landing, with the result that two Spaniards damaged their aircraft. In response, the Germans asked to be allowed to take part in military operations and, when this was granted, the squadron was moved north to Escalona del Prado, between Segovia and Cuellar. The first operation, an attack on Getafe Aerodrome on 23 August, was carried out entirely by Spanish crews in eight Ju 52/3ms and three escorting Heinkel He 51s, because it was judged politically unwise for German airmen to fly over the Madrid sector at this stage. Two He 51s were damaged on landing at Escalona, however, and this time the Germans angrily insisted that no one but themselves should fly the Heinkels. The Spaniards were constrained to agree to, this, and the Escuadrilla Rambaud, as it was called after its commander, was disbanded.

The Germans now went into action seriously for the first time, and between 25 August and 6 September 1936 claimed the destruction of five Breguet 19s, six Potez 54s, two Nieuport 52s and a Loire 46. These claims cannot be taken seriously, because only seven

A Heinkel He 51 of Spanish Nationalist ground-attack group 1-G-2. (Azaola)

Potez 54s and no Loire 46s at all had arrived in Spain by that time. One aircraft not included in their list of victories was the Nationalist de Havilland Dragon Rapide 40-5 (the D.H.89M ex-22-3 captured at Saragossa on 18 July), which the German pilots of a patrol of He 51s mistook for a Republican aircraft and shot down on 26 August. This, argued the Nationalists, would never have happened if they had been flying the Heinkels, and they painted the names of the two officers killed, Capitán Pouzo and Capitán Vela, in large letters on the fuselages of the Rapides 40-1 and 40-2 respectively as a standing reproach. The Germans got the message, and thereafter some of the best Spanish fighter pilots, including García Morato, Salvador and Salas, flew with the Germans when aircraft were available.

Meanwhile, Sonderstab W (Special Staff W), the organisation responsible for the expeditionary force to Spain, had decided to send an additional thirty-six Heinkel He 51Bs, twenty-four to the Spanish Nationalists and twelve to reinforce the German squadron. The first nine arrived, via Portugal, early in September 1936, and nine more followed at the end of the month. The result was the formation of two

German escuadrillas under the command of Oblt Eberhardt and Oblt Strumpell, and two Spanish escuadrillas of three aircraft each under the command of Capitán Montero and Capitán Martín Campos. Three of the Spanish machines were purchased by public subscription and named after the cities where the money was raised: 2-54 *Zaragoza*, 2-55 *Huesca* and 2-56 *Teruel*. On 28 September the Heinkel escuadrillas suffered their first casualty when the engine of the He 51 piloted by Lt Hefter failed after taking off from the aerodrome at Vitoria, and the machine crashed into the town square.

Although they were fighting a disorganised and poorly directed opposition, both the German and Spanish pilots were becoming aware that, as a fighter, the Heinkel He 51 left much to be desired. Only passably superior to the obsolete Nieuport 52, it was dangerously inferior to the Dewoitine D.372 and Loire 46 in level speed, manoeuvrability and, above all, climb, ill-armed though the French aircraft usually were. Particularly discomforting proof of this was seen on 17 September, when a single Dewoitine and a Hawker Spanish Fury, escorting some Breguet 19s, were able to prevent six German-flown He 51s from attacking the bombers and, indeed, to throw them all on to the defensive and scatter them. The collapse of the Republican air force

in the Madrid sector during October 1936 temporarily concealed this problem, but the arrival of the Russian I-15 and I-16 fighters in November brought it alarmingly back into focus. Serious combats began on 5 November, though the Heinkels suffered no losses until the 11th, when two were destroyed during a Republican air attack on their base at Avila. On 13 November two were shot down, Lts Eberhardt and Henrici being killed, though Henrici managed, despite a bullet lodged in his heart, to land his aircraft before dying.

The arrival of the Condor Legion, which included thirty-six new He 51Bs, in the middle of November returned the Nationalist fighters to a position of slight numerical superiority, because they now had forty-six He 51Bs and eighteen to twenty-four Fiat C.R.32s against twenty I-15s (four having been lost in the first week) and thirty-one I-16s, but did little to alleviate the problem. The He 51s were so hopelessly outclassed by the I-15s alone that they were incapable of protecting the bombers they escorted and, since there were not enough Fiat C.R.32s to provide cover for all the bomber formations, which sometimes numbered fifty aircraft at a time, daylight raids on the capital had to be abandoned after 26 November. The two Spanish escuadrillas were moved to Caudé, in what was assumed to be the quieter sector of Aragon, but on 27 December one Heinkel (piloted by Capitán Arija) was shot down, and on the 29th four more (including the three bought by public subscription) were destroyed when I-15s straffed their aerodrome. The sixth and last crashed on the same day.

The German fighter wing J/88, commanded by Hptmn Merhart, consisted of four staffeln of nine to twelve aircraft each, the fourth staffel (4.J/88) being made up of the survivors of the original Strumpell and Eberhardt escuadrillas and under the command of Oblt Knüppel. In August 1936 Knüppel had had a top hat ('Zylinder Hut') painted on his machine as a crest, and this had quickly been adopted by the rest of his escuadrilla. It now became the insignia of 4.J/88, but

Three He 51s of 1.J/88 in the summer of 1937. The nearest machine was flown by the Staffelkapitän Harro Harder. The 'Maribou' emblem is just visible between the wings.

with the dissolution of the staffel in March 1937 it was transferred to the Messerschmitt Bf 109B-equipped 2.J/88. Escuadrilla 1.J/88 adopted a diving 'Marabou', and 3.J/88 'Mickey Mouse'.

A visit by Hptmn von Moreau (see Do 17) to Berlin in December 1936 convinced the German command of the total inadequacy of the He 51B of which they had been so proud, and of the absolute necessity of committing more-modern fighters to the Spanish adventure. Meanwhile, the Germans had to make do with the Heinkel during the Battle of La Jarama in February 1937, and endure the humiliation of leaving most of the air fighting to the Italians. A Sonderstab W report described the situation as 'a farce', for, far from protecting the bombers they were escorting, as soon as the enemy appeared the He 51s were obliged to 'take refuge with the bomber formations where they hoped to seek the protection of the bombers' machine guns'.

In March 1937 the first Messerschmitt Bf 109Bs arrived to equip 2.J/88 and the Heinkels, together with those of 4.J/88, which was now disbanded, were transferred to the Spanish Nationalists. With these the Spaniards formed three escuadrillas of seven aircraft each: 1-E-2 (Manrique Montero), 2-E-2 (Ángel Salas), and 3-E-2 (César Martín Campos). After operating for three weeks over separate fronts, (1-E-2 in Aragón, 2-E-2 in the south, and 3-E-2 in the Asturias), the escuadrillas were reunited at Saragossa on 10 April. It was on 13 April, while straffing Republican positions at the Hermitage de Santa Quintera, between Tardienta and Almudévas, that they first hit on the tactic known as 'La Cadena' (the chain), inspired by the fact that the Republican trenches had thoughtlessly been dug in long straight lines. The manoeuvre was simply an adaptation of the 'Lufbery Circle'. The Heinkels would dive down in line-ahead

formation and, having machine-gunned the trench, the leader would pull up steeply, go into a half-roll, return to the end of the line and dive down again. In this way the enemy was pinned down by continuous fire until everyone's ammunition was exhausted. As a result of the first attack the Republican Karl Marx Division lost 400 men, and the unit holding the trenches was forced to abandon its lines. On 16 and 17 April, acting again as fighters, the escuadrillas engaged in a series of dogfights in which they claimed nine Republican aircraft shot down for the loss of two.

At the end of the month 2-E-2 re-equipped with Fiat C.R.32s (becoming 2-E-3), and the other two escuadrillas (3-E-2 now becoming 2-E-2) were formed into the first Spanish Heinkel He 51B grupo, 1-G-2. Escuadrilla 2-E-2 (Martín Campos) was transferred to Vitoria to join the Italian and German fighter units covering the Basque campaign, and 1-E-2 went to Escalona for the Battle of La Granja. Meanwhile, the Heinkels of J/88 were also serving chiefly in the ground-attack rôle, being employed, for example, to machine-gun the town and surrounding fields during the raid on Guernica on 26 April 1937. During the northern campaign the He 51Bs were fitted with underwing Vemag racks carrying six 10kg fragmentation bombs. In July they were transferred to Villa del Prado for the Battle of Brunete, carrying out straffing and bombing

missions several times a day under the scrutiny of Oberst von Richthofen, the Condor Legion Chief of Staff, and laying the foundations of the future Schlachtflieger of the Luftwaffe. In September 1.J/88 re-equipped with Messerschmitt Bf 109Bs and sent its Heinkels to reinforce 1-G-2.

Meanwhile, the success of the He 51B as a close-support aircraft led to the Heinkel He 51C-1, fitted with racks to carry four 50kg bombs. The production of this variant was subcontracted to the Fieseler-Flugzeugbau, and when the first batches arrived in Spain 4.J/88 was re-established in October 1937, taking as its insignia the 'Pik-As' (Ace of Spades) device. Escuadrillas 3.J/88, by then under Adolf Galland, and 4.J/88 were employed most intensively in the rapid Nationalist advance through Aragón to the Mediterranean coast, during which they learned and perfected the close-support tactics the Luftwaffe was to use so effectively in the Second World War. In the subsequent offensive towards Valencia 1-G-2 (commanded by José Mañon Jiménez, 'El Corto') underwent its sternest test, losing so many aircraft and pilots that, shortly after the start of the Battle of the Ebro (25 July 1938), it had to be temporarily withdrawn from front-line duties. At this time the second disbandment of 4.J/88 and the arrival of a second consignment of He 51C-1s enabled the Spaniards to re-equip 1-G-2 and create a second group of twenty-

A Heinkel He 59.

four aircraft, 4-G-2, commanded by Gerardo Fernández Pérez. Both groups, now the only units flying Heinkel He 51s in Spain, continued in constant action until the end of the civil war, in the last week of which 1-G-2 re-equipped with captured I-15 Chatos.

It seems that 126 Heinkel He 51s were delivered to Spain during the civil war, of which 39 (not 79, as has sometimes been published) were He 51C-1s. No accurate breakdown of losses seems possible, however, although the fact that only forty-six survived the war confirms reports that they were high. The Spanish units appear to have lost nineteen to ground fire, three shot down in combat, four destroyed on the ground and twenty-one written off as irreparable, making a total of forty-seven. This casts doubt on the German claim to have lost only six, because at least five were lost before the creation of the Condor Legion. Moreover, it is hard to believe that the twenty-seven German He 51s unaccounted for were all lost in accidents. Fifteen Heinkel He 51C-1s were delivered in May 1939, after the end of the civil war, bringing the total of He 51s on strength with the new Ejercito del Aire to sixty-one. Of these, forty were still flying in 1940, but only one remained in 1946, bearing the new type code A.1.

Span 11m; length 8.4m; height 3.2m; wing area 27.2sq m.
Empty weight 1,473kg; loaded weight 1,900kg.

Maximum speed 330km/h at sea level; climb to 1,000m in 1.4min; to 4,000m in 7.8min; ceiling 7,770m; range (at full throttle at sea level) 280km; optimum 740km.

Heinkel He 59

Despite the fact that in 1930 the Reichsmarine, or German Navy, neither had, nor was allowed to have, any aircraft, the Ernst Heinkel Flugzeugwerke at Warnemunde started work on a twin-engined biplane intended for naval co-operation, maritime reconnaissance and torpedo-bombing, the design being entrusted to Reinhold Mewes. The resulting Heinkel He 59, which was the largest aircraft produced by the company up to that time, appeared in two prototype versions: the He 59a landplane, which first flew in September 1931, and the He 59b seaplane, which first flew in January 1932. Both were described to the public as commercial freight carriers. While the He 59a had its fuel tanks in the fuselage, those of the He 59b were housed in its floats, leaving additional space in the fuselage for 'freight' (bombs), and in consequence the landplane version progressed no further than the prototype.

In 1933 twenty-one seaplanes, designated He 59B-1, were ordered as general-purpose aircraft for the projected Seefliegergruppen, as the German fleet air arm was to be named. During the course of 1935 the He 59B-1 gave way to the He 59B-2, with updated equipment,

and the He 59B-3, fitted with extra fuel tanks for long-range reconnaissance, the production of both types being subcontracted to Arado.

The He 59B had fabric-covered wooden wings braced by metal struts, and a fabric-covered welded-steel-tube fuselage. Power was provided by two BMW VI 6,0 ZU liquid-cooled engines rated at 630hp (660hp for take-off) and driving a pair of four-blade, fixed-pitch wooden airscrews, the nacelles being mounted on a pair of vertical streamlined fairings above the lower wings. There was a crew of four: a pilot, a radio-operator doubling as ventral gunner, a navigator-bombardier doubling as front gunner, and a gunner in the dorsal cockpit. The He 59B's defensive armament consisted of three 7.9mm MG 15 machine guns, one each in the nose, dorsal and ventral-step positions. Its offensive armament consisted of 1,000kg of bombs carried internally, or a single 500kg or 1,000kg torpedo carried externally.

The first five He 59B-2s arrived in Nationalist Spain in October and November 1936 and, together with four He 60s, were formed into the AS/88 (Aufklärungsgruppe See, or Sea Reconnaissance Wing) of the Condor Legion, commanded by Hptmn Karl-Heinz Wolff and based at the seaplane station at Puntales, Cádiz. The He 59B-2s were assigned the type code 71 (which was painted in black on the rear fuselage sides, but was removed after a few months) and, curiously, displayed three large white St Andrews' Crosses painted on the top surface of the upper wing, the aircraft themselves being painted light green with sky-blue undersides. The local people soon dubbed the He 59B-2s 'Zapatones' ('Big Shoes') after a popular Spanish comedian similar to the Britain's 'Little Titch'. Two Junkers Ju 52/3mW seaplanes also formed part of the staffel, but these were used only for transport and liaison work.

The He 59B-2s carried out long-distance reconnaissance missions over the western Mediterranean and Atlantic until 23 December 1936, when they were transferred to El Atalayón, a seaplane base in the Mar Chica (Little Sea) at the eastern end of Spanish Morocco, to be closer to Soviet ships bringing supplies to Cartagena. In January 1937 they were used to survey the southern Spanish coast (which is now called the 'Costa del Sol') preparatory to Gen Queipo de Llano's offensive against Málaga. Here they encountered fighter opposition for the first time, in the shape of six I-15 Chatos under the command of Boris Kosakov, based at Tabernas Aerodrome, Málaga. Frequent complaints from foreign shipping companies that their vessels were being harrassed and even attacked by Heinkel biplanes – one ship even being driven aground at Cape Scaratif on 30 January – led to strong protests from the French government, since neighbouring Algeria was then a French colony. The group was transferred to Málaga as soon as the Nationalists captured the port, and remained there until 18 May 1937, when it returned to its original base at Cádiz, Wolff having been replaced by Hptmn Küder. During the night of 24-25 May 1937 the Heinkel He 59s bombed the Republican battleship *Jaime I* in Almería harbour, and effectually put her out of action for the rest of the war. On 9 June AS/88 made its last transfer, this time to Pollensa, Mallorca, where it stayed until the end of hostilities.

From Mallorca the He 59s carried out maritime reconnaissance and attacks on ships assumed to be carrying supplies to Republican ports, and also day or night bombing, and low-level straffing, of targets on mainland Spain. At this time several of them were fitted with single MG FF (licence-built Oerlikon) 20mm cannon in place of the nose machine guns, weapons that proved extremely useful against small ships and railway locomotives. On 28 and 31 July 1937 two He 59s were forced down on the water by anti-aircraft fire, and on each occasion were successfully towed back to Pollensa by tugs, testimony to the ruggedness and seaworthiness of the aircraft. On 4 August 1937 the He 59s bombed and drove ashore a Republican merchantman, and on

11 August they set fire to and sank the Danish ship *Edith*. Other merchant ships, including two British vessels, suffered similarly during the following months. The Heinkel He 59s suffered their first combat casualty on 21 December 1937, when one was shot down by anti-aircraft fire over the coastal town of Benicarló, but a second He 59 alighted on the water beside the sinking aircraft and rescued the crew.

On 19 January 1938 Hptmn (later Major) Martin Harlinghausen took over command of AS/88, a position he kept until the end of the civil war. On 28 January a second He 59 was damaged by anti-aircraft fire, one of its engines and one float being practically shot away. The pilot managed to return to the Balearics, but was forced down in the sea between Mallorca and Republican-held Minorca. The crew was saved by a launch, but the aircraft sank. A third, wrecked by a storm, was lost on 11 February 1938. By this time the He 59s of AS/88 displayed the squadron emblem of an Ace of Spades card, on a black disc, on each side of the nose. Behind the black disc on the rear fuselage sides there was a triangular white pennant on which were painted two small black discs.

Between the middle of February and the middle of March 1938 Barcelona had, for political reasons, been granted a respite from Italian air raids. On 16 March, however, the S.79s and S.81s of the bomber groups on Mallorca launched a round-the-clock series of raids on the city, district by district, which lasted until the 18 March. These caused worldwide indignation and protests, and later both the Spanish Nationalists and the Germans tried to disassociate themselves from responsibility by claiming that they had never been informed, let alone consulted, by the Italians. All the stranger, then, that the first raids were, in fact, carried out by six He 59s, which, approaching Barcelona from the sea at high altitude under cover of darkness, cut their engines several miles out and glided over the city in silence, by then having descended to about 300m, and dropped their bombs before starting their motors

and turning out to sea to make their escape. These 'stealth' raids by night continued after the Italian raids ceased, and on 21 March the Republican fighter pilot Capitán Corral, commander of the 1ª Escuadrilla of Grupo 71, while flying a Dewoitine D.510 on night patrol, saw the sudden flares of the exhaust as the pilot of a Zapatones started his engines. Corral managed to close in and open fire before the aircraft was lost to sight. He shot it down, and the He 59 exploded in the air before hitting the ground.

The He 59s, usually in formations of three, continued their sunset, night or dawn raids on the Mediterranean ports through the summer, alternating them with daylight low-level straffing attacks on road and railway traffic near the coast. Their most successful raids were on 4 June 1938, when they sank three ships in Alicante harbour and a fourth at Denia, and on the night of 14-15 September, when they sank four ships at Barcelona. On 31 December Republican fighters shot down another He 59 over Valls, and on 5 March 1939, during the Nationalist 'Fifth Column' rising in Cartagena, Grumman GE-23 Delfines of the 2ª Escuadrilla of Grupo 28 at El Carmolí shot down another. The Heinkel managed to alight on the sea, and the crew was rescued by the *Mar Cantábrico*, which, since her capture by the Nationalists with American aircraft on board (see Appendix II and Vultee V1-A), had been converted into an auxiliary cruiser. The last casualty among the He 59s during the civil war was the result of a forced landing at sea on 22 March 1939, the crew being rescued by a Cant Z.501.

There is no agreement regarding the number of He 59s sent to Spain, some authors putting it at eight, and others at between eleven and fifteen. Since it is known that seven He 59B-2s were at Pollensa on 12 February 1939, and that ten had been lost before that date (five shot down, two damaged in action beyond repair, two wrecked in accidents, and one wrecked by a storm), the number would appear to have been seventeen. The staffel was kept at a strength of about six aircraft, and replacements from Germany, as losses occurred, were presumably flown to Mallorca individually via Italy and Sardinia. Towards the end of the war a few Spanish aircrews were taken on by AS/88 for training, and in May 1939 the five remaining He 59-2s were handed over to the Spanish navy. Three were still serving with the 52ª Escuadrilla of the 51 Grupo de Hidros in 1940, and continued flying until 1946.

Span 23.7m; length 17.4m; height 7.1m; wing area 153.2sq m.

Empty weight 6,215kg; loaded weight 9,000kg.

Maximum speed 220km/h; cruising speed 178km/h; ceiling 3,500m; range 1,750m.

Heinkel He 60E

The Heinkel He 60 was designed to meet a specification secretly (and illegally) drawn up in 1931 by the German Fliegerstab (air staff) and Reichsmarine for a two-seat naval reconnaissance seaplane stressed for catapult launching. The prototype He 60a first flew early in 1933, and the first production He 60As entered service with the Deutsche Verkehrsfliegerschulen (Civil Flying Schools), as the pretence of those years required, in 1934. The He 60 was an extremely robust, indeed heavy, unequal-span biplane, powered by a 660hp BMW VI 6,0 ZU water-cooled engine. Its oval-section fuselage was built of welded

steel tube and the wings were of wood, the whole airframe being fabric covered. As in the He 45, the pilot's cockpit was set higher than that of the observer, who was provided with a single 7.9mm MG 15 machine gun for defence. The next production models were the He 60C and He 60D, the latter being fitted with a fixed forward-firing machine gun and improved radio equipment. By July 1936 He 60s equipped three Küstenfliegergruppen (Coastal Patrol Wings) of the Luftwaffe.

In October 1936 the Spanish Nationalists requested six reconnaissance seaplanes for coastal patrol. Accordingly, with the creation of the Condor Legion, six of the last production batch of Heinkel He 60Ds (redesignated He 60Es, the 'E' denoting 'España') arrived at Cádiz. According to some sources these aircraft did not have the fixed guns fitted. The six, bearing the type code 60 and serialled 60-1 to 60-6, were incorporated into AS/88 with the He 59B-2s and based at Puntales, Cádiz, before being transferred to Atalayón in Spanish Morocco. During this period they patrolled the approaches to the Straits of Gibraltar, reporting on the movements of shipping and identifying vessels suspected of carrying supplies to Republican ports. During the Málaga campaign 60-5 and 60-6 were shot down off the Spanish coast by I-15s on 5 February 1937 (one of the He 60s had the name *Fiera del Mar* – 'Wild Beast of the Sea' – painted on its fuselage). Both managed to put down beside the Nationalist cruiser *Canarias*, which hoisted one damaged machine aboard (it was never-

theless written off) and sank the wreckage of the other. The pilot of one aircraft, Lt Dieter Leicht, was already dead.

Based at Málaga from March to June 1937, AS/88 handed over the four remaining He 60s to the Nationalists, who formed them into a single naval escuadrilla, E-60, under the command of the veteran flying-boat pilot Capitán Luis Cellier Sánchez. For the next year the squadron was based at La Canaca, near San Fernando in Cádiz bay, El Atalayón (Spanish Morocco) and Pollensa (Mallorca), beginning a mission at one base and terminating it at another, as circumstances decreed. Because only two qualified pilots were available, the aircraft flew in pairs, 60-1 usually with 60-3 and 60-2 with 60-4. It was during this period that E-60 adopted the 'Popeye' emblem (already used by other units on both sides) painted on the fuselage. On 21 August 1937 Cellier and his observer Benitez were killed when they were forced to put 60-2 down on a choppy sea off Mallorca.

In November 1937 the three remaining He 60s were transferred to the Nationalist air arm, although on 3, 4 and 5 December the naval pilot Tomás Mogano carried out a series of catapult tests at La Canaca (Cádiz) on behalf of the naval staff. On 4 December 60-1 was destroyed when failure of the oil-pressure system brought it down at sea off Cape St Vincent. An English merchant ship rescued the crew and took them to Malta, whence they returned to Spain some weeks later. In April 1938 the two remaining He 60s (60-3 and 60-4) were joined by the Fairchild 91, and carried out reconnaissance in co-operation with this machine until it was transferred to Spanish Morocco in September. In November 1938 the He 60s were transferred to Pollensa, Mallorca, which became their permanent base for the rest of the war, and were formed into the group 2-G-62-73 (62 denoting Cant Z.501s and 73 the Cant Z.506Bs). In February 1939 they were reinforced by two new He 60s, 60-5 and 60-6 (the numbers being those of the two originally lost in February 1937), bringing the total number of He 60s

The Heinkel He 60 Luis Cellier *(No 60-3) at Puntales, Cadiz, in 1937.*

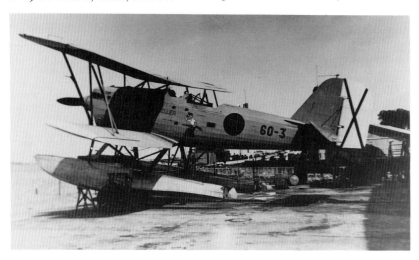

delivered to Spain to eight. The unit's last operation of the civil war was a photo-reconnaissance flight over Alicante by 60-5 on 18 March 1939. During the war He 60s had attacked thirty-five Republican ships with their machine guns and spotted about fifty vessels trying to slip through the Nationalist blockade of the Republican Mediterranean coast.

In the summer of 1939, following the establishment of the Ejercito del Aire, the four He 60s and the five remaining He 59B-2s were formed into the 52ª Escuadrilla of the 51° Grupo de Hidros (Seaplane Group) based at Pollensa, Mallorca. Constant patrols over the Mediterranean after the fall of France in June 1940, and the lack of spare parts, had their inevitable effect and, by 1942, 60-3 and 60-4 (re-serialled 52-3 and 52-4), which were suffering from corrosion, were withdrawn from service and cannibalised to keep 52-5 and 52-6 flying. In 1944 they received the new type code HR.2 and, together with six IMAM Ro 43s (HR.7) delivered in 1939, were formed into the 1ª Escuadrilla of the 2° Escuadrón of the Regimiento Núm 51. On 26 October 1945 HR.5 was destroyed in a crash, and HR.6 was sunk during a storm on the night of 27-28 August 1948.

Span 13.5m; length 11.6m; height 5.3m; wing area 56.2sq m.
Empty weight 2,775kg; loaded weight 3,400kg.
Maximum speed 240km/h; cruising speed 225km/h; ceiling 5,000m; range 950m.

Heinkel He 70

In 1931, when reports began to reach Europe of the remarkable performance of the American Lockheed Orion single-engined low-wing cantilever monoplane with a retractable undercarriage, they were greeted with a mixture of surprise and scepticism. Nevertheless, early in 1932 Deutsche Lufthansa invited both Heinkel and Junkers to design aircraft of a category and performance similar to that of the Orion, for use on express routes in Europe. As conceived on the drawing boards, the Heinkel He 65 and Junkers Ju 60 were to be aerodynamically clean low-wing monoplanes powered by the BMW-built Pratt & Whitney Hornet radial engine of 575hp, the Lockheed 9B Orion, which was the model then entering service in America, being powered by a Wright Cyclone radial of identical horsepower. However, both German designs had fixed, faired, undercarriages, because the task of

developing efficient retractable undercarriages threatened unacceptable delay.

After studying data on the Orion, Ernst Heinkel asked Lufthansa to cancel the He 65, which he felt would not be competitive. Lufthansa refused, arguing that Lockheed Orions were not likely to arrive in Europe for three or four years. Then, on Sunday 15 May 1932, Heinkel read in the newspapers that Swissair had imported two 9B Orions. He described his reaction in simple words: 'Now we're in the soup! The Orion is in Europe and with the machine we're building we can't possibly compete with it. We *must* build something faster than the Orion!' Driving his design team, led by the brilliant Siegfried and Walter Günter, almost round the clock, Heinkel had drawings prepared and submitted to Lufthansa by 14 June 1932, as well as a prototype under construction. In what must have been record time for so complex a project, the prototype was ready for its maiden flight on 1 December.

The He 70 prototype differed from the He 65 chiefly in the substitution of a 637hp BMW VI 5,5 Z twelve-cylinder glycol-cooled vee engine for the proposed radial, and in the possession of a fully retractable undercarriage. In the production models, both civil and military, this engine was replaced by a BMW VI 7,3 Z rated at 750hp. With its elliptical wings and tail surfaces and skilfully streamlined fuselage, the He 70 was an aeroplane of undeniable beauty and, in concept, appeared to be a generation ahead of most aircraft flying in Europe at that time. The fuselage was all-metal, and the wings were built of wood and covered with plywood. The

A Condor Legion Heinkel He 70 in the spring of 1937.

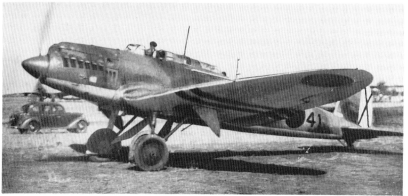

A Heinkel He 70 of the Spanish Nationalist group 7-G-14.

inverted gull form was chosen for the wings because it shortened the undercarriage legs, simplified the junction between wings and fuselage, and kept the tailplane clear of disturbed airflow. It was a tribute to the designers that *Versuchs*, or experimental, He 70s were to clock speeds of 376km/h, and that one modified He 70G, G-ADZF, bought by Rolls-Royce and fitted in England with an 875hp Peregrine engine, touched 481km/h in October 1938, a considerable achievement for an aircraft designed in 1932.

Nevertheless, the production He 70, with a top speed of 360km/h, did not achieve Heinkel's ambition of beating its American contemporaries, the Vultee V1-A and Northrop Delta, or even the older Lockheed Orion, on their own terms. Its useful load was only 100kg greater than that of the 9B Orion, and its load:tare ratio (the ratio between its useful load and its empty weight) was a wretched 26:74, compared with 33:67 for the Orion. An empty Lufthansa Heinkel He 70G (2,550kg) was 100kg heavier than a fully loaded 9B Orion (2,450kg), while its cruising speed and range were about the same. Even less pleasing was the fact that, although a Vultee could carry eight passengers in comfort, as well as its mandatory cargo of mail, for 900 miles at 320km/h, the He 70G, carrying four passengers in a cramped cabin, but no mail, could manage but 620 miles at 305km/h. Part of the blame for this lay with the engine, which, at 720kg, weighed twice as much as the 345kg Cyclone of the 9B Orion, but produced only 190hp more.

In addition to two prototypes, Deutsche Lufthansa received three He 70D-0s and ten He 70G-1s, which were commercial versions of the military He 70F. Both types were publicised in Lufthansa advertisements as the 'Heinkel Blitz' (lightning). The He 70D-0s were the first Heinkel Blitzen to appear in Spain, carrying mail from Berlin to Seville in the first stage of the airline's fortnightly service to Buenos Aires.

Having studied the military potential of the He 70, the Luftwaffe ordered two versions; the He 70E-1 light bomber carrying 300kg of bombs, and the He 70F-1, intended for reconnaissance duties and equipped with auxiliary fuel tanks and a hand-operated camera. The defensive armament of both versions was feeble, to say the least, consisting of a single 7.9mm MG 15 flexibly mounted machine gun in the observer's cockpit. Further equipment modifications, including the addition of a vertically-mounted motorised camera, produced the He 70F-2, and this was the version produced in the greatest quantity. Both types began to enter service in 1934-35, the Luftwaffe intending to replace them by the more efficient Dornier Do 17 as soon as it became available.

With the creation of the Condor Legion (7 November 1936), a squadron of twelve He 70s was dispatched to Spain, the first two aircraft arriving at the end of October and the rest during the first two weeks of November, to equip the reconnaissance unit Aufklärungsgruppe A/88. The He 70 received the type code 14. It is usually stated that these were all He 70F-2s, but according to some sources one flight of three aircraft, commanded by Lt Runze and used for high-speed light-bombing missions, was equipped with He 70E-1s. During the last week of November 1936 Runze and his 'He 70 Bomberkette' announced their presence with a low-level attack on a hydro-electric power station in northern Catalonia. A second consignment of thirteen He 70F-2s arrived between January and March 1937. During the spring of that year, the He 70s of A/88 made numerous photo-reconnaissance incursions into Republican territory. Because these flights were often undertaken by single aircraft, the He 70s were assumed to be one and the same aeroplane by the people below, who, owing to its light-coloured underside, nicknamed it *Paloma Blanca* (White Dove).

In the summer of 1937, after hard service both as bombers and reconnaissance aircraft in the Bilbao campaign, twelve He 70F-2s were transferred to Seville at the request of Gen Queipo de Llano, and 14-36, 14-45 and 14-56 were handed over to Spanish crews. The replacement of the He 70s of A/88 by Dornier Do 17s during the northern campaign was completed by September 1937, and all the remaining He 70s (four having been lost, one shot down in error by a Fiat C.R.32) were transferred to the Spaniards and formed into 7-G-14, commanded by Cdte Carlos Soler.

In Spanish service the He 70s were called 'Rayo' (lightning). Their camouflage and colouring was distinctive. While the upper surfaces were camouflaged in 'splinter' camouflage in the Condor Legion, and in wavy-band camouflage in Spanish service, the broad black streamlines on the fuselage sides, as used on the Lufthansa aircraft, were retained, the fuselage below being light blue. Some aircraft had an extraordinary 'sunbeam' pattern painted on the upper surface of the wings and the tail surfaces, though the colour of the beams cannot be ascertained.

In November 1937 two of the escuadrillas, 3-E-14 and 4-E-14, were detached, under the command of Carlos Sartorius and Antonio Rueda, to form part of the 3ª Escuadra Mixta of the 1ª Brigade Aérea Hispana, one of the two air brigades that made up the bulk of the Spanish Nationalist air arm after the summer of 1937. Another three, or six, He 70F-2s arrived in Spain during 1938, bringing the total delivered to 28 or 31. Escuadrilla 7-E-14 was occupied principally in the northern areas, taking part in the battle of Teruel, the Aragón campaign and the Battle of the Ebro, during which Sartorius became its commander. The independent escuadrillas 3-E-14 and 4-E-14, often with only two machines in each squadron, were based in Extremadura and Andalusia as a part of the Grupo Mixto 86-70, made up of He 70F-2s, Henschel Hs 123s and the two remaining Junkers Ju 86D-1s.

There are no reliable figures concerning casualties, but four were certainly lost by A/88. One was shot down over Bilbao on 15 June 1937, one, as mentioned earlier, was inadvertently shot down by an Italian fighter, and another is recorded as being lost to the Spanish units. If that is so, attrition through accidents was remarkably high, for only ten He 70F-2s survived the war. In service

Heinkel He 111Bs of 1.K/88. The nearest machine, No 25-17, is an He 111B-1 (note the deep radiator), in which the exhaust outlets have been replaced by a single collection tube, making the aircraft resemble an He 111E. (Azaola)

with the Ejercito del Aire the He 70F-2s were numbered 14-30 to 14-39, the 14 being changed to R.2 in 1945. By 1946 only six remained airworthy, and the last was withdrawn from service about 1952.

Span 14.8m; length 11.5m; height 3.1m; wing area 35.5sq m.
Empty weight 2,300kg; loaded weight 3,310kg.
Maximum speed 355km/h; cruising speed 310km/h; ceiling 6,000m; range 800km.

Heinkel He 111

The Heinkel He 111, one of the most famous, versatile and long-serving military aircraft in the history of aviation, belonged, with the Dornier Do 17 and Junkers Ju 86, to the first generation of modern bombers to equip the Luftwaffe. The manner in which this generation came into being, at a time when Germany was prohibited from having any military aircraft at all, is explained in the section on the Dornier Do 17. It will be remembered that all three were conceived as high-speed, twin-engined monoplanes that could serve either as bombers or airliners, although military requirements were always to take precedence.

Thus, of the four He 111 prototypes that first flew in 1935, two (the He 111a or V1, and the He 111b or V3) were military, and two (the He 111c or V2, and the He 111 V4) were civil machines. The Heinkel He 111 was an exceptionally graceful monoplane. Its slender fuselage, elliptical wings and tail surfaces and fishlike silhouette, based on that of its single-engined predecessor, the He 70, marked it unmistakably as the creation of its gifted designers, the brothers Siegfried and Walter Günter. In the air its handling qualities were excellent. Its only defect lay in the powerplant, two BMW VI 6,0 Z liquid-cooled engines rated at 690hp each, and this became apparent when the first of a production series of the bomber version, designated He 111A, was sent to Rechlin for trials. These showed that, with a full military load and the dorsal and ventral gun positions installed, the aeroplane was seriously underpowered, for the maximum speed of 270km/h represented little advance over existing bombers. The He 111As were rejected by the infant Luftwaffe, and six were sold to China, where, after the loss of three out of five on their first mission against the Japanese in 1937, they saw little use.

A fifth prototype (the He 111 V5 or He 111B-0), powered by two Daimler Benz DB 600 AA engines rated at 960-1,000hp each, proved highly successful, however, and the first production examples began to enter Luftwaffe service at the end of 1936. It was at this time that Oberleutnant Rudolf, Freiherr von Moreau, who had commanded the airlift across the Straits of Gibraltar and since gained distinction in the Spanish fighting, returned briefly to Germany to explain to Hermann Goering and his Luftwaffe General Staff how the air battles round Madrid had shown the German aircraft to be outclassed in all respects by their Russian opponents. In Goering's view, not only was German prestige at stake, but here was a heaven-sent opportunity to test the new generation of military aircraft, some still at prototype stage, in battle. Accordingly, among the German aircraft dispatched to Nationalist Spain early in February 1937 were four Heinkel He 111B-1s, which, together with four Do 17E-1s and four Ju 86D-1s, were formed into a separate Experimental Bomber Squadron (Versuchsbomberstaffel 88, or VB/88) in the bomber wing K/88 based at Salamanca. Under the command of Obl von Moreau, its task was to evaluate the performance of these aircraft in genuine operational conditions. The He 111s were allotted the type code 25 and, to commemorate von Moreau's original Kampfstaffel, named 'Pedros' – the Do 17s becoming 'Pablos' and the Ju 86s, which were little used, receiving no nickname.

On 7 March 1937 the Italians opened an offensive against Madrid from the north, and on the 9 March the Heinkels made their début with attacks on Republican aerodromes at Alcalá de Henares and Barajas. The Italians, however, suffered a sharp defeat north of Guadalajara, during which the Condor Legion, pleading the inclemency of the weather, signally failed to come to their assistance. After the Italians managed to dig themselves in, VB/88 resumed operations by attacking Republican troop concentrations, ironically nearly losing their first He 111 to Italian anti-aircraft fire. The Heinkels also attacked Alcalá again, but their claim to have destroyed twenty-four Russian aircraft on the ground can be dismissed as pure fantasy. On 29 March the Condor Legion was transferred to the northern front in preparation for the offensive against Bilbao, K/88 being based near Burgos on an aerodrome which, before the civil war, had been projected as the future Spanish international airport. During April the four Heinkel He 111B-1s played a small but conspicuous part in the Nationalist advance through the mountainous terrain of Vizcaya, during the course of which several Basque villages and towns – including Ochandiano, Durango and, most notoriously of all, Guernica – were heavily bombed and larged numbers of people killed. The anti-Franco and anti-Fascist press of the world named the

A Heinkel He 111B-2 is loaded with bombs.

'Heinkels' as the chief instruments of these outrages, despite the fact that most of the bombing was done by Ju 52s.

The appearance of the He 111s in March had been a complete surprise, however, and it was believed that they must have flown to Spain by night, directly across France in contempt of all international agreements (in fact, they were shipped). They were so fast that the only Republican fighters normally able to intercept them were the I-16s, which until then had had no opportunity of doing so. Thus these sleek but sinister-looking bombers came to be popularly identified as symbols of Nazi aggression, and of the fearsome innovation of concentrated terror-bombing of defenceless civilians.

Although the He 111B was fast in comparison with most bombers of its time, the drag caused by the retractable 'bin' for the ventral gunner, when extended, so seriously reduced performance that orders were given that it was to be lowered only when enemy fighters were in the immediate vicinity. Another cause of drag were the deep radiator intakes under the engine nacelles. This was rectified by installing 950hp DB 600 CG engines with shallower and more rounded intakes. Four examples of the modified version, with an improved gun mount in the nose and designated He 111B-2, were shipped to Spain in May 1937. Meanwhile, K/88 began to replace its Ju 52s with He 111B-1s, a process which was completed in October. The He 111s suffered their first casualties of the war when two were lost during the final attack on Bilbao in mid-June. After the fall of the city, VB/88 was disbanded and its

He 111B-1s and B-2s incorporated into the fourth staffel of the bomber wing, 4.K/88.

In July the Condor Legion was transferred to the central front to counter a major Republican offensive at Brunete, north-west of Madrid. On this front, however, the Republicans had a complete group of I-16 fighters, which were quite capable of tackling He 111Bs, and within a week the Heinkels, which were based at Villa del Prado, had to be withdrawn from daytime sorties. By the end of the month, however, the Condor Legion had returned north for the Nationalist offensive against Santander, where, Republican air opposition being slight, the Heinkels were able to resume daylight bombing without escort. The arrival of two squadrons of I-16s and one of I-15s, flown from the main Republican zone to aid the Basques, did little to redress the balance, for their bases were too close to the front line and were not defended by anti-aircraft guns, which made it impossible to mount an organised defence. Nevertheless, Republican fighters managed to shoot down two He 111Bs on 26 August near Gijón, and a third on 2 September. By the time the northern campaign ended with the capture of Gijón in October 1937, K/88 had about fifty He 111Bs on strength, of which twenty-two were He 111B-2s (the He 111B-1s were numbered 25-1 to 25-40, and the B-2s 25-41 to 25-62).

After several weeks of intensive attacks on Republican aerodromes, the Heinkels of K/88 entered the grim battle round Teruel, which the Republicans were besieging. Atrocious weather hindered and often defeated all air operations. On 17 December, for example, an entire formation of twenty-three He 111Bs, after taking off from Burgos de Osma, was scattered by a blizzard, one aircraft, 25-32, landing intact behind Republican lines. The Russians immediately demanded that the Heinkel, together with a captured Bf 109, be shipped to the Soviet Union for examination. The Republican defence minister, Indalecio Prieto, determined to stand up to what he regarded as Russian bullying and anxious to come to an

agreement by which the French would reopen their frontier to allow the entry of arms and supplies into Spain, secretly invited the French government to send technical specialists to test the two machines. The delegation from the CEMA at Villacoublay, headed by Capitain Constantin Rozanoff, arrived in February 1938. The take-off of the Heinkel from a small muddy field on a hillside was hazardous, but fortunately the ground fell away from the edge of the field and Rozanoff was able to gain speed by diving down and skimming the valley floor below. Before reaching Sabadell, in Catalonia, the French crew had to run a gauntlet of Republican, Nationalist and (again) Republican anti-aircraft fire. Capitán Emilio Galera, who flew on one of the subsequent test flights, told the author how, while standing directly below the dorsal gun position, he had struck his cigarette lighter and watched the flame stand straight up – proof of the superb German workmanship. When the French reports were taken back to Paris, however, they were classified so secret that the design bureaux for whom they were intended never received them. The Heinkel and Messerschmitt, meanwhile, were shipped to the USSR.

In February 1938 Spanish crews under the command of Capitán Luis Ureta Zabala were incorporated into the Condor Legion, until each patrulla of three aircraft had one Spanish-manned machine. During the massive Nationalist offensive in Aragón, which reached the Mediterranean coast on 15 April and divided the Republic in two, the Heinkels were in continuous operation against aerodromes and the retreating Republican armies. Their most ambitious effort, however, was 'Operation Neptune', from 16-18 April 1938, against the ports of Cartagena and Almería, where fresh Soviet supplies were being landed. Forty He 111Bs were employed and considerable damage was inflicted on both ports, but nine aircraft were lost, all but one in accidents caused by stormy weather, and another seven were badly damaged.

The first batches of the new He 111E-1s arrived in June 1938, allowing the Legion to transfer some of its well-worn He 111Bs to the Spanish Nationalists, who formed them into the bomber group 1-G-25 in August. The He 111E differed from the B versions chiefly in having Junkers Jumo 211A-1 engines (960hp at 1,500m), great attention having been paid to streamlining the nacelles. Maximum speeds were thereby raised to 419km/h at 4,000m and 350km/h at sea level. Another variant used in Spain was the He 111J-1, powered, like the He 111B-2, by 950hp DB 600 CG engines. It had originally been intended as a torpedo bomber, but had been converted back into an ordinary bomber in the course of production. The number of He 111J-1s sent is not recorded, but it was certainly small. Throughout the Battle of the Ebro K/88 and 10-G-25 were employed constantly in the daily tactical operations against Republican troops and in strategic raids on such ports as Barcelona and Alicante. By the end of the battle, in November 1938, only thirty He 111s were still airworthy – twenty-five at Sanjurjo (Saragossa) with K/88, and five at León with 10-G-25. The arrival of ten He 111E-3s in January 1939 enabled K/88 to hand over more He 111Bs to the Spanish Nationalists, who formed a second group, 11-G-25, in February. Meanwhile, K/88 carried out its last intensive operations of the war during the Nationalist conquest of Catalonia (23 December 1938 to 9 February 1939). During March the Spanish Heinkel groups were combined with 8-G-27 (Do 17s) to form the 8ª Escuadra Aérea under Comandante Eugenio Frutos Dieste. At this time K/88 carried out some mass-formation raids on Madrid, the last being on 27 March, four days before the end of the war.

Estimates of the number of Heinkel He 111s delivered to Spain vary between 75 and 101, but since there is record of an He 111E serialled 25-93, and another source cites a 25-98, the true figure seems to be in the region of 100. Nor is there a reliable record of their casualties. Until a few years ago, Spanish sources gave a figure of seventeen lost from all causes. From a careful examination of existing records, however, it is possible to identify twenty lost in battle, fifteen through accidents, and one through sabotage, with an additional eight 'possibles' and five 'possibles' in accidents. When the Condor Legion left Spain after the civil war, its He 111s were handed over to the newly created Spanish Ejercito del Aire, and in March 1940 fifty-eight were still in service with the 14° and 15° Regimientos at Saragossa and Logroño respectively. Meanwhile, in 1942 CASA began the production under licence of Heinkel He 111H-16s (two 1,350hp Junkers Jumo 211F-2 engines) at Seville, and these served in the Ejercito del Aire under the designation B.2H. Two hundred were built altogether. The He 111Bs and He 111Es continued in service until the 1950s. In the early 1960s a considerable number of Spanish-built He 111H-16s, repainted in Luftwaffe colours, were used for the film *The Battle of Britain*, and the type continued in Spanish service until the 1970s.

He 111B and E
Span 22.6m; length 17.5m; height 4.4m; wing area 87.598sq m.

He 111B-2
Empty equipped weight 5,840kg; loaded weight 10,000kg.

He 111E-1
Loaded weight 10,679kg.

He 111B-2
Maximum speed 370km/h; cruising speed 345km/h; ceiling 7,000m; range, with 1,500kg bomb load, 910km; with 750kg bomb load, 1,660km.

He 111E-1
Maximum speed 419km/h; cruising speed 381km/h; range, with 1,000kg bomb load, 1,500km.

Heinkel He 112 V5, He 112 V9 and He 112B

Designed by Siegfried and Walter Günter in direct competition with the Messerschmitt Bf 109, the Heinkel He 112 single-seat fighter was, like the Bf 109, a low-wing cantilever monoplane with a retractable undercarriage, but otherwise differed from its rival in every major respect. Where the Messerschmitt

The Heinkel He 112 V5 at Seville.

The Heinkel He 112 V9. (Arráez)

had a slender, straight fuselage, straight-edged narrow-chord wings, a narrow-track undercarriage and a high-angled stance on the ground, the Heinkel appeared to be all sensuous curves, with a thick inverted-gull wing of broad elliptical planform and equally broad, elliptical tail surfaces. It stood at a low ground angle on a sturdy wide-track undercarriage, and its cockpit was open. Finally, whereas the Messerschmitt was provided with automatic leading-edge slots and slotted flaps to compensate for its high wing loading and improve aileron control near the stall, the Heinkel had no slots and conventional plain flaps.

At first, the more orthodox Heinkel He 112 had the greatest appeal to the more orthodox-minded among the Luftwaffe chiefs of staff, but seemingly endless problems during its prolonged testing (it was constructionally the more complex of the two), and the superior performance and manoeuvrability of the

Messerschmitt, eventually swung the decision against it, and the Bf 109 was chosen as the Luftwaffe's future standard fighter.

Despite this, the Luftwaffe decided to send the fifth prototype, the He 112 V5 (not the He 112 V4, as asserted in previously published statements), which had a smaller fin than the earlier prototypes, to join the three Messerschmitt prototypes in Spain. It was to serve as a test bed for the experimental 20mm Motorkanone MG C/30L (20mm motor-cannon) mounted to fire through the propeller boss of the Junkers Jumo 210Da engine. After assembly, the aircraft was entrusted to Obl Günter 'Fips' Radusch, who began testing on 9 December 1936. Unfortunately no records have survived of the doubtlessly interesting career of this aircraft in Spain, when it carried the serial 5-1. In March 1937 the *Kanonvögel* (Cannon Bird), as it was called, was attached to the Bf 109-equipped staffel 2.J/88 and allegedly, while flown in rotation by Radusch, Obl Balthazar and Uffz Max Schulz, was responsible for

putting three armoured vehicles out of action during the Battle of Brunete the following July. On 19 July, however, when Schulz came in to land at Escalona Aerodrome after returning from the front, the engine suddenly cut out and the Heinkel belly-landed on a hillside, damaging its wings and breaking its back.

At this time the ninth prototype, the He 112 V9 powered by a 610hp Junkers Jumo 210 Ea engine, made its first flight. The true prototype of the He 112B series, it was an He 112 so extensively redesigned as to be a different aeroplane. The wings were of reduced span and the anhedral and dihedral angles were shallower, the fuselage was longer and straighter, the fin had a straight trailing edge, and the tailplanes and elevators were straight-edged. The cockpit was enclosed by a raised canopy with a sliding hood. The armament consisted of two fixed machine guns above the engine and two 20mm cannon in the wings. With such an engine, however, the He 112 V9 was clearly under-powered and its performance, with a top speed of 510km/h, was similar to that of the Hawker Hurricane.

With no orders from the Luftwaffe, Heinkel sought foreign purchasers, and in the autumn of 1937 secured an order for thirty He 112B fighters, essentially similar to the He 112 V9, from the Imperial Japanese Navy. Twelve were delivered to Japan in the spring of 1938, but the Sudeten crisis of September 1938, and German anxiety over a possible conflict with France and Britain, resulted in the diversion of the second batch of eighteen aircraft to the Luftwaffe. When the crisis ended with the Munich Agreement, the He 112Bs were returned to Heinkel, but by then the Japanese, disappointed by the first batch, had found pretexts for cancelling the rest of the order.

Meanwhile, the He 112 V9 was sent to Spain in April 1938, where, bearing the serial 8-2, it was flown operationally by Hptmn Harro Harder, who had led 1.J/88 through most of 1937. It was also tested by several Spanish pilots, including

A Heinkel He 112B.

Joaquín García Morato and Miguel García Pardo (see Fiat C.R.32). In their opinion it was a Rolls-Royce of an aeroplane spoilt by a bad engine, and they were none too pleased when they were offered the He 112Bs rejected by Japan, since they would have preferred, and had asked for, Messerschmitt Bf 109Es. Under the political circumstances, however, they were obliged to accept.

The first two He 112Bs arrived at Seville in November 1938, followed by six more in January 1939. With these was formed the 2ª Escuadrilla of the Grupo Mixto 5-G-5, the 1ª Escuadrilla being equipped with Messerschmitt Bf 109Bs. (The He 112 V5 had received the type code 5 and the very different He 112 V9 the type code 8, but with the arrival of the service aircraft the Nationalists reverted to the type code 5). The Heinkel squadron was led by the veteran Miguel García Pardo, and the group, commanded by José Muñoz Jiménez 'El Corto' ('The Short'), formed a part of the 7ª Escuadra de Caza led by García Morato. Based at Balaguer, the Heinkels took part in the Catalonian campaign, García Pardo himself scoring the squadron's first and only victory, over an I-16, during its first sortie on 19 January 1939. With enemy opposition eliminated, the Heinkels had little to do but escort bomber formations without incident.

On the day of the Republican surrender, 31 March 1939, García Pardo and another veteran, Rogelio García de Juan, collided during a festive aerobatic display above Almaluez aerodrome, both men being killed and the two Heinkels destroyed. The remaining nine He 112Bs arrived in Spain in April 1939, and later in the year the whole group (Grupo Mixto de Caza del Regimiento Mixto Núm 2) was transferred to Melilla in Spanish Morocco, the machines being serialled 5-50 to 5-66. Fifteen were still in service on 1 March 1940, and in December 1942, shortly after the Allied landing in Algeria, a Spanish He 112B shot down an American Lockheed P-38 Lightning which had strayed over Spanish colonial airspace. In 1945 the He 112Bs received the new type code C.5, and they continued flying into the 1950s.

He 112 V5

Span 11.5m; length 9m; height 3.7m; wing area 23.2sq m.

Empty weight 1,680kg; loaded weight 2,230kg.

Maximum speed 488km/h; climb to 1,000m in 1.57min; ceiling 8,000m.

He 112B

Span 9.1m; length 9.3m; height 3.85m; wing area 17sq m.

Empty weight 1,620kg; loaded weight 2,250kg.

Maximum speed (in Spanish service) 460km/h at 4,000m; climb to 6,000m in 11.5min; ceiling 8,200ft; range 750km.

Heinkel He 115A-0

The Heinkel He 115, one of the best seaplanes employed by any of the powers embroiled in the Second World War, first forced itself on the public consciousness during the Battle of Britain in August 1940. It was the principal layer of the notorious 'magnetic mines' – one of Hitler's 'secret weapons' – off the coast of East Anglia, in the Thames estuary, and even in the Bristol Channel. These operations were soon extended, and caused alarming damage to Allied shipping in the Atlantic and the Mediterranean. Although the He 115 was only beginning to enter Luftwaffe service when the war broke out in September 1939, two had already played a brief part in the Spanish Civil War during its final month.

Conceived as a twin-engined torpedo-bomber seaplane, the He 115 V1 prototype first flew in August 1937. It was an all-metal mid-wing monoplane, of monocoque construction, powered by two 970hp BMW 132K radial engines. In the

A Heinkel He 115A-0 at Pollensa, Mallorca, in March 1939. (Arráez)

third prototype, the He 115 V3, the angular nose section, superficially resembling that of the Junkers Ju 86, was replaced by a longer, narrower, and more extensively glazed cabin with a stepped windscreen, and the pilot's and dorsal-gunner's cockpits were combined under one long transparent canopy. In the fourth prototype, the He 115 V4, the tail surfaces were redesigned, the fin and rudder being more angular. Ten He 115A-0 pre-production aircraft, in which the float bracing wires were replaced by a system of thick stream-lined N-struts, were built in the summer of 1938.

At the beginning of March 1939 two of these, bearing the civil reg-istrations D-ANPT and D-AOHS, flew from Marienehe, via Friedrich-shafen and Italy, to Pollensa, Mal-lorca, to join the He 59s and Arado Ar 95s of Condor Legion unit AS/ 88. Painted light grey overall, with St Andrew's Crosses on rudders and wingtips and black discs on the rear fuselage sides, but with no military serials or civil markings, the two He 115s performed a few reconnaiss-ance flights over the Mediterranean. The presence of a Heinkel company representative, Dip Ing Geike, and the fact that members of the Spanish Nationalist general staff were invited as observers on these flights, sug-gests that these machines were sent to Spain as part of a Heinkel sales campaign rather than for serious military evaluation. Both aircraft, together with the Junkers Ju 87Bs, were returned to Germany with the Condor Legion in May 1939.

Span 22.28m; length 17.3m; height 6.6m; wing area 86sq m.
Empty weight 5,410kg; loaded weight 9,400kg.
Maximum speed 313km/h; cruising speed 304km/h at 4,400m; range 2,000km.

Henschel Hs 123

The Henschel Hs 123 was a singu-lar aeroplane in several respects. It was the first *Stuka* (Sturzkampfflug-zeug, or dive bomber) to be built in quantity for the Luftwaffe, yet was never used as such in war. Although it had a shorter production run than any other Luftwaffe military aircraft,

it was the longest serving of all, in the sense that the Hs 123s still fighting in Russia in 1944 differed only in minor details from those that had first entered service in 1936, or, indeed, from the original prototype that had first flown in April 1935. Finally, it was the last biplane to be retained by the Luftwaffe as a front-line aircraft.

It was often said that Ernst Udet's spectacular demonstrations of dive-bombing in a pair of Curtiss 'Helldivers' (in fact Curtiss Hawk IIs) in 1933 convinced German military and technical experts that dive-bombers would be able to hit difficult targets, such as bridges and supply columns, more accurately and at far greater range than artil-lery. In reality, during the years of covert planning under the Weimar Republic the German military had been studying the possibilities of the dive-bomber since the end of the First World War. It was the RLM (German air ministry) which pro-vided Udet with the funds to import the 'Helldivers'. These, it should be noted, were not the standard two-seat Curtiss O2C-1 Helldivers of the US Navy, but single-seat Curtiss Hawk II fighters (export versions of the Curtiss XF11C-1) fitted with bomb racks. This is an important point, because it was this fact which persuaded the Technische Amt (Technical Office) of the RLM to

A Henschel Hs 123A.

issue specifications for a single-seat dual-rôle fighter and dive-bomber to the Fieseler Flugzeugbau and the Henschel Flugzeugwerke in Febru-ary 1934.

Henschel und Sohn had been one of the world's most important builders of locomotives since 1848, and since the 1900s had extended into the production of heavy road vehicles and machine tools. Its entry into aircraft production had been extremely recent (February 1933), its primary intention having been to produce aircraft for other manufac-turers. However, Henschel had built two prototypes of its own, the Hs 121 gull-winged fighter and the Hs 122 two-seat parasol mono-plane observation aircraft. Although the first had been pronounced a failure immediately after its maiden flight, the second had showed con-siderable promise, and was even-tually to be developed into the Hs 126. Meanwhile, the Hs 123 dive-bomber was considered by the RLM to be more advanced in concept than its competitor, the Fieseler Fi 98, and three prototypes were ordered.

The prototype Hs 123 V1, D-ILUA, first flew on 1 April 1934, and was followed by the Hs 123 V2 and V3 (which had a 720hp Wright GR-1820-F52 engine in a smooth NACA cowling, in place of the blistered cowling of all other ver-sions). The Hs 123 V2 was des-troyed after failing to pull out of a terminal-velocity dive, and the V3 was badly damaged in a ground loop.

Three more prototypes (V4 to V6) and eighteen pre-series aircraft were ordered, these having modified undercarriage legs and strutted rather than wire-braced tailplanes. The V6 had an enclosed cabin, and the pre-series Hs 123A-0 an armoured headrest with a streamlined fairing. The engine was a BMW 132A-3 nine-cylinder radial rated at 630hp at sea-level (730hp for take-off), driving a two-bladed variable-pitch metal propeller.

The Hs 123A-1 (as the production aircraft was designated) was a sesquiplane of metal construction, though the upper wing was fabric-covered aft of the rear spar. The wings were braced by a pair of broad faired struts, and there were no bracing wires except in the cabane. The armament consisted of two fixed 7.9mm MG 17 machine guns mounted above the engine and four 50kg bombs on racks under the lower wings, although, in place of the 130-litre auxiliary tank usually carried, a single 250kg bomb could be installed between the undercarriage legs. The first Hs 123A-1s began to reach the Luftwaffe in the summer of 1936. Minor modifications during production, including all-metal wing covering, resulted in the Hs 123B-1, but production was cancelled in April 1937 in favour of the Junkers Ju 87. About 260 Henschel Hs 123As and 123Bs were built altogether, some of them remaining in service until the end of the Second World War.

The Henschel Hs 123 was one of the first types to be sent to Spain after the decision had been taken to expand 'Operation Magic Fire' into the Condor Legion, two aircraft being unloaded at Cádiz from the *Wigbert* during the second week of September 1936. A third aircraft arrived in October, and three more in the spring of 1937. These six all had their headrests removed. The first three, allotted the type code 24, were formed into a so-called Stuka-kette led by Lt Hein 'Rubio' Brücker, and were attached to the experimental fighter group VJ/88, which included the Heinkel He 112 V5 and Messerschmitt Bf 109 V3, V4 and V5, based at Tablada, Seville.

In January 1937 the Henschels saw their first action in support of Gen Queipo de Llano's offensive against Malaga and, after the successful conclusion of that campaign, were transferred to Vitoria for the forthcoming offensive against Bilbao. The Legion's chief of staff, Wolfram Freiherr von Richthofen, was more interested in using the Hs 123 as a close-support aircraft than as a dive-bomber (for which it was not considered steady enough in the dive), and in this rôle, although lacking R/T, it was to prove highly successful. In the course of the northern campaign four Hs 123s were lost; the first on 25 March 1937 during a brief intervention on the Madrid front, the second over Ochandiano in May, the third while attacking the 'Iron Ring' defences round Bilbao on 11 June 1937, and the fourth in an accident. The remaining two, 24-3 and 24-5, were transferred to the quieter southern front, but were brought back to the north for the Battle of Teruel. In 1938 they were transferred to the Spanish Nationalist air arm, and formed a part of the Grupo Mixto 86-70 (Junkers Ju 86D and Heinkel He 70F).

In October 1938 twelve Hs 123B-1s, with headrests, were delivered to the Spanish Nationalists and, with the serials 24-6 to 24-17, were formed into an autonomous dive-bomber group, though they saw no action in the civil war. All fourteen Henschels were still flying in March 1940, and were formed into Escuadrilla 61, based at Tablada, Seville. In 1946 they were given the new type code BV-1 (Bombardeo Vertical, tipo 1). The Hs 123s were very popular with their Spanish pilots, who, on account of their reliability and pleasant handling characteristics, called them *Angelitos* (Little Angels), a name which, in all other respects, might seem hardly appropriate. In Spain the Germans had nicknamed them *Teufelkopf* (Devil's Head), perhaps because of the fearsome noise of the engine when set back to 1,800rpm. It had been found that this created panic when the Henschels were flown a few feet above the enemy columns, and the tactic was repeated to great effect in Poland in 1939 and during the German invasion of the Low Countries and France in 1940.

Span 10.5m; length 8.66m; height 3.21m; wing area 24.85sq m.
Empty weight 1,420kg; loaded weight 2,350kg.
Maximum speed 290km/h at 2,000m; ceiling 9,000m; range 860km.

Henschel Hs 126A-1

The Henschel Hs 126, developed from the Hs 122 to take the 830hp BMW Bramo Fafnir 323A-1 radial engine, was a two-seat observation and army co-operation parasol monoplane. The crew were protected by a transparent sliding canopy with opening panels to deflect the slipstream from the

A Henschel Hs 126A-1 with a 100kg bomb fitted to a rack on the port side.

gunner/observer. An automatic Zeiss Rb camera was mounted vertically in the fuselage behind the observer's cockpit, the camera-bay doors being opened and closed by a lever operated by the observer. The offensive armament consisted of ten 100kg bombs in the bay, in place of the camera, or a single 100kg bomb carried externally on a rack on the port side of the lower fuselage. The defensive armament comprised a single forward-firing 7.9mm MG 17 machine gun mounted above the engine, and a similar, movable gun in the observer's cockpit.

The prototype Hs 126 V1 first flew in the autumn of 1936, and the first production Hs 126A-1s entered Luftwaffe service in the spring of 1938. In October 1938 six Henschel Hs 126A-1s arrived in Nationalist Spain to replace the three Heinkel He 45s still serving with 5.A/88, and were allotted the type code 19. They were christened 'Super-Pavos' (Super-Turkeys, see Heinkel He 46), and took part, with great success but with the loss of one aircraft, in the Catalonian campaign of January-February 1939. After the civil war the remaining five aircraft were handed over to the Spaniards. In 1945, bearing the new type code R.4, they were transferred to the 41 Patrulla of the Regimiento Mixto Núm 2.

Span 14.5m; length 10.8m; height 3.7m; wing area 31.6sqm.
Empty weight 2,030kg; loaded weight 3,090kg.
Maximum speed 320km/h; cruising speed 253km/h; ceiling 8,300m; range 710-730km.

Hispano E.30

Designed by Frenchman André Bedoiseaux, then resident in Spain, as an intermediate trainer for pilots, observers and gunners, the Hispano-Suiza E.30 received its designation from the simple fact that the prototype first flew in 1930. It was a two-seat parasol monoplane with the wide-track undercarriage and com-

Hispano E.30s of the Aeronáutica Naval at San Javier. The naval aircraft had uncowled engines. (Arráez)

plex strut arrangement typical of many French aircraft of that period. The first prototype, powered by a 180hp Hispano-Suiza 8Ab water-cooled engine, caught fire during a test flight and was destroyed, pilot Alejandro Gómez Spencer and passenger Gonzalo Taboada escaping by parachute. The second prototype, EC-ASS, powered by a 220hp Hispano-built Wright Whirlwind 9Qa (or 9Qd) radial engine, flew in 1931. Eighteen were built for the Aviación Militar, and seven for the Aeronáutica Naval between 1932 and 1934.

The Hispano E.30 (as it was always called) had fabric-covered wooden wings, and a metal fuselage with a metal and plywood covering.

An Hispano E.30 of the Aviación Militar, with Townend-ring cowling. (Instituto de Historia y Cultura Aeronáutica, via José Warleta)

Its tail assembly was metal, with fabric covering. The production models differed from the prototype in having a modified, triangular fin. The army version was fitted with Handley Page slots and a Townend ring round the engine, and the naval version had folding wings. The army aircraft were based at Cuatro Vientos. Two naval trainers were lost in accidents, and the five survivors were based at San Javier, Cartagena, registered EA-HAA/-H-1; 'HAB/-H-2; 'HAC/-H-3; 'HAD/-H-4; and 'HAE/-H-5.

On 18 July 1936 all but one of the Hispano E.30s were in the Republican zone. During the first weeks of the war they were employed on bombing and reconnaissance missions in Aragón and Andalucía, but with the arrival of Russian R-5s in November were relegated to training duties at the Republican flying schools round Alicante and Cartagena, receiving the type code EE.

The single E.30 in the Nationalist zone was given the type code 32. It must have been withdrawn from service by 1938, for the number 32 was then transferred to the Italian Caproni AP.1.

At the end of the war thirteen E.30s were recovered by the Nationalists and, with the type code 30, continued in service until 1945. In 1950, one, still fitted with an original Warleta bombsight, was serving at the Academia de Aviación at León. Known military serials were: 30-131, -132, -134 to -139, -161 and -185.

Span 12m; length 7.95m; height 3.53m; wing area 22.47sqm.
Empty weight 916kg; loaded weight 1,350kg; wing loading 60.1kg/sqm.
Maximum speed 225km/h; stalling speed 90km/h; climb to 3,500m in 12min, to 5,200m in 24min; ceiling 6,500m.

Hispano E.34

In 1934, as part of the re-equipment programme instigated by the Spanish Minister of War, Gil Robles, the Dirección General de Aeronáutica issued a specification for a two-seat primary and intermediate trainer to be designed around the 105hp Walter Junior inverted in-line engine. While Gil-Pazó and Loring produced low-wing monoplanes, Hispano-Suiza at Guadalajara concentrated on a biplane similar in size, performance, and appearance to the de Havilland Moth Major and Tiger Moth.

The Hispano E.34 was a single-bay, equal-span biplane with a split-axle undercarriage, its fabric-covered wooden wings being of slightly greater span and narrower chord than those of the de Havilland types. Its welded-steel-tube fuselage was faired with wooden stringers and covered with fabric. Ailerons were fitted to the lower wings, and Handley Page slots were installed along the outer leading edges of the upper wings.

In 1935 the Aeronáutica Naval ordered four E.34s, a number later raised to five, and these were assigned the provisional registrations EA-HGA to 'HGE. In the event they were powered by 130hp D.H.

An Hispano E.34. (Instituto de Historia y Cultura Aeronáutica, via José Warleta)

Gipsy Major engines. No Hispano E.34s were delivered before the outbreak of the civil war, but a few weeks previously the Aeronáutica Naval had placed a provisional order for a further twenty-five. On 18 July 1936 the prototype was at Getafe military aerodrome, Madrid. The first five production aircraft, and a number of others built after Hispano-Suiza moved to Alicante in October 1936, were delivered during 1937 and 1938, and served as primary trainers, first at Los Alcázares and later at Alcantarilla and El Palmar.

One E.34 survived the war, and, after Hispano SA moved to Seville, was rebuilt, re-engined with a new Gipsy Major, and re-designated HS-34, with the civil registration EC-AFJ, in 1942. It was evaluated by the Ejercito del Aire, but no order followed.

Span 9.1m; length 7.34m; wing area 21.5sqm.
Empty weight 523kg; loaded weight 773kg.
Maximum speed 170km/h; stalling speed 56km/h; take-off run 75m; landing run 90m; climb to 1,000m in 7min.

Hispano-Nieuport 52 and Nieuport NiD 82.

The debate over the comparative merits of the biplane and monoplane fighter was not, in the early 1920s, the matter of prime importance it was to become in the 1930s when, as a result of rapid technical progress on the one hand and the growing probability of war on the other, a country's future might have depended on making the right choice between them. Most air staffs, including the British, had settled for the biplane, believing that a monoplane was either too frail for the violent manoeuvres needed in dogfighting or, if it were sturdy enough, too heavy and slow at a time when a top speed of 240km/h was becoming standard.

In France, nevertheless, the monoplane fighter was still regarded seriously, the main reasons being that it was cheaper, had a faster climb, and offered the pilot a better all-round view. In designs where the structural weakness inherent in fast monoplanes could not be remedied, an acceptable compromise was the sesquiplane. Thus the Nieuport-Delage NiD 42C1 high-altitude fighter, based on the NiD 42S racer of 1923, first flew in 1924 as a parasol monoplane, but was ordered into production as a sesquiplane, with a pair of small auxiliary wings projecting from the lower fuselage. This machine had an unpleasant tendency to go into inadvertent spins, however, and only twenty-five were built.

There followed the Nieuport-Delage NiD 52 and NiD 62, developed in parallel, both of which had slightly reduced wing areas and enlarged tailplanes, the area of the NiD 52's auxiliary wing being reduced by 1.53sqm. The NiD 52 further differed from the NiD 42 and NiD 62 in having metal wing ribs, an all-metal fin and tailplane, and an all-metal monocoque fuselage. The most curious feature of

An Hispano-Nieuport 52 at the Hispano-Suiza factory, Guadalajara. An Hispano-built D.H.9 is in the background. (Arráez)

these Nieuport fighters was the cumbersome undercarriage, a clutter of heavy struts and a thick fairing, almost large enough to constitute a third wing, over the cross-axle. The powerplant was a 500hp Hispano-Suiza 12Hb twelve-cylinder vee engine, and the armament consisted of two fixed forward-firing 7.7mm machine guns.

The French government ordered the NiD 62, of which 725 (in the versions NiD 62, 622 and 629) provided the backbone of the French fighter forces until the advent of the Dewoitine D.500 in the early 1930s. Meanwhile, in 1928, the Spanish government selected the

NiD 52 to be built under licence by Hispano-Suiza at Guadalajara. In the Hispano-Nieuport 52 a single Corominas chin-type radiator replaced the Lamblin radiators fitted to the undercarriage legs of the French aircraft, and the armament consisted of two Vickers MkI or MkII 7.69mm machine guns. The first thirty-four aircraft were built from component kits supplied by Nieuport-Delage, the first production example being tested at Getafe by Hispano-Suiza test pilot Cdte Gómez Spencer in June 1930. Eighty-two were built entirely by Hispano-Suiza, of which the first batch of thirty or so reached Grupo Núm 11 at Getafe, commanded by

Hispano-Nieuport 52s of Grupo 11, Getafe, Madrid, before the civil war. (Azaola)

Cdte Juan Ortiz Muñoz, during the summer of 1931. Another nine were built in 1932, making 125 altogether. Late in 1931, Grupo 13 at Barcelona and Logroño began to re-equip with the new fighters, followed by Grupo 12 at Seville and Granada in 1932-33.

The 'Nieuport', as it was commonly called even on official documents, received the pre-civil-war type code 3, and the highest recorded prewar serial is 3-84 in the 1ª Escuadrilla of Grupo 11 in 1934-35. One patrulla of three Nieuports was incorporated into the Escuela de Tiro y Bombardeo (Gunnery and Bombing School) at Los Alcázares in Murcia. The Nieuports were left in plain metal finish, with the group and group serial number painted in black on the fuselage sides and the service serial number (e.g. 3-42) in black on the yellow band of the Republican tricolour on the rudder. The emblem of Grupo 11, a black panther passant, was painted on the fin, that of Grupo 12, a leaping deer in a circle, beneath the cockpit, and Grupo 13's emblem, a four-leafed clover on a red disc, appeared on the fin.

In 1931 the Spanish government purchased a Nieuport 82 parasol monoplane prototype. Its subsequent history is not recorded, but there is no evidence that it was still flying at the time of the civil war.

The Nieuport 52 was never very popular with its Spanish pilots, who found it heavy on the controls and

A Nieuport NiD 82.

'ingrato' ('ungrateful' – hard to get anything out of) and, thanks to its narrow undercarriage, liable to ground-loop at the least misjudgement on the part of the pilot when landing. Nor was its performance exhilarating. Although Nieuport-Delage claimed a maximum speed of 260km/h, no pilot had been able to coax more than 225km/h out of any machine, even during a series of controlled tests in 1932. Accidents were frequent, and there were always many machines under repair. Consequently, when the civil war started, on 18 July 1936, hardly more than fifty-six remained on the inventory, and of these about eighteen were under repair.

Most of the Nieuport 52s were in Republican hands, for the Director General de Aeronáutica, General Núñez de Prado, had been concentrating as many as possible at Getafe during the previous month. Grupo 12 at Granada had been withdrawn to Madrid, as had twelve of the Nieuports of Grupo 13 at Barcelona, leaving the Nationalists with only seven machines under repair in the workshop at Tablada, Seville, and one, damaged, at Granada. On 21 July, however, the Nationalists received a present of three Nieuport 52s when a patrulla was ill-advisedly ordered to fly to Granada aerodrome, which had fallen into Nationalist hands by the time the aircraft landed. The three pilots were imprisoned.

At Getafe there were about twenty-six serviceable Nieuports (less the three sent to Granada) equipping the 1ª and 2ª Escuadrillas of Grupo 11, at Barcelona there were nine equipping the two remaining escuadrillas of Grupo 13, and at Los Álcázares there were the three trainers. In addition, there were about ten under repair in the Hispano factory at Guadalajara. Hispano managed to put the ten

Published in the Nationalist newspapers on 8 August 1936, this photograph was said to show a 'Red fighter' shot down near Buitrago de Lozoya, about 45km north of Madrid. More probably, it shows the aircraft of Capitán Avertano González Fernández, a patrol leader of Grupo 11, who died of a stroke or heart attack while on patrol over the Sierra Guadarrama. His machine came down in Republican territory, and was found to have no bullet holes. A few days later the area was occupied by the Nationalists.

back into service, and built at least another ten aircraft from twenty sets of spare parts at the factory, delivering the finished machines to Getafe at the rate of about one a day during the latter part of August and first half of September. Thus, over the period from 18 July to 1 November 1936, the Republicans had some fifty-five Nieuport 52s to draw on, but never more than about twenty, and usually far less, at any given time.

The 2ª Escuadrilla of Grupo 11 at Getafe, commanded by Capitán Méndez Iriarte, was moved to Barajas to patrol the Sierra Guadarrama range, and especially the Somosierra Pass through which Mola's forces were attempting to advance on Madrid. The 1ª Escuadrilla remained at Getafe to cover the Alto de León heights at the southern end of the same range. On 21 July six were sent south to Los Rompedizos aerodrome, Málaga, and three to Andújar, near Córdoba. The three at Los Alcázares were apparently sent, with three de Havilland D.H.9s and (later) a single Dewoitine D.372 (which, still unarmed, was shot down on 27 August), to Guadix, east of Granada. In August another detachment was sent south to the aerodromes at Don Benito and Herrera del Duque. With the survivors from Andújar, this detachment withdrew as the Nationalists advanced, to Talavera de la Reina and finally back to Madrid in September. Of the nine airworthy Nieuports at Barcelona, at least two were detached to the *Alas Rojas* squadron at Sariñena in Aragón, and on 14 September one

Nieuport (flown by Ten Ámador Silverio, 'El Dibujante' – The Draughtsman) and three Breguet 19s flew to Bilbao across Nationalist territory to reinforce the Basques.

On the Nationalist side, the three Nieuports captured at Granada, together with the damaged machine, were transferred to Seville and put back into service, as were the seven under repair at Tablada as they became available. On 27 July 1936 two Nieuports, flown by Ten Julio Salvador and Brigada (Staff Sergeant) Ramón Senrá, took off from Seville to supply Mola at Burgos with at least a token fighter force, arriving, after an adventurous journey, two days later. On 6 August they were reinforced by a third, piloted by Ten Miguel Cuenco. Later in August Senrá was posted to Saragossa where, reinforced at different times by Ańgel Salas, Guerrero and Miguel García Pardo, he waged a somewhat lonely war against the *Alas Rojas* squadron at Sariñena. At the same time, as part of the air contingent covering the advance of Gen Franco's Army of Africa northwards through Extremadura towards Madrid, and eastwards to widen the Nationalist corridor from Jerez to Granada, such future Nationalist aces as Capitán Joaquín García Morato, Julio Salvador (who returned from the north) and Bermúdez de Castro flew Nieuport 52s when Heinkel He 51s or Fiat C.R.32s were not available. Towards the end of September the Nationalists were able to withdraw the Nieuport 52s from front-line duties.

At first, encounters between these scattered opposing fighter forces nearly always happened by chance, and the resulting combats were brief and usually indecisive. The Republicans claimed the first aerial victory, a Nationalist Breguet 19 shot down by Cdte Cascón (the *de facto* commander at Getafe) in a Nieuport on 20 July 1936, although the modest Cascón himself claimed no such thing, but merely thought he might have hit the Breguet. The first Nationalist victory, a Republican Nieuport 52 shot down over El Piñar (a mountain near Ronda) by Bermúdez de Castro on 23 July, is equally dubious, because no Repub-

lican Nieuport seems to have been lost that day. However, a Nationalist Nieuport, flown by Ten Fernández Tudela, was shot down by a Republican Douglas DC-2 near Córdoba on 31 July.

At this stage air combats were extremely confusing, because both sides flew identical types of aircraft displaying the same roundels of the Aviación Militar or Aeronáutica Naval. On 6 August a patrol of the 2ª Escuadrilla from Barajas, led by Méndez Iriarte, was mistakenly attacked by a patrol of the 1ª Escuadrilla from Getafe, during which Rafael Peña, an excellent if impulsive Republican fighter pilot who later brought down the first Junkers Ju 52/3m, shot down and killed Méndez Iriarte himself. A day or two later a Nationalist pilot in a Nieuport shot down a Nationalist Breguet 19. At the end of July both sides began to adopt distinctive markings, and such inadvertent catastrophes became rarer.

As the tempo of air fighting increased during September 1936, Republican pilots were faced with the choice of flying, on the one hand, Dewoitine D.372s and Loire 46s with a performance matching or exceeding that of the Fiat C.R.32s and Heinkel He 51s, but with defective armament, or Nieuport 52s, which had reliable armament but a performance completely outclassed by that of the Nationalist fighters. It was said that three Nieuports flown by skilful and experienced pilots might just be able to hold their own against a single Fiat C.R.32, and two against a single He 51. Because the air chiefs felt obliged to spread their poor resources over as wide an area as possible, and consequently persisted, against bitter protests, in ordering fighters out singly or in pairs, such an equalising of the odds was rarely possible. Some of the braver pilots found that the only tactic offering much chance of survival was to charge an approaching Fiat head-on, open fire at long range, and hope that the enemy pilot would turn aside first, perhaps giving the Nieuport an opportunity to escape. During a skirmish towards the end of September, Félix Urtubi, caught by two Fiats near Toledo, brought the combat, and his life, to

an end by ramming one of the Fiats.

The situation was not helped by foreign volunteers who, unfamiliar with the idosyncracies of the Nieuport 52, crashed a considerable number of machines during probation flights. As a result, not even the new and repaired machines sent down from Guadalajara by Hispano-Suiza were enough to keep pace with the attrition, and by the middle of October no airworthy Nieuport 52s remained on the Madrid aerodromes. Three were sent to Getafe from Catalonia in exchange for ammunition badly needed by Republican troops in Aragon. Two crashed on landing, however, to the relief of the Madrid pilots, who thanked the Catalonians for saving their lives, and the third crashed a few days later. Despite all that has been written regarding the hopeless inferiority of the Nieuport 52 to the Fiat C.R.32 and Heinkel He 51, the great majority of Republican Nieuport 52s were lost not in combat (only six can be accounted for with certainty), but through accidents.

During the winter of 1936-37, surviving Republican Nieuports were relegated to training and coastal patrol duties, although a few, along with almost anything else that could fly, were thrown back into action during the last days of the Battle of Guadalajara (March 1937) in an attempt to turn the Italian retreat into a rout. Nationalist Nieuport 52s received the type code 1 (later transferred to the Fiat G.50), and the Republican aircraft were given the type code CN. Not a single Hispano-Nieuport 52 on either side survived the civil war.

Span 12m; length 7.5m; height 3m; wing area 29.34sq m.
Empty weight 1,300kg; loaded weight 1,892kg.
Maximum speed 225km/h; climb to 5,000m in 13min 30sec; ceiling 8,200m.

I-15 Chato

Designed in 1933, contemporaneously with the much more advanced I-16 monoplane, by Nikolai Polikarpov and his team at the Soviet TsKB (Central Design Bureau) at Factory 36, the I-15 was a conven-

The I-15 Chato was called 'Curtiss' by the Nationalists.

tional single-seat fighter biplane. The intention was that the I-15 and I-16 would complement each other in military operations, the monoplanes tackling the enemy bombers and the biplanes using their high manoeuvrability to tackle the escorting enemy fighters.

Compact in shape and sturdily built, the I-15 ('I' denoting 'Istrebitely', or 'Fighter') had fabric-covered wooden wings braced by a pair of deep-section 'I' struts, and the upper wing centre section was gulled on to the shoulders of the fuselage to give the pilot the best possible view forwards and upwards. The fuselage was of metal, panelled with metal at the front and fabric-covered at the rear. The undercarriage consisted of a pair of cantilevered mainwheel shock-absorber legs. The intended powerplant was the M-25 radial engine, a licence-built 700hp Wright Cylcone R-1820-F3, enclosed in a narrow-chord cowling and driving a two-blade, fixed-pitch metal propeller. This engine was not available in quantity when the I-15 went into mass production in 1934, so the first production series was fitted with the 480hp M-22, a licence-built Gnome-Rhône Jupiter 9 AsB, itself a French version of the Bristol Jupiter. The I-15's armament consisted of four fixed, forward-firing PV-1 7.62mm machine guns in the fusel-

age, with provision for underwing bomb racks to carry up to 100kg of bombs.

At the beginning of 1936, after the completion of 392 I-15s powered by M-22 engines, and 59 powered by imported Wright Cyclones, production was halted owing to complaints from the squadrons regarding the high accident rate. This was attributed to the gulled upper wing, which obstructed the pilot's view forwards and downwards when landing. This resulted in the development of the I-152, a complete redesign with a cabane replacing the gulled centre section, but meanwhile production was resumed in the autumn of 1936, the new series being powered by M-25 engines driving two-pitch adjustable metal propellers.

Twenty-four I-15s were included in the first batch of Soviet aircraft sent to Spain, eighteen arriving at Cartagena on 13 or 15 October 1936 aboard the *Stari Bolshevik*, and six being trans-shipped at sea from the *Lava Mendi* and taken into Cartagena by coasters on the 16 October. The aircraft were assembled in two days, in an olive grove near Alcantarilla, and formed into two escuadrillas of twelve machines each. The 1ª Escuadrilla, under Maj 'Pablo Palan-

car' (Pavel Richagov), was based at Campo XX, a new aerodrome laid out in an estate called El Soto, near Algete, north-west of Madrid, and previously belonging to the Duque de Albuquerque (who had fled to France). The 2ª Escuadrilla, under Maj 'Antonio' (Sergei Tarkhov), was at Alcalá de Henares. Ten Andrés García Lacalle, one of four Spanish pilots who, together with the Frenchmen Jean Dary (see Dewoitine D.372 and Loire 46) and René Casteñada de Campo, joined the 1ª Escuadrilla early in November, says in his memoirs that at this time each patrulla of three aircraft had only one Russian mechanic, who had to carry out the full duties of a complete groundcrew by himself.

The first action of the I-15s, on 4 November, took the Nationalists, who assumed that Republican fighter opposition had been wiped out, by surprise. A Junkers Ju 52/3m and two Fiat C.R.32s were shot down, and another Ju 52/3m and two Fiats badly damaged, without loss in combat to the Russians, although two Russian pilots became disoriented and landed in Nationalist territory near the city of Segovia after running out of fuel. From then until 20 November the two I-15 escuadrillas, joined on 15 November by two escuadrillas of I-16s, fought two, and sometimes up to four, air battles every day. These were chiefly directed against fighters escorting the bomber formations attacking Madrid, where, on the ground, Nationalist troops were trying to work their way into the western outskirts of the city against increasingly fierce opposition. By 26 November they had forced the Nationalists to abandon daylight bombing of the capital altogether.

It has been said that the enormous boost that the dramatic arrival of these Russian fighters gave to the defenders of Madrid was the most important single factor in preventing the fall of the city to the Nationalists in November 1936. The cost in casualties was heavy, nonetheless. Nine I-15s were shot down in combat, including those of the two commanders (Tarkhov baled out over Madrid but was mortally wounded, when he came down in the Plaza Castellana, by angry Madrileños who supposed him to be German; Richagov survived), and two flown by the Spaniards Roig and Herguido, who were both killed. Beside the two lost at Segovia on 4 November, five were lost in accidents, and by 20 November only eight I-15s were still flying. Of these, three, led by Ivan Kopets, were transferred to Sariñena in Aragon, where they successfully defeated the first all-Spanish escuadrilla of six Heinkel He 51s by shooting one down and destroying four more during an attack on Caudé aerodrome, near Teruel, on 26 December 1936.

The Republicans affectionately dubbed the I-15 'Chato' (snub-nose) almost as soon as it arrived in Spain, and later adopted the name more or less officially. The Nationalists called it 'Curtiss' because, with its large radial engine, it seemed to resemble either a Curtiss F9C Sparrowhawk, which likewise had a slightly gulled upper wing, or a Hawk II, which had similar cantilevered undercarriage legs. On the Republican side French and American pilots, such as Jean Dary and Frank Tinker, believed it to be an updated Boeing F4B-4. Although it is now common knowledge that the I-15 owed nothing to any of these fighters, the story that the Russians were too backward to design their own aircraft made good propaganda, and the misnomer 'Cur-

tiss' continued in use until the 1980s.

Owing to a lack of documentation, details of the subsequent deliveries of I-15 Chatos to Spain are confused. Some authors state that, early in January 1937, an escuadrilla of Chatos commanded by Anton Kovalieski ('Casimiro') was posted to Las Tabernas aerodrome, Málaga, to counter the Nationalist offensive along the coast, and that although 'Casimiro' himself was shot down and killed, the escuadrilla acquitted itself well. However, the Republican pilot Emilio Galera, who flew with this squadron, told the author that it contained seven Russians and four Spaniards – eleven aircraft – which raises the question of where they came from. Documented deliveries of I-15 Chatos from Russia to Spain are:

1 13-16 October 1936. Twenty-four at Cartagena, on *Stari Bolshevik* and *Lava Mendi* (M-22 engines). A Russian Eskadrily consisted of thirty-one aircraft – twenty-four in the squadron, seven in reserve and one for the commander. Deliveries of Soviet aircraft to Spain were therefore usually in batches of thirty-one. For some reason, this first batch was seven aircraft short.
2 14 February 1937. Thirty-one at Cartagena, on *Aldecoa* (M-25 engines).
3 21 February 1937. Six at Cartagena, on *Warmond* (M-22 engines), and therefore probably the balance of delivery 1, but still one aircraft short.
4 1 July 1937. Twenty-three at Cartagena, on *Artea Mendi* (M-25 engines).
5 8 July 1937. Eight at Cartagena, on *Cabo Santo Tomé* (M-25 engines), balance of delivery 4.

To the Basque zone
1 1 November 1936. Fifteen at Bilbao, on *Andrei* (M-22 engines).
2 January 1937. Fifteen at Santander (M-22 engines), balance of delivery 1, to Basque zone, less one aircraft.

Leaving aside the Basque aircraft, whose history will be described separately, this puts ninety-two Chatos in the main zone, none being delivered, so far as is known at present, after 8 July 1937. However,

because in January 1937 there were eleven Chatos at Málaga, three in Aragón and others at Madrid, besides a new escuadrilla that was being formed, there must have been a delivery of thirty-one aircraft in December 1936 or very early in January 1937 which passed unrecorded. This would bring the total to 123 delivered to the main zone and 30 to the north, or 153 altogether, during the Spanish Civil War. Though this figure is larger than the 92 given with great insistence by Lacalle, it is significantly smaller than the figures found in many publications, where the number allegedly delivered is sometimes given as 'over 400' and sometimes as 550.

The deliveries of December 1936 and February 1937 resulted in the reorganisation of the existing Chato squadrons and the formation of new units. Andrés García Lacalle was appointed to command the 1ª Escuadrilla, with eight Spanish and four American pilots, and its history is told in Frank Tinker's memoir *Some Still Live* (New York, 1938). The 2ª Escuadrilla, commanded by Alonso Santamaría (who had replaced Kosakov, who in turn had replaced Tarkhov), had Spanish and Russian pilots; the 3ª, commanded by Ivan Kopets, was Russian but included the Americans Albert 'Ajax' Baumler and Charles Koch (see Seversky SEV-3); and the 4ª (not created until August 1937) was Spanish, but included the Frenchman William Labussière. At later dates other foreigners, including the Belgian André Autrique (see Avia BH-33) joined one or another of these squadrons.

The first three escuadrillas fought in all the campaigns of 1937, one of their most distinguished actions occurring in the Battle of La Jarama, in February. This was, in effect, a relentless slogging match with the Fiat C.R.32s of the Aviazione Legionaria, aided to some extent by the Heinkel He 51s of the Condor Legion and significantly by García Morato's Spanish *Patrulla Azúl* (Blue Patrol) on 18 February. At the Battle of Guadalajara the low-level attacks of the Chato and Natacha (see R-Z) squadrons were instrumental in repelling the Italian motorised offensive and turning it into a rout.

At the beginning of May 1937 it was decided to send an escuadrilla of I-15 Chatos, flown by Spaniards, to the Basque zone. A Russian eskadrily of I-15s had been delivered to the northern zone some months earlier, in fact, fifteen aircraft arriving at Bilbao on 1 November and another fifteen early in January 1937. These had been divided into four escuadrillas. Two, comprising seventeen aircraft in all, and led by Majors Naranchov and Turchansky, were based at Lamiaco, a converted polo field and racecourse south of Bilbao; one (six aircraft) was at Albericia, Santander, and one (five aircraft) was at Colunga in the Asturias. Two Chatos had been lost in accidents, but until the beginning of the Nationalist offensive, at the end of March, the Chato pilots had little to do but drive off the occasional Fokker F.XII or kette of Heinkel He 51s. Meanwhile, the Russians had taken seven Spanish pilots into the squadron, of whom the most successful was Felipe del Rio. The situation changed rapidly in April, when the Chatos found themselves hopelessly outnumbered and forced to change bases frequently, often operating from narrow valleys and almost within sight of the ever-retreating front. By the end of April barely a handful remained. Felipe del Rio had been shot down and killed by a Bf 109 on 22 April, and was replaced by Tomás Banquedano. The first two attempts to send reinforcements from the central zone failed, the aircraft being forced by storms to land in France, from where they were obliged to return to Catalonia after their guns and ammunition had been confiscated by the Non-Intervention control officials. On 24 May twelve Chatos, led by José Riverola, made a third attempt. Only one patrulla, led by Comás, reached Albericia, with empty tanks. Others lost their way, or were attacked by Fiat C.R.32s and forced down at different places. Ten were eventually recovered and these, reinforced by four more aircraft sent on 18 August and two squadrons of I-16s, continued fighting until the last days of the northern campaign, over Gijón in the Asturias, in October 1937. Three survivors managed to fly to Parme-Biarritz in France.

In May 1937 the I-15 escuadrillas in the main zone were reorganised once again, being formed into a single group, Grupo 26, under the command of Eugeni Ptukhin. The 1ª Escuadrilla was now under Eryomenko, the 2ª under Alonso Santamaría, and the 3ª under Kosakov. In July 1937 Anatoli Serov of the 1ª Escuadrilla formed a night-fighting patrol, and on the 26 July Yakushin shot down a Junkers Ju 52/3m. A second was claimed in August, and Serov himself was credited with shooting down a Savoia-Marchetti S.81 over Barcelona in March 1938. The night-fighter escuadrilla remained in existence until the collapse of Catalonia, its last commander being José Falco.

The heavy losses suffered in the battles of Brunete, Belchite and Teruel, and in the north, were made up by I-15 Chatos built in Spain. This project had been initiated by the Soviet air commander Col Jakob Smushkievich ('General Douglas') in February 1937, and two factories were requisitioned at Reus and Sabadell, being designated SAF-3 and SAF 3/16 respectively and placed under the direction of José Aguilera Cullel, a CASA engineer. The Spanish-built Chato differed from the Russian original in minor details, the chief being the provision of armour plating behind and under the pilot's seat. Production was slow at first, only forty-five being built by the end of 1937. By November 1938 the number had risen to 200, and a total of 237 was completed before the capture of the factories by the Nationalists in February 1939. Eighteen of these, however, were found by the Nationalists on Vich Aerodrome, awaiting their armaments, and were promptly employed to replace the worn-out Heinkel He 51s of 1-G-2 (which was renumbered 1-G-8).

Throughout 1938, as a result of replacements from the Catalonian factories, the four Chato escuadrillas managed to keep up a combined strength which varied, according to circumstances, between twenty-five and forty-five aircraft. Thus it can be said that, with the 153 delivered from the Soviet Union, the Spanish Republican air forces received a total of 372 Chatos during the civil war, of which 30 were delivered directly to the northern zone in November 1936 to January 1937. All four squadrons were in Catalonia during the first days of the Catalonian campaign, which began on 23 December 1938, but all but the 4ª were withdrawn to the southern zone in January 1939. The 4ª was destroyed at Vilajuiga on 6 February, although two Chatos, flown by Lacalle and José Bastida, escaped to France. At the end of the war the 1ª and 2ª Escuadrillas surrendered, but the last five Chatos of the 3ª, led by Riverola, escaped to Oran, Algeria.

In Spain the I-15 proved to be one of the outstanding fighters of its generation. During the first air battles over Madrid it was seen to be superior in all respects to the Heinkel He 51B. Slightly slower than the Fiat C.R.32 on the level, and considerably slower in a dive, it could nevertheless out-turn and out-climb the Fiat with ease. Although the two heavier-calibre 12.7mm guns of the Fiats that arrived later in the war outranged the four PV-1 7.62mm guns of the Chato, the Republican pilots firmly believed that their armament was more effective in the close, tight-manoeuvring combat in which the Chatos excelled. It was also an extremely sturdy aircraft, capable of absorbing an astonishing amount of punishment. Its only serious design fault was the proximity in the cockpit of the control lever for the engine cooling vents and the bomb-release lever. On one occasion the pilot Cuatero inadvertently released his bombs when he intended to adjust the vents while taking off. This resulted in the destruction of two aircraft, both pilots being killed, and extensive damage to a third.

During the first year of the war the I-15 Chatos and I-16 Moscas co-operated, as originally intended, whenever possible, the Mosca formations providing top cover for the Chatos and, in the event of a dogfight between the Chatos and enemy fighters, diving down and sweeping through the melée in high-speed passes, then circling round and coming in for a second attack. As Republican forces dwindled and Nationalist strength grew during the summer of 1937, the Chato squadrons often had to fend for themselves. By 1938 they were increasingly em-

An I-15 Chato of the Ejercito del Aire, after the civil war.

ployed in the ground-attack rôle, but, whenever possible, had a Mosca escort. Messerschmitt Bf 109 pilots nevertheless treated the Chato with respect, regarded it as a more dangerous opponent than the I-16 Mosca, and tried to avoid close combat with it.

The first thirty-four Chatos delivered from Russia seem to have been given the type code CC (used by the I-152 'Super-Chato' at the end of the war), but this was changed to CA. After being handed over to Spanish commanders in June 1937, the 1ª Escuadrilla adopted a circular emblem, painted below the cockpit, showing a penguin standing on a white mountain under a red sky, while the 2ª Escuadrilla adopted a Mickey Mouse and firework emblem painted on the fin. Serial numbers were painted in black or white, or both, on fuselage sides and/or fins, flight leaders' and squadron leaders' aircraft sometimes being distinguished by white or yellow triangles, circles, squares or diamonds on the fins. All Chatos were painted dull green on the upper surfaces and fuselage sides and light blue underneath, though some had light ochre patches on the top surfaces of their upper wings. Like other Republican front-line aircraft, the Chatos were constantly on the move from base to base, and the mottle may have been temporarily applied, as with the SB

Katiuskas, to harmonise with the landscape of a region where they stayed for more than a week or two.

At the end of the war the Nationalists recovered forty-four airworthy Chatos, sixty-three in various stages of construction, and a number under repair. Others had been captured during the war. In the Ejercito del Aire, where they were known as 'Curtiss' and given the type code 8, they were formed into Escuadra 32, based first at Manises (Valencia) and later at La Rabasa (Alicante). In 1940 the unit was renamed Regimiento 32. Additional I-15s completed at Sabadell after the war were formed into Regimiento 33 at Villanubla (Valladolid). In March 1940 there were 125 on the inventory, of which 53 were airworthy. In 1945 the type code was changed to A.4, and I-15s continued flying in service until the early 1950s.

Span 9.75m; length 6.3m; height 2.19m; wing area 20.8sq m.
Empty weight 1,180kg; loaded weight 1,420kg.
M-22 engine: maximum speed 347km/h; climb to 1,000m in 1.25min; ceiling 9,200m; range 480km.
M-25 engine: maximum speed 367km/h; climb to 1,000m in 1.1min; ceiling 9,800m; range 510km.

I-152 (I-15bis)

The I-152 resulted from a complete redesign of the I-15, following complaints from the Soviet fighter eskad-

rilii regarding the high landing-accident rate chiefly caused, it was alleged, by the gulled upper wing centre section. The I-152 was therefore given a straight centre section supported by a conventional cabane. The structure was strengthened throughout, as were the undercarriage legs, and the wheels were fitted with spats. The engine, an M-25V radial (an improved Wright Cyclone R-1820-F3) rated at 775hp for take-off and 750hp at 2,100rpm, was enclosed in a wide-chord cowling. The two-pitch, two-blade airscrew was fitted with a large boss. Production started in Factory No 21 in 1937, and in November of that year two I-152 eskadrilii were among the volunteer units sent to assist China against the Japanese, 186 additional I-152s being supplied to the Chinese air force.

Following appeals for more war material from the Spanish Republicans in November 1938, ninety-nine I-152s, it is believed, were among the 250 or so aircraft shipped to Spain, via France, in December 1938 and January 1939. Of all these aircraft, only thirty I-152s were able to cross the frontier in time for assembly before the collapse of Catalonia. They were given the type code CC, and were formed into a group under the command of Capitán Emilio Galera Macías. One machine was lost when its pilot failed to recover from a power dive. The remaining twenty-nine took part in a few ground-attack missions, but saw no combat with Nationalist fighters. Galera, a resident in London since 1940, told the author that, although the I-152 was semi-officially dubbed 'Super-Chato', its pilots found it less satisfactory than the I-15 in most respects, certainly in agility and sensitivity to the controls, and that its only superior characteristic was its steady and much faster dive.

On 4 February 1939 the Grupo was ordered to Vilajuiga Aerodrome for evacuation to France, and took off next morning before dawn by the light of the blaze caused by the collision of a Spartan Executive liaison monoplane and a petrol tanker. Shortly afterwards the aerodrome was attacked by the Condor Legion, and the remaining aircraft on it were destroyed. Meanwhile the I-152

An I-152 recovered from France by the Nationalists after the civil war. (Azaola)

squadron, which had strict orders to land at Toulouse-Francazal, ran into bad weather. Galera, fearing that some of his pilots, who were novices, might become lost on the longer journey and run out of fuel, brought them down instead at Carcassonne. Galera told the author that the I-152's instrumentation included a handsome and accurate clock. Before leaving their machines most of the pilots removed the clocks, intending to keep them. Galera, however, insisted that the clocks be given to him, since they were still the property of the Spanish government, and handed them over as soon as an embassy official arrived at the camp where the pilots were held.

After the civil war twenty I-152s were returned to Spain, along with some other Republican aircraft in France, in accordance with the Jordana-Bérard Agreement. These were given the type code 2W (later C.9) and formed into the Grupo de Caza Núm 24, a part of the Regimiento Mixto de Caza Núm 23 at Reus (Grupo 25 being equipped with Messerschmitt Bf 109s). They continued serving in the Ejercito del Aire until the mid-1940s.

Span 10.2m; length 6.27m; height 2.19m; wing area 22.5sq m.
Empty weight 1,310kg; loaded weight 1,834kg.
Maximum speed 364km/h; climb to 5,000m in 6.7min; ceiling 9,500m; range 450km (770km with auxiliary fuel tanks).

I-16 Mosca

Early in 1932 Professor A N Tupolev, overall head of the TsAGI (Experimental Aircraft Centre) in Moscow, began to study the feasibility of an all-metal low-wing cantilever monoplane fighter with a retractable undercarriage. Serious design work under the direction of Pavel Sukhoi and Alexandr Putylov began in July 1932, and a prototype, the ANT-31 (officially designated I-14), first flew in May 1933. By August 1933, however, Nikolai Polikarpov, who had assisted in the design of the I-14 before he was transferred to the

TsKB (Central Design Bureau) at Factory 36 to take charge of the parallel programme that produced the I-15 biplane, had become convinced that he could create a lighter and more effective fighter which retained the innovations of the I-14.

After four months of intensive work, in which Polikarpov was assisted by A G Trostyanski, a prototype, the TsKB-12 (or I-16), powered by a 480hp M-22 (licence-built Gnome-Rhône Jupiter) radial engine, made its maiden flight on 31 December 1933. A second prototype, powered by a 710hp M-25 (licence-built Wright Cyclone R-1820-F3) radial engine, flew on 18 February 1934, and during trials reached a speed of 437km/h at 3,000m, which was 80-96km/h faster than any known fighter. Because of difficulties with the I-14, the I-16 was ordered into production in August 1934, and the first examples, powered by M-22 engines, reached the V-VS (Soviet air force) in December 1934. These aircraft, of which about thirty were built, were used as conversion trainers to familiarise service pilots with the new, advanced fighter.

The first standard service version was the I-16 Type 5, which had an M-25 engine with a cowling that tapered aft into the fuselage and was perforated by eight exhaust apertures. Deliveries of this version began during the summer of 1935, a little less than two years after the first tentative delineations of the I-16 had been made on the drawing board. The extraordinary nature of this achievement becomes clear when it is

remembered that the earliest representatives in Europe of the new-style low-wing cantilever monoplane fighters, with enclosed cockpits and retractable undercarriages, had not yet flown. The Messerschmitt Bf 109 took to the air in September 1935, the Hawker Hurricane in November, and the Supermarine Spitfire in March 1936. In America the Seversky P-35, with a performance close to that of the I-16, and the marginally faster Curtiss Hawk 75, did not enter service until 1937 and 1938.

Although the Russians made no attempt to keep the existence of their fighter secret – ten I-16s took part in the May Day flypast over Moscow in 1935, and one was exhibited at the Salone Internazionale Aeronautica in Milan the following October – the aircraft aroused little interest among Western observers, many of whom dismissed the performance figures claimed for it as childish propaganda. Certainly the tubby little I-16 lacked the elegance and structural sophistication of its slightly later Western counterparts. Its wings were of metal with fabric covering, except for the metal-sheathed leading edges, and the fuselage was of wood, covered with moulded birch-ply strips. The undercarriage was raised manually, requiring forty-four turns of a crank-handle, and the front windscreen was omitted to allow for the telescopic gunsight. Instruments were rudimentary, the cockpit was cramped, and the 'transparent' canopy became nearly opaque after a short period of use and had to be left pushed forward in the open position. The armament, however, consisted of two wing-

The I-16 Type 5 was called 'Mosca' by the Republicans and 'Rata' or 'Boeing' by the Nationalists.

mounted 7.62mm ShKAS Km 35 machine guns whose high rate of fire, at 1,500-1,800 rounds per minute, gave the I-16 a hitting power greater than that of the four-gun I-15.

In the air, although it was by far the fastest service fighter in the world, the I-16 could perform loops and split-S turns with precision, had an extremely rapid rate of roll, and could dive at a sensational 600km/h. However, it verged on instability in all three axes, and was no aeroplane for an inexperienced or insensitive pilot. When used as flaps, the ailerons would throw the nose up dangerously, and the torque of the engine and propeller tended to twist the fighter on to its back, so landing the I-16 was tricky, and it had to be literally flown on to the ground at 165km/h.

Nevertheless, its high performance and structural sturdiness convinced the Russians that the 'Musha' (Fly), as it was sometimes nicknamed, was a world leader among fighter aircraft, and they were understandably keen to seize the opportunity offered by the Spanish Civil War to see how it would fare in genuine battle conditions. Accordingly, thirty-one I-16s were dispatched to Spain in October 1936 and initially formed, as a part of Grupo 12, into three escuadrillas led by A Tarasov, S Denisov and K Kolesnikov, of which one was stationed at Alcalá de Henares and another at Campo XX

(see I-15). In their first action, on 15 November 1936, they shot down two Fiat C.R.32s without loss. During the next four days, however, the Russians made the fatal mistake of engaging in close-turning dogfights with the highly manoeuvrable Fiats, and promptly lost three fighters. After this sharp lesson the I-16s flew as 'escorts' to the I-15 Chatos, sometimes above the biplanes and sometimes 1,000m or more below, when they used their rapid climb to come at the enemy from the least expected direction, in both cases confining themselves to fast, scything attacks. These tactics proved effective, and during the next three-and-a-half months only two more I-16s were shot down.

The I-16 was decisive in gaining air superiority for the Republicans, at least over the Madrid region, in November 1936, and keeping it until the late summer of 1937. The Republicans called the I-16 'Mosca' (Fly, after the Russian 'Musha', and perhaps also because the first I-16s to arrive in Spain had been built in a factory in Moscow), and later gave it the type code CM. The Nationalists called it either 'Boeing', on the nonsensical assumption that it was a Boeing P-26A with a cabin, a retractable undercarriage and added streamlining, or 'Rata' (Rat) because, during the first engagements over Madrid, the Russian fighters seemed to appear like rats out of holes in the ground. The supposed 'Boeing' origin of the I-16 was endorsed by such American pilots in Spain as Frank Tinker and Harold Dahl. As a result, even the *New York Times*, in an article

by Herbert Matthews headlined 'War Shows Lead of US Airplanes' (21 April 1937), asserted that the Russian monoplane had been built to Boeing company specifications.

A great deal has been published about the I-16 Moscas in Spain, but much of it is vague or contradictory. Even fifty years after the end of the Spanish Civil War there is still no reliable information, for the first year of the war at least, concerning the identification of the squadrons or the names of their commanders. A second batch of thirty-one I-16s arrived between mid-December 1936 and mid-February 1937, the aircraft being combined into a newly constituted Grupo 21 divided into four escuadrillas. According to some sources (but not others), these were led by Pligunov, Denisov, Kolesnikov and Boris Smirnov (but, according to yet others, Pligunov and Smirnov were one and the same person). The statement, found in some accounts, that the Grupo was commanded first by Ivan Kopets (alias 'José') and then by Ptukhin, is completely erroneous. Both were Chato pilots, and Kopets returned to Russia in April or May 1937.

The I-16s played prominent rôles in the battles of La Jarama, Guadalajara, La Granja (Segovia) and Huesca from February to May 1937. At the end of this period the first non-Russian pilots began to join two of the escuadrillas, identified by some as the 1ª and 3ª, though this is mere guesswork. These men included such experienced fighter pilots as the Spaniards Manuél Aguirre and Eduardo Claudín, the Americans Frank Tinker, Albert Baumler and (allegedly) a man who called himself 'Sinclair', and the Frenchmen William Labussière and 'Ramón Ibañez', another whose real name is unknown.

A third delivery of thirty-one Moscas arrived in two lots, seventeen on 21 May 1937 aboard the *Antonio Satrústegui*, and fourteen (plus four I-16UTI two-seat trainers) on 8 July 1937 aboard the *Cabo Santo Tomé*. These were used to form a fifth escuadrilla, and to replace losses in the other units. According to some sources this 5ª Escuadrilla was led by Valentín Ukhov, who was quickly promoted to command Grupo 21.

The nearest of these I-16 Type 6s has a Type 10 windscreen. The furthest machine is being attended to by a Hucks Starter.

According to a Russian account, Ukhov led an escuadrilla of eight Moscas to Santander on 17 June 1937 and stayed there through June and July. Tinker, however, says that Ukhov, who commanded his escuadrilla, was in action over Huesca until at least 18 June. This shows the confusion that prevails in existing published accounts, and the need for research in the Soviet archives.

During the Battle of Brunete (6-28 July 1937) the I-16s had their first serious encounters with Messerschmitt Bf 109s, and the importance of this event in the evolution of air fighting tactics is explained in the section on that aircraft.

A fourth consignment, of sixty-two I-16s, arrived aboard the *Cabo San Agustín* on 10 August 1937. This brought the total number of I-16s delivered thus far to 155, plus the four trainers. Most of the I-16s delivered in 1937 seem to have been of the Type 6 version, fitted with the 730hp M-25A engine. The increase in power, however, was more than offset by an increase in weight owing to structural strengthening and the addition of armour plating under the seat, with the result that the Type 6 was slower than the Type 5 on the level and in the climb. The sliding canopy had proved worse than useless in combat, and by now was customarily rivetted in the open, forward, position. Some of the new aircraft seem to have been delivered

without canopies and with the redesigned, wider windscreens that became standard on all later models. This modification may also have been made to some of the Type 5s and Type 6s already in Spain. The Type 6 had been fitted with flaps, but, after the death of the test pilot Romanov in a landing accident at El Carmolí, these were locked so that they could not be used for landing.

Towards the end of July 1937 the 1ª Promoción (1st Training Class) of 190 Spanish pilots returned from the USSR. Thirty had graduated on

An I-16 Type 10 of the 7ª Escuadrilla de Moscas.

I-16s and these, together with pilots trained in France (including the brilliant fighter pilot Manuel Zarauza Clavero), were incorporated into all the Escuadrillas de Moscas except the 2ª and 5ª, which remained entirely Russian. The 6ª Escuadrilla, under Gusaiev, was formed in September 1937, and on 12 October Capitán Manual Aguirre was appointed commander of the 1ª Escuadrilla. Three days later the 1ª, 2ª, 3ª, 5ª and 6ª Mosca escuadrillas, led by Aguirre, Pleshchenkov, Smirnov, Ivanov and Gusaiev, escorted two Chato escuadrillas in the attack on Garrapinillos aerodrome, Saragossa, in which three Ju 52s, two He 46s and six Fiat C.R.32s were destroyed and some twenty other aircraft damaged.

Some I-16s were sent to the northern zone. Although the exact date is in doubt, eight Russian-flown Moscas led by Ukhov landed at La Albericia aerodrome, Santander, late in June 1937, having made the flight across Nationalist territory at an altitude of 6,000m to 7,000m without oxygen. After a hasty refuelling they took off to intercept a Nationalist raid on Santander, and in the ensuing battle claimed the destruction of three 'Savoias' (S.81s or S.79s) and two Fiat C.R.32s. Ukhov seems to have returned shortly afterwards to the main zone to take command of Grupo 21, but the escuadrilla itself, under Vevseviev, remained in the north through July before returning to the south. Nothing is recorded of its actions.

The second expedition to Santander was made on 28 August 1937 by the 4ª Escuadrilla under Pligunov, the flight leaders being Russian and the rest of the pilots Spanish. Hopelessly outnumbered, and operating from primitive airstrips often within a mile or two of the front, the pilots sometimes having to dodge anti-aircraft fire as they climbed after taking off, the 4ª Escuadrilla de Moscas fought stubbornly and with ever-diminishing numbers until the end of the campaign in October. During the final days over Gijón, in the Asturias, the three or four surviving Mosca pilots, by then flying from Carreño, a tiny aerodrome on a promontory by the sea, were attacking Nationalist formations of up to seventy aircraft as a matter of course, several times a day. After the surrender, one I-16 (CM-61, piloted by Luis de Frutos) escaped to France and was returned to the main zone.

In November 1937 Zarauza was promoted to command the new, all-Spanish, 4ª Escuadrilla in the main zone and Aguirre was given command of the whole Mosca group, Grupo 21. Losses incurred during the fighting round Teruel (November 1937 to January 1938), and the rapid Nationalist advance to the Mediterranean during the spring of 1938, resulted in the temporary disbanding of the 3ª and 6ª escuadrillas and left the remaining units seriously under strength. In March 1938 thirty-one I-16 Type 10s arrived, followed in June and July by a further ninety. The Type 10, which was the sub-type produced in the largest numbers, had an open cockpit, a more powerful 750hp M-25V engine, and two additional ShKAS

After the war the Nationalists continued the production of I-16 Type 10s started by the Republicans. These machines are being assembled in a converted sherry bodega in Jerez de la Frontera.

machine guns, firing between the propeller blades. It was known in Spain as the 'Super-Mosca'. A 7ª Escuadrilla was formed, and for a time the existing squadrons were brought more or less up to strength.

During the Battle of the Ebro (25 July to 15 November 1938), the Escuadrillas de Moscas bore the brunt of the fighting on the Republican side, taking part in the largest air battles that had yet been known. Some of these involved as many as 200 aircraft, and extended from the estuary of the Ebro River over wide areas of the Costa Brava. This was a scene not equalled again until the Battle of Britain.

In August 1938 the 4ª Escuadrilla, commanded by Antonio Arias, was re-equipped with twelve Super-Moscas fitted with Wright Cyclone R-1820-F-54 engines, smuggled in from the USA, which enabled them to operate efficiently at heights up to 8,000m. Test flights showed that at −40°C the gun mechanisms froze. J-A López Smith, the chief engineer of the Escuadra de Caza, overcame this problem by passing filtered exhaust into the gun boxes, and Arias's squadron immediately made its presence felt. The Messerschmitt pilots, who had long enjoyed the pleasure of looking down on their enemies from the safety of 6,000m, now experienced the rude shock of being 'bounced' from above by fighters

with superior manoeuvrability. The 'Messerschmitt scourge' that had lasted since the previous autumn was thus abruptly ended. The 4ª Escuadrilla was nicknamed 'Nariz fria' ('cold nose') after the white propeller bosses of its machines, and 'Chupete' ('baby's dummy') from the oxygen-masks worn by the pilots. In November 1938 the last Russian pilots returned home.

Meanwhile, the production of a hundred I-16 Type 10s had begun at SAF-15, the relocated Hispano-Suiza factory at Alicante, during the summer of 1938. Great difficulty was experienced in the heat treatment of the centre-section wing spars, which were made in Alicante but had to be sent by ship, through the Nationalist blockade, to Barcelona, where the only suitable furnace was located, and returned for assembly. Nevertheless, the first four Hispano-built I-16s (serials CH-001 to CH-004) were delivered to the 1ª and 6ª escuadrillas in October 1938, CH-001 being shot down on 1 November and CH-002 on 21 December. Ten more were completed by 10 February 1939, when the loss of Catalonia brought production to a stop.

There has been much controversy, some of it acrimonious, over the number of Moscas still serving when the Nationalists launched their offensive on Catalonia on Christmas Eve 1938. Ex-Republican pilots such as Lacalle and Tarazona put the figure at between thirty and forty, and the Spanish air historian Gen Jesús Salas Larrazábal puts it at about eighty, with seventy in flying condition. Space does not permit a discussion of the conflicting evidence, but in any case, five escuadrillas of Moscas could offer poor resistance to three squadrons of Messerschmitts, one of Heinkel He 112Bs and sixteen squadrons of Fiat C.R.32s when the Republican front had collapsed and the Republican fighter squadrons were being crowded on to two or three aerodromes near the French frontier. The Moscas that were not destroyed at Figueras, Vilajuiga and Bañolas on 5 and 6 February 1939 escaped to France. After the fall of Catalonia only seven I-16 Moscas remained in the southern zone, attached to the Escuela de Alta Velocidad (High Speed Flying School) in Murcia, plus ten newly-built aircraft at Alicante, some lacking propellers and all untested. None took any part in the final phase of the war.

Of the Moscas in production at Alicante, thirty-five nearing completion were transferred to a factory in a converted sherry bodega at Jerez de la Frontera for assembly. Meanwhile, the ten finished aircraft, the seven captured at Alicante, and five others captured during the war (twenty-two in all) were formed into Grupo 26 of the Ejercito del Aire, based at Son San Juan, Mallorca. In 1941 the five that were still airworthy were transferred to Tablada, Seville, where they were joined by the twenty-three completed at Jerez, serialled 1W-23 to 1W-45 and 1W-52. In 1948 the type code was changed to C.8. The last Mosca (or Rata, as it was officially called in the Spanish air force) in flying condition, C.8-25, by then serving with the Escuela de Caza (Fighter School) at Morón de la Frontera, Seville, was withdrawn from service in 1953.

I-16 Type 5

Span 9m; length 5.9m; height 2.56m; wing area 14.5sq m.

Empty weight 1,200kg; loaded weight 1,460kg.

Maximum speed 454km/h at 3,000m; climb to 5,000m in 6.2min; ceiling 9,280m; range 820km.

I-16 Type 6

Dimensions as for Type 5.

Empty weight 1,260kg; loaded weight 1,660kg.

Maximum speed 440km/h at 3,000m; climb to 5,000m in 6.3min; ceiling 9,100m; range 800km.

I-16 Type 10

Dimensions: length increased to 5.99m.

Empty weight 1,350kg; loaded weight 1,715kg.

Maximum speed 444km/h at 3,000m; climb to 5,000m in 6.9min; ceiling 8,270m; range 800km. Performance of Type 10 with Cyclone F-54 engine unknown.

IMAM Ro 37bis

In 1936 the Romeo aircraft company became part of the Breda group and was renamed, by someone with little sense of the virtue of brevity, La Società Anonima Industrie Meccaniche e Aeronautica Meridionale. Among the various aircraft inherited by IMAM, the most successful was the Romeo Ro 37bis, a classic two-seat reconnaissance biplane of wood and metal which was being built in substantial numbers for the Regia Aeronautica. The prototype Ro 37, powered by a 550hp Fiat A-30 liquid-cooled engine, had made its maiden flight in 1934, and the first Ro 37s entered service in time to take part in the Italian invasion of Ethiopia. Meanwhile, an improved version, the Ro 37bis, powered by a 560hp Piaggio P.IX radial engine in a long-chord NACA cowling, had

An IMAM Ro 37bis.

gone into production, and it began to reach Italian squadrons by the summer of 1936. The armament consisted of two fixed forward-firing 7.7mm Breda-SAFAT machine guns in the fuselage, one movable 7.7mm gun in the rear cockpit, and twelve 12kg or 15kg bombs carried on underwing racks. Equipment included an aerial camera, which could be mounted to take photographs through an opening in the fuselage floor or over the side if oblique views were required, r/t wireless, and oxygen apparatus. Dual controls were provided to enable the observer to fly the aircraft in an emergency.

Ten Ro 37bis were unloaded from the Italian ship *Aniene* at Vigo, in Galicia, north-west Spain, on 29 September 1936, together with twelve Fiat C.R.32s, the Nationalists considering it unsafe at that time to disembark them at Cádiz. These aircraft were taken south by train, via Salamanca and Badajoz, to Tablada aerodrome, Seville, which they reached on 1 October. Assembly, supervised by Italian engineers, took less than a week, and by 8 October five of the Ro 37bis had been formed into the 1ª Squadriglia Autonoma Osservazione Aerea under the command of Capitano Colacicchi, and the remaining five into a Spanish-manned escuadrilla (1-E-12, '12' being the type code given to the Ro 37bis) commanded by Capitán José

Muñoz Jiménez, nicknamed 'el Corto' ('The Short'). After a few days of orientation and reconnaissance flights over Andalusia, both groups were sent to Talavera de la Reina, midway on the road from Badajoz to Madrid, to enable the two Spanish-manned escuadrillas of Heinkel He 46s to be transferred to the more tranquil front in Aragon. On 23 October the Ro 37bis (invariably called 'Los Romeos' in Spain) over-flew the suburbs of Madrid for the first time, taking part in the destruction by Fiats of two observation balloons moored above the Casa de Campo.

On 5-6 November the Nationalists began their direct assault on the capital, a date which coincided with the arrival, on the ground, of the first battalions of the International Brigades to defend Madrid, and, in the air, of the first two escuadrillas of Russian I-15 biplanes. The battle for, and over, Madrid turned into a grim slogging match in which, in the air at least, the Republicans soon gained the upper hand. Meanwhile, a further nine (or according to some sources, eleven) Ro 37bis had been unloaded at Cádiz, hastily assembled and rushed up to the front as a reinforcement. Perhaps the haste had been too great, for three of the 'Romeos' were damaged during test flights at Seville, and one crashed into a mountain during the flight to Talavera, killing the pilot, Tenente Fazi, and his observer, don Alonso de Orléans y Saxonia (son of don Alfonso de Orléans y Borbón, pretender to the Spanish throne and later commander of the 2ª Brigada Hispana de Aire). By this time, one Ro 37bis of the 1-E-12 Spanish escuadrilla at Talavera had been shot down and another badly damaged.

From then on the 'Romeos' operated only with adequate fighter escorts. As these were in constant demand by the bomber squadrons as well, the activities of the 'Romeos' were somewhat curtailed. Moreover, on 24 November Talavera aerodrome was shelled by Republican artillery (see Savoia-Marchetti S.81), which damaged several of the Italian-manned aircraft. The moving of the squadrons to Arenas de San Pedro and Aravaca did not end their misfortunes, for on 10 December 1936 a

A small number of Ro 37bis converted into single-seaters were used by the Aviazione Legionaria in the ground-attack rôle. (Emiliani)

German pilot in a Heinkel He 51 shot down an Ro 37bis which he had mistaken for one of the Russian R-5 biplanes that had just attacked Aravaca aerodrome. The Spanish crew of the Ro 37bis were killed. Another Ro 37bis (No. 12-14), also with a Spanish crew, was shot down on 3 January 1937 during an intense air battle between the escorting Fiat C.R.32s and a squadron of I-16 monoplanes.

The arrival in January and February 1937 of a further twenty-nine (or thirty-one) Ro 37bis, fitted with the more powerful 700hp Piaggio P.X radial engine, enabled both Italians and Spaniards to form two complete groups: the XXII Gruppo Auton. OA 'Linci' (Lynx) of two squadriglia (120ª and 128ª), and the 1-G-12 of two escuadrillas, 1-E-12 and 2-E-12. Escuadrilla 1-G-12 (redesignated 4-G-12 in June 1937) came under the command of Comandante Juan-Antonio Ansaldo, the monarchist airman who had been badly burned in the crash that had killed Gen Sanjurjo (see de Havilland Puss Moth), and who had later led the Fokker-Dragon group. For the first few days he insisted on leading the formation of Ro 37s in the de Havilland Dragon Rapide 40-2 (possibly ex-G-ADCL) which had served him so faithfully in the past.

Throughout February 1937 the Spanish 'Romeos' flew operations almost daily in the Battle of La Jarama, despite the fact that the

Italian Fiat pilots had been ordered not to cross the enemy lines (see Fiat C.R.32). Meanwhile, the Italian 'Romeos', now commanded by Maggiore Fanivia, were moved to Granada to assist in Gen Queipo de Llano's capture of Málaga (carried out largely by Italian troops), after which they returned north to take part in the Italian offensive at Gaudalajara. In April both the Italian and Spanish Ro 37bis groups were moved further north still for the Basque campaign, but in May 1-G-12 was diverted to help the Nationalist defence against a Republican attempt to capture Segovia. During this affair, now known as the Battle of La Granja, the Ro 37s had to fly daily from their northern base at Griñón and refuel at Avila before going into action. On several occasions they accompanied the Nationalist Aero A-101s on low-flying missions that took them, in single file, up the twisting and steeply ascending gorges of the Sierra Guadarrama, to harry Republican reinforcements being brought down to the front.

It was at this time that Maggiore Fanivia decided that the Ro 37bis of his group might adopt the 'cadena' ('chain') tactic of ground-straffing recently invented by the Spanish He 51 pilots of 1-G-2, although for the heavier two-seater the vertical circle of aircraft would have to become an inclined one. The manoeuvre required each aircraft to dive on the target with the engine practically idling and, as it pulled out, its pilot had to open the throttle fully to climb away at maximum speed. Unfortunately the Piaggio P.X engine of the newly-arrived Ro 37bis had an alarming tendency to cut out at this critical moment, and would restart only when the pilot closed the throttle and opened it again gradually. After Piaggio engineers failed to rectify this defect, the aircraft of the XXIIº Gruppo were redistributed. The 120ª Squadriglia, with P.X-equipped Ro 37bis, continued to be employed on reconnaissance duties, while the 128ª, with P.XI-equipped Ro 37bis, was employed on close-support and ground-attack missions. Later in the war a few of the Ro 37bis of the Spanish group 4-G-12 (including No. 12-43) were converted into single-seaters, resembling landplane versions of the Ro 43 and Ro 44 seaplanes, specifically for use as 'cadena' aircraft.

Thereafter, the Ro 37bis groups, more often separately but occasionally together, took part in every subsequent campaign of the civil war – Santander, Brunete, Belchite, the Asturias, Pozoblanco, Teruel, the Aragón offensive, the Battle of the Ebro, and the conquest of Catalonia. Command of the Italian group, which through 1938 was based at La Salada and Candasnos, fell in turn to Maggiori Franciosa and Achenza. In October 1937 Ansaldo transferred to the S.79 group and was replaced by the distinguished Nationalist pilot Comandante Manuel Negrón de las Cuevas. By this time 4-G-12 was reduced to only two airworthy machines, and was transferred to Seville for re-equipment, a further consignment of Ro 37bis having recently arrived. In December 1937 4-G-12 was stationed at Bello, south of Saragossa, for the Battle of Teruel, but on 20 February Negrón was killed by a piece of shrapnel from an anti-aircraft shell. His observer, Capitán Mira, who had never piloted an aircraft, valiantly tried to save the machine instead of baling out, but ground-looped on landing and wrecked it. (After the civil war, the Douglas DC-1 recovered from the Republicans was named in honour of Negrón.)

The next three commanders of the Spanish 'Romeos' (Cdtes Martínez de Pisón, Camacho and Cipriano Rodríguez) were also either wounded or killed in action during the Battle of the Ebro, a fact which illustrates that the vital work of the reconnaissance squadrons was perhaps the most dangerous of all. After the Catalonian campaign the XXIIº Gruppo was based at Olmedo, Castile, and 4-G-12 (Cdte Teodoro Vives) was transferred to the Córdoba front, where it remained until the end of the war.

Sixty-eight Ro 37bis appear to have been delivered to Spain, the last eight arriving in January-February 1938. There are no reliable figures regarding losses in action. The Aviazione Legionaria admitted to only two, and the Spanish Nationalists to another two, but this is hardly satisfactory, since only eighteen (eleven Italian and seven Spanish) were still airworthy on 23 December 1938.

Span 11.1m; length 8.6m; height 3.1m; wing area 31.36sq m.

Empty weight 2,040kg; loaded weight 2,400kg.

Maximum speed 320km/h at 3,000m; cruising speed 250km/h; climb to 4,000m in 9.5min; ceiling 7,200m; range 1,500km.

IMAM Ro 41

Developed in 1933-34 as a lightweight single-seat fighter, the Ro 41 was an unequal-span biplane with a gull-form upper wing, the roots of which were angled down to the shoulders of the fuselage. The bracing struts were of the Warren girder type, the undercarriage wheels were enclosed in a pair of large spats, and the 390hp Piaggio P.VII C.45 radial engine was housed in a long-chord, blistered cowling. The forward part

IMAM Ro 41s at the Escuela de Caza (Fighter School), Villanubla, near Valladolid. The nearest machine has been converted into a two-seater. (Emiliani)

of the welded-steel-tube fuselage was covered with duralumin, the aft with fabric. The wings and tail assembly were wooden, with fabric covering. The armament consisted of two fixed forward-firing Breda-SAFAT 7.7mm machine guns.

Three IMAM Ro 41s arrived at Seville in the spring of 1937, where, with the military serials 7-1 to 7-3, they formed an independent flight of the IIIº Stormo Caccia of the Aviazione Legionaria. Shortly afterwards they were handed over to the Spanish Nationalists, who used them to create a city defence patrol at Granada under the command of Emilio Jiménez Ugarte. In February 1938 there arrived a batch of sixteen Ro 41s, of which five at least were two-seat trainers. These had only a single machine gun and a removable hood over the rear cockpit for night-flying training. After these were assembled, all nineteen Ro 41s, with the new type code 37, were sent to the Escuela de Caza (Fighter School) at Villanubla, near Valladolid. A third consignment of nine Ro 41s arrived in November 1938, bringing the total delivered to twenty-eight. Some of the single-seaters featured in a propaganda film made shortly after the civil war, in which they 'stood in' for I-15 Chatos in a supposed dogfight between Fiat C.R.32s and Republican fighters. Nineteen were still in service in March 1940, and fourteen in 1945, by which time the single-seaters were designated C.7 and the two-seaters ES.3.

Span 8.81m; length 6.7m; height 2.65m; wing area 19.15sq m.

Empty weight 980kg; loaded weight 1,250kg.

Maximum speed 330km/h at 5,000m; climb 625m/min; ceiling 8,200m; range 600km.

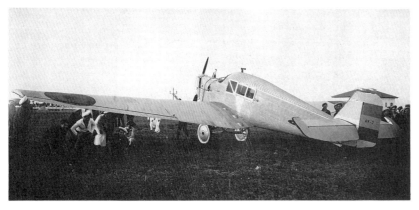

Junkers F 13

The Junkers F 13, which, as the J 13, first flew on 25 June 1919, was one of the true pioneers of commercial air transport, and the first successful all-metal cantilever passenger monoplane. It accommodated two pilots in an open cockpit and four passengers in an enclosed cabin. The airframe was covered with the characteristic Junkers corrugated duralumin skinning. Production, which continued until 1932, seems to have exceeded 350 aircraft, sold not only to Luft Hansa, but to airlines in Afghanistan, Albania, Argentina, Austria, Bolivia, Canada, China, Colombia, Hungary, Italy, Japan, Norway, Poland, Spain, the USA and the USSR. Others were shipped, as part of war reparations, to Britain, the USA and Belgium. Indeed no aeroplane, not even the Fokker F.VIIb3m, played a more important part in establishing air traffic in more quarters of the globe.

Five, or perhaps seven, Junkers F 13s (see table) were imported into Spain by Unión Aérea Española (after 13 March 1929, CLASSA).

Two F 13s were reportedly used as air ambulances by the CRE (Spanish Red Cross). Two are reported as being leased to Servicios Aereos Portugueses, and were presumably returned to Spain. One was badly damaged when, during a flight, first

The Aviación Militar's Junkers F 13, 49-2. (Arráez)

its propeller flew off and then the entire engine. The crew managed to land without injury. One F 13 was transferred to the Aviación Militar, where it was given the serial 49-2 and used as a flying laboratory by the Servicio Técnico. It was flying in 1935, but whether it was still airworthy in July 1936 is not known. The F 13 MC-CBBA (EC-BBA after 1931) was still on the LAPE inventory in July 1936, and is reported to have been on an aerodrome captured by the Nationalists. According to Victor Veniel the F 13 fell into Republican hands again when two German pilots inadvertently landed behind Republican lines in Aragón. Veniel, who was detailed to fly it to Prat de Llobregat, was surprised to be fired at by anti-aircraft guns throughout most of the journey. On landing, he discovered that, whereas the upper surfaces had been painted with Republican bands, the St Andrew's Crosses on the undersurfaces had been left unchanged. Nothing more is known of the history of either Junkers F 13 in the civil war.

F 13 with BMW IIIa engine

Span 14.82m; length 9.59m; height (tail up) 3.14m.

c/n	Date	Reg'n	Remarks
613	May 1925	MC-AAAJ	Possibly named *Marabu*. 185hp BMW IIIa engine
770	Sep 1925	MC-AJAA	185hp BMW IIIa engine
	Sep 1927	MC-CAAD	185hp BMW IIIa engine
639	Nov 1927	MC-CBBA	280/310hp Junkers L 5 engine and enlarged fin and rudder. Inherited by LAPE
2003	Feb 1930	MC-CEEA	Returned to Germany in December 1930 and became D-1203

Empty weight 1,050kg; loaded weight 1,770kg.

Maximum speed 180km/h; cruising speed 140km/h; ceiling 4,023m; endurance 7hr 35min.

F 13be with Junkers L5 engine

Loaded weight increased to 1,925kg and cruising speed to 160km/h.

Junkers G 24 and K 30

The Junkers G 24 was a three-engined low-wing monoplane transport constructed according to the system pioneered by Professor Hugo Junkers during the First World War: a metal-framed fuselage and multi-spar metal wings covered with corrugated duralumin sheets. The G 24 carried a pilot, wireless-operator and nine passengers, and power was provided by three 310hp Junkers L5 engines. It was, in short, an enlargement of the F 13 and a direct predecessor of the Junkers Ju 52/3m. Of the sixty or seventy built, at least sixteen were produced in Sweden by AB Flygindustri and, of these, five were sold to Unión Aérea Española (and, after 13 March 1929, to CLASSA) between 1926 and 1930. One (c/n 846) was sold back to Germany and became D-1091, and another (c/n 915, MC-CAFF) crashed on 17 October 1929. The remaining three, (c/n 835 EC-ADA, 914 'AAF, and 929 'FFA) passed to LAPE in 1931.

In 1935 EC-AAF and 'FFA were handed over to the Aviación Militar as trainers and general-purpose transports, though how many were still flying in July 1936 is not certain, as most of the reports of Junkers G 24s in use during the first weeks of the civil war are traceable to the single Junkers K 30 bomber based at that time at Getafe, Madrid. This aeroplane, built by AB Flygindustri in 1927 (c/n 949 S-AABH) was purchased, complete with armaments and spare parts, for 600,000 pesetas (£23,790). It arrived on 10 March 1928 at Cuatro Vientos, Madrid, where it was ceremoniously received by the Infante (Crown Prince) don Fernando and a corps of staff officers, and duly sprinkled with holy water by the attending priest. The Junkers K 30 had a crew of five, including two gunners, each operat-

ing twin machine guns in a pair of dorsal cockpits, one immediately behind the cabin and the second behind the wing trailing edge. A ventral 'dustbin' for a third gunner could be lowered under the belly. Its principal visible difference from the G 24 was the shape of its fin, which was higher and had a straight leading edge. Like the G 24, it was powered by three 310hp Junkers L5 liquid-cooled engines. For the first two years of its service the K 30 was used by the Escuadra de Instrucción and based sometimes at Alcalá de Henares and sometimes at Los Alcázares, Cartagena. About 1932 it was transferred to Escuadrá Núm 1 at Getafe, given the military serial 49-1, and placed under the charge of Capitán Manuél Cascón, who was to give distinguished service on the Republican side during the civil war.

Andrés García Lacalle writes in his memoirs that about 1933, during a debate on the effectiveness or otherwise of the 'multi-place de combat' (see Potez 54) as the supposed all-purpose warplane of the future, he argued that no large aircraft, no matter how heavily equipped with defensive armament, could be a match for single-seat interceptor fighters. The fighter pilot, he maintained, could choose his direction of attack and, by merely pointing his aircraft at the bomber, always direct a greater concentration of fire at it than its gunners could against him. Moreover, the fighter pilot enjoyed the reassuring knowledge that the bulk of his engine stood between him and enemy bullets, while the enemy gunners, often barely able to see the fighter hurtling down at them out of the sun, had no such protection. Finally, he had to hit only one vital part of the bomber to bring it down. Lacalle therefore laid a wager with

The Junkers K 30 of the Aviación Militar, 49-1. (Liron)

the crew of the Junkers K 30 that, with all its gunners and his Nieuport 52 equipped with camera-guns, he would score five hits on the Junkers for every hit they could score on his fighter. No one, he writes, was willing to accept his challenge, a fact which, he felt, settled the 'multi-place de combat' controversy once and for all.

After serving in the Sahara the K 30 was back at Getafe on 18 July 1936, and in August was transferred to the international squadron, or Escadre España, under André Malraux at Barajas, from where, with two or three of the newly arrived Potez 54s, it took part in various bombing missions. It was destroyed during one of the Nationalist bombing raids on Getafe and Barajas, probably in October 1936.

Junkers G 24

Span 29.37m; length 16.7m; wing area 101sq m.
Loaded weight 6,500kg.
Maximum speed 210km/h; cruising

A Junkers W 34.

speed 165km/h at 2,000m; ceiling 4,300m.

Junkers K 30

Span 29.37m; length 15.8m; height 5.9m; wing area 99sq m.
Empty weight 4,270kg; loaded weight 7,500kg.
Maximum speed 202km/h; cruising speed 165km/h; ceiling 4,100m; endurance 7hr.

Junkers W 34

With its all-metal construction, corrugated metal skin and nononsense, utilitarian appearance , the Junkers W 34 ('W' for Werkflugzeug, or 'general duties aeroplane') was unmistakably a member of the Junkers family and a forebear of the great Junkers Ju 52/3m. Developed from the Junkers W 33, the W 34 was a low-wing cantilever monoplane with a fixed undercarriage. It could carry a crew of two plus six passengers, or the equivalent in freight, and was powered by a 660hp BMW 132 A (licence-built Pratt & Whitney Hornet) radial engine fitted with a Townend ring. The military version, the K 43, was a trainer for night-flying, navigation, bomb-aiming and gunnery, and was fitted with a dorsal gun position. The prototype, powered by a 420hp Gnome-Rhône Jupiter VI radial, first flew in 1928, and 1,791 examples were built, the majority of them K 43s.

Operators, besides Luft Hansa and Deutsche Lufthansa, included several Latin American airlines and companies in Canada, China, South Africa and Sweden.

Three Junkers W 34s arrived in Nationalist Spain with the first contingents of the Condor Legion in

November 1936 and, bearing the military serials 43-1 to 43-3, were used for general transport duties. Aircraft 43-3 became the staff aeroplane of Gen Queipo de Llano, Commander-in-Chief of the Ejercito del Sur (Nationalist southern army). Two more (43-4 and 43-5) arrived at the end of 1937. After the civil war the W 34s continued in service until the 1950s, as it was possible to replace their engines with BMW 132As taken from Ju 52/3ms. In 1946 they were given the new type code L.14.

Span 17.76m; length 10.3m; height 3.25m; wing area 44sq m.
Empty weight 1,730kg; loaded weight 3,200kg.
Maximum speed 258km/h; cruising speed 237km/h; ceiling 6,300m; range 840km.

Junkers Ju 52/3m

Anyone compiling a list of the most famous aeroplanes ever built would surely include the Junkers Ju 52/3m without hesitation. As a versatile, long-serving and ubiquitous commercial transport its only peer has been the Douglas DC-3, and as a military transport it did more than any other type of aeroplane to shape the course of the Second World War. Its contribution to shaping the course of the Spanish Civil War was hardly less significant.

Unlike the Douglas DC-2 and DC-3, which stood at the beginning of a line of technical development which has continued until the present, the Junkers Ju 52/3m represented the end of a line of development which Professor Hugo Junkers began when he made his first tenta-

A Junkers Ju 52/3m of the Condor Legion.

tive drawings for an all-metal, thick-winged cantilever monoplane in 1909 and pursued with remarkable consistency for the next twenty years. The all-metal military aircraft he produced during the First World War embodied concepts which were astonishingly advanced for their time, and the single- and three-engined transport monoplanes of the 1920s, characterised by their corrugated duralumin skinning and a utilitarian simplicity of shape, were in demand all over the world for their ruggedness, economy and reliability.

The original Ju 52 prototype, which first flew on 13 October 1930, was a single-engined transport intended to combine the dimensions and carrying capacity of the three-engined G 24 with the later, but smaller, single-engined W 34, and was therefore designed to accommodate one or three engines, the final choice depending on the outcome of flight trials. The seventh prototype, the Ju 52/3mde, was fitted with three 525hp Pratt & Whitney Hornet radial engines, and it was an improved version of this, the Ju 52/3mge, which went into production in 1933 to meet orders both from Deutsche Lufthansa and an ever-lengthening queue of foreign purchasers. It carried a crew of three and 13-17 passengers according to requirements, and was powered by three 660hp BMW 132 radials (licence-built Pratt & Whitney Hornet S4D2), the centre engine being fitted with a Townend ring and the outboard engines having long-chord NACA cowlings. It was skinned, as usual,

with corrugated duralumin, and its four-spar tapered mainplane was of the Junkers 'double-wing' type: the entire trailing edge of each wing consisted, inboard, of a flap and, outboard, of an aileron that doubled as a flap when necessary. Its most modern-looking feature, apart from the NACA cowlings, was the pair of large streamlined wheel spats.

The Luftwaffe ordered a military version, the Ju 52/3m g3e 'Auxiliary Bomber', as a backup to the Dornier Do 11 and Do 23, which at that time were envisaged as the principal weapons of the planned German bomber force. Development troubles with the Dorniers, however, led to increased production of the Junkers, with the result that Ju 52/3m g3es equipped two-thirds of the Luftwaffe Kampfgruppen (bomber wings) by 1935. The Ju 52/3m g3e had a crew of five: a pilot, a copilot, a radio operator, a navigator who doubled as bomb-aimer and lower gunner in the retractable ventral 'dustbin', and a flight mechanic who doubled as the upper gunner in the dorsal cockpit. Each gunner was armed with a single movable 7.9mm MG 15 machine gun. Six vertical racks in a bay inside the fuselage could carry a total of 1,000kg of bombs in various mixes, the heaviest bombs being 250kg and the lightest 1kg.

Since 1934, Deutsche Lufthansa had acquired the rights to use a chain of aerodromes from the Canary Islands to Gambia on the west African coast, partly as stages of a mail service to South America, and partly for gathering naval intelligence. Thus it came about that, on 18 July 1936, the Deutsche Lufthansa Ju 52/3m D-APOK *Max von Muller*, flown by Flügkapitän Alfred Henke, was plying its regular route off Spanish Sahara when it was ordered to land at Villa Cisneros and impounded by the Nationalists who had seized control there. Apparently, their reason for doing this was to have a replacement aircraft on hand should de Havilland Dragon Rapide G-ACYR be unable to fly Gen Franco from the Canary Islands to Tetuán, a task which, in the event, the Rapide carried out successfully. However, when Franco arrived in Spanish Morocco he found that Republican ships in the Straits of Gibraltar prevented his army from crossing to southern Spain, where his colleague, Gen Queipo de Llano, had gained control of a triangle of land from Córdoba down to Cádiz and Gibraltar but lacked the troops to hold it for long. He persuaded Henke to fly two local German Nazis, Bernhardt and Langenheim, and a Spanish air force officer, Capitán Francisco Arranz, to Berlin with a request to the German government for transport aircraft and other material assistance. The Junkers Ju 52/3m arrived at Gatow, to where it had been diverted from Tempelhof to preserve secrecy, on 24 July 1936, and the two Germans were received by Hitler at Bayreuth, where he was attending the Wagner Festival, late at night on 25 July. Following Hitler's decision to aid Franco, twenty Ju 52/3ms were ordered to be dispatched as soon as possible. With Henke still as its pilot, D-APOK flew back to Spanish Morocco immediately, via Italy and Sardinia, and reached Tetuán at 1.00pm on 28 July.

The twenty Ju 52/3ms, fresh from the factory at Dessau, were formed into a bomber-transport group divided into two squadrons of ten aircraft each, under the overall command of Hauptmann Rudolph, Freiherr von Moreau. One squadron – together with the armaments and military equipment of the whole group, as well as six Heinkel He 51 fighters and ninety-five Luftwaffe and technical personnel disguised as tourists – sailed from Hanover for Cadiz, Spain, on the *Usaramo* shortly before midnight on 31 July 1936. The second squadron, led by von Moreau, flew to Spanish Morocco along the route followed by

D-APOK, departing singly or in pairs between 29 July and 9 August. These ten aircraft were given civil registrations and stripped of their military equipment, and their dorsal and ventral gun positions were faired over by metal sheets. This has given rise to the common but erroneous statement that they were civil aircraft that had been built for Deutsche Lufthansa. In fact, all twenty were military Ju 52/3m g3es built for the Luftwaffe.

On 8 August the pilot of one of the last aircraft to leave, D-AMYN, strayed off course, found himself over Spain, and landed at Barajas, Madrid, in the hope that he was in Nationalist territory. Some Lufthansa Ju 52s happened to be at Barajas that morning to evacuate German citizens from Spain, and the crew of one of these warned the pilot of his mistake. He succeeded in taking off, but lack of fuel forced him down at Azuaga, in Republican territory near the Portuguese frontier, and the Junkers and its crew were taken back to Madrid a few days later. On discovering the lack of passenger seats, the dorsal gun position beneath the upper fuselage skinning, and the provision for installing the ventral dustbin, the Spanish government protested to the German government that this was obviously a military aircraft on its way to Gen Franco. The Germans insisted it was merely a Lufthansa machine, and the British government, which was trying to persuade Germany to sign the Non-Intervention pact, pretended to agree. Eventually the Spanish government took its complaint, along with photographs of shot-down German and Italian aircraft and signed confessions of captured German and Italian airmen, to the League of Nations, but without result. The crew, meanwhile, was returned to Germany, and the Ju 52 was kept at Barajas until it was destroyed during a Nationalist air raid. Thus the number of Ju 52/3m g3es that reached Gen Franco in July and August 1936 was nineteen, plus D-APOK, but it is not clear whether the civil aircraft was later converted into a bomber or left as a transport, with its passenger seats, for staff use.

The airlifting of Franco's army from Spanish Morocco to Spain had

actually started on 20 July, using three Fokker F.VIIb3m/Ms, two Dornier Wals and, later, the Douglas DC-2 and single-engined Fokker F.VIIa. The Junkers Ju 52s greatly accelerated the operation, and by the end of August 1936 more than 8,000 troops, together with their baggage, equipment and munitions, had been flown to Tablada Aerodrome, Seville, and a newly cleared aerodrome at Jerez de la Frontera. When the airlift ended, on 11 October, the total had risen to 13,962 troops, with some 500 tons of military equipment, including 36 artillery pieces. The *puente aéreo* (aerial bridge), as it was called, was the first operation of its kind on such a scale, and the speed with which a relatively small number of aircraft had transported an entire army from its base directly to the field of battle served notice on the world that a new dimension of mobility had entered into warfare. The airlift also swung the balance of strength dramatically in favour of the Nationalists, enabling them to consolidate their precarious hold in southern Spain and begin the advance that was to carry them to the outskirts of Madrid by November. Nevertheless, when Hilter declared, 'General Franco should erect a monument to the glory of the Junkers 52; it is this aeroplane the Spanish Revolution has to thank for its victory!', he was exaggerating. If the Ju 52/3ms deserved a monument on that account, then the other aircraft that had begun the airlift in July deserved one even more, for it was the troops transported by them who established the bridgehead that made the main airlift possible.

The *Usaramo* docked at Cádiz on 6 August (see Heinkel He 51) and the Junkers were taken by rail to Tablada, Seville, for assembly next day. Nine of the aircraft were formed into three escuadrillas of three aircraft each, crewed by Spaniards, the pilots having received some hasty instruction in the type by being permitted to take part in the airlift. There is no record of what happened to the tenth machine, but it was presumably kept to assist in the airlift, replacing the aircraft lost at Madrid. At about this time the twenty Ju 52/3ms were assigned the Nationalist type code 22, the first bombers being serialled 22-61 to 22-69 (these numbers were later changed several times, which has caused some confusion, as is shown later).

On 10 August the Junkers' crews suffered their first casualty when Capitán Trechuelo, commanding the 1ª Escuadrilla, was killed by ground fire over Toledo. On the 15 August the first Ju 52 to be lost in the war crashed at Jerez, its German crew being killed. After being moved to Cáceres to cover the Nationalist advance into central Spain, the three Spanish Junkers escuadrillas were formed into a single group named Escuadra B (the Breguet 19s forming Escuadra A), and on the 23 August, escorted by three Spanish-flown Heinkel He 51s, they made their first penetration to the Madrid area with a raid on the Getafe and Barajas aerodromes. At the end of the month the 1ª Escuadrilla was moved north to León to cover the attack on Irún.

Although the German aircrews were under strict orders not to participate in military operations, on 13 August 1936 two of the Ju 52/3m transports at Tetuán, fitted with improvised bomb racks and flown by von Moreau and Henke, carried out a bombing attack on the Republican battleship *Jaime I* in the Bay of Málaga. One of the bombs dropped by Henke's aircraft hit the bridge and put the warship out of action for several months. After this the restriction was quietly lifted, and early in September three of the transports were converted into bombers and formed into an all-German kette (flight) under the command of von Moreau. It went into action on 14 September, destroyed a fuel depot at Alcázar San Juan the next day and, sometimes based at Salamanca and sometimes at León, carried out an average of two operations a day for the next eight weeks. In October three more Ju 52/3ms were formed into a second kette, commanded by Henke, the two kettes being known respectively as 'Pablos' and 'Pedros', in allusion to the Spanish *noms-de-guerre* assigned to many of the German crewmen. The first Junkers Ju 52/3m to be lost in combat in the civil war was 22-64 of the Spanish 2ª Escuadrilla, shot down on 28 September over Toledo by Rafael Peña in a Loire 46 (or perhaps Nieuport 52 – some accounts identify

it as a 'Nieuport' and others as a 'Loire-Nieuport'). All the crew were killed, among them the squadron commander Estaquio Ruiz de Alda. (His brother, Julio Ruiz de Alda, a Falangist leader murdered in the Model Prison, Madrid, in August 1936, had made the first crossing of the South Atlantic, with Ramón Franco and Pablo Rada, in the Dornier Wal *Plus Ultra* in 1927).

On 4 November 1936, as the Nationalists were deploying their forces for their attempt to break into Madrid, the Germans lost their first Ju 52/3m in combat when a formation of twelve (six German- and six Spanish-flown) with five Ro 37bis was attacked by ten I-15 Chatos, one being shot down and a second forced to crash-land. This was the first occasion that Russian fighters had been seen by the Nationalists. While continuing their intensive operations in the Madrid area during October and November, the Junkers squadrons went through several reorganisations. First, the arrival of reinforcements from Germany facilitated the creation of a 4ª Spanish Escuadrilla, which coincided with a renumbering of the individual aircraft. Thus there were (the original numbers in brackets):

1ª Escuadrilla: 22-51 (61), -52 (62), -53 (63); under Capitán Gil Mendizábal. The escuadrilla was named *Sanjurjo* in memory of Gen Sanjurjo, killed at the start of the war (see D.H. Puss Moth).

2ª Escuadrilla: 22-61 (replacing -64, shot down over Toledo on 28 September 1936), -55 (65), -56 (66); under Capitán Carrillo. Named *Toledo* in memory of the above loss.

3ª Escuadrilla: 22-60 (67), -62 (68), -63 (69); under Capitán Guerrero. Named *Las Tres Marías* after the three aircraft, *María Cruz* (-60), *María de la O* (-62) and *María Magdalena* (-63). These names had no Biblical significance, but referred to the heroines of three popular songs.

4ª Escuadrilla: Serials not known; under Capitán Luis Pardo.

In November 1936 the 1ª and 4ª escuadrillas were combined into the first Spanish grupo, 1-G-22, under Luis Pardo, the escuadrillas being renumbered 1-E-22 and 2-E-22,

and the 2ª and 3ª escuadrillas being renumbered 3-E-22 and 4-E-22. The number of Ju 52/3ms delivered in October is uncertain, but has been given as thirty-eight, some being retained as transports. They included one (or two) Ju 52/3mW seaplanes based at Atalayón in Spanish Morocco. One Ju 52/3m was lost, however, when Ananias Sanjuan, a pilot of the 1ª Escuadrilla, flew it to Alcalá de Henares and joined the Republicans, later becoming a Katiuska pilot.

With the creation of the Condor Legion in November 1936, a German bomber group (K/88) of three staffeln was formed, with nine to twelve aircraft each, receiving the serials 22-64 to 22-100. The surviving Ju 52/3ms of the Pablo and Pedro squadrons were handed over to the Spanish Nationalists and formed into two new squadrons, 5-E-22 (Luis Pardo), named *Barbarán* in honour of the Spanish transatlantic flyer, and 6-E-22 (José Larrauri), named *Navarra* (22-47 to 22-49). The first major operation of K/88 was a raid on Cartagena, intended to interrupt supplies arriving from Russia. On 15 November the whole group transferred to Melilla, in Spanish Morocco, and on the next day attacked the port in pairs throughout the day. After returning to Spain on the 18th, K/88 threw itself into the battle for Madrid, its first important mission being a combined raid with Spanish and Italian (Savoia-Marchetti S.81) bomber squadrons on the capital, about fifty aircraft taking part.

By this time, however, the Russian I-15 and I-16 fighters were gaining control of the air, and had proved themselves so superior to the Heinkel He 51 fighters escorting the slow and vulnerable Ju 52s that daylight bombing operations had to be abandoned after 26 November 1936. Moreover, the Republicans began to raid Nationalist air bases. On 4 December, for example, an attack by eighteen R-5 Rasantes on Navalmoral aerodrome put the six Ju 52/3ms of 3-E-22 (the *Tres Marías*) and 4-E-22 out of action for two months.

The hardest fighting for the Junkers came during the Battle of La Jarama in February 1937, a Nationalist attack intended to surround Madrid from the south. Spanish and Condor Legion Ju 52/3ms were to be employed in attacks on Republican aerodromes and on communications behind the front. Although these attacks were pressed home during the first days, Republican fighter opposition quickly neutralised the Nationalist fighter escorts. The Condor Legion refused to commit its He 51s any further, and the Italians prohibited their Fiat C.R.32 squadrons from crossing the lines. The German Ju 52 squadrons switched to night bombing, while the Spanish attempted to persevere with their daylight missions. However, the sight of twenty or thirty I-15s and I-16s deploying for attack, which greeted the Junkers crews on nearly every mission, forced them to turn back.

Matters came to a head on 17 February. The group commander, Capitán Calderón, had promised 'Tomorrow we bomb, and whoever falls, falls!', but his own machine was shot down in flames and another damaged beyond repair. The next day, the Spanish *Patrulla Azul* of three C.R.32s led by García Morato resolved the crisis by charging head-on into a formation of twenty I-15s, which obliged the Italian Fiat pilots, watching from the far side of the lines, to come to their rescue. The order was rescinded, but it was obvious that the slow and weakly-armed Ju 52/3ms could no longer be used in daylight, where enemy fighter opposition was strong, without complete fighter protection. The six escuadrillas were therefore reorganised into two new groups, 1-G-22 for nocturnal operations over the Madrid sector, and 2-G-22 for daylight missions over quieter fronts. From this point it is more convenient to follow the histories of the German and Spanish units separately.

In March 1937 K/88 moved to Burgos to provide bombing support to the Nationalist drive against Bilbao in the north. On 31 March it announced its presence in characteristic fashion, with attacks by twenty Ju 52/3ms (plus three He 111s and two Do 17s) on the Basque villages of Ochandiano and Durango, killing several hundred inhabitants. The unit continued similar raids throughout April, sometimes carrying out three or four missions a day, its most notorious strike being the destructive raid on Guernica on 26 April, in which twenty-three Ju 52/3ms and thirty-four other aircraft took part (one Do 17, two He 111s, three Savoia-Marchetti S.79s, ten He 51s, six Bf 109Bs and twelve C.R.32s). In July 1937 K/88, whose Ju 52/3ms were gradually being replaced by He 111s and transferred to the Spanish Nationalists, moved to Avila to help counter the Republican attack at Brunete. On 25 July, during the final phase of the battle, two Condor Legion Ju 52s were shot down over Valdemorillo. During a nocturnal raid on 26 July a third was shot down by the Russian pilot Yakushin in an I-15, and a fourth was claimed by Anatoli Serov two nights later. Also on 26 July one of the Spanish Junkers exploded in mid-air for no apparent reason, and another was lost in the same manner a few weeks later. The cause was traced not to sabotage, as was suspected, but to a fault in the electrics. The Battle of Brunete ended on 27 July 1937, and on the 29th K/88 returned to the north for the campaign against Santander and the Asturias. In October the remaining Ju 52/3ms were replaced by He 111s and transferred to Spanish units.

The first leader of 1-G-22 was the celebrated Carlos de Haya, pre-war holder of several records and chief pilot of the captured Douglas DC-2 during the early months of the civil war, who supervised its night-flying training. On his transfer to fighters, in May 1937, the command passed to Eduardo González Gallarza. The Ju 52 veteran Alfonso Carrillo commanded 2-G-22. Both groups participated in all the subsequent campaigns of the war: Santander, Belchite, the Asturias, Teruel, the Aragón breakthrough, Valencia, the Battle of the Ebro, Catalonia and Extremadura. In the autumn of 1937 1-G-22 suffered a series of setbacks. One aircraft, piloted by Muntadas and Marchenko (the White Russian often credited with inspiring the original airlift over the Straits of Gibraltar) was shot down by a night fighter. Then, on 15 October 1937, the group was attacked at its base at Garrapinillos aerodrome, Saragossa, at dawn by two squadrons of I-15s. Three Junkers Ju 52/3ms (22-49, -54 and -62), two He 46s and six Fiat C.R.32s were destroyed on the ground. At the end of 1937 both groups were incorporated into the 1ª Escuadra (González Gallarza) of the 1ª Brigada Aérea Hispana, and remained so until the end of the war. By a decree of June 1938, all aircrews who had served in the Junkers Ju 52/3m units were entitled to wear the Medalla Militar Colectiva in recognition of the services these aircraft had performed for the Nationalist cause.

Estimates of the number of Junkers Ju 52/3ms (Ju 52/3mge, Ju 52/3m g3e and Ju 52m g4e) vary between 63 and 120, and there seems to be no way of arriving at a trustworthy figure. Nor are there reliable figures regarding losses, although it has been published that twenty-two were lost by the Condor Legion alone. Sixty were handed over to the Nationalists during the civil war, but only twenty-five remained at the end of the war, of which all but one were still flying in March 1940. Although twenty-eight Spanish Ju 52 aircrews were killed in the war, we have no figures regarding aircraft lost in combat or accidents.

Finally, a number of civil Ju 52/3mges were transferred to the Nationalist internal airline Iberia, starting in August 1937. Again, there is much uncertainty regarding registrations, names etc., but those which can be identified are listed on page 210.

listed on page 210.

The first names were of fallen Nationalist heroes, the second of rivers. *Haya* seems doubtful, as that name was also given to a Douglas DC-2. In a British Civil Aviation Authority MS 'Gazetteer' ('Spain 1939-51') it is reported that, in 1940, Iberia had eight Ju 52/3ms in service and two in reserve, all of which were still in service in 1942. On 21 April 1941 Iberia had signed a contract to buy five Ju 52/3ms from Deutsche Lufthansa, but in the event only one was delivered. The document also shows that in January 1942, for instance, EC-AAL, 'AAK and 'CAJ were on the regular service from Madrid to Santa Isabel, Bata (now Gambia) in West Africa. Later in 1942 three of the military Ju 52s (22-107 to -109) were transferred to Iberia, perhaps being among those listed above. CASA built 170 examples (22-110 to -279) which entered service between 1944 and 1953.

German reg'n	First reg'n	First name	Second name	Last reg'n	Cancelled
D-AKYS	M-CABO	*Mola*	*Ebro*	EC-AAH	1947
	M-CABB	*La Cierva*(?)	*Tajo*	EC-AAC	
	M-CABA	*Sanjurjo*			
c/n 4076	M-CABC	*Morato*	*Duero*	EC-AAK	1948
	M-CABD		*Guadiana*	EC-AAI	1948
	M-CABE	*La Cierva*(?)			
c/n 7071	M-CABU	*Eugenio Gros*		EC-AAL	1947
	M-CABY	*Haya*(?)	*Guadal-quivir*(?)		
	EC-CAJ				
c/n 7196	EC-CAK			EC-ABE	1957
c/n 6725	EC-CAL			EC-AAU	1957
c/n 5386	EC-DAM			EC-ABR	1957
c/n 6015	EC-DAN			EC-ABS	1957

During the 1950s the BMW engines were replaced by E9 Beta radials built by Elizalde (which became ENMASA), which were based on the Russian M-25 (Wright Cyclone). The Junkers of the Ejercito del Aire continued in service until the 1970s, and several are still flying today.

Span 29.25m; length 18.9m; height 4.5m; wing area 110.5sq m.

Empty weight 6,610kg; loaded weight 10,00kg.

Maximum speed 290km/h; cruising speed 225km/h; at 1,000m; ceiling 5,500m; range 880km.

Junkers Ju 86D-1

The Junkers Ju 86 belonged to the same generation of German bombers as the Dornier Do 17 and Heinkel He 111 and, like them, was conceived primarily as a military aircraft which could also serve as a civil passenger or cargo transport. Indeed, it was the only one of the three in which the design seriously tried to reconcile these contradictory requirements, which may explain why,

A Junkers Ju 86D-1. (Arráez)

as a military aircraft, it never achieved the success of its competitors.

The prototype, designated Ju 86ab1, first flew on 4 November 1934, and was thus the first of the three to take to the air. Its engines, two Junkers Jumo 205C compression-ignition diesel engines rated at 592hp for take-off, were chosen for their low fuel consumption, narrow frontal area and supposed reliability in adverse conditions, but were to prove undependable in operation and difficult to maintain. Moreover, the aeroplane itself did not possess the excellent handling characteristics of the Heinkel or Dornier, a defect aggravated by the unusually narrow track of its retractable undercarriage. Nevertheless, after various modifications, the Ju 86 went into production early in 1936. One series of the civil version, the Ju 86Z-1, was produced to meet orders from Deutsche Lufthansa and abroad, and one series of Ju 86A-1 bombers was built for the Luftwaffe, the first examples reaching Kampfgeschwader 152 *Hindenburg* in the summer of that year.

The Ju 86A-1 still suffered from longitudinal instability, however,

and, after twenty or so had been built, production continued of a modified version, the Ju 86D-1, with a 42cm extension of the fuselage aft of the tail assembly. Thus it was that four Ju 86D-1s accompanied the four He 111B-1s and four Do 17E-1s when these were shipped to Spain in February 1937, to enable the most modern equipment to be evaluated in real operational conditions. The Spanish Nationalists nicknamed them 'Jumos', and assigned them the type code 26. After assembly at Tablada, Seville, one aircraft, 26-1, inadvertently strayed over Republican territory during a test flight on 23 February and crashed on the aerodrome at Andújar. One crew member was taken prisoner, and the rest were killed. Whether this was due to enemy action or engine failure is not recorded.

While serving with VB/88, the Experimental Bomber Squadron at Burgos, during the offensive against Bilbao, the three Ju 86D-1s proved inferior to the He 111Bs in nearly every respect, one more (which the Basques claimed to have shot down) catching fire in the air, and the others suffering frequent engine failures. A replacement Ju 86D-1 (26-5) arrived during the early summer of 1937, but shortly afterwards a second Ju 86D-1 was wrecked in a landing accident. The two remaining 'Jumos' were handed over to the Spaniards in June 1937 at a cost of 282,515 Reichmarks each (£22,970), making them by far the most expensive aircraft procured from Germany by the Nationalists (a Ju 52, for instance, cost 133,190 RM).

During the summer of 1938 the 'Jumos' took part in Gen Queipo de Llano's offensive in Extremadura, usually joining formations of Spanish-crewed Ju 52s. On 12 August the pilot of one, Luis Romero Girón, was wounded when his formation, escorted by two squadrons of Spanish-piloted Fiat C.R.32s, 2-E-3 and 8-E-3, was attacked by twenty-five I-15 Chatos. At the end of that month the two Ju 86D-1s, two Henschel Hs 123s and the ten He 70Fs of 4-E-14 were formed into the Grupo Mixto 86-70, commanded by Fernando Martínez Mejías, and in February 1939 were again in constant action in Extrema-

dura until the end of the civil war. Based at León after the war, and re-coded B.4, the Ju 86D-1s remained in service until January 1946.

Span 22.5m; length 17.86m; height 4.7m.

Empty equipped weight 5,800kg; loaded weight 8,000kg.

Maximum speed 325km/h at 3,000m; cruising speed 285km/h at 2,000m; ceiling 5,900m; tactical radius 570km.

Junkers Ju 87

A veteran of the International Brigades in the Spanish Civil War, who afterwards joined the British Army and was at Dunkirk, told the author that the Stukas that had pounded British troops in Belgium in 1940 had been no novelty to him, since he had experienced them before in Spain. Many would agree with him, for it is a commonplace that the German High Command regarded Spain as a testing ground for weapons and tactics in preparation for the coming war in Europe. Yet the truth is that the Germans sent only a handful of Stukas to Spain, and used them on very few occasions. The veteran was probably thinking of the 'cadenas' described in the section on the Heinkel He 51 fighter.

'Stuka', a German acronym for 'Sturzkampfflugzeug', referred to any type of dive-bomber, but to most it meant one type of dive-bomber only, the notorious Junkers Ju 87, whose menacing silhouette and wailing engine, sometimes augmented by sirens, spread terror and panic among the columns of refugees and retreating soldiers in Poland, the Low Countries and France.

Design work on the Ju 87 began in 1933 as part of the second phase of the German dive-bomber programme, the Henschel Hs 123 single-seat dive-bomber being regarded as interim equipment until a more advanced two-seater, with better performance and a heavier bomb-load, could be developed. The prototype, the Ju 87 V1, with rectangular twin fins and rudders and large undercarriage trousers, first flew in the spring of 1935. It was destroyed when the starboard fin tore off in a dive, and the subsequent prototypes had a single fin and rudder. The most

Above: *a Junkers Ju 87A.*   Below: *a Junkers Ju 87B.*

striking features of the all-metal Ju 87 were its angular inverted-gull wing, chosen to allow space for a 250kg bomb under the fuselage and to permit a shorter and lighter undercarriage, and the radiator intake under the engine. The crew of two was protected by a sliding canopy, and defensive armament consisted of a single fixed forward-firing 7.9mm MG 17 machine gun in the starboard wing and a movable MG 15 in the observer's cockpit. The entire trailing edges of the wings consisted of control surfaces, the outer being ailerons and the inner flaps and dive brakes. Power was provided by a 640hp Junkers Jumo 210 Ca liquid-cooled engine.

A pre-production batch of Ju 87A-0s was begun in the spring of 1936, and one of these was sent to Spain for evaluation in November.

After assembly it was given the military serial 29-1 and incorporated, with the Henschel Hs 123s, into VJ/88, the experimental fighter squadron then based at Tablada, Seville. It was taken in charge of Uffz Beuser, with Zitzewitz as his observer. In February 1937 VJ/88 was transferred to Vitoria, in northern Castile, in preparation for the offensive against Bilbao. The Ju 87A-0 was treated with the utmost secrecy, and nothing is known of its history in Spain. It was still at Vitoria on 7 July 1937, but seems to have been returned to Germany shortly afterwards.

At the end of the year three Junkers Ju 87A-1s, fitted with 670hp Jumo 210 D engines and broader-bladed propellers, were transferred to Spain from the 11 Staffel LG1 at Barth, and arrived at Vitoria on 15

January 1938. The three 'Stukas', which the Spaniards nicknamed 'Estupidos' ('stupid', probably from the phonetic similarity of the two words), were formed into a special Stukakette (Stuka flight) commanded by Lt Haas, and given the serials 29-4 (Lt Haas, Fw Kramer), 29-3 (Lt Wigert, Uffz Göller) and 29-2 (Uffz Bartells, Uffz Fleisch). Painted on their undercarriage trousers was an emblematic pink sow, named *Jolanthe*. On 7 February 1938 the Kette was transferred to Calamocha Aerodrome to take part in the concluding phase of the Battle of Teruel. Here it is probable that the first true dive-bombing missions were carried out, but again no records have been found. So tight was the secrecy surrounding the Ju 87s that, it is reported, not even Gen Franco himself, during a visit to the aerodrome, was allowed into the hangar where they were kept. They played some part in the Nationalist drive through Aragón to the coast in the spring of 1938, and, apparently, made a brief appearance at the Battle of the Ebro.

In October 1938 the three Ju 87A-1s were returned to Germany and replaced by five Ju 87B-1s. The Ju 87B, the classic Stuka of the first year of the Second World War, had a redesigned fuselage, undercarriage spats in place of the trousers, and was powered by a 1,000hp (1,200hp for take-off) Jumo 211 Da engine. Armament was increased by the addition of a fixed machine gun in the port wing, and a 500kg bomb could be carried between the undercarriage legs, or a 250kg bomb under the fuselage and two 50kg bombs under the wings.

The Klemm L.25

Attached to 5.K/88, the Ju 87B-1s took part in the Catalonian campaign in January and February 1939, during which one was reported to have been shot down. Whether they were employed as dive-bombers, or on close-support duties, is not recorded. At the end of the civil war, still enveloped in secrecy, they were crated and sent to Germany, without taking part in the great Victory line-up and air display at Barajas on 12 May 1939.

Ju 87A-0 and Ju 87A-1

Span 13.8m; length 10.8m; height 3.9m; wing area 31.9sq m.

Empty weight 2,315kg; loaded weight 3,400kg.

Maximum speed 320km/h; cruising speed 275km/h; ceiling 7,000m; range 1,000km.

Ju 87B-1

Span 13.8m; length 11.1m; height 4,2m; wing area 31.95sq m.

Empty weight 2,760kg; loaded weight 4,250kg.

Maximum speed 380km/h; cruising speed 340km/h; ceiling 8,100m; range 800km.

Klemm L.20 and L.25

During the 1920s the Leichtflugzeugbau Klemm factory at Sindelfingen, near Stuttgart, Germany, achieved a reputation as one of the world's leading producers of gliders and light aircraft that were inexpensive, robust, stable, and easy to fly and maintain. An early example, a Klemm L.20 (c/n 73), was presented by Esteve Fernández to the Aero Club de Cataluña, of which he was then president, on 23 May 1933. It was a two-seat, ultralight, low-wing cantilever monoplane built of wood

and powered by a 22hp Mercedes two-cylinder engine and with a narrow-track, cross-axle undercarriage. Registered EC-GGA, it was named *Max* in honour of the president's son, Maxim, who supervised its complete overhaul and flew it more than anyone else. In 1934 it was transferred to the Aero Club de Valencia, but in July 1936 was at Getafe military aerodrome, Madrid, where it was presumably destroyed by Nationalist bombing in August or September.

By far the most successful of the Klemm light aeroplanes was the L.25 of 1927. Similar in format to the L.20, it was considerably larger, more refined aerodynamically, and had a divided, wide-track undercarriage fixed to the wing spars. Its wing span was nearly twice the length of the fuselage. Like the L.20 it was of wooden construction and, except for the fabric-covered control surfaces, was skinned with plywood. It could be fitted with almost any engine of between 40 and 120hp, the most popular type in Germany being the 80hp Hirth HM 60R four-cylinder in-line engine, and in France the 45hp Salmson 9AD radial. A modified version, the British Klemm Swallow, was produced in England. At least four Klemm L.25s were in Spain in July 1936. EC-AAO (c/n 124) and 'ANA (c/n 25 or 125), both bought by the Aero Club de España, were at Getafe in 1936.

EC-DAD (c/n 111), belonging to Antonio Claros y Romero de Castilla, and 'HAH (c/n 122), belonging to Pablo Atienza Benjumea, were both at Tablada, Seville, in 1935. It is possible that 'ANA and 'HAH were at Málaga in July 1936.

All four L.25s had Salmson 9AD engines. The Klemm at Madrid remained in Republican hands and was either destroyed in 1936 or transferred to the flying schools in Murcia. Of the three at Seville or Málaga, nothing seems to have been recorded. None survived the war.

Span 13m; length 7.5m; height 2.05m; wing area 20sq m.

Empty weight 420-480kg; loaded weight 720kg.

Maximum speed 160km/h; ceiling 4,800m; range 650km.

Klemm L.32

The Klemm L.32, which appeared in 1932, was a low-wing cantilever monoplane seating a pilot and two passengers in an enclosed cabin. It was of wooden construction, with plywood covering, and had a wide-track, fixed undercarriage. The powerplant was usually an uncowled 130-150hp Siemens SH 14A radial. Three were delivered to Spain early in 1937, and, with the military serials 30-65, -66 and -68(?), were employed by the Condor Legion as liaison aircraft. In 1939 they were taken over by the Ejercito del Aire, and in 1945 their type code was changed to L.4.

Span 12m; length 7.7m; height 2.05m; wing area 17sq m.
Empty weight 575kg; gross weight 950kg.
Maximum speed 205km/h; cruising speed 180km/h; ceiling 6,600m; range 750km.

Koolhoven FK 40

The Koolhoven FK 40 was a single-engined, four- to six-passenger high-wing cantilever monoplane powered by an uncowled 230hp Gnome-Rhône Titan radial engine. It had plywood-covered wooden wings, and a welded-steel-tube fuselage with fabric covering. The tailplane was wood, and the fin and rudder were metal framed, with fabric covering. The undercarriage consisted to two Koolhoven oleo-sprung legs, each braced to the lower fuselage by a pair of V-struts. The prototype FK 40 (c/n 101, PH-AES) first flew in November 1929 and was bought by

The Klemm L.32.

KLM. No others were built, and on 5 September 1936 PH-AES was bought by E Jacobs, who is believed to have sold it to a Spanish Republican agent. Nothing is known of its history in the Spanish Civil War.

Span 14.06m; length 11.25m; height 3.4m; wing area 30sq m.
Empty weight 1,050kg; loaded weight 2,000kg.
Maximum speed 200km/h; cruising speed 180km/h; ceiling 4,400m; range 500km.

Koolhoven FK 51, FK 51bis and FK 52

Frederick ('Frits') Koolhoven established his reputation as an aircraft designer with the Armstrong Whit-

The Koolhoven FK 40.

worth and BAT aircraft companies in Britain during the First World War, but in 1926 founded his own company at Waalhaven Airport near Rotterdam, Holland. He did not achieve much success, however, until his FK 51 won a competition, against the Avro Tutor, for a new two-seat trainer for the Netherlands air force (LVA) in June 1935. The Koolhoven FK 51 was a single-bay, equal-span staggered biplane. Its wings were built of wood, with plywood covering, only the lower wings being provided with long, narrow-chord ailerons. The fuselage was a welded-steel-tube structure covered with fabric, and the tail assembly was a separate unit attached to the fuselage by four bolts. In the later production aircraft the rounded fin was replaced by a larger triangular unit. The undercarriage was of the split-axle type, comprising two oleo-sprung shock-absorber legs and two bracing struts. The FK 51 could be fitted with dual controls, night- or blind-flying equipment, or a gun mount in the rear cockpit. The prototype was powered by a 270hp Armstrong Siddeley Cheetah V radial engine in a long-chord NACA cowling, but alternative engines included the 210hp Lycoming R-670, 225hp Continental R-680-4, 215hp Armstrong Siddeley Lynx, 250hp Hispano-Suiza 9 Qa, or 330hp Lorraine-Dietrich Super Mizar.

On 16 September 1935 the celebrated Dutch pilot Dirk L Asjes demonstrated the FK 51 prototype (c/n 5101, PH-AJV) at Cuatro Vientos, Madrid, and a few days later at Getafe. Lacalle relates that, after a

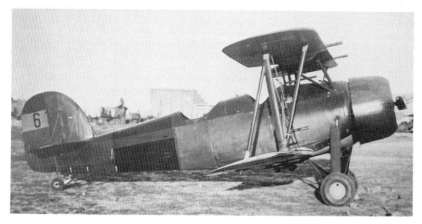

The Koolhoven FK 51 in Republican service.

brilliant display of aerobatics, Asjes landed and invited a Spanish pilot to fly with him. The invitation was accepted by Teniente Ramiro Pascual, one of the finest fighter pilots of the Aviación Militar. After a few manoeuvres Asjes, in the front cockpit, released the stick and put his hands on his head as a sign to Pascual to take over. The Koolhoven bucked and reared violently before going into a prolonged dive. Seeing the ground racing towards them, and with no indication that Pascual intended to pull out, Asjes seized the control column and, to his astonishment, found it completely free. He only managed to level the machine when its wheels were skimming the ground. Turning his head, he was surprised to see Pascual with his chin resting on his hands and quite unperturbed. The Spaniard had assumed that, by letting go the controls, Asjes was simply demonstrating the flying qualities of the aeroplane.

The Spanish government ordered twenty-eight machines, including the prototype, to be fitted with Wright Whirlwind engines. None were delivered before the Spanish Civil War broke out in July 1936, and Koolhoven feared he might be left with twenty-seven half-finished airframes on his hands until a Republican delegation visited his factory in October 1936 (probably during the same visit to Holland in which it ordered the Fokker G.1 – see Fokker D.XXI and C.X) and authorised full payment in cash through SFTA (see Appendix II). To circumvent the

June 1937; 51108 'PK, 4 July 1937; 5128 'PS and 5129 'PT, 19 July 1937; 51102 'PH, 29 July 1937; 51106 'PU, -07 'PI and -09 'PV, 2 August 1937; 51110 'PW and -11 'PX, 3 November 1937.

Aircraft c/n 5124, PH-AMT, is reported to have been a genuine single-seater. Dutch pilots flew them to the Potez aerodrome at Meaulte (Albert, France), and French pilots took them on to Toulouse-Montaudran, the Air France airport, where they were collected by Spanish

A Koolhoven FK 51 disguised as a single-seat mailplane for its transit flight across France to Spain. (Laureau)

Non-Intervention regulations, the Koolhoven FK 51s were disguised as mailplanes ordered by the King of Siam (Thailand). The rear cockpits were faired over, and the word 'POST' was stencilled on the fuselage. The prototype, re-registered PH-XYZ, was flown to Barcelona in November 1936 by a French pilot using the *non-de-guerre* 'Soufflé'. For this, an intermediary in the affair, H J van der Velde, director of the Autogiro Import Company at Hillersgeberg, was brought to trial in Holland and fined a nominal six Guilders. The next twenty-one FK 51s were struck off the Dutch register on the following dates, the actual delivery flights being several weeks earlier in every case:

c/n 5117 PH-AMK, 11 January 1937; 5118 'ML, 18 January 1937; 5120 'MO, 12 February 1937; 5121 'MP and 5122 'MR, 2 March 1937; 5123 'MS and -24 'MT, 8 March 1937; -25 'MU, 30 March 1937; 51103 'MV and -04 'MW, 26 April 1937; -05 'MX and 5127 'MY, 5

pilots. The route was changed each time, and French provincial newspapers of the day are full of reports of mysterious Dutch aircraft landing in remote fields and flying clubs and taking off again before the gendarmerie arrived. Flights were stopped by the Dutch authorities in November 1937, following denunciations in the French anti-Republican newspapers, and the last six FK 51s (51112 'ARM; -3 'N; -4 'ASE; -6 'G and -7 'H) were never delivered.

Until June 1937 the FK 51s were fitted with old, and generally worn out, 385hp Armstrong Siddeley Jaguar III and IVA radials taken from Armstrong Whitworth Argosy airliners that Imperial Airways had scrapped in 1933, but the remainder were delivered with the 425-450hp Wright Whirlwind R-975E engines contracted for, and were given the Spanish designation FK 51bis.

The first Koolhovens were used for transition training at San Javier, Cartagena, where the American mercenary pilot Frank Tinker found their control layout and handling qualities almost identical to those of the Vought Corsairs he had flown in the US Navy. Between April and June 1937 eleven FK 51s and three

FK 51bis were flown, via Catalonia and France, to the northern zone, the groups being led in each case by José Rivera Llorente. On 3 May the crew of one machine deserted at Pont Long Aerodrome, Pau, in France. In the north, the Koolhovens were used as light bombers until all but one were destroyed, the survivor crashing when its pilot tried to land at Biarritz. In the main zone the Koolhovens, with the type codes EJ (FK 51) and EK (FK 51bis), were used additionally for night-flying training at El Carmolí, Cartagena. For a time two patrullas of three aircraft each were used experimentally for the night defence of Barcelona and Valencia.

The Koolhoven FK 52 was a two-seat biplane fighter, superficially resembling an enlarged Gloster Gladiator. The prototype first flew on 9 February 1937, but crashed in August that year. It was followed by a second prototype and four production aircraft in 1938. Koolhoven always claimed that the type was a private venture, but evidence shows that it was designed, built and produced to the order of the Spanish Republican government, though it was never delivered.

After the civil war the Franco government in Spain tried to claim the four production FK 52s and six undelivered FK 51bis, but the outbreak of the Second World War curtailed negotiations. During the Soviet attack on Finland in the winter of 1939-40, Count von Rosen bought the second prototype and one of the production aircraft and presented them to the Finnish government. The others were destroyed in 1940.

Koolhoven FK 51

No figures are available for the FK 51 with the Jaguar engine, or for the FK 51bis. The following are for the FK 51 with the Armstrong Siddeley Cheetah V.

Span 9m; length 7.4m; height 2.85m; wing area 27sq m.
Empty weight 870kg; loaded weight 1,260kg.
Maximum speed 217km/h; ceiling 5,000m; range 500km.

Latécoère 28

In the years after the First World War, Les Lignes Aériennes Laté-coère, which became Aéropostale in 1927, was one of the best and most adventurous airlines in the world. Its pilots, whose hazardous mail flights over the Sahara and the Andes are unforgettably described in the books of Antoine de Saint-Exupéry, simply called it *La Ligne*, as though no other airline existed or was worth flying for. Pierre Latécoère had inherited from his father a railway rolling-stock factory which, in 1917, he had turned over to the production of one

One of the Latécoère 28s that went to Republican Spain. (Liron)

thousand Salmson biplanes for the French air force. Having created his airline after the Armistice, he decided to supply it with aircraft built by his own factory, and for the next ten years La Société Industrielle d'Aviation Latécoère (SIDAL) produced a series of biplane and monoplane single-engined transports remarkable for their ugliness.

The Latécoère 28, which first flew in 1929, was an improvement on its predecessors in this respect, despite its slab-sided fuselage, and also had a promising performance. It was a high-wing monoplane of metal and wood, with metal and fabric covering, accommodating eight to ten passengers, the pilots and navigator/radio operator being seated in a cabin placed high and forward of the wing leading edge. The wings were braced on each side by a pair of streamlined struts, and a wide-track, divided undercarriage was fitted, with its oleos attached to the forward bracing strut. Of the several versions produced, the 28/0 was powered by a 500hp Renault 12JB water-cooled engine, the 28/1 by a 500hp Hispano-Suiza 12Hbr water-cooled vee engine with a retractable radiator, and the 28/3 seaplane, with greater wing area, by a 600hp Hispano-Suiza 12Lbrx. About fifty Latécoère 28s were built altogether, including thirty-nine for Aéropostale and three or four adapted for long-distance flying. In a 28/5 named *La Frégate*, the naval pilot Lt de Vaisseau Paris

set nine speed, duration and distance records in 1930. On 12-13 May in the same year the celebrated pilot Jean Mermoz, with crew members J Dabry and L Gimié, made an historic flight from St Louis, Senegal, to Natal, Brazil, in the Latécoère 28/3 F-AJNQ *Le Comte de la Vaulx*, to test the feasibility of an airmail service from Toulouse to Buenos Aires. Off the African coast, while crossing the region known to pilots as 'the Black Hole', they had to fly through a fantastic 'forest' of waterspouts, steering the Latécoère between the undulating columns, guided only by intermittent shafts of moonlight. In all, Latécoère 28 seaplanes set fourteen world records and the landplanes set five.

In August 1933 Air France, which was created by combining five private airlines including Aéropostale, inherited the Aéropostale headquarters aerodrome at Toulouse-Montaudran and thirty-one Latécoère 28s. By 1936 about a dozen of these were still on the inventory and held in reserve at Toulouse against emergencies. Shortly after the outbreak of the Spanish Civil War, three were sent down to the Air France field at Elche, near Alicante, to fly out any French subjects who wanted to leave Spain. Although the aircraft cannot be identified with complete certainty, they were probably F-AJPG *Tornado* (c/n 922), 'PC *Sirocco* (c/n 927) and 'VB *Alizé* (c/n 933), since these were all struck off Air France strength at about this time. On 29 July 1936 the local Anarchist militia seized them on the grounds that they were more urgently needed as bombers. Pierre Cot, the French air minister, and Edouard Serre, the strongly Socialist technical director of Air France, eventually came to an agreement by which the Latécoères were sold to the Spaniards for 1,400,000 French francs (about £2,600 each in August 1936) as soon as they had completed their evacuation task.

Shortly after returning to Spain the Latécoères were converted into 'bombers' and, still displaying their Air France colours and French registrations, carried out an attack on Granada Aerodrome, an incident which provoked a loud protest from the Nationalist government.

Meanwhile, on 30 July, an Air France transport, almost certainly a Latécoère 28, made a forced landing near Alarcón, in the wilds of La Mancha. On board were two senior Comintern delegates from Moscow, Serge Rostoff (alias Michael Stefanov) and Grigori Stern, on their way from Barcelona to Madrid. Their conduct towards some Socialist militia who came to their rescue was so overbearing, however, that they were sent back to Barcelona on a lorry, the aircraft being flown to Barajas after repair. This may have been F-AJVI *Cierzo* (c/n 935), which is believed to have been the Latécoère 28 that shortly afterwards joined the *Alas Rojas* ('Red Wings') squadron at Sariñena, Aragón. Two steel tubes were slung across the passenger cabin, projecting out from each side of the fuselage, and on to each side was soldered a 'bomb rack' carrying a single 50kg bomb which could be released when the bombardier reached out and pulled a lever. On to the floor of the cabin, which had been stripped of seats, was fixed a crate containing twenty 10kg fragmentation bombs and two or three crates of incendiary bombs, which were tossed out of the windows and passenger door. For defensive armament the crew were provided with submachine guns. An attempt to mount a fixed forward-firing gun under the wing was abandoned for lack of an efficient firing device. The Latécoère carried out numerous missions with the formation nicknamed 'La Balumba' over Saragossa and Aragón until 1 September 1936, when the formation was attacked over Zuera by three Nationalist Nieuport 52s flown by Miguel García Pardo, Miguel Guerrero and Ramón Senrá. The Latécoère, piloted by Alfred Davins (a Catalonian sports flyer) and Raoul Delas (a French volunteer), was badly damaged, but was able to return to base, the only casualty being the gunner, Picanyols, whose leg had to be amputated. After this, Delas withdrew from military operations and became a transport pilot (but see Dewoitine D.53).

On 28 December 1936 a Latécoère 28 was destroyed while landing at Manises Aerodrome, Valencia, when it collided with a Nieuport 52, an incident described vividly, and for

once truthfully perhaps, by Oloff de Wet in *Cardboard Crucifix* (London, 1938). The Latécoère 28/1 F-AJHS *Tramontane* (c/n 902) was sold by Air France on 11 March 1937 to La Fédération Populaire des Sports Aéronautiques, and resold the same day to SFTA, which indicates that it almost certainly went to Republican Spain. Five other 28/1s were struck off the Air France register in 1937 and 1938, and one or more of them may have found their way to Spain as well: F-AJJF (c/n 907), 'VH *Maestral* (c/n 934), 'VJ (c/n 936), 'YM *Albrego* (c/n 938), 'MXU *Ouragan* (c/n 941) and 'MXX (c/n 944). It is possible that a single Latécoère 26/6, F-AJGH, may have been smuggled into Spain in addition to the above.

Only one Latécoère 28, based at Los Alcázares, survived the war, escaping to Oran, Algiers, with twenty-one Republican officers crammed on board, on the last day. When a Nationalist commission went to Oran in May 1939 to recover ex-Republican aircraft, they judged the 'Laté' too worn out to bother with, and merely removed some usable parts.

Span 19.25m; length 13.5m; height 3.6m; wing area 48.6sq m.
Empty weight 2,194kg; loaded weight 4,040kg.
Maximum speed 223km/h; cruising speed 220km/h; ceiling 5,500m; range 1,000km.

Letov S 231, S 331, S 431 and S 328

Between 1922 and 1936, the Vojanská továrnu na Letadla (State Aircraft Works) 'Letov' near Prague produced a series of single-seat fighters designed by Alois Smolík, of which the Letov S 20 of 1926 was the most successful. A derivative, the S 31, proved inferior to its competitor, the Avia BH-33, but was produced in small numbers to maintain employment at the state-owned factory. The S 231, an extensive redesign first flown in 1933, likewise proved inferior to its contemporary rival, the Avia B534. Nevertheless, twenty-six examples, including the prototypes, were built, and entered service with the Czechoslovakian air force in the spring and summer of 1936.

The Letov S 231 was a single-bay biplane with staggered wings of nearly equal span, powered by a 560hp Walter Merkur VS-2 (licence-built Gnome-Rhône Mercure 9Brs, itself a licence-built Bristol Mercury IV S2) in a narrow-chord cowling. It was of metal construction, the forward fuselage being skinned with metal and the rest of the airframe with fabric. The cantilever undercarriage legs had internally-sprung wheels. Armament consisted of four fixed forward-firing 7.92mm Ceska Zbrovka vz. 28 machine guns in the lower wings. In 1935 an S 231 was fitted with a 900hp Gnome-Rhône 14 K II Mistral Major radial engine in a long-chord cowling and driving a three-bladed propeller, and in May of that year, designated S 331 and registered OK-VOD, this machine set a new Czechoslovakian altitude record by attaining 10,650m. During a demonstration in Turkey, however, the fuselage suffered some damage

A Letov S 231.

The Letov S 431 (680hp Armstrong Siddeley Tiger engine) said to have been delivered with eight S 231s to Barcelona at the end of 1937.

from a power dive in which the machine touched 670km/h. Another aircraft was fitted with a 680hp Armstrong Siddeley Tiger radial and designated S 431.

The Letov S 231 was considered obsolete before it entered service, and was therefore included with the aircraft sold to the Spanish Republicans via Estonia in the winter of 1936-37. Eight machines were unloaded from the SS *Sarkani* at Sandander on 17 March 1937, and, after assembly, transferred to the Bilbao sector. Two were damaged during test flights. The story that this happened because the aircraft had been delivered without blueprints or instructions for assembly, and that the mechanics, therefore, did not know even the correct dihedral setting for the wings, is nonsense. By 8 April one had been shot down, two more lightly damaged in combat and a fourth damaged in an accident. The seventh Letov was shot down when the pilot, Juan Olmos, was bounced by Fiats while hurrying to catch up with a patrol of I-15s he had been ordered to join. The eighth was captured, more or less intact, by the Nationalists on Carreño Aerodrome, Gijón, in October 1937.

Nine Letovs arrived in Barcelona, via Estonia and France, in May and June 1938, and were assembled at Celrá. These aircraft are said to have included the S 431, despite the fact

The Letov S 331 (900hp Gnome-Rhône 14 K), said to have been shipped from Turkey in 1938.

Nationalists examine the wreckage of a Letov S 231 found in the Asturias in October 1937.

The Letov S 331 had a maximum speed of 405km/h, and could climb to 5,000m in 6.7min. Range 410km.

Lioré et Olivier LeO 20 and 213

The Lioré et Olivier LeO 20 B5, which first flew in 1926, was the standard French night bomber from about 1928 until 1937. A three-bay biplane of metal construction with fabric covering, it carried a crew of four or five, the pilot and copilot being seated in an open cockpit. Up to 500kg of bombs was carried, some internally and the rest on racks under the fuselage and wings. Its defensive armament consisted of five 7.7mm machine guns, two each in the nose and dorsal positions and one in a large ventral 'dustbin' under the fuselage. The LeO 20 was powered by two uncowled 420hp Gnome-Rhône 9 Ady radial engines, and the undercarriage legs were protected by large trousers. With its square-cut wings and tailplanes, boxy fuselage and curious projecting window in front of the nose-gunner's cockpit, it was a typical French military aircraft of the period.

In August 1926 two prototypes of a civil transport derivative, designated Lioré et Olivier LeO 21, achieved the highest score in a competition for transport aircraft organised by the Service Téchnique de l'Aéronautique. The first prototype, F-AIFD *Capitaine Ferber*, was powered by two 420hp Gnome-Rhône 9 Ab radial engines mounted on the lower wings, but the second, F-AIFE *L P Mouillard*, was re-engined with two 450hp Renault 12Ja vee engines before being intro-

that this machine is reported as having been destroyed in an accident during flight trials in the summer or autumn of 1936. They were fitted with a forward-firing Vickers gun in each lower wing and a third, synchronised, Vickers mounted in the upper fuselage. Bearing the type code CL, the Letovs were formed into the 2ª Escuadrilla of Grupo 71, led by Capitán José Bastida Porrán, and assigned to coastal patrol and city defence duties. During the night of 10 September 1938 one of these machines (CL-004) came down, unarmed, in a vineyard near Pradés, Perpignan, France, and was wrecked. The pilot, who had been flying on a mysterious errand from Toulouse to Vich (Catalonia), was whisked to hospital by the local police before being taken over the frontier. Meanwhile, the S 331 OK-VOD, after being repaired, was shipped to Barcelona directly from Istanbul. Indeed, as a Czechoslovakian aviation historian alleges that six Letov S 328 two-seat light bombers were exported to Republican Spain through a clandestine operation centred in Turkey, and as the Grumman GE-23s were (and Hawker Fury IIs would have been) imported by Republican Spain via Turkey, it seems possible that all the S 231s in the

main zone came through the intercession of Turkey as well.

Little is known of their military operations, except that several were destroyed on the ground by the Condor Legion during the Catalonian campaign. Three survived the civil war and received the type code 3W in the Ejercito del Aire. One was still flying on 1 March 1940. Of the Letov S 328s, if any were delivered, there is no surviving record.

Letov S 231

Span 10.06m; length 7.8m; height 3m; wing area 21.5sq m.

Empty weight 1,280kg; loaded weight 1,770kg.

Maximum speed 348km/h at 5,000m; climb to 5,000m in 8.2min; ceiling 9,000m; range 450km.

The ex-Armée de l'Air Lioré et Olivier LeO 213 at Los Alcázares. A Republican red band has already been painted round the fuselage. It is said to have been shot down on its first bombing raid. (Arráez)

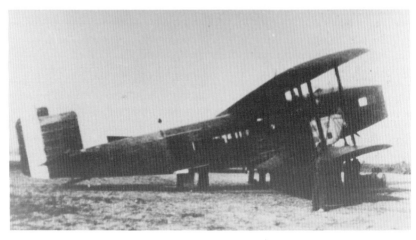

duced on the Air Union Paris–London route in July 1927. The LeO 21 accommodated a crew of two and eighteen passengers, six in the forward cabin in the nose and twelve in the main cabin behind the cockpit. The first production version, the LeO 213 (F-AIVG), appeared in 1928, and in 1929 F-AIFD was refitted internally with a bar and redesignated LeO 211. The second prototype, redesignated LeO 212, was converted, in collaboration with La Compagnie Wagons-Lits, into a twelve-seat flying restaurant, complete with bar and barman, and served what were perhaps the best luncheons ever to be offered on any airliner.

Ten further LeO 213s were built for Air Union, the whole fleet bearing the fleet title *La Rayon d'Or* on the starboard side of the nose and *The Golden Ray* on the port side, and being painted in an attractive gold, red and white scheme. Eleven of these passed to Air France after its creation in August 1933, one crashing at Croydon in May 1934. Later that year nine were transferred to the Armée de l'Air as troop-transports and parachute trainers. The remaining civil aircraft was lost in an accident. At least one LeO 213, and possibly a Leo 20, flew in the Spanish Civil War, although the evidence corroborating their presence is, as with so many of the aircraft of that war, confusing.

According to the French author Commandant Jean Gisclon (*Des avions at des hommes*, Paris, 1969; pp 165 ff), an ancient Lioré twin-engined biplane came into the possession of the international squadron at Cuatro Vientos at the end of August 1936. It was unarmed, and its bomb racks did not work. Nevertheless, a mechanic managed to install some bombs inside the fuselage, and two machine guns were fitted, one in the nose and one in the dorsal position. On returning from its first bombing raid, escorted by a de Havilland Dragon Rapide, it was attacked by a patrol of Fiat C.R.32s

and shot down, but not before its gunners had shot down one of the Fiats. The crew escaped unhurt. It is hard to judge the truth of this story. The machine Gisclon describes was apparently a LeO 20 bomber, since it had bomb racks. Nevertheless, if the French crew really used this aircraft for a bombing mission, they should be recognised as having performed a feat of extraordinary heroism.

The earliest and only record of a Lioré being flown to Spain during the civil war appeared in *L'Action française* for 3 October 1936 (a month after the episode related by Gisclon), which reported that a LeO 20, No 104, was due to leave Le Bourget that day for Barcelona, with a crew of three and carrying medical supplies. This, too, was evidently an ex-Armée de l'Air bomber from its serial 104, since the 213s in the Armée de l'Air were numbered up to '11'. However, a photograph reportedly taken at Los Alcázares, Cartagena, during the early months of the civil war shows a LeO 213 in Armée de l'Air colouring, with the French vertical tricolor on the rudder, but with what appears to be a Spanish Republican red band on the fuselage. Finally, Hilaire du Berrier, an American who flew in Spain in November 1936, showed the author a newspaper photograph of various aircraft on a Spanish Republican aerodrome in which, it is believed, a LeO 213 was visible in the middle distance. Unfortunately this photograph is now lost. All that can be said at present, therefore, is that one of each type evidently took part in the Spanish Civil War, albeit briefly.

Span 24.43m; length 15.95m; height 4.38m; wing area 105.5sq m.

Empty weight 3,487kg; loaded weight 5,700kg.

Maximum speed 190km/h at 1,000m; cruising speed 175km/h; ceiling 4,500m; range 560km.

Lockheed 5B Vega

Allan and Malcolm Loughead began building aeroplanes at Santa Barbara, California, in 1912, but were forced out of business nine years later by the hundreds of surplus military aircraft that flooded the market after the First World War. In 1926, on the basis of a design for a cantilever, high-wing four-passenger monoplane proposed by John K Northrop, the Lockheed Aircraft Company was founded. In a rented Hollywood garage work began on the Model 1 Vega, a name suggested by Northrop himself. Despite the loss of the prototype in the Dole Race from Oakland, California, to Hawaii in August 1927, the Vega was an immediate success, and 128, in five successively modernised versions, were built before production ceased in June 1934. No fewer than twelve 'aviation firsts' were achieved in Vegas, including the first transarctic and transantarctic flights, both in 1928, and the first solo flight round the world (by the *Winnie Mae*, flown by Wiley Post).

One reason for the Vega's popularity and success was its clean shape, uncluttered by struts, and its beautifully streamlined monocoque fuselage. The outer plywood shell was built in two halves, sheets of spruce being glued together by hand, and each half pressed down by inflatable bags into a large concrete mould. The Vega was the sire of a whole family of successful high-per-

A Lockheed Vega of the type sold to Spanish Republicans by the Mexican Coronel Fierro. (Bodie Archives, via R S Allen)

formance monoplanes developed by Lockheed, and set the company on the way to becoming one of the world's major aircraft manufacturers.

Only one Lockheed Vega flew in the Spanish Civil War. This was a seven-passenger Model 5B, NC534M (c/n 103), powered by a 450hp Pratt & Whitney Wasp C radial engine. It was sold in 1929 to the Mexican airline CAT (Corporación de Aeronáutica de Transportes) and re-registered XA-BHI. In 1934 it was sold to Coronel Roberto Fierro Villalobos, then Mexico's foremost pilot (see Lockheed Sirius), re-engined, and re-registered XA-AAD. In December 1936 Fierro, who was by then Director General de Aeronáutica in Mexico and a strong supporter of the Spanish Republicans, sold it to the Spanish Ambassador in Mexico. Together with a Lockheed Sirius and an Orion, both likewise supplied by Fierro, it sailed for Spain aboard the *Sil* on 22 December 1936, reaching Santander on 12 January 1937. After serving with the Basque air arm for some weeks, the Vega was flown across Nationalist territory to the main Republican zone, where it joined the ranks of LAPE. Its Spanish registration and LAPE fleet number are not recorded. The LAPE pilot José-María Carreras, who flew it frequently, told the author that it had neither engine cowling nor undercarriage spats, and that blotches of green and ochre had been painted on its original red finish by way of camouflage. Its final disposition is unknown.

Span 41ft; length 27ft 6in; height 8ft 4½in; wing area 275sq ft.
Empty weight 2,490lb; loaded weight 4,265lb.
Maximum speed 185mph; cruising speed 155mph; ceiling 27,000ft; range 690 miles.

Lockheed 8 Sirius

When John K Northrop left Lockheed, in 1928, he had already begun designing the all-metal cantilever low-wing monoplane that was to become the Northrop Alpha (see Northrop Delta). In 1929 his chief assistant at Lockheed, Gerard Vultee, met Col Charles A Lindbergh,

and in the course of discussion formulated an aeroplane of similar general design, but retaining the all-wood construction of the Vega and Lockheed Air Express, for the celebrated aviator's personal use. The result was the Lockheed Model 8 Sirius (c/n 140) in which Lindbergh broke the American transcontinental speed record in April 1930. Shortly afterwards, Lindbergh had it converted into a seaplane and, for the next four years used it for survey flights to Alaska, Japan, Africa, Greenland and South America on behalf of Pan American Airways. Fifteen Siriuses were built, most for record-breaking or experimental purposes. In September 1930 Sirius X119W (c/n 153) was used to test the first fully-retractable undercarriage, the new model being named Altair. Later, four more Siriuses (c/ns 143, 145, 152 and 165) were converted into Altairs and, of the four original Altairs also built, one (c/n 180, an experimental version with a metal fuselage) was converted into an Orion.

The third Sirius (c/n 149) was ordered from the factory by an officer of the Mexican Aviación Militar, Coronel Roberto Fierro Villalobos, who intended to 'put Mexican aviation on map', as he said, by making a long-distance flight from New York, via Mexico, to Brazil, and thence to Africa and Paris. The $25,000 for the Sirius was raised largely by public subscription and topped up by state governors and military officers, and the aeroplane, painted gleaming

Coronel Fierro's Lockheed Sirius Ana-huac, *shipped to Santander in December 1936.* (Mandrake Collection, via R S Allen)

white with light red sun-ray trim, registered X-BADA and named *Anahuac* (Aztec – 'Land of Herons'), was delivered in May 1930. It had a 450hp Pratt & Whitney Wasp C radial engine. On 23 June 1930 Fierro and Capitán Arnulfo Cortés flew 2,152 miles non-stop from New York to Mexico City in a record-breaking 16hr 30min. The flight, through several violent storms, had been perilous, however, and, although Fierro and Cortés were wildly acclaimed in Mexico, President Ortiz forbade any further long-distance attempts, and especially the flight to Africa.

The *Anahuac* thereafter became the property of the Mexican government and the pride of Mexican aviation. In 1935 it was presented to Fierro, by the Director General de Aeronáutica, for his personal use, and in December 1936 he presented it (or, as some alleged, sold it for $25,000) to the Spanish Republicans. Transported to Santander on board the Republican ship *Sil*, the Sirius is said to have been converted into a light bomber for service with the Basque air arm and to have been shot down, though there is no documented evidence of this. Its final disposition is unknown.

Span 42ft 9½in; length 27ft 6in; height 9ft 3in.
Empty weight 2,974lb; loaded weight 4,600lb.
Maximum speed 201mph; cruising speed 173mph; ceiling 19,948ft; normal range 674 miles.

Lockheed 9 Orion

The last of the wooden-airframed single-engined Lockheeds, the Model 9 Orion was also the most interesting and the one to exercise

A Republican Lockheed Orion at La Senia French military aerodrome, Oran, Algeria, after the end of the Spanish Civil War. (Arráez)

Dr Brinkley's high-speed 9F Orion. (R S Allen)

the greatest influence on designers in Europe. After trials with the retractable undercarriage on the 9A Sirius c/n 153 in May–June 1930 had proved satisfactory, the Lockheed design team, under Richard A von Hake (Gerard Vultee's successor as chief engineer), began work on a commercially exploitable development – a single-engined low-wing cantilever monoplane capable of carrying six passengers, or the equivalent in mail or cargo, at a cruising speed of at least 170mph. The prototype, at first called the 'Sirius six-passenger cabin plane' and briefly 'Altair Model D', comfortably exceeded all expectations when, powered by a 450hp Pratt & Whitney SC, it showed a top speed of 210mph and a range of 650 miles at 180mph.

A commercial aeroplane with a cruising speed which equalled the maximum speed of most fighters in service, and a maximum speed which exceeded that of the latest fighter prototypes, presented an alarming challenge to military staffs all over the world – so alarming, indeed, that many dismissed the performance claimed for the Lockheed Orion as typical 'Yankee exaggeration'. In 1932, however, two Orions, the first American commercial aircraft to be bought in Europe, were purchased by Swissair through Alfred and Ignacio Miranda (see Seversky SEV-3). 'Die rote Orions' (so called because they were painted bright red with white trim) created a sensation by cutting the schedule on the 380-mile Zurich–Munich–Vienna route from 4hr 20min to 2hr 30min.

The Orion was the first production aircraft to have a retractable undercarriage and to establish the format that has become standard for high-performance single-engined, propeller-driven aeroplanes. Thirty-six Orions were built altogether, including fourteen Model 9s, ten Model 9Ds, and a number of individual 'Specials' and conversions, including the 9C Special (c/n 180) converted from the experimental Altair with a metal fuselage. As a

result of their popularity as airliners and their achievements as record-breakers, they were among the best-known aircraft of the early 1930s.

During the Spanish Civil War, fourteen Orions (including the last three built) were bought by the Spanish Republicans:

1 9D Orion (c/n 209), F-AKHC (550hp Pratt & Whitney SID Wasp). Ordered by the French racing pilot Michel Detroyat for the Mac-Robertson England–Australia Air Race of 1934, and re-engined at the Morane-Saulnier factory with a Hispano-Suiza 9V radial of 575hp. Its performance was disappointing, and Detroyat withdrew. The Orion was acquired by the French Ministère de l'Air and tested by CEMA at Villacoublay, Paris, where the test pilot, Capitaine Vernhol, thought the aircraft nothing very special and its undercarriage, though good enough, perhaps, for the smooth tarmac runways of North America, too frail for the rough grass aerodromes of Europe. Painted silver-grey with a scarlet flash down the fuselage sides, it remained at Villacoublay, where it

was used by ministerial staff for official visits, until 25 July 1936. On that day Pierre Cot, the air minister, placed it at the disposal of André Malraux, who, with Edouard Corniglion-Molinier as pilot, was to fly to Madrid to make personal contact with members of the beleaguered Spanish government and gather intelligence on the political situation. Malraux returned in the Orion on 27 July, bringing with him the new Spanish ambassador, Alvarez de Albornoz. (The previous ambassador, Juan de Cárdenas, had joined the Nationalists.) The Orion made two more trips to Spain thereafter, the last on 12 August 1936, with Georges Cornez as pilot and passengers Lucien Vogel (editor of *Vu* magazine), Paul Ristelheuber (for *le Petit Journal*), Madeleine Jacob (the Communist *l'Humanité*) and the soon-to-be-famous photographer Robert Capa. During the flight from Barcelona to Madrid the Orion made a forced landing 52 miles south of Alcañiz, in one of the remotest parts of Aragón, and suffered some damage to the undercarriage and port wingtip. In response to urgent instructions telephoned from Madrid to bring the aeroplane to Barajas Airport, the local militia loaded the Orion on to two ox carts linked by

Laura Ingalls's custom-built 9D Special Orion Auto da Fé, *intended for the MacRobertson England-Australia Air Race. The photograph is of unusual interest since it shows the original Lockheed factory at Burbank, California.* (William T Larkins, via R S Allen)

pivoted wooden planks and set off. At the first village they found that the Orion's wings prevented it from passing between the houses. Seeing that the machine was made of wood, the militia sent for the village carpenter and told him to saw the wings off, which he did. With the wings roped to the Orion's fuselage, the militia proudly resumed their arduous journey to the capital.

2 The two Swissair 9B Orions, c/n 189 (X12231, CH-167, HB-LAH) and c/n 190 (X12232, CH-168, HB-LAJ) (575hp Wright Cyclone R-1820-E), were purchased as part of the deal that procured the Swissair Douglas DC-2 and Clark GA-43A. In Spain, one joined the LAPE fleet and the other was used by the Republican air force as a liaison and transport aircraft. In his memoirs, the American fighter pilot Frank Tinker records seeing it on 13 April 1937, piloted by another American, Joseph Rosemarin, and still in its red Swissair livery.

3 Five Orions formed part of the Wolf shipment (see Appendix II and Vultee V1-A). Seven were originally bought by Wolf, of which one (Model 9E c/n 193, NC12278, ex-TWA) crashed at Jackson, Ohio, on 18 December 1936 en route to New York, and a second (c/n 212, see **5** below) was exchanged at the last minute for the prototype Vultee V1. The Orions shipped to France by Mrs Wolf were:

Model 9 c/n 183, NC12225 (450hp Pratt & Whitney Wasp SC). This had originally belonged to Varney Air Service, and was named *North Wind* and painted white with red trim. Transferred to Varney's Mexican subsidiary Líneas Aéreas Occidentales in 1934 as XA-BHC it was sold, via Maj Ervin and Charles Babb, to Wolf.

Model 9 c/n 185, NC12227 (XA-BHD), *Winter Wind* (450hp Pratt & Whitney Wasp SC). History as above.

Model 9F c/n 196, NC12284 (645hp Wright Cyclone R-1820-F2). Bought by the celebrated Dr John R Brinkley III, a wealthy Texan surgeon specialising in 'rejuvenation' by means of goatgland transplants, and owner of a commercial radio station, it was sold to Lockheed and resold, via Ervin and Babb, to Wolf. It had a top speed of 242mph, which made it, Brinkley liked to boast, the fastest privately-owned passenger aeroplane in the world. It was painted white with black trim, and had the name *John R Brinkley* on the rear-fuselage sides.

Model 9D c/n 205, NC13747 (550hp Pratt & Whitney Wasp SIDI). Ex-Oil Field Airlines of Texas, this Orion was sold, via Ervin and Babb, to Wolf.

Model 9D Special c/n 211, NC14222 *Auto da Fé* (550hp Pratt & Whitney Wasp SIDI). Built for Laura Ingalls, with extra fuel tanks in the passenger cabin, for the MacRobertson England–Australia Air Race of 1934, this Orion was not completed in time. Painted black with scarlet trim, and with the passenger windows covered over and a cross-and-crescent emblem below the cockpit, it set several transcontinental records in 1935 and came second in the 1936 Bendix Cup race. It was sold, via Ervin and Babb, to Wolf.

As related in the section on the Vultees, the Orions were unloaded at Le Havre in January 1937, assembled at Bléville, and transferred to the two aerodromes at Toussus, Paris, of which one had been bought by SFTA (see Appendix II). It is known that c/n 183 was registered F-AQAS, c/n 185 F-AQAV, and c/n 205 F-AQAR, but it is not known how many of the five eventually reached Spain or what became of them there. In 1938 Dr Brinkley's home town of Del Rio, Texas, was disturbed by reports that his Orion had been shot down, and he himself killed in Spain, a story given some credence by the fact that he had been absent for several months. He reappeared shortly after, however, having been sailing to Newfoundland in his yacht. There is a photograph of the Republican Lockheed Orion taken at Oran, Algeria, where it had escaped at the end of the civil war, and it is said that this was c/n 196. If that is true, then his Orion was not shot down, but became the one and only Lockheed Orion recovered by the Nationalists after the war. Laura Ingalls likewise heard that her Orion had been destroyed in Spain.

4 Model 9 c/n 186, NC12228 (450hp Pratt & Whitney Wasp SC). Ex-Varney and Líneas Aéreas Occidentales; then, after other owners, sold to Charles 'Pistol Pete' Baughan (see R E G Davies, *Airlines of Latin America since 1919*, London, 1984, pp 23, 28). Bought by Fritz Bieler, this was presumably the Orion that was shipped to Santander on board the *Sil* (see Lockheed Vega and Sirius). The sale to the Spaniards was disguised by the Orion's being recorded as 'sold to Mark Wolf, from Arizona, for export, 1937'. Coronel Roberto Fierro (see Lockheed Sirius) played some part in the transaction, claiming that he mortgaged his house to pay for this aircraft, which he then gave to the Republicans. When the Orion arrived at Santander the Basque air arm used it as a light bomber. It was presumably destroyed.

5 Five Lockheed Orions, purchased on behalf of the Spanish ambassador in Mexico, were among the twenty-eight aircraft at Vera Cruz and Mexico City airports during most of 1937, awaiting shipment to Republican Spain (see Appendix II). Two Orions were bought in the USA by the Spanish Republican purchasing agent Comandante José Melendreras Sierra, though they were registered to Fritz Bieler (a German pilot resident in Mexico and a close friend of Fierro), and three were bought from Mexican owners:

9F Orion c/n 212, NC14246, XA-BDO (650hp Wright Cyclone R-1820-F2). Bought from Phillips Petroleum for $13,500. This was the Orion relinquished by Wolf in favour of the Vultee V1 prototype. Flown from Calexico, California, by Bieler on 17 December 1936. It was the last Lockheed Orion built.

9D Orion, c/n 202, NC231Y, XA-BDZ (550hp Pratt & Whitney Wasp SIDI). Bought from Carlos Panini, who ran an aerial 'bus service' between Mexico City and neighbouring mining towns. At Vera Cruz, 26 December 1936.

9D-1 Orion, c/n 204, NC232Y, XA-BDY, (550hp Pratt & Whitney Wasp SIDI). Fitted with flaps. History as c/n 202.

9 Orion, c/n 181, NC12223, XA-BEU (450hp Pratt & Whitney Wasp SC). Bought from G E Ruckstell, Grand Canyon, Arizona, via Bieler. Flown from Calexico by Cloyd Clevenger (the Spanish Ambassador's personal pilot at this time) on 28 December 1936.

9 Orion, c/n 172, NC975Y, XA-AHQ (450hp Pratt & Whitney Wasp SC). Bought from Líneas Aéreas Mineras SA (LAMSA).

This aircraft had been used for hauling gold from Mexico City to San Francisco. Arrived at Vera Cruz in January or February 1937.

The number of aircraft that sailed for Bordeaux on the *Ibai* in December 1937 is uncertain. According to the list made by the Spanish ambassador himself it included four Lockheed Orions, but according to the US Ambassador there were only two (c/n 181 and c/n 212). Presumably one or two crossed into Spain in the spring of 1938, while the frontier was open. Presumably, too, they were either destroyed during the fall of Catalonia, or flew Republican refugees into France and were never returned, for, as is said above, only one Lockheed Orion (the aircraft at Oran) was recovered by the Nationalists at the end of the war.

In 1937, after a scheme to obtain Sikorsky S-53 amphibian flying-boats came to nought, the Spanish Republican purchasing agent, Cdte Melendreras, ordered six sets of Edo floats, complete with mounting struts, to enable the Lockheed Orions in Spain to be converted into seaplanes, since coastal reconnaissance aircraft were needed urgently by the Republicans. To Melendreras's indignation, the Republican Minister for Marine and Air, Indalecio Prieto, cancelled the order because, according to Melendreras, his technical advisers had maintained that the floats would make the Orions too slow. What the technical advisers (who included the brilliant Gen Emilo Herrera) had in fact said was that the floats would not only reduce the speed of the Orions, but would make them dangerously nose-heavy, as shown by the fatal crash of the Orion-Explorer seaplane in which Wiley Post and Will Rogers had been killed during their round-the-world flight in 1935.

9 Orion
Span 42ft 9¼in; length 28ft 11in; height 9ft 8in; wing area (all versions) 294sq ft.
Empty weight 3,250lb; loaded weight 5,200lb.
Maximum speed 210mph; cruising speed 180mph; range 650 miles.

9B Orion
Dimensions as above, except length, 27ft 6in.

Empty weight 3,570lb; loaded weight 5,400lb.
Maximum speed 225mph; cruising speed 195mph; range 580 miles.

9D Orion
Dimensions as Model 9, except length, 28ft 4in.
Empty weight 3,640 lb; loaded weight 5,800lb.
Maximum speed 226mph; cruising speed 200mph; range 500 miles.

9F-1 Orion
Dimensions as above, except length, 28ft 1½in.
Empty weight 4,100lb; loaded weight 5,800lb.
Maximum speed 235mph; cruising speed 210mph.

Lockheed 10A Electra

In June 1932 the Lockheed company, which had been in a parlous state since the collapse of its parent company, the Detroit Aircraft Corporation, the year before, was refinanced and re-established as the Lockheed Aircraft Corporation by a group of airline owners and businessmen. At first they proposed to build an updated, all-metal development of the Orion, but the advent of the Boeing 247 and Douglas DC-2 in 1933, and the probability that new safety regulations would soon be introduced, making two or more engines mandatory for all commercial passenger aircraft, persuaded them to adopt a twin-engined format. After windtunnel tests the single fin and rudder was replaced by a twin-fin-and-rudder tail unit, which promised better control while flying on one engine, and on 23 February 1934 the prototype Model 10A Electra (named after the lost pleiad of the constellation Taurus) made its first flight. It was a sleek, all-metal, low-wing monoplane with a retractable undercarriage, powered by two 450hp Pratt & Whitney Wasp SB radial engines in deep-chord NACA cowlings, and had accommodation for a pilot and ten passengers (later changed to pilot, copilot and eight passengers).

The Electra was an immediate success, being ordered by more than a score of airlines and private purchasers in the USA, Canada, Latin

The Lockheed Electra (ex-NC14946) captured by the Nationalists on the Mar Cantabrico *and used by Gen Kindelán as his personal transport.*

America and Europe. Altogether, 149 were built, and of the various sub-types the most notable were the Model 10B (450hp Wright R-975-Ee engines) and Model 10E (550hp Pratt & Whitney Wasp R-1340-S3H1 engines). It was in one of the seven Lockheed Electras bought by British Airways (G-AEPR) that Neville Chamberlain made the first of his 'peace in our time' flights to Munich during the Sudetenland crisis of September 1938. From the Electra were developed the Model 12A, the Model 18 and the Hudson and Ventura bombers.

Two Lockheed Electras flew in the Spanish Civil War:

1 c/n 1033, NC14946. This aircraft was bought for the Spanish Republicans by Robert Cuse from the May Company (a chain of department stores) in December 1936. It was shipped on the *Mar Cantábrico* with seven other aircraft and captured, at sea, by the Nationalists (see Appendix II and Vultee V1-A), whose air chief, Gen Kindelán, used it as his personal transport. It survived the civil war and bore the military serial 42-2.

2 c/n 1035, NC14948. This Electra was bought by Comandante Melendreras, the Republican purchasing agent in the USA, from R W Norton of Shreveport, Los Angeles, on 24 December 1936, and flown to Mexico via San Antonio, Texas, on the same day without an export licence. Hastily re-registered XA-BDQ, it

was used a week later by the Spanish Ambassador in Mexico, don Félix Gordón Ordás, for what he intended to be a clandestine journey to Washington to discuss aircraft and arms purchases with the Spanish embassy. Unfortunately the Electra made a belly-landing in fog at Brownsville, Texas, when the pilot, Cloyd Clevenger, forgot to lower the undercarriage.

Repaired and returned to Mexico, the Electra was among the aircraft shipped to Bordeaux on the *Ibai* on 23 December 1937. It crossed to Republican Spain between 19 March and 13 June 1938 (when the Franco-Spanish frontier was opened for the passage of supplies), and served as a transport, presumably with the LAPE fleet. It is believed to have been the last aircraft to escape from Republican Spain at the end of the civil war, taking a group of senior officers (including Gen Hidalgo de Cisneros, the Republican air chief) from Los Llanos Aerodrome, Albacete, to safety in France.

Returned from France to Spain with the surviving Douglas DC-2s and other aircraft in April 1939, it was re-registered 42-4 (according to some authorities; according to others this number was given to the DC-2 c/n 1417, ex-EC-BBE *Sagitario*).

Both Electras were still flying with the Ejercito del Aire in 1940 and one, renumbered L.10, until the 1950s.

Span 55ft; length 38ft 7in; height 11ft 5½in; wing area 485.5sq ft.

Empty weight 6,720lb; loaded weight 9,737lb.

Maximum speed 208mph; cruising speed 182mph; service ceiling 21,650ft; range 810 miles.

Loire 46 C1

In the section on the Dewoitine D.372 mention is made of the uncertainties facing aircraft designers and air staffs during the early 1930s over the future of the single-seat fighter, and of how the fifteen prototypes submitted for the French C1 fighter programme of 1930 represented almost every conceivable format. Four of them (ANF Les Mureaux 170, Dewoitine D.560, Gourdou-Leseurre GL-482 and Loire 43) were gull-wing monoplanes.

The gull wing had been devised by the Polish aeronautical engineer Zygmut Pulawski to allow a fighter pilot the best possible all-round field of view. From his first prototype, the P.Z.L. P.1 of 1929, was developed the line of highly successful single-seat fighters that, for a few years, put the company in the front rank of the world's fighter manufacturers. The dramatic shape of gull-wing monoplanes also excited the imaginations of popular illustrators and such, who, ignorant of the reasons for the design, thought it 'futuristic'. Thus, in the film *Things to Come* (1936), appeared a formation of huge multi-engined bombers of the 'Pterodactyl' configuration, but with gull wings which could have served no useful purpose whatever. Nor, for that matter, did Pulawski's emulators outside Poland achieve his success. None of the four French prototypes was successful, chiefly because their wings were so thoughtfully designed that the pilot, far from enjoying an excellent field of view, was practically unable to see anything forwards, sideways or downwards. M Asselot, the chief designer of Les Ateliers et Chantiers de la Loire, an old ship-building firm that had recently amalgamated with the Nieuport company and expanded into aircraft manufacture, considered that the Loire 43 (which had been destroyed in a crash) had sufficient promise to be worth developing. A second and equally unsuccessful prototype, the Loire 45, was followed in 1934 by the Loire 46, which was such a marked improvement on its predecessors as to be almost a complete redesign.

The result, at least when seen from the front, was a beautiful and shapely aeroplane, its most obvious defect being the complex arrange-

Loire 46, showing tail assembly.

the five pre-series aircraft, since no trace of them can be found in surviving records. This possibility is supported by the assertion (believed to be uncorroborated) that they bore the construction numbers 2 to 6 inclusive. However, the fact that they arrived bearing the French military serials N-089 to N-093 (of which a photograph exists) suggests rather that they were the next batch of production examples intended for the Armée de l'Air. It is known that by November 1936 the 6me Escadre had received only twenty-two Loire 46s, and that French squadron records suggest that more Loire 46s were built than were recorded.

The details of this clandestine sale are similarly obscure, but the key figure was apparently Joseph Sadi-Lecointe. As a military pilot in the early 1920s he had gained the world speed record five times and the world altitude record twice, and until 1934 he had been chief test pilot of the Nieuport (after 1930 Loire-Nieuport) company. In 1936 he was director of APNA (the French association of pilots and navigators) and training supervisor to the state-sponsored Fédération Populaire des Sports Aéronautiques (FPSA), an

ment of struts supporting the wings. It had an elegantly spatted, wide-track undercarriage. After various modifications, which included replacing the 880hp Gnome-Rhône 14 Kes radial engine in a blistered cowling with a 930hp 14 Kfs in a smooth cowling, and changing the armament of two 20mm Oerlikon cannon for four MAC 34 7.7mm machine guns in the wings, five pre-series Loire 46s (more correctly called Loire-Nieuport 46 C1s) were ordered in January 1935. In May 1935 a further sixty were ordered for the Armée de l'Air. Like the sixty Blériot SPAD 510 biplanes ordered at the same time, the Loires were intended as stop-gaps until more modern fighters became available. By then, after so many delays in production, it was evident to all but die-hard traditionalists that, in a time of rapid development and rearmament, such fighters were already obsolescent. The first Loire 46 was delivered to the 6me Escadre at Chartres in June 1936, six months behind schedule.

A month later civil war broke out in Spain, and on 5, 6 and 7 September 1936 five Loire 46s landed on the Republican aerodrome at Prat de

A Loire 46. (Liron)

Llobregat, Barcelona. Two of the pilots who brought them were identified by the French newspaper reporters at their point of departure, Toulouse-Montaudran Airport, as a Belgian (probably André Autrique, see Avia BH-33) and Roger Nouvel, a sports pilot adding to his income by ferrying aircraft to Spain in defiance of Non-Intervention. It has been suggested that these must have been

The remains of a Loire 46 claimed as shot down by Montegnacco on 25 or 26 September 1936 over Talavera de la Reina. It may, however, be the Loire flown by Lacalle which suffered engine failure, came down between the lines, and was bombarded by artillery.

organisation active in training pilots, and procuring aircraft, for the Spanish Republic during the civil war. Early on Sunday morning, 26 July 1936, a week after the outbreak of the fighting, Sadi-Lecointe visited the Loire factory in Saint-Nazaire, ostensibly to enquire about renting a local flying field for the FPSA.

When, at the end of August 1936, an air force officer came to Villacoublay from Chartres to receive the next five Loire 46s, he was informed that they had been 'sold to the Kingdom of Hédjaz' (Saudi Arabia) as a matter of national priority. From Barcelona the Loires, their French roundels changed into red discs á la Japonaise, were flown to Cuatro Vientos, Madrid. Twenty-four MAC machine guns, plus firing mechanisms and ammunition, had been sent separately by road to evade the Non-Intervention regulations. Unfortunately the lorries were stopped in the wilds of Aragón by CNT (Anarchist) militia, who sent the guns and ammunition to the front and, not knowing what they were for, threw away the precious firing mechanisms. Thus M Midolle, an ex-air force armourer working for Air France who had been sent secretly to Spain by the technical director of the airline, the strongly pro-Republican Edouard Serre (see Gourdou-Leseurre GL-32), waited a week in vain for the guns to appear, while the Loires flew unarmed patrols to raise the morale of the Republican troops below. Eventually they were fitted with old Vickers guns and improvised firing devices, the problem of installing which was aggravated by the curvature of the gull wings.

Four Loires appeared in combat on 21 September with indecisive results, since the guns of all four jammed after a few rounds each, but over Toledo on the 25 September, Rafael Peña, flying (according to some accounts) a Loire 46, shot down a Junkers Ju 52/3m, the first of this type to be shot down in the civil war. As with the Loires in French service later, however, the Gnome-Rhône 14 Kfs engine was a cause of endless trouble, and in Spain two were lost through engine failure, the pilot on each occasion being Teniente Andrés García Lacalle. The second of these, which came

down between Republican and Nationalist lines, was later claimed by the Nationalists as an aerial victory. One Loire was certainly shot down on 16 October 1936 by the leading Nationalist air ace Joaquín García Morato, for its Yugoslav pilot, Guiseppe Krizai, baled out and was taken prisoner. (He was later exchanged, and in 1938 commanded the 1ª Escuadrilla of Grupo 72, see Dewoitine D.371.) The fourth Loire was also claimed to have been shot down near Getafe, Madrid, on 21 October. The fifth was reportedly destroyed by a bombing raid on Getafe two days later.

However, Oloff de Wet, the British volunteer pilot in Spain, whose memoirs entitled *Cardboard Crucifix* (*The Patrol is Ended* in the USA) are largely either fiction or based on secondhand experience, did seem to be speaking the truth when he told the author: 'I shall always remember the Loire because it was so pretty – far too pretty to be a fighter!' He added that he also liked it because, 'whenever the motor conked out, which was often, it glided as steady as a rock'. De Wet was not knowledgeable about aircraft types, and could hardly have remembered, forty-two years later, such details about an obscure type of aircraft from other people's conversation.

Therefore, a Loire was apparently based at Manises, Valencia, in December 1936, where de Wet was stationed (and not, as he writes, at Getafe). In that case, either the fifth Loire was transferred to the safety of

Valencia before Getafe was bombed, or a sixth Loire was delivered to Spain. Some French newspapers of September 1936 reported that six Loire 46s were sold to Spain, but that one crashed on take-off at Vilacoublay owing to the inexperience of the pilot. If that is true, it may have been repaired and sent on later.

Reports on the flying qualities of the Loire 46s in Spain are contradictory. Lacalle, who writes of all French aircraft and most of the French airmen with hostility, disliked them, and claims that everyone else disliked them too, because they were heavy on the controls (this is discussed in the section on the Dewoitine D.372). Against this we have the secret reports of Jean Dary and Victor Veniel to Pierre Cot in 1936. Dary thought the Loire more suitable than the Dewoitine for inexperienced pilots, being less tricky to fly, and believed that it would be very suitable for night fighting, being equipped with night-flying instruments and r/t radio, while Veniel thought it potentially the best fighter in Republican service until the arrival of the Russian I-16. In French service in 1937 and 1938 it was popular with its pilots, who liked its excellent rate of climb, steadiness as a gun platform and, once its engine problems were remedied, its reliability. Its chief flying defect, soon mastered, was a tendency to 'float' just before touching down. This, especially in a crosswind, could damage the undercarriage and so, owing to the arrangement of the struts, damage the wing.

The Loring E.II. (CESELSA, via José Warleta)

Span 11.8m; length 7.5m; height 4.8m; wing area 19.5sq m.

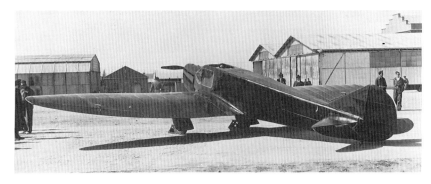

Empty weight 1,360kg; loaded weight 1,850kg.

Maximum speed 390km/h at 3,800m; stalling speed 120km/h; climb to 4,500m in 6 min; ceiling 11,750m; range 750km.

Loring E.II and Loring X

Designed by Jorge Loring Martínez and built at his aircraft factory at Carabanchel Alto, Madrid, in 1930, the Loring E.II was a two-seat parasol monoplane powered by a 110hp Elizalde A6 (licence-built Lorraine École) engine. The prototype, M-CAAM (later EC-AAM) first flew on 9 October that year, and three more examples were built in 1931, EC-AAS, 'ASA (powered by a 100hp Kinner K-5 uncowled radial engine) and 'QAQ. In July 1932 Rein Loring (see Airspeed Envoy) made a celebrated flight from Madrid to Manila in EC-ASA. The E.II EC-AAS belonged to Luis Rambaud, who was to become a distinguished Nationalist commander in the civil war (see Heinkel He 51, Cant Z.501 and Dornier Do 17) until his death in October 1938. He never saw his little aeroplane during the war, however, because it had been at Getafe, Madrid, on 18 July 1936. Neither EC-AAS nor its three stablemates survived the war.

The Loring X was a low-wing cantilever monoplane with elliptical wings and a spatted undercarriage, built in 1934-35 by Aeronáuticas Industriales SA (as the Loring company became in 1934) to compete against the Gil-Pazó GP-1 as a trainer for the Aviación Militar. It was of wooden construction, fabric covered, and was powered by a 105hp Walter Junior inverted in-line engine. The enclosed cabin seated the pilot and pupil side-by-side. The Loring X was rejected in favour of the GP-1 because its landing speed

The Loring X, unsuccessful competitor of the GP-1. (Instituto de Historia y Cultura, via José Warleta)

was considered too high. It was at Cuatro Vientos in July 1936, but nothing is known of its wartime career.

Loring E.II

Dimensions not available.
Loaded weight 689kg.
Maximum speed 185km/h; cruising speed 150km/h; range 1,500km.

Loring X

No data available.

Macchi M.18

On 15 May 1917 an Austrian Lohner L.40 two-seat flying-boat fell into Italian hands, and shortly afterwards was delivered to the SA Nieuport-Macchi with the request that a copy be built for the Italian navy. The resulting Macchi L.1, of which 139 were built, initiated the

long series of small naval flying-boats produced by Nieuport-Macchi and its successor, Aeronautica Macchi SpA, over the next fifteen years. The Macchi M.18, which first flew in 1920, was a single-seat, Warren-braced biplane of wooden construction with fabric-covered wings and tail surfaces. In the production version the engine was a 190hp Isotta-Fraschini V4b driving a two-blade wooden propeller. There was a crew of three: a pilot and copilot/navigator seated side-by-side, and an observer/gunner, equipped with a single 0.303 Vickers Mk.1 machine gun, in the bow position.

In 1922-23 the Spanish Aeronáutica Naval bought ten Macchi M.18s, of which four were used as reconnaissance aircraft aboard the aircraft transporter *Dédalo* during the Moroccan War. Between 1924 and 1935 the Talleres de la Aeronáutica Naval (Naval Aviation Workshops) at Casa Atuñez, Barcelona, built forty-four more under licence. Of these, all but four (with 300hp Hispano-Suiza V6 engines) were trainers: twelve were powered by 170hp Isotta-Fraschini V6 engines, four by 250hp V6bs, and twenty-six (designated M.18MRs) by 270hp Isotta-Fraschini Semi-Asso 220 engines. In Spanish service the M.18 acquired a bad reputation, for no fewer than eight

A Macchi M.18 of the Aeronáutica Naval at Barcelona. (Arráez)

crashed between 1924 and 1930, with a loss of fourteen lives.

By July 1936 only ten remained in service, all at the Escuela de Hidros (Seaplane Flying School) at Barcelona. Some of these made a few propaganda and morale-boosting flights over the city during the street fighting on 19-21 July. Three (Nos M-10, M-13 and M-16) were sent to accompany the Republican invasion of Mallorca in August, but were employed solely for liaison duties between the invading forces and Mahón, Menorca, one of the Balearic Islands in Republican hands. After the Republican withdrawal from Mallorca at the beginning of September 1936, the three M.18s remained at Mahón, where they soon became inoperable through lack of spare parts. By October 1936 only three of the seven remaining M.18s at Barcelona were airworthy. At the end of 1937, when only two were still serviceable, they were transferred, with the remaining Savoia-Marchetti S.62s, to the 1ª Escuadrilla of Grupo 73 at San Javier, near Cartagena. Both M.18s (with the serials HM-001 and -002) were withdrawn from service in the spring of 1938.

Span 15.8m; length 9.75m; height 3.25m; wing area 45sq m.
Empty weight 1,270kg; loaded weight 1,780kg.
Maximum speed 187km/h; cruising speed 120km/h; ceiling 5,000m; range 1,000km.

Macchi M.41

A late refinement of the Macchi small-flying-boat formula, the M.41 was an elegeant single-seat fighter

One of the three Macchi M.41 fighter flying-boats delivered to the Nationalists on Mallorca in August 1936. (Emiliani)

biplane designed by Mario Castoldi. Like its predecessors, it was of wooden construction with fabric-covered folding wings and a single pusher engine (a 420hp Fiat A-20) mounted on N struts immediately beneath the upper mainplane. Its armament consisted of two fixed forward-firing 7.7mm machine guns in the bow, and up to 60kg of bombs on racks beneath the lower mainplanes.

During the night of 27-28 August 1936, in response to an urgent appeal for help from the Nationalists on Mallorca in the face of a Republican invasion led by Comandante Bayo, the Italian ship *Emilio Morandi* arrived at Palma. It carried a cargo of arms, three Fiat C.R.32s and three Macchi M.41s, detached from the Regia Aeronautica and under the command of Comandante Leone Gallo (who was given the *nom-de-guerre* 'Cirelli' in Spain), a veteran of Gen Balbo's transatlantic formation flights. After assembly at Son San Juan, the three M.41s, flown by Tenentes Carlo Rinaldi ('Revello') and Guiseppe de Agostini, and Sergente Dante Venturini, carried out a series of low-level attacks on the Republican invading force, seriously damaging several Savoia-Marchetti S.62s moored near the ships anchored off the beach at Porto Cristo.

Shortly afterwards the M.41s were given the type code 50, numbered 50-1 to 50-3, and painted with the Nationalist St Andrew's Cross on the rudder and three black

stripes against a white ground round the rear fuselage. With their three-and-a-half hours' endurance, the M.41s gave valuable service as reconnaissance scouts, stalking Republican ships sailing to and from Menorca. On the creation of the Aviazione Legionaria in December 1936 they were formed into the 130ª Squadriglia Autonoma, Capitano Rinaldi being replaced as commander by Capitano Fabio Mannu. Lack of spares caused the Macchis to be withdrawn from flying duties by the end of May 1937 and, after more than a year parked on a quay at Pollensa, they were officially withdrawn from service at the end of 1938.

Span 11.12m; length 8.66m; height 3.12m; wing area 32sq m.
Empty weight 1,170kg; loaded weight 1,600kg.
Maximum speed 256km/h; cruising speed 227km/h; climb to 1,000m in 2.5min; ceiling 7,500m; range 700km.

Maillet-Taupin-Lignel 20 and 21

As an unintended consequence of its need to buy aircraft wherever they could be found, the Spanish Republican government became the owner of one of the largest collections of rare or curious aeroplanes that has ever existed. Among the more unusual, two strange-looking Maillet long-distance racers certainly deserve mention, even though they made no contribution whatever to the Republican war effort.

The Maillet 20 No 1 (F-ANQY) and 20 No 2 (F-AODA, which, with a modified cockpit and re-engined with a 180hp Régnier 6B-01 inverted in-line engine, became the Maillet 21 No 1) were low-wing cantilever monoplanes with fixed, spatted, undercarriages. Their most notable feature was a transparent canopy, set flush into the fuselage between the pilot's cockpit and the engine, over a cabin for two passengers (or navigator and flight mechanic). Both aircraft took part in several rallies in 1935, gaining, for example, second and fourth places in the Hélène Boucher cup. A third prototype, the 20 No 3, was fitted with a retractable undercarriage and became the Maillet 302.

In 1936 the manufacturer, Société Française de Constructions Aéronautiques (SFCA) sold the Maillet 21 F-AODA to the French government, and in September 1936 the racer was among the miscellaneous aircraft in the 'graveyard' at Villacoublay that were sold to the Spanish Republic. Bearing the temporary registration EC-72-E in white on an overall grey finish, the Maillet was flown from Villacoublay on 24 September by the American pilots Edwin Lyons (known in Spain as Ed Lebovitz) and Arthur Schapiro ('Arturo Vasnit'), both of whom flew in the Republican air force. Its propeller broke off in flight, however, and the machine came down at Grauaisson, on the French south coast near Montpellier. This incident has hitherto been confused with another concerning a B.A. Swallow.

The subsequent fate of the Maillet is not certain, although according to one account it was delivered to Spain but lost when it landed on a beach near Barcelona and was carried away by the tide. The Maillet 20 No 1 F-ANQY was sold by SFCA to a Spanish Republican agent in 1938(?). The ferry pilot, Capitain Victor Veniel, late of the Escadre André Malraux, landed it on a Republican aerodrome a few moments before the beginning of a Nationalist air raid, and the aeroplane was destroyed by a bomb.

Maillet 20

Dimensions not available.

Maximum speed 261km/h at sea level; cruising speed 250km/h; climb to 760m in 3min; ceiling 6,500m; range 916km.

The Maillet 21, with a 180hp Régnier 6B-01 engine, attained a maximum speed of about 270km/h.

Martinsyde F.4

Designed by G A Handasyde, the Martinsyde F.3 single-seat fighter first flew in November 1917. Its airframe was constructed of hickory and spruce and, except for the plywood-covered forward fuselage, all surfaces were fabric covered. Its armament consisted of two fixed

The Maillet 21 with a damaged undercarriage following a crash on 1 October 1935. (Liron)

forward-firing Vickers guns enclosed by the engine cowling. The 285hp Rolls-Royce Experimental Falcon of the prototype was replaced in the production version by the standard 275hp Falcon III, but prior claim on this engine by the Bristol Fighter F.2B resulted in production delays, and only six F.3s were built by early 1918. An alternative version designated F.4 (and later officially named 'Buzzard'), with a narrower-chord lower wing and the cockpit moved aft to improve downwards view, and powered by a 300hp Hispano-Suiza 8Fb engine, was therefore ordered into production. The first fifty-two of these had reached the RAF, though not become operational, when the First World War ended on 11 November 1918.

With its top speed of 138mph the Buzzard was one of the fastest fighters of its time, but it was not adopted by the RAF. Most of the machines were sold abroad by the Aircraft Disposal Company. Twenty were sold to Spain, and ten of these, (of which five were two-seaters with two-bay wings) were transferred, after service in the Moroccan war, to the Escuadrilla de Combate y Acompañamiento (Combat and Escort Squadron) of the Aeronáutica Naval at Barcelona in 1924. In 1933 the squadron was transferred to San Javier, Cartagena, the aircraft bearing the serials MS-1 to MS-10 (later changed to EA-EAA-1 to -EAI-10, but including -EAJ-8). All of these were officially still in service, although only seven were airworthy, on 18 July 1936.

For the next six weeks a group of naval pilots under the command of Francisco Piedra flew the Martinsydes on protection patrols over the base, which had been the scene of dramatic events before the local Nationalist uprising had been

Martinsyde F.4s of the Aeronáutica Naval at San Javier in 1935. (Arráez)

crushed, and over the port of Cartagena without, fortunately, meeting any enemy fighters. When the British mercenary pilot and confidence man Kenneth Apjohn-Carter (alias Charles Kennett, see de Havilland Puss Moth) was ordered to fly one of these, he flatly refused, and even went so far as to allege, in a newspaper article published after his return to England, that this had been part of a Spanish plot to kill foreign pilots.

At the end of August two F.4s were transferred to Málaga, but both were soon grounded by permanent engine failure. In October the remainder were transferred to the Escuela de Vuelo at El Carmolí, and were withdrawn from service as slightly more modern trainers arrived from France. The aged F.4s were flown to the Parque de Reserva (Reserve Park) at San Pedro del Pinatar nearby, after which nothing more was heard of them.

Span 32ft 9⅜in; length 25ft 5⅝in; height 8ft 10in; wing area 320sq ft.
Empty weight 1,811lb; loaded weight 2,398lb.
Maximum speed 132.5mph; climb to 10,000ft in 7min 95sec; ceiling 24,000ft.

Messerschmitt M 23b

A two-seat low-wing cantilever monoplane with a fixed undercarriage and braced tail assembly, the Messerschmitt M 23b was of wood and metal construction with plywood and fabric skinning. The powerplant could be either an 80-95hp Siemens Sh 13 radial or an 80-110hp Argus As 8 in-line engine. One M 23b, c/n

514, with an Argus engine, was bought by Pedro Balbas Vásquez in 1933, registered EC-AAP and kept at Getafe. In 1935 he sold it to the Aviación Vizcaina at Bilbao. During the early months of the civil war the Basques used it for reconnaissance and light bombing. The father of Justo Miranda, the aviation illustrator and historian, remembers that, while he was a Nationalist soldier billeted in a cottage at San Marcial in Navarra, this Messerschmitt flew over one day and the pilot dropped a number of mortar bombs, throwing them by hand over the side of the cockpit. One came down the chimney and exploded in the parlour, killing several soldiers. It was generally believed, probably without foundation, that the pilot was a Belgian woman flying for the Basques.

Span 11.8m; length 6.9m; height 2m; wing area 14.3sq m.
Empty weight 350kg; loaded weight 600kg.
Maximum speed 170km/h; cruising speed 145km/h; climb to 1,000m in 5.3min; ceiling 4,600m; endurance 5.5hr.

Messerschmitt M 35

The Messerschmitt M 35 two-seat training and touring aircraft was a handsome low-wing cantilever monoplane with open cockpits and a fixed, spatted undercarriage. It was powered by a 150hp Siemens Sh 14 radial engine in a deep-chord cowling. The fuselage was a welded-steel-tube frame, the forward part being covered with light alloy sheet-

ing and the rear with fabric. The wings, which had Handley Page slots along their leading edges, were built of wood with stressed-ply covering. The ailerons and tail surfaces were fabric covered.

An M 35 was bought in 1936 by Vicente Ríos Seguí of the Aero Club de Valencia, registered EC-BDB, and kept at Manises Aerodrome. During the civil war it was employed as a liaison aircraft and, probably, as a trainer. It was either captured or flown across the lines in 1938 and became 30-73 of the Nationalist air arm.

Span 11.57m; length 7.48m; height 2.75m; wing area 17sq m.
Empty weight 500kg; loaded weight 800kg.
Maximum speed 230km/h; cruising speed 195km/h; climb to 1,000m in 3.3min; ceiling 5,800m; range 700km.

Messerschmitt Bf 108B Taifun

When the first three places in the 3ᵐᵉ Challenge de Tourisme Internationale competition for light aircraft in 1932 were won by Polish R.W.D.6 tourers, the German Luftfahrtkommisariat (the department of the Reichluftministerium, or air ministry, responsible for policy) instructed the Bayerische Flugzeugwerke to design and build six examples of an aircraft to join the German aircraft competing in the next Challenge, set for August-September 1934. The co-director of the BFW, Dipl Ing Willy Messerschmitt, was able to adapt an existing design, the Messerschmitt M 37, with the result that the first new aeroplane, later designated Bf 108A, was able to make its maiden flight early in the spring of 1934. It was a remarkably advanced aircraft by European standards, being a sleek cantilever low-wing monoplane of all-metal, stressed skin construction, with an extremely well-designed enclosed cockpit and a fully retractable, mechanically operated, undercarriage. Notable, too, was its small, tapered, straight-edged wing, equip-

A Messerschmitt M 23b.

A Messerschmitt M 35.

ped with split flaps and Handley Page slots.

Four Bf 108As competed in the 1934 Challenge and, although none gained the first four places, they performed creditably and proved to be the fastest participants. The Bf 108B Taifun, a slightly enlarged four-seat version powered by a 240hp Argus As 10C inverted vee engine, appeared in 1935 and was ordered into series production for the Luftwaffe, for flying schools and clubs, and as a fast executive transport.

Four Bf 108B Taifuns were sent to Spain with the Condor Legion and, with the serials 44-1 to 44-4, were employed on liaison duties. A further three arrived shortly after the civil war to join the four that that had been handed over to the Ejercito del Aire. All seven were still flying in 1940, and in 1945 their type code was changed to L.15.

Span 10.6m; length 8.3m; height 2.1m; wing area 16.4sq m.
Empty weight 860kg; loaded weight 1,400kg; wing loading 85.4kg/sq m.
Maximum speed 300km/h; cruising speed 265km/h; landing speed 80km/h; climb 345m/min; ceiling 6,200m; range 950km.

Messerschmitt Bf 109

The Messerschmitt Bf 109 is generally regarded as one of the two greatest fighter aircraft ever built, the other claimant being its classical opponent in the Second World War, the Supermarine Spitfire. Designed contemporaneously with the Bf 108 cabin monoplane, with which it shared many structural and aerodynamic features, the Bf 109 was intended to meet a Luftwaffe requirement for a high-performance two-gun monoplane fighter to replace the Heinkel He 51, its competitors being the Heinkel He 112 and Arado Ar 80 low-wing cantilever monoplanes and the Focke-Wulf Fw 159 parasol monoplane.

The prototype Bf 109a (or Bf 109 V1) first flew in May 1935 ('Bf' signified Bayerische Flugzeugwerke, the 'Me' designation never

The Messerschmitt M 35 captured by the Nationalists, or brought over to them by a defector, in 1938. (Arráez)

The Messerschmitt Bf 108B Taifun.

being officially adopted for this aircraft). Its slender lines, steep ground angle, narrow-track retractable undercarriage, sideways-hinged cockpit canopy, straight-tapered slotted wings and high wing loading provoked scepticism that such a delicate-looking and sophisticated machine could ever be a fighter. During the next twelve months, however, the superiority of the Messerschmitt over its competitors, despite an influential lobby supporting the Heinkel He 112, became unde-

A Messerschmitt Bf 109B of the Condor Legion.

A Messerschmitt Bf 109D of 2.J/88, bearing the 'Zylinder Hut' (Top Hat) emblem previously used by the Heinkel He 51s of 1.J/88.

niably obvious, and the first orders were placed for quantity production. The production model Bf 109B – powered by a Junkers Jumo 210D liquid-cooled engine with a take-off rating of 720hp and a maximum continuous rating of 610hp, and driving a fixed-pitch two-bladed wooden propeller – differed remarkably little from the original prototype.

Reports of the inadequacy of the Heinkel He 51 in the Spanish Civil War persuaded the RLM (German air ministry) to send three of the prototype models, the Bf 109 V3, V4 and V5, to Spain for evaluation in the field. Although this decision was made in September 1936, the aircraft did not reach Tablada, Seville, until the beginning of December, three weeks or so after the establishment of the Condor Legion. On 9 December Lt Hannes Trautloft, at that time with the He 51 staffel 4.J/88 at Vitoria, was ordered to

Tablada to test the Bf 109 V3, but he found on arrival that it had already been flown and damaged by a inexperienced pilot. The Bf 109 V4 was not ready until 14 December, and, as a result of teething troubles (engine overheating, faulty undercarriage-locking mechanism, etc.), it was not until exactly one month later that Trautloft was able to fly the Bf 109 V4 to the Madrid sector for operational trials. Apart from the fact that the Bf 109 was assigned the Nationalist type code 6, nothing is known of the nature or results of these trials, nor is there any record that the V4 or V5 engaged in any combats. In February 1937 both aircraft, along with the V3, were returned to the Messerschmitt factory at Augsburg.

By then the first production Bf 109Bs were reaching an elite Luftwaffe fighter wing, the II Jagdgruppe of the 132 Jagdgeschwader 'Richthofen', and it was decided, in response to the pleas of Gen Sper-

rle, the Condor Legion commander, to send the first sixteen aircraft, with their pilots and maintenance crews, to Spain immediately. They arrived in March and re-equipped 2.J/88, which was now put under the command of Oblt Günther 'Franzl' Lützow. A man of strong character, Lützow supervised the conversion training of his pilots from the He 51B, a traditional biplane with an open cockpit, a fixed undercarriage and a top speed of 330km/h, to the Bf 109B, a low-wing cantilever monoplane with an enclosed cockpit, slots, a retractable undercarriage and a top speed of 465km/h, insisting that two one-hour flights were sufficient to prepare a pilot for sending to the front for formation and orientation flying. This energetic programme was frustrated by teething troubles with the aircraft, which kept eight of them at Seville for two months.

The staffel adopted the 'Zylinder Hut' (Top Hat) emblem of the disbanded 4.J/88, and it was said, with rather Teutonic jocularity, that the superior speed of the Messerschmitt was due to that 'extra zylinder'. Although it is often stated that the Messerschmitts of 2.J/88 did not join the He 51 squadrons (1. and 3.J/88) in the north until June 1937, there are documents to show that six Bf 109Bs were at Vitoria on 14 April 1937. Whether or not they took part in the notorious raid on Guernica on 26 April, however, is uncertain, for the only authors who say that they did so make too many mistakes to inspire confidence. Lützow, for example, is described as the leader of the Heinkel squadron.

Early in July 1937 2.J/88 moved to Avila to join the Nationalist air units hurriedly being deployed, under the denomination 'Grupo Aéreo Sanders' ('Sanders' being the *nom-de-guerre* of Gen Sperrle), to counter the Republican offensive at Brunete. It was in the course of this battle that the Bf 109s first encountered the equally fast Russian I-16 Moscas, and so the Battle of Brunete heralded the beginning of important changes in the tactics of air fighting. During the First World War and in the first year of the Spanish Civil War, aerial dogfights between biplanes or high-wing monoplanes had occupied fairly limited airspace, from a distance often resembling a swarm of gnats. Gradually, as both sides committed more of the fast, but less agile, low-wing monoplanes to action, air battles became vast, sprawling affairs, spread over hundreds of square miles. Such in consequence were the air battles of the Second World War, and there was to be no comparable enlargement again until jets first met in combat over the Yalu River in 1951. It was at Brunete, too, that the Messerschmitts suffered their first losses, one being shot down on 12 July 1937, and a second eight days later, both falling to I-16s. On 29 July, after the Republican army had been thrown back, 2.J/88 returned north to Herrera de Pisuerga for the Nationalist offensive against Santander, and remained to cover the campaign until the Asturias were occupied in September and October 1937. Nationalist air superiority was so overwhelming, however, that the

Bf 109s rarely met Republican fighters.

Late in September 1937 1.J/88 (commanded by Hptm Harder), which had recently re-equipped with new Bf 109Bs, had its first major engagement with six I-16s, all that remained of an escuadrilla sent from the main zone on 27 August. Both sides claimed victory, but the two Bf 109s claimed to have been shot down by a Russian, Yevseviev, and a Spaniard, Tarazona, were not admitted by the Condor Legion.

After a rest in October and the replacement of Gen Sperrle, the Legion commander, by Gen Volkmann, J/88, commanded by Maj Handrick, was reorganised once more into four staffeln: 1. and 2.J/88, with Bf 109Bs, were to be employed chiefly in air fighting, and 3. and 4.J/88, with He 51s, solely on close-support missions. In November the Jagdgruppe was moved to La Torresaviñán, in Guadalajara province, and it was during the next weeks that the Messerschmitt pilots worked out the tactics to exploit the one serious defect of their principal opponent, the I-16. Although it could be outdived by the Bf 109B up to an altitude of about 3,000m, the I-16 was equal in level speed and superior in manoeuvrability and climb. As it climbed above that altitude, however, the characteristics of its M-25 engine made the I-16 progressively more sluggish until, at about 5,000m, it had little chance against its German counterpart, which had a higher ceiling and gave optimum performance at 5,000m to 6,000m. Thus a single kette of three Messerschmitts could neutralise the effectiveness of two or three escuadrillas of I-16s simply by flying 1,000m above and behind them. It was Republican practice by now to fly in large formations with the novices at the rear. With the Bf 109s above, the formation leaders became afraid to turn, because the formation would lose its cohesion as the novices began to straggle. The Messerschmitts could pounce as soon as this occurred, and make their escape by continuing in a dive which the I-16s could not match. It sometimes happened that an I-16 squadron would return to base unaware that it had been attacked, and that one or

two of its aircraft had been shot down. As a result, the Messerschmitts had an influence on the air war quite out of proportion to their numbers.

On 4 December 1937 the Bf 109B flown by Fw Polenz (6-15) was forced down intact behind Republican lines. The Republicans had also captured a Heinkel He 111B (25-32), and both aircraft were tested at Sabadell by a French technical commission in February 1938 before being shipped to the Soviet Union. This affair is described in the section on the Heinkel He 111, but it is worth reiterating that, owing to bureaucratic incompetence at the French air ministry, the detailed reports on the Bf 109 prepared by the commission were never shown to the design teams for whom they were written.

On 15 December the Republicans opened an attack against Teruel and, after bitter fighting, captured most of the town by Christmas. Fought in appalling weather, the battle continued until February, when the Republicans were forced to withdraw. Despite high winds, blizzards and temperatures as low as −20°C, the Messerschmitts, moved to Calamocha, near the front, carried out missions whenever flying was possible, their engines being run up every night to prevent seizing. Their casualties were relatively light, and on 7 February 1938 they claimed one of their most striking successes when, led by the group commander, Hptmn Handrick, they shot down four SB bombers out of a formation of twenty-two within five minutes (the Legion claimed ten, as well as two I-16s, and this figure is still quoted in most accounts of the affray). In March 1938 the Bf 109Bs were moved to Escatrón to cover the Nationalist drive through Aragón to the coast, and were employed on a series of attacks on Republican aerodromes. Although combat losses were light, those caused by wear and tear were heavy, and by the end of this gruelling campaign the two Messerschmitt squadrons were down to half strength.

Among twenty-four Bf 109s which arrived from Germany in April 1938 were five Bf 109C-1s. This variant differed from the Bf 109B in having a Junkers Jumo 210G fuel-injection engine, rated at 720hp at 1,000m, and two additional machine guns mounted in the wings. By a coincidence, the first four-gun version of the I-16, the Type 10, was arriving in Spain at the same time. These five Bf 109Cs were allotted to 3.J/88, which transferred its He 51s to the Spaniards, and the Jagdgruppe entered into a long series of air battles which continued, with few interruptions, until November. These increased in tempo in August, during the Battle of the Ebro, and reached their climax in September.

A further reinforcement of Bf 109s during the summer included five Bf 109Ds (of an eventual thirty-five). This version reverted to the Jumo 210D engines of the Bf 109B but retained the four-gun armament of the Bf 109C. The Bf 109Ds were also incorporated into 3.J/88. Again by coincidence, a new high-altitude version of the I-16 entered the arena. Twenty-four Wright Cyclone R-1820-F54 engines had been procured in the United States by Coronel Francisco León Trejo and shipped without detection to France, crossing the frontier in June. Twelve of these had been fitted into the I-16s of the 4ª Escuadrilla under Capitán Antonio Arias, whose pilots were provided with oxygen equipment, and thereafter high-flying Messerschmitts no longer posed so great a threat to Republican formations.

During the Battle of the Ebro J/88 had adopted the tactic of flying fighters in pairs, the leader navigating and the wingman, about 200m to one side and slightly to the rear, guarding the leader from quarter or stern attack. In September Hptm Werner Mölders, Staffelkapitän of 3.J/88 and the highest-scoring Legion pilot, with thirteen claimed 'kills', modified this into the 'Vierfingerschwarm' of two pairs of Bf 109s flying in positions analagous to the finger-tips of a hand held flat. This formation, which allowed much greater flexibility than the standard vee formation then used by every air force in the world, was employed by the Luftwaffe with great success during the Second World War. It was adopted by the RAF at a rather late stage in the Battle of Britain under the name 'Finger four', and is still in use today.

The continuous fighting over the Ebro and what is now called the Costa Brava was gradually reducing the material state of the Nationalist air forces, and of the Jagdgruppe of the Condor Legion in particular, to a dangerously low level. General Volkmann's appeals for reinforcements had been ignored, for the German government, faced with the Sudeten crisis (which ended with the Munich Agreement on 29 September 1938), gave priority to building up Luftwaffe strength at home in case of a declaration of war by Britain, France and, perhaps, Soviet Russia. Germany, however, needed iron ore and such metals as wolfram, tungsten and chrome, of which Spain was a producer, and had been trying in vain, almost since the start of the civil war, to wring concessions from the Nationalist government concerning the supply of these materials.

In June 1938 the Nationalist air ace Capitán Joaquín García Morato had been alllowed to test a Bf 109C-1 at Le Cenía, the Legion headquarters aerodrome, and had recommended that the type be adopted as the future standard fighter of the Nationalist air force, and of the Spanish air force after the end of the war. In October Volkmann reported

Messerschmitt Bf 109Es of the Ejercito del Aire after the civil war.

that, without reinforcement, the Condor Legion would be unable to continue sustained operations. Of the eighty-six Bf 109s received since November 1936, barely thirty were still airworthy, a number raised to thirty-seven by the start of the Catalonian campaign on 23 December 1938. An agreement was then reached between the Spanish Nationalist and German governments that, in return for mining concessions in Spain, the Germans would re-equip the Condor Legion and the Spanish air arm with the most modern machines available, including the latest versions of the Bf 109, the Bf 109E-1 and E-3. The Bf 109E differed principally from earlier models in being powered by a fuel-injection Daimler-Benz 601 Aa twelve-cylinder inverted-vee engine rated at 1,175hp for take-off and at 775hp for maximum continuous operation. This raised the top speed of the E-1 (armed with four machine guns) from 470km/h to 570km/h at 5,000m, and of the E-3 (with two machine guns and two wing-mounted 20mm Oerlikon cannon) to 560km/h at 4,440m.

Three veteran Spanish fighter pilots, José Muñoz Jiménez ('El Corto'), Miguél García Pardo and Javier Marcía Rubio, were transferred to 3.J/88 to gain experience for the establishment of a new mixed Spanish group, 5-G-5, of which one

escuadrilla was to be equipped with Heinkel He 112s and the second with Bf 109Bs. Forty-four Bf 109E-1s and E-3s arrived in Nationalist Spain between the middle of December 1938 and the end of February 1939, but only one Legion staffel, 1.J/88, was re-equipped in time to take part in the Catalonian campaign, its Bf 109Bs being handed over to the Spaniards to form the first Messerschmitt escuadrilla, 1-E-6, based at Logroño under Javier Marcía Rubio.

Meanwhile, as the demoralised Republican armies retreated towards, and across, the French frontier, the Messerschmitts of the Condor Legion played a major rôle in the destruction of the Republican air units still in Catalonia by straffing their aerodromes after bombardment by He 111s. The most notable occasions were the attack on Bañolas on 5 February 1939 (see Dewoitine D.371), and on the crowded aerodrome at Vilajuiga on the following day, when eleven aircraft were destroyed and twenty-five badly damaged in ten minutes. During the attack, the Republican pilot José Falco managed to take off in his I-15 Chato and shoot down Bf 109E 6-98, flown by Ufw Windemuth. It crashed in the middle of the aerodrome, and the pilot was killed by German bombs before he could extricate himself. After the occupation of Catalonia, the rest of J/88 re-equipped with Bf 109Es. One of these, flown by Hptm von Bonin (who had replaced Mölders as leader of 3.J/88), scored the Legion's last victory of the war by shooting down an I-15 over Alicante on 5 March 1939. The twenty-seven remaining airworthy Bf 109s were handed over to the Spanish Nationalists.

Altogether, 131 Messerschmitt Bf 109s were delivered to Spain during the civil war. It is not possible to identify exactly which models carried which serials, and the following breakdown, based on photographs and deduction, is intended merely as a rough guide:

Bf 109 V3, V4 and **V5** appear to have carried no serial numbers.
Bf 109B: 6-1 to 6-45 (forty-five aircraft). The first sixteen of these were delivered with Schwarz fixed-pitch two-blade wooden propellers.

Thereafter aircraft began to arrive with VD (Hamilton) two-blade variable-pitch metal propellers. When available, metal propellers were fitted to the earlier aircraft. Bf 109Bs with wooden or metal propellers were retrospectively designated Bf 109B-1 and Bf 109B-2, but this differentiation was not adopted in Spain until after the civil war.
Bf 109C-1: 6-46 to 6-51 (five aircraft).
Bf 109D: 6-52 to 6-86 (thirty-five aircraft).
Bf 109E-1 and **E-3**: 6-87 to 6-131 (forty-five aircraft, of which one arrived in the autumn of 1938 and the rest between mid-December 1938 and end of February 1939).

The insignia of the various Messerschmitt units and individual machines have been a source of confusion. The prototypes were finished in light grey (RLM63) all over. All subsequent Bf 109s in Spain were finished in light grey, but with blue-white undersurfaces. The serials were painted in black behind the Nationalist black disc on the fuselage sides of the aircraft up to 6-15 at least, but on later aircraft the numerals were painted on each side of the disc, according to standard Nationalist practice. When 2.J/88 was formed in March 1937, it adopted the 'Zylinder Hut' motif of the disbanded 4.J/88 (He 51Bs) painted below and behind the cockpit in front of the black disc, or, on later aircraft, in front of the '6'. Staffel 1.J/88 abandoned the 'Maribou' and white swastika emblems of the He 51s and adopted a white Balkan Cross (a broad 'X'), which was painted on the black disc. When the staffel re-equipped with Bf 109Es this was replaced by the so-called 'Holzauge' ('Wooden Eye', a German cartoon character of the time) device on a black-ringed white disc below the cockpit. Staffel 3.J/88 took over the 'Mickey Mouse' emblem from the He 51s with which it was previously equipped.

Several Messerschmitts bore personal insignia. When 6-56 (of 2.J/88) was flown by Maj Handrick (the Kommandeur of J/88), it displayed the 1936 Olympiad emblem on its propeller boss and a cursive 'h' on its black disc. When the command, and

the machine, passed to Hptm Walter Grabmann, the 'h' was replaced by a 'g'. Hannes Trautloft's personal emblem was a large green heart, which he had painted on his He 51 and on the Bf 109 V4 while he was testing it.

In March 1940 forty-one Messerschmitt Bf 109s remained in service with Grupo 25 of the 23° Regimiento de Caza (Fighter Regiment) and as fighter trainers, and in 1942 these were reinforced by fourteen or fifteen Bf 109Fs. In the same year the Ejercito del Aire acquired a licence to produce the Bf 109G in Spain, and Hispano Aviación built 237 during the later 1940s and the 1950s. Sixty-seven, designated HA 1109, were powered by Hispano-Suiza 12.7Z engines and the rest, designated HA 1112, were powered by Rolls-Royce Merlin 500.45s.

Bf 109B

Span 9.87m; length 8.55m; height 2.45m; wing area 16.17sq m.

Empty weight 1,150kg; loaded weight 2,150kg.

Maximum speed 465km/h; climb to 6,000m in 9.8min; ceiling 8,200m; range 690km.

Bf 109C-1

Span 9.87m; length 8.55m; height 2.45m; wing area 16.17sq m.

Empty weight 1,597kg; loaded weight 2,296kg.

Maximum speed 470km/h; climb to 5,000m in 8.75min; ceiling 8,400m; range 625km.

Bf 109E-3

Span 9.87m; length 8.64m; height 2.50m; wing area 16.17sq m.

Empty weight 1,900kg; loaded weight 2,665kg.

Maximum speed 560km/h; climb to 6,000m in 7.75min; ceiling 10,500m; range 660km.

Mignet H.M.14 Pou du Ciel

Invented by Henri Mignet, the Pou du Ciel (Flying Flea) was a tiny, tandem-winged, single-seat biplane, originally powered by a 20hp Aubier et Dunne engine. Mignet's purpose was to put on the market a machine which was simple enough to be built by an amateur enthusiast in a small workshop and would be the motorcycle of the air. Accordingly he published a manual giving full instructions on how to construct and pilot his aeroplane. Between 1933 and 1936 about 120 Poux du Ciel were built, many of them in Britain, and they quickly caught the attention of the newspapers. The French authorities, however, considered the Pou du Ciel unsafe, and refused to grant certificates of airworthiness to any built in France. After a series of fatal accidents in Britain, the British authorities followed suit, and the immense popularity of the Flying Flea rapidly diminished.

In 1935 Manuel Egea, a Málaga company director and sports pilot, built a Pulga del Cielo, as it was called in Spain, at Rompedizos aerodrome, Málaga. The little machine was still there, as yet unregistered, when the civil war broke out on 18 July 1936, and it presumably passed into the hands of the Nationalists when they captured Málaga in February 1937. Whether or not anyone flew it during the civil war is not known. Republican pilots training under Lejeune Aviation at Meaux remember a Pou du Ciel in a hangar with the words 'le plus petit avion du monde' ('the smallest aeroplane in the world') stencilled along the forward wing, and it is said that a few of the Spaniards did make brief flights in it, just for fun, before returning to Spain.

Span 6m; wing 11sq m.
Empty weight 140kg.
Take-off run 100m.

A Mignet Pou du Ciel, or Flying Flea.

Miles M2F and M2H Hawk Major and M23 Hawk Speed Six

The Miles M2F Hawk Major was an aerodynamically refined development of the popular Miles M2 Hawk series of two-seat, low-wing monoplanes of the early 1930s. Constructed, like its forbears, entirely of wood with ply skinning, it was powered by a 130hp de Havilland Gipsy Major inverted in-line engine, and its wide-track undercarriage legs were faired by smart, streamlined, plywood trousers. The first M2F appeared in July 1934, and the M2H (equipped with split flaps) in November of the same year.

Six Hawk Majors flew in the Spanish Civil War. In May 1935 Luis Moroder Gómez, of the Aero Club de Valencia, bought the M2F c/n 117, G-ACYO, which was re- registered EC-ZZA. Curiously, this particular M2F had the 95hp ADC Cirrus IIIA engine of the earlier Hawks. Two months later (July 1935) another member of the Aero Club de Valencia, José Albiñana Ferrer, bought the M2H Hawk Major c/n 172 (ferry registration EC-W44), which received the registration EC-DDB.

Shortly after the outbreak of the civil war the Valencia newspapers reported that Moroder, described as a 'notorious Fascist', had escaped in his private aeroplane to Mallorca, and it has been said that this aeroplane subsequently became 30-72 in the Nationalist air arm. In fact, Moroder was in a Valencia prison in 1938 and, although he survived, he seems to have spent the war as a prisoner of the Republicans. Nor is his Hawk Major known to have been in Mallorca. Both Hawk Majors therefore were impressed into the Republican air force, and, to judge by a photograph showing EC-DDB with six 10kg fragmentation bombs on the ground beside it, they may have been used for a few military missions during the early stages of the fighting. Later, bearing the type code EN, they were used as trainers and/or liaison aircraft.

Three more M2H Hawk Majors reached the Republicans during the civil war. Union Founders Trust, a city firm acting as agent for Comandante Carlos Pastor Krauel, who had been sent by the Madrid govern-

José Rebellho's Miles M2H Hawk Major on a Nationalist aerodrome. (A J Jackson)

ment to England to buy aircraft, bought M2H c/n 138, G-ADAS, from Malcolm Farquharson Ltd at Reading Aerodrome on 9 August 1936. In company with a Miles Falcon and a General Aircraft Monospar ST-25 it was flown via France to Bilbao, arriving on 14 August 1936. It served as a general-purpose military aircraft and, on 11 December 1936, was part of a rag-tag collection of aircraft which made a desperate attack on Vitoria Aerodrome, which was being enlarged to accommodate the fighter groups of the Condor Legion and Aviazione Legionaria. The pilot on that occasion was the celebrated American flyer Bert Acosta, who later claimed that he shot down a Heinkel He 51 with his revolver during the raid, while his observer shot down two more with a hunting rifle. (For the probable origin of this tall tale, see CASA-Breguet 19.)

The other two M2H Hawk Majors, c/n 164, G-ADDC, and c/n 180, G-ADDU, were bought at Brooklands Aerodrome, Surrey, by Leslie Charles Stanynought (alias L C Lewis, see Avro 626, Spartan Cruiser *et al*), ostensibly for Lady Heath's Flying School near Dublin. However, when Stanynought and Edward Hillman (the son of the founder of Hillman's Airways – he had recently returned from flying for the Republicans) took off from Brooklands for Oxford on the first stage of their flight to Dublin, neither aeroplane was ever seen in England, or Ireland, again. In Republican Spain they presumably joined the other Miles aircraft (all with the type code EN) as trainers.

One M2H Hawk Major flew for the Nationalists. In 1934 the Portuguese airman José Rebellho bought c/n 61, G-ADEN, and, with J F Lawn, an instructor at the Royal Aero Club, flew it to Portugal, where it was registered CS-AAL. Shortly after the outbreak of the civil war Rebellho flew to Tablada, Seville, and placed himself and his machine at the service of the Nationalists. He was employed on liaison duties, and

The Hawk Speed Six, with its canopy removed, on a Republican airstrip. (Arráez)

thereafter he and his Hawk Major became a familiar sight on Nationalist aerodromes and airstrips.

Two Hawk Majors survived the war. The M2H EC-DDB became 30-145 in the postwar Ejercito del Aire before being returned to Sr Albiñana and the Aero Club de Valencia in 1946, re-registered EC-CAS. It was still flying, registered EC-ABI, in 1965. The Hawk Major 30-72 did not return to civil ownership until 1953, when it was acquired by the Aero Club de Sevilla, registered EC-AHZ, and fitted with a rather unsightly enclosed canopy over the two cockpits. It was written off after an accident in 1957. As mentioned above, it has usually been stated that EC-AHZ was originally Moroder's M2F, EC-ZZA. However-

The Miles M23 Hawk Speed Six. (A J Jackson)

er, a photograph of 'AHZ shows it with a Gipsy Major engine, whereas the M2F 'ZZA had a Cirrus IIIA of very different appearance. During the 1940s and 1950s Gipsy Major engines were in short supply in Spain, and it seems unlikely that anyone would have gone to the great expense of re-engining and re-cowling a Miles Hawk Major at such a time. There is also a puzzle over the serial 30-72. The last wartime Nationalist serial in Grupo 30 was 30-74, allotted to the Spartan Executive brought across to the Nationalists by Carrasco in December 1938. Serial 30-73 was given to the Messerschmitt M 35, which means that both this machine and the Hawk Major 30-72 came into Nationalist possession before December 1938. Since it seems likely that Rebellho's machine returned to Portugal, the most reasonable explanation is that 30-72 was one of the Hawk Majors

bought through Stanynought, and that both it and the M 35 were captured (like the Caudron C.59s) on a Republican aerodrome during the rapid Nationalist advance to the coast in the spring of 1938.

The Miles M23 Hawk Speed Six c/n 43, G-ACTE, was a special single-seat racing version of the Hawk Major custom-built for Sir Charles Rose in 1934. It was powered by a 220hp de Havilland Gipsy Six engine and fitted with a sliding, domed cockpit canopy. In 1936 Rose sold it to the racing pilot Bill Humble, who, in December, sold it to Stanynought. The sale is dated 4 January 1937, but the machine was out of England by then. Nothing is known of its service with the Republicans beyond a blurred photograph showing what appears to be this aeroplane, with mottled camouflage, standing concealed among trees.

M2H Hawk Major

Span 33ft; length 24ft; height 6ft 8in; wing area 169sq ft.

Empty weight 1,150lb; loaded weight 1,800lb.

Maximum speed 150mph; cruising speed 135mph; initial climb 1,000ft/min; ceiling 20,000ft; range 560 miles.

M23 Hawk Speed Six

Dimensions as for M2H.

Empty weight 1,355lb; loaded weight 1,900lb.

Maximum speed 185mph; cruising speed 160mph; initial climb 1,450ft/min.

Miles M3A Falcon Major and M3B Falcon Six

A three-seat cabin monoplane (pilot and two passengers) based directly on the Hawk Major, the Miles M3A, powered by a 130hp de Havilland Gipsy Major engine, first flew in 1935, and in July that year the M3B Falcon Six G-ADLC (200hp Gipsy Six engine), flown by Tommy Rose, won the King's Cup air race, with Miles Hawk Majors coming second and third. Two M3As were exported to Spain before the civil war. The first, c/n 197, was sold to Rafael de Mazarredo Trenor of the Aero Club de Valencia. It received the ferry number EC-W48, and in Spain was registered EC-BDD. The second, c/n 201, was sold to the Aero Club de

Andalucía at Tablada Aerodrome, Seville, having the ferry number EC-W45 and the registration EC-DBB.

At the start of the civil war Mazarredo escaped to the Nationalist zone and eventually became a Heinkel He 51 pilot. His Falcon Major ('BDD) passed into Republican service, being used as a trainer at Los Alcázares with the type code EN. The Falcon Major survived the war, became 30-168 in the Ejercito del Aire, and in 1940 was returned to Mazarredo for a civil career as EC-BAY(?). It was re-registered EC-CAO in 1946 and 'ACB in 1953. Meanwhile, at Seville, 'DBB was impressed by the Nationalists and, along with other light aircraft, flew on many military missions during the first few weeks of the fighting. After the war it continued as 30-55, and in 1946 became EC-BAY. In 1967 it was still flying at Seville, registered EC-ABZ.

One Miles M3B Falcon Six (200hp de Havilland Gipsy Six engine) arrived in the Basque zone on 14 August 1936. This was c/n 231, G-ADLS, belonging to Andrew Farquhar, one of four aircraft (Miles M2H Hawk Major G-ADAS, Percival Gull G-ADEP and Airspeed Envoy II G-AEBV being the other three) bought at Reading Aerodrome on 9 August by Union Founders Trust (see Miles M2H and D.H.84 Dragon) and flown out on the same day. It was converted, as far as possible, into a military aircraft, and was one of the machines flown by a group of foreign volunteer and mercenary pilots sent across from the main zone in November. On one occasion, the British pilot Walter

The Miles M3B Falcon Six G-ADLS, which flew with the Basque air arm and on one occasion was mistaken by Condor Legion pilots for a new and unknown type of fighter. (A J Jackson)

Scott Coates inadvertently flew the Falcon Six into a dogfight between a mixed Basque formation of two I-15 Chatos and a Nieuport 52 (which were escorting two Breguet 19s, a Vickers Vildebeest and a Monospar ST 25) and three Heinkel He 51s of the Condor Legion. The Germans, mistaking the Falcon Six for a new and unknown type of fighter, hastily broke off combat.

The M3B seems to have survived the northern campaign, for it was probably this machine which landed at Parme-Biarritz on 20 October 1937, piloted by Elias Hernández Camisón, who brought three Republican pilots from Gijón shortly before its capture by the Nationalists. On 7 November this aircraft was wrecked in a forced landing at Grimaud, St Tropez. The passengers were three Spaniards (perhaps the same three who had been brought from Gijón) who had been ordered to leave France.

M3A Falcon Major

Span 35ft; length 25ft 6in; height 6ft 6in; wing area 174.3sq ft.

Empty weight 1,300lb; loaded weight 2,200lb.

Maximum speed 145mph; cruising speed 125mph; initial climb 750ft/min; range 615 miles.

M3B Falcon Six

Dimensions as for M3A.

Empty weight 1,550lb; loaded weight 2,350lb.

Maximum speed 180mph; cruising speed 160mph; initial climb 1,000ft/min; range 560 miles.

Monocoupe Model 90 and 90A De Luxe

The first of the celebrated series of Monocoupe sports aeroplanes appeared in the USA in 1927, and its derivatives, all basically similar, continued in production until 1950, a record which exceeds even that of the de Havilland Moth and Tiger Moth series in Britain. During these twenty-three years the company that built the Monocoupes underwent many changes of name, ownership and location: Mono Aircraft Corporation (1927), Monocoupe Corporation (1929), Lambert Aircraft Corporation, St Louis (1934), Monocoupe Corporation (1939), Monocoupe Airplane Engine Corporation (1941) and, finally, Monocoupe Corporation again at Melbourne, Florida, to resume production of the Model 90 and 110 Special. The Monocoupes were all braced high-wing or shoulder-wing single-engined cabin monoplanes of wood and metal, seating a pilot and passenger side by side.

The most immediately recognisable feature of the Monocoupe was the rear fuselage, which in all models tapered sharply between the wing trailing edge and the tail unit. According to the designer, Donald Luscombe, this feature was inspired by the shape of the teal, the fastest of the duck family, and accounted for the remarkable top speed (104mph) of these low-powered aeroplanes. Hence the Monocoupe trademark of three stylised teal. Although they were intended simply as aircraft that were easy to fly, inexpensive and efficient, Monocoupes were widely used in air races both in the USA and in Europe. In the 1930 US National Air Races, for instance, Monocoupe 90s and 110s took first place in eleven of the fifteen events in which they were entered, second place in ten, and third place in nine.

The Model 90, of which 350 were built in different versions, was of mixed construction. The wing had a wooden spar, metal ribs and fabric covering, and there was a square cabin roof window in the centre section. The fuselage was a steel-tube frame with ply and fabric covering. The usual engine was an 80-90hp Lambert R266 radial, uncowled in the earlier Model 90s, but given a Townend ring in the 90 De Luxe, a blistered cowling in the 90A and a 'tunnel-cowling' in the 90A De Luxe. Other engines included Lycomings and Franklins of similar horsepower, and the 125hp Warner Scarab and 145hp Super Scarab.

Five Monocoupe 90s, 90As and 90A De Luxes were bought by members of the Aero Club de Andalucía, based at Tablada Aerodrome, Seville, in the 1930s:

Model 90, c/n A552, EC-MAA, Fernando Flores Solis
Model 90, c/n A566, EC-KAK, Miguel Arteman Cerdá
Model 90A, c/n 574, EC-APP, Miguel Arteman Cerdá
Model 90A De Luxe, c/n 681, EC-AZA, Luis Recasens
Model 90A De Luxe, c/n 682, EC-ZAA, Pablo Benjumea

On 18 July 1936 Señor Arteman's Monocoupe 90A, EC-APP, happened to be at Málaga, and so fell into Republican hands. It was used as a trainer (type code EQ) and as a runabout by senior officers throughout the war. On the Nationalist side, the four Monocoupes at Tablada were immediately pressed into military service, received the type code 30 (denoting single-engined light air-

The Monocoupe 90A De Luxe EC-ZAA. (John Underwood, via R S Allen)

craft) and, piloted by various members of the Aero Club de Sevilla, were used for a time as bombers, carrying single 50kg bombs on improvised racks between their undercarriage legs. On occasions they were landed behind enemy lines for rescue missions, sometimes under fire, and for dropping off intelligence agents by night.

After the civil war EQ-001 (ex-EC-APP) was recovered by the Nationalists, became 30-124 in the Ejercito del Aire, and continued flying until the 1940s. Of the Nationalist Monocoupes, Model 90 30-58 (ex-EC-KAK) was destroyed during a Republican air attack on Navalmoral aerodrome, south of Avila, in the autumn of 1936. Model 90 30-57 (ex-EC-MAA) was returned to the Aero Club de Andalucía in 1941, became EC-BAH, later 'ABT, and was scrapped in 1966. Model 90A De Luxe 30-59 (ex-EC-AZA) was used by the Condor Legion for much of the civil war and returned to Seville in 1940, becoming EC-ADN. In 1948 it was sold to J Llácer at Sabadell, Catalonia, and was scrapped in 1958. The other Model 90A De Luxe, 30-63 (ex-EC-ZAA), was returned to Seville in 1941 and became EC-ACV. After being sold to J Carmona of Madrid in 1949, and to J Picas of Manresa, near Barcelona, in 1953, it was scrapped in 1955.

Model 90A

Span 32ft; length 20ft 6in; height 6ft 11in; wing area 132sq ft.

Maximum speed (90A) 130mph (De Luxe) 135mph; cruising speed (90A) 110mph (De Luxe) 115mph; ceiling (90A) 14,000ft (De Luxe) 15,000ft; range (90A) 600 miles (De Luxe) 515 miles.

The Morane-Saulnier MS 140.
(Laureau)

Morane-Saulnier MS 60

The MS 60 was simply a de Havilland D.H.60 Moth built under licence by Morane-Saulnier. In his memoir *De la voltige aérienne a la Guerre d'Espagne* (Paris 1978), the Spanish Republican pilot Francisco Pérez Mur writes that, during a reconnaissance flight over Aragón on 26 July 1936 in a de Havilland Hornet Moth, he was obliged to land on an airstrip near Lérida through shortage of fuel. He was able to obtain 30lit of petrol from the tank of a 'Morane Moth' which had recently crashed in a nearby vegetable garden. This is the only specific reference to a Morane MS 60 in the Spanish Civil War and, since there is no record of such a type imported into Spain before the war, its presence in Catalonia at that date is a mystery. It has been asserted that a few MS 60s were smuggled into Republican Spain during the civil war, but none has yet been identified.

Morane-Saulnier MS 140

Léon Morane and Raymond Saulnier, who had been friends since childhood, exhibited their first four monoplanes at the Salon de l'Aéronautique in Paris in 1911, and in the next twenty-two years produced a series of monoplanes, mostly of the parasol type, famous for their sturdiness and superb manoeuvrability. Their Type L of 1913 was the first aircraft to have the adjective 'parasol'

Morane-Saulnier MS 181.

applied to describe that particular configuration.

The Morane-Saulnier MS 140, being a single-bay biplane, was not a typical product of the stable. Moreover, although it was not built until 1927, it seemed, from its general appearance and its 80hp Le Rhône 9C rotary engine, to belong to a generation of at least ten years earlier. It was designed as an ambulance aircraft in which a stretcher carrying one casualty could be slid through a hatch into the fuselage behind the pilot's cockpit. However, a dual control and second pilot's seat could be installed, allowing it to be used as a trainer. The MS 140 was of all-wooden construction with fabric covering. The large-area, high-lift wings were intended to enable it to operate from very small fields, and the upper wing was swept back and

the lower braced to the upper fuselage longerons by a pair of inverted vee struts. The extremely wide-track undercarriage was intended to enable the aircraft to operate from rough ground.

Only the prototype, which received no registration, was built, and ten years later it was among the assorted machines in the 'aeroplane graveyard' at Villacoublay that were sold to agents acting for the Spanish Republicans. Its fate in Spain is not recorded, but it was probably used as a trainer.

Span 11.1m; length 7.43m; height 3.13m; wing area 35sq m.
Empty weight 610kg; loaded weight 864kg.
Maximum speed 131km/h.

Morane-Saulnier MS 181

This small single-seat parasol monoplane, designed purely for aerobatic training and displays, appeared in 1929 as a scaled-down MS 230. It was built in two versions, the MS 180 with a 40hp Salmson 9Ad radial engine, and the MS 181 with a 60hp Salmson 4Ac radial. The wing, carried on an inverted-vee cabane and braced to the fuselage by metal struts, had metal spars and ailerons, with wooden ribs, and was fabric covered. The two front bays of the fuselage were built of metal, while the rest of it was of wood with fabric covering. The tail unit was of metal, again with fabric covering. Both versions were ordered by the Compagnie Française d'Aviation for its flying schools in 1930, and one MS 181, F-AJQK, was still flying at the school in the 1970s.

Four MS 181s were acquired by the Spanish Republicans:

c/n 1, F-AJQT. This machine, the prototype, was damaged at Coulommiers on 13 July 1937 while a Spanish pilot was being trained, but was repaired and thereafter disappears from the register.

c/n 6, F-AJQN. Leased by Roland Goix to Lejeune Aviation on 16 February 1937, this aircraft was used as a trainer for Spanish pilots at Isles les Villenoy. It was sold to Lejeune on 21 January 1938, but had disappeared by 21 March that year.

c/n 8, F-AJQP, and c/n 11 F-AJQS. Bought by Lejeune in September and March 1937 respectively, both aircraft were at Isles les Villenoy on 13 July 1937 and both disappeared by February 1938. In Spain, where they were allotted the type code EU, they were employed as aerobatic trainers at la Ribera (San Javier), in Murcia.

Span 9m; length 6.04m; height 2.29m; wing area 13.2sq m.
Empty weight 379kg; loaded weight 510kg.
Maximum speed 133km/h at sea level, 124km/h at 3,000m; climb to 1,000m in 11min 15sec.

Morane-Saulnier MS 230 and MS 233

This famous two-seater, of which several examples are still flying, was the most successful of all the aerobatic Morane-Saulnier parasol mono-

A Morane-Saulnier MS 230 trainer performs aerobatics.

planes. It first appeared in 1930 as a development of the MS 53 and MS 130 series, and possessed the same type of wide-track undercarriage and wood and metal construction as the MS 181. The MS 230 was powered by an uncowled 230hp Salmson 9Ab radial engine, and the MS 233 of 1931 had an uncowled 270hp Gnome-Rhône 5 Kc radial. The series was built in large numbers, production being revived in 1945 and continuing until 1947.

The MS 230 F-ALIA (c/n 183/-) was sold by Roland Coty to Lejeune Aviation on 4 February 1937, and disappeared from the Bureau Veritas register thereafter. The MS 233 F-AIID (c/n 4/2842) was a rebuilt MS 133 (c/n 8, also F-AIID and registered to Société Morane-Saulnier on 4 May 1927). Lejeune bought it in late 1936 and sent it to Spain soon afterwards, for in the first two weeks of February 1937 the Republican pilot Francisco Pérez Mur was flying it, still with its French registrations showing, at Sariñena aerodrome in Aragón. A second MS 233, F-AIKD (c/n 53), was acquired and disposed of by Lejeune in the same way and at about the same time. Later, the MS 230 and the MS 233s were transferred to La Ribera, San Javier, near Cartagena,

Morane-Saulnier MS 233 F-AIKD at El Carmolí, Cartagena, on 3 January 1937. (Arráez)

A Morane-Saulnier MS 341.

and used for aerobatic and formation training. Their type code was EU.

MS 230

Span 10.7m; length 7.00m; height 2.7m; wing area 19.7sq m.

Empty weight 793kg; loaded weight 1,150kg.

Maximum speed 205km/h at sea sevel, 193km/h at 3,000m; climb to 3,000 in 11min 18sec.

MS 233

Span 10.7m; height 2.85m; wing area 19.7sq m.

Empty weight 794kg; loaded weight 2,530kg.

Maximum speed 200km/h; ceiling 5,800m.

Morane-Saulnier MS 341 and MS 345

The Morane-Saulnier MS 340 two-seat parasol monoplane, powered by a 120hp de Havilland Gipsy III inverted in-line engine and possessing a redesigned tail unit differing markedly from those of its predecessors, was an attempt to bring the Morane-Saulnier light parasol monoplane formula into line with the standards of the 1930s. The prototype, F-AMOP, made its first flight in April 1933 and, after being re-engined with a 120hp Renault 4Pdi, was redesignated MS 341. Minor modifications led to the MS 341/2 and MS 341/3 (140hp Renault 4Pei). The MS 342 and 342/2 had 130hp de Havilland Gipsy Major

engines, and the MS 343 and 343/2 had Salmson 9Nd and 9Nc engines of 175hp and 135hp respectively. Although twelve MS 343s were built for the Armée de l'Air, the series attracted few customers.

In 1935 the company produced the altogether more elegant MS 345, powered by a 140hp Renault 4Pei. In this final version the wings had dihedral, and the clutter of bracing struts was replaced by a pair of faired Y struts connecting the wing to the undercarriage legs. The undercarriage itself was refined into a pair of broad faired cantilever legs, and the wheels were housed in large streamlined spats. The fin and rudder were made taller. All the MS 340 series used mixed wood and metal construction.

Three MS 341s and (possibly) the MS 345 ended their careers in the Spanish Civil War:

MS 341/2 F-AMBU (c/n 4/-, the prototype) was bought by Lejeune Aviation (see Appendix II) in May 1937, was last checked at Coulom-

A Morane-Saulnier MS 341 at El Carmolí. In the peaked cap is the chief instructor, Castaneda, and beside him is Gerardo Gil. Both were veterans of the Escuadrilla Lacalle I-15 Chato squadron. (Arráez)

miers on 17 July 1937, and disappeared thereafter.

MS 341/2 F-ANIE (c/n 9/-) belonged to the wife of Michel Detroyat (see Lockheed Orion), and its last Bureau Veritas check was at Villacoublay on 14 April 1937. In May it was sold to Lejeune and disappeared from view thereafter.

MS 341/3 F-ANHY (c/n 2/-) was likewise bought by Lejeune in May 1937. It was last checked at Royan on 20 July 1937, and its certificate of airworthiness was simply described as 'withdrawn', which, under the special circumstances, probably meant it was not there.

The prototype MS 345 was tested

at Villacoublay in June 1935, registered F-ANVR, and bought by Emile Rasson-Six. No production orders were received, however, and Morane-Saulnier, now busy with the MS 405/406 fighter programme, decided to abandon further development of the parasol monoplane. Lejeune bought the MS 345 at some time in 1937, and resold it to Roland Goix (see MS 181). It has been persistently reported that it then went to Republican Spain, but, since it was still at Orly on 23 July 1938, it can only have gone to Catalonia, and after that date.

Morane-Saulnier MS 341/2 and 341/3

Span 10.2m; length 6.94m; height 2.29m; wing area 15.75sq m.

Empty weight 557kg; loaded weight (MS 341/2) 917kg, (MS 341/3) 920kg.

Maximum speed (MS 341/2) 191km/h, (MS 341/3) 200km/h.

Morane-Saulnier MS 345

Span 10.2m; length 6.95m; height 2.47m; wing area 15.75sq m.

Empty weight 621kg; loaded weight 886kg.

Maximum speed 210km/h.

Moreau 10(I)

On 25 September 1937 the Spanish Nationalist newspaper *Sur* reported that a French subject named Klis had gone to Barcelona and offered a glider, which he had built himself, to the Catalonian regional government, the Generalitat. However, he had been arrested and shot by the Iberian Anarchist Federation (FAI), and his body thrown into a ditch. The author has not been able to discover the identity of 'Klis', but the story seems to be a garbled version of an incident which did indeed occur, concerning the Moreau 10(I) aircraft and its builder, Jean-Marie Moreau, a factory manager and amateur aviation enthusiast of Neuilly-sur-Seine, Paris.

In 1931 the Société Commerciale Aéronautique (SCA), which was the Fokker agent in France, built a three-seat low-wing cabin monoplane for long-distance touring. It was of wood and metal construction, with plywood covering, and powered by a 95hp Renault engine. Its de-

signation, SFR 10, referred to the three engineers who had designed and built it: Schmitt, Fleustoy and Rigaud. The machine proved to be heavy and slow, and was scrapped. The SCA, however, sold the patents and licence to Moreau, who built his own aircraft to the design and fitted it with a 135hp de Havilland Gipsy Major inverted in-line engine, which he later replaced with a 180hp Regnier 6BO-1 engine of the same configuration. This aeroplane, which he called the Moreau 10(I), passed its tests at Villacoublay and was registered F-ANNI on 6 July 1935. It was slightly damaged in an accident at Orly on 9 November 1936, and was repaired. Its last Bureau Veritas inspection at Orly on 20 October 1936 records that it had logged ninety-eight hours flying.

In an interview with M Rémy Tiger in 1978, Rémy Clément, who had been involved in the supply of aircraft to Republican Spain during the civil war (see Caudron C.510 Pélican, Farman F.190 and F.402, and other French aircraft), said that he had heard that a man named Moreau had flown his home-made aeroplane to Barcelona and had been murdered. This rumour was confirmed in October 1989 by M Jean Massé of Perpignan, who discovered a report in *l'Indépendent des Pyrénées Orientales* of 31 March 1939. Quoting a communiqué of the Sûreté Nationale, the report said that

The Moreau 10(I), whose unfortunate builder and owner was murdered in Barcelona after delivering his machine to the Republicans. (Jack Meaden)

Moreau had left France in his aeroplane at the beginning of March 1937, intending to sell it in Barcelona for 100,000 French francs (£568), a modest price compared with those being demanded from the Republicans by most vendors at that time. Nothing more was heard of him until his wife, who had been making frantic enquiries, received an anonymous letter alleging that he had been assassinated and that his body, wrapped in a sheet, had been left in a garage. Five Spaniards, including a woman, who had been among the tens of thousands who had crossed into France during the collapse of Catalonia in February 1939, had been arrested and charged with his murder. At the time of writing the circumstances and outcome of this strange affair are still not known.

Span 13.5m; length 8.3m; height 2.4m; wing area 22sq m.

Empty weight 692kg; loaded weight 1,070kg.

Maximum speed 205km/h; ceiling 5,500m; range (normal) 1,000km, (long distance) 5,000km.

Northrop Delta Models 1C and 1D, and Gamma Models 2D and 5B

The early 1930s saw the appearance of the streamlined cantilever monoplane of all-metal, stressed-skin construction and with a retractable undercarriage and enclosed accommodation for its occupants. The most significant contribution to this revolution in aircraft design was made by a number of American designers

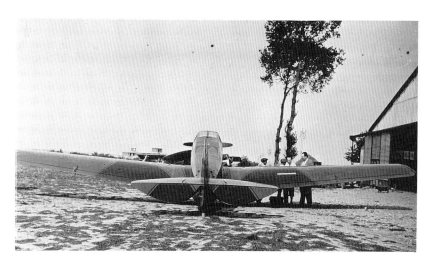

and engineers working for companies based in California (Douglas, Lockheed, Northrop and the Airplane Development Corporation, which built the Vultee V1).

John K Northrop, one of the most inventive of this gifted group, had been responsible for the Lockheed Vega and, before leaving Lockheed in 1928, had begun work, in collaboration with Gerard Vultee, on an all-metal low-wing cantilever monoplane. This became the Northrop Alpha, produced by Northrop's Avion Corporation in 1929-30, and thirteen were built for TWA and five for other clients. It was a six-passenger transport, with the pilot's cockpit to the rear of the passenger cabin. It had a fixed, unspatted, undercarriage, and was powered by a 420hp Pratt & Whitney R-1340-C Wasp C radial engine. The Northrop Beta was a scaled-down sports version with two open cockpits, an inverted in-line engine, and streamlined trousers over the undercarriage legs.

Avion was bought out by the United Aircraft Corporation, and Northrop received financial assistance to establish the Northrop Corporation as a research and development source for Douglas Aircraft. His first two creations, conceived and built more or less simultaneously, were the Model 1 Delta and Model 2 Gamma, both advanced aeroplanes incorporating the multi-cellular, stressed-skin Northrop wing to be used on the Douglas DC-1 and DC-2. Indeed, the only 'old-fashioned' feature of these aircraft was that they had fixed undercarriages, though the legs were enclosed in streamlined metal trousers.

The Delta was intended as an all-metal replacement for the Lockheed Orion, carrying a pilot (later pilot and copilot) and eight passengers, plus mail, on short-stop feeder services. It retained the fixed undercarriage not only because it was cheaper and lighter, but because it was thought to be more reliable on the small and often rough aerodromes from which it was expected to operate. Of the versions that concern us here, the 1C Delta was powered by a 700hp Pratt & Whitney TIC Wasp radial, and the 1D Delta by a 710hp Wright Cyclone R-1820-F3 radial,

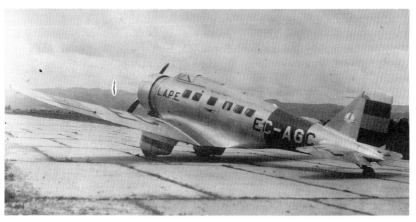

The Northrop 1C Delta ex-SE-ADI Halland *in LAPE service.* (J-M Carreras)

both being housed in wide-chord NACA cowlings.

The Gamma began as a projected series of custom-built high performance aircraft to be adapted to whatever purpose the customer had in mind. Thus, of three 2D Gammas built for TWA in 1933, two were used as mail carriers and one (c/n 4, NX13758), was fitted with a turbo-supercharged engine as an experimental high-altitude laboratory, and did much valuable research in exploring the conditions that would have to be met by later generations of high-flying commercial airliners. A Gamma was used for the Ellsworth Transantarctic Flight, and another, in Britain (registered G-AFBT), for testing the 1,400hp Bristol Hercules radial engine. The usual powerplant was the same as that of the 1D Delta.

In October 1934 new US Federal regulations were passed, stipulating that commercial passenger-carrying aircraft must have at least two engines and two pilots. This curtailed the promising career of the Delta, and in the summer of 1936 several, sold off by their operating companies, were still awaiting buyers. Accordingly, three were among the nineteen aircraft bought, through the aircraft dealer Charles Babb, by Rudolph Wolf for the Spanish Republicans in November 1936. Wolf's sudden death at the beginning of December (see Appendix II) allowed a rival buying agent, Robert Cuse, to snap up two of the Deltas (c/n 38, NC14241 and c/n 41, NC14266), which thus sailed on the *Mar Cantáb-*

rico and were captured by the Nationalists in the Bay of Biscay. In Nationalist service, after receiving much publicity for propaganda purposes, the two Deltas were employed on liaison and transport duties. Provision was made for a gunner's position midway along the roof of the passenger-cabin, but this was never used. Delta NC14266, distinguishable by its direction-finding aerial in a streamlined housing above the rear fuselage, received the military serial 43-4, and NC14241, which had a curved pylon aerial above the pilot's cabin, became 43-5. Towards the end of the civil war 43-4 was damaged by a ground loop, and it seems that 43-5 was cannibalised for its repair. At any rate, 43-4 continued flying for some years, receiving the new serial L.12 in 1940.

Wolf's third Delta, c/n 39 NC14242, which had once belonged to Hal Roach Studios, the makers of the Laurel and Hardy films, sailed with the other aircraft of the Wolf shipment at the end of December 1936, its fuselage on board the Dutch ship *Waalhaven* and its wings on board the liner *American Traveler.* After assembly it was tested by the CEMA at Villacoublay, test pilot Louis Bonte reporting that its supercharger functioned badly and caused oil and black smoke to pour from the exhaust pipes during take-off. Nonetheless, it was certificated, registered F-AQAQ, and flown to Barcelona during the night of 28-29 August 1937. On 1 November it caused local surprise, and much speculation in the French press, when it made a forced landing beside the village of St Cyprien, between Perpignan and the coast. It seems to have had no registration markings and to have been painted grey, or left in plain aluminium finish which had become weathered. The pilot, who claimed to be an American, spoke excellent French and left by road for Paris to collect a spare part. Some days later a French pilot named Marcel Finance, who may or may not have been the original pilot, appeared, carried out the repair and took off again on 9 November.

At the end of the war the Delta, now painted dark green or blue and fitted with a two-bladed propeller in place of the three-bladed Hamilton propeller it had had for a time in Spain, flew to Oran, Algeria, whence it was recovered by the Nationalists in May 1939. It served for several years in the Ejercito del Aire, with the serial 43-17 and nicknamed 'El Fabricante de Aceite' ('the Oil Maker'), before being withdrawn some time after 1946.

The fourth Delta that flew in the civil war is of particular interest. Until the late 1970s the known records seemed to show that, after serving for three years with the Swedish airline AB Aerotransport (ABA), this machine, an early Model 1C, was sold in June 1937 to Beryl Markham. After learning to fly in Kenya, where she had been brought up, Markham had achieved fame in 1936 by making the first solo east-to-west flight across the North Atlantic, flying a Percival Gull. Having declared that she had acquired the Delta for a forthcoming transatlantic flight with James Mollison, she supposedly sold it instead to the King of Iraq, in whose Royal Flight it served until it crashed in 1940. Another version of the story claimed that it never went to Iraq, but returned to Sweden, where Flygverput used it as a target-tug until 1943.

Both stories were proved false in 1976, when the ex-LAPE pilot Pedro Tonda, living in exile in Mexico, gave aeronautical historian Dr Richard K Smith a photograph of this Delta in Spanish Republican colours. There can be no doubt that this was the same aeroplane, for no other example of a 1C Delta was built. In 1977 the ex-LAPE pilot José-María Carreras gave another photograph of the same aircraft to the author. Although the story of how the Delta reached Republican Spain, and not Iraq or

Above: *Northrop 1D Delta ex-NC14242 shortly after its arrival in Republican Spain in August 1937.*

Northrop Delta ex-NC14241 in Nationalist service as 45-2. (US Air Force photo, via Dr R K Smith)

Sweden, is still unclear, it has been possible, with the help of Lennart Andersson and James Carmody, to reconstruct its history more accurately than before.

Early in 1934 AB Aerotransport bought two Northrop Deltas direct from the manufacturer, a Model 1C and a Model 1E. The 1E Delta (c/n 28, SE-ADW *Smalland*), which resembled a Gamma in configuration, crashed in July 1934. The 1C (c/n 7, SE-ADI *Halland*) was powered by a 700hp Pratt & Whitney Hornet T1C radial engine driving a two-bladed variable-pitch propeller, and still had the sliding canopy over the single-seat cockpit that was replaced, in later models, by the wider, roofed cabin to accommodate a pilot and copilot seated side by side. After a period on the Malmo-Göteborg route, it was entered for the MacRobertson England–Australia air race in October 1934, but did not compete. It then flew mail between Stockholm, Malmo and Hanover, Germany, and by January 1937 had logged 975

hours with ABA. On 22 January 1937 an application was received to export the Delta to Kenya, and this was granted on 12 February. At the beginning of May, however, the Delta was flown not to Kenya but to Croydon, London, by Capt Carl Florman, who, during the first half of 1936, had helped British Airways organise the Gatwick–Stockholm route. The airliners used for these trials had been the four Fokker F.XIIs that were sold to Gen Mola of the Spanish Nationalists in August 1936. At Croydon the Delta was kept in the hangar of Personal Airways, which, during the previous autumn, had been concerned in an attempt to sell two de Havilland Dragon Rapides (G-ACTU and 'DWZ) to French intermediaries acting for the Spanish government.

On 24 May 1937 James Mollison flew to Meaux, near Paris, in his Bellanca 28/70 *The Dorothy* in order, he said, to confer with Beryl Markham over the proposed transatlantic flight. Whether Beryl Markham flew

A Northrop 2D Gamma.

the event, rescued before it was needed. In February 1937 it was bought by Frank Cordova of Long Island, New York, who flew it to San Antonio, Texas, and sold it to Coronel Gustavo León of the Mexican air force. It reappeared at Tejeria Airport, Vera Cruz, Mexico, on

to Meaux in the Delta, or went by other means, is uncertain. Meaux, however, was the aerodrome owned by Lejeune Aviation and used for the clandestine training of pilots for, and the smuggling of aircraft to, Republican Spain. The Delta seems to have returned to Sweden some time after this, for on 26 June 1937 a new application was made to export it, this time to England. This was granted on 31 June, and a British registration, G-AEXR, was reserved for the machine. A letter in ABA files, dated 12 July 1937, states that the Delta had been sold to Beryl Markham and flown directly from Stockholm to Meaux, making the 1,000-mile journey in 4hr 40min. Its Swedish registration was cancelled on 13 July. Finally, the Delta is reported as being sold to the government of Iraq on 27 September 1937 and given the registration YI-OSF. By then, however, it had probably crossed the Pyrenees, along with Mollison's Bellanca.

About six months previously certain officials of the Iraq Legation in Paris had been discovered selling faked export licences for arms and aircraft to the Spanish Republic. One man, alleged to have earned £30,000 by this means, had fled to Lebanon, where he joined a group of Iraqi exiles hostile to King Ghasi, who ruled Iraq under a British Mandate. The British government had become alarmed and the affair had been hushed up, but it seems that, by the following September, other officials at the Legation judged it safe to revive the trade.

The appearance in this affair of familiar names – Lejeune Aviation, Personal Airways and the Fokker F.XIIs of British Airways – strengthens the suspicion that the Northrop Delta was earmarked for Republican Spain from the beginning. The story itself provides yet another example of

The Northrop 5B Gamma. (Peter Bowers, via R S Allen)

the extraordinary lengths to which the Republicans and their agents felt obliged to go to circumvent the Non-Intervention controls. Whether Beryl Markham herself was a conscious party to the subterfuge, or was unwittingly used to provide respectable cover for it, it is now impossible to say.

In Spain the Delta was registered EC-AGC and joined LAPE as Fleet No 31. It was popular with the pilots, and Carreras told the author that it was in this machine that he flew the Republican Premier, Juan Negrín, to Zurich in September 1938 for a highly secret meeting with an emissary of Hitler, to discuss possible ways of negotiating a peace with Franco. The discussions failed. Carreras did not know what became of the Delta at the end of the war, but believed it was destroyed on the ground by bombing.

Two Northrop Gammas flew in the Spanish Civil War, both with the Republicans. One, Model 2D c/n 10 NC13759, powered by a 710hp Wright Cyclone F-3 engine, was one of the three bought by TWA, which sold it in December 1935 to Texaco. Shortly thereafter it was flown to Argentina to rescue the Ellsworth Transantarctic Flight, who were, in

17 March 1937, registered XA-ABJ. It thus became part of the Spanish ambassador's collection of aircraft at Vera Cruz.

The second Gamma was the 5B c/n 188, NR14998, a prototype development of the Northrop 2E military version of the Gamma, and thus an ancestor of the Northrop A-17 and the famous Douglas SBD Dauntless dive-bomber of the Pacific War. As in the 2E, the pilot and observer were housed beneath a transparent canopy in the conventional forward position. In 1936 its 700hp Pratt & Whitney Twin Wasp Junior SAI-G engine was replaced by an 870hp Wright Cyclone G engine, and the aircraft was sent on a sales tour of Latin America. While in storage at Buenos Aires in January 1937 it was sold to Henry Fletcher of Mexico City, and brought to Mexico in February. Registered XA-ABI to Coronel Rafael Montero of the Mexican air force, it joined the Spanish ambassador's collection at Vera Cruz. Both Gammas sailed for France on board the *Ibai* (see Appendix II) on 27 December 1937, and crossed into Republican Spain in the spring of 1938. Both aircraft were allegedly incorporated into the 1ª Escuadrilla of Grupo 72, with the Vultees, and both survived the war. In the 1950s they were at Cuatro Vientos, Madrid, partially dismantled and being used for the instruction of engineering students in the Ejercito del Aire.

1C Delta

Span 47ft 9in; length 32ft 1in.

1D Delta

Span 48ft; length 33ft 1in; wing area 363sq ft.

Empty weight 4,540lb; loaded weight 7,350lb; wing loading 20.2lb/sq ft.

Maximum speed 220mph; cruising speed 200mph; range 1,550 miles.

2D Gamma

Span 47ft 10in; length 31ft 2in; height 9ft; wing area 363sq ft.

Empty weight 4,119lb; loaded weight 7,350lb,

Maximum speed 224mph at 7,000ft; cruising speed 215mph at 7,000ft; landing speed (with flaps) 62mph; initial climb 1,280ft/min; ceiling 20,000ft; range 1,700 miles with a mail cargo of 900lb.

Pallarols 40A

On 15 December 1933 two Catalonian airmen, Alfred Davins Ferrer and Emili Francesc, formed the Sirius company for the design and construction of light touring aircraft. For their premises they used a woodworking factory in Barcelona owned by Joan Pallarols Columer. Their first creation, the Pallarols 40A, was a wooden two-seat shoulder-wing monoplane with ply and fabric covering. Its most unusual feature was the placing of the two cockpits, that of the pilot being in front of the leading edge and that of the passenger behind the trailing edge. The wing was of constant chord, and was braced to the fuselage on each side by a single faired strut. The wide-track undercarriage consisted of the conventional three-strut arrangement, the two rearmost struts being faired. Power was provided by a two-cylinder, horizontally-opposed 40hp ABC Scorpion II engine.

The little aeroplane was first flown at the end of August 1934 by Guillermo Xuclá, director of the Escola d'Aviació Barcelona (Barcelona Flying School), and was found to have a promising performance and excellent handling characteristics. Registered EC-AAX, it was kept at the Aero Club Canudas, near Prat de Llobregat Airport, Barcelona, and was still there in July 1936. Nothing seems to be known of its fate in the civil war, but it was probably used during the early months as a liaison aircraft.

Dimensions not available.
Loaded weight 400kg.
Maximum speed 150km/h; cruising speed 130km/h; landing speed 65km/h; range 700km.

Percival Gull Six

One of the classic touring and sports aeroplanes of the 1930s, the Percival Gull won a name for itself almost immediately after it appeared early in

A Percival Gull, probably ex-G-ADMI, captured by the Nationalists at the end of the war. (Arráez)

1933 by being used for record-breaking flights by several prominent aviators. The most notable of these was the remarkable flight from Lympne, Kent, to Darwin, Australia, in 7 days, 4 hours and 44 minutes, made by Sir Charles Kingsford-Smith in G-ACJV *Miss Southern Cross* in December 1933, and the great flights from England to South America (Britannia Trophy) in 1935, and England to New Zealand in 1936, by Jean Batten in G-ADPR.

Designed by Capt Edgar Percival, the Gull was a low-wing cantilever monoplane of wooden construction with plywood covering. In the production aircraft the three-strut, spatted undercarriage was replaced by a pair of cantilever compression legs. The pilot and two passengers were provided with a shapely enclosed cabin. The Type D.1 Gull Four was powered by a 130hp de Havilland Gipsy Major engine, and the Type D.3 Gull Six by a 200hp Gipsy Six.

Two Percival Gull Sixes flew in the Spanish Civil War. The first was G-ADEP (c/n D.49), the machine in which, in June 1935, Edgar Percival had flown from Gravesend, Kent, to Oran, Algeria, and returned the same day in time to dine with friends in London. During the Italian invasion of Ethiopia (Abyssinia), Brian Allen Aviation at Reading had used this and two other Gulls to fly press reporters in and out of Addis Ababa. On 7 August 1936 Union Founders Trust bought G-ADEP and three other machines on Reading Aerodrome (see Airspeed Envoy, Miles Falcon and Miles Hawk Major) on

behalf of the Republican agent Comandante Carlos Pastor Krauel, and had it flown to Paris on the same day. It was flown to Spain within a day or two, probably by Edouard Corniglion-Molinier (see Lockheed Orion), who continued to fly it in Spain until his return to France in September, and described it as his favourite aeroplane. Thereafter it was employed on liaison duties by the Republicans.

The second Spanish Gull Six was G-ADMI (c/n D.54), registered to W Robertson Porter, who in August 1936 sold it to B Coyco at Orly, Paris, who in turn sold it to Lejeune Aviation at Meaux, Esbly, in October. In October 1937, Lejeune, which trained Spanish pilots in France and procured a number of aircraft for the Republicans, sold it to William Domènge (see Gourdou-Leseurre GL-32). The Gull, re-registered F-APEI, is listed, in a Nationalist report based on captured Republican documents, among aircraft delivered to Republican Spain in 1937.

One Gull Six, probably the second to arrive, survived the civil war and was recovered by the Nationalists 'in perfect condition'. It continued flying for the Ejercito del Aire, first with Grupo 30 (serial number not known) and later as L.6, until 1946.

A British police report dated 25 September 1936 includes Percival P.3 Gull Six G-ADEU among the aircraft suspected of being sold to Comandante Pastor and under guard at Croydon, but this machine does not appear in any subsequent reports.

Span 36ft 2in; length 24ft 9in; height 7ft 4½in; wing area 169sq ft.
Empty weight 1,480lb; loaded weight 2,450lb.
Maximum speed 178mph; cruising speed 158mph; ceiling 20,000ft; range 640 miles.

Potez 25

One of the most successful and versatile aircraft ever produced by the Société Henri Potez, or by France for that matter, the Potez 25 was a rugged, single-engined, two-seat, unequal-span biplane. The prototype, derived from the Potez 15S

and Potez 24, first flew in 1925, and the type was soon ordered into production. It was meant to perform the greatest possible variety of military tasks in all climates and conditions, and was therefore designed to accommodate almost any type of engine, air- or liquid-cooled, in the 420-550hp range. The Potez 25 was of wooden construction and, except for the metal skinning on the forward fuselage and round the two cockpits, was fabric covered. Although no fewer than eighty-seven experimental versions were built, those produced for the French air forces were of three principal models: the Potez 25A2 reconnaissance aircraft, equipped with a camera and radio telephony; the Potex 25B day bomber; and the Potez 25TOE (Théatre des Opérations Extérieures) for colonial and police duties, of which 2,050 were built.

In 1933 a formation of twenty-eight Potez 25TOEs (450hp Lorraine 12Eb engines) made a tour of all the French African colonies – a flight nicknamed Le Raid Nègre, or 'Black Cruise', by its commander, Général Vuillemin – and similar tests of endurance were carried out by French Potez 25TOE-equipped squadrons in the Far East. Of the 4,000 or so Potez 25s produced altogether, a considerable number was sold to, or built under licence in, foreign countries, including Romania (120), China (15), Poland (10), Sweden (10 with floats), Estonia (9), Uruguay (7), Paraguay (7), Abyssinia

One of the eight Estonian Potez 25A2s, with Gnome-Rhône Jupiter engines, shipped to the northern Republican zone in the summer of 1937. (Laureau)

(6) and one each to a dozen other countries including Spain.

The Spanish example, a 25TOE delivered in 1926 and shown at the Exposición de Aéronautica in Madrid in October that year, was a pattern aircraft for a planned series of twenty-five to be built by Hispano-Suiza. According to some questionable reports it was refurbished and pressed into service with one of the Breguet 19 units at the start of the civil war in July 1936.

Be that as it may, the first documented mention of Potez 25s in connection with the Spanish war is dated 21 July 1936, when two Spanish air force officers, Comandantes Juan Aboal and Ismael Warleta (see Douglas DC-2), arrived in Paris to arrange the purchase of military aircraft, specifically twenty Potez 54s. Only four Potez 54s were available at that date, however, and Pierre Cot, the French air minister, ordered a search of reserve stock to find other Potez aircraft that might temporarily suffice. What he found was a small series of Potez 25A2s which had been fitted with 500hp Farman 12We water-cooled engines. They had long been withdrawn from service, but seventeen were still held in a depôt in northern France. He ordered these to be transferred, by air if possible and if not by road, to the Armée de l'Air base at Mondesir, near Étampes, about 40km south of Paris, where Aboal and Warleta could inspect them. To conceal the transaction, since the French government officially rejected the Spanish appeal for help a few days later, the aircraft were to be sold to Avions Marcel Bloch (Potez and Bloch had an organisation for sharing government contracts), which would meanwhile receive an order for eight Bloch

MB 132 bombers (at that time the design existed only on the drawing boards). Bloch, it seems, was then to sell the Potez 25A2s to the Spaniards, and in due course receive a cancellation of the order for the MB 132s. The money paid by the Spaniards for the 25A2s would be paid to the French government, ostensibly as a refund (less cancellation fees and other costs) of the advance on the MB 132 order. This complicated deal fell through when the Spaniards found that only seven of the Potez 25s were airworthy. Besides, the whole affair was leaked to the Opposition French press and caused a scandal.

On the Nationalist side, according to newspaper and British consular reports, a Potez 25TOE from French Morocco landed at Tetuán on 28 August 1936, and the pilot, named Balzac, allegedly shot himself. This incident has never been satisfactorily explained, nor is it known if the Potez was returned. British newspapers also reported that two Potez 25s were 'handed over' to the Spanish Nationalists in the middle of September.

A few more Potez 25A2s may have found their way to the main Republican zone in 1937 and 1938. These had been acquired from La Société Caudron by Lejeune Aviation at Meaux (see Caudron and Morane aircraft, *inter alia*). The most likely are listed below, though how many actually reached Spain is not certain, because so many records relating to these matters were falsified.

In addition, the Potez 25/55 F-APFB (450hp Lorraine 12Eb water-cooled engine) was bought from Caudron by Lejeune on 10 September 1937(?) and struck off as 'destroyed' in December 1938. In Spain they would have been used as trainers.

As described in the section on the Bristol Bulldog II, in the spring of 1937 the Spanish Republicans

A Potez 36/21. (Liron)

Below: *a Potez 430.*

agreed to buy eight Bulldogs and eight Potez 25A2s (480hp Gnome-Rhône Jupiter radials) from Estonia in exchange for the Estonian government's acting as an ostensible buyer of aircraft in Czechoslovakia, on behalf of the Spaniards. These aircraft arrived at Gijón early in July 1937, hidden beneath potatoes on board the SS *Viuu*. Nothing is known of their service in the Basque-Asturian air arm, but none survived the northern campaign.

Span 14.14m; length 9.4m; height 3.67m; wing area 46sq m.
Empty weight 1,190kg; loaded weight 1,958-1,995kg.
Maximum speed 220-230km/h;

cruising speed 180-190km/h; ceiling 7,200-7,400m; range 500-600km.

Potez 36, 43 and 58

These three types of light aircraft were basically the same design carried through several stages of improvement. Insofar as their participation in the Spanish Civil War is concerned, they are best dealt with together.

In 1928 an English lord happened to mention to Henri Potez that there was a need for light touring aircraft equipped with comfortable cabins. This notion, perhaps inspired by a similar conversation with the same

F-AOTF (c/n 89/–)	Caudron to Lejeune	3.1937	Returned to Caudron	10.1938
F-AOTG (c/n 91/–)	Caudron to Lejeune			9.1938
F-AOTK (c/n 410/1553)	Caudron to Lejeune			9.1938
F-AOTJ (c/n 241/1265)	Caudron to Lejeune		W/o	9.1938
F-AOTI (c/n 219/1243)	Caudron to Lejeune	6.5.1937	W/o	9.1938
F-AOTH (c/n 87/1157)	Caudron to Lejeune	15.5.1937	W/o	9.1938

A Potez 58 on the Republican aerodrome at Alcantarilla, Murcia. The man on the right is José Falco, commander of the I-15 night-fighter squadron. (Arráez)

gentleman, also spurred Geoffrey de Havilland to design the D.H.80 Puss Moth, which first flew in September 1929. Potez's design, the Potez 36 high-wing, side-by-side two-seat cabin monoplane, antedated the Puss Moth by several months, but was slightly smaller and less elegant. Like the Puss Moth it was of wooden construction, with fabric-covered wings and tail and a plywood-covered fuselage. Unlike the Puss Moth it had a Handley Page slot along the whole leading edge of each wing, and it could be powered by a variety of engines, including the Salmson 7Ac radial or Renault 4Pb water-cooled engine, both of 95hp, or the 100hp Potez 6Ac radial, the variants being designated 36/13, 36/14, 36/21 and so on. Altogether, 267 Potez 36s were built, in sixteen versions.

The Potez 43 was an enlarged three-seat development of the Potez 36, and first appeared in 1932. In the Potez 43 the leading-edge slots were reduced to the same length as the ailerons, and the choice of engines was in the 100-180hp range. A total of 177 was built, in ten versions. The Potez 58, the last of the line, was an aeroplane of considerably more stylish appearance. Most of them were powered by a Potez 6B (120hp) or 6Ba (130hp) radial engine encircled by a Townend ring, and the undercarriage wheels were housed in streamlined spats. The prototype first flew in September 1934, and 203, in four versions, were built.

In July 1936 there were two Potez

36s, one Potez 43 and one Potez 58 in Spain:

Potez 36/13 EC-AUU (c/n 2018 or 2048) (95hp Salmson 7Ac radial engine). Registered to Benjamino Gutierrez Junes and kept at Llanes, in the Asturias in northern Spain.

Potez 36/14 EC-AYY (c/n unknown) (95hp Renault 4Pb water-cooled engine). Registered to the Aero Club de Sabadell in Catalonia.

Potez 431 EC-AXA (c/n 3318), (105hp Potez 6Ac radial). Registered to Carlos Coll and kept at Prat de Llobregat, Barcelona Airport. In this aeroplane Ramón Torres (see Breguet 460 Vultur) had made a remarkable 12,000km tour of Central Africa in 1934.

There are reports of a Potez 58 at Prat de Llobregat, presumably recently arrived and so unregistered.

After the outbreak of the civil war the Potez 36 and 43 in Catalonia were employed on liaison and reconnaissance duties. The much-travelled Potez 43 EC-AXA happened, unfortunately, to be at Sariñena Aerodrome on 10 August, when a violent storm destroyed most of the aircraft on the field (the Potez, a Caudron Luciole, a Vickers Vildebeest and a Nieuport 52 – only two Breguet 19s were saved). The fate of the Potez 36 is not recorded, but it did not survive the war.

On 19 December 1936 a Potez 36 (c/n 3379, F-AMJG), and two Potez 58s (c/n 3494, F-AMRG and, reportedly, c/n 3795, F-ANLK) were

stolen from the Aéro Club d'Aveyron at Millau-La Cavalerie Aerodrome, some 90km inland from Montpellier in the south of France, and flown to Barcelona by six men disguised as engineers, pilots and officials of the Ministère de l'Air who had come to inspect and test the aircraft. The affair, which resulted in several arrests, was widely reported in the press both in France and abroad. It was said that the aircraft were three 'bombers', which in turn gave rise to a long-enduring series of myths concerning the thefts of bombers in France by Spanish agents of one side or the other. To placate the Aéro Club, air minister Pierre Cot, who was himself suspected of being implicated, promised to replace the machines at government expense. His chef-de-cabinet, Jean Moulin, who had previously been a Préfet in Aveyron, was to be so again, and was to become the greatest hero of the French Resistance during the Second World War, was also under suspicion. Again, the fate of these three Potez is not recorded. There is some doubt, however, over the identity of F-ANLK, for although this was the registration reported in all the newspapers, the Bureau Veritas supplement of 1936 records that its last inspection at Millau took place on 31 December 1936, when F-ALNK was registered as present.

Two other Potez 58s which may have gone to Republican Spain were F-ANDO, sold to Rémy Clément, who procured several aircraft for the Republicans, and the Potez 585 F-AOQM (c/n 4140), which was bought by Auguste Amestoy in November 1936 and seems to have been the first aircraft acquired by Air Pyrénées (see Appendix I). Finally the Potez 36/13 F-ALJQ (c/n 2373), belonging to Le Cercle Aéronautique de Coulommiers et de la Brie (see D.H.82 and D.H.89A), disappears from the records without explanation after August 1937 – always a suspicious sign during those years. No Potez 36s, 43s or 58s survived the war.

Potez 36

Span 10.45m; length 7.5m; height 2.45m; wing area 20sq m.

Empty weight 427kg; loaded weight 770kg.

Maximum speed 150km/h; cruising speed 130km/h; ceiling 3,600m; range 690km.

Potez 43

Span 11.3m; length 7.45m; height 2.36m; wing area 19sq m.

Empty weight 470kg; loaded weight 840kg.

Maximum speed 165km/h; cruising speed 140km/h; ceiling 5,000m; range 800km.

Potez 58

Span 11.3m; length 7.45m; height 2.33m; wing area 19sq m.

Empty weight 515kg; loaded weight 906kg.

Maximum speed 190km/h; cruising speed 160km/h; ceiling 5,000m; range 1,200km.

Potez 54

The decade between 1925 and 1935 saw the appearance in France of a series of military aircraft built under the classification MC (*multi-place-de-combat* – 'multi-seat combat aircraft') and, after 1932, BCR (*bombardment-combat-reconnaissance*). The intention behind these programmes was to produce, in quantity and as cheaply as possible, one type of aeroplane to perform the duties of several, including those of long-range bomber, reconnaissance aircraft, escort fighter and, perhaps, even those of a bomber-interceptor.

During the summer of 1918 German fighter pilots had been surprised to see formations of small single-engined bombers, usually Breguet 14s, protected by formations of much larger twin-engined, two-bay biplanes. This was an unprecedented reversal of the usual order of things, but the Caudron R.11 A3, with a crew of three and armed with five machine guns, had proved itself formidable in combat. The almost identical Caudron R.11 B3 had been effective as a bomber, and there seemed no reason why an analagous aircraft should not be equally suc-

Potez 54 BP-002 'R' of Grupo 72. It has Hispano-Suiza 12 X engines, and is either one of the Potez 540s delivered in October 1937, or is the original Potez 542 'R' re-engined. Such details become important when trying to estimate the number of Potez 54s delivered to the Spanish Republicans. (Laureau)

cessful ten or fifteen years later. The Italian engineer Gen Emilio Douhet, who in 1922 had written that fast, heavily-armed aerial cruisers would win the next war almost single-handed, is often said to have influenced the French chiefs-of-staff in their thinking, but anyone who has actually read Douhet may wonder whether he could have seriously influenced anyone professionally engaged in designing military aircraft. Whatever the case, the technical advances of the early 1930s revealed fundamental flaws in the whole concept, and in 1934 the French abandoned the ideal of the all-purpose warplane. (See Junkers K 30.)

The Potez 54, a twin-engined, high-wing braced monoplane with a crew of five, was in some respects a classic BCR aeroplane, possessing the angularity, slab-sided fuselage, generous fenestration, prominent birdcage-like turrets and underbelly gondola typical of those machines. In fact, the prototype was designed and built, without a government contract, in 1932, after private conversations between Henri Potez and Général Denain (the Chief of Staff). In other respects it was a departure from the formula, being aerodynamically more pleasing and less of a 'flying castle' than its predecessors and competi-

The Potez 542 'N' of the Malraux squadron. (Azaola)

tors. The prototype, with twin fins and rudders, first flew in November 1933. After acceptance tests were completed in May 1934, as a result of which the twin rudders were replaced by a single fin and rudder, the type was ordered by the Armée de l'Air, and began to enter service in November 1934.

The production Potez 540 M5 (the first seven aircraft had a crew of four, but all subsequent examples were five-crew aircraft) was powered by two 690hp counter-rotating Hispano-Suiza 12Xjrs/Xirs liquid-cooled vee engines which were connected to the base of the fuselage by a pair of aerofoil-section stub wings, and braced by struts to the wings and upper fuselage. The wings and tail were constructed of wood with ply and fabric covering. The 1,000kg bomb load was carried partly internally, in vertical bays, and partly externally on racks beneath the stub wings. The defensive armament consisted of from three to five 7.72mm rapid-firing Darne machine guns: one in the nose turret, and single or twin guns in the dorsal turret and ventral gondola, which was semi-retractable. The Potez 540 was equipped with the latest wireless and radio communications, oxygen apparatus, night-flying instruments, and frames for installing vertical and oblique-angle aerial cameras. The nose gunner doubled as bomb-aimer/navigator, the radio-operator and flight mechanic as rear gunners, and the copilot sat behind the first pilot. A total of 189 Potez 540s was built, and the type equipped bomber-reconnaissance squadrons of the Armée de l'Air in GB/1, and GR I, GR II and GR III. In addition, fifty-one Potez 542s with 720hp Lorraine Petrel 12Hdrs/Hers liquid-cooled vee engines were built, these equipping GR I/33, I/52, II/33 and III/33 – making nineteen squadrons in all equipped with Potez 54s.

Pilots found the Potez 54s extremely pleasant to fly, and the aircraft were generally popular with their crews. Other versions were the Potez 540 M4 (seven built, as mentioned above), the Potez 540TOE (three built for colonial service), the Potez 541 and 543, both with 860hp Gnome-Rhône 14 Kdrs radial engines (one Potez 541 and eight, or perhaps ten, Potez 543s built and exported to Rumania – see below), and the Potez 542TOE (six built for colonial service) and Potez 544, with two 860hp Hispano-Suiza 12Yhs liquid-cooled vee engines. (Only one 544 was built, but some Potez 540s and 542s were converted into 544s in 1938-40.)

On 13 December 1935 a Potez 54 and an Amiot 143 visited Barajas Airport, Madrid, and were briefly examined and flown by two Spanish pilots. Several authors have claimed that twenty Potez 54s were thereupon ordered for the Aviación Militar. This is almost certainly untrue, especially since the Spanish government, already hard-pressed to meet the defence budget, had recently signed a contract to build forty-two Martin 139W bombers in Spain and to buy eight outright. What is true is that, on 21 July 1936, three days after the outbreak of fighting in Spain, the Republican government formally asked the French government for '20 avions Potez', among other armaments. This request was leaked to the Opposition press, and, to placate those who were publicly denouncing the French Premier, Léon Blum, for his friendly attitude to the Spanish Republicans, it was officially stated that the Spaniards merely wished to expedite contracts made in accordance with a Commercial Treaty signed in December 1935. This alluded to a secret clause in the treaty (in fact merely a note pencilled in the margin), which stated that the Spanish government undertook to buy 20,000,000 French francs' worth of arms in France. Such a sum would not have paid for twenty Potez 540s, whose unit cost, with engines but without armament, was 1,635,000 francs.

After much political manoeuvring and many changes of mind, Blum authorised his air minister, Pierre Cot, to send six Potez 540s and fourteen Dewoitine D.372s, all unarmed, to Barcelona, provided the business was disguised as a commercial transaction between the manufacturers and private individuals. Thus the Potez 54s were sold by Potez to the Dutch writer Edy du Perron, who in turn sold them to the Spanish writer Corpus Barga (acting, of course, for the Spanish government), and on 8 August 1936 were flown from the Air France aerodrome at Toulouse-Montaudran to Prat de Llobregat, Barcelona. Most authors assert that not six, but twelve Potez 54s were delivered that day. All contemporary sources of evidence but one agree on six, however. The Potez (and thirteen Dewoitine D.372s) were accompanied by the airmen of various nationalities who were to constitute the international Escadre España, under the command of André Malraux, who is often mistakenly credited with having purchased the aircraft for the Republicans in the first place.

The next Potez to arrive in Spain was the Potez 544 (c/n 4133) with 860hp Hispano-Suiza 12Yhs engines. This was an experimental version intended for high-altitude research and built, it is believed, to a Belgian order. However, as soon as it had made its maiden flight it was flown from the Potez factory at Meaulte (Albert) to Villacoublay on 24 August, where it was handed over to the pilot Henri Rozés (see Caudron Phalène and Dewoitine D.510), who was flying aircraft to Spain at this time. Rozés flew it to Toulouse-Montaudran and thence to Barcelona, taking as passengers the French Communist Party under-secretary, Jacques Duclos, and two of his aides. From there it was flown to Valencia and Madrid by Rozés and the Spanish pilot Ramón Torres. The Potez 544 is said to have received the French registration F-APON (though this is not in the Bureau Veritas) before leaving France, and was named *La Commune de Paris*. It was badly damaged by fighters during its first mission, the gunner Viezzoli (who had achieved fame in 1930 for his anti-Mussolini flight over Rome) being killed, and crashed on landing at Barajas. It was later repaired and returned to service.

Seven Potez 542s (c/ns 4220-6) were delivered to Republican Spain in October 1936. Air France appears to have acted in some way as an intermediary. The aircraft flew from Meaulte to Villacoublay, the national test centre, on 18 October, and thence to Teygnac-Mérignac airport, Bordeaux, where they were received by two senior airline officials, Victor Poirier and Louis de Marmier (see Bloch MB 210 and Douglas DC-2). From Bordeaux they flew to Toulouse-Montaudran, and from there, with Malraux as a passenger in the lead aircraft, to Barcelona on 20 October. Two of the pilots were Air France employees, Favreaud and Landry, and four others were Lanet (or Hanet), Roger Nouvel (a sports pilot from Gaillac who flew aircraft to Spain), Déscamps (a Potez test pilot) and Rozés. One first pilot and three copilots were Russian air force officers.

Meanwhile, on 7 September 1936, one of the Potez 540s in service with the Armée de l'Air (X-236, Potez c/n 4879, production series No 228) had been transferred to the Ministère de l'Air for special transport duties between France and Republican Spain. Its military equipment and turrets had been removed, the nose turret being replaced by a windowed fairing, and, in addition to its civil registration F-AOOO, the words *Ambassade de France* were

The Potez 542 (Lorraine Pétrél engines) 'R' of the Malraux squadron, with a 'Hammer and Sickle' emblem on its fin. (Arráez)

painted in large white capitals on the fuselage. It was the first of what was to become a ten-strong French 'ministerial squadron' of converted Potez 54s. However, on 8 December, while making a regular flight from Madrid to Toulouse with passengers on board, it was shot down by two Russian I-15s near Guadalajara. One passenger, the distinguished French journalist Louis Delaprée, was killed and another, Dr Georges Henny of the Swiss Red Cross, was wounded. The incident was widely reported, and the Spanish government tried to lay the blame on Nationalist fighters. Writing years later in his autobiography, Sefton Delmer of the *Daily Express* group alleged that the Russians had shot down the Potez deliberately to prevent Dr Henny from leaving Spain and publishing a dossier he had compiled concerning the killing of 10,000 Nationalist prisoners in Madrid by Spanish and Russian Communists. Lacalle, who was present on the aerodrome at Azuqueca when the two Russian pilots landed and shouted excitedly that they had just shot down a 'Fascist bomber', wrote that he was convinced that the catastrophe had been an innocent mistake. Some authors have referred to a second ministerial Potez 540 in Spain, F-ANJO, and have suggested it was probably the Potez 54 F-APON after it had been repaired (in France), re-registered and returned to Spain. F-ANJO, however, was a different machine

(production No 75, Armée de l'Air serial X-149), and there is no evidence to connect it with the Spanish war.

In December 1936 a Republican purchasing officer in Paris, Teniente-Coronel Juan Ortiz Muñoz, signed a contract to buy fifty Potez 540s, but, after innumerable delays and mishaps, the Republican minister for marine and air, Indalecio Prieto, stopped the transaction. Negotiations were resumed in the summer of 1937, and eventually four were bought in October 1937. During the spring of 1937 there had been plans to build Potez 54s in a factory at Sabadell, Catalonia, under the direction of Antonius Raab. During the First World War Raab had been adjutant to the famous Richthofen staffel, and during the 1920s he was partner to Gerhardt Fieseler in the Raab-Katzentstein company, builders of the excellent RK-26 biplane trainer. Married to a jewess, he had left Germany after the advent of the Nazis and in January 1937 had been invited by the Spanish Republicans to work in aircraft production. In May the Communists arrested Raab for employing Anarchists and Trotskyites in his factory. After terrible experiences under interrogation and in prison, he escaped to France and founded a company in Marseilles and Athens which, though originally intended for smuggling aircraft (including Bellanca 28/90s) into Spain, eventually grew into a major Greek airline after the Second World War. Meanwhile, the factory at Sabadell, after nearly a year's inactivity, was used for the production of I-15 Chatos.

There have been many conflicting estimates of the number of Potez 54s delivered to Republican Spain, published figures varying between sixty and six. In 1962 the Potez company itself put the number at forty-nine. In defence of the number given here (eighteen, of which fourteen arrived in 1936 and four in October 1937), three points should be mentioned. Some authors have argued that, even if only six Potez 54s were delivered on 8 August, six more must have been delivered at the end of July, a week earlier. Ex-Republican airmen I have asked about this, however, have all denied that any French military aircraft arrived at Barcelona before 8 August. It is also hard to believe that the departure of an additional six aircraft of such a size could have escaped the vigilance of the French Opposition newspapers, whose reporters were watching all the aerodromes in southern France at the time, or that their arrival at Barcelona would not have been reported to British or American officials, all of whom reported only six.

The second point concerns the frequently published assertion that some Potez 54s were delivered to the Basque zone. The origin of this seems to be that two Potez 54s, one named *¡Aquí te espero!* ('I'm waiting for you here!') and the other *¡Voy corriendo!* ('I'm hurrying!'), both usually flown by Spanish crews, carried out a number of long-distance bombing raids against the Nationalist naval base at El Ferrol, in Galicia, and against Nationalist ships in the Bay of Biscay, as well as along what is now called the Costa del Sol in the south. The raids in the north led to the belief that the Potez must be based somewhere in the Basque country, but in reality Potez 54s were delivered to, and operated from, the main Republican zone only.

The third point concerns the statement, published several times, that most or all of the Potez 543s ordered by Rumania were diverted to Spain. Newspaper reports before the Spanish Civil War show that the prototype Potez 541 arrived at Bucarest on 12 December 1935, and eight of the production Potez 543s arrived between 1 April and 31 May 1936. It is true that the French and Spanish governments secured an agreement with the Rumanian foreign minister, Titulescu, that these and other aircraft could be sold to the Spanish Republicans, but when this was discovered by King Carol, Titulescu was dismissed (opening the way to the take-over of Rumania by the Fascist Iron Guard and all the other ills that followed therefrom). The air minister, Caranfil, resigned in protest, maintaining that the money paid for the Potez 54s and other machines would have enabled Rumania to buy a squadron of Hawker Hurricanes. The problem is the lack of information concerning the number of Potez 543s orginally ordered – eight or ten – for, according to some sources, two more were delivered in 1939. These, however, may have been supplied to replace two that had been lost in accidents. Alternatively, they may have replaced two that should have been delivered in July 1936 and had gone to Spain instead. The lack of any evidence of the presence of Gnome-Rhône-engined Potez 54s in Spain, however, makes this appear unlikely. Until further evidence comes to light, therefore, it is perhaps safer to assume a total of eighteen.

As a result of an almost complete lack of Republican documentary records relating to the first six months of the air fighting in Spain, and of a surfeit of propaganda compounded by semi-fictitious accounts in memoirs, magazine articles and historical 'reconstructions' extrapolated from these same fictional pieces, similar confusion obscures every other aspect of the history of the Potez 54s in Spain, be it their military operations, the numbers lost, or their worth as military aircraft. Unless hitherto undiscovered Republican archives are found, improvement of the situation seems impossible.

At Barajas, Madrid, the first six Potez 540s were daubed with blotches of ochre over their Armée de l'Air dark green, painted with red bands on wings and fuselage, and individually identified by large white capital letters on their fins. These letters were also applied to later Potez arrivals, as well as other types of bomber such as Bloch MB 210s (and MB 200s if any were delivered), a Fokker F-VIIb3m and, possibly, the Fokker F.IX, F.XII and F.XVIII, but they do not necessarily denote a chronological order of arrival. There are twenty-eight letters in the Spanish alphabet, A–Z plus CH, LL and Ñ. Photographs (unfortunately undated) show Potez 54s with the letters A, B, D, F, L, N, Ñ, O, P, R and S – eleven of the fourteen aircraft delivered in 1936. It is known that M was a Bloch MB 210. However, S is the twenty-second letter of the Spanish alphabet, so that if the fourteen Potez 54s, four Bloch MB 210s and four Fokkers (or two MB 200s and two Fokkers, or some other combination) were identified by letters, we would have a complete series from A to S, including CH and LL. It is unlikely that the last two were employed, however, since they were confusing, and in any case they were later applied to the Aero A-101 (LL) and Hispano-built I-16 (CH).

The puzzle is complicated by the fact that the Air France director of the company aerodrome at Barcelona, Gaston Vedel, converted one or two of his hangars into workshops for the repair or rebuilding of damaged Potez 54s, but again we do not know how many were recycled in this way. For example, the two photographs of 'R' reproduced here may show two different aircraft or the same machine re-engined. Some authors have said that the first five Potez 54s were lettered E, S, P, A, Ñ, which would mean that S, far from being the last (and a 542, at that), would have been the second to be registered. Some Potez were named as well as lettered, but, apart from the three mentioned above, and another called *Jean Jaurés* after the French Socialist Party Leader, names such as *Pelikan I* and *Cocotte* cannot be confirmed. *¡Aquí te espero!* was F, but we do not know the letters of other named Potez.

During August and September 1936 the six Potez 540s were used by the international Escadre España and an all-Spanish grupo ('flight' or 'patrol' would be a better description, for it had three machines at most) commanded by Félix Sampil and, later, Antonio Martín Luna. In October and November the seven Potez 542s and the surviving, or rebuilt, 540s were still used by the two units, while the Blochs and Fokkers were commanded by José de la Roquete. Little is known of the organisational details, or whether the Potez were permanently divided between the two squadrons or kept in a pool at Barajas, and later Alcalá de Henares and Albacete, for use by either group as necessary.

In addition to the raids by *¡Aquí te espero!* and *¡Voy corriendo!*, notable exploits by the Potez 54s included an attack, in company with a Douglas DC-2 and some Breguet 19s, on a Nationalist motorised column at Medellín on 16 August 1936, an attack on Olmedo Aerodrome, the base of the Nationalist 'Fokker-Dragon' group, in September, and

some night attacks on Nationalist aerodromes in December 1936. In September 1936 a number of Russians, commanded by Maj Ernst Schacht, joined Martín Luna's squadron and carried out a series of orientation flights across Nationalist Spain in Potez 54s and, in October, made a series of bombing raids before transferring to the newly-arrived Tupolev SBs. In February 1937 the Escadre España (or Escadre André Malraux, as it was by then called) was moved to Valencia, and carried out its last serious operations during the Nationalist offensive against Málaga. Two Potez were lost, one (P) crashing on the shore beside columns of refugees fleeing eastwards along the coast, an incident vividly described in Malraux's novel *L'Espoir* (*Man's Hope* or *Days of Hope*) (Paris, 1938).

Early in May 1937 six Potez 54s, some of which must have been rebuilt machines, were formed with the Fokker F.IX, F.XII and F.XVIII into a mixed bomber group based at Lérida. On 31 May they bombed Nationalist warships at Palma, Mallorca. One Potez was shot down, the pilot, a Czech named Ferak, being captured (and later exchanged) and two other crew members, also Czechs, being killed. Thereafter, the Potez 54s seem to have been employed chiefly in night operations, not only as bombers, but for dropping agents behind Nationalist lines. At this time they were given the type code BP, and in July they were incorporated into Grupo 72, with the remaining Bloch MB 210s and, after September 1937, the newly-arrived Vultee V1-As. The four Potez 54s that arrived in October 1937 were presumably incorporated into the same group. Four Potez 54s were still flying at the end of the war. Two escaped to France with Republican VIPs on board, but, unlike the Douglas DC-2s and Lockheed Electra, were not returned. One was found on a Spanish aerodrome, though whether or not it was airworthy is not recorded. One was recovered from Oran, Algeria, and was flown back to Spain in May 1939. Nothing is known of its subsequent history.

Published figures regarding the number of Potez 54s shot down are even less reliable than those regard-

ing the number delivered. The figure generally given is fifteen, but this must include aircraft that were later repaired and put back into service, since four survived the war. The reliability of this figure is questionable because a count of Nationalist claims, added to Republican admissions, yields a total of twenty-eight in 1936 alone, when only fourteen altogether had by then been delivered. Consequently it is now almost impossible, except in a few cases, to distinguish true from untrue claims.

One well-documented episode, however, is the loss of the Potez 540 *¡Aquí te espero!* (F). On 25 September 1936, with LAPE operations director Joaquín Mellado as first pilot and an all-Spanish crew, it was sent to bomb a Nationalist target near Talavera de la Reina, and Lacalle was detailed to escort it in a Loire 46. The engine of the Loire cut out as Lacalle was taking off, and the machine crashed into a van parked at the end of the field, Lacalle surviving with cuts and bruises. The Potez continued on its mission alone, encountering two Junkers Ju 52/3ms over the lines and forcing them to turn back. A moment later the Spanish Nationalist pilot Capitán Ángel Salas, flying a Fiat C.R.32 of the Italian *La Cucaracha* squadron, saw the Potez and shot it down. It crashed in Republican territory but the crew, all of whom had survived but were injured, saw some soldiers running towards them and, supposing them to be Nationalists, committed suicide to avoid capture. From photographs, N seems to have been the Potez 54 shot down behind Nationalist lines on 16 September 1936.

According to one report, three Potez 54s were destroyed on the ground during a Nationalist air raid on Albacete aerodrome on 23 October 1936, and in a Russian account one was shot down and two badly damaged on 1 November 1936, the pilot Ghibelli (an Italian settled in the USSR) being killed. According to a recent article by Patrick Laureau (*Icare* No 130, pp.93-98), two Potez 54s of the Malraux squadron, Ñ and O, were shot down by He 51s near Valencia on 26 December 1936. The Potez 54 S, piloted by Jean Dary and with Malraux on board, crashed on take-off from La Señera Aerodrome,

Valencia, on the following day, 27 December, but may have been rebuilt. However, if six were flying in May 1937 and only fourteen had been delivered up to that time, the number totally lost cannot have exceeded eight, including the two shot down near Málaga in February 1937. This would mean that only six could have been lost in 1936.

This figure obliges us to look again at the extremely bad press the Potez 54 has received as a result of its performance in Spain. As early as December 1936 there was an acrimonious debate over Spain in the French parliament. Opposition delegates on the extreme right, who were determined to discredit Premier Léon Blum and his government at any cost, declared with thinly disguised relish that in Spain these vaunted Potez *multi-place-de-combat* aircraft, the supposed pride of the Armée de l'Air, had been 'shot down like flies', and demanded the dismissal of air minister Pierre Cot in consequence. Such allegations became commonplace, and even *Life Magazine*, in an article about Spain published on 10 April 1939, remarked that the Potez 54 had been 'a complete failure'. The harshest criticism can be found in the memoirs of the Republican fighter commander Lacalle, who states that he had been told that, in practice, a Potez 54 could not fly faster than 160km/h even at full throttle, that it was hopelessly vulnerable, that it required a crew of no fewer than seven ('a thought horrifying for any professional military pilot even to contemplate'), and that it was thus little better than a 'flying collective coffin'.

Against this we have the testimonies of Francisco Pérez Mur, who piloted one of the Potez 54s at Lérida in May-June 1937 and pays tribute to its excellent handling qualities in the air, and of Jean Dary and Victor Veniel, who wrote secret reports on the air fighting in Spain for Pierre Cot. According to them, its chief shortcoming as a bomber lay in the liquid-cooled engines, which made sudden manoeuvres, especially diving, hazardous (this was before the invention of fuel injection), and its lack of armour. Steel-tipped bullets fired from a pursuing fighter had been known to pass through the

entire length of the machine, killing the pilot and even the nose-gunner. The other faults lay not in the aeroplane itself, but in the manner it was delivered (unarmed) and used. Instead of five rapid-fire Darne machine guns, Potez 54s often went on missions with only two Lewis guns, one each in the dorsal and ventral positions, and the nose gunners armed with either nothing or a shotgun.

The lack of trained aircrew, and the multiplicity of nationalities in the Escadre España, made it rarely possible to assemble a complete crew speaking a common language. On 27 October 1936, for example, a Potez 54 carried out a bombing mission with a French first pilot, a Spanish second pilot, a Russian navigator/bomb-aimer, a Spanish flight mechanic, an Italian-Swiss front gunner, a German upper rear gunner and a French lower rear gunner, none of whom could speak any language but his own. A crew of seven, instead of five, was often unavoidable because there were not enough men available with the experience to carry out more than one duty, and there was no time to train them. Nor were there enough interpreters to make training possible.

The Hispano-Suiza 12Xjrs/Xirs engines were designed to give optimum performance at 5,000m, at which altitude a Potez 54 had a maximum speed of 294km/h and a Potez 544 a speed of about 321km/h. The Potez 54s had, however, been delivered without bombsights. The primitive bombsights hastily improvised by the Spanish mechanics, and the fact that there were no maps available, obliged the Potez 54 pilots to fly at 1,000m or lower, to enable them to locate their targets by following visible landmarks and to give them a remote chance of hitting the targets when they reached them. At that altitude the machine could barely reach 160km/h. Moreover, the Republican Jefatura (command) habitually ordered Potez 54s to carry out missions alone, or at most in pairs, with no more than a single fighter for escort, or even with no escort at all. Veniel observes that the only Potez shot down were those caught without fighter protection. To accuse the Potez 54 of 'vulnerability'

under such circumstances seems nonsensical, and one may question whether any contemporary bomber, such as the Handley Page Heyford or Dornier Do 23, could have acquitted itself better, or even as well.

Span 22.1m; length 16.2m; height 3.9m; wing area 76sq m.

Potez 540
Empty weight 3,618kg; loaded weight 5,721kg.
Maximum speed 310km/h; cruising speed 240km/h; ceiling 10,000m; range 1,200km.

Potez 542
Empty weight 3,918kg; loaded weight 5,944kg.
Maximum speed 310.5km/h; cruising speed 270km/h; ceiling 8,500m; range 1,000km.

Potez 544
Maximum speed about 340km/h.

Potez 56
Similar in size and general appearance to the Airspeed Envoy and Farman 430, the Potez 56 was a twin-engined, low-wing cantilever monoplane capable of carrying a pilot, six passengers and a small cargo of mail. Design work began in January 1934 and the prototype was ready for its maiden flight by 1 June. Based on experience gained from the Potez 53 single-engined racing monoplane, which had been built to compete in the 1933 Coupe Deutsche and from which it had derived its aerofoil section, the Potez 56 was built of wood, the wings and tail surfaces being covered with formed stressed plywood and the slab-sided fuselage with flat plywood panels. Power was provided by two 235hp Potez 9 Ab radial engines housed in wide-chord cowlings and driving Ratier electrically-adjustable two-bladed variable-pitch propellers. The undercarriage, which retracted into the engine nacelles, was found to be rather fragile in service. Mail was carried in a nose compartment.

The prototype, Potez 560 (c/n 3566) F-ANSU, was used by the Potez Aéro Service to open the Toulouse–Marseilles–Nice–Bastia (Corsica) line on 15 May 1935. The route was extended to Bordeaux, and by October 1935 four 560s were being employed. One of these, c/n 3714 F-ANMT, was rebuilt with a rather unsightly enlarged cabin which had vertical front and outward-slanting side windscreens, a small fin, an enlarged rudder and redesigned engine cowlings, and was redesignated Potez 561. Twenty-six 560s and 561s were built, though how many of each is uncertain. Three 561s are known to have been sold to Rumania, and three, including the rebuilt prototype 560 F-ANSU, are known to have flown in Spain. Other versions included the narrower-fuselaged 56E for the navy, the 566T, the 567 (240hp Potez 9E engines) and the 568 P3, of which seventy were built, eleven being captured and used by the Luftwaffe in the Second World War.

At least six Potez 56 were employed by Air Pyrénées, Air Languedoc and other ephemeral French companies providing clandestine, and of course unofficial, communication between the Spanish and Basque governments and pro-Republican members of the French government and the Spanish Embassy in Paris. Indeed, although no Potez 56 was based in Spain or incorporated into LAPE or the Republican air forces, at least two, and possibly four, became the property of the Spanish Republican government. Every effort was made to keep this fact secret, however, so that even today information regarding the mysterious comings and goings of these aircraft during the civil war is scanty.

In June 1936, a month before the outbreak of the war, Air France announced that it had ordered a small number of Potez 561s to take some of the load off larger transports during the overcrowded summer season, and that the first two would be employed on the Nice–Corsica service. These two, apparently F-APDV (c/n 4230) and 'PER (c/n 4231), were delivered on 5 August 1936. Several senior officials of Air France, including technical director Edouard Serre, operations manager Col Victor Poirier, chief test pilot Louis de Marmier and the director of Air France in Spain, Gaston Vedel, were strong supporters of the Span-

The Potez 560 prototype, F–ANSU, in its earlier configuration.

ish Republican cause, and on 14 August Serre and de Marmier flew to Madrid in one of these Potez (probably 'PDV), with Léon Jouhaud, chief of the CGT (the French General Workers' Union), his secretary, Marc Brassard, and the union secretary general, Georges Buisson, as passengers, and returned three days later.

It seems that Air France thereupon cancelled its order for, or relinquished its option on, the Potez 56s, for none was ever on the Air France inventory. By the end of September several were being used for regular flights between Paris, Toulouse, Biarritz and Bilbao, a service that was taken over by Air Pyrénées when it was founded early in 1937. On 23 October 1936, Potez 56 F-ANMV (c/n 3725) crashed at Montauban aerodrome near Toulouse (not to be confused with the Air France airport, Toulouse-Montaudran) on returning from Bilbao, and was damaged beyond repair. The passengers were Carlos Martínez, a socialist deputy in the Spanish Cortes, and several Spanish Republican officials. The mechanic, Marcel Mamet, was injured. The pilot was Ulysse Gorsse, who was later to be involved in the purchasing and ferrying to Spain of Gourdou-Leseurre GL-32s.

This Potez 56, as well as the 561 prototype F-ANMT (c/n 3741) and the 560 'NMU (c/n 3725), had been used by the Potez Aéro Service on the Biarritz–Cannes line. At the begin-

ning of October 1936 they were sold to M Deniau, who was presumably acting on behalf of the Basque government. There is no further record of either of the latter two aircraft, which are listed as 'vendu à l'étranger' in September 1936, but one report suggests that 'MT was later sold to Rumania as YR-AFF, an assertion to be treated with caution. In November 1936 the Potez Aéro Service, still the legal owners of the 561s F-APDV and 'ER, sold the aircraft to P Séguy of 3bis, rue Sicard, Paris, which was also the address of Leopold Galy, who later flew for Air Pyrénées. In fact, F-APDV was seen at Toulouse-Francazal Aerodrome bearing the Spanish registration EC-PDV on 13 January 1937, but in May, as F-APDV again, was sold by Séguy to Auguste Amestoy, the director of Air Pyrénées. It was probably the Potez 56 reported as wrecked by a forced landing in the Basque zone in March 1937. Séguy sold F-APER to SFTA (see Appendix II) in November 1936, but it is then described as 'razé' (written off) on 3 November. As for F-ANSU, the Potez 560 prototype, it was converted to 561 standard and seems to have been used during 1937 by Air Languedoc, a company similar to Air Pyrénées but covering the communications between Barcelona and Bilbao and Santander. In April 1938 it was bought by SFTA, but was at Albi (Tarn) in 1939, with only 362 hours of flying in its log book.

Span 16m; length 11.84m; height 3.1m; wing area 33sq m.

Empty weight 1,616kg; loaded weight 2,772kg.

Maximum speed 280km/h; cruising speed 250km/h; ceiling 6,000m; range 1,100km.

P.W.S.10 and P.W.S.16

Marshal Pilsudki's military government, which seized power in Poland in May 1926, encouraged the growth of the national aviation industry by insisting that the air force be equipped with indigenously designed aircraft. The P.W.S.10 was the first Polish designed single-seat fighter to be ordered in quantity by the Lotwiwo Wojskowe (Military Aviation), which at that time was equipped entirely with imported or licence-built machines such as the French Blériot SPAD 51 and Breguet 19. Design work began in 1927 at the Podlaskiej Wytwani Samelotow (Podlasian Aircraft Manufacturing Company), under the direction of A Crzedzielki and A Bobek, but was temporarily halted by the advent of the revolutionary P.Z.L. P.1 gull-winged fighter. However, as a precaution against the possible failure of the P.Z.L. fighter, work on the P.W.S.10 was resumed in 1928 and, after extensive revisions, the prototype first flew in May 1930. Before the end of the year sixty-five P.W.S.10s were ordered as a stop-gap until the production version of the P.Z.L. P.1, the P.Z.L. P.7, became available.

The P.W.S.10 was a high-wing parasol monoplane. Its two-spar wing was built of wood, with plywood and fabric covering, while the fuselage and tail assembly were of welded steel tube, fabric-covered with the exception of the metal-skinned forward fuselage. It was powered by a 450hp Skoda-built Lorraine 12E water-cooled 'W' engine driving a two-blade wooden propeller, and had a cross-axle undercarriage. Armament consisted of two fixed forward-firing 7.7m machine guns mounted above the engine. The service career of the P.W.S.10 was rather short, and by 1934 it had been replaced by the P.Z.L. P.7 and relegated to training duties.

On 23 July 1936, six days after the outbreak of civil war in Spain, the Polish government declared an embargo on the supply of arms to either side. Nevertheless, through the efforts of Comandante Carmelo de las Morenas Alcalá, the pro-Nationalist Spanish air attaché in Paris and London, a number of Polish aircraft were sold to the Spanish Nationalists via Portugal, through the Herse and SEPEWE (or SPV) export agencies, a few days after the imposition of the embargo. There is no doubt that this was done with the connivance of the Polish government, since most of the aircraft were drawn from military establishments. Among them were twenty reconditioned P.W.S.10s from the Aviation Training Centre at Deblin, of which the first fourteen were unloaded at Lisbon and transported by road to Tablada, Seville, in December 1936. These were given the type code 4 and the unflattering nickname 'Pavipollo' (Turkey Chicken), an allusion to the unpopular Heinkel He 46 'Pava', or turkey hen, and in February 1937 were formed into a fighter squadron commanded by Capitán Angél Salas Larrazábal. The P.W.S.10 was soon found to be completely inadequate as a fighter and difficult to fly, one of its vices being a tendency to drop a wing on landing, which, in combination with its narrow undercarriage, caused a series of accidents. After brief service at Léon, the escuadrilla was re-equipped with Heinkel He 51s (2-E-2), and the remaining Pavipollos were transferred to the Escuela de Transformación (Transition School) at Jerez de la Frontera. Six more P.W.S.10s arrived in 1937, but all were withdrawn from service by the end of 1938.

The P.W.S.16 was a two-seat training biplane, developed in 1933-34 and powered by a PZL- or Avia-built Wright Whirlwind J radial engine in a blistered cowling. In 1937, when the P.W.S.16 and 16bis trainers in Polish service were replaced by P.W.S.26s, twenty were sold to Portugal. It has been alleged that most of these were re-exported to the Spanish Nationalists and that a few even found their way into Republican service, though how this was managed, in view of the hostility of the Portuguese government to the

A P.W.S.10 at Tablada, Seville. (Arráez)

Spanish Republic, has never been explained. Without corroboration, the story seems as doubtful as the reported sale of ex-Polish Breguet 19s via Portugal to Nationalist Spain. As for the Republicans, it is true that, in 1938, Coronel Angél Pastor Velasco succeeded in placing an order for fifty P.Z.L. P.37 Los bombers, and it is just possible that a few obsolete P.W.S.16s were exported directly from Poland at the same time, but there is no evidence of this.

P.W.S.10

Span 11m; length 7.5m; height 2.7m; wing area 18sq m.

Empty weight 1,115kg; loaded weight 1,500kg.

Maximum speed 260km/h; climb 660m/min; ceiling 6,500m; range 300km.

P.W.S.16bis

Span 9m; length 7.03m; height 2.7m; wing area 24sq m.

Empty weight 850kg; loaded weight 1,162kg.

Maximum speed 217km/h; ceiling 4,620m; range 460km.

Renard-Stampe-Vertongen 32

In 1922 two Belgian pilots, Jean Stampe and Maurice Vertongen, and the aeronautical engineer Alfred Renard established a flying school and a small factory for the construction of training aircraft at Deurne Aerodrome on the outskirts of Antwerp. Renard later left to found his own company and achieve some fame as a builder of aircraft and aero engines, while the names of Stampe and Vertongen are remembered for the highly successful series of trainers they produced in the late 1930s, of which a few examples are still flying today.

Their first creation, which made its maiden flight in the spring of 1922, was the R.S.V.32/90, a two-bay, equal-span two-seat biplane powered by an uncowled 90hp Anzani radial engine. It was of wooden construction and, except for the metal skinning of the forward fuselage, was fabric covered. The designation 32/90 referred to the wing area (32sq m) and horsepower (90), a method used also by the

The Renard-Stampe-Vertongen 32 EC-AGG. (Arráez)

Bellanca company in America. Of the R.S.V.32s built, twenty-five have been identified: nine R.S.V.32/90s, ten R.S.V.32/100s, one R.S.V.32/105, three R.S.V.32/110s, and one R.S.V.32/120 – the last being a three-seater with either a D.H. Gipsy or a Renard engine of 120hp.

The fourth aircraft to be built, O-BADC, was sold to Narciso Carrión de Castro, of Valladolid, and was kept at Barajas with the registration EC-RAR. According to the Bureau Veritas of 1936 it was fitted with an 85hp Renard engine, and was thus, presumably, an R.S.V.32/85. It was in Republican hands throughout the civil war, and must have been transferred to one of the flying schools in Murcia. After the war it was recovered by the Nationalists and, having served in Grupo 30 (its serial is not known) was re-registered EC-AGG and returned to Senor Carrión de Castro in 1940. In 1955 he sold it to the Aero Club de Santiago de Compostela, in Galicia, and it continued flying until at least 1955.

Span 11.2m; length 7.35m; wing area 32sq m.

Empty weight 500kg; loaded weight 820kg.

Maximum speed 125km/h (with 90hp engine); ceiling 5,000m.

Romano R.82, R.83, R.92 and R.131

The Romano R.83, R.92 and R.131 were single-seat fighter biplanes specifically designed to the order of the Spanish Republican purchasing commission in Paris in 1937. Such was the secrecy surrounding their building and production that their very existence remained unknown to

aeronautical historians until very recently, the R.83 in particular not being 'rediscovered' until 1988, fifty years after six of them were tested and delivered to the Spanish Republican Fuerzas Aéreas between April and June 1938.

Etienne Romano, a man of many interests and several careers outside aviation, founded La Société Anonyme des Chantiers Aéronavales Etienne Romano (CAER) at Cannes-La-Bocca on the French Riviera in 1929. For the next eight years the company built a series of prototypes, designed by Albert Waldemann and his team, but none received orders for production. This changed in 1937, when, as a result of a Romano R.82 winning first place in an aerobatic competition at Zurich, and the influence of Romano's friend Michel Detroyat (see Lockheed Orion), CAER, which had been nationalised in December 1936 as a part of the SNCASE group of aircraft factories in south-eastern France, received an order for fifty R.82s to be built for the Armée de l'Air as advanced trainers. Further orders followed, and eventually 177 were built for the flying schools of the Armée de l'Air and Aéronavale between August 1937 and 10 May 1940. Derived from the R.80, the R.82 was a conventional two-seat biplane of wood and metal construction powered by a 280hp Salmson 9Aba radial engine in a wide-chord blistered cowling and provided with a sturdy, wide-track undercarriage. However, the wooden wings turned out to be less robust than expected, and in October 1939 the Aéronavale flying schools prohibited the use of these machines for aerobatics.

In the spring of 1937 Etienne Romano was approached by André Desmoulins, a director of Lejeune Aviation, with a request that he undertake the clandestine manufacture of aircraft for the Spanish Republican government. After consultation with Waldemann, Romano offered three types of lightweight single-seat fighter based on existing company designs. The first was the R.92. In 1934-35 Romano had built a small single-seat seaplane fighter intended for catapult launching, the R.90. The centre section of its upper wing had been gulled down on to the top of the fuselage in the style of the Russian I-15 Chato. The prototype had originally been powered by a 710hp Hispano-Suiza 9Vbrs radial engine (based on the Wright Cyclone) fitted with a Townend ring, but in October 1935 this had been replaced by a smaller-diameter 685hp Hispano-Suiza radial in a wide-chord NACA cowling. In the spring of 1936 this, in turn, had been replaced by an 835hp Hispano-Suiza 12Ycrs liquid-cooled vee engine which raised the maximum speed to a respectable (for a seaplane) 400km/h; but the R.90, although very manoeuvrable, had been consi-

One of the Romano R.82s smuggled to Republican Spain. The man in the hat and coat appears to be Etienne Romano himself. (Arráez)

dered too difficult to fly, and no order was placed. The R.92 was a landplane version, with a spatted undercarriage, of the Hispano-Suiza 12Ycrs-engined R.90, but with metal skinning replacing fabric on the rear fuselage.

The second type was the R.83, though whether this was its original or true designation is uncertain. It resembled a three-way cross between the second version of the R.90, with a wide-chord cowling; the R.82, in that the gulled centre section of the upper wing was replaced by a cabane; and the R.92, in that it had a spatted undercarriage. The cabane may have been adopted in response to criticisms from Spanish (and Russian) pilots of the shortcomings of the gull wing of the I-15 Chato. As in the R.82, R.90 and R.92, the fuselage structure consisted of a welded chrome-molybdenum steel-tube frame built up with formers and stringers to form an oval section. Light-alloy sheets covered the forward fuselage, and fabric the rear part. The intended powerplant was a 450hp Pratt & Whitney R-985 Wasp Junior radial or a 480hp Bristol Jupiter. The armament was to consist of two or four fixed forward-firing machine guns of whatever type should be available.

The third type offered to the Spanish Republicans was the R.130. This was a project which had been intended for the French C1 single-seat fighter competition of 1934, but had never progressed beyond the

drawing board. Drawings of the R.130 show a small, rather slender, equal-span staggered biplane retaining the gulled upper wing of the R.90, and powered by a 405hp Renault R.1Z.R03 inverted in-line engine. The undercarriage was to have retracted high into the fuselage beneath the upper wing, though how this was to be achieved is not clear, and the pilot was provided with an enclosed cockpit of which the roof and rear were metal covered, which would certainly have restricted his field of view. In the version offered to the Spaniards, designated R.131, the Renault engine was to be replaced by a 650hp Pratt & Whitney Twin Wasp Junior radial, which would have given the fighter a superficial resemblance to the Russian I-153.

Comandante Ángel Pastor Velasco, then in charge of the aviation procurement section of the Spanish Republican purchasing commission in Paris, ordered twenty-four R.83s and fifty R.131s off the drawing boards. Production of the R.83s was to be undertaken by the Belgian company LACEBA, reportedly established with Spanish Republican money, which was supplying components for the Spanish-built Fokker C.Xs and D.XXIs, and an assembly line was set up in a factory in Haren. The R.131 was to be produced in a disused hangar of the defunct Avions Bernard company at La Courneuve, France, under the supervision of Jean Biche, the designer of the Hanriot 110-115 pusher fighters of the early

A fighter type which remained undiscovered for half a century. One of the Romano R.83s built to the order of the Spanish Republicans by LACEBA in Belgium. (Liron)

1930s. The export of both types to Spain was to be handled through SFTA (see Appendix II).

During the spring of 1937, however, Capt Bartlett, the Bristol Aircraft Company engineer, had made his annual tour of France, and he had been shocked to hear that French aircraft were being secretly supplied to the Spanish 'Reds' with the connivance of the air minister, Pierre Cot, and in defiance of Non-Intervention. The last straw had been a personal enquiry from Etienne Romano himself, who had requested ninety Bristol radial engines – sixty for his French company and thirty for his Belgian subsidiary. When Bartlett asked what aeroplanes he could possibly want them for, Romano confessed that they were for machines being built for Spain. Bartlett indignantly reported the matter to the British government, and Anthony Eden, the British Foreign Secretary, took the matter up with the French government. Eventually, after much manoeuvring, Romano was dismissed from his position on the board of SNCASE, and Biche, who went bankrupt as a result, was obliged to stop production of the R.131s after sixteen fuselages and sets of wings had been completed. Similar press-

ure must have been put on the Belgians, for, although photographs taken at Haren show an assembly line of ten R.83s, only six were completed, fitted with 280hp Salmson 9Aba radials. They were tested in Belgium by the French CEMA test pilot Jacques Lecarme, who recalled years later that he was concerned chiefly with stability problems.

According to a post-war Spanish Nationalist report based on captured Republican documents, one R.83 was delivered to Spain on 20 April, two on 22 June, two on 28 June and one on 5 July 1938. The same report refers to eighteen Romano fuselages, making up the twenty-four ordered, costing £83,571 Sterling, and other equipment for the R.83s, costing £5,088, for which LACEBA had been paid but which it had not delivered. The loss incurred by the Spanish government over the R.131 amounted to 6,000,000 French francs, or about £57,143. Indeed, the only person to profit from the transactions was André Desmoulins, who had received 500,000 French francs commission. As for the R.92, according to Jacques Lecarme and Albert Waldemann, one example only was built (it was alleged) in a hangar belonging to the Belgian airline Sabena. After testing by Lecarme it was delivered to Barcelona in the summer of 1938.

Although many details of this affair remain hidden, one concerning the designation 'R.83' deserves mention. The Romano trainers were

designated in the sequence R.80 and R.82, and the fighters R.90 and R.92. It would therefore be logical to suppose that the R.83, being a fighter, should have been 'R.93'. During the production of the R.131s, Comandante Pastor proposed that they be fitted with low-powered engines and passed off as 'trainers' while being tested in France, to throw the Opposition press and Non-Intervention control officials off the scent. Once in Spain, the R.131s would be fitted with the 650hp Twin Wasp Junior engines intended for them. It is possible that the designation R.83 was adopted as a similar deception. The R.83s were tested and flown to Spain fitted with 280hp Salmson engines of the same type as that fitted on the R.82s. However, the reader may remember that eight Pratt & Whitney Wasp Junior engines intended for Monospar Croydons that were never built were exported to Republican Spain after May 1937. These were of the same type as those intended for the R.83, and they may well have been fitted to the six R.83s after they arrived at Barcelona.

The Bureau Veritas register of 1938, and Spanish sources, indicate that, in addition to the above aircraft, six Romano R.82 trainers, three of them ex-Armée de l'Air, were delivered to Republican Spain in 1938:

F-APEV c/n 02, kept by Etienne Romano for his own use; sold to Mme Lucienne Saby and resold to Victor Laffont on 6 February 1937. Laffont, of the Aéro Club Populaire at Villeneuve-sur-Lot, where some Spanish Republican pilots were trained, procured a number of Caudron Lucioles for the Spaniards, but later fell into a dispute with SFTA. He therefore probably exported this machine himself.

F-AQCC c/n 03, exported to Spain via Mme Saby and SFTA, after June 1937

F-AQJN c/n 135, ex-T-731, via SFTA, 14 February 1938

F-AQJO c/n 136, ex-T-732, via SFTA

F-AQJP c/n 137, via SFTA, 14

A Romeo Ro-5. (Arráez)

February 1938
F-AQJQ c/n 138, ex-T-602, via SFTA

The Romano R.83s, and presumably the R.82s, were stationed at La Ribera (San Javier) and Lorca, in Murcia, and employed as advanced trainers. The Republican pilot Emilio Galera told the author that he remembered a biplane with a blistered cowling and very like an R.82 (he had been told it was Swedish) had been used during the Catalonian campaign for liaison duties, because of its ability to take off and land in restricted areas. There is no information regarding how many of either type survived the civil war.

R.82

Span 9.88m; length 7.82m; height 3.34m; wing area 23.72sq m.
Empty weight 918kg; loaded weight 1,328kg.
Maximum speed 240km/h; ceiling 6,500m; range 660km.

R.83

No data available.

R.92

Span 8.89m; length 7.63m; height 3.1m; wing area 21sq m.
No further data available, other than a range of 600km.

R.130

Span 6m; length 7.3m; height 2.1m; wing area 11.5sq m.
Estimated: empty weight 800kg; loaded weight 1,250kg.
Estimated: maximum speed 480km/h; ceiling 10,000m; range 800km. (The maximum speed of the R.131, with a more powerful engine, would have been correspondingly higher.)

Romeo Ro-5

The Romeo Ro-5, which appeared in the late 1920s and was fairly popular with Italian flying clubs, was a single-seat light parasol monoplane with a wide-track undercarriage, powered by either a 95hp Fiat A50 or an 85hp Walter uncowled radial engine. A Fiat-powered example was bought in 1930 by Juan Canudas, proprietor of a small aerodrome near Barcelona Airport, and registered M-CAAL (EC-AAL). Although it was still flying in July 1936, nothing is known of its activities in the Spanish Civil War.

An R.W.D.9 acquired by the Spanish government in 1935. Its temporary registration was EM-W46. (Arráez)

Span 11.25m; length 7m; height 2.15m; wing area 19sq m.
Empty weight 400kg; loaded weight 680kg.
Maximum speed 180km/h; cruising speed 154km/h; landing speed 59km/h.

R.W.D.9

In 1933 the Polish-government-sponsored D.W.L. (Experimental Aviation Workshop) developed a four-seat, high-wing cabin monoplane for entry in the 4me Challenge de Tourisme Internationale to be held at Warsaw in September 1934. The resulting R.W.D.9 (R.W.D. being the initials of its three designers, Stanislaw Rogalski, Stanislaw Wigma and Jerzy Drzewiecki), powered either by a 220hp Walter Bora nine-cylinder radial engine with a Townend ring, or by a 260hp Gnome-Rhône 760 radial, was highly successful, showing a remarkable ability to operate from rough fields and restricted areas. Two R.W.D.9s took the first and second places in the competition.

Two R.W.D.9s (c/n 5, SP-DRA and c/n 97, SP-DRB) arrived in Spain in the summer of 1935 for a demonstration tour and, according to the Polish aviation historians Jerzy Cynk and Andrez Glass, both remained in Spain and took part in the civil war. Spanish researchers of the author's acquaintance tended to dismiss the last assertion as a fantasy, since there was no evidence to support it. At least one of the R.W.D.9s was evaluated by the Dirección General de Aeronáutica as a liaison aircraft for the Aviación Militar, although the provisional registration given to it, visible in the

photograph as 'EM-W4', presented a puzzle. 'EM', not seen on any other Spanish pre-civil-war aircraft, presumably denoted either 'Enlace Militar' (military liaison) or, more probably, 'España: Militar' in line with the EC classification allotted to Spanish civil aircraft, but the number 4 was hard to explain. However, in the list of EC-W' temporary registrations, which extends from EC-W10 (the Ford 4-AT-F) of 1931 to EC-W56 (a D.H. Hornet Moth) of May 1936, two of those that cannot be identified are EC-W46 and 'W50, both of the summer of 1935. It was possible, therefore, that EM-W4 was in reality EM-W46, the second digit being hidden in the photograph behind one of the spectators.

In October 1989, M Jean Massé, who has contributed several valuable items of new information to this book, found a report in the French newspaper *l'Indépendant des Pyrénées Orientales* for 1 November 1936, stating that on 31 October 'an aircraft of unknown type, registered EM-W46, proceeding from Spain and piloted by an officer, made a forced landing in the field of M Fabre, the proprietor of Ville Martin, on the common of Gaja-Villedieu', near Limoux, south of Carcassonne. The pilot was unhurt but the aircraft was badly damaged. That this was the R.W.D.9 was confirmed in January 1990, when M Massé visited the farm in question and discovered, to his astonishment, remains of the R.W.D.9 itself, which had been kept in a barn since the crash fifty-four years before. Witnesses to the accident told him that the aeroplane had been flying from Toulouse to Barcelona, not vice versa, and that the pilot had been not a Spanish but a French officer. Carrying in his hand a bottle of expensive scent, he had intended to continue his journey by train, but had been arrested before reaching the railway station. The fate of the second R.W.D.9 (EM-W50?) remains unknown at the time of writing.

Span 11.64m; length (Bora) 7.6m, (Gnome-Rhône) 8m; height 2m; wing area 16sq m.
Empty weight (Gnome-Rhône) 560kg; loaded weight (Gnome-Rhône) 930kg.

(Bora) Maximum speed 250km/h; cruising speed 210km/h; landing speed 55km/h; take-off distance to 8m, 90m; ceiling 6,000m.

R.W.D.13

Developed from the R.W.D.6, winner of the 3me Challenge Internationale de Tourisme of 1932, the R.W.D.13 was a three-seat, high-wing, cabin monoplane of similar appearance to the de Havilland Puss Moth and Caudron Phalène, but equipped with Handley Page slots along the wing leading edges to facilitate operation from restricted spaces. The prototype first flew in February 1935, and more than a hundred were built during the next four years. The R.W.D.13 was of mixed construction, and was powered by a 130hp Walter Major (licence-built D.H. Gipsy Major) inverted in-line engine driving a two-blade wooden propeller.

Shortly after the outbreak of the Spanish Civil War seven R.W.D.13s, c/ns 117, 149-53 and 155, were acquired by the Portuguese government, all being exported through the Warsaw aircraft broker Herse Company (see P.W.S.10). At least four were re-exported to the Spanish Nationalists. Bearing the military serials 30-2, -3, -4 and -14, and nicknamed 'Polacas', they were used by the Nationalist air arm for liaison duties, one being frequently flown by the air ace Capitán Joaquín García Morato. Two, 30-3 and 30-4, survived the war. In 1941 they were

Below: *an R.W.D.13 in Nationalist service.* (Arráez)

handed over to the Aero Club de Zaragoza (Saragossa), and in 1948 were transferred to the Aero Club de Logroño. Aircraft 30-3 was withdrawn in 1949, and 30-4 in 1950. Neither received civil registrations.

Span 11.5m; length 7.85m; height 2.05m; wing area 16sq m.
Empty weight 530kg; loaded weight 930kg.
Maximum speed 210km/h; cruising speed 180km/h; ceiling 4,200m; range 900km.

R-5 Rasante

The R-5 two-seat reconnaissance, day-bombing and general-purpose biplane was designed by the same team, headed by Nikolai Polikarpov, that created the famous I-15 and I-16 fighters. The prototype appeared in 1928, and in 1930 won the first place in the international competition for reconnaissance-bombers held at Teheran, in which it competed against British, French and Dutch aircraft. More than 6,000 R-5s, in many modified versions, were produced for the Soviet air force between 1931 and 1937, a number surely not exceeded by any other type of aircraft in the interwar years. It was a single-bay, unequal-span biplane built principally of wood, and was powered by an M-17 (licence-built BMW VI) water-cooled engine rated at 500hp (680hp for take-off), Its armament consisted of one fixed forward-firing 7.62mm PV-1 machine gun on the port side of the upper fuselage, and a 7.62mm DA-1 machine gun on a Scarff-type ring in the observer's cockpit. Eight 50kg bombs could be carried on

An R-5 Rasante.

R-5s of the Escuadrilla de Ataque Nocturno (Night Attack Squadron). (Arráez)

racks under the lower wings, an electric control device enabling the observer to release the bombs singly, in pairs or all together. Like most Russian aircraft, it could be fitted with skis in place of the wheels. The Po-5 and Po-5a civil versions, which served with Aeroflot until after the Second World War, had an enclosed cockpit and a cabin in place of the observer's cockpit, with room for two passengers, mail, cargo or a stretcher.

Aware of the Spanish Republicans' need to replace its Breguet 19s, the Soviets sent a complete eskadrily of thirty-one R-5s with the first consignment of aircraft in November 1936. These were formed into Grupo Núm 15 (a Russian eskadrily of thirty-one aircraft being the equivalent of a Spanish Republican Grupo) under the command of Maj Vochev. Some of the R-5s sent to Spain were fitted with M-17F engines rated at 715hp for take-off. On 2 December eighteen R-5s carried out their first mission, a low-level attack on the new aerodrome at Velada, Talavera de la Reina, to which several Italian squadrons had been withdrawn for

safety from aerodromes judged to be too near the front. Republican intelligence seems to have been good, for the R-5s made directly for a large wood beside the aerodrome, where the aircraft were hidden, and destroyed three Savoia-Marchetti S.81 bombers. One R-5 was shot down by anti-aircraft fire, and the pilot, Lt Tupicov, was taken prisoner (he was exchanged a few months later). Three Fiat C.R.32s led by Sototenente Cenni, on aerodrome protection patrol, gave chase and claimed to have shot down three more of the attackers. On 4 December the R-5s attacked Navalmoral aerodrome, severely damaging six Junkers Ju 52/3ms of the Spanish squadrons 3-E-22 and 4-E-22 (including the *Tres Marías* – see Junkers Ju 52/3m). After a few ground-straffing missions during the next week, the R-5s were judged too slow and vulnerable to operate without

strong fighter escorts, which were not available, and the group was withdrawn from action.

According to some authors, a second batch of thirty-one R-5s arrived in February 1937. These are said to have been the R-5Sht (Shtormovik) ground-attack version, fitted with four or six downward-pointing PV-1 machine guns mounted under the lower wings. They are said to have taken part in the Battle of Guadalajara, and then to have been shipped back to the Soviet Union, together with their crews and the surviving personnel of Vochev's group. The remaining R-5s of the original batch were then re-formed into a group commanded by Fernando Hernández Franch (see D.H.89) and manned by Spaniards and a few foreign volunteers, and returned to front-line close-support duties. During June 1937 two (in one of which the American Eugene Finnick was a gunner) were shot down and two were wrecked in an accident.

In July 1937 the R-5s, now bearing the type code RR and called by the Spaniards 'Rasantes' (*rasante* means 'skimming', but the name, though appropriate, may have been suggested by its closeness in sound to the Russian *radzvedchnik*, 'reconnaissance'), were re-formed into the 1ª Escuadrilla de Bombardeo Nocturno (1st Night Bombing Squadron) commanded by Walter Katz (see R-Z Natacha), a Spaniard of Ukranian-German origin. Since a squadron list names twelve Spanish pilots, all trained in the USSR, there were presumably twelve R-5s still in service at this time. Based at Caspe in Aragón, the squadron went into action during the Battle of Belchite in August 1937, carrying out night attacks on Saragossa and on Nationalist troop concentrations along the road to Quinto. Their method was to send single aircraft at twenty-minute intervals, the purpose being to keep anti-aircraft defences busy, and the citizens of Saragossa in a state of tension, from dusk to dawn. After these actions the squadron adopted as its emblem a device showing a crescent moon with the black silhouette of a bat slanting across it.

An R-Z Natacha. (Arráez)

In September Teniente Santiago Capillas (see Grumman GE-23) took over command of the squadron, which was transferred to Alcañiz, in Aragón. On 29 November 1937 one R-5, RR-006 flown by José Curta and Rafael Feito, became lost during a night raid and crash-landed at Sentein, south of St Girons (Ariege), in France. During the Battle of Teruel the squadron operated from Manises, Valencia, and in January 1938 from Bujaraloz, where two R-5s were destroyed and two wrecked in the course of a bombing raid by Heinkel He 111s. In April the squadron, now only seven aircraft strong, was moved to Alcalá de Henares, Capillas being replaced by Miguél Garcimartín, and shortly afterwards was incorporated into the 1ª Escuadrilla of Grupo 72, equipped until then solely with Vultee V1-As.

In the summer of 1938 the escuadrilla was moved to El Carmolí, near Cartagena, for coastal patrol work over the Almería region, and placed under the command of Carlos Lázaro Casajust. During the remainder of the war two more R-5s were lost, one through an accident and one to anti-aircraft fire. After a brief excursion to Manises in September 1938 for the Battle of the Ebro, the 1ª Escuadrilla returned to El Carmolí.

On 30 March 1939, the day before the civil war ended, the last seven R-5s (led by Garcimartín again), together with five Grumman GE-23s led by Ten José Riverola, flew to Oran, Algeria, the crews preferring exile to surrender. These seven aircraft were brought back to Spain in May 1939 and, with two R-5s which had been under repair, were formed into a squadron of the new Ejercito del Aire, their new type code and serials being 16W-1 to 16W-9. They were all withdrawn from service between 1940 and 1945.

Span 15.5m; length 10.5m; height 3.6m; wing area 56.2sq m.
Empty weight 1,915kg; loaded weight 2,800kg.
Maximum speed 245km/h; cruising speed 220km/h; ceiling 6,500m; range 1,100km.

R-Z Natacha

The R-Z (also known as the R-Zet or S-Z) was designed by D S Markov and A A Skarbov as a modernised and more powerful R-5. It had a 750hp (820hp for take-off) M-34RN liquid-cooled engine in place of the M-17, and other differences were the relocation of the radiator behind the undercarriage, a redesigned tail unit, a semi-enclosed cabin for the pilot and observer, and an 80cm reduction in overall length. The prototype, which first flew in 1935, showed a considerable improvement in performance over the R-5, including an increase in top speed of 44km/h, and in cruising speed of 30km/h. The armament was similar to that of the R-5: a single fixed forward-firing 7.62mm PV-1 machine gun (800 rounds per minute) mounted in the upper port side of the engine cowling, and a Shkas 7.62mm fast-firing machine gun (1,800 rounds per minute) for the observer. Up to 400kg of bombs could be carried, but in Spain loads usually consisted of 8 x 42.5kg, 8 x 37.5kg, 6 x 50kg or 4 x 75kg bombs.

The first consignment of thirty-one R-Zs arrived in Spain in January 1937, and these were formed into an all-Spanish unit, Grupo 20, commanded by Cdte Abelardo Moreno Miró. Like many Spanish airmen, Miró had started his career in the cavalry, where he had become a show-jumping instructor, before joining the Aviación Militar and rising to command a Dornier Wal escuadrilla. There followed some weeks of conversion and formation training under Russian supervision at El Carmolí, Cartagena, where Spanish pilots, mostly veterans of Breguet

19 squadrons, found that the R-Z, which they dubbed 'Natacha', had an alarming tendency to drop a wing on touchdown and to ground-loop. They all acknowledged, however, that the chief Russian instructor, Baskovi, gave them an excellent training in low-altitude formation flying and the tactics of defensive gunnery, which was to provide the foundation for their successes in the ensuing campaigns.

In March, April and May 1937 the 1ª Escuadrilla of Grupo 20, under Capitán Ramos Pérez, was employed in Andalusia to assist in halting the Nationalist forces advancing eastwards along the coast after their capture of Málaga. The 2ª Escuadrilla was sent to Madrilejos, south of Madrid, to accelerate the rout of the Italians during the Battle of Guadalajara. Here, the R-Z Natachas (officially allotted the type code LN) performed brilliantly, despite the fact that, on at least four days, the airstrips to which they were deployed were waterlogged by continual rainstorms. Operating in atrocious weather, the Natachas flew in formations of nine beneath low clouds and through heavy rain to carry out repeated attacks on the Italian columns with virtual impunity, because the weather also protected them from Nationalist Fiat C.R.32s. It is now recognised that the defeat of the Italians was brought about almost entirely by the Republican air force, and by the I-15, R-5 and R-Z squadrons in particular, and that this battle was the first in the history of warfare in which an army (and an army on the offensive, at that), had been defeated and driven back in disarray by air power alone. Towards the end of the battle the 2ª Escuadrilla was joined by the

3ª, commanded by Capitán Juan Vargas Barberán.

At this point discrepancies arise regarding the number of R-Zs supplied to the Spanish Republic. According to some authors, a second batch of thirty-one R-Zs arrived on board the merchant ship *Aldecoa* on 14 February 1937, and were formed into Grupo 25, commanded by Cdte Ricardo Monedero. According to others, Grupo 25 was not formed until June 1937, after Grupo 20 had been disbanded. Unfortunately, the only document the author has seen concerning the *Aldecoa* shipment refers merely to 'single-engined light bombers', and could well refer to the R-5Sht consignment that is said to have arrived at that time. There is no doubt, however, that one batch of thirty-one R-Zs arrived on 1 May 1937, on the *Cabo Santo Tomé*, and another on 21 May 1937 on the *Sac 2*. This makes totals of sixty-two R-5s and ninety-three R-Zs, or thirty-one R-5s and 124 R-Zs, and until further evidence is found to settle this question, it must be left open.

On 17 May 1937 the 2ª Escuadrilla of Grupo 20 joined in the abortive attempt to send aircraft to the Basque zone. Storms broke up the formations, and some of the Natachas flew back to their base in Lérida. Others landed at Pau, in France, with the two Chato squadrons and the guiding Douglas DC-2, where the Non-Intervention Control officials prohi-

R-Z Natachas taken over by the Nationalists after the civil war.

bited their continuing to Bilbao and sent them back to the main zone stripped of their armament and escorted to the frontier by French fighters.

After intensive operations in the battles of La Granja and Huesca, the Natacha units were reorganised in July 1937. Grupo 20 was reconstituted as Grupo 30, consisting of three escuadrillas, and the newly-arrived aircraft were formed into three independent escuadrillas, the 20ª, 40ª and 50ª. Cdte Moreno remained in charge of Grupo 30 until replaced by Alonso Vega, who had been wounded in the fighting over Huesca. Thenceforth the Natachas took a prominent part in every subsequent campaign of the civil war, their activities being divided between small-formation reconnaissance missions and large-formation bombing raids carried out at altitudes between 1,000m and 400m.

In September 1937, as a result of their heavy casualties during the battles of Brunete and Belchite, the three independent escuadrillas were disbanded. Their surviving machines were used to form a 4ª Escuadrilla of Grupo 30, and to bring the other three escuadrillas of the Grupo up to their proper strength of twelve aircraft, plus three in reserve, each.

The leader of the 4ª Escuadrilla, Francisco Hernández Chacón, has described in a memoir how, by flying in an asymmetrical formation of four vees, with one vee to the right and rear of the lead formation and two to the left, the gunners were able to put up such a powerful defensive cross-

fire that on many occasions they were able to beat off attacks by enemy fighters and escape by diving steeply down to ground level, still in tight formation. He emphasises that serious losses occurred only when someone panicked and caused the formation of lose its cohesion. The worst example of this occurred on 24 December 1938, when, as the Nationalist offensive began against Catalonia, nine aircraft of the 2ª Escuadrilla of Grupo 30 were attacked by eighteen Fiat C.R.32s of 3-G-3, led by the Nationalist ace Joaquín García Morato. The fighter escort of two escuadrillas of I-16 Moscas had become separated from the bombers and, in the brief interval before these could come to the rescue, the Natacha pilots, taken by surprise, broke formation and flew off in all directions, with the result that three Natachas were shot down immediately and three more were forced down in open country, only three managing to return to base.

Grupo 30 diaries of the year 1 July 1937 to 1 July 1938 show that in that period the group carried out 275 missions (2,233 sorties), and that the 1ª Escuadrilla alone changed its base of operations no fewer than 23 times, for, like other Republican air units, they were almost constantly on the move to minimise the risk of air attacks on their aerodromes. As in all reconnaissance squadrons, however, their casualties were heavy. During this period they seem to have lost thirty-six aircraft on operations and three on the ground to bombing, as well as others damaged in accidents.

Thirty-six R-Zs survived the war, which would put total losses at 57 from all causes (including rather frequent landing accidents) if 93 were delivered, and at 88 if 124 were delivered. Thirteen Natachas of the 1ª Escuadrilla, led by Cdte Romero, escaped to Oran, Algeria, on 29 March 1939, and were recovered by the Nationalists after the war. The rest were flown to Barajas and surrendered to the Nationalists. In the Ejercito del Aire the Natachas were given the type code 17W and were based in Spanish Morocco. In 1946, when twelve were still airworthy, their type code was changed to R.5.

Span 15.5m; length 9.7m; height 3.6m; wing area 42.5sq m.
Empty weight 2,430kg; loaded weight 3,500kg.
Maximum speed 290km/h; cruising speed 250km/h; ceiling 8,000m; range 1,000km.

SAB-SEMA-12

The SAB-SEMA-10 was a conventional, ruggedly-built biplane of metal construction with fabric skinning, powered by a 240hp Lorraine Mizar radial engine. It was designed by La Société d'Etudes de Materiel d'Aviation, and built by La Sté Aérienne Bordelaise (a subsidiary of the Lorraine and Amiot group of companies) to meet the requirements of a 1933 programme for an intermediate and advanced trainer, or 'avion de travail'. The competition was eventually won by the Romano R.82, and the SEMA-10, fitted with a more powerful Lorraine 9Na Algol radial engine of 300hp with a Townend ring, and with modified wings and tail, was redesignated as the SAB-SEMA-12 and registered F-APDO.

In 1936 the Société Aérienne Bordelaise was acquired by Potez, and, after a test flight on 1 October 1936 by the Air France pilot Le Chevalier, the SEMA-12 was removed from Villacoublay on the pretext that it needed further modifications. It reappeared some time later at the Republican flying school at Los Alcázares, in Murcia, bearing the type code EC.

Span 8.75m; length 6.9m; height 2.82m.

The SAB-SEMA 12 in its final configuration. (Liron)

Empty weight 1,126kg; loaded weight 1,589kg.
Maximum speed 260km/h; landing speed 85km/h; climb to 1,000m in 5min; ceiling 6,000m; range 575km.

Savoia-Marchetti S.55X

One year after being appointed chief designer of the Societá Idrovolanti Alta Italia (SIAI) in 1922, Alessandro Marchetti began work on a revolutionary flying-boat for the Italian navy. The S.55, which first flew in August 1924, was unusual in every

The Savoia-Marchetti S.55X ex-I-LONG at Palma, Mallorca, on 10 September 1936. (Arráez)

respect, having twin hulls, on top of which was mounted an extremely thick cantilever wing. Two engines in tandem, one pushing and one pulling, were housed in a nacelle mounted on an N-strut pylon arrangement above the centre-section. The pilot and copilot sat in a cabin in the wing centre-section, between the hulls and beneath the engines. A triple-rudder tail unit was carried on twin booms extending from the sterns of the hulls.

More than 200 S-55s were built in naval, military and civil versions between 1925 and 1930. The Savoia-Marchetti 'twin-hulls', as they were called, became world famous, however, as a result of a series of long-distance, mass-formation flights across the Atlantic and Siberia during the late 1920s and early 1930s, led by Italian air minister and Fascist leader Gen Italo Balbo.

The last of these was a celebrated flight by twenty-five S.55Xs (two 750hp Isotta-Fraschini Asso R eighteen-cylinder W-type liquid-cooled engines) from Rome to the Chicago World's Fair in 1933. One of the machines on this flight, I-LONG, piloted by Commandanti Largo, as well as two other S.55Xs, made a brief appearance in the Spanish Civil War.

On 16 August 1936 the Republicans attempted to capture Mallorca, which had fallen to the Nationalists immediately after the uprising on 18 July, by landing 12,000 men, led by Comandante Alberto Bayo (a Spanish air force officer who later became Fidel Castro's adviser on guerrilla warfare), at Porto Cristo on the south side of the island. The Nationalists appealed to the Italian government for help, and, while preparations were under way to send six fighter aircraft (see Fiat C.R.32 and Macchi M.41) by ship, three Savoia-Marchetti S.55Xs (MM45167, 45173 and 45175), with single movable machine guns in the gun positions in the bow and stern of each hull, took off from Orbetello, Italy, shortly after noon on 18 August. They had been paid for in cash by the Mallorquino financier Juan March, who had also paid for the twelve Savoia-Marchetti S.81 bombers sent to Spanish Morocco on 30 July. The aircraft landed at Pollensa and, as soon as their crews had been briefed on the situation, took off again and attacked the Republican ships lying off Porto Cristo beach from an altitude of 400m. All the bombs fell in the water, far from their targets. There being no more aerial bombs available, the night was spent improvising a second bomb load from hand grenades, but the raid next morning was no more effective because the bombs all fell on the beach, several hundred yards from the Republican troops. Nevertheless, the boost to the morale of the Nationalist defenders of Mallorca was as enormous as the surprise and demoralising effect on the Republicans, which were completed with the arrival of the Fiat C.R.32s.

On 20 August seven Republican Savoia-Marchetti S.62s attacked the three S.55Xs moored in Palma Harbour, one bomb scoring a direct hit on the starboard hull of I-LONG but failing to explode. Next day the crews of the two undamaged S.55Xs flew them back to Italy. Within fifteen days I-LONG was refloated and painted in Nationalist markings, with the words *MAÑANA POR LA MAÑANA* ('tomorrow morning') on the starboard hull, this being the answer invariably given to all who asked when the flying-boat would be ready for action again. Piloted by Tenente Sergio Pietralli, with a crew of four, the S.55X resumed operations on 10

September 1936, carrying out a number of bombing raids on Ibiza and transporting officers to Ibiza when the Nationalists occupied the island after the withdrawal of Bayo's forces. On 28 September the S.55X damaged its starboard hull during a landing in choppy water, and was laid up on a quay at Palma to await materials for repair. They were still awaited eight months later, when, on 26 May 1937, the S.55X was destroyed during a bombing attack by SB Katiuskas.

Span 24.1m; length 16.5m; height 5m; wing area 93sq m.
Empty weight 5,500kg; loaded weight 9,500kg.
Maximum speed 265km/h; cruising speed 170km/h; ceiling 4,500m; range 2,000km.

A Savoia-Marchetti S.62 of the Aeronáutica Naval. (Arráez)

The Savoia-Marchetti S.62P used by LAPE. (Arráez)

S.62s and a Dornier Wal at San Javier, 1935. (Arráez)

Savoia-Marchetti S.62

The small biplane flying-boat powered by a single pusher engine, strut-mounted between the wings, was a formula derived before the First World War and used successfully into the 1930s. The Savoia-Marchetti S.62 four-seat reconnaissance-bomber was a worthy, though perhaps not very inspired, example from the late 1920s, the prototype making its first flight from Lake Maggiore, in northern Italy, in 1928. Built of wood, it had a plywood-covered hull and fabric-covered wings and tail surfaces. Its engine was a 500hp water-cooled Isotta-Fraschini Asso Ri driving a four-bladed wooden propeller. The pilot and copilot sat side by side, with dual controls, and the nose cockpit was occupied by a mechanic/gunner armed with twin 7.62mm Lewis guns. A second gunner, with similar armament, occupied a position behind the wings, and 500kg of bombs could be carried on underwing racks.

Following the demonstration of an S.62 at Barcelona in March 1929, the Spanish Aeronáutica Naval, which had its own construction workshops at Barcelona and had been building Savoia-Marchetti S.13 and S.16 and Macchi M.18 flying-boats since 1921, acquired one engineless

Savoia-Marchetti S.62 S-12 was the aircraft that landed in Gibraltar bay after attacking Nationalist Dornier Wals at Algeciras on 29 July 1936. (Emiliani)

aircraft and a licence to build a maximum of 100 machines. The Spanish-built S.62s were to be fitted with 600hp Hispano-Suiza 12LB water-cooled engines built under licence by Elizalde at Barcelona. The first of the production aircraft made its maiden flight in March 1931, and during the next four years between thirty-five and forty were built, thirty-five of which were still in service on 18 July 1936, distributed as follows:

At San Javier, Cartagena, there were eighteen aircraft of the 1ª and 2ª Escuadrillas de Reconocimiento (Reconnaissance Squadrons), which had nine aircraft each. The emblem of the 1ª Escuadrilla was a dragonfly with a pair of binoculars, and that of the 2ª Escuadrilla was a witch riding a broom and looking down a telescope.

At Barcelona there were seven aircraft, of which four were under repair. There was also one civil S.62P (with an Isotta-Fraschini A50 engine) which had been bought by CLASSA in 1930 and inherited by LAPE.

At Mahón, Menorca, there were five aircraft, (Nos S-20, -22, -25, -28 and -29) of the 2ª Patrulla of the 3ª Escuadrilla de Reconocimiento.

At Marín, near Pontevedra in Galicia on the north-west Atlantic coast, there were five aircraft (S-10, -23, -33, -34 and -35). Galicia, however, was taken over by the Nationalists within a few days, and these aircraft fell into their hands.

On 19 July Gen Goded, the Military Governor of the Balearic Islands and a principal leader of the Nationalist rebellion, who had managed to secure Mallorca almost without a shot, ordered the five S.62s at Mahón, Menorca, to cross to Palma, Mallorca, and fly himself, his son and his aides to Barcelona, which he assumed was by then under the control of the military garrison. When the five machines alighted in Palma harbour S-10 developed engine trouble – at least, so claimed the pilot, Francisco Casals. On 30 July, on the pretext of trial-running the 'repaired' engine, he took off and flew to Republican-held Menorca (for Casal's later history see Sikorsky S.38B). The other four S.62s carried the general and his party to Barcelona, where they learned too late that

the rebellion, far from being successful, was collapsing amidst ferocious fighting in the city. Goded and the others were promptly seized and later tried and shot. What happened to the pilots is not recorded, but the flying-boats, contrary to some published accounts, remained at Barcelona.

The Republicans now had twenty-nine S.62s (one had crashed during fighting at San Javier air base), and the Nationalists six. While the street fighting lasted in Barcelona, the 'Savoias', as they were universally called, carried out low-level straffing attacks on buildings where the Nationalists were still holding out. When the uprising was finally crushed in Catalonia, they were employed on a series of daylight air raids on Saragossa and Huesca, in company with a few Breguet 19s, the Fokker F.VIIb3m EC-PPA converted into a bomber, some Vickers Vildebeests, and additional S.62s hastily sent up from San Javier.

Meanwhile, five S.62s at San Javier were dispatched to Málaga to attempt to disrupt the stealthy transfer, in boats, of small numbers of troops from Spanish Morocco to Spain. One aircraft, S-16, was soon put out of action by ground fire from Algeciras. On 28 July two S.62s attacked two Nationalist Dornier Wals moored off Algeciras, and one of them, S-12, came down in Gibraltarian waters. According to one account it was brought down by answering fire from the Dornier gunners; according to another, a Nationalist Nieuport 52 suddenly arrived on the scene. The British authorities, however, said that the 'enemy fighter' was a British civil aircraft which the Savoia crew mistook for a warplane and landed in panic as a result. This civil aircraft was, in fact, de Havilland D.H.84 Dragon G-ACZZ of Crilly Airways, in which Capt Donald Steele was running some secret errands for Gen Franco. On the same day, however, a Nationalist Nieuport 52 did shoot down another S.62 over Almería.

In August 1936 nine S.62s (S-1, -2, -4, -5, -17, -18, -30, -32 and -36) joined the Republican expeditionary force, under the leadership of Cdte Bayo, sent to reconquer Mallorca. They did quite well until the three Fiat C.R.32s arrived from Italy on 28

August and changed the situation dramatically within a few hours. Six S.62s were badly damaged, four of them (S-2, -5, -30 and -32) so extensively that they were abandoned on Mallorca when Republican forces withdrew from the island on 4 September.

In response to anguished pleas for aircraft from the Basque government, it was decided to send four S.62s (S-22, -24, -25 and -26) to the northern zone, together with six Breguet 19s and two Vickers Vildebeests, complete with spare parts and mechanics. The first attempt was a failure, but on 30 September, after taking off from Rosas Bay near the French frontier, the four flying-boats landed at Santander just before sundown. They were employed on reconnaissance missions through the winter, but by the time the Nationalist offensive against Bilbao started, at the end of March 1937, only one was still flying. Even this machine was grounded by the middle of April.

In October 1936 ten S.62s remained at Barcelona, and these performed reconnaissance missions and occasional attacks on Nationalist warships throughout the winter. By the end of January 1937, however, only six (S-3, -4, -10, -13, -14 and -29) were still in service. On 16 May 1937, with the creation of the FARE and the dissolution of the Aeronáutica Naval, the six Savoias and three Macchi M.18s were formed into the 1ª Escuadrilla of Grupo 73, the serials of the S.62s being changed to HS-001 to HS-006. Aircraft HS-005 and -006 were lost in 1937, one being shot down by the Nationalist cruiser *Canarias* on 15 July, and the other suffering an accident. The remaining four were relegated to training duties at San Javier, but HS-003 crashed on 24 November 1937. The last three were scrapped a year later. In the spring of 1937 it was proposed to build a series of S.62s at the new aircraft factory set up at Reus under the supervision of the anti-Nazi aircraft builder Antonius Raab (see Potez 54), but the plan was soon abandoned and the factory was devoted to building I-15 Chatos.

In the Nationalist zone, the five S.62s at Marín played an active part in putting down Republican resistance in Galicia during the first days

of the civil war, although two were soon rendered unserviceable owing to a lack of spares. On 27 July S-33, -34, and -35 were transferred to Puntales, Cádiz, to assist in the crucial events in the Straits of Gibraltar. By the end of the year only two, incorporated into the Dornier Wal squadron, were still airworthy. In 1937 S-35, attached to the He 60 kette, was still flying, but was not employed on missions of war. It was scrapped in January 1938. The two S.62s left at Marín, S-19 and S-23, were repaired and put back into service. On 13 August 1936 S-16, flown by ex-civil pilot José Brages, actually put a Republican bomber to flight, but by the spring of 1937 both aircraft had been scrapped.

Of the S.62s abandoned on Mallorca, repairs were started on S-5 and S-30, but S-30 was destroyed, along with the Savoia-Marchetti S.55X, by SB Katiuskas on 26 May 1937. Rebuilt and bearing the serial 61-5, S-5 joined the Cant Z.501 escuadrilla at Pollensa and flew missions until it was grounded by lack of spares in January 1938. While under repair it was blown out to sea and destroyed by the great storm of 11 February 1938.

Span 16m; length 12.56m; height 4.2m; wing area 69sq m.

Empty weight 2,630kg; loaded weight 4,030kg.

Maximum speed 220km/h; cruising speed 180km/h; ceiling 4,500m; range 1,200km.

Savoia-Marchetti S.79 Sparviere

Early in 1934 Alessandro Marchetti, chief designer of the Società Idrovolante Alta Italia (SIAI), began work on a fast, eight-passenger, three-engined, low-wing monoplane to compete in the MacRobertson London–Melbourne air race announced for October of that year. Although the resulting aircraft, the Savoia-Marchetti S.79, was not ready in time for the race, it revealed its potential during trials in October and November 1934 by attaining a top speed of 410km/h, demonstrating that it could easily outstrip any fighters of the Regia Aeronautica.

While the prototype, I-MAGO,

Savoia-Marchetti S.79 No 28-1 was the first of the type to arrive in Spain, and was one of the three that took part in the bombing of Guernica on 26 April 1937. (Emiliani)

fitted with more powerful Alfa-Romeo 126 RC 34 engines, was undergoing tests, SIAI developed a bomber version intended to replace the Savoia-Marchetti S.81 trimotor, which had been designed in parallel with the S.79 to meet an official specification. Believing that its high speed would protect the S.79 from a frontal attack, Marchetti insisted on retaining the trimotor configuration. However, faced with the demands of the Regia Aeronautica, he eventually compromised by installing a single fixed 12.7mm heavy-calibre machine gun in a hump above the pilot's cabin which also accommodated the dorsal gunner, equipped with a movable 12.7mm gun. Similarly, a shallow gondola added to the undersurface of

the fuselage, with a slanting window at the front, contained both the bombsight (the bombardier kneeling on two cushioned pads on the fuselage floor) and a third, movable 12.7mm ventral machine gun firing rearwards. The internal bomb bay, carrying two 500kg or five 250kg bombs suspended vertically, was offset to starboard to make room for a catwalk between the pilots' cabin and the rear fuselage, which enabled the copilot to take up his position as bomb-aimer and ventral gunner. The radio operator, who sat beside the flight engineer under the hump, doubled as dorsal gunner when necessary. In Spain, however, a crew of five was usually carried, the fifth member acting as bombardier and ventral gunner and also operating a 12.7mm machine gun mounted on a

S.79s of the 19ª Squadriglia, XXVII Gruppo Falchi delle Baleari. (Emiliani)

lateral bar which enabled him to fire out of either of the openings in the rear fuselage sides.

The S.79's fuselage was a hardened-steel-tube lattice of rectangular cross-section, the front section being skinned with duralumin and the rear with plywood and fabric. The wings were built of wood, covered by a plywood skin and laminated with doped fabric.

The Regia Aeronautica placed an initial order for ninety-six aircraft to be delivered between 1 October 1936 and 1 January 1937, but during the succeeding months a further 130 aircraft were ordered. The first S.79s to be delivered were formed into a specially created unit, the 12° Stormo Bombardamento Terrestre (the unit's emblem was a trio of green mice, 'Sorci Verdi' being an Italian expression meaning 'incredible things'), under the command of Colonnello Atillio Biseo, who had already made several record-breaking flights in the prototype, I-MAGO. Many of the pilots posted to the new Stormo were among the most experienced fighter pilots in Italy, because it was assumed that bomber pilots accustomed to slow and unwieldy Caproni Ca 73s and Ca 101s would have problems in converting to a bomber of such high wing loading and with a performance surpassing that of the fastest fighter.

Believing that the S.79 was the most advanced bomber in the world, the Italian air staff was eager to test it

under war conditions and, accordingly, two squadriglia of the 12° Stormo, the 280ª commanded by Capitano Badino and the 289ª commanded by Capitano Raina (both squadriglia being under the overall command of Maggiore Mario Aramu), were detached to join the Aviazione Legionaria as the XXIX Gruppo Bombardamento Veloce. The first three S.79s, displaying the Sorci Verdi emblem above the SIAI black flash along their fuselage sides, landed at Son San Juan Aerodrome, Mallorca, on 12 February 1937. They were joined over the next twelve weeks by eleven more aircraft in deliveries of one, nine and one. A British intelligence report from Mallorca, dated 7 May 1937, shows that, by then, twelve S.79s had flown to Tablada Aerodrome, Seville, where they received the type code 28. From Seville, three of the S.79s flew north to Soria early in April and took part in the bombing of Guernica on 26 April 1937, a detail of that notorious affair that did not become publicly known until August 1977, forty years later. The three aircraft were 28-1 (Capitano Castellani), 28-4 (Tenente Pucci) and 28-11 (Tenente Dagasso). According to Castellani's debriefing report, the thirty-six 50kg bombs which they dropped on the Renteria Bridge on the eastern outskirts of the town all missed and fell on the railway station. On 21 May five S.79s transferred to an aerodrome in the south (possibly Granada) and bombed the Republican battleship *Jaime I* at Almería. Nationalist communiqués claimed that the ship was permanently disabled, but in fact she received only a single hit on the prow, which was soon repaired.

From 24 May, and through June and early July 1937, the S.79 Gruppo, now based at Soria, took part in the offensive against Bilbao, bombing the city before it fell on 19 June. In the second week of July the S.79s were moved to the Madrid front to assist against the Republican offensive at Brunete. On 16 July they bombed the aerodrome at Alcalá de Henares, killing the base commander, Cdte Augustín Sanz Sainz (see Vultee V1-A), and on 18 July, with an escort of Messerschmitt Bf 109s, pressed home an attack on Brunete itself. By this time, owing to fierce Republican opposition, the S.79s were the only Nationalist bombers with sufficient speed to be used regularly by day. After the defeat of the Republicans at Brunete the XXIX Gruppo returned to the northern front, but in August was used in the Battle of Belchite, a Republican offensive against Saragossa intended, like that at Brunete, to draw Nationalist forces away from the north.

At this time (August 1937) five specially adapted S.79s, designated S.79C and bearing the Sorci Verdi emblem, plus a standard production bomber, took part in the 6,190km Istres–Paris–Damascus race. All six, led by Colonnello Biseo, reached Damascus within six hours, having averaged speeds of 418km/h, compared with the 349km/h of the de Havilland D.H.88 Comet racer and 299km/h of the fastest French participant. At the completion of the circuit S.79s took the first, second the third places. This was a sensational triumph for Italian aviation, and made the S.79 famous overnight.

Meanwhile, in the Spanish fighting the S.79s took part in the battles of Teruel during the winter of 1937-38, but many were frequently grounded when their engines refused to start in temperatures of –17°C. The delivery of more S.79s to Spain from August 1937 allowed the XXIX Gruppo to hand over twelve of its aircraft to the Spanish Nationalist air arm (see below). In April 1938 the arrival of a second Gruppo, the XXX (consisting of the 281ª and 285ª squadriglie) resulted in the creation of an S.79 contingent of twenty-four aircraft, the 111° Stormo *Sparvieri*. The name Sparviere (sparrowhawk), taken from the emblem of the 280ª Squadriglia, henceforth became the type-name for the S.79 itself, though crews usually called it, with less respect, 'Il Gobbo' or 'El Jorobado' (Italian and Spanish for 'hunchback').

The 111° Stormo, based at Saragossa and commanded in succession by Colonnello Gaeta and Colonnello Vetrella, took part in all of the major campaigns of the remainder of the civil war – the advance through Aragón to the coast, the unsuccessful offensive against Valencia, the Battle of the Ebro, and the conquest of Catalonia. Its high speed usually enabled the S.79 to operate without fighter escorts, but over sectors where air fighting occurred in a concentrated area, as in the Battle of the Ebro, bombing missions became a problem, because the only Nationalist fighters fast enough to keep up with the 'Sparvieri' were Messerschmitt Bf 109s, and these were often needed to escort the Condor Legion's own Heinkel He 111s.

Meanwhile, between June and November 1937, a separate S.79 Gruppo had been built up on Mallorca, the aircraft being taken from the second Italian unit to receive the type, the 8° Stormo BV. The twelve S.79s on Mallorca were formed into the XXVII Gruppo of two squadriglie (18ª and 52ª) and, taking the name from the emblem of the 18ª Squadriglia (a falcon), it was christened Gruppo *Falchi delle Baleari* ('Falcons of the Balearic Islands'). This unit was reinforced by the XXX Gruppo (10ª and 19ª Squadriglie) in March 1938, bringing the total on Mallorca to twenty-four aircraft. With the exception of the Battle of Teruel, when Mallorca-based S.79s briefly took over the bombing missions of the Spanish-based S.79s grounded by freezing conditions, the XXVII and XXX groups were employed exclusively in attacking Republican shipping and ports along the Mediterranean seaboard. During October and November 1937, while Bruno Mussolini (the dictator's son) was attached to the group, S.79s carried out a series of raids on Barcelona and Valencia, usually flying in from the sea at low level, dropping their bombs, turning out to sea again and flying off at full throttle.

After discussions on the feasibility of using the S.79 on nocturnal missions, a single S.79 based at Guidonia in Italy, with Gen Valle on board, took off by night, flew to Barcelona, dropped 800kg of bombs, and returned to Guidonia after a 2,000km round trip. There followed a series of night raids through January 1938, and on 16-18 March both groups carried out a series of savage round-the-clock attacks on Barcelona – seventeen raids in all – in which they covered the whole city district by district (see also Heinkel He 59).

These raids, which provoked public indignation and protests in Europe and the USA, were personally ordered by Mussolini without consulting Gen Franco, who, when he heard of them, is said to have been furious. With regard to the bombing of legitimate naval targets, however, the contribution of the *Falchi delle Baleari* was undoubtedly great. In 1938 alone they carried out 206 raids on Republican ports, sinking about 150,000 tons of shipping and rendering many docks unusable for weeks at a time.

The first Spanish group of six S.79s, formed in August 1937, was 3-G-28, a unit equipped previously with Junkers Ju 52/3ms, under the command of Luis Pardo, who was later replaced by J-A Ansaldo, the monarchist ex-commander of the old 'Grupo Fokker-Dragon'. In October 1937 4-G-28 was formed under the command of Luis Navarro. Meanwhile, the Spanish Nationalists negotiated the purchase of six S.79s directly from SIAI, or Savoia-Marchetti, as the company had recently been renamed, at a unit price of 2,109,600 lire (about £3,400 in 1937). These arrived in November to form 5-G-28, whose commander, Coronel José Gomá, wrote the first history of the air war in Spain in 1958. A fourth group, 6-G-28, was formed in July 1938. Based at Soria alongside the Italian S.79s, 3-G-28 took part in the Battle of Belchite. During the Battle of Teruél 3-G-28 and 4-G-28 were formed into the Escuadra Núm 2 de Bombardeo Veloz under Coronel Lacalle (not to be confused with the Republican fighter pilot, Andrés Lacalle), as part of the 1ª Brigada Hispana. Meanwhile, 5-G-28 became, with the Heinkel He 70F squadron, part of the Escuadra Núm 3 Mixta. During the Battle of the Ebro the four Spanish S.79 groups were incorporated into the 3ª and 4ª Escuadras of the 2ª Brigada Hispaña, and remained so until the end of the war.

In December 1938 3- and 4-G-28 had six aircraft each, and 5- and 6-G-28 had five aircraft each, making twenty-two in all. At that time the 111º Stormo had twenty-six aircraft in repair or detached to other units. Sixty-one S.79s (thirty-six Italian and twenty-five Spanish) were lined up for the Victory parade at Barajas Airport on 12 May 1939, which makes it doubtful that the *Falchi delle Baleari* were present. The point is significant only because it affects estimates of the total number of S.79s delivered during the civil war. From available evidence, deliveries can be itemised as follows:

Jan-Mar 1937	4
Apr-Jun 1937	10
Jul-Sep 1937	22
Oct-Dec 1937	34
Apr-Jun 1938	8
Oct-Dec 1938	12
Jan-Mar 1939	10
Total	100

After the civil war the surviving S.79s were incorporated into 11º and 12º Regimientos de Bombardeo of the Ejercito del Aire, based at Tablada and Armilla respectively. Eighty-seven were in service in 1940. In 1945 their type code was changed to B.1, and they remained in service until the early 1950s.

Span 21.1m; length 15.62m; height (tail down) 4.4m; wing area 61.7sq m.

Empty weight 6,800kg; loaded weight 10,500kg.

Maximum speed 430km/h at 4,000m; cruising speed 373km/h at 5,000m; ceiling 6,500m; range, with 1,250kg bomb-load, 1,900km.

A Savoia-Marchetti S.81 of the Aviazione Legionaria, with its escort of Fiat C.R.32s, over the target.

Savoia-Marchetti S.81 Pipistrello

Although it possessed a later type number and the characteristics of an earlier generation of aircraft, the S.81 was an exact contemporary of the much more advanced S.79. Designed in 1934 to meet a Regia Aeronautica requirement for a bomber-transport to replace the Caproni Ca 101, it was a military version of the S.73 airliner, which itself was still in the prototype stage. Retaining the wood and metal construction, with plywood and fabric skinning, of the airliner, and the trimotor configuration still favoured by the Italian air staff, it was ordered into mass production late in 1934.

Additional contracts were signed with the Piaggio and CMASA factories, and, in view of the urgency of the production programme, the series built by the different factories were to be fitted with different powerplants – notably the 650hp Alfa Romeo 125 RC 35 or 680hp 126 RC 36, the 750hp Gnome-Rhône 14 K and the 700hp Piaggio PX. RC.35, all radial engines housed in wide-chord cowlings.

The S.81's crew of five consisted of a pilot, a copilot (who doubled as bomb-aimer), a wireless operator (doubling as dorsal gunner), and an armourer and a flight engineer, who between them also manned the ventral and waist gun positions. The semi-retractable, hydraulically-powered dorsal gun turret, installed immediately behind the pilot's cabin, had twin Breda-SAFAT 7.7mm machine guns, and a second pair

were mounted to fire downwards through an opening midway along the fuselage floor. Two .303 Lewis guns were mounted to fire out of windows in the fuselage sides, and the bomb-aimer was provided with a semi-retractable gondola beneath the pilot's cabin and immediately behind the central engine. The wide-track undercarriage was fixed, and the wheels were encased in a pair of large streamlined spats. The 2,016kg bomb load usually consisted of a mix of sixteen 100kg and twenty-eight 50kg bombs, or four 250kg bombs, forty-two incendiaries (2kg) and fifty-six 15kg bombs.

Savoia-Marchetti S.81s entered Italian service in time to take part in the invasion of Abyssinia (Ethiopia), where they were often misidentified by newspaper reporters as 'Capronis', the chief type used in the fighting. Hence, when the S.81s appeared in Spain, they were almost invariably described by the world's press, during the first six months or so, as 'Capronis'.

At the start of the Nationalist rebellion, when Gen Franco arrived at Tetuán in a de Havilland Dragon Rapide on 19 July 1936 to take command of the Army of Africa, he found that there were no ships in which to carry his army across to Spain. That same day he sent Luis Bolín to Rome to request bomber-transports from Mussolini. The story of the subsequent political manoeuvrings need not be retold here, but the upshot was that, on 30 July 1936, a squadron of twelve S.81s, drawn from the 55ª, 57ª and 58ª squadriglie of the Regia Aeronautica and, according to some accounts, paid for in cash (£2,000,000 Sterling) by the Spanish financier Juán March, took off at dawn from Elmas military aerodrome, near Cagliari in Sardinia, and set course for Spanish Morocco in four flights of three aircraft each, flying in vees in line astern. The crews included a high proportion of mechanics, fitters and armourers, for it was assumed that the aircraft would soon be handed over to the Spaniards.

The S.81s, carrying full defensive armament but no bombs, retained the cream-yellow Regia Aeronautica livery, but the military insignia had been hastily and sloppily painted over. Owing to unexpectedly strong headwinds, three aircraft ran out of fuel. One crashed into the sea, all the crew being killed, a second crashed while attempting to land at Saïda, a French military aerodrome in Algeria, killing four of the crew, and the third landed safely a few yards on the French side of the border between French and Spanish Morocco. The Italian crew members were later sentenced to a month in prison and fined 200 French francs each by the French authorities. The nine surviving S.81s reached Nador, at the eastern end of Spanish Morocco, a little before noon. It was not long before their commander, Colonnello Ruggero Bonomi, learned that the 87-octane petrol needed for the Alfa Romeo 125 engines of his aircraft was not available anywhere in the colony. The remaining fuel was transferred into his machine to enable him to fly to Tetuán to confer with Gen Franco, and the other eight bombers were grounded at Nador for the next five days.

During the enforced rest period, Bonomi, discovering that there were insufficient Spanish pilots able to fly the S.81s, arranged for the Italians to be enrolled *en bloc* into the Tercio de Extranjeros (Spanish Foreign Legion) as a way of avoiding international legal difficulties. The S.81s thus equipped the first escuadrilla of the Aviación de El Tercio, which was the first air arm the Spanish Foreign Legion had ever possessed.

On 4 August a small tanker, the *Alice*, arrived at Melilla, Spanish

An S.81 during the advance through Aragón in the spring of 1938.

Morocco, with fuel, bombs, ammunition and spare parts, and the bombers immediately transferred to Tetuán. On the following day eight of the S.81s, together with two Dornier Wals, the captured Douglas DC-2 and six Breguet 19s, provided cover for a Nationalist convoy of fishing boats taking some 5,000 troops across the Straits of Gibraltar to Algeciras in Spain. Each S.81 carried one Spanish crew member as a first stage in conversion training.

On 7 August three S.81s flew back to Melilla, at the eastern end of Spanish Morocco, and from there attacked the Republican aerodrome at Guadix in the province of Granada, thus striking the first overt blow by foreign aircrews in foreign aircraft by either side in the Spanish Civil War. After an unsuccessful attack on Málaga the next day, six of the S.81s flew to Tablada, Seville, in preparation for a raid on Madrid ordered by Gen Franco. This was cancelled at the last minute, and the S.81s did not go into action until 11 August, when they bombed Republican militia retreating northwards along the roads to Badajoz and Mérida. The next three days were spent largely in flying to and fro between Tetuán and Seville to bring across the fuel, armaments and supplies that would enable them to operate from the mainland, since none of this could as yet be brought by sea.

By mid-August three of the eight S.81s (one having been wrecked on take-off) were crewed entirely by Spaniards, and on 2 September the S.81 mixed group, guided by Capitán Carlos de Haya in the Douglas DC-2, moved north to Cáceres. After a brief return south in a vain

attempt to find and sink the SS *Magellanes*, which was bringing arms for the Republicans through the Straits of Gibraltar from Mexico, the group transferred from Cáceres to Talavera de la Reina, where it remained for the assault on Madrid. During October 1936 the S.81s, staging at Granada, joined the Junkers Ju 52s in concentrated attacks on Alicante, Cartagena and the aerodrome at Hellín in an attempt to disrupt the unloading and assembly of Russian aircraft reported to be reaching Spain. By the middle of November the appearance of Russian fighters over Madrid, combined with the flooding of the aerodrome by heavy rain, obliged the S.81 group, now reduced to six aircraft, to abandon daylight operations. On 24 November the aerodrome was actually shelled by a Republican mobile column of artillery which had managed to infiltrate Nationalist lines, and the next day the aerodrome was simultaneously shelled and attacked by low-flying Russian SBs, one S.81 being destroyed.

While preparing to become a night-bomber unit, the group moved to the supposedly safer aerodrome at Veladas on 1 December, but eighteen R-5 Rasantes attacked next morning and destroyed three more aircraft. The remaining two aircraft, soon reduced to one, were moved yet again to Arenas San Pedro, and the arrival of a repaired S.81 from Seville on 20 December restored the strength to two airworthy machines, both crewed by Spaniards (Capitán Tasso and Capitán Pando). Tasso and his crew were killed when their S.81 (21-5, 21 being the code allotted to the type) was shot down by I-16s on 3 January 1937. Capitán Pando and his Spanish crew were transferred to other duties after 9 January, and the S.81, the last survivor of the original twelve, was sent to Seville for overhaul.

Meanwhile, the creation of the Aviazione Legionaria brought to Spain a new Gruppo of S.81s, the XXIV, divided into two squadriglie, the 11ª and 13ª of six aircraft each. Based at Seville, the Gruppo Bombardamento Pesato Morelli (Heavy Bomber Group *Morelli* – this being the *nom-de-guerre* of its commander, Tenento Colonnello Ferdinando

Rafaelli) took part in the Málaga campaign before being transferred to Soria, in Old Castile, to assist in the Italian attempt to encircle Madrid from the north. The offensive, which began on 7 March 1937 and became known as the Battle of Guadalajara, was defeated partly by bad weather and more specifically by the skilful straffing of the Italian motorised columns by Republican I-15 Chatos and R-Z Natachas, and by 12 March the Italians were in precipitate retreat.

As always, the weather over the areas to the north of the Sierra Guadarrama was far worse than to the south (where Republican bases were located), with the result that most of the Italian aerodromes were waterlogged. One photograph shows an S.81 up to its wings in water, from which ground crews are trying to extricate it with ropes. Nevertheless, on 18 March six S.81s managed to take off and carry out a low-level raid, under the clouds, on Guadalajara and its aerodrome. On 19 March the 11ª Squadriglia, led by Capitano Gildo Simini and escorted by Fiat C.R.32s, bombed Brihuega, and in the ensuing air battle with the Escuadrilla Lacalle (see I-15 Chato) the Republicans claimed five Fiats destroyed for the loss of one Chato. The Nationalists admitted the loss of one Fiat. On 21 March the whole group, led by Rafaelli, carried out a low-level attack on Brihuega and Torre del Burgo. Another dogfight between Fiats and Chatos resulted in the loss of one to each side.

Through April and May the S.81s, still operating from Soria, were employed in the Nationalist offensive against Bilbao, during the course of which a new consignment of S.81s was used to form the XXV Gruppo. After the Battle of Brunete (June 1937), the two groups were combined into the 21° Stormo Bombardamento Pesato, the four squadriglie being renumbered 213ª and 214ª (XXIV Gruppo) and 215ª and 216ª (XXV Gruppo).

Meanwhile, six S.81s had been delivered to Mallorca in August and September 1936, to be followed by at least four more (powered by 700hp Piaggio PX. RC 35 engines) in 1937. At the end of the northern campaign, in October 1937, the XXV Gruppo

was transferred to join them on Mallorca, to carry out night raids against Republican ports along the Mediterranean coast. It was probably at this time that the XXV Gruppo received the name *Pipistrelli* (Bats), a name soon applied to the mainland XXIV Gruppo and eventually to the Savoia-Marchetti S.81 itself. The S.81s of the XXV Gruppo were repainted with the wavy-band camouflage of the Mallorca units, but those on the mainland retained their blotched camouflage. The individual serial numbers of the XXIV Gruppo S.81s were painted not only in black on the fuselage sides, but also on white discs on the red flashes of the undercarriage spats. Thus 21-44, for example, had a '4' on the nose of each spat. During the autumn of 1937 one S.81 was employed in dropping supplies to the Nationalists beseiged in the Santuario de la Cabeza, near Córdoba. In the following winter the S.81s of XXVI Gruppo distinguished themselves in the Battle of Teruel.

After the Nationalist breakthrough to the coast in the spring of 1938, XXIV Gruppo was disbanded and its machines, together with twenty-six new (Piaggio-powered) arrivals from Italy, were handed over to the Spanish Nationalists and formed into four groups, 15-G-21, 16-G-21, 17-G-21 and 18-G-21, as parts of Escuadras 4 and 5. During the Catalonian campaign the S.81s, together with the 1ª Escuadrilla of Ju 52s, operated from Huesca and Ablitas, but in the last month of the war the S.81s were based in Andalusia and took little part in the fighting.

Between sixty-six and seventy Savoia-Marchetti S.81s were delivered to Spain during the civil war, though Nationalist claims that only four or five were lost seem suspiciously low. The survivors were formed into two Grupos, one based on Mallorca and the other at Villanubla, Valladolid, where many were destroyed by a hurricane. In March 1940 forty were still in service as transports with the Regimiento Mixto Núm 1, bearing the type code T.1 (Transporte 1).

With 650hp Alfa Romeo 125 RC.35 engines:

Span 24m; length 17.8m; height 4.4m; wing area 87sq m.

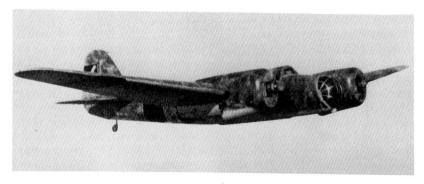

The SB Katiuska. Its full designation was SB-2M-100A.

An SB Katiuska, which the Nationalists called a 'Martin Bomber', captured and put on exhibition in San Sebastián in 1938. This particular machine had an underbelly window for aerial photography.

Empty weight 6,800kg; loaded weight 10,505kg.

Maximum speed 340km/h; cruising speed 320km/h; ceiling 7,000m; range 1,500km. (The claimed speeds seem greatly exaggerated.)

SB Katiuska

When Russian SB twin-engined bombers began their operations in the Spanish Civil War, at the end of October 1936, they took the Nationalists completely by surprise. Not only were they faster and more advanced in concept than any military aircraft hitherto seen in Spain, but they challenged the prevailing belief in the West that the Soviet aviation industry was too backward to produce modern aeroplanes of indigenous design, and that the machines equipping the large Soviet air forces were inferior and poorly manufactured copies of European or American originals. Thus, as the I-15 became a 'Curtiss' in Nationalist eyes, and the I-16 a 'Boeing', so the SB became a 'Martin Bomber', or 'Martin Bomberg' (a name initially preferred by the propaganda organs because it suggested the 'Judaic-Masonic-Bolshevik' conspiracy that the Nationalist cause was ostensibly dedicated to overthrowing). It was assumed that it must be either the Martin 139W (the export version of the Martin B-10), which CASA had been preparing to build under licence at Getafe when the civil war broke out, or a Soviet version of it. This confusion was compounded when the Republicans themselves, anxious to conceal the presence of the Russian bombers in Spain from the eyes of the world, published in their aeronautical magazine *Aire* a photograph of two United States Army Air Corps Martin B-10s, retouched with Spanish Republican markings.

Although it is true that the Russians were behind the leading Western aircraft industries in aero-engine technology and the sophisticated mass-production of airframes, they were not behind in inventive design. The SB was derived not from the Martin B-10, or even from its first prototype, the Martin 123 of 1932, but from three prototypes produced by the design bureau headed by Aleksandr Arkangelsky under the aegis of A N Tupolev at the KOSOS Ts AGI (Design Department for Experimental Aircraft at the Central Aero- and Hydrodynamic Institute in Moscow) between 1932 and 1934.

These were the ANT-21 twin-engined MI (*mnogomestnyi istrebitel*, or 'multi-seat fighter'), the ANT-29 DIP (two-seat cannon-armed fighter), and the ANT-38 SB (*skorostnoi bombarbirovshchik*, or 'fast bomber'). All were cantilever monoplanes of all-metal, stressed-skin semimonocoque construction with retractable undercarriages, the ANT-38 SB featuring full flush rivetting and enclosed accommodation for the crew. They were all extremely advanced in concept for their time.

Design work following trials of the

ANT-21 led to the ANT-40 SB, but in the meantime an interim prototype SB (it had no other designation), which was the original prototype of the Katiuska of the Spanish Civil War, made its first flight on 25 April 1934, powered by two 710hp Wright Cyclone R-1820-F3 radial engines. This aeroplane was damaged during a landing accident on 29 September 1934, and when rebuilt was fitted with two 900hp M-87 radials (licence-built Gnome-Rhône 14 Ks). Meanwhile, two more prototypes, the ANT-40 and ANT-40$_2$, were being constructed, with redesigned vertical tail surfaces and outer wing panels and 860hp Hispano-Suiza 12Ybrs water-cooled engines, for which a manufacturing licence was being negotiated. The first prototype took to the air on 7 October 1934, and the second, with further modifications, in September 1935.

Despite numerous structural problems, including frequent popping of the flush rivets, the SB (as the ANT-40$_2$ was officially designated) was considered so impressive that it was ordered into mass production. Complaints from the pilots and engineers at the NII-VVS (air force test centre) regarding these problems led to the matter being brought to the attention of Stalin, who, when Tupolev explained that there was nothing organically wrong with the SB and that its faults were 'trivialities', replied, 'There are no *trivialities* in aviation; everything is serious, and any uncorrected *triviality* could lead to the loss of an aircraft and its crew'. Such a bomber could put the Soviet Union in the lead in military aviation, and Tupolev was ordered to correct the faults come what may. He was to be arrested and gaoled a year later.

In the production SB some of the refinements had to be abandoned as too complex for mass production, and this had a detrimental effect on performance. The licence-built Hispano-Suiza 12Ybrs (M-100) engine was rated at only 730hp, and had a drag-inducing flat-fronted radiator. This, the replacement of the flush rivets by dome-headed rivets, and a poor surface finish, resulted in a lowering of the top speed to 393km/h. Some defects were never cured. For example, it was almost impossible for the navigator/ bombardier to escape by parachute, and the aircraft was vulnerable to enemy fire. The SB's bomb load of up to 500kg (stored vertically in a bay behind the pilot's cockpit) was light for a 'strategic bomber', while the twin 7.62mm ShKAS machine guns in the nose position could move only vertically. The crew sat in three separate compartments, the navigator/bombardier/gunner in the nose, the pilot in a narrow cockpit between the wing roots, and the radio operator/gunner in the rear cockpit, which was enclosed by a forward-sliding canopy which could be tilted upwards. The last was provided with an electrically-powered gun ring and movable seat, as well as a gun that could be positioned to fire through a hatch in the floor.

Although the aircraft is commonly and erroneously referred to as the Tupolev SB-2, contemporary Soviet documents invariably refer to the aircraft simply as the SB (or CB), the practice at that time being to assign an aircraft letters signifying its functions and to append numbers sequentially to successive types in the same category — hence the fighter series I-5, I-15, I-16 etc. Until this

system was changed there was no other aircraft in the SB category. However, to distinguish between SBs with different engines it was usual to add the number of engines and model, so that the SB fitted with M-100 engines could be referred to as the SB-2M-100, later variants being the SB-2M-100A, -2M-103, etcetera. This was probably the origin of the error.

Production started in 1935, the M-100 engine soon being superseded by the M-100A, which gave 830hp for take-off and raised the top speed to 423km/h. By the end of 1936 about 400 SBs had been delivered to the squadrons of the Soviet Air Force. In October 1936 thirty-one SBs and their crews were shipped to Spain with the first consignments of Soviet aircraft and, as a part of Grupo 12 under Col Arkady Zlatsostsvietov, were divided into three escuadrillas distributed among five aerodromes in La Mancha.

The 1ª Escuadrilla was based at Tomelloso under the command of Maj Ernst Schacht (see Potez 54). The 2ª and 3ª Escuadrillas, led by majors Viktor Khalzunov and Pavel Nesmeyanov, were based at two aerodromes near Albacete, Los Llanos and La Torrecica, with patrullas of two or three aircraft detached to San Clemente and Sisante. Each escuadrilla had at least one aircraft with a window in the floor, behind the pilot's cockpit, and provision for a

Photography of the Katiuskas was forbidden on pain of death, and clear photographs of them in Republican service are rare. This picture was taken after the Republic surrendered on 31 March 1939.

vertically mounted aerial camera.

Almost immediately upon its arrival in Spain the SB received the name 'Katiuska', the most common explanation being that this was the name of a Russian girl in a popular *zarzuela* (Spanish operetta) of the time. Its Republican type code, which it probably did not receive until the following spring, was BK, though the aircraft were, of course, numbered individually.

On 25 October 1936 one of the Katiuskas was badly damaged in an accident at Los Llanos and was not returned to service for several months. Three days later, however, four Katiuskas led by Ernst Schacht carried out a raid on Tablada air base, Seville, a début which, though it inflicted little material damage, caused consternation among the Nationalists. After dropping their bombs the unidentifiable aircraft had flown off at a speed which no Nationalist fighter could hope to match. One SB was hit by anti-aircraft fire and was nursed home by the other three, Schacht deliberately sacrificing the advantage of speed upon which their survival chiefly depended. Returning by a circuitous route to Tomelloso, the formation was spotted south of Madrid by the Spanish Nationalist pilot Capitán Ángel Salas, flying a Fiat C.R.32. Utilizing his high altitude, he dived and made a single firing pass, claiming later to have damaged one of the bombers, although all four returned safely to base.

On 30 October and 1 November the Katiuskas twice raided Gamonál Aerodrome, Talavera de la Reina, on the second occasion destroying or severely damaging six Fiats. The Italian commander, Colonnello

Bonomi, thereupon decided to redeploy the surviving Fiats to a new aerodrome being prepared at nearby Torrijos. During the transit flight two Fiats spotted two Katiuskas and tried to attack them, but, lacking the advantage of speed, the pursuers soon became the pursued and had to dive to ground level to escape. The next day, however, the SBs suffered their first combat loss when one was sent, alone and without fighter protection, to find the new aerodrome at Torrijos. The Russians were circling round in a vain effort to discover signs of a military aerodrome when their SB was pounced upon by a pair of Fiats which had been on standing patrol some 1,000m above. The bomber caught fire and crashed to the ground, two members of the crew escaping by parachute, and the wreckage was taken to Tablada for detailed analysis. On 12 November two more Katiuskas were lost when their pilots, Feodorov and Bakhenov, collided while returning from a mission. Shortly afterwards the 1ª Escuadrilla was moved to San Clemente, with secondary fields at Tomelloso and Argamasilla de Alba.

At this time Spanish pilots and aircrew began to be enrolled into Grupo 12, and by the end of the month they were taking part in military operations. On 7 December the first of these, Ramos, was killed when his Katiuska was shot down by Narciso Bermúdez de Castro — the first occasion on which an SB was shot down by a Spanish Nationalist pilot.

By the end of the year only six Katiuskas had been lost from all causes, and the Russian and Spanish crews still believed that they were unlikely to fall victim to Nationalist fighters in any but the most exceptional circumstances. This confidence was rudely shaken on 3 January 1937, however, when García Morato, in a Fiat C.R.32, shot down two Katiuskas returning from an attack on Córdoba railway station. The sole survivor was Ananías Sanjuan, who, on 10 November 1936, had defected from the Nationalists and landed a Ju 52/3m at Alcalá de Henares.

By 1 March 1937 Grupo 12 possessed only fifteen airworthy SBs, with four others under repair. The 3ª Escuadrilla was therefore disbanded and its aircraft and crews distributed among the 1ª and 2ª Escuadrillas. During the early part of the Battle of Guadalajara both escuadrillas were frequently grounded by the waterlogged state of their aerodromes, but from 12 March the 2ª Escuadrilla (now commanded by Schacht) at San Clemente, and the 1ª Escuadrilla (Maj Proskurov) at Alcalá de Henares, were able to rejoin the action and, often operating together, contribute to the rout of the Italian motorised columns.

Although the Katiuska squadrons, as part of the Aviación Militar, were in theory under the command of the Spanish Jefatura, in practice the choice of targets was often determined by Lt Col Jakob Shmushkievich ('General Douglas'), the C-in-C of all Russian air units in Spain. This led to accusations by some Spanish Republican commanders that the bombers were not being employed with sufficient vigour and determination, and that the targets were not always those that the Republicans would have selected. Thus disagreements over the use of the fast-bomber squadrons became entangled with political in-fighting between the Communists and other groups within the Republic. A contentious case in point was the employment of Katiuskas on low-level attacks against enemy positions on or near the front. To bomb such targets the Katiuska pilots had to fly slowly, and so make their large machines easy targets for Nationalist anti-aircraft guns. Casualties were predictably high. During an attack on the Condor Legion base a La Cenia on 2 June 1938, for example, five Katiuskas of the 3ª Escuadrilla were shot down. Nevertheless, after the RZ Natachas had proved to be too slow and vulnerable for such work, the Republicans were obliged to use the SBs in this rôle, from time to time, until the end of the war.

The camouflage used by the Katiuska squadrons was adapted to suit the landscape where a unit was based. Thus it is common to see photographs of SBs on which the dark green of the Soviet VVs has been mottled over with light ochre or brown, and others with a wave-band type of camouflage. The black serial numbers were rarely painted on the fuselage, though aircraft numbers within the group were painted in white or yellow on the fins. The Katiuska emblem of Don Quixote riding a boot was never painted on the aircraft.

On 29 May 1937 two Russian-flown Katiuskas from Los Alcázares created an international incident when, during a search for the hated Nationalist cruiser *Canarias* off Ibiza, they inadvertently bombed the German pocket battleship *Deutschland*, killing thirty-one crew members and injuring eighty-three. (The SB that scored the hit was BK-37 *El Abuelo*, 'the Grandfather'.) An infuriated Adolf Hitler ordered the *Admiral Scheer* and her escorting destroyer to bombard Almería as a reprisal, and for a few days the Spanish Republican government prepared to declare war on Germany, until wiser counsels prevailed.

A second delivery of thirty-one Katiuskas arrived in June 1937, enabling the Republicans to re-form the 3ª Escuadrilla and create a new group, Grupo 24, consisting of a single escuadrilla, later expanded to two. In Grupo 12 Zlatsostsvietov was replaced by Col A Senatarov, and Proskurov retained command of the 1ª Escuadrilla, but the other two escuadrillas were commanded by Spaniards; the 2ª by Cdte Pereira and the 3ª by Cdte Leocadio Mendiola. Grupo 24 was initially commanded by Col A Gussaev, and its escuadrillas by Maj Sergei Chernikl. In July, however, Pereira replaced Gussaev as group commander, and his 2ª Escuadrilla was formed under the command of Manuel Cremadas.

Heavy losses sustained during the battles of Brunete and Belchite (June-September 1937) resulted in the dissolution of Grupo 12, and its surviving machines were used to form a 3ª and 4ª Escuadrilla in Grupo 24, under the commands of Armado Gracia and Maximo Ricote. In November 1937 Leocadio Mendiola was promoted to command the whole Grupo, a post he retained until the end of the war. He was to become the most decorated of all Republican pilots.

The arrival of a third batch of SBs in 1938 brought the number delivered to Spain to ninety-three. The

Spanish aviation historian Gen Jesús Salas Larrazábal believes the total delivered during the civil war to have been 108, but his brother, Gen Ramón Salas Larrazábal, raises it to 155. These discrepancies arise from the ways in which certain Soviet financial documents relating to deliveries of aircraft, and some personal testimonies of Republican air force mechanics speaking from memory forty-five years later, may be interpreted. Doubt is cast on the highest figure by the fact that only nineteen Katiuskas survived the war, making the consequent loss of 136 aircraft seem excessively high. It should be emphasised that Mendiola and other ex-commanders of Katiuska squadrons insist that only ninety-three were delivered altogether, of which seventy-four were lost.

Even so, such a high rate of attrition shows that, despite its high speed and easy handling qualities, the SB Katiuska was vulnerable and not wholly satisfactory as a bomber. Its chief fault was that the unprotected fuel tanks on either side of the pilot's cockpit were certain to catch fire when either was hit by a single incendiary bullet, the pilot rarely being able to escape the almost instant conflagration on both sides of him. Moreover, the machine was very difficult to maintain and repair in the field, and, as mentioned earlier, the narrowness of the navigator/ bombardier's cabin made escape nearly impossible. The height of the undercarriage was such that, if one leg failed to lower during a landing approach, the pilot could not avoid a violent ground loop in which the unfortunate bombardier, trapped in his cabin and with little room to move, would almost invariably be killed or severely injured.

Communication between crew members was primitive. Simple words were shouted through voice pipes, or semaphore-like hand signals were used. On the bombing run the bomb-aimer used a row of three button-lights to instruct the pilot to go to port, starboard or straight ahead. As a result, co-ordination between pilot and gunners during an attack by enemy fighters was impossible. The twin front guns, which had vertical movement only, could be used for little more than ground

straffing, and the ventral gun, being so awkward to get into position, was never used at all in Spain. Thus, armed in effect with a single dorsal machine gun with a restricted field of fire, the Katiuska could hardly defend itself against enemy fighters.

On 7 February 1938 Oblt Wilhelm Balthasar, flying a Bf 109, shot down three Katiuskas in a single combat. This feat was repeated on 2 September 1938, when Capitán Ángel Salas, in a Fiat C.R.32, shot down three Katiuskas of the 4ª Escuadrilla. As a result of this loss, Teniente Jaime Mata was appointed to command the escuadrilla, although he was only nineteen years old. It was he who planned and led an audacious attack on the Condor Legion fighter base at La Cenia on 4 October 1938, which destroyed several fighters on the ground, and, on 20 November 1938, a bombing attack on a Nationalist fleet reported to be sailing from Mallorca to bombard Barcelona. Several direct hits were scored and, breaking formation, the ships returned to Mallorca.

Deprived of fighter escorts and moved from base to base to reduce the chances of their destruction on the ground, Katiuskas played little part in the last phases of the civil war, after December 1938. In January 1939, in response to Gen Hidalgo de Cisneros's visit to Stalin the previous November, ninety-three new SBs were among the quantities of war material shipped to France for transit to Republican Spain. These were SB-2M-103s, powered by M-103 engines which, with much-improved streamlined cowlings and driving three-bladed propellers, raised the top speed to 450km/h. By the time the first SB 'Super Katiuskas', as they were called, were brought by lorries across the frontier, however, half of Catalonia was already overrun by the Nationalists, and Cdte Lacalle ordered the machines to be returned to France in their crates.

When the war ended on 31 March 1939, sixteen SBs were flown to Barajas to surrender, and three others flew to Oran, Algeria, one being damaged on landing. These three were eventually recovered by the Nationalists and, on 15 August 1939, the nineteen Katiuskas, bearing the type code 20W (later B.5),

were formed into the 13 Escuadra de Bombardeo Estratégico at Los Llanos, Albacete, under Cdte Llorente Sola. In January 1940 the unit was renamed 13 Regimiento de Bombardeo. During the 1940s the number of SBs in flying condition steadily diminished, and the last were withdrawn from service in February 1946. In the official maintenance reports of the period they are still described as 'SB, Russian aircraft derived from the Martin Bomber and built under licence'.

Span 20.33m; length 12.204m; height 4.39m; wing area 56.7sq m
Empty weight 4,138kg; loaded weight 5,706kg.
Maximum speed 423km/h; cruising speed 280km/h; ceiling 9,560m; range 1,450km.

Seversky SEV-3

Shortly after the February Revolution in Russia in 1917, the new Provisional Government sent a Naval Mission to the United States of America. Among its members was Maj Alexander Procofieff de Seversky, lately commander of Naval Fighter Aviation in the Baltic Sea area and, despite the loss of a leg, the ranking ace of the Imperial Naval Air Service, with a tally of thirteen German aircraft shot down. The seizure of power by the Bolsheviks in Russia in October 1917 persuaded Seversky to stay in America, where he earned his living as a test pilot, a consultant to the US Air Service, and a tireless propagandist for air power, a subject upon which he was to write, lecture and make films for the rest of his life. In 1931, using money he had been awarded for designing an automatic bombsight, he established the Seversky Aircraft Corporation to build a 'futuristic airplane' (as he put it) which would be equipped with an amphibian landing gear he had recently invented. He was fortunate in securing as his chief designer Alexander Kartveli, a gifted Georgian emigré who was able to adapt Seversky's undeniably original, but not always sound, concepts to a practicable form.

The Seversky SEV-3 Amphibian (c/n 301, registered NX2106), in gleaming gold metallic finish, was

rolled out of a rented hangar at the Edo Aircraft Factory, Long Island, in June 1933. As the first product of a new and small company run on a shoestring, the Amphibian was as impressive as it was ambitious. It was an aerodynamically clean, though rather portly, low-wing cantilever monoplane of all-metal, semi-monocoque stressed-skin construction. The semi-elliptical one-piece wing was of the multi-cellular, five-spar type, the stressed Alclad outer skin being strengthened by reinforced corrugated sheet, and had manually-operated split trailing-edge flaps. The 350hp Wright Whirlwind R-975-ET (a modified E 2) radial engine, which had been taken from Seversky's own Laird Speed-wing, was housed in a wide-chord NACA cowling and drove a two-blade variable-pitch propeller. The pilot was protected by a shallow Plexiglas canopy and a curious, vertical, windshield. The centre of the fuselage contained a cabin, with side windows, for two people, above which was a transparent housing for entrance and egress.

Although the SEV-3 combined more innovatory features than could be found in many aeroplanes of that time, its most striking feature was Seversky's elegant twin-float amphibious landing gear, so designed that, when the wheels were extended hydraulically, the floats were automatically freed to tilt forwards to

The Seversky SEV-3 in the configuration in which it is thought to have gone to Spain. (Stephen J Hudek, via C Ackley)

allow the machine to alight on land. When the wheels were retracted, the floats were locked in the horizontal position for alighting on water. The Seversky Amphibian could be converted into a landplane by exchanging the twin struts and floats for a pair of trousered undercarriage legs, an operation which took four men a day to complete. The designation SEV-3 denoted not, as might be assumed, that this was the company's third aircraft, but that the aeroplane was equally at home on land, water or in the air.

During the next two years the Seversky Amphibian, fitted with a series of ever more powerful engines, became a familiar sight at rallies and races in America, at which it broke seven world records and won, among other things, the Thompson Trophy. On 15 September 1935 it set a world speed record for amphibians at 230·4mph, on this occasion being powered by a 710hp Wright Cyclone R-1820-F3 radial. From this original aeroplane, through a series of transformations which must be unique in the history of aviation, Kartveli evolved the long and illustrious line of military aircraft – including the BT-8 trainer, the P-35 and EP-1

single-seat fighters and the 2PA two-seat fighter – that culminated, by direct line of descent, in one of the most famous aircraft of the Second World War, the Republic P-47 Thunderbolt.

In October 1937 an attempt was made to divert three Seversky SEV-3WW militarised Amphibians, which were about to be delivered to Colombia, to Republican Spain. Although the attempt failed, it put Maj Seversky in touch with the Republican ambassador in Mexico, don Félix Gordón Ordás, to whom he made a proposal to set up a factory in Spain, complete with materials, technical instructors and supervisors. This would produce 100 single-seat fighters based on the SEV-1XP (the original prototype of the Seversky P-35) and 100 two-seat attack-bombers based on the SEV-2XP, of which a trainer version, the Seversky BT-8, was already in production for the United States Army Air Corps.

Meanwhile, in November 1936, Charles Koch, a Seversky engineer, volunteered to join the Republican air force, possibly as the result of a visit to the US factory by Coronel Francisco Léon Trejo, the head of a Spanish Republican purchasing commission which had arrived in the USA. Koch left for Spain with a group of other American volunteers under the care of Comandante Sanz Sainz (see Vultee V1-A) and arrived at Valencia in December. He took with him a portfolio of photographs, drawings and specifications of the latest Seversky aircraft, and a letter from Coronel Léon Trejo to the Republican minister for marine and air, Indalecio Prieto. Prieto became enthusiastic over the SEV-3, since amphibian aircraft would be useful for coastal patrol, and instructed the Spanish Republican ambassador in Washington to arrange for its purchase. This was done by Seversky's sales agents, the Miranda brothers (proprietors of the American Armaments Corporation – see Lockheed Orion), who sold the machine for $45,000 to Coronel Roberto Fierro (see Lockheed Sirius and Vega) on the pretext that he needed it for a trans-Caribbean record-breaking flight. Ostensibly for this purpose it was re-engined with an 810hp Wright Cyclone R-1820-G2 radial engine with reduction gear for long-distance flying.

On 24 December 1936 Maj Seversky tested this engine by flying the SEV-3 as an amphibian from New York to Miami in 5 hours 46 minutes at a cruising speed of 220mph. Back at the Seversky plant at Farmingdale, Long Island, the SEV-3 was converted once more into a landplane and, on 7 January 1937, it was flown via Brownsville to Mexico City by the company test pilot, J D Sinclair, and Seversky's general factotum, Justin Hopla. The floats, together with six Browning machine guns and ammunition, were sent by lorry. The floats arrived safely but, according to Hopla, the guns were 'hijacked' on the way. At Mexico City Airport Hopla tried to improvise mountings for six Spandau guns which he bought from a local dealer, but had to abandon the task owing to lack of time.

Since 1933 the Seversky SEV-3 prototype had been registered successively as NX2106, X2106, NR2106, X2106 again, and finally NR2106 for the second time before departure to Mexico. It had been fitted with at least five models of Wright Cyclone engine. During the same period the SEV-3 had also undergone innumerable alterations, major and minor, to canopy, cabin, windscreen, radio installation, undercarriage trousering, engine cowlings, tailwheel and, most notably, to the fin and rudder, because it had been found that a P-35-type tail was more effective when the SEV-3 was operating as a landplane.

It is believed that, when it went to Spain, the SEV-3 had the wide-diameter cowling (denoting the large G-2 engine) and the direction-finding loop at the rear of the canopy. Re-registered XA–ABG, it remained in Mexico for a year before being shipped, with other aircraft, to France on board the *Ibai* in December 1937 (see Appendix II), and crossed to Republican Spain during the period 19 March – 13 June 1938, while the French frontier was open. The floats, which had been put on board the *Ibai*, had meanwhile disappeared, but, presumably hoping (in vain) that they might reappear, the Jefatura assigned the SEV-3 to the 1ª Escuadrilla of Grupo 71, a unit detailed to coastal patrol and convoy protection duties and equipped with the remaining five Dewoitine D.371s, a Fiat C.R.32 and a Dewoitine D.510. Teniente Augusto Lecha Vilasuso, of the Pilot Class of 1925 and a veteran of the battles of Madrid and La Jarama, was instructed to take charge of the SEV-3. In all respects other than its name it remained 'un perfecto desconocido' – 'a perfect unknown', both to him and to his fellow pilots. Indeed, forty years were to pass before he was to learn what aeroplane it really was, and from where it had come. He flew the SEV-3 when duties permitted, and grew to like it, though he never got used to the flaps or propeller reduction gear, and preferred to manage without them.

In July 1938 trials were held at Sabadell to see if the SEV-3 was fast enough for use as a photo-reconnaissance aircraft in the planned offensive across the Ebro. However, since there was no means of installing armament in time, a slower but armed Grumman GE-23 was used instead.

On 5 March 1939, as the Nationalists overran Catalonia, the 1ª Escuadrilla was ordered to Bañolas, and from there to fly to France. As the squadron took off the SEV-3's Wright Cyclone failed to start, the first time this had happened since the Seversky had arrived in Spain. As a result, Lecha did not depart until ten minutes after the others. He arrived at Bañolas, with the mechanic in the observer's cockpit, to find that the Condor Legion had attacked a few moments before and destroyed all the other aircraft, and that the aerodrome was flooded. Obeying orders to land nonetheless, he touched down on the one clear path left between burning aircraft, but the wheels of the SEV-3 dug into the soft mud and the aircraft turned turtle. Lecha and the mechanic were shaken but unhurt. Because Nationalist troops were approaching a few miles away, they and the survivors on the aerodrome were obliged to make their escape at once, abandoning the SEV-3. Thus ended the career of one of the most historically interesting aeroplanes of the early 1930s.

In many books and articles on the civil war published in Spain since 1950, it has been said that there were two Serskys in the Republican air forces. The explanation offered is that they must have been the two Seversys exported to the USSR in October 1937; the SEV-XBT landplane escort fighter and the SEV-3-2PA-A Amphibian two-seat reconnaissance aeroplane c/n ?, NX1307. The belief that these machines had been sent to Spain for evaluation under operational conditions was strengthened by the type code 'CS' (Caza Seversky, or Seversky Fighter) appearing in a list of Republican aircraft found (and, apparently, subsequently lost) after the war. In fact, the celebrated Russian test pilot Maj Gen (Av) Pyotr M Stefanovsky flew one of the Serskys in the USSR in the summer of 1938, the other having already crashed during a test flight, and neither, consequently, could have been sent to Spain. The type code 'CS' must therefore have been reserved for the Seversky fighters which were going to be built in Spain.

SEV-3 with 710hp Wright Cyclone R-1820 F-3 engine, landplane configuration.

Span 36ft; length 25ft 8 in; height 9ft 9in; wing area 208sq ft.

Empty weight 2,390lb; loaded weight 3,250lb.

Maximum speed 230mph; cruising speed 190mph; ceiling 22,000ft; range 700 miles. (The manufacturer's claimed

top speed of 260mph appears to have been exaggerated).

Sikorsky S-38B

The Sikorsky S-38 belongs to that illustrious group of aeroplanes, including the Beechcraft 17, Douglas DC-2, Grumman FF-1 (see GE-23) and Seversky SEV-3, which established the success of their manufacturers. Derived from the Sikorsky S-36, the S-38A, officially named 'Amphibion' though usually called 'Ugly Duckling' or 'Flying Tadpole', appeared in May 1928. Within a year the Sikorsky Corporation, which until then had been doing rather poorly, was receiving more orders than it could handle. Initially most came from Pan American Airways, which saw the S-38 as an ideal aircraft for extending routes eastwards over the Caribbean and southwards to Central America and beyond. As Igor Sikorsky wrote later, 'It was this modest airplane which actually completed the peaceful conquest of nearly all South America'.

The S-38B, which appeared in 1929, was basically similar to the S-38A but could be converted into a freighter or 'luxury air yacht'. It had a greater fuel capacity than the S-38A and, after the eleventh production example, a sloping instead of a vertical windscreen. Of the 115 S-38s built, 14 were S-38As, 73 were S-38Bs and the rest were naval or other variants.

The Sikorsky S-38B was a short-hulled sesquiplane in which the tail assembly was supported by twin booms extending aft from the upper wing and braced by an inverted triangle of struts between the rear of the hull and the rear ends of the booms. Power was provided by a pair of uncowled 425hp Pratt & Whitney Wasp radial engines mounted on struts between the wings. The hull was built of wood and covered by Alclad sheets, while the wings and tail were of metal with fabric covering. There was accommodation for a pilot, a copilot/navigator and eight passengers. When the aircraft was operated from water the undercarriage wheels were raised outwards, hydraulically, to a position in front of the lower wing leading edge.

One S-38B participated briefly in the Spanish Civil War, although its presence was not rediscovered, or its identity established, until more than forty years afterwards. This aircraft, c/n 314-15 (NC11V), named *Silver Wings*, had been built in 1930 for Margery Durant, the daughter of an ex-president of General Motors, and had been used for pleasure flights from her home at Old Westbury, New York. She put it up for sale in 1933, and in 1934 it was bought by

Sikorsky S.38B SE-EKN Silver Wings *at Göteborg, Sweden.* (Rolf Westerberg)

two Swedes, Olaf O E Ekman and Nils F R Bernström. Re-registered SE–EKN on 15 February 1934, but retaining its American name, it was used for barnstorming and charter flights at Göteborg, Gripsholm, Sweden.

On 3 June 1936 it was taken over by Tor Eliasson, of Svensk Flygjänst, and put up for sale, an export licence being applied for on 14 June and granted on the 26 June. On 7 August, however, the Swedish Press reported that it had been sold to the Spanish Republicans, and was about to be flown to France by Hugo Fredikson, a freelance pilot and and NCO in the Swedish air force reserve. When the Swedish government refused permission for its export, the ardently pro-Spanish Nationalist editor of *The Aeroplane*, C G Grey, commented on 12 August: 'Poor thing. Probably its last chance'.

The next report was that it had been sold to a 'French airline in Africa' — in other words SFTA (see Appendix II) – and on 20 October 1936 Fredikson applied for the export licence (now with 'England' named as the destination) to be extended. Although this was not granted until 11 December 1936, the Sikorsky arrived at Schiphol, Holland, on 22 October, flown by Tor Eliasson, Hugo Fredikson and Gerhard Hedström, who took off next day at 11.18am, bound for Paris. Running almost immediately into thick fog, Eliasson was forced to put down on one of the new artificial lagoons (or polders) near Groningen, and he returned the aircraft to Schiphol a week later.

In December the S-38B was collected by A Boyer, a French volunteer with the Basque air arm, and flown, via Toulouse, to Bilbao, where it was damaged during a Nationalist air raid on the day of its arrival. After emergency repairs it was flown to Santander by Francisco Casals, an experienced pilot of the Savoia-Marchetti S.62 squadron. Owing to a shortage of spares and more pressing duties, the mechanics could not complete the repair until 30 July 1937, when Casals, with four passengers, took it on a test flight along the coast towards Bilbao. Unfortunately the pilots of a passing patrol of I-15 Chatos, never having seen such an odd-looking aircraft before and not knowing whether it were friend or foe, shot it down to be on the safe side. The only survivor was a young boy, the son of a hotel proprietor of Santander, who had been invited along for the ride.

Span (upper wing) 71ft 8in; (lower wing) 36ft; length 40ft 3in; height in water 10ft 2in; wing area 720sq ft.

Empty weight 6,550lb; loaded weight 10,480lb.

Maximum speed 125mph; cruising speed 110mph; ceiling 18,000ft; range 750 miles.

Spartan Cruiser II

During the 1970s a gentleman who had been engaged in procuring aircraft for both sides in the Spanish Civil War told the author that he had personally delivered three Spartan Cruisers to Spain, and that they had been converted into bombers, albeit in a primitive fashion. It seems, however, that only one Spartan Cruiser was in any way involved in the war, and only for a single week. While it is true that those who research into the aircraft of the Spanish Civil War are often misled

Spartan Cruiser II G-ACBM wearing its Iraqi registration. (A J Jackson)

by faked records and other devices by which the entrepreneurs of those days sought to cover their tracks, it really does appear that all of the other fifteen Spartan Cruisers that were built (types I, II and III), can be accounted for satisfactorily.

The Spartan Cruiser was a three-engined, eight-passenger monoplane of wood and metal construction and of somewhat sedate, even antique, appearance, which was used by several small airlines in Britain and abroad during the 1930s. The machine that went to Spain was the first of the production series, the Cruiser II c/n 2 G-ACBM, powered by three 130hp Cirrus Hermes IV water-cooled engines. This aircraft had been sold to Airwork Iraq (a subsidiary of Airwork Ltd of Heston) in 1933 and re-registered YI-AAA, becoming the first aeroplane to receive an Iraqi civil registration. After the crash of the Spartan Cruiser G-ACDX, belonging to Spartan Airways, in 1935, YI-AAA was brought back as a replacement and had its original registration restored.

In August 1937 Charles Leslie Stanynought, alias L C Lewis, who had been procuring aircraft for Spain since the previous autumn (see Avro 626, Miles M2H Hawk Major, *et al*), bought G-ACBM through a chain of deals which are listed as having taken place on the same day, 27 August 1937: the Straight Corporation to Airwork Ltd, to Nash Aircraft Sales and Hire Ltd, Croydon, and to Stanynought. In fact the aircraft had left England a week earlier, for on 19 August C E Eckersley-Maslin, acting on behalf of an employee of the Straight Corporation, flew it to Le Bourget.

There exists a letter, dated 20 August 1937, from the Basque Secretary of Defence to Comandante Antonio Martín Luna, the Jefe de las Fuerzas Aéreas en la Zona del Norte (chief of the air forces in the northern zone), warning him that an aircraft registered G-ACBM was to arrive that day and must not be fired upon. Whether the Cruiser made that flight is uncertain, for on 24 August it was at Le Bourget Airport undergoing taxiing tests and servicing under the supervision of Abel Guidez, late of the International Squadron and now flying for Air Pyrénées (see Appendix I).

On 26 August a British registered 'avionette' (light aircraft), which may have been the Spartan Cruiser or a Monospar, landed at Biscarosse, south of Arcachon, France, after coming from Santander, which was on the point of falling to the Nationalists. The French police arrested the passengers and pilot, who was named as 'Hashin' or 'Haskin' (perhaps a mis-spelling of Maslin). In September the Cruiser was at Orly, Paris, and it was still there on 7 December 1937. After that, nothing more is heard of it. It may have gone to the Republican main zone in 1938, but more probably it was scrapped.

Span 54ft; length 39ft 2in; wing area 436sq ft.

Empty weight 3,650lb; loaded weight 6,200lb.

Maximum speed 133mph; cruising speed 115mph; ceiling 15,000ft; range 310 miles.

Spartan 7-W Executive

In 1934 the directors of the Spartan Aircraft Company of Wichita, Kansas, decided that the best way to survive the Depression that was ruining so many manufacturers in

The Spartan 7W Executive EC-AGM in LAPE service. It was destroyed in a crash at Vilajuiga on 5 February 1939. (Azaola)

America would be to build an expensive and luxuriously appointed single-engined cabin monoplane for multi-millionaires and the chiefs of the wealthiest industrial corporations. To attract such clients, the machine had to embody the very latest in aeronautical technology and refinements in comfort, and thus be a complete departure from everything the company had built before. It is hardly surprising, therefore, that the design and building of the prototype Spartan 7-X (X13984) by James B Ford and his team, which took eighteen months, and the maiden flight on 1 January 1936, were carried out with as little publicity as possible. The 285hp Jacobs L-5 radial engine was judged insufficiently powerful for a machine which showed such promise on its initial tests, however, and a second prototype Model 7-W (NC13992), fitted with a nine-cylinder Pratt & Whitney Wasp Junior SB in a wide-chord NACA cowling, rated at 400hp at 2,200rpm (450hp at 2,300rpm for take-off), made its maiden flight on 14 September 1936.

The Spartan Executive, as it was appropriately named, accommodated a pilot, copilot and three passengers, or a pilot and four passengers, in a spacious soundproofed cabin upholstered with Laidlow cloth and provided with a sofa-type seat at the rear. Its cabin door was made unusually large to allow the entry of corpulent passengers with as little loss of dignity as possible. The semi-monocoque fuselage and monospar cantilever wings were all-metal, with an Alclad stressed skin, and the cantilever tail assembly was a multi-cellular structure. The ailerons, flaps, elevators and rudder were fabric covered. The undercarriage was fully retractable.

Despite its excellent performance and delightful handling qualities, the superb craftsmanship exercised in its construction and the striking beauty of its gleaming surfaces and sculptured contours, the Executive failed to attract an immediate rush of orders. Of the thirty-four eventually built, only twenty-four were sold in the USA. Consequently, when the Spanish Republican purchasing agent Comandante José Melendreras Sierra made his hurried tour of American aerodromes in search of aircraft, in December 1936, he was able to buy three brand new machines direct from the company: the 7-W-1 NC13992 (the second prototype), the 7-W-3 NC13994, and the 7-W-4 NC13997. The ostensible buyer of these aircraft was

Coronel Roberto Fierro (see Lockheed Sirius, Seversky SEV-3 *et al*), and they were ferried to Mexico, one at a time, via Brownsville, Texas, by the Mexican pilot 'Doc' de Selles on 23 December 1936, 13 February, and 20 February, 1937 respectively, and given the Mexican registrations XA-BES, 'BEW and 'BEX.

After a year's delay they were shipped to France aboard the *Ibai* on 27 December 1937, and crossed into Spain in the spring of 1938. One, registered EC-AGM, joined the LAPE fleet, where it was immensely popular with the pilots and was often flown by Pepa Columer, the wife of José-María Carreras and the first Spanish woman to become a pilot. The other two, with the serials TP-01 and TP-02, were used as liaison aircraft by the FARE.

On 7 December 1938 Capitán Carrasco Martínez, pilot to Coronel Núñez Maza, the air forces Chief of Staff, defected to the Nationalists in one of these machines (probably TP-02). In his memoirs, the Duque de Lerma (José Larios) has described how, shortly afterwards, he and three fellow pilots from the Morato Fiat group (3-G-3) flew from Aragón to Seville in this Spartan and nearly crashed it when it ran out of fuel, the engine stopping as it touched down.

One Spartan was destroyed on 5 February 1939 at Vilajuiga, where the remains of the Republican air forces in Catalonia were being mustered before escaping to France. It was returning from France, and the director of LAPE, Comandante Juan Quintana y Ladrón de Guerra, a Señor Arnold (a LAPE official) and Lucio González (a LAPE mechanic) intended to fly it on to Madrid before dawn on the 5th. Taking off, overloaded, in the pitch dark, the Spartan struck a petrol tanker which someone had foolishly parked at the end of the runway. Quintana was killed and the other two were badly burned. The light of the conflagration, however, enabled the squadron of I-152 fighters led by Capitán Emilio Galera to take off and fly to France.

It has been said that the LAPE Executive, EC-AGM, survived the war and became 30-74 (later L.6) in the Ejercito del Aire. Since Quintana was on board the machine destroyed at Vilajiuga, it would be more logical to assume that this was the LAPE aircraft, and that 30-74 was the Executive (TP-02?) taken over to the Nationalists by Carrasco the previous December. This theory is supported by the generally agreed assertion that 30-74 was also the last wartime Nationalist military serial given to the Grupo 30 of single-engined light aircraft. Whatever the truth, 30-74 continued serving until 1950.

It has been said that four Spartan 7-WP Zeus (militarised Executives fitted with a dorsal gun position, two fixed forward-firing machine guns and bomb racks) were purchased by the Spanish Republicans in 1938, but

The Stinson SR Reliant EC-SAS, owned by José-María de la Cuesta. (John W Underwood, via R S Allen)

were lost when the ship carrying them to Alicante was intercepted and sunk by the Nationalists. The story seems unlikely to be true, for it is hard to see how such a shipment could have been made without being detected eventually by the United States authorities. It is yet another case which must remain open pending conclusive evidence.

Span 39ft; length 26ft 10in; height 8ft; wing area 250sq ft.
Empty weight 2,987lb; loaded weight 4,400lb.
Maximum speed 212mph at 5,000ft; cruising speed 208mph at 9,600ft; ceiling 24,200ft; range 850 miles.

Stinson SR Reliant

The Stinson SR Reliant was a redesign of the Stinson S Junior and the Stinson Model R, intended to combine the best features of both. Like its predecessors, it was a radial-engined, high-wing cabin monoplane intended for use as an air taxi, a business executive transport, a comfortable tourer, a sports aeroplane or a general-purpose aircraft. It could be fitted with wheels, floats or skis. The prototype, powered by a 215hp Lycoming R-680 radial engine in a wide-chord, blistered cowling, appeared in May 1933. Its spacious cabin accommodated a pilot, three passengers and 75lb of baggage. The strut-braced wings were of wood and metal construction, covered, except for the duralumin leading edges, by fabric. The fuselage was based on a framework of steel tubing, its forepart covered by metal and the rear by fabric. The tailplane was adjustable in flight, and the wide-track under-

carriage consisted of a pair of cantilever legs with streamlined spats over the wheels. The Reliant, which was sturdy, easy to fly and maintain, and of attractive appearance, proved extremely successful, and there was a long series of variants with more powerful engines and aerodynamic improvements. Those from the Model SR-7 onwards had tapered wings.

Two Stinson SR Reliants were in Spain in July 1936. One was c/n 8743 (ex-NC13489), bought from the Société Caudron by Enrique Cera of the Aero Club de Barcelona in April 1935, re-registered EC-BCB and painted blue. During the first weeks of the civil war it was used for liaison, reconnaissance, and even light bombing missions over the Aragón sector, until Capitań Sanchís took it over on 27 October 1936 and used it for reconnaissance flights over the Balearic Islands. Early in November 1936 Capitán Juan Senén Varela, with Enrique Cera as passenger, escaped in this Reliant to Mallorca. Based at San Bonet, probably with the military serial 30-55, it was used for liaison and training. However, on 8 June 1937 it crashed into the sea shortly after taking off on a flight in which two officials of the Nationalist part of the Banco de España (more than half the staff had joined the Nationalists during the uprising) were carrying four million pesetas to the Ibiza branch. Although the pilot and passengers were saved, the aircraft and money were lost.

The second Reliant was almost certainly c/n 8737, bought directly from the Stinson Aircraft Corporation in 1933 by José-María de la Cuesta and his brother for a long-distance flight to Egypt and back. It was registered EC-SAS, and at the same time was re-engined with a 250hp Hispano-Suiza 9Qd radial engine. During the civil war it served as the personal transport (with the type code TS) of Teniente Coronel Alfonso Reyes, the Deputy Chief, and later Chief, of the air forces in Catalonia during the first six months of the fighting. It survived the civil war, and in 1943 was returned to civil flying with the new registration EC-AAT. In 1948 it was acquired by the CETFA for photographic survey work. The often published statement

that FC-SAS/'AAT was a Stinson S Junior or Model R (c/n 8522) is an error, probably originating in confusion with another Stinson that may have visited Spain during the 1930s.

Two other Stinsons should be mentioned here. The Model S Junior c/n 8066 (ex-NC10897) was brought to England in November 1931 and re-registered G-ABSU. In July 1936 or later its owner, Lt Col E P Johnston, sold it abroad and, since there is no further trace of it, it was suspected of having been sold to Spain. This is possible, but it seems unlikely because no one remembers any Stinsons other than the two above. The second Stinson is the SR-2 Reliant G-ACSV (ex-NC3824, 250hp Lycoming), also wrongly identified as a Stinson Junior in UK Air Ministry records. This belonged for a time to Brian Allen Aviation at Croydon (see Airspeed Envoy, Miles Falcon *et al*), and during the summer of 1937 an agent acting for the Spanish Republicans

attempted to buy it. The Air Ministry revoked its General Licence, however, and the Reliant remained at Croydon until the end of the Spanish war. By then it was registered to Eric Gerald Hayes of Basingstoke.

SR Reliant with 215hp Lycoming R-680 engine.

Span 43ft 3in; length 27ft, height 8ft 5in; wing area 235sq ft.

Empty weight 2,070lb; loaded weight 3,155lb.

Maximum speed 130mph; cruising speed 115mph; ceiling 14,000ft; range 460 miles.

Vultee V1, V1-A, V11-GB and Breese Model 1 Racer

The five short years between January 1930 and December 1934 saw momentous changes in the science and art of aeronautical engineering, and nowhere was this more evident than in the evolution of commercial

transport aircraft in the United States. The Northrop Alpha and Boeing Monomail single-engined, all-metal, monocoque cantilever monoplanes first flew in 1930, and both, perhaps, were too far ahead of their time for their own good. There followed the Lockheed Orion in 1931, the Northrop Delta and Clark GA 43 in 1932, and the Vultee V1 in February 1933.

These aircraft, whose revolutionary 'new look' provoked much scepticism in Europe, raised the normal operating speeds of the time from about 150mph to about 200mph, an increase of twenty-five per cent. They also offered a significant improvement in that most vital of all the statistics of an aeroplane, its load:tare ratio, or the ratio between the useful load (fuel, crew, changeable equipment and furnishings, as well as its payload of passengers, cargo or armament) and its empty weight.

The careers of these high-performance single-engined airlin-

The much-travelled Vultee V1-A NC14256 at Hanworth, England, in the autumn of 1936, shortly before it was sold to the Spanish Republicans. (John W Underwood, via R S Allen)

The celebrated Vultee V1-A NR13770 Lady Peace *during a rather undignified interlude in its career, as the property of an advertising agency.* (Roger Besecker, via R S Allen)

ers, however, were curtailed by a safety regulation introduced in October 1934, which made it mandatory for all commercial passenger aircraft in the USA to have two or more engines, as well as a pilot and copilot, and to be able to maintain level flight on one engine, or on two engines in the case of trimotors. By then, in any case, the new and even more advanced twin-engined Boeing 247 ('the first truly modern airliner'), Lockheed 10 Electra and Douglas DC-2 were already in service. By then, too, in Europe work had already begun on the design of new generations of fighters and bombers, such as the Messerschmitt Bf 109, Hawker Hurricane, Supermarine Spitfire and Heinkel He 111, while in the Soviet Union the ANT 40$_2$, the prototype of the SB-2M-100A Katiuska, had been undergoing trials for five months and the I-16 fighter, a low-wing cantilever monoplane with a retractable undercarriage, had been in squadron service for eight months.

Despite its brief commercial career, the Vultee V1-A (the production version of the V1) represented a significant step in the formulation of the modern aeroplane, in that it was the last and most advanced of the American single-engined transports that were to give such a stimulus to aircraft design all over the world. By the summer of 1936 most of the single-engined transports in the USA had been withdrawn from airline service and placed on the

secondhand market, and, as a fortuitous result, many of them ended their days in Spain. Of the twenty-six Vultee V1-As built, for example, no fewer than nineteen were bought by the Spanish Republicans. Of these, seven (and the V1) eventually reached Republican Spain, where, of all the scores of assorted civil aircraft bought for hasty conversion, where possible, into bombers, they proved to be the most brilliantly successful. Four others reached the Nationalists.

Gerard Vultee, a gifted young engineer who had previously worked for Douglas Aircraft and as assistant to John K Northrop at Lockheed (see Lockheed Vega and Northrop Delta), began design work on a six-passenger monoplane, embodying the latest concepts and construction techniques, in 1931. A year later he was appointed vice-president and chief engineer of the Airplane Development Corporation, a company founded by the automobile tycoon E L Cord, who had recently bought a number of aircraft manufacturers and airlines. The success of the prototype V1 brought an order from American Airlines for twenty V1-As, a modified version with lengthened fuselage and greater wing span, at $30,000 each.

The V1-A, powered by a 700hp

A Republican Vultee V1-A after conversion into a bomber by SAF-15, at La Rabasa, Alicante.

Wright Cyclone R-1820 F-2 radial engine in a wide-chord NACA cowling, was an all-metal low-wing cantilever monoplane with a fully-retractable undercarriage. The covering of its monocoque fuselage was unusual in that it comprised narrow strips of flat Alclad sheets rivetted on to the elliptical frames so that they overlapped like shingles, a system which greatly facilitated maintenance. Another unusual feature was the windscreen, which was raked forward to protect the pilot and copilot from glare while landing. Eight passengers sat in a sound-proofed cabin, and were provided with a lavatory installed against the bulkhead behind the pilots' cabin. The V1-A possessed a remarkable range, for its time, of 900 miles at a cruising speed of just over 200mph. Its load:tare ratio of 37.6:62.4 compared very favourably with the 30:70 of the other type of airliner then operated by American Airlines, the twin-engined, much larger and much slower Curtiss Condor biplane.

When the first Vultees entered service, in the summer of 1934, they gained immediate popularity by cutting the flying time on the Dallas-Chicago route by half, and national fame when James Doolittle set a new transcontinental speed record in NC13770 (c/n 8) in January 1935. Nevertheless, following the safety regulation of October 1934, American Airlines decided to replace the Vultees with Douglas DC-2s. It

cancelled its order after receiving thirteen aircraft (plus the prototype V1, which was employed as a mail-plane only), and began phasing them out of service in January 1936. Thus it was that, shortly after the outbreak of civil war in Spain, Capitán Augustin Sanz Sainz of the Aviación Militar, who had been authorised by the Republican government to buy aircraft in the USA, was offered nine of the American Airlines Vultees by Charles Babb, a well-known aircraft dealer, for $22,000 each. The price included the cost of complete refurbishing, a generous supply of spares, and Babb's ten per cent commission.

The sale, arranged ostensibly on behalf of 'an airline in French Africa' through T H Chamberlain (a London salesman known as 'the flying commercial traveller') and Henri Pieck, a Dutch-Swiss artist who ran a Soviet spy ring in Britain, fell through in October 1936 when the Spanish government, faced with the calculated obstruction of certain banks in London and New York, was unable to transfer the requisite funds to America. An attempt was then made to export the Vultees to Spain via Aéronaves de Mexico, which was at that time a small air-taxi service between Mexico City and Acapulco, but this failed when the US State Department objected that such a company could not possibly need so many large aircraft.

In November 1936 the deal was taken over by Daniel Wolf, director of the Holland-based Hunzedal trading company and an important procurer of supplies for the Spanish Republicans, and his uncle Rudolf Wolf, a Wall Street commission agent and dealer in jute and similar goods. This time, despite the sudden death of Rudolf Wolf in the middle of the proceedings (see Appendix II), the attempt was successful. At the end of December the entire American Airways stock of Vultees, including the Vultee V1 prototype, sailed for France (the nineteen aircraft of the Wolf shipment are listed in Appendix II: one V1, nine V1-As, five Lockheed Orions, three Consolidated 20A Fleetsters and a Northrop Delta), together with an American test pilot, a Vultee company engineer, and a representative of Hunzedal. After unloading and

assembly at Bléville Aerodrome, near Le Havre, the aircraft were sold by Wolf to SFTA (see Appendix II) and transferred to two aerodromes near Paris, Toussus-le-Noble, which had been bought by SFTA, and Toussus-Paris. All were given French registrations, but since the entire block of letters from F-AQAD to 'AV in the Bureau Veritas register has been left blank, complete identification is not possible. It is known, however, that the prototype V1 became F-AQAP, c/n 10 (NC13772) became F-AQAO, c/n 19 (NC 14253) became 'AK and one other 'AL. Of these, F-AQAK was tested at Villacoublay by CEMA.

On 17 August 1937 six of the Vultees and the Northrop Delta, flown by French pilots, took off together from Toussus-le-Noble. One Vultee crashed on take-off and a second, F-AQAL, crashed near Versailles, the pilot, Pierre Matheron, being killed. A fortnight later two of the remaining Vultees (including 'AK) were lost when a group of French Fascist terrorists, nicknamed 'Cagoulards' ('Hooded Ones'), raided a hangar at Toussus-Paris during the night of 29 August and planted *plastique* explosive (the first recorded use of this material) in canisters under the aircraft. On 2 September the last two Vultees, and one other aircraft, were flown to Barcelona by Robert Aimé, Robert Cury and Roger Nouvel, pilots who had been ferrying aircraft to Spain since the start of the civil war. Thus six of the original ten Vultees of the Wolf shipment reached Republican Spain, where they joined a Vultee V1-A which had arrived at Barcelona the previous February.

This machine, c/n 22, NC14256, had been converted into a luxurious executive transport for E L Cord, who in 1935 had leased it to the Standard Oil salesman Benjamin ('Sell 'em Ben') Smith for oil-deposit surveying in Ethiopia. During the Italian invasion the Vultee (now registered to a British oil man, Francis Rickett) allegedly flew arms and journalists into Addis Ababa. After much travelling about the Middle East, it landed at Croydon in September 1936 and soon caught the attention of the authorities as a likely aircraft to be sold to Spain. For this

reason it was flown to Le Bourget, where it was indeed bought for $56,000 (£11,400) by Comandante José Jácome of the Spanish Republican purchasing commission in Paris. The French authorities locked it in a hangar, but on 10 February 1937 Vincent Schmidt, an American mercenary pilot and painter who had already, he later maintained, ferried a Bloch 'night bomber' to Barcelona, entered the hangar while the guard was in the toilet, started the engine, and took off on a cold motor. Keeping above the clouds until he was out of France, Schmidt found Barcelona Airport by means of some Air France maps lent to him by his fellow-American pilot, Hilaire du Berrier. After returning to Paris he described to du Berrier his pleasure in flying such a 'beautiful 'plane', which had 'leapt forward' as soon as he had got the undercarriage up.

For a time, bearing the government registration EC-48-E, this Vultee was used for transport and liaison duties. In September 1937 however, this machine and the five recently-arrived V1-As were taken to SAF-15 at La Rabasa, Alicante, for conversion into attack-bombers. Each aircraft had a smooth curved metal hood built behind the pilot's cabin to protect the dorsal gunner, two fixed forward-firing machine guns were mounted in each wing, and bomb racks were fitted under the wings and fuselage. The V1 prototype remained in its civil configuration and was used as a trainer. The six Vultee V1-As, with the military serials BV-1 to BV-6, were incorporated into the 1ª Escuadrilla of Grupo 72, commanded by Capitán Lázaro Casajust (succeeded by Cdte Macho Juárez) and based at Los Alcázares, Cartagena. Little is recorded of their military operations, though they were employed intensively. The diary of Francisco Tarazona records that, on 28 April 1938, his squadron of I-16s escorted six Vultees on a low-level bombing mission against the port of Viñaroz, recently captured by the Nationalists. The squadron was moved to Valdepeñas in 1938, and from there to El Carmolí and then back to Los Alcázares.

Meanwhile, a seventh V1-A had arrived at Barcelona via France. This machine, c/n 12 (NC13774), had belonged to Phillips Petroleum, from which it had been bought, along with a Lockheed Orion, by Cdte Melendreras, a member of the Republican purchasing commission in the USA and Mexico, on 17 December 1936. A price of $32,000 was paid for each aircraft. Melendreras and Billy Parks, the Phillips company pilot, flew it out from Calexico, California, the same day, without an export licence. Bearing the Mexican registration XA-BET, it was among the aircraft loaded aboard the *Ibai* on 27 December 1937 for Le Havre, and crossed into Spain at some time between 19 March and 13 June 1938, when the French government kept the frontier open for the passage of arms. It seems to have been the V1-A that was converted into a photo-reconnaissance aircraft.

No Republican Vultees were shot down during the civil war, but two were destroyed (together with three I-16s and a GP-1 trainer) when the hangar in which they were undergoing repair at La Rabasa collapsed on 19 November 1938 – a disaster attributed to sabotage. As day bombers they were superior to the Nationalist Heinkel He 70Fs, their nearest contemporaries. Although they were more heavily armed, they could carry nearly twice the bomb load over twice the range at the same high cruising speed of 200mph. After the war five were recovered by the Nationalists (three at Oran, Algeria, one at Los Alcázares, and one at La Rabasa).

In addition, four Vultee V1-As flew on the Nationalist side. They were among the eight aircraft purchased by Robert Cuse, of the Vimalert Co, New Jersey, and shipped for Santander on board the *Mar Cantabrico* in January 1937 (see Appendix II), and so passed into Nationalist hands when the vessel was intercepted in the Bay of Biscay on 8 March. Of these four V1-As (c/n 8, NR13770; c/n 15, NC14251; c/n 21, NC14255; and c/n 24, NC17325), the first was the most historically interesting. Built originally to the order of Col G R Hutchinson for the MacRobertson England–Australia air race of 1934 and for subsequent use on a proposed USA-USSR airline, it was retained by the manufacturer when

Hutchinson's funds failed to materialize, and used by Doolittle for his transcontinental flight in January 1935 (see above).

After brief use by the United States Army Air Corps and, after that, by an advertising agency which covered it with stickers, it was bought on hire purchase in 1936 by the Broadway entertainer Harry Richman (chiefly remembered for his song 'Puttin' on the Ritz'). Richman planned to attempt, with the pilot Richard Merrill, the first 'double-crossing of the Atlantic', a phrase which caused much hilarity among political commentators of the day. The aircraft was fitted with astro-navigation equipment and a reduction-geared Wright Cyclone R-1820-G2 engine for long-distance cruising, and 30,000 ping-pong balls were put in the wings to give buoyancy should the machine come down in the sea. Named *Lady Peace* because of the menacing political climate in Europe, the Vultee took nearly a mile to become airborne at Floyd Bennett Field, New York, and managed to leave the ground only by scraping between two hangars. Richman and Merrill broke the transatlantic record on 7-8 September 1936 by crossing in 18 hours 38 minutes at an average speed of 210mph, but, after losing their bearings, landed in a field near Llwyncelyn, Wales. During the return flight on 14 September a fuel valve jerked loose from an auxiliary tank, forcing them down in Newfoundland. Unable to complete his hire-purchase payments, Richman sold the *Lady Peace* to Cuse in December 1936, only to learn, to his chagrin, that it was intended for use in the Spanish Civil War.

According to some Spanish authors, the Nationalists originally proposed to form the Vultees into a reconnaissance-bomber flight, attached to the Condor Legion and designated Grupo 18 (a type code later given the the Caproni Ca 310s). If this was the plan it was soon abandoned, for by the summer of 1937 the four Vultees, still bearing the military serials 18-6 to 18-9, were distributed among various Nationalist squadrons as 'aviones nodrizos' ('midwife aeroplanes'), or general-purpose transports. The *Lady Peace* seems to have been 18-7.

In the summer of 1938 all single-engined transport aircraft, including the Vultees, the two Northrop Deltas, and four Junkers W 34s handed over by the Condor Legion, were formed into Grupo 43: 18-6 became 43-13; 18-7, 43-14; 18-8, 43-15; and 18-9, 43-16. Of these, we know that 43-14 (ex-*Lady Peace* and renamed *Capitán Haya*) was attached to the 3-G-3 Fiat C.R.32 fighter group, and at the end of the war served as an altar for the celebration of mass on the Feast of Our Lady of Loreto, the Spanish patroness of aviation. Vultee 43-15 was attached to 1-G-2 (Heinkel He 51s) until it was damaged in a belly-landing in December 1938 (possibly caused by a saboteur putting sugar in the petrol tank). On being returned to service after the war it was attached to the 32 Regimiento de Caza of the new Ejercito del Aire, a group equipped with I-15s recovered from the defeated Republicans.

The five Vultees recovered after the war were likewise assigned to various units (43-12 went to the 4-G-2 He 51 group, and 43-18 to the 1-G-12 Ro 37 group), and in 1948 they were all given the single military serial L.13. In 1950 the Vultees were withdrawn from service and sold for scrap.

The Breese-and-Dallas Model 1 Racer was designed byVance Breese, Gerard Vultee's co-designer on the prototype Vultee V1, as a scaled-down V1-A to carry five passengers. Powered by a 450hp Pratt & Whitney Wasp SC-1 radial engine in a wide-chord NACA cowling, it first flew in April 1933, and was registered NX12899. After it had been re-engined with an 800hp Pratt & Whitney Twin Wasp and converted into a racing aeroplane (NR replacing the NX prefix of the registration), it was sold to Jacqueline Cochrane on 3 October 1936. On 6 January 1937 she sold it to the Hollywood pilot and 'aerial choreographer' for films, Paul Mantz, who, with the German pilot/adventurer Fritz Bieler, sold it to Coronel Roberto Fierro of the Mexican air force (see Lockheed Vega and Orion, Seversky SEV-3 *et al*). Mantz flew it to Mexico without an export licence on 10 January 1937, and, with the Mexican registration XA-ABH, the Breese Racer became

The Breese-Dallas Racer (John Underwood, via R S Allen)

one of the 'Spanish Ambassador's Collection' of aircraft waiting at Vera Cruz for shipment to Republican Spain. To confuse reporters from anti-Spanish-Republican newspapers, FBI agents and the like, these aircraft were flown from aerodrome to aerodrome in Mexico, and on one of these flights the Breese Racer, piloted by Cloyd Clevenger, made a forced landing and was wrecked beyond repair.

In May 1938 Capitán Santiago Capillas, then in command of a squadron of R-5 biplanes (see also Grumman GE-23), was ordered to Barcelona to supervise the unloading and assembly of twenty-eight Vultee V11-GB attack-bombers purchased in the USA. After waiting three weeks in vain, he was told that the ship supposedly bringing these aircraft had been sunk, that in any case there had been no Vultees on board, and that once again some arms dealer must have swindled the Spanish Republican government.

The origins of this story are curious. In November 1936 Richard Dinely, a San Francisco arms dealer of dubious reputation, offered Cdte

Melendreras (see above) six Vultee V11-GBs from a consignment of thirty being built for the Kwuomintang government of China, together with forty-three other aircraft. The offer was accepted by the Spanish Republican ambassador in Mexico, Félix Gordón Ordás, but in January 1937 he was warned by the US State Department that Dinely planned to swindle the Spanish government by not delivering the aircraft, and that, in fact, he had not even bought them. The figure twenty-eight told to Capillas seems to have been the result of confusion, somewhere in the Spanish Republican bureaucracy, of the six V11-GBs with Ambassador Gordón's twenty-eight aircraft in Mexico, some of which had been shipped on the *Ibai* and were then

(May 1938) crossing from France into Spain.

Vultee V1

Span 48ft; length 35ft 6in; height 9ft 3in; wing area 361sq ft.

Empty weight 4,275lb; loaded weight 7,250lb.

Maximum speed 225mph.

Vultee V1-A

Span 50ft; length 37ft; height 10ft 2in; wing area 384sq ft.

Empty weight 5,302lb; loaded weight 8,500lb.

Maximum speed 225mph; cruising speed 205mph; landing speed with flaps down 63mph; service ceiling 20,000ft; cruise range with 1,649lb payload, 1,000 miles.

Appendices

Appendix I
Civil War Airlines

LAPE

During the first few weeks of the civil war the Douglas DC-2s of LAPE were employed both as transports, especially for flying gold to Paris, and as bombers. After December 1936 LAPE became the transport service of the Aviación Militar (and of the FARE after May 1937), and several of its older aircraft were transferred to the training schools in Murcia. Although it is known that LAPE received about sixteen additional aircraft from abroad during the civil war, it has not been possible to identify all of their registrations and fleet numbers. The adjacent table is a tentative list compiled from photographic or hearsay evidence.

Air Pyrénées

Air Pyrénées was founded in December 1936 by Spanish and French Basques to reopen rapid communication between France and the Republican (Basque-Asturian) zone in the north of Spain, which was by then cut off from land contact with the outside world and could otherwise be reached only by sea or by flying 240km over Nationalist territory. There were, in fact, two sister companies, La Société Air Pyrénées, at 32 Quai de Galupérie, Biarritz, and Lignes Aériennes Pyrénées et

LAPE fleet list

Type	c/n	Registration	Fleet number
Douglas DC-2	1527	EC-BBE(?)	26
Douglas DC-2	1320	EC-AGA	27
Northrop 1C Delta	7	EC-AGC	31
Airspeed Envoy II	72	EC-AGE	32
Caudron Göeland	6/7349	EC-AGF	33
Caudron Göeland	5/7348	EC-AGG	34
GA Clark GA-43A	2022		
Breguet 470T	1	EC-AHC	
Avia 51			
Breguet 670T	01	EC-AGI(?)	
Fokker F.XX	5347	EC-45-E	
Spartan Executive		EC-AGM	
Douglas DC-1	1137	EC-AGN	39
De Havilland D.H.89		EC-AGO	41
D.H.89		EC-AGP	
D.H.89			
D.H.89			

Espagne, at 55 Avenue George V, Paris (which was also the address of the Spanish Republican purchasing commission in Paris). The directors were Auguste Amestoy, a native of Briscous, and M Legumbéry, a Basque businessman. Technical assistance was given by Air France and air ministry officials such as Edouard Serre and André Labarthe. Several of the pilots, such as Jean Dary and Abel Guidez, were veterans of the Escadre España. Georges Lebeau, a staunch pro-Basque Frenchman (but not, apparently, a Basque himself) flew many dangerous missions along the Biscay coast, usually in the Beechcraft 17 nicknamed the 'Avión Negus' (see Beechcraft 17). Several aircraft, including the two Airspeed Envoys F-APPQ and 'AQCS, were

shot down. Indeed, the exploits of this little airline deserve a book to themselves. Its fleet, so far as is known, is listed on page 292.

Iberia

In August 1937 the Nationalists created Iberia, an internal airline transport service, taking the name from the defunct Spanish airline of the 1920s, La Compañía Aérea de Transportes Iberia SA (CATISA). In 1929 CATISA and the Compañía Española de Tráfico Aéreo (CETA) were combined with Unión Aérea Española (UAE) to form Concesionaria de Líneas Aéreas SA (CLASSA), which in turn became LAPE in 1931. The 1937 Iberia was subsidised according to the number

Air Pyrénées fleet list

Type	Quantity	Remarks
Airspeed Envoy III	6	c/ns 69-74) F-APPQ, 'QAA, 'D, 'CR, 'CS and 'CT
Beechcraft BR 17	1	c/n 66, ex-NC15811, F-APFD, *El Avión Negus*
Beechcraft BL 17	1	c/n 83, ex-NC15813, painted light blue
Caudron C.440 Göeland	1	c/n 6905, F-ANKV
Caudron C.440 Göeland	1	c/n 6906, F-ANNX
Caudron C.448 Göeland	1	c/n 7272, F-AOMX
Caudron C.635 Simoun	1	F-ANCG. Registered to Jean Dary
Potez 561	2-5	See Potez 56 for details
Potez 58	1	c/n 4140, F-AOQM. Sold by Leopold Galy, an Air Pyrénées pilot, to Amestoy, and probably the first aircraft acquired by Air Pyrénées

of kilometres flown, and was initially equipped with Junkers Ju 52/3ms bought from Deutsche Lufthansa, which also supplied the German pilots. The aircraft are listed under 'Junkers Ju 52/3m', but in October 1937 only one was in service. The airline's central airport was at first the newly laid-out aerodrome at Matacán, Salamanca, which later became a training base, and services were opened to Tetuán, Vitoria, Burgos, Cáceres and Seville, a return flight from Salamanca to Seville costing 360 pesetas in those days.

After the civil war the Sociedad Anónima Española de Transporte Aéreo (SAETA) was created to use all surviving Republican transport aircraft. On 12 April 1940 SAETA became Tráfico Aéreo Español (TAE), but this was closed in December 1940 and its aircraft handed over to Iberia. Deutsche Lufthansa and Ala Littoria had each held a 12.5 per cent share of TAE, and during the next two years DLH made strenuous efforts to gain control of Iberia, which were no less strenuously resisted by the Spanish government.

By January 1941 Iberia possessed ten Ju 52s, four DC-2s, the DC-1, three He 111s, six D.H.89 Dragon Rapides, one or two Savoia-Marchetti S.73s and possibly one or two D.H.84 Dragons. To these was added the Ford 4-AT Trimotor EC-BAB in February 1941, though this was returned to the Ejercito del Aire in 1942. During the fuel shortage of 1941-42 only the D.H.89s, whose engines could run on automobile petrol, were able to continue regular services. The first infusion of new equipment came in 1946, when Iberia was able to purchase nineteen aircraft from the US Surplus War Property Administration, and began to grow into one of the world's great airlines.

Appendix II
The clandestine importation of aircraft into Spain during the civil war of 1936-39

While it is true that all the aircraft used in the Spanish Civil War, excepting the 533-550 in Spain when the fighting started, were imported behind curtains of secrecy to flout the Non-Intervention Agreement, this section is concerned with those bought for cash in countries other than Germany, Italy and the USSR. Between 500 and 600 were purchased, or ordered, altogether. Of these, between 394 and 453 were delivered to the Republicans and between 37 and 67 to the Nationalists, besides 30 more found on board Republican ships captured by the Nationalists. Gun-running is an ancient trade, but aircraft-smuggling was then something wholly new, and most of the elaborate subterfuges employed today by 'sanctions-busters' and other illicit traffickers in aircraft were devised during the Spanish Civil War. It was during the Spanish Civil War, too, that the US Government, followed later by other governments, first introduced the so-called 'End User's Certificate' to prevent arms dealers from circumventing an embargo by exporting war material to a proscribed country through a chain of intermediate countries.

The Nationalists

During the first month or so of the war the Nationalists bought between thirty-seven and sixty-seven aircraft in Britain, France, Holland, Poland and Portugal. The purchases were made through existing companies such as Airwork at Heston and the SEPEWE (or SPV) agency in Warsaw. Ten British-registered aircraft (one Airspeed Envoy II, four de Havilland D.H.89 Dragon Rapides, four Fokker F.XIIs and one General Aircraft Monospar ST-12) and two Dutch-registered Fokker F.VIIb3ms left aerodromes in southern England for Burgos in the first fortnight of August 1936, although two of the F.XIIs crashed en route. At the same time the Nationalists bought twenty P.W.S.10 fighters in Poland and, according to Polish air historians, twenty Breguet 19s. From France they acquired a Fokker F.VIIa and possibly the Farman F.193 F-AMXL, the F.391 F-AMTH and the Caudron Aiglon F-APCE, and from Portugal the Farman F.191 *Aquila Branca*. By the middle of September, when it became clear that they would receive all they needed from Germany and Italy on credit, the Nationalists ceased buying aircraft abroad for cash, although in 1937 and 1938 they did obtain four Polish R.W.D.13s and possibly a number of P.W.S.16 and 16bis trainers via Portugal. The Miles Hawk Major that the Portuguese airman

Rebellho placed at their service in July 1936 was probably bought by them eventually as well. In addition, as mentioned above, they captured twenty-two Aero A-101s and eight American aircraft (see later) on ships sailing to Republican ports.

The Republicans

On 25 July 1936 the French government announced that, although it would refuse any request from the Spanish government for armed military aircraft, it would allow unarmed military aircraft to be sold by commercial companies to private Spanish citizens resident in France. Thus, early in August 1936, fourteen unarmed Dewoitine D.372s and six Potez 54s were 'sold' by l'Office Générale de l'Air, a selling organisation for the Potez and Bloch companies, to the Spanish journalist Andrés García de la Barga (better known as 'Corpus Barga'). In England, Cdte Carlos Pastor Krauel of the Aviación Militar bought between thirty and forty aircraft, some of them through Union Founders Trust, a City trading company, and others direct from aircraft dealers such as Rollason of Croydon and charter companies such as Air Dispatch. The Airspeed aircraft were bought direct from the Airspeed company, as were a few Dragons and Dragon Rapides from de Havilland (though this sale was quickly cancelled).

The departure of thirteen of these aircraft from Britain during the first fortnight of August 1936, as well as eleven aircraft to the Nationalists, provoked H M Government to amend the law to prohibit the export of all aircraft to either side in Spain, and by the end of the month every government in Europe (including, it must be emphasised, Germany and Italy) had signed the International Non-Intervention Agreement to prevent the export of all war materials to Spain. A few more machines were smuggled out, but most were kept in England by having their General Licences suspended and, in some cases, their propellers removed. For a period, no fewer than nineteen aircraft were kept in this condition and under police guard at Croydon and at the Airspeed factory at Portsmouth.

Meanwhile, other Spanish officers were sent on peregrinations round Europe in search of aircraft. Incredible as it may seem, Teniente Coronel Luis Riaño was even sent to Nazi Germany. Republican attempts to buy aircraft and arms abroad during the first months of the civil war were ill-organised and often amateurish. Dozens of 'agents', few with business experience or technical knowledge and some barely literate, arrived in France from Spain, provided with money by one or another of the many political or regional committees that had become the only authorities in some areas of Republican Spain during the confusion and violence of the first weeks of the war. Such agents were easily deceived by professional arms dealers, who played one against the other to raise prices and get rid of aircraft previously earmarked for scrap. The Spanish embassy in Paris was besieged by every kind of dealer and entrepreneur who saw, in the desperate plight of the Republic, a unique opportunity to make a killing.

Pierre Cot, the French air minister, was the most resolute opponent of Non-Intervention in the French cabinet and, through a small number of trusted aides in the Ministère de l'Air, facilitated as far as he could the surreptitious export of occasional unarmed aircraft to Republican Spain. The organising of the means was delegated to his chef-de-cabinet for civil aviation, Jean Moulin, later to become the foremost hero and martyr of the Résistance during the Second World War. Others who played active parts were Joséph Sadi-Lecointe, Director of Training at the Fédération Populaire des Sports Aéronautiques (FPSA), the French equivalent of the British Civil Flying Training Scheme, and four senior officials of Air France: Edouard Serre, the technical director; Louis de Marmier, chief test pilot; Victor Poirier and Gaston Vedel, chief of the Air France airport at Barcelona.

At the end of September 1936 the new Spanish Republican ambassador to France, Luis Araquistain, created a central Comisión de Compras (Purchasing Commission) through which all purchases of war material were henceforth to be made. Its head office, disguised as the Mexican

export firm Socimex, was at 55 Avenue George V, near the embassy, with subsidiary offices at 64 Avenue Victor Emmanuel and elsewhere in the city. At the end of October a second purchasing commission was established in Prague and a third in New York. Operations in Europe were directed by Dr Alejandro Otero, a gynaecologist and Socialist Deputy of the Cortes (Spanish Parliament). Aviation purchases were the responsibility of Ten Cor Luis Riaño and, in his absence, Cdte Jácome.

Legally, the presence of this purchasing commission in Paris contravened Non-Intervention, and its existence was always a potential source of embarrassment to the French and Spanish governments, and a constant target of vituperation from the French anti-Republican press, the Italian and German propaganda ministries and, of course, from the Spanish Nationalists and their supporters all over the world. Indeed, the Czechoslovakian government, although it was sympathetic to the Spanish Republican cause, was obliged to close down the office in Prague and expel its members from the country. Coronel Ángel Pastor Velasco, the head of the commission, took over the commission in Paris when Otero returned to Spain to become Sub-Secretary for Armaments.

Meanwhile, between September and December 1936, the Spanish government supplied funds to set up four principal companies through which to buy aircraft and aviation equipment, or to place production orders with aircraft and component manufacturers:

La Société Française des Transports Aérien (SFTA)

Formed on 28 September 1936, at 78 Avenue des Champs-Elysées, Paris, SFTA had a nominal capital of 12 million French francs. Its first director was Alfred Pilain, who oversaw the purchase of the four Fokker trimotors (F.IX, F.XII, F.XVIII and F.XX) from KLM, for which it used the name 'Air Tropic'. On 2 December 1936 Pilain was succeeded by Edouard Godillot, a 54-year-old French airman. Jean Godillot, perhaps a brother, seems to have acted as secretary. Because it was prudently kept small, SFTA was able to guard its secrets very effectively, although it soon became known to the French Right-wing press and to the Non-Intervention Committee in London as a major supplier of aircraft and arms to the Spanish Republic. Through French records, however, it is possible to trace at least 120 (and perhaps another 70) aircraft exported through SFTA to Republican Spain. At the end of the civil war its assets were frozen pending a settlement with the Spanish Republican government in exile, but the Second World War ended the proceedings. The company was officially dissolved in 1946.

Les Ateliers de Construction et d'Exploitation des Brevets Aéronautiques (LACEBA)

This company had workshops in the Rue Martin Lietard, Brussels, and at Haren, Belgium. Jean Bastin, the director, had moved from the directorship of LACAB (builder of the LACAB GR.8 fighter-bomber prototype, which at one time was sold to the Spanish Republicans but not delivered) to found this company, which was allegedly created with money supplied by the Spanish government, an allegation later disputed even though it was confirmed by captured Spanish Republican documents. LACEBA built the Romano R.83 fighter for Spain and supplied the undercarriages and other components for the Fokker C.Xs and D.XXIs under construction at Alicante.

Société d'Exploitations Téchniques et Aériens (SETA)

Headquartered at 3 Phillellion, Athens, SETA was formed to acquire the Bellanca 28/90s from the USA. There seems to have been a connection between this company and Antonius Raab, late of Raab-Katzenstein and once a friend of Hermann Goering (see I-15 Chato, Potez 54 and Savoia-Marchetti S.62), whose company, SA pour la Fabrication et l'Expoitation des Avions at 19-21 Bvde Miaouli, Piraeus (Greece), and with a branch at 25 Rue des Fabres, Marseilles, attempted to purchase aircraft, aero

engines and aircraft parts on behalf of the Spanish Republicans.

Hanover Sales Corporation (see below)

Several ephemeral export–import companies were created for the purchase of aircraft: Arc-en-Ciel, Merklafirma (the Swissair Douglas DC-2, Lockheed Orions and Clark GA-43A), Air Languedoc and others. Some of the flying schools and clubs where Spanish pilots were trained in France were also used as purchasing agencies before reselling to Spain through SFTA, Lejeune Aviation at Esbly, south of Meaux near Paris, Victor Laffont of Aéro Populaire (Agen), and Le Cercle Aéronautique des Coulommiers et de la Brie being the most prominent.

Space does not permit a description of the numerous individuals who took part in these enterprises, except to say that the unscrupulous villainy of some was more than offset by the disinterested courage of others (for example Réné Clément, another figure of the Résistance). Finally, it should be noted that an important contribution was made by Soviet agents of the GRU (external military intelligence service) and the NKVD (predecessor of the KGB), who organised networks of front-companies across Europe and the Middle East. Despite what has been published by such defectors as Walter Krivitsky, there is little factual information about their activities.

Aircraft shipments from the USA, Canada and Mexico

On the outbreak of the Spanish Civil War the United States government refrained from signing the International Non-Intervention Agreement, and President Franklin D Roosevelt contented himself by declaring a 'moral embargo', by which companies were to be trusted to refuse orders for war material from agents acting on behalf of either side in Spain. The following autumn the US State Department frequently declared its satisfaction that the entire US aircraft industry was observing the 'moral embargo', but the Spanish

Republican ambassador in Mexico, don Félix Gordón Ordás, was receiving offers of copious quantities of aircraft and armaments from numerous agencies and manufacturers.

Unfortunately, the lack of cohesion that bedevilled the Republican war effort in Spain obtained on the far side of the Atlantic as well. As a result, Comandante Augustín Sanz Sainz, a Republican air force officer empowered to purchase aircraft in the USA, and Gordón in Mexico, acted without one another's knowledge and, occasionally, even competed for the same aircraft, an absurd situation which American aircraft dealers and brokers were able to exploit with relish.

Because the Spanish ambassador in Washington had joined the Nationalists, a new ambassador, Fernando de los Ríos (who had been in charge of the first aircraft purchase in Paris in July and August 1936) arrived in October, accompanied by a purchasing commission under Coronel Francisco León Trejo, assisted by Comandante José Melendreras Sierra and Capitán Francisco Corral. This was followed by a second commission in November, under Dr Alejandro Otero (see Grumman GE-23). All of the initial purchases, including that of the nine Vultee V1-As from American Airlines, had to be cancelled owing to the action of banks in Paris, London and New York, which obstructed the transfer of funds from Spain. When some money, originally sent from Madrid at the beginning of September 1936, finally arrived in Mexico at the end of November, Melendreras and Corral made a rapid tour of American airports and aerodromes and purchased about thirty aircraft, of which twenty-eight reached Mexico before (and, in some cases, after) the embargo resulting from the Cuse affair (see below) came into effect.

Meanwhile, in November, Dr Otero and his financial adviser, Martin Licht, established the Hanover Sales Corporation at 30 Broad Steet (and 165 Broadway), New York, as a transatlantic equivalent of SFTA. Under the presidency of Miles Sherover, Hanover Sales handled the export of all supplies to Republican Spain from the USA during the rest of the civil war.

*Northrop Delta ex-NC14242 at Oran,
Algeria, 30 March 1939.* (Arráez)

The Wolf shipment

Daniel Wolf owned a number of shipping and trading companies, of which the most important were the N V Hunzedal at the Hague and SOCDECO at Antwerp. During the autumn of 1936 he began to procure supplies for the Spanish Republicans, basing himself at the Ritz Hotel in Paris. He proved to be so efficient that, after the failure to purchase the nine Vultee V1-As, the problem was turned over to him. He placed the American end of the transaction in the hands of his uncle, Rudolph Wolf, a Manhattan commission-agent and broker in jute and burlap, and, to allay the suspicions of the State Department, enrolled the help of his friend Anthony Fokker, who in turn enlisted the help of his friends, Hall Roosevelt, brother-in-law to the American President, and Brigadier-General Richard Coke Marshall. In the meantime, Maj R G Ervin, an ex-Shell executive and the president of the P&E Corporation in New York, bought ten aircraft (seven Lockheed Orions and three Northrop Deltas) from various owners – a course possibly suggested by his friend James Haizlip (see Beechcraft 17) and sold them, through Charles Babb (see Vultee V1-A) to Rudolph Wolf. Wolf thereupon bought the nine Vultees and applied for licences to export the nineteen aircraft.

Partly due to the intercession of Hall Roosevelt and Fokker, the licences were granted on 5 December 1936. Unhappily, after a celebratory dinner with Babb in Washington, Rudolph Wolf collapsed and died that night, the licences were revoked, and the aircraft were put back on the market. His widow, Rachel Wolf, promptly formed a new company and spent two weeks fighting off other dealers who were trying to buy the aircraft to sell them to the Spaniards at higher prices. She lost two Deltas to Robert Cuse (see below) and an Orion, c/n 193 NC12278, which was wrecked when Robert Blair, a well-known charter pilot, landed badly at Jackson Airport, Ohio. These were replaced by three Consolidated 20A Fleetsters. At the last moment she exchanged

another Orion (c/n 212, NC14248, which was quickly bought by Melendreras and flown to Mexico on 17 December 1936) for the prototype Vultee V1. The nineteen aircraft were granted export licences by a reluctant State Department, there being no legal grounds for withholding them because the aircraft were ostensibly intended for speculative resale in any country except Spain, and the machines were loaded aboard the *Waalhaven* and the *President Harding*, which left New York on 28 December 1936. The wings of the Delta followed on the *American Traveler* on 30 December, accompanied by an Amercian test pilot, Clell Ernest Powell, a Vultee engineer, Jack A Martin, and a Mr Couwenhoven of Hunzedal. The aircraft are listed below.

Consolidated 20A Fleetsters

c/n	Registration	Name	Previous owner
1	NC13708	—	TWA
4	NC13211	—	TWA
6	NC13213	—	TWA

Lockheed Orions

Model	c/n	Registration	Name	Previous owner
9	183	NC12225		C A Collins, Palm Springs
9	185	NC12227	*El Marelto*	C A Collins, Air Transport Corp
9F	196	NC12284	*J D Brinkley MD*	Dr J D Brinkley sold the aircraft to Lockheed, who sold it to Ervin, who sold it to Babb, who sold it to Wolf
9D	205	NC13747		Oil Field Airlines Dallas, Texas
9D Special	211	NC14222	*Auto da Fé*	Laura Ingalls

Continued

Northrop Delta

Model	c/n	Registration	Previous owner
1D	39	NC14242	Hal Roach Studios 1934–35 Erle P Haliburton Inc

Vultees

Model	c/n	Registration	Previous owner	Fleet No.
V1	1	NC12293	American Airlines	A-180
V1-A	2	NC13764	American Airlines	A-181
V1-A	3	NC13765	American Airlines	A-182
V1-A	4	NC13766	American Airlines	A-183
V1-A	6	NC13768	American Airlines	A-185
V1-A	7	NC13769	American Airlines	A-186
V1-A	10	NC13772	American Airlines	A-187
V1-A	11	NC13773	American Airlines	A-188
V1-A	17	NC14248	American Airlines	A-189
V1-A	19	NC14253	American Airlines	A-190

c/n 5, NC13767, A-184, had crashed in January 1936, and the above therefore comprised the entire American Airlines fleet of Vultees.

The Cuse shipment

Robert Cuse, a Lithuanian-born engineer and president of the Vimalert Corporation, Jersey City, had exported reconditioned aero engines and other equipment to the USSR through Amtorg, the Soviet trading organisation in the USA, since the 1920s. In September 1936 Amtorg (it seems) provided Cuse with several million pounds Sterling with which to buy aircraft and other material for Republican Spain. On 24 December 1936 he applied for a licence to export 18 aircraft, plus 411 aero engines and parts to make a further 150 engines, direct to Bilbao. The aircraft were as follows.

Although the sums paid were probably much higher, the valuations on the export certificates were: Douglas DC-1, $70,000; Fairchild 91, $60,000; Lockheed 10A Electra, $60,000, Boeing 247, $35,000 each; Northrop Delta, $30,000 each; new Vultee V1-A, $40,000 each; secondhand Vultee, $35,000 each. It is interesting to compare these figures with the price charged by Cyrus Smith, of American Airlines, for secondhand Vultee V1-As identical to those sold by Cuse – $22,000 each, including a complete refurbishing and a supply of spare parts. Smith seems to have been one of the very

Type	c/n	Registration	Previous owner
Douglas DC-1	1137	NC223Y	Howard Hughes
Fairchild 91	9401	NC14743	Fairchild Aircraft Corp
Lockheed Electra	1033	NC14946	May Co department store
Northrop 1D Delta	38	NC14241	Crosley Radio
Northrop 1D Delta	41	NC14266	May Co department store
Boeing 247	1684	NC13303	Pennsylvania Airlines
Boeing 247	1689	NC13308	Pennsylvania Airlines
Boeing 247	1692	NC13311	Pennsylvania Airlines
Boeing 247	1713	NC13331	Pennsylvania Airlines
Boeing 247	1726	NC13344	Pennsylvania Airlines
Boeing 247	1738	NC13356	Pennsylvania Airlines
Vultee V1-A	8	NR13770	Harry Richman
Vultee V1-A	9	NC13771	Idaho Maryland Mines
Vultee V1-A	15	NC14251	Nevada Gas, Lang
Vultee V1-A	21	NC14255	Richardson & Watts
Vultee V1-A	23	NC16000	ADC (Vultee)
Vultee V1-A	24	NC17325	ADC (Vultee)
Vultee V1-A	26	NC17326	ADC (Vultee)

few vendors who treated the Spanish Republicans honorably, although he had little patience with the Spanish Republicans themselves. Cuse's two Northrop Deltas had been snapped up during the confusion following Rudolph Wolf's death and resold to the Spaniards at a higher price.

Cuse's application to export directly to Republican Spain in defiance of the 'moral embargo' raised a tremendous political storm, and provoked Roosevelt and Congress to introduce legislation prohibiting the export of war material, including civil aircraft, to either side in Spain. Cuse was thus obliged to embark such aircraft as he could on board the *Mar Cantábrico* while the debates were in progress. The ship sailed out of territorial waters moments before the resolution was passed, but ten aircraft were left behind on the quay. The aircraft that sailed were the four secondhand Vultees (c/ns 8 (*Lady Peace*), 9, 15 and 21), the two Northrop Deltas, the Lockheed Electra and the Fairchild 91. The *Mar Cantábrico* was intercepted by Nationalist warships in the Bay of Biscay, however, and the aircraft passed into Nationalist hands.

The Sil shipment

The Republican ship *Sil* sailed from Vera Cruz, Mexico, on 22 December 1936, and arrived at Santander on 12 January 1937. On board were three aircraft procured through the Mexican Director General de Aeronáutica, Coronel Roberto Fierro Villalobos: a Lockheed Vega, the Lockheed Sirius X-BADA *Anahuac* and a Lockheed Orion (c/n 186), of which the details are given under the types concerned.

The Grumman shipment

The details are given under Grumman GE-23.

The *Ibai* shipment

In December 1936 and January 1937 Comandante José Melendreras Sierra and Capitán Francisco Corral bought twenty-eight aircraft in the United States, and they were flown to Mexico on the following dates:

11 December 1936
Buhl CA-6 Air Sedan, c/n 58, NC8452, 300hp Wright J6 engine.
Lockheed 10A Electra, c/n 1035,

NC14948, XA-BDQ. From Joe Reed, via Carlos Panini.

17 December 1936
Vultee V1-A, c/n 12, NC13774, XA-BET.
Lockheed 9F Orion, c/n 212, NC14246, XA-BDO.
Both bought from Phillips Petroleum, the Orion being the machine exchanged by Rachel Wolf for the prototype Vultee V1-A.
Consolidated 20A Fleetster, c/n 7, NC13214, XA-BEB, from TWA, via Morgan T Hackman.

23 December 1936
Spartan 7-W-1 Executive, c/n –, NC13992, XA-BES, from Spartan Aircraft.

24 December 1936
Curtiss T-32 Condor, c/n 43, NC12391, XA-BDR, from American Airlines.

25 December 1936
Curtiss T-32 Condor, c/n 40, NC12399, XA-BDV, from American Airlines.
Curtiss T-32 Condor, c/n 48, NC12396, XA-BDP, from American Airlines.
Curtiss T-32 Condor, c/n 50, NC12383, XA-BDU, from American Airlines.

26 December 1936
Curtiss T-32 Condor, c/n 25, NC12365, XA-BDS, from American Airlines.
Curtiss T-32 Condor, c/n 51, NC12398, XA-BDT, from American Airlines.
Lockheed 9D Orion, c/n 202, NC231Y, XA-BDZ, from Byrd-Frost Air Transport.
Lockheed 9D-1 Orion, c/n 204, NC232Y, XA-BDY, from General Development Co, Tulsa Oklahoma, via Panini.

28 December 1936
Lockheed 9 Orion c/n 181, NC12223, XA-BEU, from G E Ruckstell, Grand Canyon, Arizona.

30 December 1936
Consolidated TM23, c/n 1, NR33Y, XA-BDX, via Morgan Hackman.

1 January 1937
Beechcraft 17, c/n 52, NC15403 (or 15413), XA-BEV ('BEY?'), from Lion Oil Refining Co, Eldorado, Arkansas. This may have been one of two Beechcraft bought by Francisco Corral on 21 November 1936, ostensibly for an ambulance service

Six ex-American Airlines Curtiss Condors at Grand Central Air Terminal, Los Angeles, in 1939. Bought through Charles Babb by the Spanish Republicans, they had been unable to leave Mexico during the Spanish Civil War. In 1939 they were shipped back to Los Angeles and sold to the Chinese government to raise money for Republican refugees in Latin America. (W T Larkins, via R S Allen)

at Tabasco. However, Lion Oil reported this aircraft to be at Eldorado on 28 April 1937, which, since the Spanish ambassador mentioned a Beechcraft in his collection of aircraft awaiting shipment to Spain, suggests it may have been delivered after that date.

7 January 1937
Seversky SEV-3, c/n 301, NR2106 (see Seversky SEV-3).

10 January 1937
Breese Racer (see Vultee V1 and V1-A)

– January 1937
Lockheed 9D Special Orion, c/n 172, NC975Y, XA-AHQ, from Líneas Aéreas Mineras, but based at San Francisco.

14 February 1937
Spartan 7-W-3 Executive, NC13994, XA-BEW, from Spartan Aircraft.

21 February 1937
Spartan 7-W-4 Executive, NC13997, XA-BEX, as above.
Northrop 2D Gamma, c/n 10, NC13759 (see Northrop Delta and Gamma).

22 February 1937
Northrop 5B Gamma, c/n 188, NR14998, XA-ABI (see Northrop Delta and Gamma).

– February 1937
Bellanca CH-300 Pacemaker, c/n 202, NC10792, XA-AAI(?), from Aéronaves de Mexico, but at Los Angeles when bought.

14 March 1937
Boeing 247, c/n 1738, NC13356.

17 March 1937
Boeing 247, c/n 1713, NC13331.
Boeing 247, c/n 1684, NC13303.
These three Boeing 247s were bought from Cuse after the departure of the *Mar Cantábrico*.

After the most extraordinary tribulations through most of 1937, the Spanish ambassador in Mexico, Félix Gordón Ordás, managed to embark about a dozen aircraft on the *Ibai* on 29 December 1937. Although it is not possible to give an exact list, they included the Consolidated Fleetster, Lockheed Electra, Vultee V1-A, Seversky SEV-3, both Northrops, the three Spartan Executives and two Lockheed Orions. They may also have included the Consolidated TM23 biplane, two more Orions and a machine mysteriously described as a 'De Price' (possibly the Bellanca Pacemaker, which had been sold to Coronel Fierro by Edward Brice of Boston, Massachusetts). The aircraft left behind, which included the six Curtiss Condors and three Boeing 247s, were later sold to pay for the support of Spanish Republican refugees arriving in Mexico. The Curtiss Condors ended their careers in China.

Aircraft not delivered

A considerable number of aircraft were bought or ordered by the Spanish Republicans but, for various reasons, not delivered.

From Belgium

Dewoitine D.9	1	via Armande Gavage, an arms dealer.
Fokker F.VIIb3m	3	OO-AIK, 'AIR and 'AIS, from Sabena.
LACAB GR.8	1	From the manufacturer.
Renard R-32	1	From the manufacturer.
Romano R.83	18	Six delivered out of twenty-four (see text).

From Czechoslovakia

Aero A-330	15	Reason unknown.
Avia 51	2	Ship delivering them reportedly lost at sea – unconfirmed.
Avia B.534/II	20	Train carrying them to Gdynia stopped by Polish authorities.

From France

Romano R.131	50	Production prohibited after completion of sixteen airframes (see Romano R.82 and R.83).

Other aircraft, mostly foreign machines in transit through France, are mentioned throughout the text

From the Netherlands

Fokker F.VIIb3m	2	Mentioned in French air ministry letter.
Fokker G.1	26	Ordered October 1936; production not complete when civil war ended.
Koolhoven FK 51bis	6	(see Koolhoven FK 51)
Koolhoven FK 52	4	(see Koolhoven FK 51)

From Poland

P.Z.L. P.37 Los	50	Ordered late 1937 or early 1938. No examples built by the time the civil war ended.

From the United Kingdom

Airspeed Courier	5	G-ACLF, 'LT, 'SZ, 'VE, 'UF.
Airspeed Envoy	8	G-ADCA, 'AZ, 'BZ, 'BA, 'EXE, c/ns 61, 62 and 69.
Armstrong Whitworth Atlas	18	(Ex-RAF. Trainers: K1176, -8, K1454, -5, -90, K2524, -39; army co-operation versions: K1536, -64, -76, -79, -83, -95, K1600, -01, -02.)
Avro 626	3	G-AEVI, 'J and 'K.
Avro 652 Anson I	2	G-ACRM *Avalon* and 'N *Ava*.
Beechcraft 17	2	G-ADLE, 'ESJ (see text).
De Havilland D.H. 84 Dragon	10	G-ACBW, 'DN, 'EK, 'HV, 'KB, 'KU, 'MC, 'EMI, 'J and 'K.
De Havilland D.H.89 Dragon Rapide	4	G-ACTU, 'DAK, 'DWZ, 'EMH.
De Havilland D.H.85 Leopard Moth	1	G-ACSH.
General Aircraft Monospar ST-25	3	G-AEVN, 'WN, 'EYF.
Lockheed 12	1	G-AEMZ.
Hawker Tomtit	1	G-AEVU.
Short Scion	1	G-ADDN.
Stinson Reliant	1	G-ACSV (see text).

From the United States

In addition to the aircraft left in Mexico (see above), there were the sixteen Grumman GE-23s impounded in Canada, six aircraft from the Cuse shipment, three Curtiss Condors destroyed by fire, forty-two Bellanca 28/90s, and possibly four Spartan Zeus (see Spartan Executive). In their memoirs and reports Félix Gordón Ordás (the Republican ambassador in Mexico) and José Melendreras (a purchasing officer in the USA) both mention contracts for, and offers of, eighteen Martin 139s (later increased to fifty), three Seversky SEV-3MWWs, twenty-eight Sikorsky S-53s, and individual aircraft too numerous to list here. A later scheme to export 100 aircraft, including Douglas DC-3s and Stearman 'O' reconnaissance monoplanes, came to nothing.

Even the types listed total 362 aircraft, of which about 100 are known to have been paid for.

Problematical aircraft

There are a number of types of aircraft often alleged to have flown in the Spanish Civil War, but which evidence now shows did not. The American military attaché at Valencia, Col Stephen Fuqua, mentions the Amiot 143 and ANF Les Mureaux 115 and 117 as being among the types used by the Spanish Republicans. Six Amiot 143s were ordered at the beginning of the civil war, but the order was cancelled when the Amiot company refused to sell to the Republicans. In a report to the Catalonian Generalitat (regional government), dated 30 October 1936, the purchasing agent F F Guardiola mentions a 'Les Mureaux monoplane' armed with a cannon and two machine guns for the pilot and a gun for the observer, on offer and ready for immediate delivery. This was obviously the prototype Mureaux 180C2 gull-wing monoplane two-seat fighter, which on that same day had arrived at CEMA, Villacoublay, for new trials after extensive modifications. It was still at Villacoublay in March 1937, and is reported to have been scrapped. In June 1937 the extreme Right Wing French newspaper *Candide* reported the delivery of three Mureaux 115R2s to Spain,

The Renard R.32 prototype, sold to the Republicans in August 1936 but kept in Belgium.

but *Candide's* reports were notoriously unreliable.

The fighter most persistently reported as having flown in Spain is the Fairey Fantôme. The story originates from the fact that, on 20 August 1936, the two existing Fairey Fantômes assembled at Gosselies, Belgium, which had been purchased by the Soviet government, were loaded aboard the *Tovarich Stalin* at Antwerp. It was alleged that the ship had sailed not to Russia, but to Republican Spain. *Lloyds Shipping Index* (18 August 1936) shows that the ship sailed to Leningrad, however. Moreover, the test pilot Maj Gen Pyotr Stepanovich flew one of the Fantômes in Russia in the summer of 1938.

A photograph of some damaged P.Z.L. P.23 Karas army co-operation monoplanes allegedly in Spanish Republican service clearly shows Polish aircraft, the picture obviously having been taken by a German in Poland in September 1939. Other reports have referred to a Levasseur P.L.110 (probably confused with a Breguet 19), a Miles Sparrowhawk and a Rohrbach Roland. No Sparrowhawks reached Spain, and all Rohrbach Rolands were scrapped some years before the civil war. Similarly, the I-153 in the French Musée de l'Air is often said to have escaped from Spain at the end of the civil war. It appears to have been built, however, about six months after the Spanish war ended, and must therefore be a Russian machine captured in 1941 and brought to France by a Luftwaffe pilot. Nor does it appear, contrary to numerous assertions, that any Fiat C.R.42 fighters were delivered to Spain.

A Spanish mechanic who had served in the Republican air force told the French aviation enthusiast Rémy Tiger that he remembered having seen three gull-wing single-seat fighters, similar to the Loire 46, at Barcelona in 1938. They were not Loires, he insisted, since he had worked on that type in 1936. The author can offer no solution to this puzzle, apart from suggesting a con-

The Fokker G.1. 'Le Faucheur' ('Grim Reaper'). Twenty-six were ordered by the Spanish Republicans, to be imported via Estonia, but only one or two were completed, and none delivered, when the civil war ended in March 1939.

fusion of memory after forty-five years. The only fighters in Europe resembling the Loire were the P.Z.L. P.11 and P.24, and the Aero A-102. Had any P.Z.L. P.24s reached Republican Spain, the fact would certainly be known by now, since they were formidable fighting aircraft. Only one Aero A-102 seems to have been built. It suffered two crashes, one in 1934 and the second in 1936.

It was exhibited in the Great Aviation Exhibition in Prague in 1937, after which it was rejected by the Czech air force in favour of the Avia B.35 low-wing monoplane. It is just possible, therefore, that one Aero A-102 (or two, if two were built) was sent to Spain with the Aero A-101s later in 1937. Regarding the P.Z.L. P.24, there are stories that one did indeed

The LACAB GR-8 multi-place de combat biplane, obsolete in concept before it flew, was another Belgian prototype bought for the Spanish Republicans by an arms-dealing group. It never left Belgium, and was destroyed during the Second World War.

The Breguet 230 prototype during a visit to San Javier in 1935. (Arráez)

The Loire 25o No 1. (Liron)

Below: *The Fairey Fantôme.*

fly with the Nationalist air force. The prototype is said to have been in Turkey when the Italians invaded Ethiopia, and to have been delivered to the Emperor Haile Selasse. It was captured by the Italians, who then transferred it to Spain for trials. There is no confirmation of this, and the tale seems improbable.

An aircraft to be included in this apocryphal list is the Breguet 230. This was a three-seat bomber bi-plane powered by a 650hp Hispano-Suiza water-cooled engine, and featuring a peculiar canopy over the middle cockpit. The aircraft was obsolete before it was built, in 1931. Only one was produced, registered F-AMGR, and the story that it flew in the Spanish Civil War seems to have originated from the fact that it visited Spain in the summer of 1935. It disappears from the records after the autumn of 1936, but, had it returned to Spain, it is unlikely that so strange a machine would not have been remembered by somebody.

Finally, one aeroplane that has hitherto escaped notice and may have flown in Spain was the Loire 250, a prototype radial-engined single-seat low-wing monoplane fighter which proved to have a disappointing per-formance. Its career can be followed in some detail from its first flight in October 1935 until its dismantling and overhauling in November 1936. On 6 May 1937 *Les Ailes* reported that the Loire 250 was no longer being kept by SNCAO (the group of aircraft manufacturers in western France into which the Loire company had recently been nationalised), and was in a hangar at Villacoublay. After that, nothing more is heard of it. Since so many aircraft that apparent-ly vanished without trace during this period were found, after research thirty or forty years later, to have ended their careers in Spain, the possibility that this was the fate of the Loire 250 is by no means remote.

Appendix III
Types and numbers of aircraft used by the opposing sides, 1936-39

The Republicans

From before the war

Military

Boeing 281	1
CASA-Breguet 19	60-70
CASA-Breguet 26T ambulance	1
Cierva Autogiro	3 (1 C.19 Mk IV and 2 C.30A)
De Havilland D.H.89M	2
Dornier Wal	8 (plus 5 under repair on 18 July 1936).
Fokker F.VIIb3m	2, transferred from LAPE
Fokker F.VIIb3m/M	1
Hawker Spanish Fury	3
Hispano-Nieuport 52	35 (plus 10 under repair and 10 built from parts). 55 in all
Junkers F 13 (HQ aircraft)	1
Junkers K 30	1
Nieuport NiD 82	1 (unconfirmed)
Potez 25A2	1 (unconfirmed)

Naval

CASA-Vickers Vildebeest	27 (2 as seaplanes)
Cierva C.30A	2
Dornier Wal	8
Hawker Osprey	1
Macchi M.18	10
Martinsyde F.4	9 (7 airworthy on 18 July 1936)
Savoia-Marchetti S.62	30

Military trainers

De Havilland D.H.9	22
De Havilland D.H.60G-IIIA Moth Major	11
De Havilland D.H.60M Metal Moth	2
De Havilland D.H.82A Tiger Moth	5
Fleet 10	2
Hispano E.30	17
Hispano E.34	1

Naval trainers

CASA III	1
Avro 504K	2
De Havilland D.H.60G-IIIA Moth Major	1
Hispano E.30	5

Civil transport aircraft

De Havilland D.H.84 Dragon	1
De Havilland D.H.89 Dragon Rapide	1
Douglas DC-2	3
Fokker F.VIIb3m	5
Ford 4-AT	1
Junkers-G 24	1 (unconfirmed)
Savoia-Marchetti S.62P	1

Light and miscellaneous aircraft

Adaro 1.E.7 Chirta	1
Aeronca C-3	1
American-Eagle-Lincoln Eaglet	1
Avro 594 Avian	11
Avro 631 Cadet	1 (unconfirmed)
B.A. L25C Swallow	1
B.A. Eagle 2	1
Beechcraft 17L	1
Blackburn L.1C Bluebird IV	1
Blériot SPAD 51	1
Bristol F2B	6
CASA III	6
Caudron C.272 Luciole	7
Cierva Autogiro	2 (1.C19 Mk IV and 1 C.30A)
Comper Swift	1
De Havilland D.H.60X Moth	6
De Havilland D.H.60G Gipsy Moth	20
De Havilland D.H.60M Metal Moth	1
De Havilland D.H.60G-III Gipsy Moth	1
De Havilland D.H.60G-IIIA Moth Major	4
De Havilland D.H.80A Puss Moth	2
De Havilland D.H.83 Fox Moth	6
De Havilland D.H.85 Leopard Moth	1
De Havilland D.H.87A and 87B Hornet Moth	6
Farman F.194	1
Farman F.200	1
Farman F.354	1
Fiat A.S.1	2
Freüller Valls MA	1
General Aircraft Monospar ST-12	1
González Gil-Pazó GP-1	1
González Gil-Pazó GP-2	1
González Gil-Pazó GP-4	1
Guinea-Severt 2DDM	1
Hanriot HD-14	2
Klemm L.20	1
Klemm L.25	2
Loring E.II	4
Loring X	1
Messerschmitt M 23b	1
Messerschmitt M 35	1
Mignet H.M.14 Pou du Ciel	1
Miles M2F and M2H Hawk Major	2
Miles M3A Falcon	1
Pallarols 40A	1

Potez 36	2
Potez 43	1
Potez 58	1
Renard-Stampe-Vertongen 32/85	1
Romeo Ro-5	1
R.W.D.9	1-2
Stinson SR Reliant	2

TOTAL: 412-427 aircraft, of which 118-130 were military and 86 naval, plus 15 under repair and 10 built in the autumn of 1936.

Imported during the civil war

Belgium

Avia BH-33	1
De Havilland D.H.89 Dragon Rapide	1

Czechoslovakia

Aero A-101 and Ab 101	25 (out of 47 sent)
Avia 51	1 (out of 3 sent)
Letov S 231, 331, 431	17-21
Letov S 328	6 (unconfirmed)

Estonia

Bristol Bulldog	8-11 (11 unconfirmed)
Potez 25A2	8

France

Beechcraft 17	1-2
Blériot SPAD 51	1
Blériot SPAD 56/6	1
Blériot SPAD 91/6	1
Blériot SPAD 111/3	1
Blériot SPAD 111/6	1
Bloch MB 200	1-2
Bloch MB 210	4-7
Bloch 300	1
Breguet 27S	1 (unconfirmed)
Breguet 460	1
Breguet 470	1
Breguet 670T	1
Caudron C.59	9-10
Caudron C.490	3
Caudron Luciole	14-19
Caudron C.510 Pélican	1
Caudron Göeland	6-10
Caudron C.600 Aiglon	20-30
Caudron C.635 Simoun	1
Couzinet 101	1
Dewoitine D.27/53	2-3
Dewoitine D.31	1 (unconfirmed)
Dewoitine D.35	1 (unconfirmed)
Dewoitine D.370-01	1
Dewoitine D.371-01	1
Dewoitine D.371	10
Dewoitine D.372	13-14
Dewoitine D.510TH	2
Farman F.190	4
Farman F.192/1	1
Farman F.193	1
Farman F.197	1
Farman F.291/1	1

Farman F.354	1
Farman F.401/402	5
Farman F.430, 431, 432	4
Farman F.481 Alizé	12
Fokker F.VIIb3m (F-AJCH)	1
Gourdou-Lesuerre GL-32	15-20
Gourdou-Lesuerre GL-410	1
Gourdou-Lesuerre GL-482	1
Gourdou-Leseurre GL-633	6
Hanriot H-437	1
Hanriot H-439	6
Hanriot H-182	6-10
Latécoère 28	4-7
Lioré et Olivier 20 and 213	1-2
Loire 46	5-6
Loire 250	1 (unconfirmed)
Maillet 20 and 21	2
Morane-Saulnier MS 60	1 (but probably more)
Morane-Saulnier MS 146	1
Morane-Saulnier MS 181	4
Morane-Saulnier MS 230	1
Morane-Saulnier MS 233	2
Morane-Saulnier MS 341	3
Morane-Saulnier MS 345	1
Moreau 10	1
Potez 25A2	5-7 (unconfirmed)
Potez 36	1
Potez 56	6
Potez 58	2-5
Potez 540	10 (6 in 1936, 4 in 1937)
Potez 542	7
Potez 544	1
Romano R.82	6
Romano R.83	6
SAB-SEMA-12	1

Italy

De Havilland D.H.89 Dragon Rapide	(I-DRAG) 1

The Netherlands

Fokker C.X	1
Fokker D.XXI	1
Fokker F.VIIa	1
Fokker F.IX	1
Fokker F.XII	1
Fokker F.XVIII	1
Fokker F.XX	1
Koolhoven FK 40	1 (unconfirmed)
Koolhoven FK 51	22

Sweden

Northrop 1C Delta	1
Sikorsky S-38B	1

Switzerland

Douglas DC-2	1
General Aviation Clark GA 43A	1
Lockheed 9B Orion	2

United Kingdom

Airspeed Envoy I and II	3 (out of 4 sent)

Airspeed Envoy III	6
Airspeed Viceroy	1
Avro 626	1
Avro 643 Cadet	1
B.A. L25 Swallow	1 (unconfirmed)
Bellanca 28/70 *The Dorothy*	1
De Havilland D.H.84 Dragon	4 (out of 5 sent)
De Havilland D.H.82A Tiger Moth	(out of 14 sent) 12
De Havilland D.H.90 Dragonfly	3
De Havilland D.H.85 Leopard Moth	(captured) 1
Douglas DC-1	1
Focke-Wulf Fw 56 Stösser	3 (see text)
General Aircraft Monospar ST-25	10
Miles M2H Hawk Major	3
Miles M23 Hawk Speed Six	1
Miles M3b Falcon	1
Percival Gull Six	1
Spartan Cruiser II	1

United States, Canada and Mexico

Consolidated 20A Fleetster	4
Douglas DC-2	1
Grumman GE-23	34
Lockheed Vega	1

Lockheed Sirius	1
Lockheed Orion	3-7 (out of 12 bought)
Northrop 1D Delta	1
Northrop 2D Gamma	1
Northrop 5B Gamma	1
Seversky SEV-3	1
Spartan Executive	3
Vultee V1	1
Vultee V1-A	7

USSR

I-15	153
I-152	30
I-16	276
R-5	31-62
R-Z	93-124
SB 2M-100A	93-108
I-16UTI trainers	4

Russian aircraft built in Spain

I-15 Chato	237 (of which 219 reached the squadrons)
I-16 Mosca	14 (of which about 10 reached the squadrons)

The only figure concerning deliveries of aircraft to Republican Spain which the Soviet authorities have ever published appears on Page 329 of *International Solidarity with the Spanish Republic* (Moscow 1975), where a total of 806 is given without any comment or details. There seems to be no way of bringing the above totals of 680-757 up to this number unless we assume that it includes the aircraft dispatched to Spain at the end of the civil war, between the middle of December 1938 and the beginning of February 1939. During a meeting with General Hidalgo de Cisneros in Moscow in November 1938, Stalin promised to send 250 more aircraft. Of these, however, only thirty I-152 fighters reached the Republican air force before the collapse of Catalonia, other aircraft being sent back in their crates across the French frontier. If, therefore, we transfer these thirty I-152s to the 250 aircraft promised, where they belong, and assume the total number of Soviet aircraft that reached Spain before them to have been 680, which agrees more closely with the estimates given by ex-Republican airmen, then the figure of 806 becomes intelligible, since it would mean that, of the 250 promised, 126 were actually dispatched before the fall of Catalonia persuaded the Russians to cancel further deliveries.

TOTALS

Imported from:

Belgium	2
Czechoslovakia	43-53 (42-53 military)
Estonia	16-19 (all military)
France	237-287 (60-69 military, unarmed)
Italy	1
The Netherlands	30 (24 military, unarmed)
Sweden	2
Switzerland	4
United Kingdom	55-56
United States, Canada and Mexico	59-63 military) (6 converted into

USSR	680-757 (680 probably being more accurate), of which all were military and armed, except the four I-16UTIs

Built in Spain:

I-15 Chato	219 (out of 237 built)
I-16 Mosca	about 10 (out of 14 built)

The Republicans can thus be seen to have imported between 1,124 and 1,272 aircraft during the civil war, of which 806-887 could be classed as military. To these should be added the 229 fighters built in Spain.

The Nationalists

From before the war

Military

CASA-Breguet 19	63
De Havilland D.H.89M Dragon Rapide	1
Dornier Wal	3 (plus 10 under repair)
Fokker F.VIIb3m/M	3
Hispano-Nieuport 52	3 (plus 7 under repair)

Naval

Savoia-Marchetti S.62	5

Military trainers

De Havilland D.H.9	18
Hispano E.30	1

Civil transport aircraft

Douglas DC-2	1
Junkers F 13	1

Light and miscellaneous aircraft

Avro 594 Avian	2
B.A. L25 Swallow	1
Caudron C.282 Phalène	2
De Havilland D.H.60X Moth	1
De Havilland D.H.60G Gipsy Moth	9
De Havilland D.H.80A Puss Moth	1
De Havilland D.H.85 Leopard Moth	1
Fairchild K.R.22	1
Fiat A.S.1	1
General Aircraft Monospar ST-25	1
Klemm L.25	2
Miles M3A Falcon	1
Monocoupe 90, 90A & 90A De Luxe	5
R.W.D.9	1 (unconfirmed)

TOTAL
128 aircraft, of which 78 were military and naval.

Imported during the civil war

France

Caudron C.600	1
Farman F.193	1 (unconfirmed)
Farman F.391	1 (unconfirmed)
Fokker F.VIIa *Carlanco*	1

Germany
Military, naval and transport

Arado Ar 68E-1	3
Arado Ar 95A	9
Dornier Do 17	31-47
Fieseler Fi 156 Storch	4
Heinkel He 45	36-41
Heinkel He 46	30-46
Heinkel He 51	126
Heinkel He 59	17
Heinkel He 60E	8
Heinkel He 70	28-31
Heinkel He 111	about 100
Heinkel He 112 V5 and He 112 V9	2
Heinkel He 112B	8
Heinkel He 115A-0	2
Henschel Hs 123	18
Henschel Hs 126	6
Junkers Ju 52/3m	60-120
Junkers Ju 86D	5
Junkers Ju 87A	3
Junkers Ju 87B	5
Messerschmitt Bf 109	131

Trainers and miscellaneous

Arado Ar 66C-1	6
Bücker Bü 131 Jungmann	50
Bücker Bü 133 Jungmeister	20
Gotha Go 145A	21
Heinkel He 50G	1
Junkers W 34	5
Klemm L.32	3
Messerschmitt Bf 108	4

Italy
Military, naval and transport

Breda 64	1
Breda 65	23
Cant Z.501	9
Cant Z.506B	4
Caproni Ca 135S	2 (out of 7 sent)
Caproni Ca 310	10
Fiat B.R.20	13-19
Fiat C.R.32	377
Fiat G.50	10
IMAM Ro 37Bis	68
Macchi M.41	3
Savoia-Marchetti S.55X	3
Savoia-Marchetti S.79	100
Savoia-Marchetti S.81	66-70

Trainers and miscellaneous

Breda 25	1 (possibly more)
Breda 28	6
Breda 33	1
Breda 39	1
Caproni Ca 100	2
Caproni AP.1	10
Fiat C.R.20	6
Fiat C.R.30	2
IMAM Ro 41	28

The Netherlands

Fokker F.VIIb3m	2

Poland and Portugal

Breguet 19	20 (unconfirmed)
Farman F.191 *Aquila Branca*	1
Miles M2H Hawk Major	1
P.W.S.10	20
P.W.S.16	16 (unconfirmed)
R.W.D.13	4

United Kingdom

Airspeed Envoy II	1 (plus 1 from the Republicans)
De Havilland D.H.89 Dragon Rapide	4
General Aircraft Monospar ST-12	1
Fokker F.XII	2 (out of 4 sent)

Captured at sea on Republican ships

Aero A-101	22 (on *Hordena*)
Fairchild 91	1 (on *Mar Cantabrico*)
Lockheed 10A Electra	1 (on *Mar Cantabrico*)
Northrop 1D Delta	2 (on *Mar Cantabrico*)
Vultee V1-A	4 (on *Mar Cantabrico*)

The Nationalists thus imported 1,526-1,623 aircraft, of which 1,321-1,431 were military aircraft from Germany (632-732) and Italy (689-699), plus 22 Czechoslovakian military aircraft captured at sea, and 8 convertible transports from the UK.

Summary

Of the 400 or so aircraft retained by the Republicans at the start of the war, the only four potentially effective fighters (the Boeing 281 and the three Hawker Spanish Furies) were without armament, and were not armed until the middle of August. The French aircraft were likewise unarmed, and of the 444-515 assorted aircraft imported from countries other than the USSR, only the thirty-four Grumman GE-23s were both reasonably modern and delivered with their armament. The Republicans can therefore be said to have had between 950 and 1,060 effective combat aircraft at their disposal during the civil war, of which 676 (or at most 753) came from the Soviet Union. Over the same period, the Nationalists disposed of 1,429-1,539 effective combat aircraft, of which 1,321-1,431 came from Germany and Italy.

Index of Aircraft

Index of Engines

Sub-types (e.g. Salmson 9 Ab, 9 Aba, 9 Ac etc.) are not listed in the index but are given in the text when known.

General Index